Existing
An Introduction to Existential Thought

Steven Luper
Trinity University

Mayfield Publishing Company
Mountain View, California
London • Toronto

For Ann Marie

Library of Congress Cataloging-in-Publication Data
Existing : an introduction to existential thought / edited by Steven
   Luper.
       p.   cm.
   Includes bibliographical references.
   ISBN 0-7674-0587-0
   1. Existentialism.   I. Luper, Steven.
B819.E95   1999
142′.78 — dc21   98-52827
                                                    CIP

Manufactured in the United States of America
10   9   8   7   6   5   4   3   2   1

Mayfield Publishing Company
1280 Villa Street
Mountain View, California 94041

Sponsoring editor, Kenneth King; *production editor,* Carla White
Kirschenbaum; *manuscript editor,* Patricia Ohlenroth; *text and cover
designer,* Linda Robertson; *design manager,* Jean Mailander; *manufac-
turing manager,* Randy Hurst. This text was set in 10/11.5 Minion by
G & S Typesetters, and printed on 45# Chromotone Matte by Banta
Book Group, Harrisonburg.

Cover art © Estate of Hans Hofmann / Licensed by VAGA, New York, NY

Contents

Preface

In this volume I have gathered together a wide variety of materials for readers who wish to become acquainted with existentialist thought. The reader will also find much material by phenomenologists, to the extent that existentialist work by Heidegger and his successors overlapped with work in the phenomenological movement initiated by Heidegger's teacher, Edmund Husserl. However, the topic of this volume is existentialist thought, and phenomenology is covered only insofar as is necessary for an understanding of existentialist work.

The volume begins with an essay (Chapter 1) that introduces existentialist thought, and each chapter except the last is preceded by an introductory essay. In addition, each chapter, with the exception of the last, ends with a set of questions for further reflection, together with suggested works to which the reader might turn for additional study.

The selections are arranged so that each will be accessible if read in order. However, the reader might consider beginning with the materials in Chapter 7, devoted to existentialist literature, since it is far more accessible than the philosophical essays. And, of course, instructors who use *Existing* as a text will want to assign some selections throughout the book and not others. As an instructor I have always preferred to have a wealth of material to select from, so that I can use different materials and emphasize different things during different semesters. Perhaps others will have this preference as well.

Chapters 2 through 6 include the core writings of the four main figures in existentialism—Søren Kierkegaard, Friedrich Nietzsche, Martin Heidegger, and Jean-Paul Sartre—and generous selections from the work of several other important twentieth-century existentialist thinkers. These latter include excerpts from Miguel de Unamuno's *Tragic Sense of Life*, Ga-

briel Marcel's *Being and Having*, Karl Jaspers' *Philosophy*, Maurice Merleau-Ponty's *Phenomenology of Perception* and his essay "The Metaphysical in Humanity," Simone de Beauvoir's *The Ethics of Ambiguity*, Albert Camus' *The Myth of Sisyphus*, Martin Buber's *I and Thou*, and Paul Tillich's *The Courage to Be*. Where possible I have selected translations that are especially accessible. In particular, I have used Joan Stambaugh's new translation of Heidegger's *Being and Time*. Very brief excerpts from the writings of four philosophers who had a profound influence on the development of existentialism are also included. These are Blaise Pascal, whose *Pensées* are excerpted; G. W. F. Hegel, from whose *Logic, Phenomenology of Spirit*, and *Philosophy of Right* I have taken very brief selections, including "Master and Slave"; Arthur Schopenhauer, from whose *World as Will and Idea* I have taken "Section 68"; and Edmund Husserl, whose *Logical Investigations* and "Paris Lectures" I have excerpted. Pascal's and Hegel's ideas were important to many of the existentialists, but I have grouped their work with Kierkegaard's under the heading Precursors. Schopenhauer, on the other hand, I have grouped with Nietzsche's work, because much of Nietzsche's work was a response to Schopenhauer's.

The final chapter consists of literary works that deal with existential themes. Some of these are written by existentialist philosophers. Thus excerpts from Sartre's *Nausea* and *No Exit* are included. Other selections are written by literary figures, some well known, and some not so well known. These works include Fyodor Dostoevsky's "The Grand Inquisitor" from *The Brothers Karamazov* as well as his *Notes from Underground,* Franz Kafka's "An Imperial Message," Jorge Borges' "Everything and Nothing," Philip K. Dick's "The Imposter," Flannery O'Connor's "A Good Man Is Hard to Find," and John Barth's *The End of the Road*.

An anthology devoted to a subject as controversial as existentialist thought is bound to have flaws, and no doubt many instructors will think of ways in which *Existing* can be improved. I would appreciate any advice others are willing to give me. Hence, I would like to invite people to send constructive criticism to me at *sluper@trinity.edu,* or at Trinity University, 715 Stadium Drive, San Antonio, TX 78212.

It is with pleasure that I acknowledge the help of several people who have contributed to this volume. First, I would like to thank Ken King, who suggested the project and who provided a great deal of help and encouragement along the way. The team at Mayfield Publishing Company runs a first-rate operation. I would also like to thank my colleague Judith Norman who provided a fresh translation of Hegel's "Master and Slave." I am also grateful to several reviewers for very helpful suggestions: Thomas Vician, DeAnza College; Sami Hawi, University of Wisconsin-Milwaukee; Susan Rouse, Kennesaw State University; Ted Humphrey, Arizona State University; Cathryn Bailey, Mankato State University; and Javier Ibanez-Noe, Marquette University. Special thanks go to Yolanda Estes at the University of Colorado-Boulder and Paul Haanstad at the University of Utah, both of whom provided detailed and insightful comments on an earlier draft. Finally, I am grateful to Margaret Carrasco for the efficient way in which she handled the manuscript and permissions.

CHAPTER 1

Introduction

Human beings have always shared their lives with others. We are social animals, as Aristotle claimed (or "herding animals," as Nietzsche preferred to say), and we identify ourselves, at least in part, with various groups such as families, teams, nations, and so on. We might even say that while community life has always been prominent, the life of the individual has been largely nonexistent, until the last several centuries. In recent history the urge to develop and cultivate our own separate lives has been felt more and more profoundly. It works against our default practice of remaining immersed in the group, but for most of us both forces are at work in our psyches; sometimes one dominates, sometimes the other. A similar pattern can be found in the history of ideas. During some periods of time there are writers who recommend individuality, while during other periods there is a return to the comforting view that in truth the self just *is* the community, so to "strike out on our own" is to pursue a lifestyle in which we are alienated from ourselves.

So far as the history of ideas goes, it is probably accurate to say that force is gathering behind the view that individuals derive their identities from the group. In the last several decades, writers identified with the label "communitarianism" (Roberto Unger, Alasdair MacIntyre, Charles Taylor, Michael Sandel, and others) have been busy rediscovering the ancient view that our identities are deeply rooted in the community. It is an idea whose time has come, gone, and is on its way back again. But it is remarkable that the communitarian comeback is facing resistance. The ancient emphasis on the importance of the community at the expense of the individual has been reversed, at least for the time being, and communitarians are unable simply to presuppose the preeminence of the community. They find themselves carrying the burden of showing that the individual should defer to the community. In an individualistic age like ours, the communitarians must also show how a community identity might be created. It is one thing to remain immersed in (that is, to refrain from distinguishing oneself as against) a close-knit community such as a Greek *polis,* which was shaped by ancient forces. One does this by not acting, by not choosing to cultivate individuality. But how does one go about creating unity within a nation such as the United States, in which very different people are intent on going in very different directions?

That the communitarian-style view needs defense is remarkable when we consider how little challenge it received until very recently in human affairs. There was always some opposition from religious and philosophical traditions that posited the existence of the individual soul, but this opposition has developed very slowly. Over the centuries the belief that each of us has a soul gave rise to the idea that each of us, and not some authority such as a Church leader, is the custodian of his or her individual soul. That idea, in turn, led some to think of people as self-determining and as individually responsible (to God) for their own decisions and beliefs. Not until roughly the seventeenth century did these ideas really take life, however. At that time influential thinkers began to spell out reasons people have for taking charge of their lives, and reasons others have for letting people take charge of their lives. One seventeenth-century writer of the first sort, Blaise Pascal, was especially important in the development of existentialism, for reasons I shall sketch out. First, however, let us consider a strand of seventeenth-century political philosophy that indirectly contributed to the advent of existentialism by helping to create the climate of opinion in which people were allowed control over their lives.

INDIVIDUALIST POLITICS

Seventeenth-century political philosophers such as John Locke began to defend the individual's moral right to freedom from governmental restraint. Roughly until Locke's day it was assumed that the state had legitimate authority to rule over the individual. This presumption had many sources of support, not least among them the Platonic-Aristotelian idea that only a few people know the nature of the good life, and it is they who should run human affairs. But Locke suggested that each of us is as well positioned as anyone else to run our own affairs because everyone (except children and the mentally incompetent) is capable of identifying the requirements of morality and abiding by them. Hence, all should have the freedom (from restraint) necessary for self-determination and individual responsibility. We should all take responsibility for our own lives and should be free to do so.

The politics of individualism were endorsed by Immanuel Kant in the eighteenth century but also drew powerful opposition from others. In his own style the French philosopher Jean-Jacques Rousseau defended the predominance of the community over the individual, as did the British writer Edmund Burke, and in the early nineteenth century the German philosopher G. W. F. Hegel gave the communitarian view one of the most influential defenses it has ever received. Nor are communitarians the only thinkers that drew from Hegel. As is well known, Karl Marx also owed much to Hegel's writings, and some of the twentieth-century existentialists found the ideas of Hegel and Marx as attractive as the ideas of Kierkegaard and Nietzsche and worked hard to achieve a reconciliation. But the individualist political philosophy initiated in the seventeenth century gained momentum in the following century in spite of the backlash against it, and prominent philosophers such as John Stuart Mill carried it into the nineteenth century.

It was in this climate that the first genuinely existentialist thinkers began to write: the Danish philosopher Søren Kierkegaard and the German philosopher Friedrich Nietzsche. Writing in the mid-nineteenth century, Kierkegaard had been influenced by Hegelianism but firmly opposed himself to Hegel's philosophy. By contrast, Nietzsche, whose work appeared at about the same time as Kierkegaard's, largely ignored the work of Hegel. Nietzsche began his work influenced by and then radically opposed to the writings of the German philosopher Arthur Schopenhauer, a contemporary of Hegel's who had also constructed a powerful attack on the importance of the individual.

Now, existentialism is not a form of political philosophy, or at least not directly so. And although much in the Hegelian system of thought was political philosophy, it was not specifically to Hegel's political views that Kierkegaard reacted. What drew Kierkegaard's fire was the invisibility of the individual and the individual life within Hegel's system. Writing in his *Journals*, Kierkegaard said:

> The thing is to understand myself, to see what God really wishes me to do; the thing is to find a truth which is true for me, to find the idea for which I can live and die. . . . What good would it do me to be able to develop a theory of the state and combine all the details into a single whole, and so construct a world in which I did not live . . . ; what good would it do me if truth stood before me, cold and naked, not caring whether I recognized her or not, and producing in me a shudder of fear rather than a trusting devotion?[1]

A similar point can be made about Nietzsche: He was not a political philosopher, or in any case not primarily so. (Indeed, neither was Schopenhauer.) Instead, a great deal of Nietzsche's work was written in opposition to Schopenhauer's unfavorable assessment of the individual and the individual's life. In their ways, both Hegel and Schopenhauer supported the idea that in its most important sense our identity is the identity we share with others, and life as an individual is at best of derivative importance. Nietzsche and Kierkegaard both argued that just the opposite is the case.

While existentialism is not political philosophy, individualist political philosophy helped create the climate necessary for existentialism to flourish, for individualist political philosophy suggested that people should be responsible for their own lives and argued that self-determination should be protected. The suggestion that our self-determination should be protected does not tell us what we should do with our lives after they are left in our hands, however, and the individualist political philosophers had little to say about the matter, having assumed that the individual's affairs are a private matter. But the existentialists are very much interested in the private affairs of people. In particular, they want to convince people to take charge of their own lives, and they want to help people overcome obstacles barring the way.

The reader might well find the proposition that we should seize life banal. The reader might also think that seizing life is a straightforward matter. Why, you might ask, do such obvious matters need discussing? In response, the existentialists would attempt to convince you that there are powerful mechanisms in play that prevent individuals from recognizing the nature and importance of their existence. To get an idea of how this argument might go, let us refer to the writings of Blaise Pascal, a seventeenth-century figure who seems to have been the first to argue in this way.

PASCAL AND SEIZING LIFE

It was Pascal who first defended a point that would later be developed in detail by the existentialists: The remarkable fact that many, if not most, people do not even value, much less take charge of, their own existence. Instead, they are filling their lives with various activities so as to divert their attention away from their own unfavorable attitude toward individual existence:

> Diversion.—When I have occasionally set myself to consider the different distractions of men, the pains and perils to which they expose themselves at court or in war, . . . I have discovered that all the unhappiness of men arises from one single fact, that they cannot stay quietly in their own chamber. . . .
>
> But on further considerations, when, after finding the cause of all our ills, I have sought to discover the reason of it, I have found that there is one very real reason, namely, the natural poverty of our feeble and mortal condition, so miserable that nothing can comfort us when we think of it closely.[2]

According to Pascal, most people lose themselves in "diversions" so as to avoid thinking about "the natural poverty of [their] feeble and mortal condition. . . ." By doing this, they escape the necessity of explicitly deciding whether their lives are worth living. Escaping this judgment is important to them because it seems overwhelmingly clear that their lives are not

worth living. Pascal went on to point out an important upshot of diversion: In escaping the necessity of evaluating their lives, people also abandon themselves in an important sense; they give up any chance they might have of approaching life in such a way that they can affirm and embrace it.

> Here is no real and lasting satisfaction; . . . our evils are infinite. . . . Let us reflect on this, and then say whether it is not beyond doubt that there is no good in this life but in the hope of another. . . .[3]

Now, Pascal himself believed that "there is no good in this life but in the hope of another." The only worthwhile existence was one centered in the afterlife in his view. The reader may well find this assessment extreme. But notice that Pascal's main point stands even if his assessment is exaggerated: If we fear that we might be in for substantial misfortune in the course of life, and our fear leads us to divert ourselves from facing life and the question of its value, we will never overcome that fear and never embrace life.

Pascal did not initiate existentialism, but his *Pensées* helped to usher it in. Both Kierkegaard and Nietzsche agreed with Pascal's point that people typically conceal from themselves the importance of their own existence and end up not owning their lives. But Kierkegaard's story about the way the diversion works differs sharply from Nietzsche's. As a Christian, Kierkegaard's story was naturally closer to Pascal's. Kierkegaard thought that many different sorts of reasons lead people to the despair of not valuing their existence and prevent people from arriving at the religious faith that is necessary for overcoming despair. Nietzsche, by contrast, would have said that religious faith itself is perhaps the most powerful cause of contempt for existence.

In spite of the considerable differences between them, both Nietzsche and Kierkegaard emphasized that people are immersed in inaccurate views about human existence, and both emphasized the importance of uncovering the truth about ourselves. Our surface beliefs and values cannot be trusted, for they are often the products of despair or the effort to avoid despair or other mechanisms that mislead people. Hence, both philosophers launched into two of Pascal's projects: clarifying these mechanisms and accurately portraying human existence. The completion of both projects would then make it possible to get an accurate view of the type of human existence worth having and pave the way for self-determination.

THE UNACKNOWLEDGED MALLEABILITY OF NATURE AND THE SELF

Much of the work of Kierkegaard and Nietzsche was devoted to Pascal's two projects. Yet the pursuit of these projects is not really what made their work distinctively existential. Of course, the term "existentialism" is notoriously difficult to define, for the views of writers who called themselves existentialists differ in important ways and in some cases are closely aligned with the views of writers who spurned the label. Nonetheless, Pascal was not an existentialist in spite of his groundbreaking work in *Pensées*. It is true that *Pensées* was an incomplete manuscript; he was working on it when he died. But there is no reason to think that he would have been an existentialist even if he had had time to complete his work. The point is that his work completely lacked an element present in the writings of Kierkegaard and Nietzsche, the first existentialist philosophers. It was after taking on Pascal's projects that Kierkegaard and Nietzsche were led to the view that lies at the heart of existentialism.

While analyzing the psychology of self-deception, each was struck by the facility with which people change their fundamental values, commitments, and beliefs when such changes appear to help them avoid suffering. And while attempting to uncover the true nature of human existence, each was struck by the fact that our conception of human nature and our identities vary depending on our fundamental values, commitments, and beliefs. Already these observations suggested something Pascal did not see: human nature and individual identities are to some extent matters we freely decide for ourselves.

Further lines of thought reinforced the suggestion that much about the nature of people is determined by our free choice. These lines of thought were outgrowths of the work of Immanuel Kant, who himself was influenced by David Hume, an eighteenth-century Scotsman.

Hume had demolished the ordinary conception of the self, demoted reason from master to servant of the passions, and reduced knowledge to mere belief caused by the observation of repeated patterns. Moreover, Hume had offered the most persuasive argument yet that the real nature of the world and of the self are beyond our ken. In response to Hume, Kant maintained that the world of things *as they are in themselves* is not knowable, but we can know the world and the self *as they inevitably will appear* (as phenomena) because "the mind" is active in giving them the shape they take. Is Kant's idea that the mind shapes the world and the self a subjectivist view, according to which the features of the world depend on minds, or an objectivist view, according to which the features of the world are independent of minds? The answer is that Kant's "Copernican revolution" blurred the line between subjective and objective accounts of the world. It is possible to argue that Kant's revolutionary idea is consistent with both subjectivist and objectivist accounts of the world. The perceivable world can be viewed subjectively, as mind-dependent, because the mind is indeed active in ordering the experienced world. Nonetheless, the world can be viewed objectively, given the specific way in which it is shaped by the mind: The mind orders experience along causal, spatial, and temporal lines, and the world one individual perceives is structured in the same ways as the world another individual perceives. Hence, the perceivable or phenomenal world presents itself to each individual as a spatio-temporal manifold of causally interacting objects. The world the mind shapes is a uniform causal order, and it is the same causal order for each of us—in this sense "mind" shapes an "objective" world.

Not long after Kant introduced his revolutionary idea, others began to modify it to support further subjectivist ideas. From Kantianism short steps led first to the view that individual minds shape individual worlds-as-they-appear-to-the-individual and then to the view that the world and the human being could be shaped, interpreted, and assigned significance or value in multiple ways that vary from person to person. Moreover, none of these individual perspectives is rationally defensible against the others. These ideas suggested to some existentialist thinkers that not just human nature but all of nature is malleable in a way that is entirely inconsistent with the classical objectivist view that facts and values are determined by features of the world itself, not shaped by minds and human interests.

Nietzsche and Kierkegaard were familiar with the work of Hume and Kant, but neither unequivocally accepted the view we just sketched in all its subjectivist radicalness. From the start both Nietzsche and Kierkegaard were committed to uncovering the truth about human beings, a commitment that carried a powerful realist presumption, although this presumption was undermined more and more as each explored ways in which human reality is a human creation. Later phenomenalist existentialists emphasized the malleability of the natural world far more than did Nietzsche or Kierkegaard. Nietzsche and Kierkegaard both held that there are dimensions of persons that cannot be altered by individuals. Kierkegaard claimed, for example, that our dependence upon God is an inescapable element of our identities, and Nietzsche suggested that human beings have in-built motivations with which we must identify and for which we must find outlets or else they will find their own outlets and influence our lives in ways we do not control. These essential dimensions simply must be accepted if we are to affirm our existence. Nonetheless, both Kierkegaard and Nietzsche found themselves inclined to think that human nature and the identities of people are malleable, and later existentialists cultivated the seeds of this radical view. The human being, it turns out, is largely free to create the human being. Largely, people are freely self-creating beings—here, finally, is the insight that is most characteristic of existentialism, an insight absent from the writings of Pascal. By contrast, the idea that the entire natural world is largely shaped by the human mind is the central idea of phenomenalism, a philosophical approach initiated in the early twentieth century by Edmund Husserl that developed alongside of, and merged with, twentieth-century existential thought.

That existentialism as a philosophy is centered around the view that we are freely self-creating beings can be confirmed by the influential definition of "existentialism" given by Jean-Paul Sartre. According to Sartre, existentialism is the doctrine that our existence precedes our essence. It is the view that we are alive long before we acquire an essence. Now, to say that something has an essence is to say that it has a definitive attribute or a feature that makes it the kind of thing it is. In the case of a human being, our essence would be the attributes by virtue of which we are human beings. However, it is the existentialist's view that each of us freely defines human nature; we decide what our essence is.

EXISTENCE

After the introduction of the idea that people are largely freely self-creating, existentialist writers led by Martin Heidegger drew on the work of Husserl in order to give the term "existence" an entirely new meaning. The notion of existence has varied over the years. Throughout much of Western history, people have been influenced by the neo-Platonic idea that some things are more real than others, starting with God, who has the greatest degree of reality of all. Famously, this spectrum is described by Arthur Lovejoy as "the great chain of being." But twentieth-century readers are unlikely to think of being in this grandiose way. For most of us, to be is to be an object or an attribute of an object, so that everything that is real has one of these two familiar kinds of reality.

But the existentialists argue that this modern view is an oversimplification. They attempt to carve out a sense in which human existence is unlike that of other items in the world. Existentialists remind us that most things in the world are not free. Most things are incapable of choice and hence incapable of choosing their essential attributes. Such things are passive with respect to their defining attributes, and they exist by default—they exist so long as nothing outside of them deprives them of their essential attributes. Some things have an essence before they exist. For example, tools are designed so as to play some preconceived role, and that role is their essence. Thus, a knife's essential attribute is the capacity to cut, and it exists just so long as that attribute remains intact. Break a knife into small pieces, or melt it down, and the knife ceases to exist. But human beings, according to existentialists, are permanently capable of deciding, at least in part, what constitutes the nature of a human being; that is, which attributes are definitively important for being a human being. And this permanent capacity is so basic to humanity that we should mark it off by saying that people exist in a different sense than other sorts of beings. The definitively important attribute of humanity is our freedom largely to decide what shall be the definitively important attribute of humanity.

Consider an application of this conception of human existence. Suppose we say, as some of the existentialists urge us to, that human beings are creatures with individual identities, that having an individual identity or self is what is definitively important if we are to be a human being. In that case we will say that to exist as a human being is to exist as an individual self, and we will understand the nature of human existence in terms of the existence of the individual self. Our attention will then turn to the concept of the self; to analyze human existence any further, we must grapple with identity.

Now, when existentialist writers such as Kierkegaard and Jean-Paul Sartre examine the nature of the self, they come to a conclusion that might surprise the modern reader. According to Kierkegaard and Sartre, our identities are something we must construct. Different existentialist writers say different things about how this construction works, but most existentialists agree that a being who fails to construct an identity may be alive, but does not exist as a self. Unlike most things, an individual self does not exist by default; indeed, the default would be *not* to exist as an individual self. To exist as an individual self requires an effort: the effort of constructing an identity and freely reaffirming it over time.

Notice what happens when we add this view of the self to the conception of human existence as we are attempting to understand it, namely, as having an identity, or being someone. According to this view, we do not exist unless we are individuals. So far as human existence is concerned, unless we are someone, we simply are not there.

Let us immediately add that some of us might have a different view about being human. Perhaps something other than being someone is definitively important if we are to be a human being. Various views are possible. Consider just one alternative. If we live in a community that provides clearly specified social roles, we might take playing our appointed role, and thus participating in the group, as what makes us human. If we take this collectivist attitude, then we will understand human existence in terms of participating in the community rather than as being an individual, and our conception of existence will be radically opposed to the conception of existence as being an individual. In fact, using the collectivist approach, those who attempt to separate themselves from the community and cultivate individuality are trying to end their existence. Anyone who succeeds in becoming a separate individual simply *would not be there.*

Having noticed that many views of human existence are possible, the existentialists speak of the alternatives as individually possible (but mutually exclusive) modes of human existence. Thus, for example, while the collectivist's view is incompatible with the individualist's stance, both define possible modes of human existence. However, the fact that a mode of existence is possible does not entail that it is desirable, and some of the existentialists, such as Kierkegaard and Nietzsche, are deeply critical of some modes of existence. Others, such as Martin Heidegger, are officially neutral on the relative value of competing modes of existence. But all of the existentialists emphasize two things about making a conscious, individual decision about our mode of existence: we are permanently free to make this decision and permanently responsible for doing so.

ANGST, ABSURDITY, AND AUTHENTICITY

In saying that we are responsible for deciding what is definitively important in human existence, the existentialists mean to emphasize that whatever our view about what is important it is we who choose to adopt that view. We are the cause of our own decision, and however we decide, we are free to choose differently. But this is not all existentialists have in mind. They mean to say that it is important for us to embrace our distinctive form of being, to self-consciously choose for ourselves what is definitively important in human existence, and to live accordingly. They mean to condemn those who refuse to face the decision, and even Heidegger says that unless we make a conscious, individual choice as to our mode of existence, our existence will be "inauthentic."

The existentialists go out of their way to condemn the inauthentic way of life for much the same reason that Pascal condemned the life lost in diversion: When we live inauthentically, we fail to make our lives our own. Like Pascal, the existentialists also say that an inauthentic existence is likely to result from fleeing anxiety. But what did Pascal and the existentialists think we are so anxious about? What are we ignoring so intently that we end up ignoring the fact that we exist?

As I have said, Pascal himself had already pointed out features of the human situation that lead people away from life because they refuse to notice them. These features include our mortality and the transience of human affairs. They also include the apparent insignificance and meaninglessness of life as viewed from the objective, impersonal perspective reached by abstracting away from the subjective, personal point of view. Like Pascal, the existentialists believe that these aspects of life cause *Angst,* or anxiety, which we escape ultimately by escaping life. And they want to show that even these aspects of life can be dealt with in an honest way that is consistent with affirming our existence. But existentialists also think that the challenges identified by Pascal are not our only sources of anxiety. Our very nature as self-creating beings is also a source of *Angst,* and hence, something people refuse to notice. This anxiety, too, must be assimilated if we are to affirm life. But why is our own nature so alarming?

To say that we are by nature freely self-defining is to say that we are permanently confronted with the decision as to what shall be definitively important in human existence and in our own lives in particular. But this decision is like no other we face, for it cannot be grounded. Normally decisions are made on the basis of assumptions and values we take for granted. When I decide to write a paragraph, for example, my decision comes in the context of ongoing projects whose importance I take for granted. Having assumed that it is important to work out the implications of my mortality, I decide to put together a book about existentialism, and in the midst of putting together that book, I decide to write a paragraph. Each decision provides a sensible rationale for the next. But my decision as to what shall be definitively important in human existence is not like these derivative ones. It is the decision that establishes the context for all other decisions. In making it, I freely decide what finally is important, and then other decisions can fall into place.

The decision is made especially difficult if we follow most of the existentialists and say that there are no such things as objective values and that there are only values we create ourselves by freely deciding what finally we shall regard as important. If objective values do not exist, my decision cannot be based on them, and then the decision can rest on nothing. In that sense it must be arbitrary. If our most basic, life-guiding

decision is arbitrary, then it can be hard to resist saying that our lives are absurd or ultimately senseless: they are the result of a complex web of decisions that ultimately rest on nothing. This encounter with the absurd causes us anxiety, according to the existentialists.

Another daunting aspect of human existence results from the facts that (1) we are permanently free to change our decisions and that (2) our identities are inextricably bound up with these decisions. If who we are is determined by what we take to be important, and we are permanently free to change our minds about the latter, then our very existence as individuals is insecure. Being who we are is not only something we must decide for ourselves, but also something we must continuously reaffirm, or else we cease to be. It is anguishing to know that our freedom is so far-reaching as to leave our existence permanently unsettled in this way.

It is sometimes said that the existentialists are a morbid bunch, dwelling as they do on such themes as death, despair, anxiety, anguish, nausea, dread, absurdity, meaninglessness, nothingness, and so on, while ignoring the majestic aspects of life. This criticism is misguided. Their ambition is to enable us to embrace our existence while honestly facing up to the entirety of the human situation no matter how disappointing it might seem initially. Life is full of grandeur and mystery, and the existentialists know this well, but it is not the uplifting aspects of life that make it difficult to affirm. If the existentialists are correct, most people lose their grip on life long before they appreciate its splendor; they do so because they are determined to ignore what seems negative. The seemingly rosy advice "always look at the bright side of life" conceals the unstated judgment that it is too dangerous to look at the dark side, for if we do we will be horrified; and when we recall that life has the one side as fully as it has the other, we risk having to conclude that life in all of its shades, bright and dark, is not worth having.

NOTES

1. Søren Kierkegaard, *The Journals,* trans. Alexander Dru (Oxford: Oxford University Press, 1938), 15.
2. Blaise Pascal, *Pensées,* trans. W. F. Trotter (New York: E. P. Dutton & Co., Inc., 1958), sec. 139, 39.
3. Ibid., sec. 194, 55.

FURTHER READINGS

Introductory Works on Existentialism

Barrett, William. *Irrational Man: A Study in Existential Philosophy.* New York: Doubleday Anchor Books, 1962.

Blackham, J. J. *Six Existentialist Thinkers.* London: Routledge & Kegan Paul, 1952.

Cooper, David. *Existentialism: A Reconstruction.* Oxford: Blackwell, 1991.

Macquarrie, John. *Existentialism.* London: Penguin Books, 1973.

Olafson, Frederick. *Principles and Persons: An Ethical Interpretation of Existentialism.* Baltimore, Md.: Johns Hopkins University Press, 1967.

Solomon, Robert. *From Rationalism to Existentialism.* Lanham: University Press of America, 1985.

Warnock, Mary. *Existentialism.* Oxford: Oxford University Press, 1970.

Contemporary Analytic Work on Existentialist Themes

ON DEATH

Fischer, J. M., ed. *The Metaphysics of Death.* Stanford: Stanford University Press, 1993.

Nagel, Thomas. "Death." In *Mortal Questions.* Cambridge: Cambridge University Press, 1979.

FREEDOM OF THE WILL

Frankfurt, Harry. *The Importance of What We Care About.* Cambridge: Cambridge University Press, 1988.

Watson, Gary. *Free Will.* Oxford: Oxford University Press, 1982.

ON SELF-DECEPTION

Fingarette, Herbert. *Self-Deception.* London: Routledge & Kegan Paul, 1969.

Haight, M. R. *A Study of Self-Deception.* Brighton: Harvester, 1980.

ON SELF-CREATION

Dennett, Daniel. "Self-Made Selves." In *Elbow Room.* Cambridge: MIT Press, 1984.

ON CONTINGENCY AND ABSURDITY

Nagel, Thomas. "Birth, Death, and the Meaning of Life." In *The View from Nowhere.* New York: Oxford University Press, 1986.

CHAPTER 2

Søren Kierkegaard (1813–1855)

The Danish philosopher Søren Aabye Kierkegaard was the last child of a successful businessman named Michael Kierkegaard. Only two of Michael Kierkegaard's seven children survived, and one of them—Søren—was born with a hunchback. Although Michael Kierkegaard was a devout Lutheran, he believed that he and his family were cursed by God, perhaps as a result of an incident reported by his son: "as a small boy tending sheep on the Jutland heath, suffering many ills, famished and exhausted [he] stood up on a hill and cursed God! And that man was never able to forget it, not even at the age of 82."[1] Kierkegaard took his father's idea seriously, saying, "I suspected that my father's ripe old age was not a divine blessing, but rather a curse; . . . in my father I saw a doomed man destined to survive us all. . . ."[2] But the idea was proven false when his father died in 1838, well before his two sons. Kierkegaard was led to "regard his death as the last sacrifice he made to his love for me, for he died . . . in order that perhaps something might still come of me."[3] Under the force of this conviction, Kierkegaard began an immense intellectual effort. His formerly desultory academic studies were focused and renewed; he was awarded a degree in theology in 1840 and went on to write and publish an impressive amount of work. Many of these works were published under various pseudonyms, such as "Johannes de Silentio," "Frater Taciturnus," and "Anti-Climacus." Also in 1840 Kierkegaard became engaged to Regine Olsen, only to break off the engagement about a year later. Kierkegaard described the episode in a passage in his *Diary:*

I asked for an appointment and received it for the afternoon of September 10. I have not uttered a single word to beguile her—her answer was yes.

Instantly I initiated relations with the entire family. . . . But inwardly . . . ! the second day I saw that I had made a mistake. A person like myself, doing penance, my [former way of life], my melancholy . . . that was all it took.

I suffered indescribably during that time.

If I had not been a penitent . . . , then the bond with her would have made me as happy as I could never hitherto have dreamed of becoming. . . . But as I understood it, there was a divine protest against our union. . . . To step out of the relationship as a cad, perhaps as an arch-cad, was the only thing to do; . . . but at the same time it was exquisite chivalry. . . . *A Seducer's Diary* was written for her sake, to help push her boat from ashore.[4]

Kierkegaard alludes to his painful break with Olsen time and again both in his private journal and in his published writings, which include passages that were meant to be read by her.

Kierkegaard is considered the father of existentialism, and for good reason: He pursued virtually every existentialist theme, and often his treatments of the subject were the best. A useful way to begin study of Kierkegaard's wide-ranging writings is to read Pascal, who anticipated Kierkegaard's style of philosophizing, and then Hegel, against whom Kierkegaard reacted. Selections from both of these writers are provided in this chapter.*

I already discussed Pascal's relevance to existentialism in the general introduction to the book. Pascal argued in his *Pensées* that our fear of facing tragic

---

*The reader might also wish to examine selections by Fyodor Dostoevsky, a Russian who pursues some of the themes of religious existentialism.

aspects of life leads us to divert ourselves from the whole question of life's value, and we end up unable to embrace life. Pascal's suggestion is expanded upon by Kierkegaard and later existentialists. The relevance of Hegel for Kierkegaard will require a more extensive discussion, to which we turn next.

THE HEGELIAN BACKGROUND

Like the other great rationalists, such as René Descartes (1596–1650), Benedict Spinoza (1632–1677), and G. W. Leibniz (1646–1716), the German philosopher G. W. F. Hegel (1770–1831) maintained that the world is entirely intelligible or rational and that its nature is, in principle, knowable. He arrived at his view by modifying Immanuel Kant's (1724–1804) conception of the mind.

Kant had initiated a "Copernican revolution" in response to David Hume's (1711–1776) skepticism concerning our knowledge of the external world. The revolution consisted in rejecting Hume's view of knowledge, according to which the mind is passive in experience, and replacing it with the view that the mind is active in experience. If our beliefs about the world are based on the study of images passively received through experience, then doubt about the accuracy of those images leads to doubt about the accuracy of beliefs based on them—such is the heart of Hume's skepticism. According to Kant's revolutionary idea, we may know that various things must be true of the experienced world because the mind itself shapes the world as it is experienced. While the "noumenal" world—the world of things as they are in themselves—is forever shut away from the knowing subject, knowledge is possible because forms and categories supplied by the mind are constitutive of the phenomenal world, the world as it appears to us. Thus, sensibility or the capacity for sensation is possible because the forms of sensibility—namely, space and time—are imposed by the mind. And understanding or the capacity to make judgments about the experienced world is possible because the mind imposes concepts (such as substance, causality, and unity) in the course of generating experience. Kant had also said that pure reason or the capacity to draw inferences generates certain ideas—freedom, God, and immortality—that are merely regulative in the sense that they guide human conduct but are not constitutive of the experienced world.

Like Kant, Hegel did not want to accept Hume's skepticism about the possibility of knowledge, and Hegel thought that Kant's way of dealing with skepticism was basically correct: knowledge is possible because the mind actively structures the world we experience. Hegel's main innovation was a modification of Kantianism: the ideas of pure reason as well as the categories are constitutive of the world.

Even the consciousness that experiences the world is a possible subject of knowledge, according to Hegel, but our knowledge of this consciousness is limited to what we can infer on the basis of contrasting consciousness with what it is not. To see how this contrastive knowledge works, consider a typical experience. When I experience the keyboard on which I am typing, I experience it as *not me*. But in this experience is an awareness of consciousness, an awareness captured in the fact that the keyboard, and everything else I am conscious of, is *other* than consciousness. Thus, my knowledge of consciousness is my knowledge of an element in experience other than the object experienced. Nonetheless, according to Hegel, consciousness and the objects of consciousness are inseparable, for objects are accessible only to consciousness, and consciousness is detectable only as that which is other than objects.

Because the world is shaped by mental operations, and those mental operations constitute a rational thought process, the world itself is rational. However, when Hegel says that the world is rational, he does not mean to say that the world as it is at a particular moment of time is rational. Unlike Kant, Hegel did not view the mind as static, as shaping the world all at once and once and for all. The mind's shaping process is developmental, and the world is a world that is unfolding. In fact, at particular points in time the world includes features that clash with each other in the sense that it is impossible to form an intelligible conception of the way those features all fit together. Some of the features are "opposites" of others. However, even these features of the world are intelligible in the context of what precedes them and what follows them. The world is becoming, and it is the world of becoming that is wholly intelligible.

Moreover, there is a way in which the world may develop so that even at a particular time it forms an intelligible whole, and a process is under way that will bring about this harmony. Guiding that development is an underlying mental or spiritual process that strives to become aware of the way the world must be developed so as to be fully rationally coherent, and that progressively actualizes this ideal world. The world's development is the expression of this underlying rational thought process. Eventually the process will produce an awareness of a fully rational interpretation of the world, and the world, in turn, will take shape as a fully intelligible whole. At that point it will be clear that "what is rational is actual and what is actual is rational," as Hegel said in the preface to his *Philosophy of Right*.

In constructing its fully rational vision, the world's guiding thought process always emphasizes the universal over the particular, and the group over the individual, for coherence at these highest levels of abstraction ensures coherence throughout the vision. Individuals are important only insofar as they are instances of universals or members of groups who conform to the group order, and therefore ought to identify as much as possible with the universal (humanity) and the group (their nation, community, family). Moreover, according to Hegel's ethics of *Sittlichkeit*, our moral duties are derived from our group's order. So that the nation, community, and family may take their distinctive shapes, individuals must play certain roles, such as that of parent, legislator, and so on. Individuals meet their moral responsibilities by playing these roles.

Hegel associated the underlying rational thought process and its concrete expression with human beings and the social orders they fashion. As human beings develop a more rational vision of themselves and the world, they become more conscious, and they order their communities and states in a more rational way. Hegel also associated the thought process with something that he variously called 'Geist' or the 'Absolute' or 'God.' In some sense, he thought, our improving consciousness of ourselves and the world order constituted *Geist*'s improving consciousness.

People—and through us *Geist*—increase their consciousness through something Hegel calls the dialectical process. We begin by focusing on some particular and attempting to understand it. Invariably our interpretation proves to be incomplete or otherwise inadequate because our interpretation is overly narrow and not couched in concepts of universal scope. But in the process of discovering the weak-

nesses of our interpretation, we generate a less limited alternative. The alternative itself will have its weaknesses, however, and the dialectical process will cycle through again and again, always producing a more encompassing interpretation with which to inform consciousness.

Through the dialectical process human beings and *Geist* are also developing an interpretation of ourselves and the world order. Eventually, Hegel assumes, *Geist* will arrive at an interpretation that is fully coherent. For the first time *Geist* will be completely conscious, and its interpretation will correctly express its nature. Insofar as *Geist* is defined as a consciousness that is entirely lucid to itself, it will not fully exist until it is fully aware of itself. As Hegel puts it, it will not have fully 'actualized' itself until it creates a final interpretation that then expresses the truth about itself. Notoriously Hegel supposed that *Geist* had arrived at full knowledge of itself through the medium of Hegel's own philosophy.

Kierkegaard believed that Hegel's rationalism was at odds with Christianity. In Hegel's view Christianity had expressed important insights into the nature of the world but had done so in mythical terms that Hegel's philosophy would surpass and correct. The improved form of Christianity would not be a matter of pure faith, inasmuch as Hegel's system was rationally defensible. But Kierkegaard emphasized aspects of the Christian view that suggest that God and the world are entirely beyond the grasp of human beings. Hence, some of the most important truths must simply be accepted on faith. Moreover, an objective conception of the world, like Hegel's, will ignore individuals and their relationship to God: From the objective view, subjective matters have little importance, and individuals have little importance because the facts about individuals are subjective facts. From the subjective point of view, however, it is the objective that has little importance, as Kierkegaard urges.

Hegel's suggestion that individuals participate in the identity of God conflicts with traditional Christianity, and Kierkegaard criticized him on this point as well. Hegel was aware of his departure, however. In fact, in his *Phenomenology of Spirit* Hegel criticized Christianity for creating an "unhappy consciousness" by supposing that God exists in a supernatural realm that is entirely separate from humanity. In so doing, Christianity separates people from an essential aspect of their own nature, for God's spiritual qualities are really the spiritual qualities of people. In identifying these qualities with God, and locating God in the beyond, Christianity encourages us to think that our spiritual potential cannot be developed in the material world in which we live and is not part of who we are. In this sense we are alienated from our own spirituality.

I have offered this brief examination of Hegel's views because Kierkegaard can be better understood when we see the sort of philosophy he rejected. Now it is time to turn our attention to a positive characterization of Kierkegaard's philosophy. To that end I will begin with the point that he was drawn into existentialism out of concerns that were closely related to those of his predecessor Pascal. Kierkegaard suggested that many of the strategies that people use to make themselves happy backfire, and those people end up in despair, in not really wanting to exist. Kierkegaard wished to clarify these strategies and show how they backfire. He also wanted to clarify the nature of existence, for like later existentialists, he came to think that a fully human form of existence involved self-creation. Finally, Kierkegaard wanted to describe how Christianity, properly understood, enables us to avoid despair. People in despair do not embrace their existence, but through Christianity people are able to overcome despair. As he says near the beginning of *The Sickness Unto Death*:

> Is despair an excellence or a defect? Purely dialectically, it is both. . . . The possibility of this sickness is man's superiority over the animal; to be aware of this sickness is the Christian's superiority over the natural man; to be cured of this sickness is the Christian's blessedness.[5]

HAPPINESS AND MISFORTUNE

To see how despair can result from the attempt to make ourselves happy, consider the fact that if something is important to you, it can give you a reason to live. But it might also give you a reason not to want to exist. Let us consider these points in turn.

Suppose that you care deeply about the child you are raising or that you have an intense desire to fashion a particular form of sculpture. You must remain in existence in order to satisfy these desires; existing is a necessary condition for satisfying them. So, be-

cause you want to satisfy the desires, you will want to remain in existence. In this sense satisfying the desires constitutes a reason to live.

Not all desires can function in this way. The desires that the sun continues to shine and that God exists are desires you can do nothing to satisfy. In no way does their satisfaction depend on your existence. Therefore, such desires will not supply you a reason to live. By contrast, desires whose satisfaction depend on your existence supply a reason for you to live that is as powerful as the importance you attribute to satisfying the desire.

If something is important to you, it can also set you up for misfortune; for it is a misfortune to be unable to do or have what you take to be important. It will be tragic to lose a beloved child or to fail in an ambition that you take to be your life's work. The thwarting of a desire that is important to you is a misfortune, and if the thwarted desire is a desire whose satisfaction depends on your existence, the misfortune will be compounded, for you will have lost one of your reasons to live.

Needless to say, suffering a misfortune is a grave matter. If we can avoid tragic loss, we will want to do so. But is it possible to arrange to go through life entirely unscathed? Many people seem to think so. Some think that we can avoid tragic loss by eliminating conditions that make tragedy possible. Assuming that the possibility of tragedy can be linked to not getting what is important to us, we are faced with two main options. First, we might adjust what we care about so that, whatever happens, no desires that are important to us will be thwarted. Second, we can attempt to secure sufficient power over the world to ensure that we will always get what is important to us.

In order to implement the first strategy, we might sort through our scheme of desires and either eliminate all desires whose satisfaction we cannot ensure or at least stop regarding the satisfaction of such vulnerable desires as important. If in this way we can adapt our scheme of desires to ensure that all desires that are important to us will be satisfied, it seems we will have placed ourselves out of the reach of misfortune.

However, it is crucial to see how few desires would be left if we limited ourselves to desires whose satisfaction we could ensure. Anytime the satisfaction of a desire requires that we take action, our desire is at risk for we cannot be sure that our actions will succeed. For example, despite our best efforts to ensure the well-being of our children, they might fall victim to a deadly accident or disease. A market crash or war might destroy our life's work. And virtually any desire we might have would be left unsatisfied if we were to die prematurely. Hence, adapting our desires to ensure the satisfaction of all those that are important to us will require a drastic step. If we are serious about placing ourselves out of the reach of misfortune by eliminating vulnerable desires, we will have to abandon all of those desires whose satisfaction requires that we exist. Yet these desires supply our reason to exist.

Our strategy for avoiding misfortune seems to have backfired. We wanted an approach to life that would free us from the possibility of misfortune. But our approach then deprived us of the very concerns that gave us a reason to live. In theory we might be able to drift through life caring only about things such as the sun's shining—things that we can do nothing about. But is life worth living if we do not even care whether we exist?

If applying our first strategy results in a life about whose continuation we are indifferent, perhaps we should abandon that strategy in favor of the second strategy I mentioned earlier: securing sufficient power over the world to ensure that our desires will be satisfied. If we are threatened by disease, we hire competent medical help; if threatened by thieves, we surround ourselves with protection, and so on.

Unfortunately the control people are able to exert over the world is limited, so much so that Kierkegaard will urge us to believe that it is negligible. Perhaps we can take steps that will make it less likely that we will suffer significant losses, and with luck we might succeed for long stretches of time. But given typical human concerns, ensuring that we will avoid tragic losses seems out of the question. As a way to eliminate the very possibility of misfortune, the second strategy will not succeed. Neither of our two strategies for insulating ourselves from the possibility of misfortune is acceptable.

That neither strategy is acceptable is one of Kierkegaard's themes. According to him, there is nothing people may do through their own efforts to insulate themselves from the possibility of misfortune, and if they try, their efforts will backfire. Kierkegaard illustrates approaches to life taken by people doubting that they will achieve what is important to them, and he tries to show that these approaches end up depriving people of a worthwhile life by depriving them of a reason to exist. He suggests that the victims of these approaches are in this sense in despair and are able to

persist in life only by deceiving themselves about what they are doing.

Like Pascal, Kierkegaard considered despair to be a grave matter. In the introduction to the *Concluding Unscientific Postscript*, he says that "it is not impossible that the individual who is infinitely interested in his own eternal happiness can some day become eternally happy; on the other hand it is certainly impossible that the person who has lost a sense for it . . . can become eternally happy." Achieving any real happiness, let alone eternal happiness, entails a passion for existing, so if we do not even want to live, we cannot be called happy.

DESPAIR

In *The Sickness Unto Death* Kierkegaard says that we are in despair when we fail to want to exist, and adds that despair is the worst fate that can befall a person: "to be in despair is not only the worst misfortune and misery—no, it is ruination. . . ."[6] Thus, despair is no ordinary setback. It might be brought on by a tragedy, but misery caused by losses or setbacks in life is not itself despair and need not result in despair. Suffering will bring us to despair only if it makes us fail to want to exist, for despair is precisely this failure.

Despair will occur when people actually desire that they not exist, but it might also occur in the absence of such a desire for it occurs whenever people lack the positive desire to exist. If I do not care whether I exist, then I do not desire not to exist, but I am in despair anyway for I fail to want to exist. Kierkegaard speaks of two main forms of despair: "to will to do away with oneself" and "in despair to will to be oneself." But he reduces the second of these to the first[7]: "the other form of despair, in despair to will to be oneself, can be traced back to the first." To see that the one reduces to the other, we must realize that it is misleading to say that people despairingly wish to be themselves. In fact, truly wishing to be or exist as ourselves "is the very opposite of despair. . . ." The despair Kierkegaard calls willing to be oneself is actually wishing to be someone (or something) whom we mistakenly take to be ourselves. Suppose that Brutus wishes to be Caesar so badly that he begins to think of himself as Caesar. It might be tempting for Brutus to say "I wish to be myself!" in order to express the desire to be Caesar. But, in fact, what his desire to be Caesar really means is that he does not desire to be or exist as himself. As Kierkegaard would say, "The self that he despairingly wants to be is a self that he is not. . . ."

Virtually everyone is to some extent in despair, according to Kierkegaard. But those who are in despair do not necessarily know it. Avoiding despair requires lucid knowledge of the nature of ourselves for without that knowledge we cannot want our true selves to exist. Yet people who are ignorant about themselves can also be ignorant about their ignorance. That ignorance, in turn, might help them to sustain a tranquil indifference about continuing to exist. Hence, they might be ignorant about their despair and not suffer from their ignorance. This unconscious despair is the most pernicious form, for becoming conscious of the fact that we fail to want to exist is the first step to consciously wanting to exist. Kierkegaard maintained that "[t]he person who without affection says that he is in despair is still a little closer . . . to being cured than all those who . . . do not regard themselves as being in despair."

According to Kierkegaard, we avoid despair when, and only when, we know our nature and we want to (continue to) exist. But might we not believe that everyone is mortal, and thus believe that our existence will not continue, even though we want it to? And shouldn't this be described as a case of despair? This is not ordinary Kierkegaardian despair because the desire to exist is intact. But Kierkegaard would say that it is indeed despair because it involves the mistaken belief that the self is mortal. The self or "spirit" has an immortal existence that depends upon the power of God, he says, and people must realize this if they are to truly know and value themselves. If people genuinely are immortal and dependent upon God, then they must acknowledge and affirm their immortality and dependence, or else they will be in despair.

THE SELF AND HUMAN EXISTENCE

Kierkegaard offers his most detailed characterization of the self in *The Sickness unto Death*. There he says that "the self is a relation that relates itself to itself or is the relation's relating itself to itself in the relation; the self is not the relation but is the relation's relating itself to itself." He goes on to add to this perplexing account, saying that human selves did not "establish" themselves, and their relationship to whoever (or

whatever) did establish them is also part of their identity. Because it is God who established us, our relationship to God is part of our identity.

When Kierkegaard says that selves relate themselves to themselves, he implies that selves freely choose to be reflexively self-aware. Reflexive awareness is the capacity to be aware of oneself and simultaneously to be aware of that very awareness. It is largely through reflexive self-awareness that selves relate to themselves. "Self-consciousness . . . is decisive with regard to the self." Hence, a failure in consciousness interferes with our being selves, and when we fail to choose to be reflexively self-aware, we are not selves in the fullest way. "The more consciousness, the more self; the more consciousness, the more will; the more will, the more self." [8]

Kierkegaard makes some points about the essential features of the self. The first point is just that there *are* essential features: If the self is changed in certain ways, it ceases to be the self. These features whose loss the self would not survive Kierkegaard calls "necessary" aspects of the self. Now, some of these necessary features of our identity are in our control while others are not; that is, it is up to us to make some features necessary to our identity, while other features just are necessary to our identity. Emphasizing our control over some of the necessary features of the self Kierkegaard says: "The self is . . . just as possible as it is necessary, for it is indeed itself, but it has the task of becoming itself." [9]

Consider some examples. One essential feature over which we have no control is that we are not entirely self-creating. Our existence was established by and is maintained by God. Our dependence on God is a permanent, ineradicable part of our identity. An essential feature that we can give to ourselves is a basic commitment or project. When we choose to make such a commitment so important to us that we define ourselves in terms of it, it is then essential to us. To fail in our commitment, or to abandon it, is to cease to be who we are. One of Kierkegaard's examples of a definitive commitment is a marriage. Human beings are free to take on such definitive projects and free to avoid them, but unless they do, they are not really selves, according to Kierkegaard, and a passionate, earnest pursuit of the things that life makes possible will be lost to them.

The Kierkegaardian self "has the task of becoming itself." Among other things, this task entails pursuing the project that we have chosen to take as essential to us. Largely by making progress toward the completion of our definitive project, we develop or "become ourselves," pulling the disparate events of our lives into a coherent, meaningful whole. But to fully become ourselves, we must also develop our self-awareness, including our awareness of what is entailed by our dependence on God.

According to Kierkegaard, we decide at least part of what it takes for us to continue to exist as selves by making decisions about how we must be related to future stages of our lives if we are to count as being the same self or person. In view of this uniquely human capacity to define ourselves, Kierkegaard sometimes speaks of the human *mode of existence.* He also speaks of three main "spheres" of existence—the esthetic, the ethical, and the religious—which differ in that the people involved relate to future stages of their lives in fundamentally distinct ways. That is, when the people in one sphere make a decision about what it takes to remain the same continuing, developing person, their decision is of a fundamentally different sort as compared to the decision made by people in another sphere. Let us consider these three spheres of existence.

THE ESTHETIC

In *Either/Or,* one of his early writings, Kierkegaard is especially concerned to expose the flawed nature of something he calls the *esthetic* approach to life. He suggests that a second approach, called the *ethical,* is superior to the esthetic, although in the final analysis the ethical approach, like the esthetic, leaves people in despair.

The esthetic approach is much like that of hedonists (such as the ancient Greek philosopher Epicurus), who assume that whatever causes them pleasure is good, that whatever causes them pain is bad, and that whatever causes them neither pleasure nor pain is a matter of indifference, and who then devote their lives to the pursuit of pleasurable experiences while risking as little pain as possible.

In "Rotation of Crops" Kierkegaard imagines the advice that would be given by an experienced practitioner of the esthetic way of life, and in "The Seducer's Diary" he describes how the esthetic way of life would work out in romantic encounters. At the initial stages, we are told, we must contend with the fact that pleasurable experiences tend to be short-lived, and the activity that first generates pleasure tends to generate far less pleasure when repeated. It may be thrilling to ride a bicycle the first few times you do it, but after a while it will become routine and far less pleasurable. Repeated often enough, it becomes boring, and boredom is an unpleasant experience. To achieve the pleasure you experienced 'the first time,' you will have to do something you have not done before. You must pursue novelty, and the pursuit of novelty precludes concerning yourself in any serious way with anything in particular, for each concern is apt to become stale. You must develop the hedonist's reserve: from the start hedonists who take an interest in some person or activity are prepared to turn to something else when that person or activity becomes boring. Prudent hedonists will even avoid experiences that are likely to be extraordinarily pleasant, for later they will be unable to achieve the same level of pleasure and will be tormented by the memory of their previous high. "From the beginning," Kierkegaard points out, "one curbs the enjoyment and does not hoist full sail on any decision; one indulges with a certain mistrust." Hence, determined hedonists will never develop true friendships or marriages, both of which entail a lasting commitment that is inconsistent with the hedonist's reserve. Because they are unwilling to make lasting commitments, they do not give themselves an identity.

Truly sophisticated hedonists will go a step further. They will cultivate the ability to control by their own willpower whether they are experiencing pleasure, and they will try to acquire the ability to select the things that will trigger the sensation of pleasure. With these abilities they can arbitrarily select certain features of their circumstances and simply *decide* that these features are pleasantly interesting, thus ensuring themselves a steady flow of pleasant experiences.

Kierkegaard is deeply critical of the esthetic approach to life. The strategy that sophisticated esthetes would pursue if they were able reveals in a perspicuous way the truth about all esthetes: they do not think that anything that is happening in the world around them has any importance in its own right. The only thing that stops them from being completely indifferent to what is going on around them is the fact that they must manipulate the world in order to control their mood. From their perspective it would be best if they could cut that last bond, freeing themselves from any need to manipulate the world, and under their own willpower sustain the pleasure that is really their only concern. At that point esthetes might *appear* to take the attitude that anything that happens is good and interesting. But that is not really their attitude. In fact, their view is that nothing aside from pleasure matters in the least.

They are in despair, whether they know it or not, for esthetes do not make the sort of commitment that would give them an identity, and they lack the desire to live (as B tells A early in "The Esthetic Validity of Marriage," which is a part of *Either/Or* that is not included in these readings). This latter fact can be brought out clearly if we recall that esthetes are indifferent about anything that causes them neither pleasure nor pain. As Epicurus pointed out, ceasing to exist is something that causes neither pleasure nor pain, for one must exist if one is to feel anything at all. Hence, the esthetic approach leads people to become indifferent about ceasing to exist, which entails becoming indifferent about existing.

THE ETHICAL AND RESIGNATION

Kierkegaard discusses the ethical sphere of existence in "The Esthetic Validity of Marriage," where he brings out some of the ways in which it is superior to the esthetic approach to life. But in "Becoming Subjective" there is a more revealing account of the ethical. There we learn that people are initiated into the ethical sphere when they come to realize how little power they have over the world outside of their own minds. Control over the "internal," over our beliefs, desires and intentions, is one thing, but control over the "external," over what happens when we attempt to act on our intentions or satisfy our desires, is quite another, and we are never in a position to think that we can control the latter. Say, for example, I intend to save a drowning man and decide to extend an oar out towards him. I might slip in the boat and end up knocking him on the head, thus ensuring the drowning I was attempting to avert.

In response to this knowledge of our impotence, we may form the conviction that we cannot bring about what we intend to, and even if things go as we planned, we cannot take credit for that coincidence. Kierkegaard calls the conviction that we have no control over the events that occur when we attempt to pursue our plans *resignation.* The resigned are said to *renounce* these events. They do not control them so they cannot take responsibility for them.

Some desires about the external will be completely nonsensical for resigned people. For example, if I am resigned, I will not desire to win the love of Regine, since I do not think that I can control external events, as would be required by the very nature of "winning" her love. But other desires concerning the external are not wholly nonsensical. For example, I might well desire that Regine love me, and I might well love her. This desire might lead me to wish that I had some power to influence her, but I will be convinced that nothing I can do will have any effect on her.

However, while allowing myself desires concerning the external is not always absurd, it *is* always imprudent, precisely because I believe that I can do nothing to satisfy them. Hence, there will be powerful rational (prudential) grounds for resigned people to cut loose entirely from the "external"—to cease caring about the "external." Simultaneously they are likely to embrace the "inner" with greater emphasis than before for they may still think that they have a good deal of control over their inner lives and can take responsibility for what they do with their inner lives. They are likely to enter the ethical sphere, which they do when they adopt the attitude that what is important is arranging the "inner" as it ought to be— that is, forming the desires, beliefs, and intentions they ought to form:

> A truly great ethical individuality would consummate his life as follows: he would develop himself to the utmost of his capacity; in the process he perhaps would produce a great effect in the external world, but this would not occupy him at all, because he would know that the external is not in his power and therefore means nothing either *pro* or *contra.*[10]

Notice that resigned people who are willing to resist the counsel of prudence might well hold onto desires concerning the "external" and refuse to enter completely into the ethical sphere. Suppose, once again, that I desire the love of Regine, which I might do even though I do not believe that I can win her love. Then my desire for her love precludes my complete immersion into the ethical sphere. The knights of resignation whom Kierkegaard discusses in *Fear and Trembling* are in precisely this situation. As *knights* of resignation, they are not wedded to acting prudently and persist in their commitments to the external even though doing so brings them pain. Knights of resignation refuse to cross over to the ethical stage for they have not ceased to care about all matters external. Concerning such a knight who desires someone, Kierkegaard writes that "there may be someone who found it quite convenient that the desire was no longer alive and that the arrow of his pain had grown dull, but such a person is no knight." Such knights are melancholy for while they have a strong desire, they believe that they may do nothing to satisfy it. Nonetheless, they have a degree of peaceful self-sufficiency because they have no expectations about the "external," and since they may take solace in meeting "inner" demands.

While resigned people might be tempted to enter entirely into the ethical sphere, they find that they cannot. The problem is that they are entirely unable to live up to the ethical ideal; they cannot form the intentions they ought to form. They can meet some "inner" demands, but fall far short of meeting them all. According to Kierkegaard, this inability to will what we ought to will cannot be overcome; it is an inherent flaw in human nature, which he signals with the term "sinfulness."

Because we cannot live up to the ethical ideal, we are unable to embrace an existence in which our defining project is being ethical. Such an existence is beyond us, and those who tell themselves that they are in the ethical form of existence are in despair.

RELIGIOUSNESS A AND THE TELEOLOGICAL SUSPENSION OF THE ETHICAL

Resignation need not lead us to attempt to enter the ethical sphere. Nor need it cause us to drift through life like a knight of resignation. Another possibility, Kierkegaard suggests, is that resignation will initiate people into the religious sphere of existence, the generic form of which he calls religiousness A and the specifically Christian form of which he calls religiousness B.

Our powerlessness over both the "inner" and "external" precludes our making ourselves happy through our own efforts, but in the religious sphere we are able to confront our impotence yet resist the urge to simply stop caring about our existence. This is done by adopting the belief that God will give us eternal happiness and will do so even though we are inherently flawed; that is, God will not hold our

flawed nature against us and will ensure that we will have whatever is important for us to have. Thus, if the love of someone is fundamentally important to us (hence "essential" to us), as religious persons we will be convinced that God will find a way to ensure that we receive that love. Because of our conviction that God will intervene, we are able to take a fearless, passionate interest in things even while we realize that those things are not in our control. In all of these matters we will give God the credit, not ourselves.

This acknowledgement that in the final analysis we cannot take responsibility for our lives is at least part of what Kierkegaard has in mind when he says that "self-annihilation before God" is essential to religiousness. In emphasizing self-annihilation before God, Kierkegaard might also mean to refer to the claim that the highest priority of religious people must be pleasing God. If pleasing God takes priority over everything else, then it is even more important than meeting any commitment other than pleasing God that we might have taken to be essential to our identity. Therefore, to be Christian is to stand prepared to sacrifice our very identity in preference to doing God's will.

That people place their highest priority on pleasing God has another important consequence. It means that they must be willing to do anything that God requires, even if God requires conduct that is morally wrong. Kierkegaard emphasizes this point in *Fear and Trembling,* in which he discusses the Biblical story of Abraham and speaks of a "teleological suspension of the ethical." Abraham "suspended" his commitment to morality in order to please God, but what he intended to do was still murder from the standpoint of morality. Kierkegaard implies that all religious people must be prepared to follow Abraham's example.

RELIGIOUSNESS B, THE LEAP OF FAITH, AND TRUTH AS SUBJECTIVITY

In religiousness B our belief in God takes a specifically Christian form: We believe that God the eternal appeared in time, and that this historically situated being will give us eternal happiness. We adopt our belief through a "leap of faith," and we sustain our faith through a passionate interest in existing: "faith is the contradiction between the infinite passion of inwardness and the objective uncertainty."[11] On one side of the "contradiction" of faith is our passion for eternal happiness ("the infinite passion of inwardness"), which prompts us to believe that God will sustain us in our existence, and on the other side is our awareness that our belief in God is completely absurd ("the objective uncertainty"). Kierkegaard calls Christianity *paradoxical-religiousness* because he thinks that its dogma involves a contradiction that places Christianity entirely beyond comprehension and bases it on the absurd. The contradiction is that God (the infinite, the eternal) became finite (a human being) and existed in time.

But if Christianity is absurd, isn't Kierkegaard advocating an approach to life that involves self-deception? Since the avoidance of self-deception is a central concern of Kierkegaard's, this is a serious charge indeed. I must add that it is not entirely clear what Kierkegaard's response to the charge would be. There are at least two possibilities, which are not mutually exclusive.

At times he appears to think that his belief in God does not involve self-deception because he is fully aware that his belief flies in the face of reason. In *Fear and Trembling* he refers to the Christian as a knight of faith and says that "if [the knight of faith] wants to imagine that he has faith without passionately acknowledging the impossibility with his whole heart and soul, he is deceiving himself." Here and elsewhere he insists that it is no more reasonable to believe in the Christian God than it is to believe any other contradiction. Being Christian without realizing that Christianity is absurd would involve self-deception. But being Christian need not involve self-deception, Kierkegaard seems to think, for if Christians are fully aware that their belief is absurd, then they are not deceiving themselves.

To decide whether or not the charge of self-deception remains plausible, we would have to work out a clear account of self-deception. Not every false belief results from self-deception, of course. Some false beliefs are rational beliefs that are based on misleading evidence: we might think a claim is true on very good evidence when in fact it is false. And not every irrational belief results from self-deception: we might simply have made a mistake in the reasoning leading up to our belief. The question for Kierkegaard is this: Is it self-deception to assent to a belief when we know that it is irrational?

There is a second response to the charge of self-deception. At times Kierkegaard relies on the suggestion that adopting the Christian approach to life will ensure that Christianity is true in a subjective sense of 'true.' That is, if we adopt the Christian approach, we will experience life just as if Christianity were true, even if Christianity is objectively false. Thus, in "Subjective Truth, Inwardness; Truth Is Subjectivity," he offers the following claim:

> When the question about truth is asked subjectively, the individual's relation [to the truth] is reflected upon subjectively. If only the how of this relation is in truth, the individual is in truth, even if he in this way were to relate himself to untruth.

A bit later he adds:

> If someone objectively inquires into immortality, and someone else stakes the passion of the infinite on the uncertain—where, then, is there more truth, and who has more certainty? The one has once and for all entered upon an approximation that never ends . . . ; the other is immortal and therefore struggles by contending with the uncertainty.

The 'how' of Christianity is to unleash in ourselves the unrestricted desire for eternal happiness, a desire that can only be satisfied by people who have eternity at their disposal and who believe that God will give them that happiness. But people who in this sense have the "passion of the infinite" are already unreservedly helping themselves to life as immortals would; their subjective point of view is exactly the same as that of immortals—so long as they continue to exist. By contrast, those who refuse to live except in ways that are reasonable end up living like "slugs."

NOTES

1. Peter Rohde, ed., *The Diary of Søren Kierkegaard* (New York: Carol Publishing Group, 1990), entry 44, 33.
2. Ibid., entry 38, 30–31.
3. Ibid., entry 37, 30.
4. Ibid., entry 51, 37–38.
5. Søren Kierkegaard, "Despair Is the Sickness Unto Death" in *The Sickness Unto Death* (hereafter *Sickness*), trans. and ed. H. Hong and E. Hong (Princeton: Princeton University Press, 1980), part 1, sec. A,

14–15.

6. Ibid., part 1, sec. A, 15.
7. Ibid., part 1, sec. A.
8. Søren Kierkegaard, "The Forms of This Sickness," *Sickness*, 29.
9. Ibid., sec. A, 35.
10. Søren Kierkegaard, "Becoming Subjective" in *Concluding Unscientific Postscript to* Philosophical Fragments (hereafter *Postscript*), trans. and ed. H. Hong and E. Hong (Princeton: Princeton University Press, 1992), 135.
11. Søren Kierkegaard, "Subjective Truth, Inwardness; Truth Is Subjective" in *Postscript*, part 2, 204.

PRECURSORS

BLAISE PASCAL

 Pensées

139

Diversion.—When I have occasionally set myself to consider the different distractions of men, the pains and perils to which they expose themselves at court or in war, whence arise so many quarrels, passions, bold and often bad ventures, etc., I have discovered that all the unhappiness of men arises from one single fact, that they cannot stay quietly in their own chamber. A man who has enough to live on, if he knew how to stay with pleasure at home, would not leave it to go to sea or to besiege a town. A commission in the army would not be bought so dearly, but that it is found insufferable not to budge from the town; and men only seek conversion and entering games, because they cannot remain with pleasure at home.

But on further consideration, when, after finding the cause of all our ills, I have sought to discover the reason of it, I have found that there is one very real reason, namely, the natural poverty of our feeble and mortal condition, so miserable that nothing can comfort us when we think of it closely.

Whatever condition we picture to ourselves, if we muster all the good things which it is possible to possess, royalty is the finest position in the world. Yet, when we imagine a king attended with every pleasure he can feel, if he be without diversion, and be left to consider and reflect on what he is, this feeble happiness will not sustain him; he will necessarily fall into

forebodings of dangers, of revolutions which may happen, and, finally, of death and inevitable disease; so that if he be without what is called diversion, he is unhappy, and more unhappy than the least of his subjects who plays and diverts himself.

. . .

146

Man is obviously made to think. It is his whole dignity and his whole merit; and his whole duty is to think as he ought. Now, the order of thought is to begin with self, and with its Author and its end.

Now, of what does the world think? Never of this, but of dancing, playing the lute, singing, making verses, running at the ring, etc., fighting, making oneself king, without thinking what it is to be a king and what to be a man.

147

We do not content ourselves with the life we have in ourselves and in our own being; we desire to live an imaginary life in the mind of others, and for this purpose we endeavour to shine. We labour unceasingly to adorn and preserve this imaginary existence, and neglect the real. And if we possess calmness, or generosity, or truthfulness, we are eager to make it known, so as to attach these virtues to that imaginary existence. We would rather separate them from ourselves to join them to it; and we would willingly be cowards in order to acquire the reputation of being brave. A great proof of the nothingness of our being, not to be satisfied with the one without the other, and to renounce the one for the other! For he would be infamous who would not die to preserve his honour.

. . .

168

Diversion.—As men are not able to fight against death, misery, ignorance, they have taken it into their heads, in order to be happy, not to think of them at all.

169

Despite these miseries, man wishes to be happy, and only wishes to be happy, and cannot wish not to be so. But how will he set about it? To be happy he would have to make himself immortal; but, not being able to do so, it has occurred to him to prevent himself from thinking of death.

170

Diversion.—If man were happy, he would be the more so, the less he was diverted, like the Saints and Gods.—Yes; but is it not to be happy to have a faculty of being amused by diversion?—No; for that comes from elsewhere and from without, and thus is dependent, and therefore subject to be disturbed by a thousand accidents, which bring inevitable griefs.

171

Misery.—The only thing which consoles us for our miseries is diversion, and yet this is the greatest of our miseries. For it is this which principally hinders us from reflecting upon ourselves, and which makes us insensibly ruin ourselves. Without this we should be in a state of weariness, and this weariness would spur us to seek a more solid means of escaping from it. But diversion amuses us, and leads us unconsciously to death.

172

We do not rest satisfied with the present. We anticipate the future as too slow in coming, as if in order to hasten its course; or we recall the past, to stop its too rapid flight. So imprudent are we that we wander in the times which are not ours, and do not think of the only one which belongs to us; and so idle are we that we dream of those times which are no more, and thoughtlessly overlook that which alone exists. For the present is generally painful to us. We conceal it from our sight, because it troubles us; and if it be delightful to us, we regret to see it pass away. We try to sustain it by the future, and think of arranging matters which are not in our power, for a time which we have no certainty of reaching.

Let each one examine his thoughts, and he will find them all occupied with the past and the future. We scarcely ever think of the present; and if we think of it, it is only to take light from it to arrange the future. The present is never our end. The past and the present are our means; the future alone is our end. So we never live, but we hope to live; and, as we are always preparing to be happy, it is inevitable we should never be so.

. . .

190

To pity atheists who seek, for are they not unhappy enough? To inveigh against those who make a boast of it.

191

And will this one scoff at the other? Who ought to scoff? And yet, the latter does not scoff at the other, but pities him.

. . .

194

. . . Let them at least learn what is the religion they attack, before attacking it. If this religion boasted of having a clear view of God, and of possessing it open and unveiled, it would be attacking it to say that we see nothing in the world which shows it with this clearness. But since, on the contrary, it says that men are in darkness and estranged from God, that He has hidden Himself from their knowledge, that this is in fact the name which He gives Himself in the Scriptures, *Deus absconditus;* and finally, if it endeavours equally to establish these two things: that God has set up in the Church visible signs to make Himself known to those who should seek Him sincerely, and that He has nevertheless so disguised them that He will only be perceived by those who seek Him with all their heart; what advantage can they obtain, when, in the negligence with which they make profession of being in search of the truth, they cry out that nothing reveals it to them; and since that darkness in which they are, and with which they upbraid the Church, establishes only one of the things which she affirms, without touching the other, and, very far from destroying, proves her doctrine?

In order to attack it, they should have protested that they had made every effort to seek Him everywhere, and even in that which the Church proposes for their instruction, but without satisfaction. If they talked in this manner, they would in truth be attacking one of her pretensions. But I hope here to show that no reasonable person can speak thus, and I venture even to say that no one has ever done so. We know well enough how those who are of this mind behave. They believe they have made great efforts for their instruction, when they have spent a few hours in reading some book of Scripture, and have questioned some priest on the truths of the faith. After that, they boast of having made vain search in books and among men. But, verily, I will tell them what I have often said, that this negligence is insufferable. We are not here concerned with the trifling interests of some stranger, that we should treat it in this fashion; the matter concerns ourselves and our all.

The immortality of the soul is a matter which is of so great consequence to us, and which touches us so profoundly, that we must have lost all feeling to be indifferent as to knowing what it is. All our actions and thoughts must take such different courses, according as there are or are not eternal joys to hope for, that it is impossible to take one step with sense and judgment, unless we regulate our course by our view of this point which ought to be our ultimate end.

Thus our first interest and our first duty is to enlighten ourselves on this subject, whereon depends all our conduct. Therefore among those who do not believe, I make a vast difference between those who strive with all their power to inform themselves, and those who live without troubling or thinking about it.

I can have only compassion for those who sincerely bewail their doubt, who regard it as the greatest of misfortunes, and who, sparing no effort to escape it, make of this inquiry their principal and most serious occupations.

But as for those who pass their life without thinking of this ultimate end of life, and who, for this sole reason that they do not find within themselves the lights which convince them of it, neglect to seek them elsewhere, and to examine thoroughly whether this opinion is one of those which people receive with credulous simplicity, or one of those which, although obscure in themselves, have nevertheless a solid and immovable foundation, I look upon them in a manner quite different.

This carelessness in a matter which concerns themselves, their eternity, their all, moves me more to anger than pity; it astonishes and shocks me; it is to me monstrous. I do not say this out of the pious zeal of a spiritual devotion. I expect, on the contrary, that we ought to have this feeling from principles of human interest and self-love; for this we need only see what the least enlightened persons see.

We do not require great education of the mind to understand that here is no real and lasting satisfac-

tion; that our pleasures are only vanity; that our evils are infinite; and, lastly, that death, which threatens us every moment, must infallibly place us within a few years under the dreadful necessity of being for ever either annihilated or unhappy.

There is nothing more real than this, nothing more terrible. Be we as heroic as we like, that is the end which awaits the noblest life in the world. Let us reflect on this, and then say whether it is not beyond doubt that there is no good in this life but in the hope of another; that we are happy only in proportion as we draw near it; and that, as there are no more woes for those who have complete assurance of eternity, so there is no more happiness for those who have no insight into it.

Surely then it is a great evil thus to be in doubt, but it is at least an indispensable duty to seek when we are in such doubt; and thus the doubter who does not seek is altogether completely unhappy and completely wrong. And if besides this he is easy and content, professes to be so, and indeed boasts of it; if it is this state itself which is the subject of his joy and vanity, I have no words to describe so silly a creature.

How can people hold these opinions? What joy can we find in the expectation of nothing but hopeless misery? What reason for boasting that we are in impenetrable darkness? And how can it happen that the following argument occurs to a reasonable man?

"I know not who put me into the world, nor what the world is, nor what I myself am. I am in terrible ignorance of everything. I know not what my body is, nor my senses, nor my soul, not even that part of me which thinks what I say, which reflects on all and on itself, and knows itself no more than the rest. I see those frightful spaces of the universe which surround me, and I find myself tied to one corner of this vast expanse, without knowing why I am put in this place rather than in another, nor why the short time which is given me to live is assigned to me at this point rather than at another of the whole eternity which was before me or which shall come after me. I see nothing but infinites on all sides, which surround me as an atom, and as a shadow which endures only for an instant and returns no more. All I know is that I must soon die, but what I know least is this very death which I cannot escape.

"As I know not whence I come, so I know not whither I go. I know only that, in leaving this world, I fall for ever either into annihilation or into the hands of an angry God, without knowing to which of these two states I shall be for ever assigned. Such is my state, full of weakness and uncertainty. And from all this I conclude that I ought to spend all the days of my life without caring to inquire into what must happen to me. Perhaps I might find some solution to my doubts, but I will not take the trouble, nor take a step to seek it; and after treating with scorn those who are concerned with this care, I will go without foresight and without fear to try the great event, and let myself be led carelessly to death, uncertain of the eternity of my future state."

Who would desire to have for a friend a man who talks in this fashion? Who would choose him out from others to tell him of his affairs? Who would have recourse to him in affliction? And indeed to what use in life could one put him?

. . .

Nothing is so important to man as his own state, nothing is so formidable to him as eternity; and thus it is not natural that there should be men indifferent to the loss of their existence, and to the perils of everlasting suffering. They are quite different with regard to all other things.

. . .

G. W. F. HEGEL

Preliminary Notion and Sections 81 and 140, from Logic

19

Logic is the science of the pure Idea; pure, that is, because the Idea is in the abstract medium of Thought. . . .

It is universally agreed that thought is the object of Logic. But of thought our estimate may be very mean, or it may be very high. On one hand, people say: 'It is *only* a thought.' In their view thought is subjective, arbitrary and accidental—distinguished from the thing itself, from the true and the real. On the other hand, a very high estimate may be formed of thought;

when thought alone is held adequate to attain the highest of all things, the nature of God, of which the senses can tell us nothing. God is a spirit, it is said, and must be worshipped in spirit and in truth. But the merely felt and sensible, we admit, is not the spiritual; its heart of hearts is in thought; and only spirit can know spirit. . . . The world of spiritual existences, God himself, exists in proper truth, only in thought and as thought. If this be so, therefore, thought, far from being a mere thought, is the highest and, in strict accuracy, the sole mode of apprehending the eternal and absolute. . . .

. . . If the science of Logic then considers thought in its action and its productions (and thought being no resultless energy produces thoughts and the particular thought required), the theme of Logic is in general the supersensible world, and to deal with that theme is to dwell for a while in that world. Mathematics is concerned with the abstractions of time and space. But these are still the object of sense, although the sensible is abstract and idealized. Thought bids adieu even to this last and abstract sensible: it asserts its own native independence, renounces the field of the external and internal sense, and puts away the interests and inclinations of the individual. . . .

20

If we take our prima facie impression of thought, we find on examination first (a) that, in its usual subjective acceptation, thought is one out of many activities or faculties of the mind, co-ordinate with such others as sensation, perception, imagination, desire, volition, and the like. The product of this activity, the form or character peculiar to thought, is the UNIVERSAL, or, in general the abstract. Thought, regarded as an *activity*, may be accordingly described as the *active* universal, and, since the deed, its product, is the universal once more, may be called a self-actualizing universal. Thought conceived as a *subject* (agent) is a thinker, and the subject existing as a thinker is simply denoted by the term 'I'. . . .

. . . Now language is the work of thought: and hence all that is expressed in language must be universal. What I only mean or suppose is mine: it belongs to me—this particular individual. But language expresses nothing but universality; and so I cannot say what I merely *mean*. And the unutterable—feeling or sensation—far from being the highest truth, is the most unimportant and untrue. If I say 'the individual', 'this individual', 'here', 'now', all these are universal terms. Everything and anything is an individual, a 'this', and if it be sensible, is here and now. Similarly when I say 'I', I *mean* my single self to the exclusion of all others; but what I *say*, viz. 'I', is just every 'I', which in like manner excludes all others from itself. In an awkward expression which Kant used, he said that I *accompany* all my conceptions—sensations, too, desires, actions, etc. 'I' is in essence and act the universal: and such partnership is a form, though an external form, of universality. All other men have it in common with me to be 'I'; just as it is common to all my sensations and conceptions to be mine. But 'I', in the abstract, as such, is the mere act of self-concentration or self-relation, in which we make abstraction from all conception and feeling, from every state of mind and every peculiarity of nature, talent, and experience. To this extent, 'I' is the existence of a wholly *abstract* universality, a principle of abstract freedom. Hence thought, viewed as a subject, is what is expressed by the word 'I'; and since I am at the same time in all my sensations, conceptions, and states of consciousness, thought is everywhere present, and is a category that runs through all these modifications. . . .

21

Thought was described as active. We now, in the second place, consider this action in its bearings upon objects, or as reflection upon something. In this case the universal or product of its operation contains the value of the thing—is the essential, inward, and true.

. . .

23

The real nature of the object is brought to light in reflection; but it is no less true that this exertion of thought is *my* act. If this be so, the real nature is a *product* of *my* mind, in its character of thinking subject—generated by me in my simple universality, self-collected and removed from extraneous influences—in one word, in my Freedom.

'Think for yourself' is a phrase which people often use as if it had some special significance. The fact is, no man can think for another, any more than he can eat or drink for him and the expression is a pleonasm.

To think is in fact *ipso facto* to be free, for thought as the action of the universal is an abstract relating of self to self, where, being at home with ourselves, and as regards our subjectivity utterly blank, our consciousness is, in the matter of its contents, only in the fact and its characteristics. If this be admitted, and if we apply the term humility or modesty to an attitude where our subjectivity is not allowed to interfere by act or quality, it is easy to appreciate the question touching the humility or modesty and pride of philosophy. For in points of contents, thought is only true in proportion as it sinks itself in the facts; and in point of form it is no private or particular state or act of the subject, but rather that attitude of consciousness where the abstract self, freed from all the special limitations to which its ordinary states or qualities are liable, restricts itself to that universal action in which it is identical with all individuals. . . .

24

. . . Animal, *qua* animal, does not exist: it is merely the universal nature of the individual animals, while each existing animal is a more concretely defined and particularized thing. But to be an animal—the law of kind which is the universal in this case—is the property of the particular animal, and constitutes its definite essence. Take away from the dog its animality, and it becomes impossible to say what it is. All things have a permanent inward nature, as well as an outward existence. They live and die, arise and pass away; but their essential and universal part is the kind; and this means much more than something *common* to them all.

If thought is the constitutive substance of external things, it is also the universal substance of what is spiritual. In all human perception thought is present; so too thought is the universal in all the acts of conception and recollection; in short, in every mental activity, in willing, wishing, and the like. All these faculties are only further specializations of thought. When it is presented in this light, thought has a different part to play from what it has if we speak of a faculty of thought, one among a crowd of other faculties, such as perception, conception, and will, with which it stands on the same level. When it is seen to be the true universal of all that nature and mind contain, it extends its scope far beyond all these, and becomes the basis of everything. From this view of thought, in its objective meaning as νοῦς, we may next pass to consider the subjective sense of the term. We say first, Man is a being that thinks; but we also say at the same time, Man is a being that perceives and wills. Man is a thinker, and is universal; but he is a thinker only because he feels his own universality. The animal too is by implication universal, but the universal is not consciously felt by it to be universal: it feels only the individual. The animal sees a singular object, for instance, its food, or a man. For the animal all this never goes beyond an individual thing. Similarly, sensation has to do with nothing but singulars, such as *this* pain or *this* sweet taste. Nature does not bring its νοῦς into consciousness: it is man who first makes himself double so as to be a universal for a universal. This first happens when man knows that he is 'I'. By the term 'I' I mean myself, a single and altogether determinate person. And yet I really utter nothing peculiar to myself, for *every one* else is an 'I' or 'Ego', and when I call myself 'I', though I indubitably mean the single person myself, I express a thorough universal. 'I', therefore, is mere being-for-self, in which everything peculiar or marked is renounced and buried out of sight; it is as it were the ultimate and unanalysable point of consciousness. We may say 'I' and thought are the same, or, more definitely, 'I' is thought as a thinker. What I have in my consciousness is for me. 'I' is the vacuum or receptacle for anything and everything: for which everything is and which stores up everything in itself. Every man is a whole world of conceptions, that lie buried in the night of the 'Ego'. It follows that the 'Ego' is the universal in which we leave aside all that is particular, and in which at the same time all the particulars have a latent existence. In other words, it is not a mere universality and nothing more, but the universality which includes in it everything. . . .

· · ·

In common life truth means the agreement of an object with our conception of it. We thus presuppose an object to which our conception must conform. In the philosophical sense of the word, on the other hand, truth may be described, in general abstract terms, as the agreement of a thought-content with itself. This meaning is quite different from the one given above. At the same time the deeper and philo-

sophical meaning of truth can be partially traced even in the ordinary usage of language. Thus we speak of a true friend; by which we mean a friend whose manner of conduct accords with the notion of friendship. In the same way we speak of a true work of Art. Untrue in this sense means the same as bad, or self-discordant. In this sense a bad state is an untrue state; and evil and untruth may be said to consist in the contradiction subsisting between the function or notion and the existence of the object. Of such a bad object we may form a correct representation, but the import of such representation is inherently false. Of these correctnesses, which are at the same time untruths, we may have many in our heads. God alone is the thorough harmony of notion and reality. All finite things involve an untruth: they have a notion and an existence, but their existence does not meet the requirements of the notion. For this reason they must perish, and then the incompatibility between their notion and their existence becomes manifest. It is in the kind that the individual animal has its notion; and the kind liberates itself from this individuality by death.

· · ·

81

. . . It is of the highest importance to ascertain and understand rightly the nature of Dialectic. Wherever there is movement, wherever there is life, wherever anything is carried into effect in the actual world, there Dialectic is at work. It is also the soul of all knowledge which is truly scientific. In the popular way of looking at things, the refusal to be bound by the abstract deliverances of understanding appears as fairness, which, according to the proverb Live and let live, demands that each should have its turn; we admit the one, but we admit the other also. But when we look more closely, we find that the limitations of the finite do not merely come from without; that its own nature is the cause of its abrogation, and that by its own act it passes into its counterpart. We say, for instance, that man is mortal, and seem to think that the ground of his death is in external circumstances only; so that if this way of looking were correct, man would have two special properties, vitality and—also—mortality. But the true view of the matter is that life, as life, involves the germ of death, and that the finite, being radically self-contradictory, involves its own self-suppression.

.   .   .

. . . We are aware that everything finite, instead of being stable and ultimate, is rather changeable and transient; and this is exactly what we mean by that Dialectic of the finite, by which the finite, as implicitly other than what it is, is forced beyond its own immediate or natural being to turn suddenly into its opposite. We have before this identified Understanding with what is implied in the popular idea of the goodness of God; we may now remark of Dialectic, in the same objective signification, that its principle answers to the idea of his power. All things, we say—that is, the finite world as such—are doomed; and in saying so, we have a vision of Dialectic as the universal and irresistible power before which nothing can stay, however secure and stable it may deem itself. The category of power does not, it is true, exhaust the depth of the divine nature or the notion of God; but it certainly forms a vital element in all religious consciousness.

Apart from this general objectivity of Dialectic, we find traces of its presence in each of the particular provinces and phases of the natural and spiritual world. Take as an illustration the motion of the heavenly bodies. At this moment the planet stands in this spot, but implicitly it is the possibility of being in another spot; and that possibility of being otherwise the planet brings into existence by moving. Similarly the 'physical' elements prove to be Dialectical. The process of meteorological action is the exhibition of their Dialectic. It is the same dynamic that lies at the root of every natural process, and, as it were, forces nature out of itself. To illustrate the presence of Dialectic in the spiritual world, especially in the provinces of law and morality, we have only to recollect how general experience shows us the extreme of one state or action suddenly shifting into its opposite: a Dialectic which is recognized in many ways in common proverbs. Thus *summum jus summa injuria*, which means that to drive an abstract right to its extremity is to do a wrong. In political life, as every one knows, extreme anarchy and extreme despotism naturally lead to one another. The perception of Dialectic in the province of individual Ethics is seen in the well-known adages: Pride comes before a fall; Too

much wit outwits itself. Even feeling, bodily as well as mental, has its Dialectic. Every one knows how the extremes of pain and pleasure pass into each other: the heart overflowing with joy seeks relief in tears, and the deepest melancholy will at times betray its presence by a smile.

140

If the essence of nature is ever described as the inner part, the person who so describes it only knows its outer shell. In Being as a whole, or even in mere sense-perception, the notion is at first only an inward, and for that very reason is something external to Being, a subjective thinking and being, devoid of truth. In Nature as well as in Mind, so long as the notion, design, or law are at first the inner capacity, mere possibilities, they are first only an external, inorganic nature, the knowledge of a third person, alien force, and the like. As a man is outwardly, that is to say in his actions (not of course in his merely bodily outwardness), so is he inwardly: and if his virtue, morality, etc. are only inwardly his—that is if they exist only in his intentions and sentiments, and his outward acts are not identical with them—the one half of him is as hollow and empty as the other.

.   .   .

So long as understanding keeps the Inward and Outward fixed in their separation, they are empty forms, the one as null as the other. Not only in the study of nature, but also of the spiritual world, much depends on a just appreciation of the relation of inward and outward, and especially on avoiding the misconception that the former only is the essential point on which everything turns, while the latter is unessential and trivial. We find this mistake made when, as is often done, the difference between nature and mind is traced back to the abstract difference between inner and outer. As for nature, it certainly is in the gross external, not merely to the mind, but even on its own part. But to call it external 'in the gross' is not to imply an abstract externality—for there is no such thing. It means rather that the Idea which forms the common content of nature and mind, is found in nature as outward only, and for that very reason only inward. The abstract understanding, with its 'either-or', may struggle against this conception of nature. It is none the less obviously found in our other modes of consciousness, particularly in religion. It is the lesson of religion that nature, no less than the spiritual world, is a revelation of God: but with this distinction, that while nature never gets so far as to be conscious of its divine essence, that consciousness is the express problem of the mind, which in the matter of that problem is as yet finite. Those who look upon the essence of nature as mere inwardness, and therefore inaccessible to us, take up the same line as that ancient creed which regarded God as envious and jealous; a creed which both Plato and Aristotle pronounced against long ago. All that God is, he imparts and reveals; and he does so, at first, in and through nature.

Any object indeed is faulty and imperfect when it is only inward, and thus at the same time only outward, or (which is the same thing) when it is only an outward and thus only an inward. For instance, a child, taken in the gross as human being, is no doubt a rational creature; but the reason of the child as child is at first a mere inward, in the shape of his natural ability or vocation, etc. This mere inward, at the same time, has for the child the form of a mere outward, in the shape of the will of his parents, the attainments of his teachers, and the whole world of reason that environs him. The education and instruction of a child aim at making him actually and for himself what he is at first potentially and therefore for others, viz. for his grown-up friends. The reason, which at first exists in the child only as an inner possibility, is actualized through education: and conversely, the child by these means becomes conscious that the goodness, religion, and science which he had at first looked upon as an outward authority, are his own and inward nature. As with the child so it is in this matter with the adult, when, in opposition to his true destiny, his intellect and will remain in the bondage of the natural man. Thus, the criminal sees the punishment to which he has to submit as an act of violence from without: whereas in fact the penalty is only the manifestation of his own criminal will.

From what has now been said, we may learn what to think of a man who, when blamed for his shortcomings, or, it may be, his discreditable acts, appeals to the (professedly) excellent intentions and sentiments of the inner self he distinguishes therefrom. There certainly may be individual cases where the malice of outward circumstances frustrates well-meant designs, and disturbs the execution of the best-laid plans. But in general even here the essential unity between inward and outward is maintained. We are thus justified in saying that a man is what he does; and the lying vanity which consoles itself with the feeling of inward excellence may be confronted with the words of the Gospel: 'By their fruits ye shall know them.' That grand saying applies primarily in a moral and religious aspect, but it also holds good in reference to performances in art and science. The keen eye of a teacher who perceives in his pupil decided evidences of talent, may lead him to state his opinion that a Raphael or a Mozart lies hidden in the boy: and the result will show how far such an opinion was well-founded. But if a daub of a painter, or a poetaster, soothe themselves by the conceit that their head is full of high ideals, their consolation is a poor one; and if they insist on being judged not by their actual works but by their projects, we may safely reject their pretensions as unfounded and unmeaning. The converse case however also occurs. In passing judgment on men who have accomplished something great and good, we often make use of the false distinction between inward and outward. All that they have accomplished, we say, is outward merely; inwardly they were acting from some very different motive, such as a desire to gratify their vanity or other unworthy passion. This is the spirit of envy. Incapable of any great action of its own, envy tries hard to depreciate greatness and to bring it down to its own level. Let us, rather, recall the fine expression of Goethe, that there is no remedy but Love against great superiorities of others. We may seek to rob men's great actions of their grandeur, by the insinuation of hypocrisy; but, though it is possible that men in an instance now and then may dissemble and disguise a good deal, they cannot conceal the whole of their inner self, which infallibly betrays itself in the *decursus vitae*. Even here it is true that a man is nothing but the series of his actions.

What is called the 'pragmatic' writing of history has in modern times frequently sinned in its treatment of great historical characters, and defaced and tarnished the true conception of them by this fallacious separation of the outward from the inward. Not content with telling the unvarnished tale of the great acts which have been wrought by the heroes of the world's history, and with acknowledging that their inward being corresponds with the import of their acts, the pragmatic historian fancies himself justified and even obliged to trace the supposed secret motives that lie behind the open facts of the record. The historian, in that case, is supposed to write with more depth in proportion as he succeeds in tearing away the aureole from all that has been heretofore held grand and glorious, and in depressing it, so far as its origin and proper significance are concerned, to the level of vulgar mediocrity. To make these pragmatic researches in history easier, it is usual to recommend the study of psychology, which is supposed to make us acquainted with the real motives of human actions. The psychology in question however is only that petty knowledge of men, which looks away from the essential and permanent in human nature to fasten its glance on the casual and private features shown in isolated instincts and passions. A pragmatic psychology ought at least to leave the historian, who investigates the motives at the ground of great actions, a choice between the 'substantial' interests of patriotism, justice, religious truth, and the like, on the one hand, and the subjective and 'formal' interests of vanity, ambition, avarice, and the like, on the other. The latter, however, are the motives which must be viewed by the pragmatist as really efficient, otherwise the assumption of a contrast between the inward (the disposition of the agent) and the outward (the import of the action) would fall to the ground. But inward and outward have in truth the same content; and the right doctrine is the very reverse of this pedantic judiciality. If the heroes of history had been actuated by subjective and formal interests alone, they would never have accomplished what they have. And if we have due regard to the unity between the inner and the outer, we must own that great men willed what they did, and did what they willed.

G. W. F. HEGEL
Master and Slave
from Phenomenology of Spirit*

Self-consciousness is, to begin with, simple being-for-self. It is equal to itself by virtue of excluding everything else. Its essence and its absolute object is the 'I';

---

*Translated by Judith Norman.

and it is an *individual* in this immediacy (or being) of its being-for-self. Anything it considers as 'other' is inessential, and characterized negatively. But the other is a self-consciousness too; an individual is confronting an individual. Confronting each other *immediately* in this manner, they are like ordinary objects to each other, independent forms [of consciousness] subsisting at the level of mere life—for the existing object has determined itself as life. They are consciousnesses immersed [in the immediacy of life], and have not completed for each other the movement of absolute abstraction in which immediate being is eradicated, and only the purely negative being of self-identical consciousness remains. They have not yet presented themselves to each other as pure *being-for-self*, that is, as *self-consciousness*. Each one is fully certain of itself, but not of the other, and therefore its own self-certainty has no truth yet; for such truth would only come if its own being-for-self presented itself as an independent object, or, in other words, if the object presented itself as pure self-certainty. But according to the concept of recognition, this is only possible if each is for the other as the other is for it; it is only possible when each one, in itself through its own action, and again through the action of the other, achieves this pure abstraction of being-for-self.

However, the presentation of itself as the pure abstraction of self-consciousness consists of showing itself as pure negation of its objective manner, or showing that it is not attached to any definite *existence*, certainly not to the general individuality of existence; [showing, in other words,] that it is not attached to life. This is a *two-fold* action: an action of the other, and an action through itself. Insofar as it is an action of the *other*, each one seeks the death of the other. But this involves the second type of action, *the action through itself* as well; for the first action entails the risking of one's own life. The relation of both self-consciousnesses thus dictates that they must *prove* themselves and each other through a struggle of life and death.— They must enter into this struggle, for they must raise the certainty of *being for themselves* to truth, both for the other as well as for themselves. Freedom is proven worthwhile only by risking one's life; such a risk also proves that the essence of self-consciousness is not [just] *being*, that it is not *immediate* as it appears to be, that it is not this submersion in the expansion of life; rather, it proves that it contains only vanishing moments, that it is simply pure *being-for-self.* The individual who has not wagered its life can indeed be recognized as a *person,* but it has not achieved the truth of this recognition by being recognized as an independent self-consciousness. Likewise, each must pursue the death of the other, just as each risks its own life; for it values the other no more than it values itself. Its essence is presented to it as an other. It is outside of itself, and its exteriority must be overcome. The other is a consciousness entangled in a variety of ways; it must regard its otherness as pure being-for-self or as absolute negation.

But this trial by death destroys the truth that was supposed to come from it, and in so doing it destroys the certainty of itself in general. For, just as life is the *natural* position of consciousness, independence without absolute negativity, likewise, death is the *natural* negation of consciousness, negation without independence, and consequently remains without the meaning required of recognition. Death has indeed shown with certainty that both risked their lives, disregarding both their own deaths as well as that of the other; but this has not been shown for those who survive the struggle. They overcome their consciousness to the extent that it has been placed in this alien element of natural existence; or, they overcome and are overcome as *extremes* that want to be for themselves. But the essential moment thereby disappears from the game, the moment of decomposition into extremes of opposing determinations; and the middle falls into a dead unity, which is decomposed in dead extremes that merely lie side by side without opposition; there is no interchange between them through consciousness. Instead, they are indifferent to each other like mere things, and leave each other alone. Their action is that of abstract negation; it is not a negation from consciousness that *overcomes* itself so that it *retains* and *preserves* the elements that are overcome, and thereby survives its own overcoming.

In this experience, self-consciousness learns that life is as essential to it as pure self-consciousness. The simple I is the absolute object in immediate self-consciousness; for us or in itself, however, this object is the absolute mediator, and has steadfast independence as an essential moment. The result of this first experience is the dissolution of that simple unity [of the simple I]; through [this dissolution,] a pure self-consciousness is posited, as well as a consciousness that is not purely for itself, but is rather for another; that is, as *existing* consciousness or consciousness in the shape proper to *things.* Both moments are essential; since they are at first unequal and opposed, and their reflection has not yet submitted to the unity, they are like two opposed forms of consciousness; the first is independent and its essence is being-for-self; the other is dependent, and its essence is life or existing for an other. The former is the *master,* the latter is the *slave.*

The master is the consciousness that is *for itself,* and no longer merely the concept of such a consciousness; rather, he is consciousness existing for itself and mediated by an *other* consciousness, one whose essence involves being synthesized with independent *being* or objects in general. The master is in a relation to both these moments: first, to the object, which he desires, and second, to the consciousness whose essence is bound up with objects. And to the extent that (a) as concept of self-consciousness he is an immediate relation of *being-for-itself,* but (b) henceforth concurrently as mediator, or as a being-for-self that is for itself only through an other, he is related (a) immediately to both, and (b) mediately to each through the other. The master is related *mediately* to the slave through the *independent object,* because the slave is held fast to such an object; it is the chain from which he could not break free in the struggle, thereby proving that he is dependent and has his independence in objects. But the master is the one with power over this being, since he proved in struggle that he can regard it as merely negative. By having power over this being which has power over the other [the slave], the outcome is that he subordinates the slave to himself. Likewise the master relates to the thing *mediately, through agency the slave.* The slave, as self-consciousness in general, relates to the thing negatively as well, and overcomes it; but from his perspective, the thing is also independent. For this reason, he cannot fully annihilate it through his negation. In other words, he only *labors* on it. For the lord, on the other hand, the *immediate* relation *becomes* pure negation itself, or *enjoyment,* due to the mediating agency [of the slave]. He can achieve what desire failed to do—to have done with [the thing], and to satisfy himself by enjoying it. Desire could not achieve this, due to the thing's independence. But the master, with the slave interposed in between him and the thing, appropriates only the dependent aspect of the thing, and enjoys it fully; he leaves the independent side of the thing to the slave, who labors upon it.

In both of these moments, the master achieves recognition by way of an other consciousness, since this other posits himself as unessential in both moments: first, in laboring on the thing, and second, in his dependence upon a particular being. In neither of these moments can this other consciousness become master over this being and achieve absolute negation. A moment of recognition is thus at hand, because the other consciousness suppresses its being-for-self, and thereby does to itself what the first consciousness does to it. In the same way, the other moment is also at hand, in that the second consciousness' action [of self-suppression] is the first's own action; for what the slave does is actually the deed of the master. The master's essence is only being-for-self; he is the purely negative power and for him the thing is nothing; for this reason, he is the purely essential action in this relationship. The slave, on the other hand, is an impure, unessential action. But [this situation cannot be one of] genuine recognition, since it is missing the moment in which the master does to himself what he does to the slave, and the slave does to the master what [the slave] does to himself. Therefore, the result is a one-sided and unequal recognition.

In this [failed] recognition, the unessential consciousness is the object that constitutes the *truth* of the master's self-certainty. But it is clear that this object does not correspond to its concept; instead the object that the master has mastered is not an independent consciousness at all. The master is confronted with a dependent rather than an independent consciousness. Consequently, he is not certain of *being-for-self* as the truth; instead, his truth is in fact the unessential consciousness and its unessential action.

As a result, the *truth* of the independent consciousness is the *slavish consciousness*. To be sure, this slavish consciousness first appears *outside* itself and not as the truth of self-consciousness. But just as the master's experience has demonstrated that his essence is the reverse of what he would have it be, slavery also ultimately proves to be the opposite of what it is immediately; as a consciousness *that has been forced back* upon itself, it will return into itself and change into a truly independent self-consciousness.

We have seen only what slavery is in relation to mastery. But it is a self-consciousness [in its own right], and we must now observe what it is in and of itself. At first, the master is the essence of being a slave; thus the consciousness *that exists independently and for itself* is the *truth* for [the slave], but nonetheless it is not apparent to the slave that this is its

truth. The slave alone has the truth of pure negativity and of *being-for-self in fact in itself*. This is because the slave *experienced* this in its own self. [The slave's] consciousness was not afraid of this thing or that, at some time or another; instead, it feared for its entire being, because it has felt the fear of death, of the absolute master. It has been seized with terror, shaken to its very core; it has lost all its bearings. But this purely abstract moment where everything stable becomes fluid—this moment is the simple essence of self-consciousness, the absolute negativity, *the pure being-for-self*, that is consequently part of this consciousness [an diesem Bewusstsein]. This moment of pure being-for-self is *for* this consciousness as well, because this consciousness has this being-for-self as an *object* in the [form of the] master. Furthermore, it is not merely this abstract dissolution *in general;* it is actually achieved in servitude. Through his slavery he gets rid of all *particular* moments of his attachment to natural existence and labors his way through it.

But the feeling of absolute power, both in general and in the particulars of servitude, is only implicitly dissolution; and although fear of the lord is indeed the beginning of wisdom, consciousness is not aware [at first] that it is a *being-for-self.* But such awareness is gained through labor. In the moment that corresponds to desire in the master's consciousness, it seemed that the side of the unessential relation to the thing had indeed devolved upon the servile consciousness, since the thing retains its independence. Desire reserved for itself the [right to a] pure negation of the object, and consequently to an unadulterated feeling of self. But the satisfaction [gained by desire] is accordingly merely transient, for it is missing the *object-like* side, or *endurance.* Labor, to the contrary, is *repressed* desire, transience *delayed,* or a *formation.* The negative relation to the object becomes the *form* of the object, and becomes an [element of] *permanence,* because it is precisely to the laborer that the object has independence. This *negative medium* or the formative *action* is at the same time the *particularity* or the pure being-for-self of the consciousness, which now, in the labor outside of it, gains an element of permanence. The laboring consciousness can thereby perceive in independent being *its own self.*

But the formative activity does not only have the positive meaning that the servile consciousness, as pure *being-for-self*, gains an existence. In contrast to its first moment, it also has the negative meaning of fear. This is because, in producing the thing, his own negativity—his being-for-self—becomes an object for him only by canceling out the existing *form* confronting him. But this object-like *negative* is precisely the alien essence that it had feared. But now it destroys this alien negative, and posits *itself* as such in the element of permanence, and thereby becomes *for itself* something that *exists for itself*. In the master, the being-for-self is an 'other' for the slave, or is only *for him;* in fear, the being-for-self is *in the slave himself.* In producing, the being-for-self becomes *his own* for him, and it occurs to consciousness that it is in and for itself. The form does not thereby become for him, since it is *externalized,* something other than himself; for precisely the form is his pure being-for-self, that becomes the truth for him. Through this rediscovery of himself by himself, the slave realizes that it is through his labor—where he seemed to have only an aliened existence—that his spirit is his own.

G. W. F. HEGEL

Ethical Life
from Philosophy of Right

150. Virtue is the ethical order reflected in the individual character so far as that character is determined by its natural endowment. When virtue displays itself solely as the individual's simple conformity with the duties of the station to which he belongs, it is rectitude.

151. But when individuals are simply identified with the actual order, ethical life (*das Sittliche*) appears as their general mode of conduct, i.e. as custom (*Sitte*), while the habitual practice of ethical living appears as a second nature which, put in the place of the initial, purely natural will, is the soul of custom permeating it through and through, the significance and the actuality of its existence. It is mind living and present as a world, and the substance of mind thus exists now for the first time as mind.

152. In this way the ethical substantial order has attained its right, and its right its validity. That is to say, the self-will of the individual has vanished together with his private conscience which had claimed independence and opposed itself to the ethical substance. For, when his character is ethical, he recognizes as the end which moves him to act the univer-

sal which is itself unmoved but is disclosed in its specific determinations as rationality actualized. He knows that his own dignity and the whole stability of his particular ends are grounded in this same universal, and it is therein that he actually attains these. Subjectivity is itself the absolute form and existent actuality of the substantial order, and the distinction between subject on the one hand and substance on the other, as the object, end, and controlling power of the subject, is the same as, and has vanished directly along with, the distinction between them in form. . . .

153. The right of individuals to be subjectively destined to freedom is fulfilled when they belong to an actual ethical order, because their conviction of their freedom finds its truth in such an objective order, and it is in an ethical order that they are actually in possession of their own essence or their own inner universality.

· · ·

257. The state is the actuality of the ethical Idea. It is ethical mind *qua* the substantial will manifest and revealed to itself, knowing and thinking itself, accomplishing what it knows and in so far as it knows it. The state exists immediately in custom, mediately in individual self-consciousness, knowledge, and activity, while self-consciousness in virtue of its sentiment towards the state finds in the state, as its essence and the end and product of its activity, its substantive freedom. . . .

WORKS BY SØREN KIERKEGAARD

Rotation of Crops
from Either/Or

Idleness, we are accustomed to say, is the root of all evil.* To prevent this evil, work is recommended. But it is just as easy to see from the dreaded occasion as from the recommended remedy that this whole view

———

*Footnotes omitted—ed.

is of very plebian extraction. Idleness as such is by no means a root of evil; on the contrary, it is a truly divine life, if one is not bored. To be sure, idleness may be the occasion of losing one's property etc., but the noble nature does not fear such things but does indeed fear being bored. The Olympian gods were not bored; happy they lived in happy idleness. A female beauty who neither sews nor spins nor irons nor reads nor plays an instrument is happy in idleness, for she is not bored. Idleness, then, is so far from being the root of evil that it is rather the true good. Boredom is the root of evil; it is that which must be held off. Idleness is not the evil; indeed, it may be said that everyone who lacks a sense for it thereby shows that he has not raised himself to the human level. There is an indefatigable activity that shuts a person out of the world of spirit and places him in a class with the animals, which instinctively must always be in motion. There are people who have an extraordinary talent for transforming everything into a business operation, whose whole life is a business operation, who fall in love and are married, hear a joke, and admire a work of art with the same businesslike zeal with which they work at the office. The Latin proverb *otium est pulvinar diaboli* [idleness is the devil's pillow] is quite correct, but the devil does not find time to lay his head on this pillow if one is not bored. But since people believe that it is man's destiny to work, the antithesis idleness/work is correct. I assume that it is man's destiny to amuse himself, and therefore my antithesis is no less correct.

. . .

Now, if boredom, as discussed above, is the root of all evil, what then is more natural than to seek to conquer it? But here, as everywhere, it is primarily a matter of calm deliberation, lest, demonically possessed by boredom in an attempt to escape it, one works one's way into it. All who are bored cry out for change. In this, I totally agree with them, except that it is a question of acting according to principle.

My deviation from popular opinion is adequately expressed by the phrase "rotation of crops." There might seem to be an ambiguity in this phrase, and if I were to find room in this phrase for a designation of the ordinary method I would have to say that rotation of crops consists in continually changing the soil. But the farmer does not use the expression in this way.

For a moment, however, I will use it in this way to discuss the rotation of crops that depends upon the boundless infinity of change, its extensive dimension.

This rotation of crops is the vulgar, inartistic rotation and is based on an illusion. One is weary of living in the country and moves to the city; one is weary of one's native land and goes abroad; one is *europamüde* [weary of Europe] and goes to America etc.; one indulges in the fanatical hope of an endless journey from star to star. Or there is another direction, but still extensive. One is weary of eating on porcelain and eats on silver; wearying of that, one eats on gold; one burns down half of Rome in order to visualize the Trojan conflagration. This method cancels itself and is the spurious infinity. . . .

The method I propose does not consist in changing the soil but, like proper crop rotation, consists in changing the method of cultivation and the kinds of crops. Here at once is the principle of limitation, the sole saving principle in the world. The more a person limits himself, the more resourceful he becomes. A solitary prisoner for life is extremely resourceful; to him a spider can be a source of great amusement. Think of our school days; we were at an age when there was no esthetic consideration in the choosing of our teachers, and therefore they were often very boring—how resourceful we were then! What fun we had catching a fly, keeping it prisoner under a nutshell, and watching it run around with it! What delight in cutting a hole in the desk, confining a fly in it, and peeking at it through a piece of paper! How entertaining it can be to listen to the monotonous dripping from the roof! What a meticulous observer one becomes, detecting every little sound or movement. Here is the extreme boundary of that principle that seeks relief not through extensity but through intensity.

The more resourceful one can be in changing the method of cultivation, the better, but every particular change still falls under the universal rule of the relation between *recollecting* and *forgetting*. It is in these two currents that all life moves, and therefore it is a matter of having them properly under one's control. Not until hope has been thrown overboard does one begin to live artistically; as long as a person hopes, he cannot limit himself. It is indeed beautiful to see a person put out to sea with the fair wind of hope; one may utilize the chance to let oneself be towed along, but one ought never have it on board one's craft, least of all as pilot, for it is an untrustworthy shipmaster. For this reason, too, hope was one of Prometheus's dubious gifts; instead of giving human beings the foreknowledge of the immortals, he gave them hope.

To forget—this is the desire of all people, and when they encounter something unpleasant, they always say: If only I could forget! But to forget is an art that must be practiced in advance. To be able to forget always depends upon how one remembers, but how one remembers depends upon how one experiences actuality. The person who runs aground with the speed of hope will recollect in such a way that he will be unable to forget. Thus *nil admirari* [marvel at nothing] is the proper wisdom of life. No part of life ought to have so much meaning for a person that he cannot forget it any moment he wants to; on the other hand, every single part of life ought to have so much meaning for a person that he can remember it at any moment. The age that remembers best is also the most forgetful: namely, childhood. The more poetically one remembers, the more easily one forgets, for to remember poetically is actually only an expression for forgetting. When I remember poetically, my experience has already undergone the change of having lost everything painful. In order to be able to recollect in this way, one must be very much aware of how one lives, especially of how one enjoys. If one enjoys indiscriminately to the very end, if one continually takes the utmost that enjoyment can give, one will be unable either to recollect or to forget. That is, one has nothing else to recollect than a satiation that one only wishes to forget but that now torments with an involuntary recollection. Therefore, if a person notices that enjoyment or a part of life is carrying him away too forcefully, he stops for a moment and recollects. There is no better way to give a distaste for going on too long. From the beginning, one curbs the enjoyment and does not hoist full sail for any decision; one indulges with a certain mistrust. Only then is it possible to give the lie to the proverb that says that one cannot eat one's cake and have it, too.

. . .

The art of recollecting and forgetting will also prevent a person from foundering in any particular relationship in life—and assures him complete suspension.

Guard, then, against *friendship*. . . . What are the sure signs of friendship? Antiquity answers: *idem velle, idem nolle, ea demum firma amicitia* [agreement in likes and dislikes, this and this only is what constitutes true friendship]—and is also extremely boring. What is the meaning of friendship? Mutual assistance with counsel and action. Two friends form a close alliance in order to be everything to each other, even though no human being can be anything for another human being except to be in his way. Well, we can help each other with money, help each other into and out of our coats, be each other's humble servants, gather for a sincere New Year's congratulation, also for weddings, births, and funerals.

But just because one stays clear of friendship, one will not for that reason live without contact with people. On the contrary, these relationships can take a deeper turn now and then, provided that one always —even though keeping the same pace for a time— has enough reserve speed to run away from them.

. . .

Never become involved in *marriage*. Married people pledge love for each other throughout eternity. Well, now, that is easy enough but does not mean very much, for if one is finished with time one is probably finished with eternity. If, instead of saying "throughout eternity," the couple would say "until Easter, until next May Day," then what they say would make some sense, for then they would be saying something and also something they perhaps could carry out. What happens in marriage? First, one of them detects after a short time that something is wrong, and then the other one complains and screams: Faithlessness! Faithlessness! After a while, the other one comes to the same conclusion and a state of neutrality is inaugurated through a balancing of accounts by mutual faithlessness, to their common satisfaction and gratification. But it is too late now, anyway, because a divorce involves all kinds of huge problems.

Since marriage is like that, it is not strange that attempts are made in many ways to shore it up with moral props. If a man wants to be separated from his wife, the cry goes up: He is a mean fellow, a scoundrel, etc. How ridiculous, and what an indirect assault upon marriage! Either marriage has intrinsic reality, and then he is adequately punished by losing it, or it has no reality, and then it is unreasonable to vilify him because he is wiser than others. If someone became weary of his money and threw it out the window, no one would say he is a mean fellow, for either money has reality, and then he is adequately punished by not having it anymore, or it has no reality, and then, of course, he is indeed wise.

One must always guard against contracting a life relationship by which one can become many. That is why even friendship is dangerous, marriage even more so. They do say that marriage partners become one, but this is very obscure and mysterious talk. If an individual is many, he has lost his freedom and cannot order his riding boots when he wishes, cannot knock about according to whim. If he has a wife, it is difficult; if he has a wife and perhaps children, it is formidable; if he has a wife and children, it is impossible.

. . .

Just because one does not become involved in marriage, one's life need not for that reason be devoid of the erotic. The erotic, too, ought to have infinity—but a poetic infinity that can just as well be limited to one hour as to a month.

. . .

Never take any *official post*. If one does that, one becomes just a plain John Anyman, a tiny little cog in the machine of the body politic. The individual ceases to be himself the manager of the operation, and then theories can be of little help. One acquires a title, and implicit in that are all the consequences of sin and evil. The law under which one slaves is equally boring no matter whether advancement is swift or slow. A title can never be disposed of; it would take a criminal act for that, which would incur a public whipping, and even then one cannot be sure of not being pardoned by royal decree and acquiring the title again.

Even though one stays clear of official posts, one should nevertheless not be inactive but attach great importance to all the pursuits that are compatible with aimlessness; all kinds of unprofitable pursuits may be carried on. Yet in this regard one ought to develop not so much extensively as intensively and, although mature in years, demonstrate the validity of the old saying: It doesn't take much to amuse a child.

Just as one varies the soil somewhat, in accordance with the theory of social prudence (for if one were to live in relation to only one person, rotation of crops would turn out badly, as would be the case if a farmer had only one acre of land and therefore could never let it lie fallow, something that is extremely important), so also must one continually vary oneself, and this is the real secret. To that end, it is essential to have control over one's moods. To have them under control in the sense that one can produce them at will is an impossibility, but prudence teaches us to utilize the moment. Just as an experienced sailor always scans the sea and detects a squall far in advance, so one should always detect a mood a little in advance. Before entering into a mood, one should know its effect on oneself and its probable effect on others. The first strokes are for the purpose of evoking pure tones and seeing what is inside a person; later come the intermediate tones. The more practice one has, the more one is convinced that there is often much in a person that was never imagined. When sentimental people, who as such are very boring, become peevish, they are often amusing. Teasing in particular is an excellent means of exploration.

Arbitrariness is the whole secret. It is popularly believed that there is no art to being arbitrary, and yet it takes profound study to be arbitrary in such a way that a person does not himself run wild in it but himself has pleasure from it. One does not enjoy the immediate object but something else that one arbitrarily introduces. One sees the middle of a play; one reads the third section of a book. One thereby has enjoyment quite different from what the author so kindly intended. One enjoys something totally accidental; one considers the whole of existence from this standpoint; one lets its reality run aground on this.

. . .

Baggesen tells somewhere that a certain man is no doubt a very honest fellow but that he has one thing against him: nothing rhymes with his name. It is very advantageous to let the realities of life be undifferentiated in an arbitrary interest like that. Something accidental is made into the absolute and as such into an object of absolute admiration. This is especially effective when the feelings are in motion. For many people, this method is an excellent means of stimulation. Everything in life is regarded as a wager etc. The more consistently a person knows how to sustain his arbitrariness, the more amusing the combinations become.

Preface
from Fear and Trembling

Not only in the business world but also in the world of ideas, our age stages *ein wirklicher Ausverkauf* [a real sale]. Everything can be had at such a bargain price that it becomes a question whether there is finally anyone who will make a bid. Every speculative monitor who conscientiously signals the important trends in modern philosophy, every assistant professor, tutor, and student, every rural outsider and tenant incumbent in philosophy is unwilling to stop with doubting everything but goes further. Perhaps it would be premature and untimely to ask them where they really are going, but in all politeness and modesty it can probably be taken for granted that they have doubted everything, since otherwise it certainly would be odd to speak of their having gone further. They have all made this preliminary movement and presumably so easily that they find it unnecessary to say a word about how, for not even the person who in apprehension and concern sought a little enlightenment found any, not one suggestive hint or one little dietetic prescription with respect to how a person is to act in carrying out this enormous task. "But did not Descartes do it?" Descartes, a venerable, humble, honest thinker, whose writings no one can read without being profoundly affected—he did what he said and said what he did. Alas! Alas! Alas! That is a great rarity in our day! As Descartes himself so frequently said, he did not doubt with respect to faith.

. . .

What those ancient Greeks, who after all did know a little about philosophy, assumed to be a task for a whole lifetime, because proficiency in doubting is not acquired in days and weeks, what the old veteran disputant attained, he who had maintained the equilibrium of doubt throughout all the specious arguments, who had intrepidly denied the certainty of the senses and the certainty of thought, who, uncompromising, had defied the anxiety of self-love and the insinuations of fellow feeling—with that everyone begins in our age.

In our age, everyone is unwilling to stop with faith but goes further. It perhaps would be rash to ask where they are going, whereas it is a sign of urbanity and culture for me to assume that everyone has faith, since otherwise it certainly would be odd to speak of going further. It was different in those ancient days. Faith was then a task for a whole lifetime, because it was assumed that proficiency in believing is not acquired either in days or in weeks. When the tried and tested oldster approached his end, had fought the good fight and kept the faith, his heart was still young enough not to have forgotten the anxiety and trembling that disciplined the youth, that the adult learned to control, but that no man outgrows—except to the extent that he succeeds in going further as early as possible. The point attained by those venerable personages is in our age the point where everyone begins in order to go further.

The present author is by no means a philosopher. He has not understood the system, whether there is one, whether it is completed; it is already enough for his weak head to ponder what a prodigious head everyone must have these days when everyone has such a prodigious idea.

Exordium*
from Fear and Trembling

Once upon a time there was a man who as a child had heard that beautiful story of how God tempted Abraham and of how Abraham withstood the temptation, kept the faith, and, contrary to expectation, got a son a second time.[†] When he grew older, he read the same story with even greater admiration, for life had fractured what had been united in the pious simplicity of the child. The older he became, the more often his thoughts turned to that story; his enthusiasm for it became greater and greater, and yet he could understand the story less and less. Finally, he forgot everything else because of it; his soul had but one wish, to see Abraham, but one longing, to have witnessed that event. His craving was not to see the beautiful regions of the East, not the earthly glory of the promised land, not that God-fearing couple whose old age God

---

*mood.

[†]Reading footnotes omitted—ed.

had blessed, not the venerable figure of the aged patriarch, not the vigorous adolescence God bestowed upon Isaac—the same thing could just as well have occurred on a barren heath. His craving was to go along on the three-day journey when Abraham rode with sorrow before him and Isaac beside him. His wish was to be present in that hour when Abraham raised his eyes and saw Mount Moriah in the distance, the hour when he left the asses behind and went up the mountain alone with Isaac—for what occupied him was not the beautiful tapestry of imagination but the shudder of the idea.

That man was not a thinker. He did not feel any need to go beyond faith; he thought that it must be supremely glorious to be remembered as its father, an enviable destiny to possess it, even if no one knew it.

That man was not an exegetical scholar. He did not know Hebrew; if he had known Hebrew, he perhaps would easily have understood the story and Abraham.

1

"And God tempted Abraham and said to him, take Isaac, your only son, whom you love, and go to the land of Moriah and offer him there as a burnt offering on a mountain that I shall show you."

It was early in the morning when Abraham arose, had the asses saddled, and left his tent, taking Isaac with him, but Sarah watched them from the window as they went down the valley—until she could see them no longer. They rode in silence for three days. On the morning of the fourth day, Abraham said not a word but raised his eyes and saw Mount Moriah in the distance. He left the young servants behind and, taking Isaac's hand, went up the mountain alone. But Abraham said to himself, "I will not hide from Isaac where this walk is taking him." He stood still, he laid his hand on Isaac's head in blessing, and Isaac kneeled to receive it. And Abraham's face epitomized fatherliness; his gaze was gentle, his words admonishing. But Isaac could not understand him, his soul could not be uplifted; he clasped Abraham's knees, he pleaded at his feet, he begged for his young life, for his beautiful hopes; he called to mind the joy in Abraham's house, he called to mind the sorrow and the solitude. Then Abraham lifted the boy up and walked on, holding his hand, and his words were full of comfort and ad-

monition. But Isaac could not understand him. Abraham climbed Mount Moriah, but Isaac did not understand him. Then Abraham turned away from him for a moment, but when Isaac saw Abraham's face again, it had changed: his gaze was wild, his whole being was sheer terror. He seized Isaac by the chest, threw him to the ground, and said, "Stupid boy, do you think I am your father? I am an idolater. Do you think it is God's command? No, it is my desire." Then Isaac trembled and cried out in his anguish: "God in heaven, have mercy on me, God of Abraham, have mercy on me; if I have no father on earth, then you be my father!" But Abraham said softly to himself, "Lord God in heaven, I thank you; it is better that he believes me a monster than that he should lose faith in you."

When the child is to be weaned, the mother blackens her breast. It would be hard to have the breast look inviting when the child must not have it. So the child believes that the breast has changed, but the mother—she is still the same, her gaze is tender and loving as ever. How fortunate the one who did not need more terrible means to wean the child!

2

It was early in the morning when Abraham arose: he embraced Sarah, the bride of his old age, and Sarah kissed Isaac, who took away her disgrace, Isaac her pride, her hope for all the generations to come. They rode along the road in silence, and Abraham stared continuously and fixedly at the ground until the fourth day, when he looked up and saw Mount Moriah far away, but once again he turned his eyes toward the ground. Silently he arranged the firewood and bound Isaac; silently he drew the knife—then he saw the ram that God had selected. This he sacrificed and went home.—From that day henceforth, Abraham was old; he could not forget that God had ordered him to do this. Isaac flourished as before, but Abraham's eyes were darkened, and he saw joy no more.

When the child has grown big and is to be weaned, the mother virginally conceals her breast, and then the child no longer has a mother. How fortunate the child who has not lost his mother in some other way!

3

It was early in the morning when Abraham arose: he kissed Sarah, the young mother, and Sarah kissed Isaac, her delight, her joy forever. And Abraham rode thoughtfully down the road; he thought of Hagar and the son, whom he drove out into the desert. He climbed Mount Moriah, he drew the knife.

It was a quiet evening when Abraham rode out alone, and he rode to Mount Moriah; he threw himself down on his face, he prayed God to forgive him his sin, that he had been willing to sacrifice Isaac, that the father had forgotten his duty to his son. He often rode his lonesome road, but he found no peace. He could not comprehend that it was a sin that he had been willing to sacrifice to God the best that he had, the possession for which he himself would have gladly died many times; and if it was a sin, if he had not loved Isaac in this manner, he could not understand that it could be forgiven, for what more terrible sin was there?

When the child is to be weaned, the mother, too, is not without sorrow, because she and the child are more and more to be separated, because the child who first lay under her heart and later rested upon her breast will never again be so close. So they grieve together the brief sorrow. How fortunate the one who kept the child so close and did not need to grieve any more!

4

It was early in the morning, and everything in Abraham's house was ready for the journey. He took leave of Sarah, and Eliezer, the faithful servant, accompanied him along the road until he turned back again. They rode along in harmony, Abraham and Isaac, until they came to Mount Moriah. Abraham made everything ready for the sacrifice, calmly and gently, but when he turned away and drew the knife, Isaac saw that Abraham's left hand was clenched in despair, that a shudder went through his whole body—but Abraham drew the knife.

Then they returned home again, and Sarah hurried to meet them, but Isaac had lost the faith. Not a word is ever said of this in the world, and Isaac never talked to anyone about what he had seen, and Abraham did not suspect that anyone had seen it.

When the child is to be weaned, the mother has stronger sustenance at hand so that the child does not perish. How fortunate the one who has this stronger sustenance at hand.

Thus and in many similar ways did the man of whom we speak ponder this event. Every time he returned from a pilgrimage to Mount Moriah, he sank down wearily, folded his hands, and said, "No one was as great as Abraham. Who is able to understand him?"

Eulogy on Abraham
from Fear and Trembling

If a human being did not have an eternal consciousness,* if underlying everything there were only a wild, fermenting power that writhing in dark passions produced everything, be it significant or insignificant, if a vast, never appeased emptiness hid beneath everything, what would life be then but despair? If such were the situation, if there were no sacred bond that knit humankind together, if one generation emerged after another like forest foliage, if one generation succeeded another like the singing of birds in the forest, if a generation passed through the world as a ship through the sea, as wind through the desert, an unthinking and unproductive performance, if an eternal *oblivion,* perpetually hungry, lurked for its prey and there were no power strong enough to wrench that away from it—how empty and devoid of consolation life would be! But precisely for that reason it is not so, and just as God created man and woman, so he created the hero and the poet or orator. The poet or orator can do nothing that the hero does; he can only admire, love, and delight in him. Yet he, too, is happy—no less than that one is, for the hero is, so to speak, his better nature, with which he is enamored—yet happy that the other is not himself, that his love can be admiration. He is recollection's genius. He can do nothing but bring to mind what has been done, can do nothing but admire what has been done; he takes nothing of his own but is zealous for what has been entrusted. He follows his heart's desire, but when he has found the object of his search, he roams about to every man's door with his song and speech so that all may admire the hero as he does, may be proud of the hero as he is. This is his occupation, his humble task; this is his faithful service in the house of the hero. If he remains true to his love in this

---

*Footnotes omitted—ed.

way, if he contends night and day against the craftiness of oblivion, which wants to trick him out of his hero, then he has fulfilled his task, then he is gathered together with the hero, who has loved him just as faithfully, for the poet is, so to speak, the hero's better nature, powerless, to be sure, just as a memory is, but also transfigured just as a memory is. Therefore, no one who was great will be forgotten, and even though it takes time, even though a cloud of misunderstanding takes away the hero, his lover will nevertheless come, and the longer the passage of time, the more faithfully he adheres to him.

No! No one who was great in the world will be forgotten, but everyone was great in his own way, and everyone in proportion to the greatness of that which *he loved*. He who loved himself became great by virtue of himself, and he who loved other men became great by his devotedness, but he who loved God became the greatest of all. Everyone shall be remembered, but everyone became great in proportion to his *expectancy*. One became great by expecting the possible, another by expecting the eternal; but he who expected the impossible became the greatest of all. Everyone shall be remembered, but everyone was great wholly in proportion to the magnitude of that with which he *struggled*. For he who struggled with the world became great by conquering the world, and he who struggled with himself became great by conquering himself, but he who struggled with God became the greatest of all. Thus did they struggle in the world, man against man, one against thousands, but he who struggled with God was the greatest of all. Thus did they struggle on earth: there was one who conquered everything by his power, and there was one who conquered God by his powerlessness. There was one who relied upon himself and gained everything; there was one who in the security of his own strength sacrificed everything; but the one who believed God was the greatest of all. There was one who was great by virtue of his power, and one who was great by virtue of his wisdom, and one who was great by virtue of his hope, and one who was great by virtue of his love, but Abraham was the greatest of all, great by that power whose strength is powerlessness, great by that wisdom whose secret is foolishness, great by that hope whose form is madness, great by the love that is hatred to oneself.

By faith Abraham emigrated from the land of his fathers and became an alien in the promised land. He left one thing behind, took one thing along: he left behind his worldly understanding, and he took along his faith. Otherwise he certainly would not have emigrated but surely would have considered it unreasonable. By faith he was an alien in the promised land, and there was nothing that reminded him of what he cherished, but everything by its newness tempted his soul to sorrowful longing. And yet he was God's chosen one in whom the Lord was well pleased! As a matter of fact, if he had been an exile, banished from God's grace, he could have better understood it—but now it was as if he and his faith were being mocked. There was also in the world one who lived in exile from the native land he loved. He is not forgotten, nor are his dirges of lamentation when he sorrowfully sought and found what was lost. There is no dirge by Abraham. It is human to lament, human to weep with one who weeps, but it is greater to have faith, more blessed to contemplate the man of faith.

By faith Abraham received the promise that in his seed all the generations of the earth would be blessed. Time passed, the possibility was there, Abraham had faith; time passed, it became unreasonable, Abraham had faith. There was one in the world who also had an expectancy. Time passed, evening drew near; he was not so contemptible as to forget his expectancy, and therefore he will not be forgotten, either. Then he sorrowed, and his sorrow did not disappoint him as life had done, it did everything it could for him; in the sweetness of his sorrow he possessed his disappointed expectancy. It is human to sorrow, human to sorrow with the sorrowing, but it is greater to have faith, more blessed to contemplate the man of faith. We have no dirge of sorrow by Abraham. As time passed, he did not gloomily count the days; he did not look suspiciously at Sarah, wondering if she was not getting old; he did not stop the course of the sun so she would not become old and along with her his expectancy; he did not soothingly sing his mournful lay for Sarah. Abraham became old, Sarah the object of mockery in the land, and yet he was God's chosen one and heir to the promise that in his seed all the generations of the earth would be blessed. Would it not have been better, after all, if he were not God's chosen? What does it mean to be God's chosen? Is it to be denied in youth one's youthful desire in order to have it fulfilled with great difficulty in one's old age? But Abraham believed and held to the promise. If Abraham had wavered, he would have given it up. He would have said to God, "So maybe it is not your will that this should be; then I will give up my wish. It was my one and only wish, it was my blessedness. My soul is open and sincere; I am hiding no secret resentment because you denied me this." He would not have been forgotten, he would have saved many by his example, but he still would not have become the father of faith, for it is great to give up one's desire, but it is greater to hold fast to it after having given it up; it is great to lay hold of the eternal, but it is greater to hold fast to the temporal after having given it up.

Then came the fullness of time. If Abraham had not had faith, then Sarah would surely have died of sorrow, and Abraham, dulled by grief, would not have understood the fulfillment but would have smiled at it as at a youthful dream. But Abraham had faith, and therefore he was young, for he who always hopes for the best grows old and is deceived by life, and he who is always prepared for the worst grows old prematurely, but he who has faith—he preserves an eternal youth. So let us praise and honor that story! For Sarah, although well advanced in years, was young enough to desire the pleasure of motherhood, and Abraham with his gray hairs was young enough to wish to be a father. Outwardly, the wonder of it is that it happened according to their expectancy; in the more profound sense, the wonder of faith is that Abraham and Sarah were young enough to desire and that faith had preserved their desire and thereby their youth. He accepted the fulfillment of the promise, he accepted it in faith, and it happened according to the promise and according to his faith. Moses struck the rock with his staff, but he did not have faith.

So there was joy in Abraham's house when Sarah stood as bride on their golden wedding day.

But it was not to remain that way; once again Abraham was to be tried. He had fought with that crafty power that devises all things, with that vigilant enemy who never dozes, with that old man who outlives everything—he had fought with time and kept his faith. Now all the frightfulness of the struggle was concentrated in one moment. "And God tempted Abraham and said to him, take Isaac, your only son, whom you love, and go to the land of Moriah and offer him as a burnt offering on a mountain that I shall show you."

So everything was lost, even more appallingly than if it had never happened! So the Lord was only mocking Abraham! He wondrously made the preposterous come true; now he wanted to see it annihilated. This was indeed a piece of folly, but Abraham did not laugh at it as Sarah did when the promise was announced. All was lost! Seventy years of trusting expectancy, the brief joy over the fulfillment of faith. Who is this who seizes the staff from the old man, who is this who demands that he himself shall break it! Who is this who makes a man's gray hairs disconsolate, who is this who demands that he himself shall do it! Is there no sympathy for this venerable old man, none for the innocent child? And yet Abraham was God's chosen one, and it was the Lord who imposed the ordeal. Now everything would be lost! All the glorious remembrance of his posterity, the promise in Abraham's seed—it was nothing but a whim, a fleeting thought that the Lord had had and that Abraham was now supposed to obliterate. That glorious treasure, which was just as old as the faith in Abraham's heart and many, many years older than Isaac, the fruit of Abraham's life, sanctified by prayer, matured in battle, the blessing on Abraham's lips—this fruit was now to be torn off prematurely and rendered meaningless, for what meaning would it have if Isaac should be sacrificed! That sad but nevertheless blessed hour when Abraham was to take leave of everything he held dear, when he once more would raise his venerable head, when his face would shine as the Lord's, when he would concentrate all his soul upon a blessing that would be so powerful it would bless Isaac all his days—this hour was not to come! For Abraham would indeed take leave of Isaac, but in such a way that he himself would remain behind; death would separate them, but in such a way that Isaac would become its booty. The old man would not, rejoicing in death, lay his hand in blessing on Isaac, but, weary of life, he would lay a violent hand upon Isaac. And it was God who tested him! Woe to the messenger who brought such news to Abraham! Who would have dared to be the emissary of this sorrow? But it was God who tested Abraham.

Yet Abraham had faith, and had faith for this life. In fact, if his faith had been only for a life to come, he certainly would have more readily discarded everything in order to rush out of a world to which he did not belong. But Abraham's faith was not of this sort, if there is such a faith at all, for actually it is not faith but the most remote possibility of faith that faintly sees its object on the most distant horizon but is separated from it by a chasmal abyss in which doubt plays its tricks. But Abraham had faith specifically for this life—faith that he would grow old in this country, be honored among the people, blessed by posterity, and unforgettable in Isaac, the most precious thing in his life, whom he embraced with a love that is inadequately described by saying he faithfully fulfilled the father's duty to love the son, which is indeed stated in the command: the son, whom you love. Jacob had twelve sons, one of whom he loved; Abraham had but one, whom he loved.

But Abraham had faith and did not doubt; he believed the preposterous. If Abraham had doubted, then he would have done something else, something great and glorious, for how could Abraham do anything else but what is great and glorious! He would have gone to Mount Moriah, he would have split the firewood, lit the fire, drawn the knife. He would have cried out to God, "Reject not this sacrifice; it is not the best that I have, that I know very well, for what is an old man compared with the child of promise, but it is the best I can give you. Let Isaac never find this out so that he may take comfort in his youth." He would have thrust the knife into his own breast. He would have been admired in the world, and his name would never be forgotten; but it is one thing to be admired and another to become a guiding star that saves the anguished.

But Abraham had faith. He did not pray for himself, trying to influence the Lord; it was only when righteous punishment fell upon Sodom and Gomorrah that Abraham came forward with his prayers.

We read in sacred scripture: "And God tempted Abraham and said: Abraham, Abraham, where are you? But Abraham answered: Here am I." You to whom these words are addressed, was this the case with you? When in the far distance you saw overwhelming vicissitudes approaching, did you not say to the mountains, "Hide me," and to the hills, "Fall on me"? Or, if you were stronger, did your feet nevertheless not drag along the way, did they not long, so to speak, for the old trails? And when your name was called, did you answer, perhaps answer softly, in a whisper? Not so with Abraham. Cheerfully, freely, confidently, loudly he answered: Here am I. We read on: "And Abraham arose early in the morning." He hurried as if to a celebration, and early in the morning he was at the appointed place on Mount Moriah. He said nothing to Sarah, nothing to Eliezer—who, after all, could understand him, for did not the nature of the temptation extract from him the pledge of silence? "He split the firewood, he bound Isaac, he lit the fire, he drew the knife." My listener! Many a father has thought himself deprived of every hope for the future when he lost his child, the dearest thing in the world to him; nevertheless, no one was the child of promise in the sense in which Isaac was that to Abraham. Many a father has lost his child, but then it was God, the unchangeable, inscrutable will of the Almighty, it was his hand that took it. Not so with Abraham! A harder test was reserved for him, and Isaac's fate was placed, along with the knife, in Abraham's hand. And there he stood, the old man with his solitary hope. But he did not doubt, he did not look in anguish to the left and to the right, he did not challenge heaven with his prayers. He knew it was God the Almighty who was testing him; he knew it was the hardest sacrifice that could be demanded of him; but he knew also that no sacrifice is too severe when God demands it—and he drew the knife.

Who strengthened Abraham's arm, who braced up his right arm so that it did not sink down powerless! Anyone who looks upon this scene is paralyzed. Who strengthened Abraham's soul lest everything go black for him and he see neither Isaac nor the ram! Anyone who looks upon this scene is blinded. And yet it perhaps rarely happens that anyone is paralyzed or blinded, and still more rarely does anyone tell what happened as it deserves to be told. We know it all—it was only an ordeal.

If Abraham had doubted as he stood there on Mount Moriah, if irresolute he had looked around, if he had happened to spot the ram before drawing the knife, if God had allowed him to sacrifice it instead of Isaac—then he would have gone home, everything would have been the same, he would have had Sarah, he would have kept Isaac, and yet how changed! For his return would have been a flight, his deliverance an accident, his reward disgrace, his future perhaps perdition. Then he would have witnessed neither to his faith nor to God's grace but would have witnessed to how appalling it is to go to Mount Moriah. Then Abraham would not be forgotten, nor would Mount Moriah. Then it would not be mentioned in the way Ararat, where the ark landed, is mentioned, but it would be called a place of terror, for it was here that Abraham doubted.

Venerable Father Abraham! When you went home from Mount Moriah, you did not need a eulogy to comfort you for what was lost, for you gained everything and kept Isaac—was it not so? The Lord did not take him away from you again, but you sat happily together at the dinner table in your tent, as you do in the next world for all eternity. Venerable Father Abraham! Centuries have passed since those days, but you have no need of a late lover to snatch your memory from the power of oblivion, for every language calls you to mind—and yet you reward your lover more gloriously than anyone else. In the life to come you make him eternally happy in your bosom; here in this life you captivate his eyes and his heart with the wonder of your act. Venerable Father Abraham! Second Father of the race! You who were the first to feel and to bear witness to that prodigious passion that disdains the terrifying battle with the raging elements and the forces of creation in order to contend with God, you who were the first to know that supreme passion, the holy, pure, and humble expression for the divine madness that was admired by the pagans—forgive the one who aspired to speak your praise if he has not done it properly. He spoke humbly, as his heart demanded; he spoke briefly, as is seemly. But he will never forget that you needed 100 years to get the son of your old age against all expectancy, that you had to draw the knife before you kept Isaac; he will never forget that in 130 years you got no further than faith.

ᴏ Preliminary Expectoration
from Fear and Trembling

From the external and visible world there comes an old adage: "Only one who works gets bread."* Oddly enough, the adage does not fit the world in which it is most at home, for imperfection is the fundamental law of the external world, and here it happens again and again that he who does not work does get bread, and he who sleeps gets it even more abundantly than he who works. In the external world, everything belongs to the possessor. It is subject to the law of indifference, and the spirit of the ring obeys the one who has the ring, whether he is an Aladdin or a Noured-

---

*Most footnotes omitted—ed.

din, and he who has the wealth of the world has it regardless of how he got it.

It is different in the world of the spirit. Here an eternal divine order prevails. Here it does not rain on both the just and the unjust; here the sun does not shine on both good and evil. Here it holds true that only the one who works gets bread, that only the one who was in anxiety finds rest, that only the one who descends into the lower world rescues the beloved, that only the one who draws the knife gets Isaac. He who will not work does not get bread but is deceived just as the gods deceived Orpheus with an ethereal phantom instead of the beloved, deceived him because he was soft, not boldly brave, deceived him because he was a zither player and not a man. Here it does not help to have Abraham as father or to have seventeen ancestors. The one who will not work fits what is written about the virgins of Israel: he gives birth to wind—but the one who will work gives birth to his own father.

There is a knowledge that presumptuously wants to introduce into the world of spirit the same law of indifference under which the external world sighs. It believes that it is enough to know what is great—no other work is needed. But for this reason it does not get bread; it perishes of hunger while everything changes to gold. And what in fact does it know? There were many thousands of Greek contemporaries, countless numbers in later generations, who knew all the triumphs of Miltiades, but there was only one who became sleepless over them. There were countless generations who knew the story of Abraham by heart, word for word, but how many did it render sleepless?

The story about Abraham is remarkable in that it is always glorious no matter how poorly it is understood, but here again it is a matter of whether or not we are willing to work and be burdened. But we are unwilling to work, and yet we want to understand the story. We glorify Abraham, but how? We recite the whole story in clichés: "The great thing was that he loved God in such a way that he was willing to offer him the best." This is very true, but "the best" is a vague term. Mentally and orally we homologize Isaac and the best, and the contemplator can very well smoke his pipe while cogitating, and the listener may very well stretch out his legs comfortably. If that rich young man whom Jesus met along the way had sold all his possessions and given the money to the poor, we would praise him as we praise every great deed, even if we could not understand him without working, but he still would not become an Abraham, even though he sacrificed the best. What is omitted from Abraham's story is the anxiety, because to money I have no ethical obligation, but to the son the father has the highest and holiest. We forget it and yet want to talk about Abraham. So we talk and in the process of talking interchange the two terms, Isaac and the best, and everything goes fine. But just suppose that someone listening is a man who suffers from sleeplessness—then the most terrifying, the most profound, tragic, and comic misunderstanding is very close at hand. He goes home, he wants to do just as Abraham did, for the son, after all, is the best. If the preacher found out about it, he perhaps would go to the man, he would muster all his ecclesiastical dignity and shout, "You despicable man, you scum of society, what devil has so possessed you that you want to murder your son." And the pastor, who had not noticed any heat or perspiration when preaching about Abraham, would be surprised at himself, at the wrathful earnestness with which he thunders at the poor man. He would be pleased with himself, for he had never spoken with such emphasis and emotion. He would say to himself and his wife, "I am an orator—what was lacking was the occasion. When I spoke about Abraham on Sunday, I did not feel gripped at all." If the same speaker had a little superfluity of understanding to spare, I am sure he would have lost it if the sinner had calmly and with dignity answered: But, after all, that was what you yourself preached about on Sunday. How could the preacher ever get such a thing in his head, and yet it was so, and his only mistake was that he did not know what he was saying. And to think that there is no poet who could bring himself to prefer situations such as this to the nonsense and trumpery with which comedies and novels are stuffed! The comic and the tragic make contact here in absolute infinitude. By itself, the preacher's discourse was perhaps ludicrous enough, but it became infinitely ludicrous through its effect, and yet this was quite natural. Or suppose that the unprotesting sinner is convinced by the pastor's severe lecture, suppose that the zealous pastor goes home happy—happy in the consciousness that he not only was effective in the pulpit but above all had irresistible power as a spiritual counselor, inasmuch as on Sunday he inspired the congregation, while on Monday, like a cherub with a flaming sword, he placed himself in front of the person whose actions would give the lie to the old saying that things do not go in the world as the preacher preaches.[‡‡]

But if the sinner remains unconvinced, his situation is really tragic. Then he probably will be executed or sent to the madhouse. In short, in relation to so-called reality, he became unhappy; in another sense, I am sure, Abraham made him happy, for he who works does not perish.

How is a contradiction such as that of the speaker to be explained? Is it because Abraham has gained a prescriptive right to be a great man, so that what he does is great and when another man does the same thing it is a sin, an atrocious sin? In that case, I do not wish to participate in such empty praise. If faith cannot make it a holy act to be willing to murder his son, then let the same judgment be passed on Abraham as on everyone else. If a person lacks the courage to think his thought all the way through and say that Abraham was a murderer, then it is certainly better to attain this courage than to waste time on unmerited eulogies. The ethical expression for what Abraham did is that he meant to murder Isaac; the religious expression is that he meant to sacrifice Isaac—but precisely in this contradiction is the anxiety that can make a person sleepless, and yet without this anxiety Abraham is not who he is. Or if Abraham perhaps did not do at all what the story tells, if perhaps because of the local conditions of that day it was something entirely different, then let us forget him, for what is the value of going to the trouble of remembering that past which cannot become a present. Or perhaps the speaker forgot something equivalent to the ethical oversight that Isaac was the son. In other words, if faith is taken away by becoming *Nul* and *Nichts,* all that remains is the brutal fact that Abraham meant to murder Isaac, which is easy enough for anyone to imitate if he does not have faith—that is, the faith that makes it difficult for him.

[‡‡] In the old days, people said: It is too bad that things do not go in the world as the preacher preaches. Maybe the time will come, especially with the aid of philosophy, when they can say: Fortunately things do not go as the preacher preaches, for there is still some meaning in life, but there is none in his sermons.

As for me, I do not lack the courage to think a complete thought. Up to now I have feared none, and if I should encounter such a one, I hope that I at least will have the honesty to say: This thought makes me afraid, it shocks me, and therefore I will not think it. If I am wrong in so doing, my punishment will not fail to come. If I had acknowledged as true the judgment that Abraham was a murderer, I am not sure that I would have been able to silence my reverence for him. But if I did think that, I probably would have said nothing, for one should not initiate others into such thoughts. But Abraham is no illusion, he did not sleep his way to fame, he does not owe it to a whim of fate.

Is it possible to speak unreservedly about Abraham without running the risk that some individual will become unbalanced and do the same thing? If I dare not, I will say nothing at all about Abraham, and the last thing I will do is to scale him down in such a way that he thereby becomes a snare for the weak. As a matter of fact, if one makes faith everything—that is, makes it what it is—then I certainly believe that I dare to speak of it without danger in our day, which is scarcely prodigal in faith. It is only by faith that one achieves any resemblance to Abraham, not by murder. If one makes love into a fleeting mood, a sensual feeling in a person, then one only lays snares for the weak by talking about the achievements of love. Everyone, to be sure, has momentary feelings, but if everyone therefore would do the dreadful thing that love has sanctified as an immortal achievement, then everything is lost, both the achievement and the one led astray.

It is permissible, then, to speak about Abraham, for whatever is great can never do damage when it is understood in its greatness; it is like a two-edged sword that kills and saves. If it fell to my lot to speak about him, I would begin by showing what a devout and God-fearing man Abraham was, worthy of being called God's chosen one. Only a person of that kind is put to such a test, but who is such a person? Next I would describe how Abraham loved Isaac. For that purpose I would call upon all the good spirits to stand by me so that what I said would have the glow of fatherly love. I hope to describe it in such a way that there would not be many a father in the realms and lands of the king who would dare to maintain that he loved in this way. But if he did not love as Abraham loved, then any thought of sacrificing Isaac would surely be a spiritual trial. On this point alone, one

could talk for several Sundays—after all, one does not need to be in a great hurry. If it were done properly, the result would be that some of the fathers would by no means demand to hear more but for the time being would be pleased if they actually succeeded in loving as Abraham loved. But if there was one who, having heard the greatness as well as the dreadfulness in Abraham's deed, ventured to proceed along that path, I would saddle my horse and ride along with him. At every station before coming to Mount Moriah, I would explain to him that he still could turn around, could repent of the misunderstanding that he was called to be tried in such a conflict, could confess that he lacked the courage, so that God himself would have to take Isaac if he wanted to have him. It is my conviction that such a man is not repudiated, that he can be blessed along with all the others, but not within time. Even in the periods of the greatest faith, would not such a judgment be passed on a man like that? I knew a man who once could have saved my life if he had been magnanimous. He spoke bluntly, "I see very well what I could do, but I dare not; I fear that eventually I shall lack strength, that I shall regret it." He was not magnanimous, but who would therefore not go on loving him?

Having spoken thus, having stirred the listeners to an awareness of the dialectical struggles of faith and its gigantic passion, then I would not become guilty of an error on the part of the listeners, so they would think, "He has faith to such a degree that all we have to do is hang onto his coattails." I would add, "By no means do I have faith. By nature I am a shrewd fellow, and shrewd people always have great difficulty in making the movement of faith, but I do not attribute per se *any worth to the difficulty that brought the shrewd person further in the overcoming of it than to the point at which the simplest and most unsophisticated person arrives more easily.*"

Love indeed has its priests in the poets, and occasionally we hear a voice that knows how to honor it, but not a word is heard about faith. Who speaks to the honor of this passion? Philosophy goes further. Theology sits all rouged and powdered in the window and courts its favor, offers its charms to philosophy. It is supposed to be difficult to understand Hegel, but to understand Abraham is a small matter. To go beyond Hegel is a miraculous achievement, but to go beyond Abraham is the easiest of all. I for my part have applied considerable time to understanding Hegelian philosophy and believe that I have understood it fairly well; I am sufficiently brash to think that when I cannot understand particular passages despite all my pains, he himself may not have been entirely clear. All this I do easily, naturally, without any mental strain. Thinking about Abraham is another matter, however; then I am shattered. I am constantly aware of the prodigious paradox that is the content of Abraham's life, I am constantly repelled, and, despite all its passion, my thought cannot penetrate it, cannot get ahead by a hairsbreadth. I stretch every muscle to get a perspective, and at the very same instant I become paralyzed.

I am not unfamiliar with what the world has admired as great and magnanimous. My soul feels its kinship with it and in all humility is certain that the cause for which the hero strives is also my cause, and when I consider it, I cry out to myself: *jam tua res agitur* [now your cause is at stake]. I *think* myself *into* the hero; I cannot think myself into Abraham; when I reach that eminence, I sink down, for what is offered me is a paradox. I by no means conclude that faith is something inferior but rather that it is the highest, also that it is dishonest of philosophy to give something else in its place and to disparage faith. Philosophy cannot and must not give faith, but it must understand itself and know what it offers and take nothing away, least of all trick men out of something by pretending that it is nothing. I am not unfamiliar with the hardships and dangers of life. I fear them not and approach them confidently. I am not unfamiliar with the terrifying. My memory is a faithful spouse, and my imagination, unlike myself, is a busy little maid who sits all day at her work and in the evening can coax me so charmingly that I have to look at it, even though it is not always landscapes or flowers or *Schäfer-Historier* [pastoral idylls] that she paints. I have seen the terrifying face to face, and I do not flee from it in horror, but I know very well that even though I advance toward it courageously, my courage is still not the courage of faith and is not something to be compared with it. I cannot make the movement of faith, I cannot shut my eyes and plunge confidently into the absurd; it is for me an impossibility, but I do not praise myself for that. I am convinced that God is love; for me this thought has a primal lyrical validity. When it is present to me, I am unspeakably happy; when it is absent, I long for it more vehemently than the lover for the object of his love. But I do not have

faith; this courage I lack. To me God's love, in both the direct and the converse sense, is incommensurable with the whole of actuality. Knowing that, I am not so cowardly that I whimper and complain, but neither am I so perfidious as to deny that faith is something far higher. I can bear to live in my own fashion, I am happy and satisfied, but my joy is not the joy of faith, and by comparison with that, it is unhappy. I do not trouble God with my little troubles, details do not concern me; I gaze only at my love and keep its virgin flame pure and clear. Faith is convinced that God is concerned about the smallest things. I am satisfied with a left-handed marriage in this life; faith is humble enough to insist on the right hand, for I do not deny that this is humility and will never deny it.

I wonder if anyone in my generation is able to make the movements of faith? If I am not mistaken, my generation is rather inclined to be proud of doing what it probably does not even believe me capable of—that is, the imperfect. My soul balks at doing what is so often done—talking inhumanly about the great, as if a few centuries were an enormous distance. I prefer to speak humanly about it, as if it happened yesterday, and only let the greatness itself be the distance that either elevates or judges. If I (*in the capacity of tragic hero,* for higher I cannot come) had been ordered to take such an extraordinary royal journey as the one to Mount Moriah, I know very well what I would have done. I would not have been cowardly enough to stay at home, nor would I have dragged and drifted along the road or forgotten the knife in order to cause a delay. I am quite sure that I would have been punctual and all prepared—more than likely, I would have arrived too early in order to get it over sooner. But I also know what else I would have done. The moment I mounted the horse, I would have said to myself: Now all is lost, God demands Isaac, I sacrifice him and along with him all my joy—yet God is love and continues to be that for me, for in the world of time God and I cannot talk with each other, we have no language in common. Perhaps someone in our time would be so foolish, so envious of the great, as to want to delude himself and me into believing that if I had actually done this I would have done something even greater than what Abraham did, for my immense resignation would be far more ideal and poetic than Abraham's small-mindedness. But this is utterly false, for my immense resignation would be a substitute for faith. I would not be able to do more than make the infinite movement in order to find myself and again rest in myself. Neither would I have loved Isaac as Abraham loved him. That I was determined to make the movement could prove my courage, humanly speaking—that I loved him with my whole soul is the presupposition without which the whole thing becomes a misdeed—nevertheless I would not love as Abraham loved, for then I would have held back at the very last minute, without, however, arriving too late at Mount Moriah. Furthermore, by my behavior I would have spoiled the whole story, for if I had gotten Isaac again, I would have been in an awkward position. What was the easiest for Abraham would have been difficult for me—once again to be happy in Isaac!—for he who with all the infinity of his soul, *proprio motu et propriis auspiciis* [of his own accord and on his own responsibility], has made the infinite movement and cannot do more, he keeps Isaac only with pain.

But what did Abraham do? He arrived neither too early nor too late. He mounted the ass, he rode slowly down the road. During all this time he had faith, he had faith that God would not demand Isaac of him, and yet he was willing to sacrifice him if it was demanded. He had faith by virtue of the absurd, for human calculation was out of the question, and it certainly was absurd that God, who required it of him, should in the next moment rescind the requirement. He climbed the mountain, and even in the moment when the knife gleamed he had faith—that God would not require Isaac. No doubt he was surprised at the outcome, but through a double-movement he had attained his first condition, and therefore he received Isaac more joyfully than the first time. Let us go further. We let Isaac actually be sacrificed. Abraham had faith. He did not have faith that he would be blessed in a future life but that he would be blessed here in the world. God could give him a new Isaac, could restore to life the one sacrificed. He had faith by virtue of the absurd, for all human calculation ceased long ago. It is evident that sorrow can make a man mentally ill, and that is hard enough; it is also evident that there is a willpower that can haul to the wind so drastically that it rescues the understanding, even though a person becomes a little odd (and I do not intend to disparage this). But to be able to lose one's understanding and along with it everything finite, for which it is the stockbroker, and then to win the very same finitude again by virtue of the absurd—this

appalls me, but that does not make me say it is something inferior, since, on the contrary, it is the one and only marvel. It is commonly supposed that what faith produces is no work of art, that it is a coarse and boorish piece of work, only for the more uncouth natures, but it is far from being that. The dialectic of faith is the finest and the most extraordinary of all; it has an elevation of which I can certainly form a conception, but no more than that. I can make the mighty trampoline leap whereby I cross over into infinity; my back is like a tightrope dancer's, twisted in my childhood, and therefore it is easy for me. One, two, three—I can walk upside down in existence, but I cannot make the next movement, for the marvelous I cannot do—I can only be amazed at it. Indeed, if Abraham, the moment he swung his leg over the ass's back, had said to himself: Now Isaac is lost, I could just as well sacrifice him here at home as ride the long way to Moriah—then I do not need Abraham, whereas now I bow seven times to his name and seventy times to his deed. This he did not do, as I can prove by his really fervent joy on receiving Isaac and by his needing no preparation and no time to rally to finitude and its joy. If it had been otherwise with Abraham, he perhaps would have loved God but would not have had faith, for he who loves God without faith reflects upon himself; he who loves God in faith reflects upon God.

This is the peak on which Abraham stands. The last stage to pass from his view is the stage of infinite resignation. He actually goes further and comes to faith. All those travesties of faith—the wretched, lukewarm lethargy that thinks: There's no urgency, there's no use in grieving beforehand; the despicable hope that says: One just can't know what will happen, it could just possibly be—those travesties are native to the paltriness of life, and infinite resignation has already infinitely disdained them.

Abraham I cannot understand; in a certain sense I can learn nothing from him except to be amazed. If someone deludes himself into thinking he may be moved to have faith by pondering the outcome of that story, he cheats himself and cheats God out of the first movement of faith—he wants to suck worldly wisdom out of the paradox. Someone might succeed, for our generation does not stop with faith, does not stop with the miracle of faith, turning water into wine—it goes further and turns wine into water.

Would it not be best to stop with faith, and is it not shocking that everyone wants to go further? Where will it all end when in our age, as declared in so many ways, one does not want to stop with love? In worldly shrewdness, in petty calculation, in paltriness and meanness, in everything that can make man's divine origin doubtful. Would it not be best to remain standing at faith and for him who stands to see to it that he does not fall, for the movement of faith must continually be made by virtue of the absurd, but yet in such a way, please note, that one does not lose the finite but gains it whole and intact. For my part, I presumably can describe the movements of faith, but I cannot make them. In learning to go through the motions of swimming, one can be suspended from the ceiling in a harness and then presumably describe the movements, but one is not swimming. In the same way I can describe the movements of faith. If I am thrown out into the water, I presumably do swim (for I do not belong to the waders), but I make different movements, the movements of infinity, whereas faith makes the opposite movements: after having made the movements of infinity, it makes the movements of finitude. Fortunate is the person who can make these movements! He does the marvelous, and I shall never weary of admiring him; it makes no difference to me whether it is Abraham or a slave in Abraham's house, whether it is a professor of philosophy or a poor servant girl—I pay attention only to the movements. But I do pay attention to them, and I do not let myself be fooled, either by myself or by anyone else. The knights of the infinite resignation are easily recognizable—their walk is light and bold. But they who carry the treasure of faith are likely to disappoint, for externally they have a striking resemblance to bourgeois philistinism, which infinite resignation, like faith, deeply disdains.

I honestly confess that in my experience I have not found a single authentic instance, although I do not therefore deny that every second person may be such an instance. Meanwhile, I have been looking for it for many years, but in vain. Generally, people travel around the world to see rivers and mountains, new stars, colorful birds, freakish fish, preposterous races of mankind; they indulge in the brutish stupor that gawks at life and thinks it has seen something. That does not occupy me. But if I knew where a knight of faith lived, I would travel on foot to him, for this marvel occupies me absolutely. I would not leave him for a second, I would watch him every minute to see how he made the movements; I would consider myself

taken care of for life and would divide my time between watching him and practicing myself, and thus spend all my time in admiring him. As I said before, I have not found anyone like that; meanwhile, I may very well imagine him. Here he is. The acquaintance is made, I am introduced to him. The instant I first lay eyes on him, I set him apart at once; I jump back, clap my hands, and say half aloud, "Good Lord, is this the man, is this really the one—he looks just like a tax collector!" But this is indeed the one. I move a little closer to him, watch his slightest movement to see if it reveals a bit of heterogeneous optical telegraphy from the infinite, a glance, a facial expression, a gesture, a sadness, a smile that would betray the infinite in its heterogeneity with the finite. No! I examine his figure from top to toe to see if there may not be a crack through which the infinite would peek. No! He is solid all the way through. His stance? It is vigorous, belongs entirely to finitude; no spruced-up burgher walking out to Fresberg on a Sunday afternoon treads the earth more solidly. He belongs entirely to the world; no bourgeois philistine could belong to it more. Nothing is detectable of that distant and aristocratic nature by which the knight of the infinite is recognized. He finds pleasure in everything, takes part in everything, and every time one sees him participating in something particular, he does it with an assiduousness that marks the worldly man who is attached to such things. He attends to his job. To see him makes one think of him as a pen-pusher who has lost his soul to Italian bookkeeping, so punctilious is he. Sunday is for him a holiday. He goes to church. No heavenly gaze or any sign of the incommensurable betrays him; if one did not know him, it would be impossible to distinguish him from the rest of the crowd, for at most his hearty and powerful singing of the hymns proves that he has good lungs. In the afternoon, he takes a walk to the woods. He enjoys everything he sees, the swarms of people, the new omnibuses, the Sound. Encountering him on Strandveien, one would take him for a mercantile soul enjoying himself. He finds pleasure in this way, for he is not a poet, and I have tried in vain to lure the poetic incommensurability out of him. Toward evening, he goes home, and his gait is as steady as a postman's. On the way, he thinks that his wife surely will have a special hot meal for him when he comes home—for example, roast lamb's head with vegetables. If he meets a kindred soul, he would go on talking all the way to Østerport about this delicacy with a passion befitting a restaurant operator. It so happens that he does not have four shillings to his name, and yet he firmly believes that his wife has this delectable meal waiting for him. If she has, to see him eat would be the envy of the elite and an inspiration to the common man, for his appetite is keener than Esau's. His wife does not have it—curiously enough, he is just the same. On the way he passes a building site and meets another man. They converse for a moment; in an instant he erects a building, and he himself has at his disposition everything required. The stranger leaves him thinking that he surely is a capitalist, while my admired knight thinks: Well, if it came right down to it, I could easily get it. He sits at an open window and surveys the neighborhood where he lives: everything that happens—a rat scurrying under a plank across the gutter, children playing—engages him with an equanimity akin to that of a sixteen-year-old girl. And yet he is no genius, for I have sought in vain to spy out the incommensurability of genius in him. In the evening, he smokes his pipe; seeing him, one would swear it was the butcher across the way vegetating in the gloaming. With the freedom from care of a reckless good-for-nothing, he lets things take care of themselves, and yet every moment of his life he buys the opportune time at the highest price, for he does not do even the slightest thing except by virtue of the absurd. And yet, yet—yes, I could be infuriated over it if for no other reason than envy—and yet this man has made and at every moment is making the movement of infinity. He drains the deep sadness of life in infinite resignation, he knows the blessedness of infinity, he has felt the pain of renouncing everything, the most precious thing in the world, and yet the finite tastes just as good to him as to one who never knew anything higher, because his remaining in finitude would have no trace of a timorous, anxious routine, and yet he has this security that makes him delight in it as if finitude were the surest thing of all. And yet, yet the whole earthly figure he presents is a new creation by virtue of the absurd. He resigned everything infinitely, and then he grasped everything again by virtue of the absurd. He is continually making the movement of infinity, but he does it with such precision and assurance that he continually gets finitude out of it, and no one ever suspects anything else. It is supposed to be the most difficult feat for a ballet dancer to leap into a specific posture in such a way that he never once strains for the posture but in the very leap assumes the posture. Perhaps there is no ballet dancer who can do it—but this knight does it. Most people live completely absorbed in worldly joys and sorrows; they are benchwarmers who do not take part in the dance. The knights of infinity are ballet dancers and have elevation. They make the upward movement and come down again, and this, too, is not an unhappy diversion and is not unlovely to see. But every time they come down, they are unable to assume the posture immediately, they waver for a moment, and this wavering shows that they are aliens in the world. It is more or less conspicuous according to their skill, but even the most skillful of these knights cannot hide this wavering. One does not need to see them in the air; one needs only to see them the instant they touch and have touched the earth—and then one recognizes them. But to be able to come down in such a way that instantaneously one seems to stand and to walk, to change the leap into life into walking, absolutely to express the sublime in the pedestrian—only that knight can do it, and this is the one and only marvel.

Nevertheless, this marvel can so easily deceive that I shall describe the movements in a specific case that can illuminate their relation to actuality, for this is the central issue. A young lad falls in love with a princess, and this love is the entire substance of his life, and yet the relation is such that it cannot possibly be realized, cannot possibly be translated from ideality into reality.[§§] Of course, the slaves of the finite, the frogs in the swamp of life, scream: That kind of love is foolishness; the rich brewer's widow is just as good and solid a match. Let them go on croaking in the swamp. The knight of infinite resignation does not do any such thing; he does not give up the love, not for all the glories of the world. He is no fool. First of all, he assures himself that it actually is the substance of his life, and his soul is too healthy and too proud to waste the least of it in an intoxication. He is not cowardly; he is not

---

[§§] It goes without saying that any other interest in which an individual has concentrated the whole reality [*Realitet*] of actuality [*Virkelighedens*] can, if it proves to be unrealizable, prompt the movement of resignation. I have chosen a love affair to show the movements, because this interest is far easier to understand and thus frees me from all preliminary considerations that in a deeper sense could be of concern only to very few individuals.

afraid to let it steal into his most secret, his most remote thoughts, to let it twist and entwine itself intricately around every ligament of his consciousness—if his love comes to grief, he will never be able to wrench himself out of it. He feels a blissful delight in letting love palpitate in every nerve, and yet his soul is as solemn as the soul of one who has drunk the poisoned cup and feels the juice penetrate every drop of blood—for this is the moment of crisis. Having totally absorbed this love and immersed himself in it, he does not lack the courage to attempt and to risk everything. He examines the conditions of his life, he convenes the swift thoughts that obey his every hint, like well-trained doves, he flourishes his staff, and they scatter in all directions. But now when they all come back, all of them like messengers of grief, and explain that it is an impossibility, he becomes very quiet, he dismisses them, he becomes solitary, and then he undertakes the movement. If what I say here is to have any meaning, the point is that the movement is carried out normatively.## In the first place, the knight will then have the power to concentrate the whole substance of his life and the meaning of actuality into one single desire. If a person lacks this concentration, this focus, his soul is dissipated in multiplicity from the beginning, and then he never manages to make the movement; he acts as shrewdly in life as the financiers who put their resources into

---

This requires passion. *Every movement of infinity is carried out through passion, and no reflection can produce a movement. This is the continual leap in existence that explains the movement, whereas mediation is a chimera, which in Hegel is supposed to explain everything and which is also the only thing he never has tried to explain.* Just to make the celebrated Socratic distinction between what one understands and what one does not understand requires passion; and even more, of course, [passion is necessary in order] to make the authentic Socratic movement, the movement of ignorance. What our generation lacks is not reflection but passion. In one sense, therefore, our age is actually too tenacious of life to die, for dying is one of the most remarkable leaps, and a little poem has always appealed to me very much because the poet, after beautifully and simply expressing his desire for the good things of life in five or six lines, ends thus:

ein seliger Sprung in die Ewigkeit
[a blessed leap into eternity].

widely diversified investments in order to gain on one if they lose on another—in short, he is not a knight. In the next place, the knight will have the power to concentrate the conclusion of all his thinking into one act of consciousness. If he lacks this focus, his soul is dissipated in multiplicity from the beginning, and he will never find the time to make the movement; he will continually be running errands in life and will never enter into eternity, for in the very moment he approaches it, he will suddenly discover that he has forgotten something and therefore must go back. In the next moment, he thinks, it will be possible, and this is quite true, but with such observations one will never come to make the movement but with their help will sink deeper and deeper into the mire.

The knight, then, makes the movement, but which one? Will he forget it all, for this, too, constitutes a kind of concentration? No, for the knight does not contradict himself, and it is a contradiction to forget the whole substance of his life and yet remain the same. He feels no inclination to become another person, by no means regards that as something great. Only the lower natures forget themselves and become something new. The butterfly, for example, completely forgets that it was a caterpillar, and may in turn so completely forget that it was a butterfly that it may become a fish. The deeper natures never forget themselves and never become anything other than what they were. The knight, then, will recollect everything, but this recollection is precisely the pain, and yet in infinite resignation he is reconciled with existence. His love for that princess would become for him the expression of an eternal love, would assume a religious character, would be transfigured into a love of the eternal being, which true enough denied the fulfillment but nevertheless did reconcile him once more in the eternal consciousness of its validity in an eternal form that no actuality can take away from him. Fools and young people say that everything is possible for a human being. But that is a gross error. Spiritually speaking, everything is possible, but in the finite world there is much that is not possible. The knight, however, makes this impossibility possible by expressing it spiritually, but he expresses it spiritually by renouncing it. The desire that would lead him out into actuality but has been stranded on impossibility is now turned inward, but it is not therefore lost, nor is it forgotten. Sometimes it is the vague emotions of desire in him that awaken recollection; sometimes he awakens it himself, for he is too proud to be willing to let the whole substance of his life turn out to have been an affair of the fleeting moment. He keeps this love young, and it grows along with him in years and in beauty. But he needs no finite occasion for its growth. From the moment he has made the movement, the princess is lost. He does not need the erotic titillation of seeing the beloved etc., nor does he in the finite sense continually need to be bidding her farewell, because in the eternal sense he recollects her, and he knows very well that the lovers who are so bent on seeing each other for the last time in order to say farewell once again are justified in their eagerness, justified in thinking it to be the last time, for they forget each other very quickly. He has grasped the deep secret that even in loving another person one ought to be sufficient to oneself. He is no longer finitely concerned about what the princess does, and precisely this proves that he has made the movement infinitely. Here one has occasion to see whether the movement in an individual is authentic or feigned. There was one who also believed that he had made the movement; but look, time passed, the princess did something else—she married, for example, a prince—and his soul lost the resilience of resignation. He thereby demonstrated that he had not made the movement properly, for one who has resigned infinitely is sufficient to oneself. The knight does not cancel his resignation, he keeps his love just as young as it was in the first moment; he never loses it simply because he has made the movement infinitely. What the princess does cannot disturb him; it is only the lower natures who have the law for their actions in someone else, the premises for their actions outside themselves. If, however, the princess is similarly disposed, something beautiful will emerge. She will then introduce herself into the order of knighthood into which one is not taken by election but of which everyone is a member who has the courage to enroll oneself, the order of knighthood that proves its immortality by making no distinction between male and female. She, too, will keep her love young and sound; she, too, will have overcome her agony, even though she does not, as the ballad says, lie by her lord's side every night. These two will in all eternity be compatible, with such a rhythmical *harmonia præstabilita* that if the moment ever came—a moment, however, that does not concern them finitely, for then they

would grow old—if the moment ever came that allowed them to give love its expression in time, they would be capable of beginning right where they would have begun if they had been united in the beginning. The person who understands this, whether man or woman, can never be deceived, for it is only the baser natures that fancy that they are deceived. No girl who does not have this pride actually understands what it means to love, but if she does have this pride, the craftiness and cunning of the whole world cannot deceive her.

In infinite resignation there is peace and rest; every person who wills it, who has not debased himself by self-disdain—which is still more dreadful than being too proud—can discipline himself to make this movement, which in its pain reconciles one to existence. Infinite resignation is that shirt mentioned in an old legend. The thread is spun with tears, bleached with tears; the shirt is sewn in tears—but then it also gives protection better than iron or steel. The defect in the legend is that a third person can work up this linen. The secret in life is that each person must sew it himself, and the remarkable thing is that a man can sew it fully as well as a woman. In infinite resignation there is peace and rest and comfort in the pain, that is, when the movement is made normatively. I could easily write a whole book if I were to expound the various misunderstandings, the awkward positions, the botched up movements I have encountered in just my own little experience. There is little belief in spirit, and yet the essential thing in making this movement is spirit. It is essential that it not be a unilateral result of a *dira necessitas* [cruel constraint of necessity], and the more this is present, the more doubtful it always is that the movement is normal. Thus, if one believes that cold, barren necessity must necessarily be present, then one is declaring thereby that no one can experience death before one actually dies, which to me seems to be cross materialism. But in our age people are less concerned about making pure movements. If someone who wanted to learn to dance were to say: For centuries, one generation after the other has learned the positions, and it is high time that I take advantage of this and promptly begin with the quadrille—people would presumably laugh a little at him, but in the world of spirit this is very plausible. What, then, is education? I believed it is the course the individual goes through in order to catch up with himself, and the person who will not go through this course is not much helped by being born in the most enlightened age.

Infinite resignation is the last stage before faith, so that anyone who has not made this movement does not have faith, for only in infinite resignation do I become conscious of my eternal validity, and only then can one speak of grasping existence by virtue of faith.

Now let us meet the knight of faith on the occasion previously mentioned. He does exactly the same as the other knight did: he infinitely renounces the love that is the substance of his life, he is reconciled in pain. But then the marvel happens; he makes one more movement even more wonderful than all the others, for he says: Nevertheless I have faith that I will get her —that is, by virtue of the absurd, by virtue of the fact that for God all things are possible. The absurd does not belong to the differences that lie within the proper domain of the understanding. It is not identical with the improbable, the unexpected, the unforeseen. The moment the knight executed the act of resignation, he was convinced of the impossibility, humanly speaking; that was the conclusion of the understanding, and he had sufficient energy to think it. But in the infinite sense it was possible, that is, by relinquishing it [*resignere derpaa*], but this having, after all, is also a giving up. Nevertheless, to the understanding this having is no absurdity, for the understanding continues to be right in maintaining that in the finite world where it dominates this having was and continues to be an impossibility. The knight of faith realizes this just as clearly; consequently, he can be saved only by the absurd, and this he grasps by faith. Consequently, he acknowledges the impossibility, and in the very same moment he believes the absurd, for if he wants to imagine that he has faith without passionately acknowledging the impossibility with his whole heart and soul, he is deceiving himself and his testimony is neither here nor there, since he has not even attained infinite resignation.

Precisely because resignation is antecedent, faith is no esthetic emotion but something far higher; it is not the spontaneous inclination of the heart but the paradox of existence. If, for example, in the face of every difficulty, a young girl still remains convinced that her desire will be fulfilled, this assurance is by no means the assurance of faith, even though she has been brought up by Christian parents and perhaps has had confirmation instruction from the pastor for a whole year. She is convinced in all her childlike naiveté and innocence, and this assurance ennobles her nature and gives her a supranatural magnitude so that like a thaumaturge she can invoke the finite powers of existence and bring the very stones to tears, while on the other hand in her perplexity she can just as well run to Herod as to Pilate and move the whole world with her pleas. Her assurance is most captivating, and one can learn much from her, but there is one thing that cannot be learned from her—how to make movements—for her assurance does not dare, in the pain of resignation, to look the impossibility in the eye.

So I can perceive that it takes strength and energy and spiritual freedom to make the infinite movement of resignation; I can also perceive that it can be done. The next [movement] amazes me, my brain reels, for, after having made the movement of resignation, then by virtue of the absurd to get everything, to get one's desire totally and completely—that is over and beyond human powers, that is a marvel. But this I can perceive: that the young girl's assurance is nothing but rashness compared with the unshakability of faith in the full recognition of the impossibility. Every time I want to make this movement, I almost faint; the very same moment I admire absolutely, I am seized with great anxiety. For what is it to tempt God? And yet this is the movement of faith and continues to be that, even though philosophy, so as to confuse the concepts, wants to delude us into thinking it has faith, even though theology is willing to sell it off at a low price.

The act of resignation does not require faith, for what I gain in resignation is my eternal consciousness. This is a purely philosophical movement that I venture to make when it is demanded and can discipline myself to make, because every time some finitude will take power over me, I starve myself into submission until I make the movement, for my eternal consciousness is my love for God, and for me that is the highest of all. The act of resignation does not require faith, but to get the least little bit more than my eternal consciousness requires faith, for this is the paradox. The movements are often confused. It is said that faith is needed in order to renounce everything. Indeed, one hears what is even more curious: a person laments that he has lost his faith, and when a check is made to see where he is on the scale, curiously enough, he has only reached the point where he is to make the infinite movement of resignation. Through resignation I renounce everything. I make this movement all by myself, and if I do not make it, it is because I am too cowardly and soft and devoid of enthusiasm and do not feel the significance of the high dignity assigned to every human being, to be his own censor, which is far more exalted than to be the censor general of the whole Roman republic. This movement I make all by myself, and what I gain thereby is my eternal consciousness in blessed harmony with my love for the eternal being. By faith I do not renounce anything; on the contrary, by faith I receive everything exactly in the sense in which it is said that one who has faith like a mustard seed can move mountains. It takes a purely human courage to renounce the whole temporal realm in order to gain eternity, but this I do gain and in all eternity can never renounce—it is a self-contradiction. But it takes a paradoxical and humble courage to grasp the whole temporal realm now by virtue of the absurd, and this is the courage of faith. By faith Abraham did not renounce Isaac, but by faith Abraham received Isaac. By virtue of resignation, that rich young man should have given away everything, but if he had done so, then the knight of faith would have said to him: By virtue of the absurd, you will get every penny back again—believe it! And the formerly rich young man should by no means treat these words lightly, for if he were to give away his possessions because he is bored with them, then his resignation would not amount to much.

Temporality, finitude—that is what it is all about. I can resign everything by my own strength and find peace and rest in the pain; I can put up with everything—even if that dreadful demon, more horrifying than the skeletal one who terrifies men, even if madness held its fool's costume before my eyes and I understood from its face that it was I who should put it on—I can still save my soul as long as my concern that my love of God conquer within me is greater than my concern that I achieve earthly happiness. In his very last moment, a person can still concentrate his whole soul in one single look to heaven, from whence come all good gifts, and this look will be understood by himself and by him whom it seeks to mean that he has been true to his love. Then he will calmly put on the costume. He whose soul lacks this romanticism has sold his soul, whether he gets a kingdom or a wretched piece of silver for it. By my own strength I

cannot get the least little thing that belongs to finitude, for I continually use my strength in resigning everything. By my own strength I can give up the princess, and I will not sulk about it but find joy and peace and rest in my pain, but by my own strength I cannot get her back again, for I use all my strength in resigning. On the other hand, by faith, says that marvelous knight, by faith you will get her by virtue of the absurd.

But this movement I cannot make. As soon as I want to begin, everything reverses itself, and I take refuge in the pain of resignation. I am able to swim in life, but I am too heavy for this mystical hovering. To exist in such a way that my contrast to existence constantly expresses itself as the most beautiful and secure harmony with it—this I cannot do. And yet, I repeatedly say, it must be wonderful to get the princess. The knight of resignation who does not say this is a deceiver; he has not had one single desire, and he has not kept his desire young in his pain. There may be someone who found it quite convenient that the desire was no longer alive and that the arrow of his pain had grown dull, but such a person is no knight. A free-born soul who caught himself doing this would despise himself and begin all over again, and above all would not allow his soul to be self-deceived. And yet it must be wonderful to get the princess, and the knight of faith is the only happy man, the heir to the finite, while the knight of resignation is a stranger and an alien. To get the princess this way, to live happily with her day after day (for it is also conceivable that the knight of resignation could get the princess, but his soul had full insight into the impossibility of their future happiness), to live happily every moment this way by virtue of the absurd, every moment to see the sword hanging over the beloved's head, and yet not to find rest in the pain of resignation but to find joy by virtue of the absurd—this is wonderful. The person who does this is great, the only great one; the thought of it stirs my soul, which never was stingy in admiring the great.

If everyone in my generation who does not wish to stop with faith is actually a person who has grasped the horror of life, has grasped the meaning of Daub's statement that a soldier standing alone with a loaded rifle at his post near a powder magazine on a stormy night thinks strange thoughts; if everyone who does not wish to stop with faith is actually a person who has the spiritual power to comprehend that the wish was an impossibility and then to take time to be alone with the thought; if everyone who does not wish to stop with faith is a person who in pain is reconciled and is reconciled through pain; if everyone who does not wish to stop with faith is a person who subsequently (and if he has not done all the foregoing, then he should not trouble himself when the issue is that of faith) performed the marvel and grasped existence in its totality by virtue of the absurd—then what I am writing is the loftiest eulogy upon the generation by its most inferior member, who could make only the movement of resignation. But why are they not willing to stop with faith? Why do we sometimes hear that people are ashamed to acknowledge that they have faith? I cannot comprehend it. If I ever manage to be able to make this movement, I will in the future drive with four horses.

Is it actually the case that all the bourgeois philistinism I see in life—which I do not permit myself to condemn with my words but with my deeds—is actually not what it seems, is the marvel? It is indeed conceivable, for that hero of faith did, after all, have a striking resemblance to it, for that hero of faith was not even an ironist and humorist but something much higher. There is a lot of talk these days about irony and humor, especially by people who have never been able to practice them but nevertheless know how to explain everything. I am not completely unfamiliar with these two passions; I know a little more about them than is found in German and German-Danish compendiums. Therefore I know that these two passions are essentially different from the passion of faith. Irony and humor are also self-reflective and thus belong to the sphere of infinite resignation; their elasticity is owing to the individual's incommensurability with actuality.

Be it a duty or whatever, I cannot make the final movement, the paradoxical movement of faith, although there is nothing I wish more. Whether a person has the right to say this must be his own decision; whether he can come to an amicable agreement in this respect is a matter between himself and the eternal being, who is the object of faith. Every person can make the movement of infinite resignation, and for my part I would not hesitate to call a coward anyone who imagines that he cannot do it. Faith is another matter, but no one has the right to lead others to believe that faith is something inferior or that it is an easy matter, since on the contrary it is the greatest and most difficult of all.

The story of Abraham is understood in another way. We praise God's mercy, that he gave him Isaac again and that the whole thing was only an ordeal. An ordeal, this word can say much and little, and yet the whole thing is over as soon as it is spoken. We mount a winged horse, and in the same instant we are on Mount Moriah, in the same instant we see the ram. We forget that Abraham only rode an ass, which trudges along the road, that he had a journey of three days, that he needed some time to chop the firewood, to bind Isaac, and to sharpen the knife.

And yet we pay tribute to Abraham. The speaker can just as well sleep until the last quarter hour before he has to speak; the listener can just as well go to sleep during the speech, for everything goes along splendidly without any trouble on either side. If someone were present who suffered from sleeplessness, he would perhaps go home, sit down in a corner, and think: The whole thing is over in a moment; all you have to do is wait for a minute and you will see the ram, and the ordeal will be over. If the speaker were to meet him in this situation, I think he would step up to him in all his dignity and say, "What a wretched man, to let your soul sink into such foolishness; no miracle takes place, and all life is an ordeal." As the speaker grew more effusive, he would become more and more emotional, more and more pleased with himself, and although he noticed no gorged blood vessels when he was talking about Abraham, he now would feel the veins on his forehead swell. Perhaps he would be dumbfounded if the sinner quietly and with dignity answered: After all, that was what you preached about last Sunday.

Let us then either cancel out Abraham or learn to be horrified by the prodigious paradox that is the meaning of his life, so that we may understand that our age, like every other age, can rejoice if it has faith. If Abraham is not a nobody, a phantom, a showpiece used for diversion, then the sinner can never err in wanting to do likewise, but the point is to perceive the greatness of what Abraham did so that the person can judge for himself whether he has the vocation and the courage to be tried in something like this. The comic contradiction in the speaker's behavior was that he made a nonentity of Abraham and yet wanted to forbid the other to conduct himself in the same way.

Should we, then, not dare to speak about Abraham? I surely think we can. If I were to speak about him, I would first of all describe the pain of the ordeal. To that end, I would, like a leech, suck all the anxiety and distress and torment out of a father's suffering in order to describe what Abraham suffered, although under it all he had faith. I would point out that the journey lasted three days and a good part of the fourth; indeed, these three and a half days could be infinitely longer than the few thousand years that separate me from Abraham. I would point out—and this is my view—that every person may still turn back before he begins such a thing and at any time may repentantly turn back. If one does this, I am not apprehensive; I do not fear arousing a desire in people to be tried as Abraham was. But to sell a cheap edition of Abraham and yet forbid everyone to do likewise is ludicrous.

In order to perceive the prodigious paradox of faith, a paradox that makes a murder into a holy and God-pleasing act, a paradox that gives Isaac back to Abraham again, which no thought can grasp, because faith begins precisely where thought stops—in order to perceive this, it is now my intention to draw out in the form of problemata the dialectical aspects implicit in the story of Abraham.

Problema I
from Fear and Trembling

IS THERE A TELEOLOGICAL SUSPENSION OF THE ETHICAL?

The ethical as such is the universal,* and as the universal it applies to everyone, which from another angle means that it applies at all times. It rests immanent in itself, has nothing outside itself that is its τέλος [end, purpose] but is itself the τέλος for everything outside itself, and when the ethical has absorbed this into itself, it goes not further. The single individual, sensately and psychically qualified in immediacy, is the individual who has his τέλος in the universal, and it is his ethical task continually to express himself in this, to annul his singularity in order

––––––––––
*Footnotes omitted—ed.

to become the universal. As soon as the single individual asserts himself in his singularity before the universal, he sins, and only by acknowledging this can he be reconciled again with the universal. Every time the single individual, after having entered the universal, feels an impulse to assert himself as the single individual, he is in a spiritual trial, from which he can work himself only by repentantly surrendering as the single individual in the universal. If this is the highest that can be said of man and his existence, then the ethical is of the same nature as a person's eternal salvation, which is his τέλος forevermore and at all times, since it would be a contradiction for this to be capable of being surrendered (that is, teleologically suspended), because as soon as this is suspended it is relinquished, whereas that which is suspended is not relinquished but is preserved in the higher, which is its τέλος.

If this is the case, then Hegel is right in "The Good and Conscience," where he qualifies man only as the individual and considers this qualification as a "moral form of evil" (see especially *The Philosophy of Right*), which must be annulled in the teleology of the moral in such a way that the single individual who remains in that stage either sins or is immersed in spiritual trial. But Hegel is wrong in speaking about faith; he is wrong in not protesting loudly and clearly against Abraham's enjoying honor and glory as a father of faith when he ought to be sent back to a lower court and shown up as a murderer.

Faith is namely this paradox that the single individual is higher than the universal—yet, please note, in such a way that the movement repeats itself, so that after having been in the universal he as the single individual isolates himself as higher than the universal. If this is not faith, then Abraham is lost, then faith has never existed in the world precisely because it has always existed. For if the ethical—that is, social morality—is the highest and if there is in a person no residual incommensurability in some way such that this incommensurability is not evil (i.e., the single individual, who is to be expressed in the universal), then no categories are needed other than what Greek philosophy had or what can be deduced from them by consistent thought. Hegel should not have concealed this, for, after all, he had studied Greek philosophy.

People who are profoundly lacking in learning and are given to clichés are frequently heard to say that a light shines over the Christian world, whereas a darkness enshrouds paganism. This kind of talk has always struck me as strange, inasmuch as every more thorough thinker, every more earnest artist still regenerates himself in the eternal youth of the Greeks. The explanation for such a statement is that one does not know what one should say but only that one must say something. It is quite right to say that paganism did not have faith, but if something is supposed to have been said thereby, then one must have a clearer understanding of what faith is, for otherwise one falls into such clichés. It is easy to explain all existence, faith along with it, without having a conception of what faith is, and the one who counts on being admired for such an explanation is not such a bad calculator, for it is as Boileau says: *Un sot trouve toujours un plus sot, qui l'admire* [One fool always finds a bigger fool, who admires him].

Faith is precisely the paradox that the single individual as the single individual is higher than the universal, is justified before it, not as inferior to it but as superior—yet in such a way, please note, that it is the single individual who, after being subordinate as the single individual to the universal, now by means of the universal becomes the single individual who as the single individual is superior, that the single individual as the single individual stands in an absolute relation to the absolute. This position cannot be mediated, for all mediation takes place only by virtue of the universal; it is and remains for all eternity a paradox, impervious to thought. And yet faith is this paradox, or else (and I ask the reader to bear these consequences *in mente* [in mind] even though it would be too prolix for me to write them all down) or else faith has never existed simply because it has always existed, or else Abraham is lost.

It is certainly true that the single individual can easily confuse this paradox with spiritual trial, but it ought not to be concealed for that reason. It is certainly true that many persons may be so constituted that they are repulsed by it, but faith ought not therefore to be made into something else to enable one to have it, but one ought rather to admit to not having it, while those who have faith ought to be prepared to set forth some characteristics whereby the paradox can be distinguished from a spiritual trial.

The story of Abraham contains just such a teleological suspension of the ethical. There is no dearth of keen minds and careful scholars who have found analogies to it. What their wisdom amounts to is the beautiful proposition that basically everything is the same. If one looks more closely, I doubt very much that anyone in the whole wide world will find one single analogy, except for a later one, which proves nothing if it is certain that Abraham represents faith and that it is manifested normatively in him, whose life not only is the most paradoxical that can be thought but is also so paradoxical that it simply cannot be thought. He acts by virtue of the absurd, for it is precisely the absurd that he as the single individual is higher than the universal. This paradox cannot be mediated, for as soon as Abraham begins to do so, he has to confess that he was in a spiritual trial, and if that is the case, he will never sacrifice Isaac, or if he did sacrifice Isaac, then in repentance he must come back to the universal. He gets Isaac back again by virtue of the absurd. Therefore, Abraham is at no time a tragic hero but is something entirely different, either a murderer or a man of faith. Abraham does not have the middle term that saves the tragic hero. This is why I can understand a tragic hero but cannot understand Abraham, even though in a certain demented sense I admire him more than all others.

In ethical terms, Abraham's relation to Isaac is quite simply this: the father shall love the son more than himself. But within its own confines the ethical has various gradations. We shall see whether this story contains any higher expression for the ethical that can ethically explain his behavior, can ethically justify his suspending the ethical obligation to the son, but without moving beyond the teleology of the ethical.

When an enterprise of concern to a whole nation is impeded, when such a project is halted by divine displeasure, when the angry deity sends a dead calm that mocks every effort, when the soothsayer carries out his sad task and announces that the deity demands a young girl as sacrifice—then the father must heroically bring this sacrifice. He must nobly conceal his agony, even though he could wish he were "the lowly man who dares to weep" and not the king who must behave in a kingly manner. Although the lonely agony penetrates his breast and there are only three persons in the whole nation who know his agony, soon the whole nation will be initiated into his agony and also into his deed, that for the welfare of all he will sacrifice her, his daughter, this lovely young girl. O bosom! O fair cheeks, flaxen hair. And the daughter's tears will agitate him, and the father will turn away his face, but the hero must raise the knife. And when the news of it reaches the father's house, the beautiful Greek maidens will blush with enthusiasm, and if the daughter was engaged, her betrothed will not be angry but will be proud to share in the father's deed, for the girl belonged more tenderly to him than to the father.

When the valiant judge who in the hour of need saved Israel binds God and himself in one breath by the same promise, he will heroically transform the young maiden's jubilation, the beloved daughter's joy to sorrow, and all Israel will sorrow with her over her virginal youth. But every freeborn man will understand, every resolute woman will admire Jephthah, and every virgin in Israel will wish to behave as his daughter did, because what good would it be for Jephthah to win the victory by means of a promise if he did not keep it—would not the victory be taken away from the people again?

When a son forgets his duty, when the state entrusts the sword of judgment to the father, when the laws demand punishment from the father's hand, then the father must heroically forget that the guilty one is his son, he must nobly hide his agony, but no one in the nation, not even the son, will fail to admire the father, and every time the Roman laws are interpreted, it will be remembered that many interpreted them more learnedly but no one more magnificently than Brutus.

But if Agamemnon, while a favorable wind was taking the fleet under full sail to its destination, had dispatched that messenger who fetched Iphigenia to be sacrificed; if Jephthah, without being bound by any promise that decided the fate of the nation, had said to his daughter: Grieve now for two months over your brief youth, and then I will sacrifice you; if Brutus had had a righteous son and yet had summoned the lictors to put him to death—who would have understood them? If, on being asked why they did this, these three men had answered: It is an ordeal in which we are being tried—would they have been better understood?

When in the crucial moment Agamemnon, Jephthah, and Brutus heroically have overcome the agony, heroically have lost the beloved, and have only to complete the task externally, there will never be a noble soul in the world without tears of compassion for their agony, of admiration for their deed. But if in the crucial moment these three men were to append to the heroic courage with which they bore the agony the little phrase: But it will not happen anyway—who then would understand them? If they went on to

explain: This we believe by virtue of the absurd—who would understand them any better, for who would not readily understand that it was absurd, but who would understand that one could then believe it?

The difference between the tragic hero and Abraham is very obvious. The tragic hero is still within the ethical. He allows an expression of the ethical to have its τέλος in a higher expression of the ethical; he scales down the ethical relation between father and son or daughter and father to a feeling that has its dialectic in its relation to the idea of moral conduct. Here there can be no question of a teleological suspension of the ethical itself.

Abraham's situation is different. By his act he transgressed the ethical altogether and had a higher τέλος outside it, in relation to which he suspended it. For I certainly would like to know how Abraham's act can be related to the universal, whether any point of contact between what Abraham did and the universal can be found other than that Abraham transgressed it. It is not to save a nation, not to uphold the idea of the state that Abraham does it; it is not to appease the angry gods. If it were a matter of the deity's being angry, then he was, after all, angry only with Abraham, and Abraham's act is totally unrelated to the universal, is a purely private endeavor. Therefore, while the tragic hero is great because of his moral virtue, Abraham is great because of a purely personal virtue. There is no higher expression for the ethical in Abraham's life than that the father shall love the son. The ethical in the sense of the moral is entirely beside the point. Insofar as the universal was present, it was cryptically in Isaac, hidden, so to speak, in Isaac's loins, and must cry out with Isaac's mouth: Do not do this, you are destroying everything.

Why, then, does Abraham do it? For God's sake and—the two are wholly identical—for his own sake. He does it for God's sake because God demands this proof of his faith; he does it for his own sake so that he can prove it. The unity of the two is altogether correctly expressed in the word already used to describe this relationship. It is an ordeal, a temptation. A temptation—but what does that mean? As a rule, what tempts a person is something that will hold him back from doing his duty, but here the temptation is the ethical itself, which would hold him back from doing God's will. But what is duty? Duty is simply the expression for God's will.

Here the necessity of a new category for the understanding of Abraham becomes apparent. Paganism does not know such a relationship to the divine. The tragic hero does not enter into any private relationship to the divine, but the ethical is the divine, and thus the paradox therein can be mediated in the universal.

Abraham cannot be mediated; in other words, he cannot speak. As soon as I speak, I express the universal, and if I do not do so, no one can understand me. As soon as Abraham wants to express himself in the universal, he must declare that his situation is a spiritual trial, for he has no higher expression of the universal that ranks above the universal he violates.

Therefore, although Abraham arouses my admiration, he also appalls me. The person who denies himself and sacrifices himself because of duty gives up the finite in order to grasp the infinite and is adequately assured; the tragic hero gives up the certain for the even more certain, and the observer's eye views him with confidence. But the person who gives up the universal in order to grasp something even higher that is not the universal—what does he do? Is it possible that this can be anything other than a spiritual trial? And if it is possible, but the individual makes a mistake, what salvation is there for him? He suffers all the agony of the tragic hero, he shatters his joy in the world, he renounces everything, and perhaps at the same time he barricades himself from the sublime joy that was so precious to him that he would buy it at any price. The observer cannot understand him at all; neither can his eye rest upon him with confidence. Perhaps the believer's intention cannot be carried out at all, because it is inconceivable. Or if it could be done but the individual has misunderstood the deity— what salvation would there be for him? The tragic hero needs and demands tears, and where is the envious eye so arid that it could not weep with Agamemnon, but where is the soul so gone astray that it has the audacity to weep for Abraham? The tragic hero finishes his task at a specific moment in time, but as time passes he does what is no less significant: he visits the person encompassed by sorrow, who cannot breathe because of his anguished sighs, whose thoughts oppress him, heavy with tears. He appears to him, breaks the witchcraft of sorrow, loosens the bonds, evokes the tears, and the suffering one forgets his own sufferings in those of the tragic hero. One cannot weep over Abraham. One approaches him with a *horror religiosus,* as Israel approached Mount Sinai. What if he himself is distraught, what if he had made a mistake, this lonely man who climbs Mount Moriah, whose peak towers sky-high over the flatlands of Aulis,

what if he is not a sleepwalker safely crossing the abyss while the one standing at the foot of the mountain looks up, shakes with anxiety, and then in his deference and horror does not even dare to call to him?— Thanks, once again thanks, to a man who, to a person overwhelmed by life's sorrows and left behind naked, reaches out the words, the leafage of language by which he can conceal his misery. Thanks to you, great Shakespeare, you who can say everything, everything, everything just as it is—and yet, why did you never articulate this torment? Did you perhaps reserve it for yourself, like the beloved's name that one cannot bear to have the world utter, for with his little secret that he cannot divulge the poet buys this power of the word to tell everybody else's dark secrets. A poet is not an apostle; he drives out devils only by the power of the devil.

But if the ethical is teleologically suspended in this manner, how does the single individual in whom it is suspended exist? He exists as the single individual in contrast to the universal. Does he sin, then, for from the point of view of the idea, this is the form of sin. Thus, even though the child does not sin, because it is not conscious of its existence as such, its existence, from the point of view of the idea, is nevertheless sin, and the ethical makes its claim upon it at all times. If it is denied that this form can be repeated in such a way that it is not sin, then judgment has fallen upon Abraham. How did Abraham exist? He had faith. This is the paradox by which he remains at the apex, the paradox that he cannot explain to anyone else, for the paradox is that he as the single individual places himself in an absolute relation to the absolute. Is he justified? Again, his justification is the paradoxical, for if he is, then he is justified not by virtue of being something universal but by virtue of being the single individual.

How does the single individual reassure himself that he is legitimate? It is a simple matter to level all existence to the idea of the state or the idea of a society. If this is done, it is also simple to mediate, for one never comes to the paradox that the single individual as the single individual is higher than the universal, something I can also express symbolically in a statement by Pythagoras to the effect that the odd number is more perfect than the even number. If occasionally there is any response at all these days with regard to the paradox, it is likely to be: One judges it by the result. Aware that he is a paradox who cannot be understood, a hero who has become a σχάνδαλον [offense] to his age will shout confidently to his contemporaries: The result will indeed prove that I was justified. This cry is rarely heard in our age, inasmuch as it does not produce heroes—this is its defect—and it likewise has the advantage that it produces few caricatures. When in our age we hear these words: It will be judged by the result—then we know at once with whom we have the honor of speaking. Those who talk this way are a numerous type whom I shall designate under the common name of assistant professors. With security in life, they live in their thoughts: they have a *permanent* position and a *secure* future in a well-organized state. They have hundreds, yes, even thousands of years between them and the earthquakes of existence; they are not afraid that such things can be repeated, for then what would the police and the newspapers say? Their life task is to judge the great men, judge them according to the result. Such behavior toward greatness betrays a strange mixture of arrogance and wretchedness—arrogance because they feel called to pass judgment, wretchedness because they feel that their lives are in no way allied with the lives of the great. Anyone with even a smattering *erectioris ingenii* [of nobility of nature] never becomes an utterly cold and clammy worm, and when he approaches greatness, he is never devoid of the thought that since the creation of the world it has been customary for the result to come last and that if one is truly going to learn something from greatness one must be particularly aware of the beginning. If the one who is to act wants to judge himself by the result, he will never begin. Although the result may give joy to the entire world, it cannot help the hero, for he would not know the result until the whole thing was over, and he would not become a hero by that but by making a beginning.

Moreover, in its dialectic the result (insofar as it is finitude's response to the infinite question) is altogether incongruous with the hero's existence. Or should Abraham's receiving Isaac by a *marvel* be able to prove that Abraham was justified in relating himself as the single individual to the universal? If Abraham actually had sacrificed Isaac, would he therefore have been less justified?

But we are curious about the result, just as we are curious about the way a book turns out. We do not want to know anything about the anxiety, the distress, the paradox. We carry on an esthetic flirtation with the result. It arrives just as unexpectedly but also just as effortlessly as a prize in a lottery, and when we

have heard the result, we have built ourselves up. And yet no manacled robber of churches is so despicable a criminal as the one who plunders holiness in this way, and not even Judas, who sold his Lord for thirty pieces of silver, is more contemptible than someone who peddles greatness in this way.

It is against my very being to speak inhumanly about greatness, to make it a dim and nebulous far-distant shape or to let it be great but devoid of the emergence of the humanness without which it ceases to be great, for it is not what happens to me that makes me great but what I do, and certainly there is no one who believes that someone became great by winning the big lottery prize. A person might have been born in lowly circumstances, but I would still require him not to be so inhuman toward himself that he could imagine the king's castle only at a distance and ambiguously dream of its greatness, and destroy it at the same time he elevates it because he elevated it so basely. I require him to be man enough to tread confidently and with dignity there as well. He must not be so inhuman that he insolently violates everything by barging right off the street into the king's hall—he loses more thereby than the king. On the contrary, he should find a joy in observing every bidding of propriety with a happy and confident enthusiasm, which is precisely what makes him a free spirit. This is merely a metaphor, for that distinction is only a very imperfect expression of the distance of spirit. I require every person not to think so inhumanly of himself that he does not dare to enter those palaces where the memory of the chosen ones lives or even those where they themselves live. He is not to enter rudely and foist his affinity upon them. He is to be happy for every time he bows before them, but he is to be confident, free of spirit, and always more than a charwoman, for if he wants to be no more than that, he will never get in. And the very thing that is going to help him is the anxiety and distress in which the great were tried, for otherwise, if he has any backbone, they will only arouse his righteous envy. And anything that can be great only at a distance, that someone wants to make great with empty and hollow phrases—is destroyed by that very person.

Who was as great in the world as that favored woman, the mother of God, the Virgin Mary? And yet how do we speak of her? That she was the favored one among women does not make her great, and if it would not be so very odd for those who listen to be able to think just as inhumanly as those who speak, then every young girl might ask: Why am I not so favored? And if I had nothing else to say, I certainly would not dismiss such a question as stupid, because, viewed abstractly, vis-à-vis a favor, every person is just as entitled to it as the other. We leave out the distress, the anxiety, the paradox. My thoughts are as pure as anybody's, and he who can think this way surely has pure thoughts, and, if not, he can expect something horrible, for anyone who has once experienced these images cannot get rid of them again, and if he sins against them, they take a terrible revenge in a silent rage, which is more terrifying than the stridency of ten ravenous critics. To be sure, Mary bore the child wondrously, but she nevertheless did it "after the manner of women," and such a time is one of anxiety, distress, and paradox. The angel was indeed a ministering spirit, but he was not a meddlesome spirit who went to the other young maidens in Israel and said: Do not scorn Mary, the extraordinary is happening to her. The angel went only to Mary, and no one could understand her. Has any woman been as infringed upon as was Mary, and is it not true here also that the one whom God blesses he curses in the same breath? This is the spirit's view of Mary, and she is by no means— it is revolting to me to say it but even more so that people have inanely and unctuously made her out to be thus—she is by no means a lady idling in her finery and playing with a divine child. When, despite this, she said: Behold, I am the handmaid of the Lord— then she is great, and I believe it should not be difficult to explain why she became the mother of God. She needs worldly admiration as little as Abraham needs tears, for she was no heroine and he was no hero, but both of them became greater than these, not by being exempted in any way from the distress and the agony and the paradox, but became greater by means of these.

It is great when the poet in presenting his tragic hero for public admiration dares to say: Weep for him, for he deserves it. It is great to deserve the tears of those who deserve to shed tears. It is great that the poet dares to keep the crowd under restraint, dares to discipline men to examine themselves individually to see if they are worthy to weep for the hero, for the slop water of the snivellers is a debasement of the sacred. —But even greater than all this is the knight of faith's daring to say to the noble one who wants to weep for him: Do not weep for me, but weep for yourself.

We are touched, we look back to those beautiful times. Sweet sentimental longing leads us to the goal of our desire, to see Christ walking about in the promised land. We forget the anxiety, the distress, the paradox. Was it such a simple matter not to make a mistake? Was it not terrifying that this man walking around among the others was God? Was it not terrifying to sit down to eat with him? Was it such an easy matter to become an apostle? But the result, the eighteen centuries—that helps, that contributes to this mean deception whereby we deceive ourselves and others. I do not feel brave enough to wish to be contemporary with events like that, but I do not for that reason severely condemn those who made a mistake, nor do I depreciate those who saw what was right.

But I come back to Abraham. During the time before the result, either Abraham was a murderer every minute or we stand before a paradox that is higher than all mediations.

The story of Abraham contains, then, a teleological suspension of the ethical. As the single individual he became higher than the universal. This is the paradox, which cannot be mediated. How he entered into it is just as inexplicable as how he remains in it. If this is not Abraham's situation, then Abraham is not even a tragic hero but a murderer. It is thoughtless to want to go on calling him the father of faith, to speak of it to men who have an interest only in words. A person can become a tragic hero through his own strength— but not the knight of faith. When a person walks what is in one sense the hard road of the tragic hero, there are many who can give him advice, but he who walks the narrow road of faith has no one to advise him— no one understands him. Faith is a marvel, and yet no human being is excluded from it; for that which unites all human life is passion, and faith is a passion.

Problema II
from Fear and Trembling

IS THERE AN ABSOLUTE DUTY TO GOD?*

The ethical is the universal, and as such it is also the divine. Thus it is proper to say that every duty is essentially duty to God, but if no more can be said than this, then it is also said that I actually have no

*Most footnotes have been omitted—ed.

duty to God. The duty becomes duty by being traced back to God, but in the duty itself I do not enter into relation to God. For example, it is a duty to love one's neighbor. It is a duty by its being traced back to God, but in the duty I enter into relation not to God but to the neighbor I love. If in this connection I then say that it is my duty to love God, I am actually pronouncing only a tautology, inasmuch as "God" in a totally abstract sense is here understood as the divine—that is, the universal, that is, the duty. The whole existence of the human race rounds itself off as a perfect, self-contained sphere, and then the ethical is that which limits and fills at one and the same time. God comes to be an invisible vanishing point, an impotent thought; his power is only in the ethical, which fills all of existence. Insofar, then, as someone might wish to love God in any other sense than this, he is a visionary, is in love with a phantom, which, if it only had enough power to speak, would say to him: I do not ask for your love—just stay where you belong. Insofar as someone might wish to love God in another way, this love would be as implausible as the love Rousseau mentions, whereby a person loves the Kaffirs instead of loving his neighbor.

Now if this train of thought is sound, if there is nothing incommensurable in a human life, and if the incommensurable that is present is there only by an accident from which nothing results insofar as existence is viewed from the idea, then Hegel was right. But he was not right in speaking about faith or in permitting Abraham to be regarded as its father, for in the latter case he has pronounced judgment both on Abraham and on faith. In Hegelian philosophy, *das Äussere* (*die Entäusserung*) [the outer (the externalization)] is higher than *das Innere* [the inner]. This is frequently illustrated by an example. The child is *das Innere,* the adult *das Äussere,* with the result that the child is determined by the external and, conversely, the adult as *das Äussere* by the inner. But faith is the paradox that interiority is higher than exteriority, or, to call to mind something said earlier, the uneven number is higher than the even.

Thus in the ethical view of life, it is the task of the single individual to strip himself of the qualification of interiority and to express this in something external. Every time the individual shrinks from it, every time he withholds himself in or slips down again into the qualifications of feeling, mood, etc. that belong to interiority, he trespasses, he is immersed in spiritual trial. The paradox of faith is that there is an interiority that is incommensurable with exteriority, an interiority that is not identical, please note, with the first but is a new interiority. This must not be overlooked. Recent philosophy has allowed itself simply to substitute the immediate for "faith." If that is done, then it is ridiculous to deny that there has always been faith. This puts faith in the rather commonplace company of feelings, moods, idiosyncrasies, *vapeurs* [vagaries], etc. If so, philosophy may be correct in saying that one ought not to stop there. But nothing justifies philosophy in using this language. Faith is preceded by a movement of infinity; only then does faith commence, *nec opinate* [unexpected], by virtue of the absurd. This I can certainly understand without consequently maintaining that I have faith. If faith is nothing more than philosophy makes it out to be, then even Socrates went further, much further, instead of the reverse—that he did not attain it. In an intellectual sense, he did make the movement of infinity. His ignorance is the infinite resignation. This task alone is a suitable one for human capabilities, even though it is disdained these days; but only when this has been done, only when the individual has emptied himself in the infinite, only then has the point been reached where faith can break through.

The paradox of faith, then, is this: that the single individual is higher than the universal, that the single individual—to recall a distinction in dogmatics rather rare these days—determines his relation to the universal by his relation to the absolute, not his relation to the absolute by his relation to the universal. The paradox may also be expressed in this way: that there is an absolute duty to God, for in this relationship of duty the individual relates himself as the single individual absolutely to the absolute. In this connection, to say that it is a duty to love God means something different from the above, for if this duty is absolute, then the ethical is reduced to the relative. From this it does not follow that the ethical should be invalidated; rather, the ethical receives a completely different expression, a paradoxical expression, such as, for example, that love to God may bring the knight of faith to give his love to the neighbor—an expression opposite to that which, ethically speaking, is duty.

If this is not the case, then faith has no place in existence, then faith is a spiritual trial and Abraham is lost, inasmuch as he gave in to it.

This paradox cannot be mediated, for it depends specifically on this: that the single individual is only the single individual. As soon as this single individual wants to express his absolute duty in the universal, becomes conscious of it in the universal, he recognizes that he is involved in a spiritual trial, and then, if he really does resist it, he will not fulfill the so-called absolute duty, and if he does not resist it, then he sins, even though his act *realiter* [as a matter of fact] turns out to be what was his absolute duty. What should Abraham have done, for instance? If he had said to someone: I love Isaac more than anything in the world and that is why it is so hard for me to sacrifice him—the other person very likely would have shaken his head and said: Why sacrifice him, then? Or, if the other had been smart, he probably would have seen through Abraham and perceived that he was manifesting feelings that glaringly contradicted his action.

The story of Abraham contains such a paradox. The ethical expression for his relation to Isaac is that the father must love the son. This ethical relation is reduced to the relative in contradistinction to the absolute relation to God. To the question "Why?" Abraham has no other answer than that it is an ordeal, a temptation that, as noted above, is a synthesis of its being for the sake of God and for his own sake. In fact, these two determinants correspond in ordinary language. For instance, if we see someone doing something that does not conform to the universal, we say that he is hardly doing it for God's sake, meaning thereby that he is doing it for his own sake. The paradox of faith has lost the intermediary, that is, the universal. On the one side, it has the expression for the highest egotism (to do the terrible act, do it for one's own sake), on the other side, the expression for the most absolute devotion, to do it for God's sake. Faith itself cannot be mediated into the universal, for thereby it is canceled. Faith is this paradox, and the single individual simply cannot make himself understandable to anyone. People fancy that the single individual can make himself understandable to another single individual in the same situation. Such a view would be unthinkable if in our day we were not trying in so many ways to sneak slyly into greatness. The one knight of faith cannot help the other at all. Either the single individual himself becomes the knight of faith by accepting the paradox or he never becomes one. Partnership in these areas is utterly unthinkable. Only the single individual can ever give himself a more explicit explanation of what is to be understood by Isaac. And even though an ever so precise determination could be made, generally speaking, of what is to

be understood by Isaac (which, incidentally, would be a ridiculous self-contradiction—to bring the single individual, who in fact stands outside the universal, under universal categories when he is supposed to act as the single individual who is outside the universal), the single individual would never be able to be convinced of this by others, only by himself as the single individual. Thus, even if a person were craven and base enough to want to become a knight of faith on someone else's responsibility, he would never come to be one, for only the single individual becomes that as the single individual, and this is the greatness of it—which I certainly can understand without becoming involved in it, since I lack the courage—but this is also the terribleness of it, which I can understand even better.

As we all know, Luke 14:26 offers a remarkable teaching on the absolute duty to God: "If any one comes to me and does not hate his own father and mother and wife and children and brothers and sisters, yes, and even his own life, he cannot be my disciple." This is a hard saying. Who can bear to listen to it? This is the reason, too, that we seldom hear it. But this silence is only an escape that is of no avail. Meanwhile, the theological student learns that these words appear in the New Testament, and in one or another exegetical resource book he finds the explanation that μισεῖν [to hate] in this passage and in a few other passages *per* μείωσιν [by weakening] means: *minus diligo, posthabeo, non colo, nihili facio* [love less, esteem less, honor not, count as nothing]. The context in which these words appear, however, does not seem to confirm this appealing explanation. In the following verse we are told that someone who wants to erect a tower first of all makes a rough estimate to see if he is able to finish it, lest he be mocked later. The close proximity of this story and the verse quoted seems to indicate that the words are to be taken in their full terror in order that each person may examine himself to see if he can erect the building.

If that pious and accommodating exegete, who by dickering this way hopes to smuggle Christianity into the world, succeeded in convincing one person that grammatically, linguistically, and χατ' ἀναλογίαν [by analogy] this is the meaning of that passage, then it is to be hoped that he at the same time would succeed in convincing the same person that Christianity is one of the most miserable things in the world. The teaching that in one of its most lyrical outpourings, in which the consciousness of its eternal validity overflows most vigorously, has nothing to offer except an overblown word that signifies nothing but only suggests that one should be less kind, less attentive, more indifferent, the teaching that in the moment it gives the appearance of wanting to say something terrible ends by slavering instead of terrifying—that teaching certainly is not worth standing up for.

The words are terrible, but I dare say that they can be understood without the necessary consequence that the one who has understood them has the courage to do what he has understood. One ought to be sufficiently honest, however, to admit what it says, to admit that it is great even though one himself lacks the courage to do it. Anyone who acts thus will not exclude himself from participation in this beautiful story, for in a way it does indeed have a kind of comfort for the person who does not have the courage to begin construction of the tower. But honest he must be, and he must not speak of this lack of courage as humility, since, on the contrary, it is pride, whereas the courage of faith is the one and only humble courage.

It is easy to see that if this passage is to have any meaning it must be understood literally. God is the one who demands absolute love. Anyone who is demanding a person's love believes that this love is demonstrated by his becoming indifferent to what he otherwise cherished is not merely an egotist but is also stupid, and anyone demanding that kind of love simultaneously signs his own death sentence insofar as his life is centered in this desired love. For example, a man requires his wife to leave her father and mother, but if he considers it a demonstration of her extraordinary love to him that she for his sake became an indifferent and lax daughter etc., then he is far more stupid than the stupid. If he had any idea of what love is, he would wish to discover that she was perfect in her love as a daughter and sister, and he would see therein that she would love him more than anyone in the kingdom. Thus what would be regarded as a sign of egotism and stupidity in a person may by the help of an exegete be regarded as a worthy representation of divinity.

But how to hate them [Luke 14:26]? I shall not review here the human distinction, either to love or to hate, not because I have so much against it, for at least it is passionate, but because it is egotistic and does not fit here. But if I regard the task as a paradox, then I understand it—that is, I understand it in the way one can understand a paradox. The absolute duty

can lead one to do what ethics would forbid, but it can never lead the knight of faith to stop loving. Abraham demonstrates this. In the moment he is about to sacrifice Isaac, the ethical expression for what he is doing is: he hates Isaac. But if he actually hates Isaac, he can rest assured that God does not demand this of him, for Cain and Abraham are not identical. He must love Isaac with his whole soul. Since God claims Isaac, he must, if possible, love him even more, and only then can he *sacrifice* him, for it is indeed this love for Isaac that makes his act a sacrifice by its paradoxical contrast to his love for God. But the distress and the anxiety in the paradox is that he, humanly speaking, is thoroughly incapable of making himself understandable. Only in the moment when his act is in absolute contradiction to his feelings, only then does he sacrifice Isaac, but the reality of his act is that by which he belongs to the universal, and there he is and remains a murderer.

Furthermore, the passage in Luke must be understood in such a way that one perceives that the knight of faith can achieve no higher expression whatsoever of the universal (as the ethical) in which he can save himself. Thus if the Church were to insist on this sacrifice from one of its members, we would have only a tragic hero. The idea of the Church is not qualitatively different from the idea of the state. As soon as the single individual can enter into it by a simple mediation, and as soon as the single individual has entered into the paradox, he does not arrive at the idea of the Church; he does not get out of the paradox, but he must find therein either his salvation or his damnation. A Church-related hero such as that expresses the universal in his act, and there will be no one in the Church, not even his father and mother, who does not understand him. But a knight of faith he is not, and in fact he has a response different from Abraham's; he does not say that this is an ordeal or a temptation in which he is being tried.

As a rule, passages such as this one in Luke are not quoted. We are afraid to let people loose; we are afraid that the worst will happen as soon as the single individual feels like behaving as the single individual. Furthermore, existing as the single individual is considered to be the easiest thing in the world, and thus people must be coerced into becoming the universal. I can share neither that fear nor that opinion, and for the same reason. Anyone who has learned that to exist as the single individual is the most terrible of all will not be afraid to say that it is the greatest of all, but he must say this in such a way that his words do not become a pitfall for one who is confused but instead help him into the universal, although his words could create a little room for greatness. Anyone who does not dare to mention such passages does not dare to mention Abraham, either. Moreover, to think that existing as the single individual is easy enough contains a very dubious indirect concession with respect to oneself, for anyone who actually has any self-esteem and concern for his soul is convinced that the person who lives under his own surveillance alone in the big wide world lives more stringently and retired than a maiden in her virgin's bower. It may well be that there are those who need coercion, who, if they were given free rein, would abandon themselves like unmanageable animals to selfish appetites. But a person will demonstrate that he does not belong to them precisely by showing that he knows how to speak in fear and trembling, and speak he must out of respect for greatness, so that it is not forgotten out of fear of harm, which certainly will not come if he speaks out of a knowledge of greatness, a knowledge of its terrors, and if one does not know the terrors, one does not know the greatness, either.

Let us consider in somewhat more detail the distress and anxiety in the paradox of faith. The tragic hero relinquishes himself in order to express the universal; the knight of faith relinquishes the universal in order to become the single individual. As said previously, everything depends on one's position. Anyone who believes that it is fairly easy to be the single individual can always be sure that he is not a knight of faith, for fly-by-nights and itinerant geniuses are not men of faith. On the contrary, this knight knows that it is glorious to belong to the universal. He knows that it is beautiful and beneficial to be the single individual who translates himself into the universal, the one who, so to speak, personally produces a trim, clean, and, as far as possible, faultless edition of himself, readable by all. He knows that it is refreshing to become understandable to himself in the universal in such a way that he understands it, and every individual who understands him in turn understands the universal in him, and both rejoice in the security of the universal. He knows it is beautiful to be born as the single individual who has his home in the universal, his friendly abode, which immediately receives him with open arms if he wants to remain in it. But

he also knows that up higher there winds a lonesome trail, steep and narrow; he knows it is dreadful to be born solitary outside of the universal, to walk without meeting one single traveler. He knows very well where he is and how he relates to men. Humanly speaking, he is mad and cannot make himself understandable to anyone. And yet "to be mad" is the mildest expression. If he is not viewed in this way, then he is a hypocrite, and the higher he ascends this path, the more appalling a hypocrite he is.

The knight of faith knows that it is inspiring to give up himself for the universal, that it takes courage to do it, but that there also is a security in it precisely because it is a giving up for the universal. He knows that it is glorious to be understood by everyone of noble mind and in such a way that the observer himself is ennobled thereby. This he knows, and he feels as if bound; he could wish that this was the task that had been assigned to him. In the same way, Abraham now and then could have wished that the task were to love Isaac as a father would and should, understandable to all, memorable for all time; he could have wished that the task were to sacrifice Isaac to the universal, that he could inspire fathers to laudable deeds —and he is almost shocked at the thought that for him such wishes constitute a spiritual trial and must be treated as such, for he knows that he is walking a lonesome path and that he is accomplishing nothing for the universal but is himself only being tried and tested. What did Abraham accomplish for the universal? Let me speak humanly about it, purely humanly! It takes him seventy years to have the son of old age. It takes him seventy years to get what others get in a hurry and enjoy for a long time. Why? Because he is being tested and tempted. Is it not madness! But Abraham had faith, and only Sarah vacillated and got him to take Hagar as concubine, but this is also why he had to drive her away. He receives Isaac—then once again he has to be tested. He knew that it is glorious to express the universal, glorious to live with Isaac. But this is not the task. He knew that it is kingly to sacrifice a son like this to the universal; he himself would have found rest therein, and everybody would have rested approvingly in his deed, as the vowel rests in its quiescent letter. But that is not the task—he is being tested. That Roman commander widely known by his nickname Cunctator stopped the enemy by his delaying tactics—in comparison with him, what a procrastinator Abraham is—but he does not save the state.

This is the content of 130 years. Who can endure it? Would not his contemporaries, if such may be assumed, have said, "What an everlasting procrastination this is; Abraham finally received a son, it took long enough, and now he wants to sacrifice him—is he not mad? If he at least could explain why he wants to do it, but it is always an ordeal." Nor could Abraham explain further, for his life is like a book under divine confiscation and never becomes *publice juris* [public property].

This is the terrifying aspect of it. Anyone who does not perceive this can always be sure that he is no knight of faith, but the one who perceives it will not deny that even the most tried of tragic heroes dances along in comparison with the knight of faith, who only creeps along slowly. Having perceived this and made sure that he does not have the courage to understand it, he may then have an intimation of the wondrous glory the knight attains in becoming God's confidant, the Lord's friend, if I may speak purely humanly, in saying "You" to God in heaven, whereas even the tragic hero addresses him only in the third person.

The tragic hero is soon finished, and his struggles are soon over; he makes the infinite movement and is now secure in the universal. The knight of faith, however, is kept in a state of sleeplessness, for he is constantly being tested, and at every moment there is the possibility of his returning penitently to the universal, and this possibility may be a spiritual trial as well as the truth. He cannot get any information on that from any man, for in that case he is outside the paradox.

First and foremost, then, the knight of faith has the passion to concentrate in one single point the whole of the ethical that he violates, in order that he may give himself the assurance that he actually loves Isaac with his whole soul.* If he cannot, he is under-

going spiritual trial. Next, he has the passion to produce this assurance instantaneously and in such a way that it is fully as valid as in the first moment. If he cannot do this, then he never moves from the spot, for then he always has to begin all over again. The tragic hero also concentrates in one point the ethical he has teleologically overstepped, but in that case he has a stronghold in the universal. The knight of faith has simply and solely himself, and therein lies the dreadfulness. Most men live in adherence to an ethical obligation in such a way that they let each day have its cares, but then they never attain this passionate concentration, this intense consciousness. In achieving this, the tragic hero may find the universal helpful in one sense, but the knight of faith is alone in everything. The tragic hero does it and finds rest in the universal; the knight of faith is constantly kept in tension. Agamemnon gives up Iphigenia and thereby finds rest in the universal, and now he proceeds to sacrifice her. If Agamemnon had not made the movement, if at the crucial moment his soul, instead of being passionately concentrated, had wandered off into the usual silly talk about having several daughters and that *vielleicht das Ausserordentliche* [perhaps the extraordinary] still could happen—then, of course, he is no hero but a pauper. Abraham, too, has the concentration of the hero, although it is far more difficult for him, since he has no stronghold at all in the universal, but he makes one movement more, whereby he gathers his soul back to the marvel. If Abraham had not done this, he would have been only an Agamemnon, insofar as it can be otherwise explained how wanting to sacrifice Isaac can be justified when the universal is not thereby benefited.

Whether the single individual actually is undergoing a spiritual trial or is a knight of faith, only the single individual himself can decide. But from the paradox itself several characteristic signs may be inferred

---

*May I once again throw some light on the distinction between the collisions of the tragic hero and of the knight of faith. The tragic hero assures himself that the ethical obligation is totally present in him by transforming it into a wish. Agamemnon, for example, can say: To me the proof that I am not violating my fatherly duty is that my duty is my one and only wish. Consequently we have wish and duty face to face with each other. Happy is the life in which they coincide, in which my wish is my duty and the reverse, and for most men the task in life is simply to

adhere to their duty and to transform it by their enthusiasm into their wish. The tragic hero gives up his wish in order to fulfill this duty. For the knight of faith, wish and duty are also identical, but he is required to give up both. If he wants to relinquish by giving up his wish, he finds no rest, for it is indeed his duty. If he wants to adhere to the duty and to his wish, he does not become the knight of faith, for the absolute duty specifically demanded that he should give it up. The tragic hero found a higher expression of duty but not an absolute duty.

that are understandable also to someone not in it. The true knight of faith is always absolute isolation; the spurious knight is sectarian. This is an attempt to jump off the narrow path of the paradox and become a tragic hero at a bargain price. The tragic hero expresses the universal and sacrifices himself for it. In place of that, the sectarian Punchinello has a private theater, a few good friends and comrades who represent the universal just about as well as the court observers in *Gulddaasen* represent justice. But the knight of faith, on the other hand, is the paradox; he is the single individual, simply and solely the single individual without any connections and complications. This is the dreadfulness the sectarian weakling cannot endure. Instead of learning from this that he is incapable of doing the great and then openly admitting it—naturally something I cannot but approve, since it is what I myself do—the poor wretch thinks that by joining up with other poor wretches he will be able to do it. But it does not work; in the world of spirit cheating is not tolerated. A dozen sectarians go arm in arm with one another; they are totally ignorant of the solitary spiritual trials that are in store for the knight of faith and that he dares not flee precisely because it would be still more dreadful if he presumptuously forced his way forward. The sectarians deafen one another with their noise and clamor, keep anxiety away with their screeching. A hooting carnival crowd like that thinks it is assaulting heaven, believes it is going along the same path as the knight of faith, who in the loneliness of the universe never hears another human voice but walks alone with his dreadful responsibility.

The knight of faith is assigned solely to himself; he feels the pain of being unable to make himself understandable to others, but he has no vain desire to instruct others. The pain is his assurance; vain desire he does not know—for that his soul is too earnest. The spurious knight quickly betrays himself by this expertise that he has acquired instantly. He by no means grasps what is at stake: that insofar as another individual is to go the same path he must become the single individual in the very same way and then does not require anyone's advice, least of all the advice of one who wants to intrude. Here again, unable to endure the martyrdom of misunderstanding, a person jumps off this path and conveniently enough chooses the worldly admiration of expertise. The true knight of faith is a witness, never the teacher, and therein lies the profound humanity, which has much more to it

than this trifling participation in the woes and welfare of other people that is extolled under the name of sympathy, although, on the contrary, it is nothing more than vanity. He who desires only to be a witness confesses thereby that no man, not even the most unimportant man, needs another's participation or is to be devalued by it in order to raise another's value. But since he himself did not obtain at bargain price what he obtained, he does not sell it at bargain price, either. He is not so base that he accepts the admiration of men and in return gives them his silent contempt; he knows that true greatness is equally accessible to all.

Therefore, either there is an absolute duty to God—and if there is such a thing, it is the paradox just described, that the single individual as the single individual is higher than the universal and as the single individual stands in an absolute relation to the absolute—or else faith has never existed because it has always existed, or else Abraham is lost, or else one must interpret the passage in Luke 14 as did that appealing exegete and explain the similar and corresponding passages in the same way.

An Expression of Gratitude to Lessing
from Concluding Unscientific Postscript to *Philosophical Fragments*

. . . [Lessing] understood, and knew how to maintain, that the religious pertained to Lessing and Lessing alone, just as it pertains to every human being in the same way, understood that he had infinitely to do with God, but nothing, nothing to do directly with any human being.* See, this is the object of my expression, the object of my gratitude. . . .

But now his result! Has he accepted Christianity, has he rejected it, has he defended it, has he attacked it? . . . Wonderful Lessing! He has none, none at all; there is not the slightest trace of any result. . . .

The world has perhaps always had a lack of what could be called authentic individualities, decisive subjectivities, those artistically permeated with reflec-

———————
*Many footnotes have been omitted—ed.

tion, the independent thinkers who differ from the bellowers and the didacticizers. . . .

But with regard to actually becoming subjective, it is again a matter of what reflective presuppositions the subject has to penetrate, what ballast of objectivity he must dispose of, and what infinite conception he has of the significance of this turning, its responsibility and its *discrimen* [distinctive mark]. Even though this way of looking at the matter implies a requirement that drastically reduces the number of individualities among whom a choice could be made, even though Lessing, it seems to me, is the only one, I do not put him forward in order to appeal to him (ah, if only one dared to do that, if only one dared to establish an immediate relation to him, one would surely be helped!). It also occurs to me that it would be rather dubious, because with such an appeal I would also have contradicted myself and canceled everything. If the subjective individual himself has not worked himself through and out of his objectivity, all appeal to another individuality will be only a misunderstanding. And if the subjective individual has done that, he will certainly know his own course and the dialectical presuppositions in and according to which he has his religious existence. The course of development of the religious subject has the peculiar quality that the pathway comes into existence for the single individual and closes up behind him. And why should the Deity not know how to maintain his price!

. . . And the Deity certainly does possess what is the most precious of all, but also knows how to safeguard himself in a way entirely different from all earthly supervision, knows in an entirely different way how to prevent anyone from slipping in world-historically, objectively, and scholarly-scientifically by utilizing the jostling crowd. . . .

Possible and Actual Theses by Lessing
from Concluding Unscientific Postscript to *Philosophical Fragments*

. . . I now intend to present something that I shall, what the deuce, ascribe to Lessing, without being certain that he would acknowledge it, something that I in

teasing exuberance could easily be tempted to want to foist upon him as something he said, although not directly.*. . .

1. *The subjective existing thinker is aware of the dialectic of communication.* Whereas objective thinking is indifferent to the thinking subject and his existence, the subjective thinker as existing is essentially interested in his own thinking, is existing in it. Therefore, his thinking has another kind of reflection, specifically, that of inwardness, of possession, whereby it belongs to the subject and to no one else. . . .

The reflection of inwardness is the subjective thinker's double-reflection. In thinking, he thinks the universal, but, as existing in this thinking, as acquiring this in his inwardness, he becomes more and more subjectively isolated.

The difference between subjective and objective thinking must also manifest itself in the form of communication.† This means that the subjective thinker

------

*Most footnotes have been omitted—ed.
†Double-reflection is already implicit in the idea of communication itself: that the subjective individual (who by inwardness wants to express the life of the eternal, in which all sociality and all companionship are inconceivable because the existence-category, movement, is inconceivable here, and hence essential communication is also inconceivable because everyone must be assumed to possess everything essentially), existing in the isolation of inwardness, wants to communicate himself, consequently that he simultaneously wants to keep his thinking in the inwardness of his subjective existence and yet wants to communicate himself. It is not possible (except for thoughtlessness, for which all things are indeed possible) for this contradiction to become manifest in a direct form.—It is not so difficult, however, to understand that a subject existing in this way may want to communicate himself. A person in love, for instance, to whom his erotic love is his very inwardness, may well want to communicate himself, but not directly, just because the inwardness of erotic love is the main thing for him. Essentially occupied with continually acquiring the inwardness of erotic love, he has no result and is never finished, but he may nevertheless want to communicate; yet for that very reason he can never use a direct form, since that presupposes results and completion. So it is also in a God-relationship. Just because he himself is continually in the process of becoming in an inward direction, that is, in inwardness, he can never communicate himself directly, since the

must promptly become aware that the form of communication must artistically possess just as much reflection as he himself, existing in his thinking, possesses. Artistically, please note, for the secret does not consist in his enunciating the double-reflection directly, since such an enunciation is a direct contradiction. . . .

Therefore, the subjective religious thinker, who has comprehended the duplexity of existence in order to be such a thinker, readily perceives that direct communication is a fraud toward God (which possibly defrauds him of the worship of another person in truth), a fraud toward himself (as if he had ceased to be an existing person), a fraud toward another human being (who possibly attains only a relative God-relationship), a fraud that brings him into contradiction with his entire thought. . . .

Objective thinking is completely indifferent to subjectivity and thereby to inwardness and appropriation; its communication is therefore direct. . . .

2. *In his existence-relation to the truth, the existing subjective thinker is just as negative as positive, has just as much of the comic as he essentially has of pathos, and is continually in a process of becoming, that is, striving.* Since the existing subject is existing (and that is the lot of every human being, except the objective ones, who have pure being to be in), he is indeed in the process of becoming. Just as his communication must in form essentially conform to his own existence, so his thought must correspond to the form of existence. Through Hegel, everyone is now familiar with the dialectic of becoming. That which in the process of becoming is the alternation between being and nonbeing (a category that is nevertheless somewhat un-

clear, inasmuch as being is itself also the continuity in the alternation) is later the negative and the positive. . . .

That the existing subjective thinker is continually striving does not mean, that in a finite sense he has a goal toward which he is striving, where he would be finished when he reached it. No, he is striving infinitely, is continually in the process of becoming, something that is safeguarded by his being just as negative as positive and by his having just as much of the essentially comic as of the essentially pathos-filled, and that has its basis in the circumstance that he is existing and renders this in his thinking. The process of becoming is the thinker's very existence, from which he can indeed thoughtlessly abstract and become objective. How far the subjective thinker might be along that road, whether a long way or a short, makes no essential difference (it is, after all, just a finitely relative comparison); as long as he is existing, he is in the process of becoming.

Existence itself, existing, is a striving and is just as pathos-filled as it is comic: pathos-filled because the striving is infinite, that is, directed toward the infinite, is a process of infinitizing, which is the highest pathos; comic because the striving is a self-contradiction. From a pathos-filled perspective, one second has infinite value; from a comic perspective, ten thousand years are but a prank, like a yesterday, and yet the time the existing individual is in does consist of such parts. When ten thousand years are simply and directly declared to be a prank, many a fool will go along and find it to be wisdom but forget the other, that a second has infinite value. When a second is said to have infinite value, someone or other will be startled and better understand that ten thousand years have infinite value. And yet the one is just as difficult to understand as the other if only one takes time to understand what is to be understood, or if in another way one is seized so infinitely by the thought of having no time to waste, not one second, that a second acquires infinite value.

This nature of existence calls to mind the Greek conception of Eros as found in the *Symposium* and which Plutarch correctly explains in his work on Isis and Osiris (§57). The parallel with Isis, Osiris, and Typhon does not concern me, but when Plutarch calls to mind that Hesiod assumed Chaos, Earth, Tartarus, and Eros to be primordial entities, it is very correct in this connection to recall Plato. Here erotic love

---

movement is here the very opposite. Direct communication requires certainty, but certainty is impossible for a person in the process of becoming, and it is indeed a deception. Thus, to employ an erotic relationship, if a maiden in love yearns for the wedding day because this would give her assured certainty, if she wanted to make herself comfortable in legal security as a spouse, if she preferred marital yawning to maidenly yearning, then the man would rightfully deplore her unfaithfulness, although she indeed did not love anyone else, because she would have lost the idea and actually did not love him. And this, after all, is the essential unfaithfulness in an erotic relationship; the incidental unfaithfulness is to love someone else.

manifestly means existence or that by which life is in everything, the life that is a synthesis of the infinite and the finite. According to Plato, Poverty and Plenty begot Eros, whose nature is made up of both. But what is existence? It is that child who is begotten by the infinite and the finite, the eternal and the temporal, and is therefore continually striving. This was Socrates' view—therefore love is continually striving, that is, the thinking subject is existing. Only the systematicians and the objectivists have ceased to be human beings and have become speculative thought, which dwells in pure being. Of course, the Socratic is not to be understood finitely as a continued and perpetually continued striving toward a goal without reaching it. No, but however much the subject has the infinite within himself, by existing he is in the process of becoming.

The thinker who in all his thinking can forget to think conjointly that he is existing does not explain existence; he makes an attempt to cease to be a human being, to become a book or an objective something that only a Münchhausen can become. That objective thinking has its reality is not denied, but in relation to all thinking in which precisely subjectivity must be accentuated it is a misunderstanding. Even if a man his whole life through occupies himself exclusively with logic, he still does not become logic; he himself therefore exists in other categories. Now, if he finds that this is not worth thinking about, then let him have his way. It will scarcely be a pleasure for him to learn that existence mocks the one who keeps on wanting to become purely objective. . . .

3. *Lessing has said that contingent historical truths can never become a demonstration of eternal truths of reason, also that the transition whereby one will build an eternal truth on historical reports is a leap.* . . .

Everything that becomes historical is contingent, inasmuch as precisely by coming into existence, by becoming historical, it has its element of contingency, inasmuch as contingency is precisely the one factor in all coming into existence. —And therein lies again the incommensurability between a historical truth and an eternal decision.

Understood in this way, the transition whereby something historical and the relation to this becomes decisive for an eternal happiness is a μετάβασις εἰς ἄλλο γένος [shifting from one genus to another] (Lessing even says that if it is not that, then I do not

know what Aristotle has understood by it, . . .), a leap for both the contemporary and the one who comes later. It is a leap, and this is the word that Lessing has employed within the accidental limitation that is characterized by an illusory distinction between contemporaneity and noncontemporaneity. His words read as follows: *Das, das ist der garstige breite Graben, über den ich nicht kommen kann, so oft und ernstlich ich auch den Sprung versucht habe* [That, that is the ugly broad ditch that I cannot cross, however often and however earnestly I have tried to make the leap]. Perhaps that word "leap" is only a stylistic turn. Perhaps that is why the metaphor is expanded for the imagination by adding the predicate *breit* [broad], as if even the smallest leap did not possess the quality of making the ditch infinitely broad, as if it would not be equally difficult for the one who *cannot* leap *at all*, whether the ditch is broad or narrow, as if it were not the dialectically passionate loathing of a leap that makes the ditch infinitely broad, just as Lady Macbeth's passion makes the blood spot so immensely large that the ocean cannot wash it away. Perhaps it is also cunning on Lessing's part to employ the word *ernstlich* [earnestly], because with regard to what it means to leap, especially when the metaphor is developed for the imagination, earnestness is droll enough, inasmuch as it stands in no relation, or in a comic relation, to the leap, since it is not the breadth of the ditch in an external sense that prevents it but the dialectical passion in an internal sense that makes the ditch infinitely broad. To have been very close to doing something already has its comic aspect, but to have been very close to making the leap is nothing whatever, precisely because the leap is the category of decision. And now in utmost earnestness to have wanted to make the leap—yes, that Lessing is indeed a rogue, for surely he has, if anything, with the utmost earnestness made the ditch broad—is that not just like making fun of people! Yet, as is well known, with regard to the leap it is also possible to make fun of people in a more popular manner: one closes one's eyes, grabs oneself by the neck *à la* Münchhausen, and then— then one stands on the other side, on that other side of sound common sense in the promised land of the system. . . .

This is almost all that can be said about Lessing's relation to the leap. . . . Before getting a chance to read that volume by Lessing, I had read *Fear and Trembling* by Johannes de Silentio. In that book I had perceived how the leap, according to the author, as the decision χατ᾽ ἐξοχήν [par excellence] becomes specifically decisive for what is Christian and for every dogmatic category. This can be achieved neither through Schelling's intellectual intuition nor through what Hegel, flouting Schelling's idea, wants to put in its place, the method, because the leap is the most decisive protest against the inverse operation of the method. All Christianity is rooted in the paradox, according to *Fear and Trembling*—yes, it is rooted in fear and trembling (which are specifically the desperate categories of Christianity and the leap)—whether one accepts it (that is, is a believer) or rejects it (for the very reason that it is the paradox). . . .

4. Lessing has said: *Wenn Gott in seiner Rechten alle Wahrheit, und in seiner Linken den einzigen immer regen Trieb nach Wahrheit, obschon mit dem Zusatze, mich immer und ewig zu irren, verschlossen hielte, und spräche zu mir: wähle! Ich fiele ihm mit Demuth in seine Linke, und sagte: Vater, gieb! die reine Wahrheit ist ja doch nur für dich allein [If God held all truth enclosed in his right hand, and in his left hand the one and only ever-striving drive for truth, even with the corollary of erring forever and ever, and if he were to say to me: Choose!—I would humbly fall down to him at his left hand and say: Father, give! Pure truth is indeed only for you alone]!* When Lessing said these words, the system was presumably not finished; alas, and now he is dead! If he were living now, now when the system has been completed for the most part or is at least in the works and will be finished by next Sunday, believe me, Lessing would have clutched it with both hands. He would not have had the time and the propriety and the elation to play in jest, as it were, odds and evens with God and to choose in earnest the left hand. But the system also has more to offer than what God has in both his hands; even at this very moment it has more, not to mention next Sunday, when it will definitely be finished. . . .

[A]n assurance here regarding my own lowly person. I am as willing as anyone to fall down in worship before the system if I could only catch a glimpse of it. So far I have not succeeded, and although I do have young legs, I am almost worn out by running from Herod to Pilate. A few times I have been very close to worshiping, but behold, at the very moment I had already spread my handkerchief on the ground, so as to avoid dirtying my trousers by kneeling, when I for the last time very innocently said to one of the initiates, "Now, tell me honestly, is it indeed completely finished, because if that is the case, I will prostrate myself, even if I should ruin a pair of trousers" (on account of the heavy traffic to and from the system, the road was rather muddy)—I would invariably receive the answer, "No, it is not entirely finished yet." And so the system and the kneeling were postponed once again.

System and conclusiveness are just about one and the same, so that if the system is not finished, there is not any system. Elsewhere I have already pointed out that a system that is not entirely finished is a hypothesis, whereas a half-finished system is nonsense. If someone were to declare that this is mere word-splitting, that on the contrary the systematicians themselves say that the system is not finished, I would merely ask: Why do they call it a system? Why speak with a forked tongue at all? . . .

On the other hand, a continued striving for a system is indeed a striving, and a striving, yes, a continued striving, is indeed what Lessing is talking about. But certainly not a striving for nothing! On the contrary, Lessing speaks of a striving for truth; and he uses a peculiar phrase regarding this urge for truth: *den einzigen immer regen Trieb* [the one and only ever-striving drive]. This word *einzig* [one and only] can scarcely be understood as meaning anything other than the infinite in the same sense as it is higher to have one thought, one only, than to have many thoughts. So these two, Lessing and the systematician, both speak of a continued striving—the only difference is that Lessing is obtuse or truthful enough to call it a continued striving, the systematician sagacious or untruthful enough to call it the system. How would this difference be judged in another context? When commission agent Behrend had lost a silk umbrella, he advertised for a cotton umbrella, because he thought this way: If I say that it is a silk umbrella, the finder will be more easily tempted to keep it. Perhaps the systematician thinks this way: If on the title page or in the newspaper I call my production a continued striving for the truth, alas, who will buy it or admire me; but if I call it the system, the absolute system, everyone will buy the system—if only the difficulty did not remain that what the systematician is selling is not the system.

Let us then proceed, but let us not make sport of each other. I, Johannes Climacus, am neither more nor less than a human being; and I assume that the one with whom I have the honor of conversing is also a human being. If he wants to be speculative thought, pure speculative thought, I must give up conversing with him, because at that moment he becomes invisible to me and to the weak mortal eye of a human being.

Consequently, *(a) a logical system can be given; (b) but a system of existence cannot be given.*

a.

α. If, however, a logical system is to be constructed, special care must be taken not to incorporate anything that is subject to the dialectic of existence, accordingly, anything that is solely by existing or by having existed, not something that is simply by being. It follows quite simply that Hegel's matchless and matchlessly admired invention—the importation of movement into logic (not to mention that in every other passage one misses even his own attempt to make one believe that it is there)—simply confuses logic.* It is indeed curious to make movement the

---

*The light-mindedness with which systematicians admit that Hegel has perhaps not been successful everywhere in importing movement into logic, much like the grocer who thinks that a few raisins do not matter when the purchase is large—this farcical docility is, of course, contempt for Hegel that not even his most vehement attacker has allowed himself. There have certainly been logical attempts prior to Hegel, but his method is everything. For him and for everyone who has intelligence enough to comprehend what it means to will something great, the absence of it at this or that point cannot be a trivial matter, as when a grocer and a customer bicker about whether there is a little underweight or overweight. Hegel himself has staked his whole reputation on the point of the method. But a method possesses the peculiar quality that, viewed abstractly, it is nothing at all; it is a method precisely in the process of being carried out; in being carried out it is a method, and where it is not carried out, it is not a method, and if there is no other method, there is no method at all. To turn Hegel into a rattlebrain must be reserved for his admirers; an attacker will always know how to honor him for having willed something great and having failed to achieve it.

basis in a sphere in which movement is inconceivable or to have movement explain logic, whereas logic cannot explain movement. . . .

In a logical system, nothing may be incorporated that has a relation to existence, that is not indifferent to existence. The infinite advantage that the logical, by being the objective, possesses over all other thinking is in turn, subjectively viewed, restricted by its being a hypothesis, simply because it is indifferent to existence understood as actuality. This duplexity distinguishes the logical from the mathematical, which has no relation whatever toward or from existence but has only objectivity—not objectivity and the hypothetical as unity and contradiction in which it is negatively related to existence.

The logical system must not be a mystification, a ventriloquism, in which the content of existence emerges cunningly and surreptitiously, where logical thought is startled and finds what the Herr Professor or the licentiate has had up his sleeve. Judging between the two can be done more sharply by answering the question: In what sense is a category an abbreviation of existence, whether logical thinking is abstract after existence or abstract without any relation to existence. . . .

β. The dialectic of the beginning must be clarified. The almost amusing thing about it, that the beginning is and then in turn is not, because it is the beginning—this true dialectical remark has long enough been like a game that has been played in Hegelian society.

The system, so it is said, begins with the immediate; some, failing to be dialectical, are even oratorical enough to speak of the most immediate of all, although the comparative reflection contained here might indeed become dangerous for the beginning.† The system begins with the immediate and therefore without presuppositions and therefore abso-

---

†To show how would become too prolix here. Frequently it is not worth the trouble either, because, after a person has laboriously advanced an objection sharply, from a philosopher's rejoinder he discovers that his misunderstanding was not that he could not understand the idolized philosophy but rather that he had allowed himself to be persuaded to believe that the whole thing was supposed to be something—and not flabby thinking concealed by the most overbearing expressions.

lutely, that is, the beginning of the system is the absolute beginning. This is entirely correct and has indeed also been adequately admired. But why, then, before the system is begun, has that other equally important, definitely equally important, question not been clarified and its clear implications honored: *How does the system begin with the immediate, that is, does it begin with it immediately?* The answer to this must certainly be an unconditional no. If the system is assumed to be after existence (whereby a confusion with a system of existence is created), the system does indeed come afterward and consequently does not begin immediately with the immediate with which existence began, even though in another sense existence did not begin with it, because the immediate never is but is annulled when it is. The beginning of the system that begins with the immediate *is then itself achieved through reflection.*

Here is the difficulty, for if one does not let go of this one thought, deceptively or thoughtlessly or in breathless haste to have the system finished, this thought in all its simplicity is capable of deciding that there can be no system of existence and that a logical system must not boast of an absolute beginning, because such a beginning is just like pure being, a pure chimera. . . .

The expression "to begin with nothing," even apart from its relation to the infinite act of abstraction, is itself deceptive. That is, to begin with nothing is neither more nor less than a new paraphrasing of the very dialectic of beginning. The beginning is and in turn is not, simply because it is the beginning, something that can also be expressed in this way: the beginning begins with nothing. It is merely a new expression, not a single step ahead. In the one instance, I only think a beginning *in abstracto;* in the other instance, I think the relation of the equally abstract beginning to a something with which a beginning is made. Now it is quite properly manifest that this something, indeed, the only something that corresponds to such a beginning, is nothing. But this is merely a tautological paraphrasing of the second thesis: the beginning is not. "The beginning is not" and "the beginning begins with nothing" are altogether identical theses, and I do not move from the spot.

What if, rather than speaking or dreaming of an absolute beginning, we speak of a leap? To want to be satisfied with a "mostly," an "as good as," a "one can almost say that," an "if you sleep on it until tomorrow, you may well say that" merely shows that one is related to Trop, who little by little went so far as to assume that having almost taken the bar examination was the same as having taken it. Everyone laughs at this, but when one chatters speculatively in the same manner in the realm of truth, in the shrine of science and scholarship, then it is good philosophy—genuine speculative philosophy. Lessing was no speculative philosopher; therefore he assumed the opposite, that an infinitely little distance makes the ditch infinitely broad, because the leap itself makes the ditch that broad. . . .

. . . If the individual does not stop reflection, he will be infinitized in reflection, that is, no decision is made.[*] By thus going astray in reflection, the individual really becomes objective; more and more he loses the decision of subjectivity and the return into himself. Yet it is assumed that reflection can stop itself objectively, whereas it is just the other way around; reflection cannot be stopped objectively, and when it is stopped subjectively, it does not stop of its own accord, but it is the subject who stops it. . . .

γ. In order to shed light on logic, it might be desirable to become oriented psychologically in the state of mind of someone who thinks the logical—what kind of dying to oneself is required for that purpose, and to what extent the imagination plays a part in it. The following is again another meager and very simple comment, but it may be quite true and not at all superfluous: a philosopher has gradually come to be such a marvelous creature that not even the most prodigal imagination has invented anything quite so fabulous. How, if at all, is the empirical *I* related to the pure *I-I*?[†] Whoever wants to be a philosopher

---

[*]Perhaps the reader will recall that when the issue becomes objective, there is no question of an eternal happiness, because this lies precisely in subjectivity and in decision.

[†]See, for example, J. G. Fichte, *Grundlage der gesammten Wissenschaftslehre, Johann Gottlieb Fichte's sämmtliche Werke,* I–VIII, ed. Immanuel Hermann Fichte (Berlin, Bonn: 1845–46; *ASKB* 492–99), I, p. 94; *Fichte: Science of Knowledge,* tr. Peter Heath and John Lachs (New York: Meredith, 1970), pp. 95–96:

Thus the self asserts, by means of X, that *A* exists *absolutely for the judging self, and that simply in virtue of its being posited in the self as such;* which is to say, it is

will certainly also want to be somewhat informed on this point and above all not want to become a ludicrous creature by being transmogrified—*eins, zwei, drei, kokolorum* [one, two, three, hocus pocus]—into speculative thought. If the person occupied with logical thought is also human enough not to forget that he is an existing individual, even if he has finished the system, the fantasticality and the charlatanry will gradually vanish. . . .

b.

A system of existence cannot be given. Is there, then, not such a system? That is not at all the case. Neither is this implied in what has been said. Existence itself is a system—for God, but it cannot be a system for any existing spirit. System and conclusiveness correspond to each other, but existence is the very opposite. Abstractly viewed, system and existence cannot be thought conjointly, because in order to think existence, systematic thought must think it as annulled and consequently not as existing. Existence is the spacing that holds apart; the systematic is the conclusiveness that combines.

Actually there now develops a deception, an illusion, which *Fragments* has attempted to point out. I must now refer to this work, namely, to the question of whether the past is more necessary than the future. That is, when an existence is a thing of the past, it is indeed finished, it is indeed concluded, and to that extent it is turned over to the systematic view. Quite so—but for whom? Whoever is himself existing cannot gain this conclusiveness outside existence, a conclusiveness that corresponds to the eternity into which the past has entered. Even if a good-natured thinker is so absentminded as to forget that he himself is existing, speculative thought and absentmindedness are still not quite the same thing. On the contrary, that he himself is existing implies the claim of existence upon him and that his existence, yes, if he is a great individual, that his existence at the present time may, as past, in turn have the validity of conclu-

siveness for a systematic thinker. But who, then, is this systematic thinker? Well, it is he who himself is outside existence and yet in existence, who in his eternity is forever concluded and yet includes existence within himself—it is God. So why the deception! Just because the world has lasted now for six thousand years, does existence therefore not have the very same claim upon the existing individual that it has always had, which is not that he in make-believe should be a contemplating spirit but that he in actuality should be an existing spirit. All understanding comes afterward. Whereas an individual existing now undeniably comes afterward in relation to the six thousand years that preceded, the curiously ironic consequence would emerge—if we assumed that he came to understand them systematically—that he would not come to understand himself as an existing being, because he himself would acquire no existence, because he himself would have nothing that should be understood afterward. It follows that such a thinker must be either the good Lord or a fantastical *quodlibet* [anything]. Certainly everyone will perceive the immorality in this, and certainly everyone will also perceive that what another author has observed regarding the Hegelian system is entirely in order: that through Hegel a system, the absolute system, was brought to completion—without having an ethics. By all means, let us smile at the ethical-religious fantasies of the Middle Ages in asceticism and the like, but above all let us not forget that the speculative, farcical exaggeration of becoming an *I-I*—and then *qua* human being often such a philistine that no enthusiast would have cared to lead such a life—is equally ludicrous.

So let us ask very simply, as a Greek youth would ask his master (and if the lofty wisdom can explain everything else but cannot answer a simple question, one surely sees that the world is out of joint), about the impossibility of a system of existence: Who is supposed to write or finish such a system? Surely a human being, unless we are to resume the peculiar talk about a human being's becoming speculative thought, a subject-object. Consequently, a human being—and surely a living, that is, an existing, human being. Or if the speculative thought that produces the system is the joint effort of these various thinkers, in what final conclusion does this fellowship combine? How does it come to light? Surely through a human being? And how, in turn, do the individual thinkers relate themselves to this effort; what are the middle terms be-

---

asserted that within the self—whether it be specifically positing, or judging, or whatever it may be—there is something that is permanently uniform, forever one and the same; and hence the X that is absolutely posited can also be expressed as I = I; I am I.

tween the particular and the world-historical; and in turn what sort of being is the one who is stringing it all on the systematic thread? Is he a human being or is he speculative thought? But if he is a human being, then he is indeed existing. Now, all in all, there are two ways for an existing individual: either he can do everything to forget that he is existing and thereby manage to become comic (the comic contradiction of wanting to be what one is not, for example, that a human being wants to be a bird is no more comic than the contradiction of not wanting to be what one is, as *in casu* [in this case] an existing individual, just as in the use of language it is comic when someone forgets his name, which signifies not so much forgetting his name as the singularity of his nature), because existence possesses the remarkable quality that an existing person exists whether he wants to or not; or he can direct all his attention to his existing. It is from this side that an objection must first be made to modern speculative thought, that it has not a false presupposition but a comic presupposition, occasioned by its having forgotten in a kind of world-historical absentmindedness what it means to be a human being, not what it means to be human in general, for even speculators might be swayed to consider that sort of thing, but what it means that we, you and I and he, are human beings, each one on his own.

The existing individual who directs all his attention to the actuality that *he* is existing will approvingly look upon those words of Lessing about a continued striving as a beautiful saying, not as something that gained its author immortal fame, because the saying is so very simple, but as something every attentive person must certify. The existing individual who forgets that he is existing will become more and more absentminded, and just as people occasionally set down the fruits of their *otium* [leisure] in books, so we may expect the expected existential system as the fruit of his absentmindedness—well, not all of us, but only those who are as absentminded as he is. Whereas the Hegelian system in absentmindedness goes ahead and becomes a system of existence, and what is more, is finished—without having an ethics (the very home of existence), that other simpler philosophy, presented by an existing individual for existing individuals, is especially intent upon advancing the ethical.

As soon as it is remembered that philosophizing is not speaking fantastically to fantastical beings but speaking to existing individuals, consequently that a decision about whether a continued striving is somewhat inferior to systematic conclusiveness is not to be made fantastically *in abstracto,* but that the question is what existing beings have to be satisfied with insofar as they are existing—then the continued striving will be unique in not involving illusion. Even if a person has achieved the highest, the repetition by which he must indeed fill out his existence, if he is not to go backward (or become a fantastical being), will again be a continued striving, because here in turn the conclusiveness is moved ahead and postponed. This is just like the Platonic conception of love; it is a want, and not only does that person feel a want who craves something he does not have but also that person who desires the continued possession of what he has. In the system and in the fifth act of the drama, one has a positive conclusiveness speculatively-fantastically and esthetically-fantastically, but such a conclusiveness is only for fantastical beings.

The continued striving is the expression of the existing subject's ethical life-view. The continued striving must therefore not be understood metaphysically, but neither is there any individual who exists metaphysically. Thus through a misunderstanding a contrast could be drawn between systematic conclusiveness and the continued striving for truth. One might then be able, and perhaps has even tried, to bear in mind the Greek notion of continually wanting to be a learner. But that is only a misunderstanding in this sphere. On the contrary, ethically understood, the continued striving is the consciousness of being an existing individual, and the continued learning the expression of the perpetual actualization, which at no moment is finished as long as the subject is existing; the subject is aware of this and is therefore not deluded. But Greek philosophy had a continual relation to ethics. That was why continually wanting to be a learner was not regarded as a great discovery or the inspired undertaking of an exceptional individual, since it was neither more nor less than the understanding that one is existing and that to be conscious of this is no merit but to forget it is thoughtlessness.

So-called pantheistic systems have frequently been cited and attacked by saying that they cancel freedom and the distinction between good and evil. This is perhaps expressed just as definitely by saying that every such system fantastically volatilizes the concept *existence.* But this should be said not only of pantheistic systems, for it would have been better to show that every system must be pantheistic simply because of the conclusiveness. Existence must be annulled in the eternal before the system concludes itself. No existing remainder may be left behind, not even such a tiny little dingle-dangle as the existing Herr Professor who is writing the system. . . .

The systematic idea is subject-object, is the unity of thinking and being; existence, on the other hand, is precisely the separation. From this it by no means follows that existence is thoughtless, but existence has spaced and does space subject from object, thought from being. Objectively understood, thinking is pure thinking, which just as abstractly-objectively corresponds to its object, which in turn is therefore itself, and truth is the correspondence of thinking with itself. This objective thinking has no relation to the existing subjectivity, and while the difficult question always remains—namely, how the existing subject gains entrance into this objectivity in which subjectivity is pure abstract subjectivity (which again is an objective qualification and does not signify any existing human being)—it is certain that the existing subjectivity evaporates more and more. And finally, if it is possible that a human being can become such a thing and that all this is not something of which he at best can become cognizant through imagination, this existing subjectivity becomes a pure abstract co-knowledge in and knowledge of this pure relation between thinking and being, this pure identity, indeed this tautology, because here being does not mean that the thinking person is, but basically only that he is a thinker.

The existing subject, however, is existing, and so indeed is every human being. Yet let us not do the wrong of calling the objective tendency impious, pantheistic self-worship but rather view it as a venture in the comic, because the idea that from now on to the end of the world nothing should be said except what would suggest a further improvement in a nearly finished system is simply a systematic consequence for systematizers.

By beginning straightway with ethical categories against the objective tendency, one does wrong and fails to hit the mark, because one has nothing in common with the attacked. But by remaining within the metaphysical, one can employ the comic, which also is in the metaphysical sphere, in order to overtake such a transfigured professor. If a dancer could leap very high, we would admire him, but if he wanted to give the impression that he could fly—even though he could leap higher than any dancer had ever leapt be-

fore—let laughter overtake him. Leaping means to belong essentially to the earth and to respect the law of gravity so that the leap is merely the momentary, but flying means to be set free from telluric conditions, something that is reserved exclusively for winged creatures, perhaps also for inhabitants of the moon, perhaps—and perhaps that is also where the system will at long last find its true readers. To be a human being has been abolished, and every speculative thinker confuses himself with humankind, whereby he becomes something infinitely great and nothing at all. In absentmindedness, he confuses himself with humankind, just as the opposition press uses "we" and the skippers say "the devil take me." But having cursed for a long time, one finally returns to the direct statement, because all swearing cancels itself; and when one has learned that every urchin can say "we," one learns that it nevertheless means a little more to be *one*; and when one sees that every cellar dweller can play the game of being humankind, one finally perceives that to be simply and solely a human being means something more than playing party games this way. And one thing more—when a cellar dweller plays this game, everyone thinks it ludicrous; and yet it is just as ludicrous when the greatest human being does it. And in that regard one may laugh at him and, as is fitting, still have respect for his abilities, his learning, etc.

Becoming Subjective
from Concluding Unscientific Postscript to Philosophical Fragments

Objectively, one continually speaks only about the case in point; subjectively, one speaks about the subject and subjectivity—and see, the subjectivity itself is the case in point.* It must continually be insisted upon that the subjective issue is not something about the case in point but is the subjectivity itself. In other words, since the issue is the decision and all decision, as shown previously, is rooted in subjectivity, it is important that objectively there be no trace what-

---

*Most footnotes have been omitted—ed.

ever of any case in point, because at that very moment the subjective individual wants to evade some of the pain and crisis of decision, that is, wants to make the issue somewhat objective. If the introductory intellectual discipline is waiting for one more book before the matter is submitted to judgment, if the system lacks one more paragraph, if the speaker holds one more argument in reserve—then the decision is postponed. Thus there is not a question of the truth of Christianity here in the sense that if this was decided the subjective individual would then be ready and willing to accept it. No, the question is about the subject's acceptance of it. And here it must be regarded as perdition's illusion (which has remained ignorant of the fact that the decision is rooted in subjectivity) or as an equivocation of illusiveness (which shoves off the decision by objective treatment in which there is no decision in all eternity) to assume that this transition from something objective to a subjective acceptance follows directly of its own accord, since precisely this is the decisive point and an objective acceptance (*sit venia verbo* [pardon the expression]) is paganism or thoughtlessness.

Christianity wants to give the single individual an eternal happiness, a good that is not distributed in bulk but only to one, and to one at a time. Even though Christianity assumes that subjectivity, as the possibility of appropriation, is the possibility of receiving this good, it nevertheless does not assume that as a matter of course the subjectivity is all set, as a matter of course has even an actual idea of the significance of this good. This development or remaking of the subjectivity, its infinite concentration in itself under a conception of the infinite's highest good, an eternal happiness, is the developed possibility of the subjectivity's first possibility. Christianity, therefore, protests against all objectivity; it wants the subject to be infinitely concerned about himself. What it asks about is the subjectivity; the truth of Christianity, if it is at all, is only in this; objectively, it is not at all. And even if it is only in one single subject, then it is only in him, and there is greater Christian joy in heaven over this one than over world history and the system, which as objective powers are incommensurate with the essentially Christian.

It is generally thought that to be subjective is no art. Well, of course, every human being is something of a subject. But now to become what one is as a matter of course—who would waste his time on that? That would indeed be the most dispensable of all tasks in life. Quite so. But that is why it is already so very difficult, indeed, the most difficult of all, because every human being has a strong natural desire and drive to become something else and more. . . .

The objective orientation (which wants to turn everyone into an observer and at its maximum into such an observer that, almost like a ghost, he is easily confused with the prodigious spirit of ages past) naturally wants to hear nothing and know nothing except that which stands in relation to itself. If within the given presupposition a person is fortunate enough to be able to be of service with some information regarding a perhaps previously unknown tribe that now, aided by a flag, will join the paragraph parade, if within the given presupposition he is competent to assign China a place other than the one it has hitherto occupied in the systematic procession, then he is welcome. Anything else is normal-school rigmarole, inasmuch as it is supposed to be certain that the objective trend toward becoming an observer is in modern linguistic usage the *ethical* answer to the question of what I am to do ethically. (To be an observer, that is the ethical! That a person ought to be an observer is the *ethical* answer—otherwise one is compelled to assume that there is no question whatever about the ethical and hence no answer either.) And it is supposed to be certain that world history is the task assigned to our observing nineteenth century—the objective orientation is the way and the truth.

Let us, however, very simply review for ourselves a little moot point of subjectivity regarding the objective orientation. Just as *Fragments* called attention to a little introductory observation before proceeding to point out the idea's world-historical process *in concreto*—what it means that the idea becomes historical—so I, too, shall now pause with a few introductory observations regarding the objective orientation: *what ethics would have to judge if becoming a subjective individual were not the highest task assigned to every human being.* What must it judge? Well, it must, of course, be driven to despair, but what does the system care about that? It is indeed consistent enough not to allow ethics to enter into the system.

The world-historical idea increasingly concentrates everything systematically. What a Sophist once said, that he could carry the whole world in a nutshell, now seems to be accomplished in modern surveys of world history: they are becoming more and more compendious. It is not my intention to point out the comic in this. However, through various thoughts leading to the same goal, I shall attempt to clarify what ethics and the ethical object to in this entire order of things. In our day, it is not a matter of a particular scholar's or thinker's occupying himself with world history; no, the whole age is clamoring for world history. Yet ethics and the ethical, by being the essential stronghold of individual existence, have an irrefutable claim upon every existing individual, an irrefutable claim of such a nature that whatever a person achieves in the world, even the most amazing thing, is nevertheless dubious if he himself has not been ethically clear when he chose and has not made his choice ethically clear to himself. The ethical quality is jealous of itself and spurns the most amazing quantity.

Therefore ethics looks with a suspicious eye at all world-historical knowledge, because this easily becomes a trap, a demoralizing esthetic diversion for the knowing subject, because the distinction between what does and does not become world-historical is quantitative-dialectical. That is also why the absolute ethical distinction between good and evil is world-historically-esthetically neutralized in the esthetic-metaphysical category of "the great," "the momentous," to which the bad and the good have equal access. In the world-historical, an essential role is played by factors of another kind, different from the ethical-dialectical: namely, the accidental, circumstances, that play of forces in which the reshaping totality of historical life absorbs the individual's action in order to transform it into something different that does not directly belong to him. Neither by willing the good to the utmost of his ability nor by willing evil with diabolical callousness is a person assured of becoming world-historical; even in the case of misfortune, it holds true that it takes luck to become world-historical. How, then, does an individual become world-historical? Ethically viewed, he becomes world-historical by accident. But ethics also considers unethical the transition whereby a person abandons the ethical quality in order to try his hand, cravingly, wishfully, etc., at the quantifying other.

An age and a person can be immoral in various ways, but it is also immoral or at least a temptation to consort too much with world history, a temptation that can easily lead a person to want also to be world-historical when the time comes that he himself is going to act. By continually being occupied as an observer of the accidental, that *accessorium* [addition] by which world-historical figures become world-historical, a

person is easily misled into confusing this *accessorium* with the ethical and easily misled, unhealthily, flirtingly, and cowardly, to being concerned about the accidental, instead, himself existing, of being infinitely concerned about the ethical. Perhaps the reason our age is dissatisfied when it is going to act is that it has been coddled by observing. That is perhaps why there are so many fruitless attempts to become something more than one is by lumping together socially in the hope of impressing the spirit of history numerically. Spoiled by constant association with world history, people want the momentous and only that, are concerned only with the accidental, the world-historical outcome, instead of being concerned with the essential, the innermost, freedom, the ethical.

In other words, continual association with the world-historical makes a person incompetent to act. True ethical enthusiasm consists in willing to the utmost of one's capability, but also, uplifted in divine jest, in never thinking whether or not one thereby achieves something. As soon as the will begins to cast a covetous eye on the outcome, the individual begins to become immoral—the energy of the will becomes torpid, or it develops abnormally into an unhealthy, unethical, mercenary hankering that, even if it achieves something great, does not achieve it ethically—the individual demands something other than the ethical itself. A truly great ethical individuality would consummate his life as follows: he would develop himself to the utmost of his capability; in the process he perhaps would produce a great effect in the external world, but this would not occupy him at all, because he would know that the external is not in his power and therefore means nothing either *pro* or *contra*. He would remain in ignorance about it, lest he be delayed by the external and fall into its temptation, because that which a logician fears most, an erroneous inference, a μετάβασις εἰς ἄλλο γένος [shifting from one genus to another], the ethicist equally fears drawing a conclusion or making a transition from the ethical to something other than the ethical. He would, then, remain in ignorance about it through a resolution of the will, and even in death he would *will* not to know that his life had had any significance other than that of having ethically prepared the development of his soul. Then if the power governing all things would want to dispose circumstances so that he became a world-historical figure— well, that is something he would first inquire about jestingly in eternity, for not until then is there time for the light-minded questions of carelessness.

In other words, if a person cannot by his own efforts, in freedom, by willing the good, become a world-historical figure—which is impossible precisely because it is only possible, that is, perhaps possible, that is, dependent on something else—then it is unethical to be concerned about it. And when, instead of renouncing this concern and tearing himself loose from its temptation, a person prinks it up with the pious appearance of benefiting others, he is immoral and wants sneakily to insinuate into his account with God the thought that God nevertheless does need him just a little bit. But this is obtuseness, for God needs no human being. How highly embarrassing to be Creator if it turned out that God came to need the creature. On the contrary, God can require everything of every human being, everything and for nothing, since every human being is an unworthy servant, and the ethically inspired person is different from others only in knowing this and in hating and loathing all deception.

When a headstrong person is battling with his contemporaries and endures it all but also shouts, "Posterity, history will surely make manifest that I spoke the truth," then people believe that he is inspired. Alas, no, he is just a bit smarter than the utterly obtuse people. He does not choose money and the prettiest girl or the like; he chooses world-historical importance—yes, he knows very well what he is choosing. But in relation to God and the ethical, he is a deceitful lover; he is also one of those for whom Judas became a guide (Acts 1:16)—he, too, is selling his relationship with God, though not for money. And although he perhaps reforms an entire age through his zeal and teaching, he confounds existence *pro virili* [to the very extent of his powers], because his own form of existence is not adequate to his teaching, because by excepting himself he establishes a teleology that renders existence meaningless.

A king or a philosopher can perhaps be served in a finite sense by a sagacious, talented fellow who safeguards the king's power and upholds the philosopher's teaching and binds everyone in submission to the king and the philosopher, although he himself is neither a good subordinate nor a true adherent. But in relation to God this is rather obtuse. The deceitful lover who does not want to be faithful as lover, but only as world-historical entrepreneur, will not be

faithful to the utmost. He does not want to understand that there is nothing between him and God but the ethical; he does not want to understand that he ought to be made enthusiastic by it; he does not want to understand that God, without doing any injustice and without denying his nature, which is love, could create a human being endowed with capacities unmatched by all others, place him in a remote spot, and say to him, "Now go and live the human life through with a strenuousness unmatched by all others; work so that one-half would be sufficient to transform an age, but you and I are alone in this. All your effort will have no importance whatever for any other human being, and yet you shall, do you understand, you shall will the ethical, and you shall, do you understand, you shall be enthusiastic, because this is the highest."

The deceitful lover does not understand this. Even less does he understand the next thing, when a truly enthusiastic ethical individuality, moved in earnestness, elevated in the holy jest of divine madness, says, "Let me be as if created for the sake of a whim; this is the jest. Yet I shall with utmost strenuousness will the ethical; this is the earnestness. I want nothing else, nothing. O insignificant importance, O jesting earnestness, O blessed fear and trembling! How blessed to be able to fulfill God's requirements while smiling at the demands of the times. How blessed to despair over not being able to do it as long as one does not let go of God!" Only such an individuality is ethical, but he has also comprehended that the world-historical is a composite that is not directly dialectical for the ethical.

The longer life goes on and the longer the existing person through his action is woven into existence, the more difficult it is to separate the ethical from the external, and the easier it seems to corroborate the metaphysical tenet that the outer is the inner, the inner the outer, the one wholly commensurate with the other. This is precisely the temptation, and the ethical becomes more difficult day by day, because it consists in infinity's true hypertension, which is the beginning, where it therefore is most clearly manifest.

Let us imagine an individual who stands at the beginning of life. He now resolves, for example, to spend his whole life pursuing the truth and actualizing known truth. So in the moment of resolution he rejects everything, everything, including, of course, world-historical importance. But now, what if momentous importance comes to him little by little as the fruit of his labor? Well, if it comes as the fruit of his labor—but it never does that. If it comes, then it is Governance who adds it to his ethical striving in itself, and consequently it is not the fruit of his labor. It is a *pro* that must be regarded as a temptation just as much as any *contra*. It is the most dangerous of all temptations, and many a glorious beginning in the hypertension of the infinite has grown slack in what for the fallen one became a soft, effeminate embrace.

But back to the beginning. With the true ethical hypertension of the infinite, he rejects everything. In fables and fairy tales there is a lamp called the wonderful lamp; when it is rubbed, the spirit appears. Jest! But freedom, that is the wonderful lamp. When a person rubs it with ethical passion, God comes into existence for him. And look, the spirit of the lamp is a servant (so wish for it, you whose spirit is a wish), but the person who rubs the wonderful lamp of freedom becomes a servant—the spirit is the Lord. This is the beginning. Let us now see if it will do to add something else to the ethical. So the resolving person says: I will—but I also want to have world-historical importance—*aber* [but]. So there is an *aber*—and the spirit vanishes again, because the rubbing has not been done properly, and the beginning does not occur. But if it has occurred or has been done properly, every subsequent *aber* must again be renounced, even if existence in the most flattering and inveigling way did everything to force it upon one.

Or the resolved person says: I will this, but I also will that my efforts shall benefit other people, because, just between us, I am such a good person that I want to benefit, if possible, all of humankind. Even if the spirit did appear when the rubbing is done this way, I think it would rise up in wrath and say: "Obtuse fellow, do I not exist, I, the Almighty, and even if human beings—all of whom I created and counted, I, who count the hairs on a person's head—were as countless as the sands of the sea, am I still not able to help everyone just as I am helping you? You presumptuous fellow! Can you demand anything? But I can demand everything. Do you have anything of which you could give me some? Or when doing your utmost, are you not simply returning my property to me, and perhaps in rather poor condition?"

So here the beginner stands—the slightest trace of an *aber,* then the beginning miscarries. But if it is this way at the beginning, the continuation must fully correspond to it. If that beginner began well, if he also achieved something amazing, if all his contemporaries were much indebted to him and thanked him, then it is indeed important for him to understand in jest what jest is. The earnestness is his own inner life; the jest is that it pleases God to attach this importance to his striving, to the striving of one who is only an unworthy servant. When a mirage in its absolute transforming power picks up a person and shows him in preternatural magnitude to the astonished observer: is it that person's merit? Likewise, when Governance arranges things so that a person's inner striving is reflected magically in the shadow play of world history: is that his merit? I should think that the true ethicist to whom this happened, if he were to speak of it, would waggishly recall a certain Don Quixote. He would say that just as that knight, perhaps as payment for wanting to be world-historical, was persecuted by a nisse, who spoiled everything for him, so he also had to have a nisse who played his game with him in reverse—for only obtuse schoolmasters and just as obtuse geniuses make the mistake of believing that it is they themselves [who do it] and forget themselves over their great consequence in world history. . . .

. . . O singular power that resides in the ethical! If a king were to say to his enemies: Do as I command; if not, tremble before my scepter, which will remain as a terror over you—unless it should please Governance to take my throne away from me this very day and make a swineherd my successor! Why do we so seldom hear this "if," this "unless," this last part of the speech, which is the ethical truth? It is indeed truth—and the art is only this, to be enthusiastic, or as another author has said: to be happy out on 70,000 fathoms of water. And the person who, himself existing, has understood life in this way will not be mistaken about world history, which in the foggy vision of speculative thought only runs together into something quite different, about which the speculative thinker becomes profoundly wise afterward. . . .

α. *We must disregard,* as already suggested, *the idea that access to becoming world-historical is quantitatively dialectical, so that what has become world-historical has gone through this dialectic.* That there is no such distinction for the omniscient God cannot console a finite mind, because, well, I dare not say aloud what I mean; that would not do in the world-historical nineteenth century. But I probably dare to whisper it in the ear of the systematician: There is a difference between King Solomon and Jørgen Hattemager—but do not breathe a word about this to anyone else. For God the conception of the world-historical is infused by and with his co-knowledge of the innermost secret in the conscience of the greatest and of the lowliest human being. If a human being wants to take this position, he is a fool; but if he does not want this, he will have to be satisfied with a survey that looks for salient points, and that is precisely why it is quantity that tips the scale. That the ethical is present in world history, just as it is present wherever God is, is therefore not denied, but rather that a finite spirit can in truth see it; wanting to see it there is a presumptuous and risky undertaking that can easily end with the observer's losing the ethical in himself.

In order to study the ethical, every human being is assigned to himself. In that regard, he himself is more than enough for himself; indeed, he is the only place where *he* can with certainty study it. . . .

The ethical as the absolute is infinitely valid in itself and does not need embellishment in order to look better. But the world-historical is just such a dubious embellishment (when it is not the eye of an omniscient one but the eye of a human being that is to see through it), and in world history, the ethical, just like nature, according to the poet, serves *knechtisch dem Gesetz der Schwere* [the law of gravity slavishly], since the differential of quantity is also a law of gravity. The more the ethical can be simplified, the better one sees it. Thus it is not the case, as is deceitfully imagined, that the ethical is seen better in world history, where everything involves millions, than in a person's own poor life. On the contrary, it is just the opposite; he sees it better in his own life simply because he makes no mistake about substance and mass. The ethical is inwardness, and the smaller the range in which one sees it, if one does see it in its infinity, the better one sees it; whereas the person who thinks he must have world-historical embellishments in order thereby to see it better shows in doing so that he is ethically immature. The person who does not comprehend the infinite validity of the ethical, even if it pertained to him alone in the whole world, does not really comprehend the ethical; that it pertains to all human beings is in a certain sense none of his business, except as a shadow that accompanies the ethical clarity in which he lives. . . .

World-historically, the individual subject certainly is a trifle, but the world-historical is, after all, an addendum; ethically, the individual subject is infinitely important. — *Against Hegelian view.*

Take any human passion and have it be related to the ethical in the individual; ethically viewed, this will have great significance; world-historically, perhaps none at all or perhaps very great significance, for the world-historical, viewed ethically, enters by way of a "perhaps." Whereas that relation between passion and the ethical occupies the existing individual to the utmost (it is this that the mocker calls nothing and speculative thought speculatively ignores with the help of immanence), world-historical Governance perhaps shapes a reflecting context for this individual, whereby his life-situation acquires widespread world-historical importance. He does not have it, but Governance adds it to him. . . .

. . . Therefore venture, says the ethical, dare to renounce everything, including also that highly ranked yet delusive association with world-historical observation; dare to become nothing at all, to become a single individual from whom God ethically requires everything, but without daring for all that to cease being enthusiastic—see, that is the venturesome deed! But then your gain is also that God in all eternity cannot get rid of you, for your eternal consciousness is only in the ethical—see, that is the reward! World-historically, to be a single individual is nothing at all, infinitely nothing—and yet this is a human being's only true and highest significance, and thus higher than any other significance, which is a phantom, not, to be sure, in itself, but always a phantom if it is supposed to be the highest.

γ. . . .

If world history is the history of the human race, it follows automatically that I do not come to see the ethical in it. What I do come to see must correspond to the abstraction that the human race is, must be something just as abstract. The ethical, on the other hand, is predicated on individuality and to such a degree that each individual actually and essentially comprehends the ethical only in himself, because it is his co-knowledge with God. In other words, although in a certain sense the ethical is infinitely abstract, in another sense it is infinitely concrete, indeed, the most concrete of all, because it is dialectical for every human being as this individual human being.

Thus the observer sees world history in purely metaphysical categories, and he sees it speculatively as the immanence of cause and effect, ground and consequent. Whether he is able to discern a τέλος [end, goal] for the whole human race, I do not decide, but that τέλος is not the ethical τέλος, which is for individuals, but is a metaphysical τέλος. Insofar as the individuals participate in the history of the human race by their deeds, the observer does not see these deeds as traced back to the individuals and to the ethical but sees them as traced away from the individuals and to the totality. Ethically, what makes the deed the individual's own is the intention, but this is precisely what is not included in world history, for here it is the world-historical intention that matters. World-historically, I see the effect; ethically, I see the intention. But when I ethically see the intention and understand the ethical, I also see that every effect is infinitely indifferent, that what the effect was is a matter of indifference, but then of course I do not see the world-historical. . . .

δ. If becoming subjective were not the task, that is, the highest task assigned to every human being, a task that can indeed be sufficient for even the longest life, since it has the singular quality that it is not over until life is over—if this were not the case with becoming subjective, then a difficulty would remain that must, it seems to me, so press down like a leaden weight upon every human being's troubled conscience that he would wish himself dead today rather than tomorrow. This objection is not mentioned in our objective and yet liberal age, which is much too busy with the system and with forms to bother about human life. The objection is this: *If one posits only the development of the generation or the race or at least posits it as the highest, how does one explain the divine squandering that uses the endless host of individuals of one generation after the other in order to see the world-historical development in motion?* The world-historical drama proceeds extremely slowly. Why does God not make haste if that is all he wants? What undramatic forbearance or, more correctly, what a prosaic and boring spinning-out process! And if that is all he wants, how horrible, tyrannically to squander myriads of human lives. But what does the observer care about that? The observer world-historically catches a glimpse of the play of colors in the generations, just like a shoal of herring in the sea—the individual herring is not

worth much. The observer stares numbly into the immense forest of the generations, and like someone who cannot see the forest for the trees, he sees only the forest, not a single tree. He hangs up curtains systematically and uses people and nations for that purpose—individual human beings are nothing to him; even eternity itself is draped with systematic surveys and ethical meaninglessness. Poetry squanders poetically, but, far from fasting itself, it does not dare to presuppose the divine frugality of the infinite that ethically-psychologically does not need many human beings but needs the idea all the more. No wonder, then, that one even admires the observer when he is noble, heroic, or, perhaps more correctly, absentminded enough to forget that he, too, is a human being, an existing individual human being! By steadily staring into that world-historical drama, he dies and departs; nothing of him remains, or he himself remains like a ticket the usher holds in his hand as a sign that now the spectator has gone.

If, however, becoming subjective is the highest task assigned to a human being, then everything turns out beautifully. From this it first follows that he no longer has anything to do with world history but in that respect leaves everything to the royal poet. Second, there is no squandering, for even though individuals are as innumerable as the sands of the sea, the task of becoming subjective is indeed assigned to every person. Finally, this does not deny the reality of the world-historical development, which, reserved for God and eternity, has both its time and its place.

ε. First, then, the ethical, to become subjective, then the world-historical. Surely even the most objective person is basically in secret agreement with what has been stated here, that first of all the wise person ought to understand the same thing that the simple person understands and ought to feel bound to the same thing that binds the simple person—and that only then should he pass on to the world-historical. First, then, the simple. . . .

If only, even for a moment, I might engage the wise person in conversation, because I would gladly be the simple one who stops him with the following simple observation: *Is it not precisely the simple that is most difficult for the wise man to understand?* The simple person understands the simple directly, but when the wise person is to understand it, it becomes infinitely difficult. . . .

That the simple can be so protracted is indeed very strange. Let us take an example from the religious sphere (to which the ethical lies so close that they continually communicate with each other). To pray is, of course, a very simple matter; one would think it to be as easy as buttoning one's trousers, and if nothing else stood in the way, one could promptly tackle the world-historical. And yet how difficult! Intellectually, I must have an altogether clear conception of God, of myself, and of my relationship with him, and of the dialectic of the relationship of prayer—lest I confuse God with something else so that I do not pray to God, and lest I confuse myself with something else so that I do not pray—so that in the relationship of prayer I maintain the distinction and the relationship. Reasonable married people confess that they need months and years of daily life together in order to learn to know each other, and yet God is much more difficult to know. God is not something external, as is a wife, whom I can ask whether she is now satisfied with me. If in my relationship with God I regard what I am doing as good and do not keep watch over myself with the infinite's mistrust of me, then it is just as if God, too, were content with me, because God is not something external, but is the infinite itself, is not something external that quarrels with me when I do wrong but the infinite itself that does not need scolding words, but whose vengeance is terrible—the vengeance that God does not exist for me at all, even though I pray. . . .

Consequently, to become subjective should be the highest task assigned to every human being, just as the highest reward, an eternal happiness, exists only for the subjective person or, more correctly, comes into existence for the one who becomes subjective. Moreover, becoming subjective should give a person plenty to do as long as he lives; thus it should not happen to the zealous person but only to the busy trifler that he will be finished with life before life is finished with him. And he should not be entitled to ignore life but should instead be obliged to understand that he very likely had not comprehended life's task correctly, since it otherwise would follow as a matter of course that the task of life would last as long as life lasts, that is, the task of living. Consequently, if the individual comprehends that to become subjective is his highest task, then, in the carrying out of that task, issues should become manifest to him that in turn

could suffice for the subjective thinker fully as well as the objective issues that the objective thinker has at hand suffice for him, this person who goes further and further, who, scorning repetition's ever-deepening absorption in the one thought, never repeats himself but astounds the age first by being a systematician, then a world historian, then an astronomer, veterinarian, waterworks inspector, geographer, etc.

Amazing! But why should it not be sufficient when one, from the Socratic wisdom that discovers one's own disposition to all evil before one begins with being finished as a good person, learns to make a similar discovery: that to finish too quickly is the greatest danger of all. . . .

That is how the matter stands. Believe me, I, too, am one of those who have power, even though I do say so myself, although ordinarily I would be ranked with normal-school graduates and village parish clerks. I am one of those who have power; yet my power is not that of a ruler or a conqueror, for the only power I have is the power to restrain. My power, however, is not extensive, for I have power only over myself, and I do not have even that if I do not exercise restraint every moment. I do not have time to try to exercise restraint directly upon the age in which I live, and furthermore I think that trying to restrain the age directly is as futile as for a passenger on a train to try to stop it by clutching the seat ahead of him—he identifies himself directly with the age and yet he wants to restrain it. No, the only thing to do is to get off the train and restrain oneself.

If one gets off the train (and especially in our day, when one is keeping up with the age, one is continually *auf der Eisenbahn* [on the railway]) and never forgets that the task is to exercise restraint, since the temptation is to finish too quickly, then nothing is more certain than that the task is enough for a lifetime. . . .

Here are a few examples that in all brevity show how the simplest issue is changed by restraint into the most difficult. Thus there is no reason for hastily choosing astronomy, veterinary science, and the like if one has not understood the simple. Here brevity cannot be a hindrance, for the issues are not finished.

For example, *what it means to die*. On that topic I know what people ordinarily know: that if I swallow a dose of sulfuric acid I will die, likewise by drowning myself or sleeping in coal gas etc. I know that Napoleon always carried poison with him, that Shakespeare's Juliet took it; that the Stoics regarded suicide as a courageous act and others regard it as cowardice, that one can die from such a ludicrous trifle that the most solemn person cannot help laughing at death, that one can avoid certain death, etc. . . .

However, despite this almost extraordinary knowledge or proficiency of knowledge, I am by no means able to regard death as something I have understood. So before I move on to world history, about which I still must always say: God knows if it actually does concern you; I think it would be better to consider this, lest existence mock me for having become so erudite that I had forgotten to understand what will happen to me and every human being sometime— sometime, but what am I saying! Suppose death were insidious enough to come tomorrow! Just this uncertainty, if it is to be understood and held firm by an existing person and consequently be thought into everything precisely because it is uncertainty, even into my beginning with world history, so that I make it clear to myself whether I am beginning something worth beginning if death should come tomorrow— this uncertainty already gives rise to unbelievable difficulties, of which not even the orator is aware. . . .

If death is always uncertain, if I am mortal, then this means that this uncertainty cannot possibly be understood in general if I am not also such a human being in general. But this I am not. That is something only absentminded people are, for example, Soldin, the bookseller. And even if I am that at my beginning, the life-task is indeed to become subjective, and to the same degree the uncertainty becomes more and more dialectically penetrating in relation to my personality. Therefore it becomes more and more important to me to think it into every moment of my life, because, since its uncertainty is at every moment, this uncertainty is vanquished only by my vanquishing it every moment.

If, however, the uncertainty of death is something in general, then my dying is also something in general. Perhaps dying is also something in general for systematicians, for absentminded people. For the late bookseller Soldin, dying is said to have been something in general—"When he was going to get up in the morning, he was not aware that he was dead." But for me, *my* dying is by no means something in general; for others, my dying is some such thing. Nor am *I* for myself some such thing in general; perhaps for others I am some such thing in general. But if the task

is to become subjective, then every subject becomes *for himself* exactly the opposite of some such thing in general. . . .

See, when dying is to be placed in relation to the subject's whole life in this way, I am, even if my life were at stake, very far indeed from having comprehended death, and even less have I existentially carried out my task. And yet I have thought again and again, have sought guidance in books—and found none.*

For example, *what it means to be immortal*. . . .

The difficulty in the question arises precisely when it is made simple, not in the way a well-trained assistant professor inquires about the immortality of human beings, abstractly understood as humankind in general, and thus about the immortality of human beings in general, fantastically understood as the race, and thus about the immortality of the human race. . . .

Objectively the question cannot be answered at all, because objectively the question of immortality cannot be asked, since immortality is precisely the intensification and highest development of the developed subjectivity. Not until one rightly wills to become subjective can the question rightly arise—how, then, could it be answered objectively?

Socially the question cannot be answered at all, because socially it cannot be enunciated, since only the subject who wills to become subjective can grasp the question and rightly ask: Do *I* become immortal or am *I* immortal? See, people can very well join to-

---

*Although it has been said frequently, I wish to repeat it again here: What is developed here by no means pertains to the simple folk, whom the god will preserve in their lovable simplicity (although they sense the pressure of life in another way), the simplicity that feels no great need for any other kind of understanding, or, insofar as it is felt, humbly becomes a sigh over the misery of this life, while this sigh humbly finds comfort in the thought that life's happiness does not consist in being a person of knowledge. On the other hand, it does pertain to the person who considers himself to have the ability and the opportunity for deeper inquiry, and it pertains to him in such a way that he does not thoughtlessly settle down to world history but first of all calls to mind that being an existing human being is such a strenuous and yet natural task for every human being that one naturally chooses it first and in this strenuous effort most likely finds enough for a lifetime.

gether in various things. For example, several families can join together for a box at the theater, and three single gentlemen can join together for a riding horse so that each one rides every third day. But this is not the way it is with immortality; the consciousness of my immortality belongs simply and solely to me. The very moment I am conscious of my immortality, I am completely subjective, and I cannot become immortal in partnership in rotation with two other single gentlemen. . . .

Immortality cannot be demonstrated systematically, either. The defect is not in the demonstrations but in the refusal to understand that, viewed systematically, the whole question is nonsense; thus, instead of seeking further demonstrations, one should rather seek to become a little subjective. Immortality is the subjective individual's most passionate interest; the demonstration lies precisely in the interest. . . .

Subjective Truth, Inwardness; Truth Is Subjectivity

from Concluding Unscientific Postscript to Philosophical Fragments

Whether truth is defined more empirically as the agreement of thinking with being or more idealistically as the agreement of being with thinking, the point in each case is to pay scrupulous attention to what is understood by being and also to pay attention to whether the knowing human spirit might not be lured out into the indefinite and fantastically become something such as no *existing* human being has ever been or can be, a phantom with which the individual busies himself on occasion, yet without ever making it explicit to himself by means of dialectical middle terms how he gets out into this fantastical realm, what meaning it has for him to be there, whether the entire endeavor out there might not dissolve into a tautology within a rash, fantastical venture.*

If, in the two definitions given, being is understood as empirical being, then truth itself is transformed into a *desideratum* [something wanted] and

_____

*Most footnotes have been omitted—ed.

everything is placed in the process of becoming, because the empirical object is not finished, and the existing knowing spirit is itself in the process of becoming. Thus truth is an approximating whose beginning cannot be established absolutely, because there is no conclusion that has retroactive power. On the other hand, every beginning, when it is *made* (if it is not arbitrariness by not being conscious of this), does not occur by virtue of immanental thinking but *is made* by virtue of a resolution, essentially by virtue of faith. That the knowing spirit is an existing spirit, and that every human being is such a spirit existing for himself, I cannot repeat often enough, because the fantastical disregard of this has been the cause of much confusion. May no one misunderstand me. I am indeed a poor existing spirit like all other human beings, but if in a legitimate and honest way I could be assisted in becoming something extraordinary, the pure *I-I*, I would always be willing to give thanks for the gift and the good deed. If, however, it can occur only in the way mentioned earlier, by saying *eins, zwei, drei, kokolorum* or by tying a ribbon around the little finger and throwing it away in some remote place when the moon is full—then I would rather remain what I am, a poor existing individual human being.

The term "being" in those definitions must, then, be understood much more abstractly as the abstract rendition or the abstract prototype of what being *in concreto* is as empirical being. If it is understood in this way, nothing stands in the way of abstractly defining truth as something finished, because, viewed abstractly, the agreement between thinking and being is always finished, inasmuch as the beginning of the process of becoming lies precisely in the concretion that abstraction abstractly disregards.

But if being is understood in this way, the formula is a tautology; that is, thinking and being signify one and the same, and the agreement spoken of is only an abstract identity with itself. Therefore, none of the formulas says more than that truth is, . . .

When for the existing spirit *qua* existing there is a question about truth, that abstract reduplication of truth recurs; but existence itself, existence itself in the questioner, who does indeed exist, holds the two factors apart, one from the other, and reflection shows two relations. To objective reflection, truth becomes something objective, an object, and the point is to disregard the subject. To subjective reflection, truth becomes appropriation, inwardness, subjectivity, and the point is to immerse oneself, existing, in subjectivity. . . .

Now, then, which of the ways is the way of truth for the existing spirit? Only the fantastical *I-I* is simultaneously finished with both ways or advances methodically along both ways simultaneously, which for an existing human being is such an inhuman way of walking that I dare not recommend it.

Since the questioner specifically emphasizes that he is an existing person, the way to be commended is naturally the one that especially accentuates what it means to exist.

The way of objective reflection turns the subjective individual into something accidental and thereby turns existence into an indifferent, vanishing something. The way to the objective truth goes away from the subject, and while the subject and subjectivity become indifferent, the truth also becomes indifferent, and that is precisely its objective validity, because the interest, just like the decision, is subjectivity. The way of objective reflection now leads to abstract thinking, to mathematics, to historical knowledge of various kinds, and always leads away from the subjective individual, whose existence or nonexistence becomes, from an objective point of view, altogether properly, infinitely indifferent, altogether properly, because, as Hamlet says, existence and nonexistence have only subjective significance. . . .

But the objective way is of the opinion that it has a security that the subjective way does not have (of course, existence, what it means to exist, and objective security cannot be thought together). It is of the opinion that it avoids a danger that lies in wait for the subjective way, and at its maximum this danger is madness. In a solely subjective definition of truth, lunacy and truth are ultimately indistinguishable, because they may both have inwardness.* But one does not become lunatic by becoming objective. At this point I might perhaps add a little comment that does

---

*Even this is not true, however, because madness never has the inwardness of infinity. Its fixed idea is a kind of objective something, and the contradiction of madness lies in wanting to embrace it with passion. The decisive factor in madness is thus not the subjective, but the little finitude that becomes fixed, something the infinite can never become.

not seem superfluous in an objective age. Is the absence of inwardness also lunacy? The objective truth as such does not at all decide that the one stating it is sensible; on the contrary, it can even betray that the man is lunatic, although what he says is entirely true and especially objectively true. . . .

Don Quixote is the prototype of the subjective lunacy in which the passion of inwardness grasps a particular fixed finite idea. But when inwardness is absent, parroting lunacy sets in, which is just as comic, and it would be desirable for an imaginatively constructing psychologist to depict it by taking a handful of such philosophers and putting them together. When the insanity is a delirium of inwardness, the tragic and the comic are that the something that infinitely pertains to the unfortunate person is a fixed detail that pertains to no one else. But when the insanity is the absence of inwardness, the comic is that the something known by the blissful person is the truth, truth that pertains to the whole human race but does not in the least pertain to the highly honored parroter. This kind of insanity is more inhuman than the other. One shrinks from looking the first one in the eye, lest one discover the depth of his frantic state, but one does not dare to look at the other at all for fear of discovering that he does not have proper eyes but glass eyes and hair made from a floor mat, in short, that he is an artificial product. . . .

Subjective reflection turns inward toward subjectivity and in this inward deepening will be of the truth, and in such a way that, just as in the preceding, when objectivity was advanced, subjectivity vanished, here subjectivity as such becomes the final factor and objectivity the vanishing. Here it is not forgotten, even for a single moment, that the subject is existing, and that existing is a becoming, and that truth as the identity of thought and being is therefore a chimera of abstraction and truly only a longing of creation, not because truth is not an identity, but because the knower is an existing person, and thus truth cannot be an identity for him as long as he exists. If this is not held fast, then with the aid of speculative thought we promptly enter into the fantastical *I-I* that recent speculative thought certainly has used but without explaining how a particular individual relates himself to it, and, good Lord, of course no human being is more than a particular individual.

If the existing person could actually be outside himself, the truth would be something concluded for him. But where is this point? The *I-I* is a mathematical point that does not exist at all; accordingly anyone can readily take up this standpoint—no one stands in the way of anyone else. Only momentarily can a particular individual, existing, be in a unity of the infinite and the finite that transcends existing. This instant is the moment of passion. Modern speculative thought has mustered everything to enable the individual to transcend himself objectively, but this just cannot be done. Existence exercises its constraint, and if philosophers nowadays had not become pencil-pushers serving the trifling busyness of fantastical thinking, it would have discerned that suicide is the only somewhat practical interpretation of its attempt. But pencil-pushing modern speculative thought takes a dim view of passion, and yet, for the existing person, passion is existence at its very highest—and we are, after all, existing persons. In passion, the existing subject is infinitized in the eternity of imagination and yet is also most definitely himself. The fantastical *I-I* is not infinitude and finitude in identity, since neither the one nor the other is actual; it is a fantastical union with a cloud. . . .

All essential knowing pertains to existence, or only the knowing whose relation to existence is essential is essential knowing. Essentially viewed, the knowing that does not inwardly in the reflection of inwardness pertain to existence is accidental knowing, and its degree and scope, essentially viewed, are a matter of indifference. That essential knowing is essentially related to existence does not, however, signify the above-mentioned abstract identity between thinking and being, nor does it signify that the knowledge is objectively related to something existent as its object, but it means that the knowledge is related to the knower, who is essentially an existing person, and that all essential knowing is therefore essentially related to existence and to existing. Therefore, only ethical and ethical-religious knowing is essential knowing. But all ethical and all ethical-religious knowing is essentially a relating to the existing of the knower.

Mediation is a mirage, just as the *I-I* is. Viewed abstractly, everything *is* and nothing becomes. Mediation cannot possibly find its place in abstraction, since it has *movement* as its presupposition. Objective knowledge can certainly have the existent as its object, but since the knowing subject is existing and himself in the process of becoming by existing, speculative thought must first explain how a particular existing

subject relates himself to the knowledge of mediation, what he is at the moment, whether, for example, he is not at that very moment rather absentminded, and where he is, whether he is not on the moon. . . .

In order to clarify the divergence of objective and subjective reflection, I shall now describe subjective reflection in its search back and inward into inwardness. At its highest, inwardness in an existing subject is passion; truth as a paradox corresponds to passion, and that truth becomes a paradox is grounded precisely in its relation to an existing subject. In this way the one corresponds to the other. In forgetting that one is an existing subject, one loses passion, and in return, truth does not become a paradox; but the knowing subject shifts from being human to being a fantastical something, and truth becomes a fantastical object for its knowing.

When the question about truth is asked objectively, truth is reflected upon objectively as an object to which the knower relates himself. What is reflected upon is not the relation but that what he relates himself to is the truth, the true. If only that to which he relates himself is the truth, the true, then the subject is in the truth. When the question about truth is asked subjectively, the individual's relation is reflected upon subjectively. If only the how of this relation is in truth, the individual is in truth, even if he in this way were to relate himself to untruth.*

Let us take the knowledge of God as an example. Objectively, what is reflected upon is that this is the true God; subjectively, that the individual relates himself to a something *in such a way* that his relation is in truth a God-relation. Now, on which side is the truth? Alas, must we not at this point resort to mediation and say: It is on neither side; it is in the mediation? Superbly stated, if only someone could say how an existing person goes about being in mediation, because to be in mediation is to be finished; to exist is to become. An existing person cannot be in two places at the same time, cannot be subject-object. When he is closest to being in two places at the same time, he is in passion; but passion is only momentary, and passion is the highest pitch of subjectivity.

---

*The reader will note that what is being discussed here is essential truth, or the truth that is related essentially to existence, and that it is specifically in order to clarify it as inwardness or as subjectivity that the contrast is pointed out.

The existing person who chooses the objective way now enters upon all approximating deliberation intended to bring forth God objectively, which is not achieved in all eternity, because God is a subject and hence only for subjectivity in inwardness. The existing person who chooses the subjective way instantly comprehends the whole dialectical difficulty because he must use some time, perhaps a long time, to find God objectively. He comprehends this dialectical difficulty in all its pain, because he must resort to God at that very moment, because every moment in which he does not have God is wasted.* At that very moment he has God, not by virtue of any objective deliberation but by virtue of the infinite passion of inwardness. The objective person is not bothered by dialectical difficulties such as what it means to put a whole research period into finding God, since it is indeed possible that the researcher would die tomorrow, and if he goes on living, he cannot very well regard God as something to be taken along at his convenience, since God is something one takes along *à tout prix* [at any price], which, in passion's understanding, is the true relationship of inwardness with God.

It is at this point, dialectically so very difficult, that the road swings off for the person who knows what it means to think dialectically and, existing, to think dialectically, which is quite different from sitting as a fantastical being at a desk and writing about something one has never done oneself, quite different from writing *de omnibus dubitandum* and then as an existing person being just as credulous as the most sensate human being. It is here that the road swings off, and the change is this: whereas objective knowledge goes along leisurely on the long road of approximation, itself not actuated by passion, to subjective knowledge every delay is a deadly peril and the decision so infinitely important that it is immediately

urgent, as if the opportunity had already passed by unused.

Now, if the problem is to calculate where there is more truth (and, as stated, simultaneously to be on both sides equally is not granted to an existing person but is only a beatifying delusion for a deluded *I-I*), whether on the side of the person who only objectively seeks the true God and the approximating truth of the God-idea or on the side of the person who is infinitely concerned that he in truth relate himself to God with the infinite passion of need—then there can be no doubt about the answer for anyone who is not totally botched by scholarship and science. If someone who lives in the midst of Christianity enters, with knowledge of the true idea of God, the house of God, the house of the true God, and prays, but prays in untruth, and if someone lives in an idolatrous land but prays with all the passion of infinity, although his eyes are resting upon the image of an idol—where, then, is there more truth? The one prays in truth to God although he is worshiping an idol; the other prays in untruth to the true God and is therefore in truth worshiping an idol.

If someone objectively inquires into immortality, and someone else stakes the passion of the infinite on the uncertainty—where, then, is there more truth, and who has more certainty? The one has once and for all entered upon an approximation that never ends, because the certainty of immortality is rooted in subjectivity; the other is immortal and therefore struggles by contending with the uncertainty.

Let us consider Socrates. These days everyone is dabbling in a few proofs or demonstrations—one has many, another fewer. But Socrates! He poses the question objectively, problematically: if there is an immortality. So, compared with one of the modern thinkers with the three demonstrations, was he a doubter? Not at all. He stakes his whole life on this "if"; he dares to die, and with the passion of the infinite he has so ordered his whole life that it might be acceptable—*if* there is an immortality. Is there any better demonstration for the immortality of the soul? But those who have the three demonstrations do not order their lives accordingly. If there is an immortality, it must be nauseated by their way of living—is there any better counterdemonstration to the three demonstrations? The "fragment" of uncertainty helped Socrates, because he himself helped with the

---

*In this way God is indeed a postulate, but not in the loose sense in which it is ordinarily taken. Instead, it becomes clear that this is the only way an existing person enters into a relationship with God: when the dialectical contradiction brings passion to despair and assists him in grasping God with "the category of despair" (faith), so that the postulate, far from being the arbitrary, is in fact *necessary* defense [*Nød værge*], self-defense; in this way God is not a postulate, but the existing person's postulating of God is— a necessity [*Nødvendighed*].

passion of infinity. The three demonstrations are of no benefit whatever to those others, because they are and remain slugs and, failing to demonstrate anything else, have demonstrated it by their three demonstrations.

In the same way a girl has perhaps possessed all the sweetness of being in love through a weak hope of being loved by the beloved, because she herself staked everything on this weak hope; on the other hand, many a wedded matron, who more than once has submitted to the strongest expression of erotic love, has certainly had demonstrations and yet, strangely enough, has not possessed *quod erat demonstrandum* [that which was to be demonstrated]. The Socratic ignorance was thus the expression, firmly maintained with all the passion of inwardness, of the relation of the eternal truth to an existing person, and therefore it must remain for him a paradox as long as he exists. Yet it is possible that in the Socratic ignorance there was more truth in Socrates than in the objective truth of the entire system that flirts with the demands of the times and adapts itself to assistant professors.

Objectively the emphasis is on **what is said***; subjectively the emphasis is on* **how** *it is said.* This distinction applies even esthetically and is specifically expressed when we say that in the mouth of this or that person something that is truth can become untruth. Particular attention should be paid to this distinction in our day, for if one were to express in a single sentence the difference between ancient times and our time, one would no doubt have to say: In ancient times there were only a few individuals who knew the truth; now everyone knows it, but inwardness has an inverse relation to it.* Viewed esthetically, the contradiction that emerges when truth becomes untruth in this and that person's mouth is best interpreted comically. Ethically-religiously, the emphasis is again on: *how.* But this is not to be understood as manner, modulation of voice, oral delivery, etc., but it is to be understood as the relation of the existing person, in his very existence, to what is said. Objectively, the question is only about categories of thought; subjectively, about inwardness. At its maximum, this "how" is the passion of the infinite, and the passion of the infinite is the very truth. But the passion of the infinite is pre-

_____

*See *Stages on Life's Way,* p. 366 fn.

cisely subjectivity, and thus subjectivity is truth. From the objective point of view, there is no infinite decision, and thus it is objectively correct that the distinction between good and evil is canceled, along with the principle of contradiction, and thereby also the infinite distinction between truth and falsehood. Only in subjectivity is there decision, whereas wanting to become objective is untruth. The passion of the infinite, not its content, is the deciding factor, for its content is precisely itself. In this way the subjective "how" and subjectivity are the truth.

But precisely because the subject is existing, the "how" that is subjectively emphasized is dialectical also with regard to time. In the moment of the decision of passion, where the road swings off from objective knowledge, it looks as if the infinite decision were thereby finished. But at the same moment, the existing person is in the temporal realm, and the subjective "how" is transformed into a striving that is motivated and repeatedly refreshed by the decisive passion of the infinite, but it is nevertheless a striving.

When subjectivity is truth, the definition of truth must also contain in itself an expression of the antithesis to objectivity, a memento of that fork in the road, and this expression will at the same time indicate the resilience of the inwardness. Here is such a definition of truth: *An objective uncertainty, held fast through appropriation with the most passionate inwardness, is the truth,* the highest truth there is for an *existing* person. At the point where the road swings off (and where that is cannot be stated objectively, since it is precisely subjectivity), objective knowledge is suspended. Objectively he then has only uncertainty, but this is precisely what intensifies the infinite passion of inwardness, and truth is precisely the daring venture of choosing the objective uncertainty with the passion of the infinite. I observe nature in order to find God, and I do indeed see omnipotence and wisdom, but I also see much that troubles and disturbs. The *summa summarum* [sum total] of this is an objective uncertainty, but the inwardness is so very great, precisely because it grasps this objective uncertainty with all the passion of the infinite. In a mathematical proposition, for example, the objectivity is given, but therefore its truth is also an indifferent truth.

But the definition of truth stated above is a paraphrasing of faith. Without risk, no faith. Faith is the contradiction between the infinite passion of inward-

[handwritten margin notes: Christianity / Protestant(ism) / objective object]

ness and the objective uncertainty. If I am able to apprehend God objectively, I do not have faith; but because I cannot do this, I must have faith. If I want to keep myself in faith, I must continually see to it that I hold fast the objective uncertainty, see to it that in the objective uncertainty I am "out on 70,000 fathoms of water" and still have faith. . . .

When subjectivity, inwardness, is truth, then truth, objectively defined, is a paradox; and that truth is objectively a paradox shows precisely that subjectivity is truth, since the objectivity does indeed thrust away, and the objectivity's repulsion, or the expression for the objectivity's repulsion, is the resilience and dynamometer of inwardness. The paradox is the objective uncertainty that is the expression for the passion of inwardness that is truth. . . .

Introduction
from The Sickness Unto Death

"This sickness is not unto death" (John 11:4).* And yet Lazarus did die; when the disciples misunderstood what Christ added later, "Our friend Lazarus has fallen asleep, but I go to awaken him out of sleep" (11:11), he told them flatly "Lazarus is dead" (11:14). So Lazarus is dead, and yet this sickness was not unto death; he was dead, and yet this sickness is not unto death. We know that Christ had in mind the miracle that would permit his contemporaries, "if they would believe, to see the glory of God" (11:40), the miracle by which He raised Lazarus from the dead; therefore "this sickness" was not only not unto death, but, as Christ predicted, was "for the glory of God, so that the Son of God may be glorified by means of it" (11:4). But even if Christ did not resurrect Lazarus, is it not still true that his sickness, death itself, is not unto death? When Christ approaches the grave and cries out with a loud voice, "Lazarus, come out" (11:43), is it not plain that "this" sickness is not unto death? But even if Christ had not said that, does not the mere fact that He who is "the resurrection and the life" (11:25) approaches the grave signify that this sick-

ness is not unto death: the fact that Christ exists, does it not mean that *this* sickness is not unto death! What good would it have been to Lazarus to be resurrected from the dead if ultimately he had to die anyway—of what good would it have been to Lazarus if He were not He who is the resurrection and the life for everyone who believes in Him! No, it may be said that *this* sickness is not unto death, not because Lazarus was raised from the dead, but because He exists; therefore this sickness is not unto death. Humanly speaking, death is the last of all, and, humanly speaking, there is hope only as long as there is life. Christianly understood, however, death is by no means the last of all; in fact, it is only a minor event within that which is all, an eternal life, and, Christianly understood, there is infinitely much more hope in death than there is in life—not only when in the merely human sense there is life but this life in consummate health and vitality.

Christianly understood, then, not even death is "the sickness unto death"; even less so is everything that goes under the name of earthly and temporal suffering: need, illness, misery, hardship, adversities, torments, mental sufferings, cares, grief. And even if such things were so hard and painful that we human beings or at least the sufferer, would declare, "This is worse than death"—all those things, which, although not sickness, can be compared with a sickness, are still, Christianly understood, not the sickness unto death.

That is how sublimely Christianity has taught the Christian to think about earthly and worldly matters, death included. It is almost as if the Christian might become haughty because of this proud elevation over everything that men usually call misfortune or the worst of evils. Nevertheless, Christianity has in turn discovered a miserable condition that man as such does not know exists. This miserable condition is the sickness unto death. What the natural man catalogs as appalling—after he has recounted everything and has nothing more to mention—this to the Christian is like a jest. Such is the relation between the natural man and the Christian; it is like the relation between a child and an adult: what makes the child shudder and shrink, the adult regards as nothing. The child does not know what the horrifying is; the adult knows and shrinks from it. The child's imperfection is, first, not to recognize the horrifying, and then, implicit in this, to shrink from what is not horrifying. So it is also

———
*Footnotes omitted—ed.

with the natural man: he is ignorant of what is truly horrifying, yet is not thereby liberated from shuddering and shrinking—no, he shrinks from that which is not horrifying. It is similar to the pagan's relationship to God: he does not recognize the true God, but to make matters worse, he worships an idol as God.

Only the Christian knows what is meant by the sickness unto death. As a Christian, he gained a courage that the natural man does not know, and he gained this courage by learning to fear something even more horrifying. This is the way a person always gains courage; when he fears a greater danger, he always has the courage to face a lesser one; when he is exceedingly afraid of one danger, it is as if the others did not exist at all. But the most appalling danger that the Christian has learned to know is "the sickness unto death."

The Sickness Unto Death Is Despair

from The Sickness Unto Death

DESPAIR IS THE SICKNESS UNTO DEATH

A.

Despair is a sickness of the spirit, of the self, and accordingly can take three forms: in despair not to be conscious of having a self (not despair in the strict sense); in despair not to will to be oneself; in despair to will to be oneself

A human being is spirit.* But what is spirit? Spirit is the self. But what is the self? The self is a relation that relates itself to itself or is the relation's relating itself to itself in the relation; the self is not the relation but is the relation's relating itself to itself. A human being is a synthesis of the infinite and the finite, of the temporal and the eternal, of freedom and necessity, in short, a synthesis. A synthesis is a relation between

_____

*Most footnotes have been omitted—ed.

two. Considered in this way, a human being is still not a self.

In the relation between two, the relation is the third as a negative unity, and the two relate to the relation and in the relation to the relation; thus under the qualification of the psychical the relation between the psychical and the physical is a relation. If, however, the relation relates itself to itself, this relation is the positive third, and this is the self.

Such a relation that relates itself to itself, a self, must either have established itself or have been established by another.

If the relation that relates itself to itself has been established by another, then the relation is indeed the third, but this relation, the third, is yet again a relation and relates itself to that which established the entire relation.

The human self is such a derived, established relation, a relation that relates itself to itself and in relating itself to itself relates itself to another. This is why there can be two forms of despair in the strict sense. If a human self had itself established itself, then there could be only one form: not to will to be oneself, to will to do away with oneself, but there could not be the form: in despair to will to be oneself. This second formulation is specifically the expression for the complete dependence of the relation (of the self), the expression for the inability of the self to arrive at or to be in equilibrium and rest by itself, but only, in relating itself to itself, by relating itself to that which has established the entire relation. Yes, this second form of despair (in despair to will to be oneself) is so far from designating merely a distinctive kind of despair that, on the contrary, all despair ultimately can be traced back to and be resolved in it. If the despairing person is aware of his despair, as he thinks he is, and does not speak meaninglessly of it as of something that is happening to him (somewhat as one suffering from dizziness speaks in nervous delusion of a weight on his head or of something that has fallen down on him, etc., a weight and a pressure that nevertheless are not something external but a reverse reflection of the internal) and now with all his power seeks to break the despair by himself and by himself alone— he is still in despair and with all his presumed effort only works himself all the deeper into deeper despair. The misrelation of despair is not a simple misrelation but a misrelation in a relation that relates itself to itself and has been established by another, so that the misrelation in that relation which is for itself also reflects itself infinitely in the relation to the power that established it.

The formula that describes the state of the self when despair is completely rooted out is this: in relating itself to itself and in willing to be itself, the self rests transparently in the power that established it.

B.

THE POSSIBILITY AND THE ACTUALITY OF DESPAIR

Is despair an excellence or a defect? Purely dialectically, it is both. If only the abstract idea of despair is considered, without any thought of someone in despair, it must be regarded as a surpassing excellence. The possibility of this sickness is man's superiority over the animal, and this superiority distinguishes him in quite another way than does his erect walk, for it indicates infinite erectness or sublimity, that he is spirit. The possibility of this sickness is man's superiority over the animal; to be aware of this sickness is the Christian's superiority over the natural man; to be cured of this sickness is the Christian's blessedness.

Consequently, to be able to despair is an infinite advantage, and yet to be in despair is not only the worst misfortune and misery—no, it is ruination.

Despair is the misrelation in the relation of a synthesis that relates itself to itself. But the synthesis is not the misrelation; it is merely the possibility, or in the synthesis lies the possibility of the misrelation. If the synthesis were the misrelation, then despair would not exist at all, then despair would be something that lies in human nature as such. That is, it would not be despair; it would be something that happens to a man, something he suffers, like a disease to which he succumbs, or like death, which is everyone's fate. No, no, despairing lies in man himself. If he were not a synthesis, he could not despair at all; nor could he despair if the synthesis in its original state from the hand of God were not in the proper relationship.

Where, then, does the despair come from? From the relation in which the synthesis relates itself to itself, inasmuch as God, who constituted man a relation, releases it from his hand, as it were—that is, inasmuch as the relation relates itself to itself. And because the relation is spirit, is the self, upon it rests the re-sponsibility for all despair at every moment of its existence, however much the despairing person speaks of his despair as a misfortune and however ingeniously he deceives himself and others, confusing it with that previously mentioned case of dizziness, with which despair, although qualitatively different, has much in common, since dizziness corresponds, in the category of the psychical, to what despair is in the category of the spirit, and it lends itself to numerous analogies to despair.

Once the misrelation, despair, has come about, does it continue as a matter of course? No, it does not continue as a matter of course; if the misrelation continues, it is not attributable to the misrelation but to the relation that relates itself to itself. That is, every time the misrelation manifests itself and every moment it exists, it must be traced back to the relation. For example, we say that someone catches a sickness, perhaps through carelessness. The sickness sets in and from then on is in force and is an *actuality* whose origin recedes more and more into the *past*. It would be both cruel and inhuman to go on saying, "You, the sick person, are in the process of catching the sickness right now." That would be the same as perpetually wanting to dissolve the actuality of the sickness into its possibility. It is true that he was responsible for catching the sickness, but he did that only once; the continuation of the sickness is a simple result of his catching it that one time, and its progress cannot be traced at every moment to him as the cause; he brought it upon himself, but it cannot be said that he *is bringing* it upon himself. To despair, however, is a different matter. Every actual moment of despair is traceable to possibility; every moment he is in despair he *is bringing* it upon himself. It is always the present tense; in relation to the actuality there is no pastness of the past: in every actual moment of despair the person in despair bears all the past as a present in possibility. The reason for this is that to despair is a qualification of spirit and relates to the eternal in man. But he cannot rid himself of the eternal—no, never in all eternity. He cannot throw it away once and for all, nothing is more impossible; at any moment that he does not have it, he must have thrown it or is throwing it away—but it comes again, that is, every moment he is in despair he is bringing his despair upon himself. For despair is not attributable to the misrelation but to the relation that relates itself to itself. A person cannot rid himself of the relation to himself any more than he can rid himself of his self, which, after all, is one and the same thing, since the self is the relation to oneself.

C.

DESPAIR IS "THE SICKNESS UNTO DEATH"

This concept, the sickness unto death, must, however, be understood in a particular way. Literally it means a sickness of which the end and the result are death. Therefore we use the expression "fatal sickness" as synonymous with the sickness unto death. In that sense, despair cannot be called the sickness unto death. Christianly understood, death itself is a passing into life. Thus, from a Christian point of view, no earthly, physical sickness is the sickness unto death, for death is indeed the end of the sickness, but death is not the end. If there is to be any question of a sickness unto death in the strictest sense, it must be a sickness of which the end is death and death is the end. This is precisely what despair is.

But in another sense despair is even more definitely the sickness unto death. Literally speaking, there is not the slightest possibility that anyone will die from this sickness or that it will end in physical death. On the contrary, the torment of despair is precisely this inability to die. Thus it has more in common with the situation of a mortally ill person when he lies struggling with death and yet cannot die. Thus to be sick *unto* death is to be unable to die, yet not as if there were hope of life; no, the hopelessness is that there is not even the ultimate hope, death. When death is the greatest danger, we hope for life; but when we learn to know the even greater danger, we hope for death. When the danger is so great that death becomes the hope, then despair is the hopelessness of not even being able to die.

It is in this last sense that despair is the sickness unto death, this tormenting contradiction, this sickness of the self, perpetually to be dying, to die and yet not die, to die death. For to die signifies that it is all over, but to die death means to experience dying, and if this is experienced for one single moment, one thereby experiences it forever. If a person were to die of despair as one dies of a sickness, then the eternal in him, the self, must be able to die in the same sense as the body dies of sickness. But this is impossible; the dying of despair continually converts itself into a living. The person in despair cannot die; "no more than the dagger can slaughter thoughts" can despair consume the eternal, the self at the root of despair, whose worm does not die and whose fire is not quenched. Nevertheless, despair is veritably a self-consuming, but an impotent self-consuming that cannot do what it wants to do. What it wants to do is to consume itself, something it cannot do, and this impotence is a new form of self-consuming, in which despair is once again unable to do what it wants to do, to consume itself; this is an intensification, or the law of intensification. This is the provocativeness or the cold fire in despair, this gnawing that burrows deeper and deeper in impotent self-consuming. The inability of despair to consume him is so remote from being any kind of comfort to the person in despair that it is the very opposite. This comfort is precisely the torment, is precisely what keeps the gnawing alive and keeps life in the gnawing, for it is precisely over this that he despairs (not as having despaired): that he cannot consume himself, cannot get rid of himself, cannot reduce himself to nothing. This is the formula for despair raised to a higher power, the rising fever in this sickness of the self.

An individual in despair despairs over *something*. So it seems for a moment, but only for a moment; in the same moment the true despair or despair in its true form shows itself. In despairing over *something*, he really despaired over *himself*, and now he wants to be rid of himself. For example, when the ambitious man whose slogan is "Either Caesar or nothing" does not get to be Caesar, he despairs over it. But this also means something else: precisely because he did not get to be Caesar, he now cannot bear to be himself. Consequently he does not despair because he did not get to be Caesar but despairs over himself because he did not get to be Caesar. This self, which, if it had become Caesar, would have been in seventh heaven (a state, incidentally, that in another sense is just as despairing), this self is now utterly intolerable to him. In a deeper sense, it is not his failure to become Caesar that is intolerable, but it is this self that did not become Caesar that is intolerable; or, to put it even more accurately, what is intolerable to him is that he cannot get rid of himself. If he had become Caesar, he would despairingly get rid of himself, but he did not become Caesar and cannot despairingly get rid of himself. Essentially, he is just as despairing, for he does not have his self, is not himself. He would not have become himself by becoming Caesar but would have been rid of himself, and by not becoming Caesar he despairs over not being able to get rid of himself. Thus it is superficial for someone (who probably has never seen anyone in despair, not even himself) to say of a person in despair: He is consuming himself. But this is precisely what he in his despair [wants] and this is precisely what he to his torment cannot do, since the despair has inflamed something that cannot burn or be burned up in the self.

Consequently, to despair over something is still not despair proper. It is the beginning, or, as the physician says of an illness, it has not yet declared itself. The next is declared despair, to despair over oneself. A young girl despairs of love, that is, she despairs over the loss of her beloved, over his death or his unfaithfulness to her. This is not declared despair; no, she despairs over herself. This self of hers, which would have been rid of or would have lost in the most blissful manner had it become "his" beloved, this self becomes a torment to her if it has to be a self without "him." This self, which would have become her treasure (although, in another sense, it would have been just as despairing), has now become to her an abominable void since "he" died, or it has become to her a nauseating reminder that she has been deceived. Just try it, say to such a girl, "You are consuming yourself," and you will hear her answer, "O, but the torment is simply that I cannot do that."

To despair over oneself, in despair to will to be rid of oneself—this is the formula for all despair. Therefore the other form of despair, in despair to will to be oneself, can be traced back to the first, in despair not to will to be oneself, just as we previously resolved the form, in despair not to will to be oneself, into the form, in despair to will to be oneself (see A). A person in despair despairingly wills to be himself. But if he despairingly wills to be himself, he certainly does not want to be rid of himself. Well, so it seems, but upon closer examination it is clear that the contradiction is the same. The self that he despairingly wants to be is a self that he is not (for to will to be the self that he is in truth is the very opposite of despair), that is, he wants to tear his self away from the power that established it. In spite of all his despair, however, he cannot manage to do it; in spite of all his despairing efforts, that power is the stronger and forces him to be the self he does not want to be. But this is his way of willing to get rid of himself, to rid himself of the self that he is in order to be the self that he has dreamed up. He would

be in seventh heaven to be the self he wants to be (although in another sense he would be just as despairing), but to be forced to be the self he does not want to be, that is his torment—that he cannot get rid of himself.

Socrates proved the immortality of the soul from the fact that sickness of the soul (sin) does not consume it as sickness of the body consumes the body. Similarly, the eternal in a person can be proved by the fact that despair cannot consume his self, that precisely this is the torment of contradiction in despair. If there were nothing eternal in a man, he could not despair at all; if despair could consume his self, then there would be no despair at all.

Such is the nature of despair, this sickness of the self, this sickness unto death. The despairing person is mortally ill. In a completely different sense than is the case with any illness, this sickness has attacked the most vital organs, and yet he cannot die. Death is not the end of the sickness, but death is incessantly the end. To be saved from this sickness by death is an impossibility, because the sickness and its torment—and the death—are precisely this inability to die.

This is the state in despair. No matter how much the despairing person avoids it, no matter how successfully he has completely lost himself (especially the case in the form of despair that is ignorance of being in despair) and lost himself in such a manner that the loss is not at all detectable—eternity nevertheless will make it manifest that his condition was despair and will nail him to himself so that his torment will still be that he cannot rid himself of his self, and it will become obvious that he was just imagining that he had succeeded in doing so. Eternity is obliged to do this, because to have a self, to be a self, is the greatest concession, an infinite concession, given to man, but it is also eternity's claim upon him.

THE UNIVERSALITY OF THIS SICKNESS (DESPAIR)

Just as a physician might say that there very likely is not one single living human being who is completely healthy, so anyone who really knows mankind might say that there is not one single living human being who does not despair a little, who does not secretly harbor an unrest, an inner strife, a disharmony, an anxiety about an unknown something or a something he does not even dare to try to know, an anxiety about some possibility in existence or an anxiety about himself, so that, just as the physician speaks of going around with an illness in the body, he walks around with a sickness, carries around a sickness of the spirit that signals its presence at rare intervals in and through an anxiety he cannot explain. In any case, no human being ever lived and no one lives outside of Christendom who has not despaired, and no one in Christendom if he is not a true Christian, and insofar as he is not wholly that, he still is to some extent in despair.

No doubt this observation will strike many people as a paradox, an overstatement, and also a somber and depressing point of view. But it is none of these things. It is not somber, for, on the contrary, it tries to shed light on what generally is left somewhat obscure; it is not depressing but instead is elevating, inasmuch as it views every human being under the destiny of the highest claim upon him, to be spirit; nor is it a paradox but, on the contrary, a consistently developed basic view, and therefore neither is it an overstatement.

The customary view of despair does not go beyond appearances, and thus it is a superficial view, that is, no view at all. It assumes that every man must himself know best whether he is in despair or not. Anyone who says he is in despair is regarded as being in despair, and anyone who thinks he is not is therefore regarded as not. As a result, the phenomenon of despair is infrequent rather than quite common. That one is in despair is not a rarity; no, it is rare, very rare, that one is in truth not in despair.

The common view has a very poor understanding of despair. Among other things, it completely overlooks (to name only this, which, properly understood, places thousands and thousands and millions in the category of despair), it completely overlooks that not being in despair, not being conscious of being in despair, is precisely a form of despair. In a much deeper sense, the position of the common view in interpreting despair is like that of the common view in determining whether a person is sick—in a much deeper sense, for the common view understands far less well what spirit is (and lacking this understanding, one cannot understand despair, either) than it understands sickness and health. As a rule, a person is considered to be healthy when he himself does not say that he is sick, not to mention when he himself says that he is well. But the physician has a different view of sickness. Why? Because the physician has a defined and developed conception of what it is to be healthy and ascertains a man's condition accordingly. The physician knows that just as there is merely imaginary sickness there is also merely imaginary health, and in the latter case he first takes measures to disclose the sickness. Generally speaking, the physician, precisely because he is a physician (well informed), does not have complete confidence in what a person says about his condition. If everyone's statement about his condition, that he is healthy or sick, were completely reliable, to be a physician would be a delusion. A physician's task is not only to prescribe remedies but also, first and foremost, to identify the sickness, and consequently his first task is to ascertain whether the supposedly sick person is actually sick or whether the supposedly healthy person is perhaps actually sick. Such is also the relation of the physician of the soul to despair. He knows what despair is; he recognizes it and therefore is satisfied neither with a person's declaration that he is not in despair nor with his declaration that he is. It must be pointed out that in a certain sense it is not even always the case that those who say they despair are in despair. Despair can be affected, and as a qualification of the spirit it may also be mistaken for and confused with all sorts of transitory states, such as dejection, inner conflict, which pass without developing into despair. But the physician of the soul properly regards these also as forms of despair; he sees very well that they are affectation. Yet this very affectation is despair: he sees very well that this dejection etc. are not of great significance, but precisely this— that it has and acquires no great significance—is despair.

The common view also overlooks that despair is dialectically different from what is usually termed a sickness, because it is a sickness of the spirit. Properly understood, this dialectic again brings thousands under the definition of despair. If at a given time a physician has made sure that someone is well, and that person later becomes ill, then the physician may legitimately say that this person at one time was healthy but now is sick. Not so with despair. As soon as despair becomes apparent, it is manifest that the individual was in despair. Hence, at no moment is it possible to decide anything about a person who has not been saved by having been in despair, for whenever that which triggers his despair occurs, it is immediately apparent that he has been in despair his whole life. On the other hand, when someone gets a fever, it can by no means be said that it is now apparent that he has had a fever all his life. Despair is a qualification of the spirit, is related to the eternal, and thus has ~~something of the eternal in its dialectic.~~

Despair is not only dialectically different from a sickness, but all its symptoms are also dialectical, and therefore the superficial view is very easily deceived in determining whether or not despair is present. Not to be in despair can in fact signify precisely to be in despair, and it can signify having been rescued from being in despair. A sense of security and tranquillity can signify being in despair; precisely this sense of security and tranquillity can be the despair, and yet it can signify having conquered despair and having won peace. Not being in despair is not similar to not being sick, for not being sick cannot be the same as being sick, whereas not being in despair can be the very same as being in despair. It is not with despair as with a sickness, where feeling indisposed is the sickness. By no means. Here again the indisposition is dialectical. Never to have sensed this indisposition is precisely to be in despair.

This means and has its basis in the fact that the condition of man, regarded as spirit (and if there is to be any question of despair, man must be regarded as defined by spirit), is always critical. We speak of a crisis in relation to sickness but not in relation to health. Why not? Because physical health is an immediate qualification that first becomes dialectical in the condition of sickness, in which the question of a crisis arises. Spiritually, or when man is regarded as spirit, both health and sickness are critical; there is no immediate health of the spirit.

As soon as man ceases to be regarded as defined by spirit (and in that case there can be no mention of despair, either) but only as psychical-physical synthesis, health is an immediate qualification, and mental or physical sickness is the only dialectical qualification. But to be unaware of being defined as spirit is precisely what despair is. Even that which, humanly speaking, is utterly beautiful and lovable—a womanly youthfulness that is perfect peace and harmony and joy—is nevertheless despair. To be sure, it is happiness, but happiness is not a qualification of spirit, and deep, deep within the most secret hiding place of happiness there dwells also anxiety, which is despair; it very much wishes to be allowed to remain there, because for despair the most cherished and desirable place to live is in the heart of happiness. Despite its illusory security and tranquillity, all immediacy is anxiety and thus, quite consistently, is most anxious about nothing. The most gruesome description of something most terrible does not make immediacy as anxious as a subtle, almost carelessly, and yet deliberately and calculatingly dropped allusion to some indefinite something—in fact, immediacy is made most anxious by a subtle implication that it knows very well what is being talked about. Immediacy probably does not know it, but reflection never snares so unfailingly as when it fashions its snare out of nothing, and reflection is never so much itself as when it is—nothing. It requires extraordinary reflection, or, more correctly, it requires great faith to be able to endure reflection upon nothing—that is, infinite reflection. Consequently, even that which is utterly beautiful and lovable, womanly youthfulness, is still despair, is happiness. For that reason, it is impossible to slip through life on this immediacy. And if this happiness does succeed in slipping through, well, it is of little use, for it is despair. Precisely because the sickness of despair is totally dialectical, it is the worst misfortune never to have had that sickness: it is a true godsend to get it, even if it is the most dangerous of illnesses, if one does not want to be cured of it. Generally it is regarded as fortunate to be cured of a sickness; the sickness itself is the misfortune.

Therefore, the common view that despair is a rarity is entirely wrong; on the contrary, it is universal. The common view, which assumes that everyone who does not think or feel he is in despair is not or that only he who says he is in despair is, is totally false. On the contrary, the person who without affectation says that he is in despair is still a little closer, is dialectically closer, to being cured than all those who are not regarded as such and who do not regard themselves as being in despair. The physician of souls will certainly agree with me that, on the whole, most men live without ever becoming conscious of being destined as spirit—hence all the so-called security, contentment with life, etc., which is simply despair. On the other hand, those who say they are in despair are usually either those who have so deep a nature that they are bound to become conscious as spirit or those whom bitter experiences and dreadful decisions have assisted in becoming conscious as spirit: it is either the one or the other; the person who is really devoid of despair is very rare indeed.

There is so much talk about human distress and wretchedness—I try to understand it and have also had some intimate acquaintance with it—there is so much talk about wasting a life, but only that person's life was wasted who went on living so deceived by life's joys or its sorrows that he never became decisively and eternally conscious as spirit, as self, or, what amounts to the same thing, never became aware and in the deepest sense never gained the impression that there is a God and that "he," he himself, his self, exists before this God—an infinite benefaction that is never gained except through despair. What wretchedness that so many go on living this way, cheated of this most blessed of thoughts! What wretchedness that we are engrossed in or encourage the human throng to be engrossed in everything else, using them to supply the energy for the drama of life but never reminding them of this blessedness. What wretchedness that they are lumped together and deceived instead of being split apart so that each individual may gain the highest, the only thing worth living for and enough to live in for an eternity. I think that I could weep an eternity over the existence of such wretchedness! And to me an even more horrible expression of this most terrible sickness and misery is that it is hidden—not only that the person suffering from it may wish to hide it and may succeed, not only that it can so live in a man that no one, no one detects it, no, but also that it can be so hidden in a man that he himself is not aware of it! And when the hourglass has run out, the hourglass of temporality, when the noise of secular life has grown silent and its restless or ineffectual activism has come to an end, when everything around you is still, as it is in eternity, then—whether you were man or woman, rich or poor, dependent or independent, fortunate or unfortunate, whether you ranked with royalty and wore a glittering crown or in humble obscurity bore the toil and heat of the day, whether your name will be remembered as long as the world stands and consequently as long as it stood or you are nameless and run nameless in the innumerable multitude, whether the magnificence encompassing you surpassed all human description or the most severe and ignominious human judgment befell you—eternity asks you and every individual in these millions and millions about only one thing: whether you have lived in despair or not, whether you have despaired in such a way that you did not realize that you were in despair, or in such a way that you covertly carried this sickness inside of you as your gnawing secret, as a fruit of sinful love under your heart, or in such a way that you, a terror to others, raged in despair. And if so, if you have lived in despair, then, regardless of whatever else you won or lost, everything is lost for you, eternity does not acknowledge

you, it never knew you—or, still more terrible, it knows you as you are known and it binds you to yourself in despair.

THE FORMS OF THIS SICKNESS (DESPAIR)

The forms of despair may be arrived at abstractly by reflecting upon the constituents of which the self as a synthesis is composed. The self is composed of infinitude and finitude. However, this synthesis is a relation, and a relation that, even though it is derived, relates itself to itself, which is freedom. The self is freedom. But freedom is the dialectical aspect of the categories of possibility and necessity.

However, despair must be considered primarily within the category of consciousness; whether despair is conscious or not constitutes the qualitative distinction between despair and despair. Granted, all despair regarded in terms of the concept is conscious, but this does not mean that the person who, according to the concept, may appropriately be said to be in despair is conscious of it himself. Thus, consciousness is decisive. Generally speaking, consciousness—that is, self-consciousness—is decisive with regard to the self. The more consciousness, the more self; the more consciousness, the more will; the more will, the more self. A person who has no will at all is not a self; but the more will he has, the more self-consciousness he has also.

A.

DESPAIR CONSIDERED WITHOUT REGARD TO ITS BEING CONSCIOUS OR NOT, CONSEQUENTLY ONLY WITH REGARD TO THE CONSTITUENTS OF THE SYNTHESIS

a. Despair as Defined by Finitude/Infinitude

The self is the conscious synthesis of infinitude and finitude that relates itself to itself, whose task is to become itself, which can be done only through the relationship to God. To become oneself is to become concrete. But to become concrete is neither to become finite nor to become infinite, for that which is to become concrete is indeed a synthesis. Consequently, the progress of the becoming must be an infinite moving away from itself in the infinitizing of the self, and an infinite coming back to itself in the finitizing process. But if the self does not become itself, it is in despair, whether it knows that or not. Yet every moment that a self exists, it is in a process of becoming, for the self κατὰ δύναμιν [in potentiality] does not actually exist, is simply that which ought to come into existence. Insofar, then, as the self does not become itself, it is not itself; but not to be itself is precisely despair.

α. Infinitude's Despair Is to Lack Finitude

That this is so is due to the dialectic inherent in the self as a synthesis, and therefore each constituent is its opposite. No form of despair can be defined directly (that is, undialectically), but only by reflecting upon its opposite. The condition of the person in despair can be described directly, as the poet in fact does by giving him lines to speak. But the despair can be defined only by way of its opposite, and if the lines are to have any poetic value, the coloring of the expression must contain the reflection of the dialectical opposite. Consequently, every human existence that presumably has become or simply wants to be infinite, in fact, every moment in which a human existence has become or simply wants to be infinite, is despair. For the self is the synthesis of which the finite is the limiting and the infinite the extending constituent. Infinitude's despair, therefore, is the fantastic, the unlimited, for the self is healthy and free from despair only when, precisely by having despaired, it rests transparently in God.

The fantastic, of course, is most closely related to the imagination, but the imagination in turn is related to feeling, knowing, and willing; therefore a person can have imaginary feeling, knowing, and willing. As a rule, imagination is the medium for the process of infinitizing; it is not a capacity, as are the others—if one wishes to speak in those terms, it is the capacity *instar omnium* [for all capacities]. When all is said and done, whatever of feeling, knowing, and willing a person has depends upon what imagination he has, upon how that person reflects himself—that is, upon imagination. Imagination is infinitizing reflection, and therefore the elder Fichte quite correctly assumed that even in relation to knowledge the categories derive from the imagination. The self is reflection, and the imagination is reflection, is the rendition of the self as the self's possibility. The imagination is the possibility of any and all reflection, and the intensity of this medium is the possibility of the intensity of the self.

The fantastic is generally that which leads a person out into the infinite in such a way that it only leads him away from himself and thereby prevents him from coming back to himself.

When feeling becomes fantastic in this way, the self becomes only more and more volatilized and finally comes to be a kind of abstract sentimentality that inhumanly belongs to no human being but inhumanly combines sentimentally, as it were, with some abstract fate—for example, humanity *in abstracto*. Just as the rheumatic is not master of his physical sensations, which are so subject to the wind and weather that he involuntarily detects any change in the weather etc., so also the person whose feeling has become fantastic is in a way infinitized, but not in such a manner that he becomes more and more himself, for he loses himself more and more.

So also with knowing, when it becomes fantastic. The law for the development of the self with respect to knowing, insofar as it is the case that the self becomes itself, is that the increase of knowledge corresponds to the increase of self-knowledge, that the more the self knows, the more it knows itself. . . .

When feeling or knowing or willing has become fantastic, the entire self can eventually become that, whether in the more active form of plunging headlong into fantasy or in the more passive form of being carried away, but in both cases the person is responsible. The self, then, leads a fantasized existence in abstract infinitizing or in abstract isolation, continually lacking its self, from which it only moves further and further away. Take the religious sphere, for example. The God-relationship is an infinitizing, but in fantasy this infinitizing can so sweep a man off his feet that his state is simply an intoxication. To exist before God may seem unendurable to a man because he cannot come back to himself, become himself. Such a fantasized religious person would say (to characterize him by means of some lines): "That a sparrow can live is comprehensible; it does not know that it exists before God. But to know that one exists before God, and then not instantly go mad or sink into nothingness!"

But to become fantastic in this way, and thus to be in despair, does not mean, although it usually becomes apparent, that a person cannot go on living fairly well, seem to be a man, be occupied with temporal matters, marry, have children, be honored and esteemed—and it may not be detected that in a deeper sense he lacks a self. Such things do not create much of a stir in the world, for a self is the last thing the world cares about and the most dangerous thing of all for a person to show signs of having. The greatest hazard of all, losing the self, can occur very quietly in the world, as if it were nothing at all. No other loss can occur so quietly; any other loss—an arm, a leg, five dollars, a wife, etc.—is sure to be noticed.

β. *Finitude's Despair Is to Lack Infinitude*

That this is so is due, as pointed out under α, to the dialectic inherent in the self as a synthesis, and therefore each constituent is its opposite.

To lack infinitude is despairing reductionism, narrowness. . . .

Despairing narrowness is to lack primitivity or to have robbed oneself of one's primitivity, to have emasculated oneself in a spiritual sense. Every human being is primitively intended to be a self, destined to become himself, and as such every self certainly is angular, but that only means that it is to be ground into shape, not that it is to be ground down smooth, not that it is utterly to abandon being itself out of fear of men, or even simply out of fear of men not to dare to be itself in its more essential contingency (which definitely is not to be ground down smooth), in which a person is still himself for himself. But whereas one kind of despair plunges wildly into the infinite and loses itself, another kind of despair seems to permit itself to be tricked out of its self by "the others." Surrounded by hordes of men, absorbed in all sorts of secular matters, more and more shrewd about the ways of the world—such a person forgets himself, forgets his name divinely understood, does not dare to believe in himself, finds it too hazardous to be himself and far easier and safer to be like the others, to become a copy, a number, a mass man. . . .

. . . The despair that not only does not cause one any inconvenience in life but makes life cozy and comfortable is in no way, of course, regarded as despair. That this is the world's view is borne out, for example, by practically all the proverbs, which are nothing more than rules of prudence. For example, we say that one regrets ten times for having spoken to once for having kept silent—and why? Because the external fact of having spoken can involve one in difficulties, since it is an actuality. But to have kept silent! And yet this is the most dangerous of all. For by maintaining silence, a person is thrown wholly upon himself; here actuality does not come to his aid by punishing him, by heaping the consequences of his speaking upon him. No, in this respect it is easy to keep silent. But the person who knows what is genuinely appalling fears most of all any mistake, any sin that takes an inward turn and leaves no outward trace. The world considers it dangerous to venture in this way—and why? Because it is possible to lose. Not to venture is prudent. And yet, precisely by not venturing it is so terribly easy to lose what would be hard to lose, however much one lost by risking, and in any case never this way, so easily, so completely, as if it were nothing at all—namely, oneself. . . .

b. Despair as Defined by Possibility/Necessity

α. *Possibility's Despair Is to Lack Necessity*

. . . The self is κατὰ δύναμιν [potentially] just as possible as it is necessary, for it is indeed itself, but it has the task of becoming itself. Insofar as it is itself, it is the necessary, and insofar as it has the task of becoming itself, it is a possibility.

But if possibility outruns necessity so that the self runs away from itself in possibility, it has no necessity to which it is to return; this is possibility's despair. . . .

Thus possibility seems greater and greater to the self; more and more becomes possible because nothing becomes actual. Eventually everything seems possible, but this is exactly the point at which the abyss swallows up the self. . . . The instant something appears to be possible, a new possibility appears, and finally these phantasmagoria follow one another in such rapid succession that it seems as if everything were possible, and this is exactly the final moment, the point at which the individual himself becomes a mirage.

What the self now lacks is indeed actuality, and in ordinary language, too, we say that an individual has become unreal. However, closer scrutiny reveals that what he actually lacks is necessity. The philosophers are mistaken when they explain necessity as a unity of possibility and actuality—no, actuality is the unity of possibility and necessity. When a self becomes lost in possibility in this way, it is not merely because of a lack of energy; at least it is not to be interpreted in the usual way. What is missing is essentially the power to obey, to submit to the necessity in one's life, to what may be called one's limitations. Therefore, the tragedy is not that such a self did not amount to something in the world; no, the tragedy is that he did not become aware of himself, aware that the self he is is a very definite something and thus the necessary. . . .

β. *Necessity's Despair Is to Lack Possibility*

The believer has the ever infallible antidote for despair—possibility—because for God everything is possible at every moment. This is the good health of faith that resolves contradictions. The contradiction here is that, humanly speaking, downfall is certain, but that there is possibility nonetheless. . . .

To lack possibility means either that everything has become necessary for a person or that everything has become trivial.

The determinist, the fatalist, is in despair and as one in despair has lost his self, because for him everything has become necessity. He is like that king who starved to death because all his food was changed to gold. Personhood is a synthesis of possibility and necessity. Its continued existence is like breathing (respiration), which is an inhaling and exhaling. The self of the determinist cannot breathe, for it is impossible to breathe necessity exclusively, because that would utterly suffocate a person's self. The fatalist is in despair, has lost God and thus his self, for he who does not have a God does not have a self, either. But the fatalist has no God, or, what amounts to the same thing, his God is necessity; since everything is possible for God, then God is this—that everything is possible. . . .

It is quite different with the philistine-bourgeois mentality, that is, triviality, which also essentially lacks possibility. The philistine-bourgeois mentality is spiritlessness; determinism and fatalism are despair of spirit, but spiritlessness is also despair. The philistine-bourgeois mentality lacks every qualification of spirit and is completely wrapped up in probability, within which possibility finds its small corner; therefore it lacks the possibility of becoming aware of God. Bereft of imagination, as the philistine-bourgeois always is, whether alehouse keeper or prime minister, he lives within a certain trivial compendium of experiences as to how things go, what is possible, what usually happens. In this way, the philistine-bourgeois has lost his self and God. In order for a person to become aware of his self and of God, imagination must raise him higher than the miasma of probability, it must tear him out of this and teach him to hope and to fear—or to fear and to hope—by rendering possible that

which surpasses the *quantum satis* [sufficient standard] of any experience. . . .

. . . The philistine-bourgeois mentality thinks that it controls possibility, that it has tricked this prodigious elasticity into the trap or madhouse of probability, thinks that it holds it prisoner; it leads possibility around imprisoned in the cage of probability, exhibits it, imagines itself to be the master, does not perceive that precisely thereby it has imprisoned itself in the thralldom of spiritlessness and is the most wretched of all. The person who gets lost in possibility soars high with the boldness of despair; he for whom everything became necessity overstrains himself in life and is crushed in despair; but the philistine-bourgeois mentality spiritlessly triumphs.

B.

DESPAIR AS DEFINED BY CONSCIOUSNESS

The ever increasing intensity of despair depends upon the degree of consciousness or is proportionate to its increase: the greater the degree of consciousness, the more intensive the despair. . . .

a. The Despair That Is Ignorant of Being Despair, or the Despairing Ignorance of Having a Self and an Eternal Self

. . . [I]f a man is presumably happy, imagines himself to be happy, although considered in the light of truth he is unhappy, he is usually far from wanting to be wrenched out of his error. On the contrary, he becomes indignant, he regards anyone who does so as his worst enemy, he regards it as an assault bordering on murder in the sense that, as is said, it murders his happiness. Why? Because he is completely dominated by the sensate and the sensate-psychical, because he lives in sensate categories, the pleasant and the unpleasant, waves goodbye to spirit, truth, etc., because he is too sensate to have the courage to venture out and to endure being spirit. . . .

Therefore, it makes no difference whether the person in despair is ignorant that his condition is despair—he is in despair just the same. . . .

. . . [P]aganism and likewise the natural man make the distinction between being in despair and not being in despair—that is, they talk about despair as if only some individuals despaired. Nevertheless, this distinction is just as misleading as the distinction that paganism and the natural man make between love and self-love, as if all this love were not essentially self-love. Beyond this misleading distinction, however, paganism and also the natural man cannot possibly go, because to be ignorant of being in despair is the specific feature of despair.

It is easy to see from all this that the esthetic conception of spiritlessness by no means provides the criterion for judging what is despair and what is not, which, incidentally, is quite in order, for if what is spirit cannot be defined esthetically, how can the esthetic answer a question that simply does not exist for it! . . . No, the esthetic category of spiritlessness does not provide the criterion for what is and what is not despair; what must be applied is the ethical-religious category: spirit or, negatively, the lack of spirit, spiritlessness. Every human existence that is not conscious of itself as spirit or conscious of itself before God as spirit, every human existence that does not rest transparently in God but vaguely rests in and merges in some abstract universality (state, nation, etc.) or, in the dark about his self, regards his capacities merely as powers to produce without becoming deeply aware of their source, regards his self, if it is to have intrinsic meaning, as an indefinable something—every such existence, whatever it achieves, be it most amazing, whatever it explains, be it the whole of existence, however intensively it enjoys life esthetically—every such existence is nevertheless despair. . . .

b. The Despair That Is Conscious of Being Despair and Therefore Is Conscious of Having a Self in Which There Is Something Eternal and Then Either in Despair Does Not Will to Be Itself or in Despair Wills to Be Itself

α. *In Despair Not to Will to Be Oneself: Despair in Weakness*

To call this form despair in weakness already casts a reflection on the second form, β, in despair to will to be oneself. . . .

(1) DESPAIR OVER THE EARTHLY OR OVER SOMETHING EARTHLY

This is pure immediacy or immediacy containing a quantitative reflection. . . .

. . . Immediacy actually has no self, it does not know itself; thus it cannot recognize itself and therefore generally ends in fantasy. When immediacy despairs, it does not even have enough self to wish or dream that it had become that which it has not become. The man of immediacy helps himself in another way: he wishes to be someone else. This is easily verified by observing immediate persons; when they are in despair, there is nothing they desire more than to have been someone else or to become someone else. In any case, it is difficult to keep from smiling at one who despairs in this way, who, humanly speaking and despite being in despair, is so very innocent. As a rule, one who despairs in this way is very comical. Imagine a self (and next to God there is nothing as eternal as a self), and then imagine that it suddenly occurs to a self that it might become someone other —than itself. And yet one in despair this way, whose sole desire is this most lunatic of lunatic metamorphoses, is infatuated with the illusion that this change can be accomplished as easily as one changes clothes. The man of immediacy does not know himself, he quite literally identifies himself only by the clothes he wears, he identifies having a self by externalities (here again the infinitely comical). There is hardly a more ludicrous mistake, for a self is indeed infinitely distinct from an externality. . . .

When immediacy is assumed to have some reflection, the despair is somewhat modified; a somewhat greater consciousness of the self comes about, and thereby of the nature of despair and of one's condition as despair. It means something for such an individual to talk about being in despair, but the despair is essentially despair in weakness, a suffering, and its form is: in despair not to will to be oneself. . . .

. . . When the self with a certain degree of reflection in itself wills to be responsible for the self, it may come up against some difficulty or other in the structure of the self, in the self's necessity. For just as no human body is perfect, so no self is perfect. This difficulty, whatever it is, makes him recoil. Or something happens to him that breaks with the immediacy in him more profoundly than his reflection had done, or his imagination discovers a possibility that, if it eventuated, would thus become the break with immediacy.

So he despairs. In contrast to the despair of self-assertion, his despair is despair in weakness, a suffering of the self; but with the aid of the relative reflection that he has, he attempts to sustain his self, and this constitutes another difference from the purely immediate man. He perceives that abandoning the self is a transaction, and thus he does not become apoplectic when the blow falls, as the immediate person does; reflection helps him to understand that there is much he can lose without losing the self. He makes concessions; he is able to do so—and why? Because to a certain degree he has separated his self from ex-ternalities, because he has a dim idea that there may even be something eternal in the self. Nevertheless, his struggles are in vain; the difficulty he has run up against requires a total break with immediacy, and he does not have the self-reflection or the ethical reflec-tion for that. He has no consciousness of a self that is won by infinite abstraction from every externality, this naked abstract self, which, compared with imme-diacy's fully dressed self, is the first form of the infi-nite self and the advancing impetus in the whole pro-cess by which a self infinitely becomes responsible for its actual self with all its difficulties and advantages.

So he despairs, and his despair is: not to will to be himself. But he certainly does not entertain the ludi-crous notion of wanting to be someone else; he keeps up the relation to his self—reflection has attached him to the self to that extent. His relation to the self is like the relation a person may have to his place of res-idence (the comic aspect is that the self certainly does not have as contingent a relation to itself as one has to a place of residence), which becomes an abomination because of smoke fumes or something else, whatever it might be. So he leaves it, but he does not move away, he does not set up a new residence; he continues to regard the old one as his address, he assumes that the problem will disappear. So also with the person in de-spair. As long as the difficulty lasts, he does not dare, as the saying so trenchantly declares, "to come to himself," he does not will to be himself; presumably this will pass, perhaps a change will take place, this gloomy possibility will probably be forgotten. So as long as it lasts, he visits himself, so to speak, only oc-casionally, to see whether the change has commenced. As soon as it commences, he moves home again, "is himself once again," as he says; but this simply means that he begins where he left off—he was a self up to a point and he went no further than that. . . .

(2) Despair of the Eternal or over Oneself

. . . If the preceding despair was *despair in weakness,* then this is *despair over his weakness,* while still re-maining within the category: despair in weakness as distinct from despair in defiance (β). Consequently, there is only a relative difference, namely, that the

previous form has weakness's consciousness as its final consciousness, whereas here the consciousness does not stop with that but rises to a new consciousness—that of his weakness. The person in despair himself understands that it is weakness to make the earthly so important, that it is weakness to despair. But now, instead of definitely turning away from despair to faith and humbling himself under his weakness, he entrenches himself in despair and despairs over his weakness. In so doing, his whole point of view is turned around: he now becomes more clearly con-scious of his despair, that he despairs of the eternal, that he despairs over himself, over being so weak that he attributes such great significance to the earthly, which now becomes for him the despairing sign that he has lost the eternal and himself.

β. *In Despair to Will to Be Oneself: Defiance*

. . . The kind of despair described in α(2) was over one's weakness; the despairing individual does not will to be himself. But if the person in despair goes one single dialectical step further, if he realizes why he does not will to be himself, then there is a shift, then there is defiance, and this is the case precisely because in despair he wills to be himself.

First comes despair over the earthly or over some-thing earthly, then despair of the eternal, over one-self. Then comes defiance, which is really despair through the aid of the eternal, the despairing misuse of the eternal within the self to will in despair to be oneself. But just because it is despair through the aid of the eternal, in a certain sense it is very close to the truth; and just because it lies very close to the truth, it is infinitely far away. The despair that is the thor-oughfare to faith comes also through the aid of the eternal; through the aid of the eternal the self has the courage to lose itself in order to win itself. Here, how-ever, it is unwilling to begin with losing itself but wills to be itself. . . .

In order in despair to will to be oneself, there must be consciousness of an infinite self. This infinite self, however, is really only the most abstract form, the most abstract possibility of the self. And this is the self that a person in despair wills to be, severing the self from any relation to a power that has established it, or severing it from the idea that there is such a power. With the help of this infinite form, the self in despair wants to be master of itself or to create itself, to make his self into the self he wants to be, to determine what he will have or not have in his concrete self. His concrete self or his concretion certainly has necessity and limitations, is this very specific being with these natural capacities, predispositions, etc. in this specific concretion of relations etc. But with the help of the infinite form, the negative self, he wants first of all to take upon himself the transformation of all this in order to fashion out of it a self such as he wants, produced with the help of the infinite form of the negative self—and in this way he wills to be himself. In other words, he wants to begin a little earlier than do other men, not at and with the beginning, but "in the beginning"; he does not want to put on his own self, does not want to see his given self as his task—he himself wants to compose his self by means of being the infinite form.

If a generic name for this despair is wanted, it could be called stoicism, but understood as not referring only to that sect. To elucidate this kind of despair more precisely, it is best to distinguish between an acting self and a self acted upon and to show how the self, when it is acting, relates itself to itself, and how the self, when it is acted upon, in being affected, relates itself to itself—and thus to show that the formula always is: in despair to will to be oneself.

If the self in despair is an *acting self,* it constantly relates itself to itself only by way of imaginary constructions, no matter what it undertakes, however vast, however amazing, however perseveringly pursued. It recognizes no power over itself; therefore it basically lacks earnestness and can conjure forth only an appearance of earnestness, even when it gives its utmost attention to its imaginary constructions. This is a simulated earnestness. Like Prometheus stealing fire from the gods, this is stealing from God the thought—which is earnestness—that God pays attention to one; instead, the self in despair is satisfied with paying attention to itself, which is supposed to bestow infinite interest and significance upon his enterprises, but it is precisely this that makes them imaginary constructions. For even if this self does not go so far into despair that it becomes an imaginatively constructed god—no derived self can give itself more than it is in itself by paying attention to itself—it remains itself from first to last; in its self-redoubling it becomes neither more nor less than itself. In so far as the self in its despairing striving to be itself works itself into the very opposite, it really becomes no self. In the whole dialectic within which it acts there is nothing steadfast; at no moment is the self steadfast,

that is, eternally steadfast. The negative form of the self exercises a loosening power as well as a binding power; at any time it can quite arbitrarily start all over again, and no matter how long one idea is pursued, the entire action is within a hypothesis. The self is so far from successfully becoming more and more itself that the fact merely becomes increasingly obvious that it is a hypothetical self. The self is its own master, absolutely its own master, so-called; and precisely this is the despair, but also what it regards as its pleasure and delight. On closer examination, however, it is easy to see that this absolute ruler is a king without a country, actually ruling over nothing; his position, his sovereignty, is subordinate to the dialectic that rebellion is legitimate at any moment. Ultimately, this is arbitrarily based upon the self itself.

Consequently, the self in despair is always building only castles in the air, is only shadowboxing. All these imaginatively constructed virtues make it look splendid; like oriental poetry, they fascinate for a moment; such self-command, such imperturbability, such ataraxia, etc. practically border on the fabulous. Yes, they really do, and the basis of the whole thing is nothing. In despair the self wants to enjoy the total satisfaction of making itself into itself, of developing itself, of being itself; it wants to have the honor of this poetic, masterly construction, the way it has understood itself. And yet, in the final analysis, what it understands by itself is a riddle; in the very moment when it seems that the self is closest to having the building completed, it can arbitrarily dissolve the whole thing into nothing.

If the self in despair is *acted upon,* the despair is nevertheless: in despair to will to be oneself. Perhaps such an imaginatively constructing self, which in despair wills to be itself, encounters some difficulty or other while provisionally orienting itself to its concrete self, something the Christian would call a cross, a basic defect, whatever it may be. The negative self, the infinite form of the self, will perhaps reject this completely, pretend that it does not exist, will having nothing to do with it. But it does not succeed; its proficiency in imaginary constructing does not stretch that far, and not even its proficiency in abstracting does. In a Promethean way, the infinite, negative self feels itself nailed to this servitude. Consequently, it is a self acted upon. What, then, are the manifestations of this despair that is: in despair to will to be oneself?

In the preceding pages, the form of despair that despairs over the earthly or something earthly was understood basically to be—and it also manifests itself as being—despair of the eternal, that is, an unwillingness to be comforted by and healed by the eternal, an overestimation of the things of this world to the extent that the eternal can be no consolation. But this is also a form of the despair, to be unwilling to hope in the possibility that an earthly need, a temporal cross, can come to an end. The despairing person who in despair wills to be himself is unwilling to do that. He has convinced himself that this thorn in the flesh gnaws so deeply that he cannot abstract himself from it (whether this is actually the case or his passion makes it so to him*), and therefore he might as well accept it forever, so to speak. He is offended by it, or, more correctly, he takes it as an occasion to be offended at all existence; he defiantly wills to be himself, to be himself not in spite of it or without it (that would indeed be to abstract himself from it, and that he cannot do, or that would be movement in the direction of resignation)—no, in spite of or in defiance of all existence, he wills to be himself with it, takes it along, almost flouting his agony. Hope in the possibility of help, especially by virtue of the absurd, that for God everything is possible—no, that he does not want. And to seek help from someone else—no, not for all the world does he want that. Rather than to seek help, he prefers, if necessary, to be himself with all the agonies of hell.

That popular notion that "of course, a person who suffers wants to be helped if only someone is able to help him" is not really so, is far from true, even though the contrary instance is not always as deep in despair as the one above. This is how things go. A sufferer usually has one or several ways in which he might want to be helped. If he is helped in these ways, then he is glad to be helped. But when having to be helped becomes a profoundly earnest matter, especially when it means being helped by a superior, or by the supreme one, there is the humiliation of being obliged to accept any kind of help unconditionally, of becoming a nothing in the hand of the "Helper" for whom all things are possible, or the humiliation of simply having to yield to another person, of giving up being himself as long as he is seeking help. Yet there is undoubtedly much suffering, even prolonged and agonized suffering, in which the self nevertheless is not pained in this way, and therefore it fundamentally prefers the suffering along with the retention of being itself.

The more consciousness there is in such a sufferer who in despair wills to be himself, the more his despair intensifies and becomes demonic. It usually originates as follows. A self that in despair wills to be itself is pained in some distress or other that does not allow itself to be taken away from or separated from his concrete self. So now he makes precisely this torment the object of all his passion, and finally it becomes a demonic rage. By now, even if God in heaven and all the angels offered to help him out of it—no, he does not want that, now it is too late. Once he would gladly have given everything to be rid of this agony, but he was kept waiting; now it is too late, now he would rather rage against everything and be the wronged victim of the whole world and of all life, and it is of particular significance to him to make sure that he has his torment on hand and that no one takes it away from him—for then he would not be able to demonstrate and prove to himself that he is right. . . .

We began in α(1) with the lowest form of despair: in despair not to will to be oneself. Demonic despair is the most intensive form of the despair: in despair to will to be oneself. It is not even in stoic self-infatuation and self-apotheosis that this despair wills to be itself; it does not will to be itself as that does which, mendaciously to be sure, yet in a certain sense, wills it according to its perfection. No, in hatred toward existence, it wills to be itself, wills to be itself in accordance with its misery. Not even in defiance or defiantly does it will to be itself, but for spite; not even in defiance does it want to tear itself loose from the

---

*Moreover, lest it be overlooked, from this point of view one will see that much of what in the world is dressed up under the name of resignation is a kind of despair: in despair to will to be one's abstract self, in despair to will to make the eternal suffice, and thereby to be able to defy or ignore suffering in the earthly and the temporal. The dialectic of resignation is essentially this: to will to be one's eternal self and then, when it comes to something specific in which the self suffers, not to will to be oneself, taking consolation in the thought that it may disappear in eternity and therefore feeling justified in not accepting it in time. Although suffering under it, the self will still not make the admission that it is part of the self, that is, the self will not in faith humble itself under it. Resignation viewed as despair is thus essentially different from the despair of not willing in despair to be oneself, for in despair one does will to be oneself, but with the exclusion of something specific in regard to which one in despair does not will to be oneself.

power that established it, but for spite wants to force itself upon it, to obtrude defiantly upon it, wants to adhere to it out of malice—and, of course, a spiteful denunciation must above all take care to adhere to what it denounces. Rebelling against all existence, it feels that it has obtained evidence against it, against its goodness. The person in despair believes that he himself is the evidence, and that is what he wants to be, and therefore he wants to be himself, himself in his torment, in order to protest against all existence with this torment. Just as the weak, despairing person is unwilling to hear anything about any consolation eternity has for him, so a person in such despair does not want to hear anything about it, either, but for a different reason: this very consolation would be his undoing—as a denunciation of all existence. Figuratively speaking, it is as if an error slipped into an author's writing and the error became conscious of itself as an error—perhaps it actually was not a mistake but in a much higher sense an essential part of the whole production—and now this error wants to mutiny against the author, out of hatred toward him, forbidding him to correct it and in maniacal defiance saying to him: No, I refuse to be erased; I will stand as a witness against you, a witness that you are a second-rate author.

QUESTIONS FOR REFLECTION

1. Why does Pascal think that "There is no good in this life but in the hope of another . . ."? (sect. 194) Is the problem mortality, so that the problem would be solved for Pascal if he had an elixir that gave him an immortal life on earth? If not, then how does the afterlife solve Pascal's problem?

2. How might Hegel respond to Kierkegaard's claim that the subjective view is more important than the objective view?

3. Would God's existence be a subjective truth or an objective truth?

4. Describe a form of religiousness A that is not religiousness B. Would Kierkegaard say there is any reason to prefer religiousness B over religiousness A? What is your view?

5. What is self-deception? (For help with this question, you might wish to read the books cited at the end of Chapter 1.) Is it important to avoid self-deception? Why?

6. What is Kierkegaard's attitude about self-deception (does he criticize any views on the ground that they involve self-deception)? Does Kierkegaard's approach to life, with its emphasis on believing an absurdity, involve self-deception? If so, is that grounds for rejecting Kierkegaard's approach?

7. One important aspect of Kierkegaard's writing is his emphasis on the importance of the individual. Can that emphasis be reconciled with the "self-annihilation before God" required by paradoxical-religiousness? Clarify.

8. Is placing my highest priority on pleasing God compatible with defining my identity in terms of a relationship with another person? If pleasing God is my highest priority, what attitude must I have about the possibility that God may allow that relationship to be destroyed?

9. What is Kierkegaard's conception of the ethical? How is it related to Kantian and Hegelian ethics?

10. What precisely is meant by the "teleological suspension of the ethical"? Would it have been ethically wrong for Abraham to kill his son for God or not? If it was right in some higher sense but wrong in the ethical sense, shouldn't we say that the ethical applied to Abraham the whole time, rather than saying that the ethical was "suspended"? (Suppose God had said "Abraham, do something that is horribly unethical," and Abraham set out to comply. Would his compliance have involved a "teleological suspension of the ethical"?)

11. Does Kierkegaard's suggestion that we cannot control the "external" encourage us not to take responsibility for the welfare of others? How would Kierkegaard defend himself from the charge that avoiding this responsibility is morally wrong?

FURTHER READINGS

Works by Pascal

Pensées (1670). New York: E. P. Dutton & Co., 1958.

Works by Hegel

Early Theological Writings (1793–1800). Translated by T. M. Knox. Philadelphia: University of Pennsylvania Press, 1971.

Hegel's Phenomenology of Spirit (1807). Translated by A. V. Miller. Oxford: Oxford University Press, 1977.

Hegel's Science of Logic (1812–1816). Translated by A. V. Miller. London: George Allan & Unwin, 1969.

Philosophy of Right (1821). Translated by T. M. Knox. Oxford: Clarendon Press, 1942.

Hegel's Philosophy of Mind (1832–1845). Part Three of *The Encyclopaedia of the Philosophical Sciences* (1830). Translated by William Wallace. Oxford: Clarendon Press, 1971.

Lectures on the History of Philosophy (1832–1845). Translated by J. Sibree. New York: Dover, 1956.

The Logic of Hegel (1832–1845). Part One of *The Encyclopaedia of the Philosophical Sciences.* Translated by William Wallace. Oxford: Clarendon Press, 1975.

Hegel's Philosophy of Nature (1832–1845). Part Two of *The Encyclopaedia of the Philosophical Sciences.* Translated by A. V. Miller. Oxford: Clarendon Press, 1970.

Selections. Edited by J. Loewenberg. New York: Willey Book Co., 1944.

Works by Kierkegaard

The Concept of Irony with Continual Reference to Socrates (1841) together with *Notes of Schelling's Berlin Lectures.* Edited and translated by H. Hong and E. Hong. Princeton: Princeton University Press, 1989.

Either/Or (1843). 2 vols. Edited and translated by H. Hong and E. Hong. Princeton: Princeton University Press, 1987.

Fear and Trembling (1843) together with *Repetition* (1843). Edited and translated by H. Hong and E. Hong. Princeton: Princeton University Press, 1983.

The Concept of Anxiety (1844). Edited and translated by H. Hong and E. Hong. Princeton: Princeton University Press, 1980.

Philosophical Fragments or a Fragment of Philosophy (1844). Edited and translated by H. Hong and E. Hong. Princeton: Princeton University Press, 1985.

Stages on Life's Way (1845). Edited and translated by H. Hong and E. Hong. Princeton: Princeton University Press, 1988.

Concluding Unscientific Postscript to Philosophical Fragments (1846). Edited and translated by H. Hong and E. Hong. Princeton: Princeton University Press, 1992.

Works of Love (1847). Translated by H. Hong and E. Hong. New York: Harper Torchbook, 1962.

Purity of Heart Is to Will One Thing (1847). New York: Harper Torchbooks, 1938.

Christian Discourses (1848). Translated by Walter Lowrie. Princeton: Princeton University Press, 1971.

The Sickness Unto Death (1849). Edited and translated by H. Hong and E. Hong. Princeton: Princeton University Press, 1980.

Works on Pascal

Krailsheimer, A. *Pascal.* Oxford: Past Masters, 1980.

Metzer, S. E. *Discourses of the Fall: A Study of Pascal's Pensées.* Berkeley: University of California Press, 1967.

Parish, R. *Pascal's Lettres Provinciales: A Study in Polemic.* Oxford: Oxford University Press, 1989.

Works on Hegel

Beiser, F. C., ed. *The Cambridge Companion to Hegel.* Cambridge: Cambridge University Press, 1993.

Findlay, J. N. *Hegel: A Re-examination.* London: Allen & Unwin, 1958.

Kojève, Alexandre. *Introduction to the Reading of Hegel.* New York: Basic Books, Inc., 1969.

MacIntyre, A., ed. *Hegel: A Collection of Critical Essays.* New York: Anchor, 1972.

Marcuse, H. *Reason and Revolution: Hegel and the Rise of Social Theory.* London: Oxford University Press, 1941.

McLellan, David. *The Young Hegelians and Karl Marx.* London: Macmillan, 1969.

Norman, Richard. *Hegel's Phenomonology: A Philosophical Introduction.* Brighton: Sussex University Press, 1976.

Solomon, Robert. *In the Spirit of Hegel: A Study of Hegel's Phenomenology.* New York: Oxford University Press, 1983.

Taylor, Charles. *Hegel.* Cambridge: Cambridge University Press, 1975.

———. *Hegel and Modern Society.* Cambridge: Cambridge University Press, 1979.

Wood, Allen. *Hegel's Ethical Theory.* Cambridge: Cambridge University Press, 1990.

Works on Kierkegaard

Collins, J. *The Mind of Kierkegaard.* Princeton: Princeton University Press, 1983.

Gardiner, Patrick. *Kierkegaard.* Oxford: Oxford University Press, 1988.

Hannay, Alastair. *Kierkegaard.* London: Routledge & Kegan Paul, 1982.

Hannay, Alastair and Gordon Marino, eds. *The Cambridge Companion to Kierkegaard.* Cambridge University Press, 1998.

Mackey, Louis. *Kierkegaard: A Kind of Poet.* Philadelphia: University of Pennsylvania Press, 1971.

Pojman, Louis. *The Logic of Subjectivity.* Alabama: University of Alabama Press, 1984.

Rudd, Anthony. *Kierkegaard and the Limits of the Ethical.* Oxford: Clarendon Press, 1993.

CHAPTER 3

Friedrich Nietzsche (1844–1900)

Friedrich Wilhelm Nietzsche was born in Prussia. His father was a Lutheran pastor and his mother was the daughter of a Lutheran vicar. (Nietzsche himself was confirmed in 1861.) Five years after Nietzsche's birth his father died from complications of a brain disease or injury. As a youth Nietzsche received a classical education and studied philology at the Universities of Bonn and Leipzig. More than once he attempted military service, but this was made impossible by his health, which was never robust (he had poor vision and suffered severe migraine headaches). When his attempt to join the cavalry failed, he volunteered as a medical orderly and became severely ill after being trapped behind enemy lines with patients. His undistinguished military career was offset by his brilliant—if brief—scholarly career. At the extraordinarily early age of twenty-five he was offered a professorship in classical philology at the University of Basel. Most of Nietzsche's work was written during a sixteen-year period that began in 1872. About halfway through this period his failing health forced him to resign his teaching position. After that he traveled extensively, hoping to find a climate suitable to his poor constitution. Nietzsche's one serious marriage proposal (to Lou von Salomé) was rejected. In 1889 he collapsed in the streets of Turin and never regained lucidity. He was cared for by his mother and then by his sister Elizabeth Förster, an antisemite and proto-Nazi who attempted to use her brother's writings for her cause in spite of his own vehement rejection of antisemitism and German nationalism.

Much of Nietzsche's work was influenced by and a response to the writings of the German philosopher Arthur Schopenhauer (1788–1860). Hence, before we examine Nietzsche's philosophy, it is best to consider Schopenhauer's views. To facilitate our discussion the reader may wish to read the excerpt from Schopenhauer's *The World as Will and Representation* (1818) provided in this chapter.

SCHOPENHAUER

Arthur Schopenhauer developed a Kantian perspective according to which the perceivable, phenomenal "objective" world is structured by the mind or "subject" according to various categories. For Schopenhauer these categories were time, space, and causality, and as the result of their imposition, the phenomenal world is a world of diversity and plurality. Because the subject or knower does the structuring, the subject is prior to the world of diversity and is something indefinite—neither a unity nor a diversity. As Schopenhauer says, "neither plurality nor its opposite, namely unity, belongs to [the knower]."[1] This is not to say that we have no access to the world of things as they are in themselves; Schopenhauer rejected Kant's claim that this world is forever beyond our grasp. In Schopenhauer's view the reality behind the phenomenal world is *will;* the thing-in-itself is *will.* Each of us has access to will through intuition, and the will you intuit is the same will that I intuit.

Schopenhauer portrays the will as a blind, irrational force. Showing the influence of David Hume's (1711–1776) claim that reason is the servant of the passions, Schopenhauer portrayed reason as an instrument shaped by will to accomplish its ends. Moreover, anticipating Sigmund Freud (1856–1939), Schopenhauer emphasized that will often pursues goals that are hidden from consciousness.

One of the things the will tends to keep hidden is that our existence—indeed, the existence of everything there is—is pointless because it is willed finally for no reason at all. To a large extent the will keeps us from noticing that existence is pointless by filling our lives with consuming ambitions that feel important because they feel urgent. These ambitions, including the craving for life itself, give us the illusion that life's purpose is to attain happiness. On closer examination, however, we can see that all of our desires are the product of will, and because will is baseless, so are our ambitions. Unthinkingly, we take it for granted that the ends we will to achieve, including our desire to exist, have objectively given value, and then we go about seeking the means to achieve our ends. In doing so, we never question whether the things we want really are good. If we did, we would find that the only reason we think that the things we desire are good is that we desire them. If nothing has objective value, however, there is nothing to pursue for its own sake, nothing that is capable of inspiring our lives, for example. Will is blind in that it wills the continuation of existence for no reason. Existence is not for the sake of anything, and thus it and the will for existence are meaningless. Our lives are like those of other animals who struggle desperately. In the end these animals are attempting to perpetuate their kind, yet their existence comes to nothing except a new generation of animals engaged in the same pointless struggle.

Not only is our existence pointless, but what goes by the name of happiness is not worth having. For happiness consists in the satisfaction of desires, but neither desiring nor satisfying a desire is worthwhile. To desire is to be in the unpleasant condition of wanting and craving—the condition of being incomplete. To desire is for us to perceive ourselves as insufficient, inadequate, and wanting. When we desire, we strive to find something to fill the void. But the attempt to fill the void is in vain. We perceive the short-lived satisfaction as our finally being released from craving, but immediately we find ourselves in the grip of another craving. The pursuit of happiness amounts to a series of experiences of emptiness and inadequacy that is never ended, and so the pursuit of happiness is really a form of suffering. Indeed, will itself is suffering.

Nonetheless, reason enables will to grasp will's nature and realize the inescapable truth about the nature of will; namely, that it is suffering. This suffering manifests itself in the life of each individual. Salvation for each of us requires that (1) we identify with the will that manifests itself in each of us, thus ceasing to take seriously our individuality, (2) we see that will is suffering, (3) we see that the best thing would be for

will not to exist, and so (4) we (will that will) cease to will. In this way we become passive, indifferent pure intellects that mirror the world around us. Such indifference is about the best we can hope for.

SCHOPENHAUER AND NIETZSCHE

Nietzsche's earliest works include much generous praise for Schopenhauer and show that initially his approach to philosophy was heavily influenced by his predecessor's. In Nietzsche's first book, *The Birth of Tragedy Out of the Spirit of Music* (1872), Schopenhauer's influence is at its strongest. In this book Nietzsche attempts to explain why the ancient Greeks were fascinated by tragedy as a form of art. At one level Nietzsche's answer is that the Greeks were drawn to tragedy because of their joy, strength, and overflowing health. Secure in their affirmation of life, the Greeks found it challenging and rewarding to seek out and face the harshest truths about human existence. Nietzsche's more developed explanation traces art in general and tragedy in particular to the "opposition, in origin and aims, between the Apollinian art of sculpture, and the nonimagistic, Dionysian art of music" that "appear coupled with each other, and through this coupling ultimately generate an equally Dionysian and Apollinian form of art—Attic tragedy."[2] In coining the terms *Dionysian* and *Apollinian*, Nietzsche alludes to Dionysus, the god of fertility and wine whose retinue included satyrs, nymphs, and maenads, and to Apollo, the god of light. Nietzsche aligns the Apollinian element in art with an element in Schopenhauer's philosophy; namely, the structuring activity of the mind by which we perceive a world of diversity and plurality, a world that conforms to Schopenhauer's *principium individuationis,* or principle of individuation. The Dionysian corresponds to a second Schopenhauerean element: namely, the primordial will that lies beneath the world of appearance. For Schopenhauer the world as it is experienced is a dreamlike world of illusion concealing the will-like world as it is in itself, and Nietzsche offers a similar view: the Apollinian is a dreamlike, illusory veil over the Dionysian, the sensuous yet cruel will that constitutes the "ground of our being,"[3] the world as it is in itself. Under the influence of the Dionysian, people experience an intoxicating, "mysterious primordial unity" normally concealed from us by the influence of the Apollinian.

In a second early work, "Schopenhauer as Educator," essay 3 of *Untimely Meditations* (1873–1876), Nietzsche reveals what drew him to the work of Schopenhauer. Schopenhauer suggested that through saintly, self-abnegating individuals the surging and pointless natural order can be seen as having finally produced the reflective capacity needed to realize its meaning: existence is not worthwhile. His view was grim indeed, but Schopenhauer had the honesty and strength of mind to accept the ugly truth as he saw it and was not prompted to overcome his despair with some sort of evasion. Thus, Nietzsche attributed to Schopenhauer the same strength of mind he found in the ancient Greeks.

However, even in his early writings Nietzsche rejected Schopenhauer's pessimism. Life has aspects that can be horrifying, but the best response is not to reject life. Rather, gifted people should respond by reaching new heights of grandeur. By doing so, they redeem a world that might otherwise be condemned. Nietzsche himself undertakes this project of advocating and pursuing excellence. According to Nietzsche, the people who matter are the great individuals—the geniuses who turn their creative efforts to fashioning wholly new and remarkable lives. From the vantage point of the lives they create, such geniuses are capable of the "profound [Dionysian] feeling of oneness and identity with all living things," insofar as they see themselves as "the mankind towards which all nature presses for its redemption."[4] Everything else—an ordinary person, people in general, the state—matters only insofar as it helps to create conditions favorable to the advent of great redemptive individuals. Again and again in his writings Nietzsche expresses this idea that we should strive to be great so that life can be seen as worth embracing. For example, in *Genealogy of Morals,* second essay, sec. 24, he says that the "man of the future" will "redeem us" from "the will to nothingness."

In writings that follow "Schopenhauer as Educator," Nietzsche registers a new, more critical understanding of Schopenhauer, and already in *The Joyful Wisdom,* sec. 370, Nietzsche no longer understands Schopenhauer's work as an honest and courageous (if misguided) attempt to set out the truth about human existence. He portrays Schopenhauer much as Schopenhauer had portrayed the wicked person in the latter's own writings, namely, as "one who suffers deeply, who struggles, is tormented, and would like to turn what is most personal, singular, and narrow, the real idiosyncrasy of his suffering, into a binding law and compulsion—one who, as it were, revenges himself on all things by forcing his own image, the image of his torture, on them, branding them with it." Nietzsche soon comes to see vengefulness behind many of Schopenhauer's themes and expresses his suspiciousness of the vengefulness of Schopenhauer's pessimistic philosophy in more concrete terms. Thus, he focuses on the striking fact that Schopenhauer embraces fairly traditional moral principles in spite of his pessimism. This suggests that morality can be used against life, according to Nietzsche, and he launches an investigation of moral philosophy as a species of pessimism.

Soon Nietzsche's suspicions about Schopenhauerean philosophy grow into suspicions about the thought of many other figures, and he launches a massive project in which he attempts to show that seemingly innocuous religious and philosophical perspectives actually encourage people to deplore human existence and stifle the development of great individuals. He explains asceticism, another Schopenhauerean theme, as self-hatred, as vengefulness turned inward upon the self, and emphasizes the opposite of ascetism: egoism, or the affirmation of the self. In *The Joyful Wisdom* he attributes to Socrates the idea that life is a disease, and in various works, including *The Genealogy of Morals,* he explores ways in which religion and moral philosophy ally themselves against life.

ETERNAL RECURRENCE

After turning against his mentor, Nietzsche shaped some of his views in self-conscious opposition to Schopenhauer's. One example in particular should be emphasized. In *Beyond Good and Evil,* sec. 56, Nietzsche says a correct assessment of Schopenhauer's views may open our "eyes to the opposite idea: the ideal of the most high-spirited, alive, and world-affirming human being who has not only come to terms and learned to get along with whatever was and is, but who wants to have what was and is repeated into all eternity. . . ." In view of this passage, it is reasonable to suppose that Nietzsche is interested in the doctrine of eternal recurrence—the ancient stoic idea that history repeats itself in all particulars—because he thinks that anyone who affirms human existence just as it is would be happy to see it repeated forever. The desire for recurrence is then the test of whether or not we affirm life as much as Schopenhauer condemned it.

Of course, one might argue that the opposite of Schopenhauer's *condemnation* of existence in all of its particulars is the *affirmation* of existence in all of its particulars, rather than the desire to "have what was and is repeated." In any case, Nietzsche certainly advocates affirming existence as it is, hiding nothing from ourselves, and at the end of the second chapter of *Ecce Homo,* he formulates his ideal without referring to eternal recurrence: "My formula for greatness in a human being is *amor fati* [love of fate]: that one wants nothing to be different, not forward, not backward, not in all eternity."

THE ÜBERMENSCH

Introduced in *Thus Spoke Zarathustra* (1883–1885), Nietzsche's ideal of the *Übermensch** is best understood in light of his view that it is the great individual who redeems life. The *Übermensch* is a person who sheds traditional values and re-creates himself or herself in light of a new vision of human excellence. Moreover, the *Übermensch* is never satisfied with the new level of excellence he introduces; instead, he is constantly on the way to overcoming himself and creating ever higher forms of excellence. The *Übermensch* is always a work in progress.

WILL TO POWER AND MORALITY

According to Nietzsche, the most important human motivation is the will to power, which takes various forms. More often than not, Nietzsche understands it to be the desire for excellence or greatness, but while everyone wants to excel, different people interpret excellence in different ways. Those whom Nietzsche praises in the highest terms are people who create the very terms under which they excel. They create their own values in an attempt to define and achieve higher excellence. They constantly reinvent human excellence; although they affirm themselves, they are never

satisfied with themselves and constantly strive to outdo themselves and others.

Using his theory of human motivation, Nietzsche develops positive portrayals of human characteristics that most people despise. Such despised qualities as egoism, unconventionality, cruelty, and the desire to exploit others he portrays as natural features of great individuals. A high self-regard is simply a mark of a healthy affirmation of life. Furthermore, the great are entitled to see themselves as superior to others *because* they excel. Finally, given the logic of comparative concepts such as "superior," "excellent," "above average," and so on, becoming great requires that we outdo others. Yet when we desire to outdo others, and they us, we are interested in depriving them of something they value; we want to exploit them. The great will also tend to be "free spirits" who set aside the restraints of social convention and hold themselves only to values and laws that they give themselves.

Not only does Nietzsche positively portray human characteristics that are usually despised, he also devotes a great deal of space to negative portrayals of traditional human virtues. By combining these two reevaluations, Nietzsche intends to combat the idea that human existence is a thing to be deplored. He elevates the status of "bad" human characteristics by welding them to "good" characteristics. "Man needs what is most evil in him for what is best in him," he says in *Zarathustra*, part 3, sec. 13. Pity he links to people like Schopenhauer who actually loath humanity, and Nietzsche emphasizes that improving ourselves in particular or humanity in general requires harsh discipline and the willingness to neglect those who embrace mediocrity. Moreover, he suggests that "slave morality," or egalitarian, democratic values, are the creations of weak, mediocre people who envy powerful, great individuals who straightforwardly value power and being powerful. Slave moralists take their revenge on the powerful by adopting a value scheme by which the powerful are portrayed as "evil" and the importance of excelling is denied.

> The slave revolt in morality begins when *ressentiment* itself becomes creative and gives birth to values. . . . Slave morality from the outset says No to what is 'outside,' what is 'different,' what is 'not itself'; and *this* No is its creative deed. This inversion of the value-positing eye . . . is of the essence of *ressentiment* . . . its action is

---

*Sometimes translated as "superman" or "overman."

fundamentally reaction. The reverse is the case with the noble mode of valuation: it acts and grows spontaneously, it seeks its opposite only so as to affirm itself more gratefully and triumphantly. . . .[5]

Nietzsche suggests that "slave morality" is unnatural and unhealthy in that it is an inversion of the natural will to power that seduces us to life. Also, "slave morality" requires self-deception. Unlike the powerful, the weak refuse to acknowledge the importance of relative standing against others, yet the weak are deeply concerned about their relative standing, as is betrayed by their emphasis on equality—equality is *itself* a measure of relative standing. If we are honest with ourselves, Nietzsche thinks, we will acknowledge the force of "master morality." We will acknowledge values such as self-regard and superiority, which are affirmed by great individuals.

GOD IS DEAD

In pronouncing God dead, Nietzsche meant to suggest that the concept of God no longer plays a useful role in human progress and serves only to hinder people. Nietzsche attempted to bring out many ways in which the world's religions and otherworldly philosophies such as Platonism have turned people against life, and he singled out Christianity (which he calls "Platonism for the masses") for his most biting invective. To express their disappointment with human existence, religious people denigrate the actual world by contrasting it with an imaginary supernatural world of their own creation. The more gloriously the supernatural world is portrayed, the less valuable the actual world seems, and the less attached to human existence people find themselves. Nietzsche also suggests (in *Genealogy of Morals,* second essay, sec. 22) that the idea of God is a projection by the person who is looking for relief from self-torment: "He ejects from himself all his denial of himself . . . in the form of an affirmation, as something existent, corporeal, real, as God, . . . as the beyond. . . ." Nietzsche urges people to expend their creative efforts on making the actual world more remarkable by making their own lives more remarkable. We should not aspire to the supernatural world contemplated by Christianity. As Nietzsche's character says in part 2, sec. 2 of *Thus*

Spoke Zarathustra, "God is a conjecture; but . . . your conjectures should be limited by what is thinkable."

A great number of beliefs rest on assumptions about the otherworldly; hence, as it comes to lose its grip on us, we will have to reject those further beliefs as well. In particular, people have long assumed that valuation is made possible because God makes some things objectively good or right and others objectively bad or wrong. Hence, Nietzsche believed that a wave of nihilism would result from the death of God; he believed that many would echo Dostoyevski's claim that if God does not exist, then all is permitted (*Will to Power,* Book One). However, Nietzsche himself rejected nihilism. Valuing does not require an objective basis, for people may invent values. They may devise new visions of human excellence and affirm the achievement of excellence.

TRUTH AND PERSPECTIVISM

Nietzsche's understanding of, and attitude about, truth took various turns during his career. Throughout his career he emphasized the importance of accepting the truth about human existence, for we must grasp the nature of the world if we are truly to affirm existence. To affirm existence, which is one of the marks of greatness (*Beyond Good and Evil,* sec. 39), we must also affirm our natural interest in power, and our values and identities must be healthy outgrowths of our will to power. But Nietzsche's emphasis on the importance of the truth was not unequivocal. In fact, he grew more and more suspicious of the unqualified commitment to truth. For example, in *The Joyful Wisdom,* sec. 344, he linked this commitment to the ancient Greek religious belief that truth is divine, and in *Beyond Good and Evil,* sec. 34, he said that "it is no more than a moral prejudice that truth is worth more than mere appearance."

Increasingly, Nietzsche's emphasis on the importance of not deceiving ourselves was undermined by his own analyses of truth and reason. Soon after his earliest writings he began to criticize the idea of truth as the portrayal of facts about things-in-themselves, facts dealing with an otherworldly metaphysical realm. Reason Nietzsche understood as the instrument of the desires, so that a disinterested objective form of reason was not possible. Truth Nietzsche sometimes analyzed as useful lies, as calcified prejudice, and as worn-out metaphors, although he also says in several places that beliefs that are very harmful can be true and that "renouncing false judgements would mean renouncing life and a denial of life." He also experimented with *perspectivism,* which some commentators erroneously interpret as the view that truth is relative to perspective. In fact, Nietzsche's perspectivism is the view that people's interpretations of the world will vary depending on what they desire, that many different interpretations will be defensible from the point of view of many different value orientations, and that none of these interpretations will be more plausible than *all* of the others. Nonetheless, some interpretations will be more plausible than *some* others, and presumably among the most plausible interpretations will be those defended by people who will power and affirm life. Perspectivism led Nietzsche to suggest that people abandon the idea that the objective, scientific view is the only interpretation of the world and that they experiment with more life-affirming views of the world.

THE SELF

Nietzsche questions virtually all of the traditional, Cartesian views about ourselves. He says that we do not have direct access to ourselves as conscious subjects. The conscious subject is an inferred entity, something we posit in order to explain what we can perceive. Moreover, and as a consequence of the inferential status of the conscious subject, all aspects of the psyche are questionable. For instance, the idea that the subject is a thinking substance is simply a questionable hypothesis. A related point is that Nietzsche, like Schopenhauer, takes very seriously the idea of the unconscious. In fact, Nietzsche suggests that our mental life is largely hidden from us; our conscious life reaches only to the outer skin of the psyche.

While Nietzsche rejects the Cartesian view of the self, it is by no means clear what Nietzsche means to put in its place. In various places he experiments with several interesting alternatives. In *The Joyful Wisdom* he sketches a view that suggests that individuals should not be closely identified with their conscious life. He suggests that the capacity for consciousness goes hand in hand with the capacity for language and that the latter is a social device, so that "consciousness does not really belong to man's individual existence but

rather to his social or herd nature." In other places, such as *Will to Power,* secs. 480–492, Nietzsche questions the idea of a unified self or subject and suggests that while we attempt to create a unity out of the disparate elements of the psyche, there is no reason to think that we will always succeed. He experiments with the idea that within the psyche is a "multiplicity" of subjects struggling for domination over each other. In some passages, such as *The Joyful Wisdom,* sec. 110, he challenges the claim that the will is free, saying that the doctrine of free will is a device designed to make people feel guilty for their actions, while in others, such as in the second essay of *Genealogy of Morals,* he suggests that it can be free.

NOTES

1. Arthur Schopenhauer, *The World as Will and Representation,* trans. E. F. J. Payne (New York: Dover Publications, Inc., 1918), p. 5.
2. Friedrich Nietzsche, *The Birth of Tragedy Out of the Spirit of Music* in *The Birth of Tragedy and The Case of Wagner* (hereafter *Tragedy*), trans. Walter Kaufmann (New York: Vintage Books, 1967), sec. 1.
3. *Tragedy,* sec. 4.
4. Nietzsche, "Schopenhauer as Educator" in *Untimely Meditations,* trans. R. J. Hollingdale (Cambridge: Cambridge University Press, 1983), sec. 5.
5. Nietzsche, *Genealogy of Morals* in *On the Genealogy of Morals and Ecce Homo,* trans. Walter Kaufmann (New York: Vintage Books, 1969), sec. 10.

PRECURSOR

ARTHUR SCHOPENHAUER

From The World as Will and Representation

68.

I take up again the thread of our discussion of the ethical significance of conduct, to show how, from the same source from which all goodness, affection, virtue, and nobility of character spring, there ultimately arises also what I call denial of the will-to-live.*

---

*Some footnotes have been omitted—ed.

Just as previously we saw hatred and wickedness conditioned by egoism, and this depending on knowledge being entangled in the *principium individuationis,* so we found as the source and essence of justice, and, when carried farther to the highest degrees, of love and magnanimity, that penetration of the *principium individuationis.* This penetration alone, by abolishing the distinction between our own individuality and that of others, makes possible and explains perfect goodness of disposition, extending to the most disinterested love, and the most generous self-sacrifice for others.

Now, if seeing through the *principium individuationis,* if this direct knowledge of the identity of the will in all its phenomena, is present in a high degree of distinctness, it will at once show an influence on the will which goes still farther. If that veil of Maya, the *principium individuationis,* is lifted from the eyes of a man to such an extent that he no longer makes the egoistical distinction between himself and the person of others, but takes as much interest in the sufferings of other individuals as in his own, and thus is not only benevolent and charitable in the highest degree, but even ready to sacrifice his own individuality whenever several others can be saved thereby, then it follows automatically that such a man, recognizing in all beings his own true and innermost self, must also regard the endless sufferings of all that lives as his own, and thus take upon himself the pain of the whole world. No suffering is any longer strange or foreign to him. All the miseries of others, which he sees and is so seldom able to alleviate, all the miseries of which he has indirect knowledge, and even those he recognizes merely as possible, affect his mind just as do his own. It is no longer the changing weal and woe of his person that he has in view, as is the case with the man still involved in egoism, but, as he sees through the *principium individuationis,* everything lies equally near to him. He knows the whole, comprehends its inner nature, and finds it involved in a constant passing away, a vain striving, an inward conflict, and a continual suffering. Wherever he looks, he sees suffering humanity and the suffering animal world, and a world that passes away. Now all this lies just as near to him as only his own person lies to the egoist. Now how could he, with such knowledge of the world, affirm this very life through constant acts of will, and precisely in this way bind himself more and more firmly to it, press himself to it more and more closely? Thus, whoever is still involved

in the *principium individuationis,* in egoism, knows only particular things and their relation to his own person, and these then become ever renewed *motives* of his willing. On the other hand, that knowledge of the whole, of the inner nature of the thing-in-itself, which has been described, becomes the *quieter* of all and every willing. The will now turns away from life; it shudders at the pleasures in which it recognizes the affirmation of life. Man attains to the state of voluntary renunciation, resignation, true composure, and complete willlessness. At times, in the hard experience of our own sufferings or in the vividly recognized suffering of others, knowledge of the vanity and bitterness of life comes close to us who are still enveloped in the veil of Maya. We would like to deprive desires of their sting, close the entry to all suffering, purify and sanctify ourselves by complete and final resignation. But the illusion of the phenomenon soon ensnares us again, and its motives set the will in motion once more; we cannot tear ourselves free. The allurements of hope, the flattery of the present, the sweetness of pleasures, the well-being that falls to the lot of our person amid the lamentations of a suffering world governed by chance and error, all these draw us back to it, and rivet the bonds anew. Therefore Jesus says: "It is easier for a camel to go through the eye of a needle, than for a rich man to enter into the Kingdom of God." *

If we compare life to a circular path of red-hot coals having a few cool places, a path that we have to run over incessantly, then the man entangled in delusion is comforted by the cool place on which he is just now standing, or which he sees near him, and sets out to run over the path. But the man who sees through the *principium individuationis,* and recognizes the true nature of things-in-themselves, and thus the whole, is no longer susceptible of such consolation; he sees himself in all places simultaneously, and withdraws. His will turns about; it no longer affirms its own inner nature, mirrored in the phenomenon, but denies it. The phenomenon by which this becomes manifest is the transition from virtue to *asceticism.* In other words, it is no longer enough for him to love others like himself, and to do as much for them as for himself, but there arises in him a strong aversion to the

---

*Matthew xix, 24. [Tr.]

inner nature whose expression is his own phenomenon, to the will-to-live, the kernel and essence of that world recognized as full of misery. He therefore renounces precisely this inner nature, which appears in him and is expressed already by his body, and his action gives the lie to his phenomenon, and appears in open contradiction thereto. Essentially nothing but phenomenon of the will, he ceases to will anything, guards against attaching his will to anything, tries to establish firmly in himself the greatest indifference to all things. His body, healthy and strong, expresses the sexual impulse through the genitals, but he denies the will, and gives the lie to the body; he desires no sexual satisfaction on any condition. Voluntary and complete chastity is the first step in asceticism or the denial of the will-to-live. It thereby denies the affirmation of the will which goes beyond the individual life, and thus announces that the will, whose phenomenon is the body, ceases with the life of this body. Nature, always true and naïve, asserts that, if this maxim became universal, the human race would die out; and after what was said in the second book about the connexion of all phenomena of will, I think I can assume that, with the highest phenomenon of will, the weaker reflection of it, namely the animal world, would also be abolished, just as the half-shades vanish with the full light of day. With the complete abolition of knowledge the rest of the world would of itself also vanish into nothing, for there can be no object without a subject. . . . Sacrifice signifies resignation generally, and the rest of nature has to expect its salvation from man who is at the same time priest and sacrifice.

· · ·

Asceticism shows itself further in voluntary and intentional poverty, which arises not only *per accidens,* since property is given away to alleviate the sufferings of others, but which is here an end in itself; it is to serve as a constant mortification of the will, so that satisfaction of desires, the sweet of life, may not again stir the will, of which self-knowledge has conceived a horror. He who has reached this point still always feels, as living body, as concrete phenomenon of will, the natural tendency to every kind of willing; but he deliberately suppresses it, since he compels himself to refrain from doing all that he would like to do, and on the other hand to do all that he would not like to do, even if this has no further purpose than that of serving to mortify the will. As he himself denies the will

that appears in his own person, he will not resist when another does the same thing, in other words, inflicts wrong on him. Therefore, every suffering that comes to him from outside through chance or the wickedness of others is welcome to him; every injury, every ignominy, every outrage. He gladly accepts them as the opportunity for giving himself the certainty that he no longer affirms the will, but gladly sides with every enemy of the will's phenomenon that is his own person. He therefore endures such ignominy and suffering with inexhaustible patience and gentleness, returns good for all evil without ostentation, and allows the fire of anger to rise again within him as little as he does the fire of desires. Just as he mortifies the will itself, so does he mortify its visibility, its objectivity, the body. He nourishes it sparingly, lest its vigorous flourishing and thriving should animate afresh and excite more strongly the will, of which it is the mere expression and mirror. Thus he resorts to fasting, and even to self-castigation and self-torture, in order that, by constant privation and suffering, he may more and more break down and kill the will that he recognizes and abhors as the source of his own suffering existence and of the world's. Finally, if death comes, which breaks up the phenomenon of this will, the essence of such will having long since expired through free denial of itself except for the feeble residue which appears as the vitality of this body, then it is most welcome, and is cheerfully accepted as a longed-for deliverance. It is not merely the phenomenon, as in the case of others, that comes to an end with death, but the inner being itself that is abolished; this had a feeble existence merely in the phenomenon. This last slender bond is now severed; for him who ends thus, the world has at the same time ended.

And what I have described here with feeble tongue, and only in general terms, is not some philosophical fable, invented by myself and only of today. No, it was the enviable life of so many saints and great souls among the Christians, and even more among the Hindus and Buddhists, and also among the believers of other religions. Different as were the dogmas that were impressed on their faculty of reason, the inner, direct, and intuitive knowledge from which alone all virtue and holiness can come is nevertheless expressed in precisely the same way in the conduct of life. For here also is seen the great distinction between intuitive and abstract knowledge, a distinction of such importance and of general application in the whole of our discussion, and one which hitherto has received too little no-tice. Between the two is a wide gulf; and, in regard to knowledge of the inner nature of the world, this gulf can be crossed only by philosophy. Intuitively, or *in concreto,* every man is really conscious of all philo-sophical truths; but to bring them into his abstract knowledge, into reflection, is the business of the philosopher, who neither ought to nor can do more than this.

Thus it may be that the inner nature of holiness, of self-renunciation, of mortification of one's own will, of asceticism, is here for the first time expressed in abstract terms and free from everything mythical, as *denial of the will-to-live,* which appears after the com-plete knowledge of its own inner being has become for it the quieter of all willing. On the other hand, it has been known directly and expressed in deed by all those saints and ascetics who, in spite of the same inner knowledge, used very different language accord-ing to the dogmas which their faculty of reason had accepted, and in consequence of which an Indian, a Christian, or a Lamaist saint must each give a very different account of his own conduct; but this is of no importance at all as regards the fact. A saint may be full of the most absurd superstition, or, on the other hand, may be a philosopher; it is all the same. His con-duct alone is evidence that he is a saint; for, in a moral regard, it springs not from abstract knowledge, but from intuitively apprehended, immediate knowledge of the world and of its inner nature, and is expressed by him through some dogma only for the satisfaction of his faculty of reason.

.   .   .

. . . We saw above that the wicked man, by the vehe-mence of his willing, suffers constant, consuming, in-ner torment, and finally that, when all the objects of willing are exhausted, he quenches the fiery thirst of his wilfulness by the sight of others' pain. On the other hand, the man in whom the denial of the will-to-live has dawned, however poor, cheerless, and full of priva-tion his state may be when looked at from outside, is full of inner cheerfulness and true heavenly peace. It is not the restless and turbulent pressure of life, the jubilant delight that has keen suffering as its preced-ing or succeeding condition, such as constitute the conduct of the man attached to life, but it is an un-shakable peace, a deep calm and inward serenity, a state that we cannot behold without the greatest long-

ing, when it is brought before our eyes or imagination, since we at once recognize it as that which alone is right, infinitely outweighing everything else, at which our better spirit cries to us the great *sapere aude.** We then feel that every fulfilment of our wishes won from the world is only like the alms that keep the beggar alive today so that he may starve again tomorrow. Res-ignation, on the other hand, is like the inherited estate; it frees its owner from all care and anxiety for ever.

It will be remembered from the third book that aesthetic pleasure in the beautiful consists, to a large extent, in the fact that, when we enter the state of pure contemplation, we are raised for the moment above all willing, above all desires and cares; we are, so to speak, rid of ourselves. We are no longer the individ-ual that knows in the interest of its constant willing, the correlative of the particular thing to which objects become motives, but the eternal subject of knowing purified of the will, the correlative of the Idea. And we know that these moments, when, delivered from the fierce pressure of the will, we emerge, as it were, from the heavy atmosphere of the earth, are the most bliss-ful that we experience. From this we can infer how blessed must be the life of a man whose will is si-lenced not for a few moments, as in the enjoyment of the beautiful, but for ever, indeed completely extin-guished, except for the last glimmering spark that maintains the body and is extinguished with it. Such a man who, after many bitter struggles with his own nature, has at last completely conquered, is then left only as pure knowing being, as the undimmed mirror of the world. Nothing can distress or alarm him any more; nothing can any longer move him; for he has cut all the thousand threads of willing which hold us bound to the world, and which as craving, fear, envy, and anger drag us here and there in constant pain. He now looks back calmly and with a smile on the phan-tasmagoria of this world which was once able to move and agonize even his mind, but now stands before him as indifferently as chess-men at the end of a game, or as fancy dress cast off in the morning, the form and figure of which taunted and disquieted us on the car-nival night. Life and its forms merely float before him as a fleeting phenomenon, as a light morning dream to one half-awake, through which reality already

––––––––
*"Bring yourself to be reasonable!" [Tr.]

shines, and which can no longer deceive; and, like this morning dream, they too finally vanish without any violent transition. . . .

However, we must not imagine that, after the denial of the will-to-live has once appeared through knowledge that has become a quieter of the will, such denial no longer wavers or falters, and that we can rest on it as on an inherited property. On the contrary, it must always be achieved afresh by constant struggle. For as the body is the will itself only in the form of objectivity, or as phenomenon in the world as representation, that whole will-to-live exists potentially so long as the body lives, and is always striving to reach actuality and to burn afresh with all its intensity. We therefore find in the lives of saintly persons that peace and bliss we have described, only as the blossom resulting from the constant overcoming of the will; and we see the constant struggle with the will-to-live as the soil from which it shoots up; for on earth no one can have lasting peace. We therefore see the histories of the inner life of saints full of spiritual conflicts, temptations, and desertion from grace, in other words, from that kind of knowledge which, by rendering all motives ineffectual, as a universal quieter silences all willing, gives the deepest peace, and opens the gate to freedom. Therefore we see also those who have once attained to denial of the will, strive with all their might to keep to this path by self-imposed renunciations of every kind, by a penitent and hard way of life, and by looking for what is disagreeable to them; all this in order to suppress the will that is constantly springing up afresh. Finally, therefore, because they already know the value of salvation, their anxious care for the retention of the hard-won blessing, their scruples of conscience in the case of every innocent enjoyment or with every little excitement of their vanity; this is also the last thing to die, the most indestructible, the most active, and the most foolish of all man's inclinations. By the expression *asceticism,* which I have already used so often, I understand in the narrower sense this *deliberate* breaking of the will by refusing the agreeable and looking for the disagreeable, the voluntarily chosen way of life of penance and self-chastisement, for the constant mortification of the will.

Now, if we see this practised by persons who have already attained to denial of the will, in order that they may keep to it, then suffering in general, as it is inflicted by fate, is also a second way . . . of attaining to that denial. Indeed, we may assume that most men can reach it only in this way, and that it is the suffer-

ing personally felt, not the suffering merely known, which most frequently produces complete resignation, often only at the approach of death. For only in the case of a few is mere knowledge sufficient to bring about the denial of the will, the knowledge namely that sees through the *principium individuationis,* first producing perfect goodness of disposition and universal love of mankind, and finally enabling them to recognize as their own all the sufferings of the world. Even in the case of the individual who approaches this point, the tolerable condition of his own person, the flattery of the moment, the allurement of hope, and the satisfaction of the will offering itself again and again, i.e., the satisfaction of desire, are almost invariably a constant obstacle to the denial of the will, and a constant temptation to a renewed affirmation of it. For this reason, all those allurements have in this respect been personified as the devil. Therefore in most cases the will must be broken by the greatest personal suffering before its self-denial appears. We then see the man suddenly retire into himself, after he is brought to the verge of despair through all the stages of increasing affliction with the most violent resistance. We see him know himself and the world, change his whole nature, rise above himself and above all suffering, as if purified and sanctified by it, in inviolable peace, bliss, and sublimity, willingly renounce everything he formerly desired with the greatest vehemence, and gladly welcome death. . . .

In real life we see those unfortunate persons who have to drink to the dregs the greatest measure of suffering, face a shameful, violent, and often painful death on the scaffold with complete mental vigour, after they are deprived of all hope; and very often we see them converted in this way. We should not, of course, assume that there is so great a difference between their character and that of most men as their fate seems to suggest; we have to ascribe the latter for the most part to circumstances; yet they are guilty and, to a considerable degree, bad. But we see many of them converted in the way mentioned, after the appearance of complete hopelessness. They now show actual goodness and purity of disposition, true abhorrence of committing any deed in the least degree wicked or uncharitable. They forgive their enemies, even those through whom they innocently suffered; and not merely in words and from a kind of hypocritical fear of the judges of the nether world, but in reality and with inward earnestness, and with no wish for revenge. Indeed, their suffering and dying in the end become agreeable to them, for the denial of the will-to-live has made its appearance. They often decline the deliverance offered them, and die willingly, peacefully, and blissfully. The last secret of life has revealed itself to them in the excess of pain, the secret, namely, that evil and wickedness, suffering and hatred, the tormented and the tormentor, different as they may appear to knowledge that follows the principle of sufficient reason, are in themselves one, phenomenon of the one will-to-live that objectifies its conflict with itself by means of the *principium individuationis*. They have learned to know both sides in full measure, the wickedness and the evil; and since they ultimately see the identity of the two, they reject them both at the same time; they deny the will-to-live.

. . .

Since all suffering is a mortification and a call to resignation, it has potentially a sanctifying force. By this is explained the fact that great misfortune and deep sorrow in themselves inspire one with a certain awe. But the sufferer becomes wholly an object of reverence to us only when, surveying the course of his life as a chain of sorrows, or mourning a great and incurable pain, he does not really look at the concatenation of circumstances which plunged just his life into mourning; he does not stop at that particular great misfortune that befell him. For up till then, his knowledge still follows the principle of sufficient reason, and clings to the particular phenomenon; he still continues to will life, only not on the conditions that have happened to him. He is really worthy of reverence only when his glance has been raised from the particular to the universal, and when he regards his own suffering merely as an example of the whole and for him; for in an ethical respect he becomes inspired with genius, one case holds good for a thousand, so that the whole of life, conceived as essential suffering, then brings him to resignation.

WORKS BY FRIEDRICH NIETZSCHE

The Birth of Tragedy

I

We will have gained much for the science of esthetics, when once we have perceived not only by logical inference, but by the immediate certainty of intuition, that the continuous development of art is bound up with the duality of the *Apollonian* and the *Dionysian*: in like manner as procreation is dependent on the duality of the sexes, involving perpetual conflicts with only periodically intervening reconciliations. These names we borrow from the Greeks, who disclose to the intelligent observer the profound mysteries of their view of art, not in concepts, but in the impressively clear figures of their world of deities. It is in connection with Apollo and Dionysus, the two Greek deities of art, that we learn that there existed in the Grecian world a profound tension in origin and aims between the art of the sculptor, the Apollonian, and the non-plastic art of music, that of Dionysus. Both of these so heterogeneous tendencies run parallel to each other, for the most part openly at variance and continually inciting each other to new and more powerful births, to perpetuate in them the strife of this antithesis, which is seemingly bridged over by their mutual term "Art"; until at last, by a metaphysical miracle of the Hellenic will, they appear paired with each other; and through this pairing they eventually generate the equally Dionysian and Apollonian artwork of Attic tragedy.

In order to bring these two tendencies within closer range, let us conceive them first of all as the separate artworlds of *dreamland* and *intoxication;* between which physiological phenomena and contrast may be observed analogous to that existing between the Apollonian and the Dionysian. In dreams, according to the conception of Lucretius, the glorious divine figures first appeared to the souls of men; in dreams the great shaper beheld the charming corporeal structure of superhuman beings, and the Hellenic poet, if consulted on the mysteries of poetic inspiration, would likewise have suggested dreams and would have offered an explanation resembling that of Hans Sachs in the Meistersingers:

Mein Freund, das grad' ist Dichters Werk,
dass er sein Träumen deut' un merk'.
Glaubt mir, des Menschen wahrster Wahn
wird ihm im Traume aufgethan:
all' Dichtkunst und Poëterei
ist nichts als Wahrtraum-Deuterei.*

_____

*My friend, just this is the poet's task
His dreams to read and to unmask.

The beautiful appearance of the dream-worlds, in the production of which every man is a perfect artist, is the presupposition of all sculpture, and as we shall see, of an important part of poetry also. We take delight in the immediate apprehension of form: All forms speak to us; there is nothing indifferent, nothing superfluous. But in this dream-reality we also have the sensation that it is nothing more than appearance glimmering through it. Such at least is my experience, and for its frequency, indeed, normality I could adduce many proofs, as also the sayings of the poets. Indeed, the man with philosophic tendencies has a foreboding that this reality in which we live and have our being is an appearance and beneath it another and altogether different reality lies concealed. Schopenhauer actually designates the gift of occasionally regarding men and things as mere phantoms and dream images as the criterion of philosophical ability. Accordingly, the man who is sensitive to art stands in the same relation to the reality of dreams as the philosopher to the reality of existence; he is a close and willing observer, for from these images he reads the meaning of life, and by these processes he trains himself for life. And it is perhaps not only the agreeable and friendly images that he realizes about himself with such perfect understanding: the earnest, the troubled, the dreary, the gloomy, the sudden checks, the tricks of fortune, the uneasy presentiments; in short, the whole "Divine Comedy" of life, and the Inferno, also pass before him; not merely like pictures on the wall—for he too lives and suffers in these scenes—and yet not without that fleeting sensation of appearance. And perhaps many a person will, like myself, recollect that amid the dangers and terrors of dream-life they sometimes tried to check themselves and not without success by calling out "It is a dream! I will dream on!" I have likewise been told of persons capable of continuing the causality of one and the same dream for three and even more successive nights—all of which clearly testifies that our innermost being, the common substratum of all of us, experiences our dreams with deep joy and cheerful acquiescence.

This cheerful acquiescence in the dream-experience has likewise been embodied by the Greeks in their Apollo: For Apollo, as the god of all shaping energies, is also the soothsaying god. He, who (as the etymology of the name indicates) is the "shining one," the deity of light, also rules over the fair appearance of the inner world of fantasies. The higher truth, the perfection of these states in contrast to the only partially intelligible everyday world, ay, the deep consciousness of nature, healing and helping in sleep and dream, is at the same time the symbolic analog of the ability of soothsaying and, in general, of the arts, through which life is made possible and worth living. But also that delicate line, which the dream-image must not overstep—lest it act pathologically (in which case appearance, being reality pure and simple, would impose upon us)—must not be wanting in the picture of Apollo: that measured limitation, that freedom from the wilder emotions, that philosophical calmness of the sculptor god. His eye must be "sunlike," according to his origin; even when it is angry and looks displeased, the sacredness of his beautiful appearance is still there. And so we might apply to Apollo, in an eccentric sense, what Schopenhauer says of the man wrapped in the veil of Mâyâ:* *Welt als Wille und Vorstellung:* "Just as in a stormy sea, limitless in every direction, rising and falling with howling mountainous waves, a sailor sits in a boat and trusts in his frail sailing vessel: so in the midst of a world of sorrows the individual sits quietly supported by and trusting in his *principium individuationis.*" Indeed, we might say of Apollo that in him the unshaken faith in this *principium* and the quiet sitting of the man wrapped therein have received their sublimest expression; and we might even designate Apollo as the glorious divine image of the *principium individuationis,* from out of the gestures and looks of which all the joy and wisdom of "appearance," together with its beauty, speak to us.

In the same work Schopenhauer has described to us the stupendous *awe* which seizes a man, when all of a sudden he is at a loss to account for the cognitive forms of a phenomenon, in that the principle of sufficient reason, in some one of its manifestations, seems to admit of an exception. Add to this awe the blissful ecstasy which rises from the innermost depths of man, ay, of nature, at this same collapse of the *principium*

Trust me, illusion's truths thrice sealed
In dream to man will be revealed.
All verse-craft and poetization
Is but true dreams' interpretation.

---

*Cf. *World and Will as Idea,* 1.455 ff., trans. by Haldane and Kemp.

individuationis, and we shall gain an insight into the being of the *Dionysian,* whose closest analogy is perhaps *intoxication.* It is either under the influence of the narcotic draught, of which the hymns of all primitive men and peoples tell us, or by the powerful approach of spring penetrating all nature with joy, that those Dionysian emotions awake, in the augmentation of which the subjective vanishes to complete self-forgetfulness. So also in the German Middle Ages singing and dancing crowds, ever increasing in number, were borne from place to place under this same Dionysian power. In these St. John's and St. Vitus's dancers we again perceive the Bacchic choruses of the Greeks, with their previous history in Asia Minor as far back as Babylon and the orgiastic Sacæa. There are some, who, from lack of experience or obtuseness, will turn away from such phenomena as "folk-diseases" with a smile of contempt or pity prompted by the consciousness of their own health. Of course, the poor wretches do not divine what a cadaverous-looking and ghastly aspect this very "health" of theirs presents when the glowing life of the Dionysian revellers rushes past them.

Under the charm of the Dionysian not only is the union between one person and another again established, but also estranged, hostile or subjugated nature again celebrates her reconciliation with her lost son, man. Of her own accord earth proffers her gifts, and peacefully the beasts of prey approach from the desert and the rocks. The chariot of Dionysus is covered with flowers and garlands: panthers and tigers pass beneath his yoke. Change Beethoven's "Ode to Joy" into a painting, and, if your imagination be equal to the occasion when the awestruck millions sink into the dust, you will then be able to approach the Dionysian. Now is the slave a free man, now all the stubborn, hostile barriers, which necessity, caprice, or "shameless fashion" have set up between people, are broken down. Now, at the evangel of cosmic harmony, each one feels himself not only united, reconciled, blended with his neighbor, but as one with him, as if the veil of Mâyâ had been torn and were now merely fluttering in tatters before the mysterious Primordial Unity. In song and in dance man exhibits himself as a member of a higher community: he has forgotten how to walk and speak, and is on the point of taking a dancing flight into the air. His gestures speak of enchantment. Even as the animals now talk, and as the earth yields milk and honey, so also something supernatural sounds forth from him. He feels himself a god, he himself now walks about enchanted and elated like the gods whom he saw walking about in his dreams. Man is no longer an artist; he has become a work of art: the artistic power of all nature reveals itself here in the tremors of intoxication with the highest gratification of the Primordial Unity. The noblest clay, the costliest marble, namely man, is here kneaded and cut, and the chisel strokes of the Dionysian artist are accompanied with the cry of the Eleusinian mysteries: "Ihr stürzt nieder, Millionen? Ahnest du den Schöpfer, Welt?" *

. . .

5

This entire antithesis, according to which, as according to some standard of value, Schopenhauer, too, still classifies the arts, the antithesis between the subjective and the objective, is quite out of place in esthetics, inasmuch as the subject, *i.e.,* the desiring individual who furthers his own egoistic ends, can be conceived only as the adversary, not as the origin of art. In so far as the subject is the artist, however, he has already been released from his individual will and has become the medium through which the one existent Subject celebrates his redemption in appearance. For this one thing must above all be clear to us, to our humiliation *and* exaltation, that the entire comedy of art is not at all performed, say, for our betterment and culture, and that we are just as little the true authors of this art-world: Rather, we may assume with regard to ourselves that its true author uses us as images and artistic projections and that we have our highest dignity in our significance as works of art—for only as an *esthetic phenomenon* is existence and the world eternally *justified*—while of course our consciousness of our specific significance hardly differs from the kind of consciousness which the soldiers painted on canvas have of the battle represented there. And so, all our knowledge of art is basically quite illusory because as knowing persons we are not one and the same with the Being who, as the sole author and spectator of this comedy of art, prepares a perpetual entertainment for

---

*Do you bow in the dust, oh millions?
Do you divine your creator?

Cf. Schiller's "Ode to Joy"; and Beethoven, Ninth Symphony.— Tr.

himself. Only in so far as the genius in the act of artistic production coalesces with this primordial artist of the world, does he get a glimpse of the eternal essence of art, for in this state he is, in a marvelous manner, like the weird picture of the fairy tale which can at will turn its eyes and behold itself. He is now at once subject and object; at once poet, actor, and spectator.

Schopenhauer as Educator
from Untimely Meditations

I

When the traveler, who had seen many countries and nations and continents, was asked what common attribute he had found everywhere existing among men, he answered, "They have a tendency to sloth." Many may think that the fuller truth would have been, "They are all timid. They hide themselves behind manners and opinions. Basically, every man knows well enough that he is a unique being, only once on this earth; and by no extraordinary chance will such a marvelously picturesque piece of diversity in unity as he is, ever be put together a second time. He knows this, but hides it like an evil conscience. And why? From fear of his neighbor, who demands the latest conventionalities in him and is wrapped up in them himself. But what is it that forces the man to fear his neighbor, to think and act with his herd, and not seek his own joy? Shyness perhaps, in a few rare cases, but in the majority it is idleness; the "taking things easily," in a word the "tendency to sloth," of which the traveler spoke. He was right; men are more slothful than timid, and their greatest fear is of the burdens that an uncompromising honesty and nakedness of speech and action would lay on them. It is only the artists who hate this lazy wandering in borrowed manners and ill-fitting opinions, and discover the secret of the evil conscience, the truth that each human being is a unique marvel. They show us how in every little movement of his muscles the man is an individual self, and further— as an analytical deduction from his individuality—a beautiful and interesting object, a new and incredible phenomenon (as is every work of nature) that can never become tedious. If the great thinker despises mankind, it is for their laziness; they seem mere in-

different bits of pottery, not worth any commerce or improvement. The man who will not belong to the general mass has only to stop "taking himself easily"; to follow his conscience, which cries out to him, "Be yourself! All that you do and think and desire, is not— you yourself!"

Every youthful soul hears this cry day and night, and quivers to hear it: For she divines the sum of happiness that has been from eternity destined for her if she think of her true deliverance; and toward this happiness she can in no way be helped, so long as she lies in the chains of opinion and of fear. . . .

. . . The wonderful fact of our existing at this present moment of time gives us the greatest encouragement to live after our own rule and measure; so inexplicable is it, that we should be living just today, though there has been an infinite amount of time in which we might have arisen; that we own nothing but a span's length of it, this "today," and must show in it from where and into what we have arisen. We have to answer for our existence to ourselves; and will therefore be our own true pilots and not admit that our being resembles a blind fortuity. One must take a rather impudent and reckless way with the riddle; especially as the key is apt to be lost, however things turn out. Why cling to your bit of earth, or your little business, or listen to what your neighbor says? It is so provincial to bind oneself to views which are no longer binding a couple of hundred miles away. East and West are signs that somebody chalks up in front of us to fool such cowards as we are. "I will make the attempt to gain freedom," says the youthful soul; and will be hindered just because two nations happen to hate each other and go to war, or because there is a sea between two parts of the earth, or a religion is taught in the vicinity that did not exist two thousand years ago. "And this is not you," the soul says. "No one can build you the bridge, over which you must cross the river of life, save yourself alone. . . ."

But how can we "find ourselves" again, and how can man "know himself"? He is a thing obscure and veiled: If the hare has seven skins, man can cast from him seventy times seven and yet will not be able to say "Here you are in truth; this is outer shell no more." Also this digging into one's self, this straight, violent descent into the pit of one's being, is a troublesome and dangerous business to start. A man may easily incur such an injury so that no physician can heal him.

And again, what would be the use, because everything bears witness to our essence—our friendships and enmities, our looks and greetings, our memories and forgetfulnesses, our books and our writing! This is the most effective way: To let the youthful soul look back on life with the question, "What have you up to now truly loved? What has drawn your soul upward, mastered it, and blessed it, too?" Erect these things that you have honored before yourself, and, maybe, they will show you, in their being and their order a law that is the fundamental law of your own self. Compare these objects. Consider how one completes and broadens and transcends and explains another; how they form a ladder on which you have always been climbing to yourself: for your true being lies not deeply hidden in yourself, but an infinite height above you, or at least above that which you commonly take to be yourself. The true educators and molders reveal to you the real groundwork and import of your being, something that in itself cannot be educated, and that in any case is difficult of approach, bound and crippled: your educators can be nothing but your liberators. And that is the secret of all culture: It does not supply artificial limbs, wax noses, or spectacles for the eyes—what could provide such gifts is but a sham of education. But it is rather a liberation, a removal of all the weeds and rubbish and vermin that attack the delicate shoots, the streaming forth of light and warmth, the tender dropping of the night rain. It is the imitation and the adoring of nature when she is as merciful as a mother—her completion, when it deflects before her fierce and ruthless blasts and turns them to good, and draws a veil over all expression of her tragic lack of understanding—for she is a stepmother too, sometimes.

There are other means of "finding ourselves," of coming to ourselves out of the confusion in which we all wander as in a dreary cloud. But I know of no means better than to think about our educators. So I will today take as my theme the hard teacher Arthur Schopenhauer.

. . .

IV

. . . To be honest, it is necessary to become really angry in order that things may be better. The image of Schopenhauer's man can help us here. *Schopenhauer's man*

voluntarily takes upon himself the pain of telling the truth: This pain serves to quench his individual will and makes him ready for the complete transformation of his being, which is the inner meaning of life to realize. This truthfulness in him appears to other men to be an effect of malice for they think the preservation of their inadequacies and pretenses is the first duty of humanity, and anyone who destroys their playthings is merely malicious. They are tempted to cry out to such a man, in Faust's words to Mephistopheles:

> "So to the active and eternal
> Creative force,
> You now oppose the cold fist of the Devil"

[A]nd he who would live according to Schopenhauer would seem to be more like a Mephistopheles than a Faust—that is, to our weak modern eyes, which always discover signs of malice in any negation. But there is a kind of denial and destruction that is the effect of that strong aspiration after holiness and deliverance, which Schopenhauer was the first philosopher to teach our profane and worldly generation. Everything that can be denied deserves to be denied; and real sincerity means the belief in a state of things which cannot be denied or in which there is no lie. The sincere man feels that his activity has a metaphysical meaning. It can only be explained by the laws of a different and a higher life. It is in the deepest sense an affirmation: even if everything that he does seems utterly opposed to the laws of our present life. It must lead therefore to constant suffering; but he knows, as Meister Eckhard did, that "the quickest beast that will carry you to perfection is suffering." Every one, I should think, who has such an ideal before him, must feel a wider sympathy; and he will have a burning desire to become a "Schopenhauer man"—pure and wonderfully patient; on his intellectual side full of a devouring fire and far removed from the cold and contemptuous "neutrality" of the so-called scientific man; so high above any warped and morose outlook on life as to offer himself as the first victim of the truth he has won with a deep consciousness of the sufferings that must spring from his sincerity. His courage will destroy his happiness on earth; he must be an enemy to the men he loves and the institutions in which he grew up; he must spare neither person nor thing; however it may hurt him, he will be misunderstood and thought an ally of forces that he abhors; in his search for righteousness he will seem unrighteous by human standards. But he must comfort himself with the words that his teacher Schopenhauer once used: "A happy life is impossible. The highest thing that man can aspire to is a *heroic* life; such as one that a man lives who is always fighting against unequal odds for the good of others and wins in the end without any thanks. After the battle is over, he stands like the Prince in the *re corvo* of Gozzi, with dignity and nobility in his eyes but turned to stone. His memory remains and will be reverenced as a hero's; his will, that has been mortified all his life by toiling and struggling, by evil payment and ingratitude, is extinguished in Nirvana." Such a heroic life, with its full "mortification," corresponds very little to the paltry ideas of the people who talk most about it and make festivals in memory of great men in the belief that a great man is great in the same way as they are small, either through exercise of his gifts to please himself or by a blind mechanical obedience to this inner force; so that the man who does not possess the gift or feel the compulsion has the same right to be small as the other to be great. But "gift" and "compulsion" are contemptible words, mere means of escape from an inner voice, a slander on him who has listened to the voice—the great man. He least of all will allow himself to be given gifts or compelled to anything: for he knows as well as any smaller man how easily life can be taken and how soft the bed is on which he might lie if he went the pleasant and conventional way with himself and his fellow creatures. All human affairs are organized to distract people from life so that we cease to be aware of life. Now why will he so strongly choose the opposite, namely, to be aware of life and to suffer from it? Because he sees that men will betray himself and that there is a kind of agreement to draw him from his den. He will prick up his ears and gather himself together and say, "I will remain my own." He gradually comes to understand what a fearful decision it is. For he must go down into the depths of existence with a string of curious questions on his lips—"Why am I alive? What lesson do I have to learn from life? How have I become what I am, and why do I suffer from what I am?" He is troubled and sees that no one is troubled in the same way; but rather that the hands of his fellow men are passionately stretched out toward the fantastic drama of the political theater, or they themselves are treading the boards under many disguises—youths, men and graybeards, fathers, citizens, priests, merchants and officials—busy with the comedy they are all playing and never thinking of their own selves. To the question "Why do you live?" they would all immediately answer with pride, "To *become* a good citizen or professor or statesman," and yet they *are* something which can never be changed. And why are they just this? Ah, and why nothing better? The man who only regards his life as a moment in the evolution of a race or a state or a science, and thus thinks he belongs merely to the history of "becoming," has not understood the lesson of existence and must learn it over again. This eternal "becoming something" is a lying puppet show, in which man has forgot himself; it is the distraction that scatters the individual to the four winds, the eternal childish game that the great child time, is playing in front of us—and with us. The heroism of truthfulness lies in ceasing to be the plaything of time. Everything in the process of "becoming" is a hollow sham, contemptible and shallow: man can only find the solution of his riddle in "being" something definite and unchangeable. He begins to test how deep both "becoming" and "being" are rooted in him; and a fearful task is before his soul: to destroy the first and bring all the falsity of things to the light. He wishes to know everything, but not, like Goethe's man, to feed a delicate taste, to take delight, from a safe place, in the multiplicity of existence; he himself is the first sacrifice that he brings. The heroic man does not think of his happiness or misery, his virtues or his vices, or of his being the measure of things; he has no further hopes of himself and will accept the utter consequences of his hopelessness. His strength lies in his ability to forget himself: if he has a thought for himself, it is only to measure the vast distance between himself and his aim and to view what he has left behind himself as so much dross. The old philosophers sought for happiness and truth with all their strength: and there is an evil principle in nature that not one shall find that which he cannot help seeking. But the man who looks for a lie in everything, and becomes a willing friend to unhappiness, shall have a marvelous disillusioning: There hovers near him something unutterable, of which truth and happiness are but idolatrous images born of the night; the earth loses her dragging weight, the events and powers of earth become as a dream, and a gradual clearness widens around him like a summer evening. It is as though the beholder of these things began to awaken, and it had only been the clouds of a passing dream that had been weaving about him. They will at some time disappear; and then it will be day.

V

But I have promised to speak of Schopenhauer, as far as my experience goes, as an *educator,* and it is far from being sufficient to paint the ideal humanity which is the "Platonic idea" in Schopenhauer; especially as my representation is an imperfect one. The most difficult task remains—to say how a new circle of duties may spring from this ideal and how one can reconcile such a transcendent aim with ordinary action; to prove, in short, that the ideal *educates.* One might otherwise think that it is merely the blissful or intoxicating vision of a few rare moments that leaves us afterward the prey of a deeper disappointment. It is certain that the ideal begins to affect us in this way when we come suddenly to distinguish light and darkness, bliss and abhorrence; this is an experience that is as old as ideals themselves. . . .

The deeper minds of all ages have had pity for animals because they suffer from life and have not the power to turn the sting of the suffering against themselves, and understand their being metaphysically. The sight of blind suffering is the spring of the deepest emotion. And in many quarters of the earth men have supposed that the souls of the guilty have entered into beasts and that the blind suffering which at first sight calls for such pity has a clear meaning and purpose to the divine justice—of punishment and atonement. And a heavy punishment it is, to be condemned to live in hunger and need, in the shape of a beast, and to reach no consciousness of one's self in this life. I can think of no harder lot than the wild beast's. He is driven to the forest by the fierce pang of hunger that seldom leaves him at peace; and peace is itself a torment, the surfeit after horrid food, won, maybe, by a deadly fight with other animals. To cling to life, blindly and madly, with no other aim, to be ignorant of the reason, or even the fact, of one's punishment, nay, to thirst after it as if it were a pleasure, with all the perverted desire of a fool, this is what it means to be an animal. If universal nature leads up to man, it is to show us that he is necessary to redeem her from the curse of the beast's life, and that in him

existence can find a mirror of itself wherein life appears, no longer blind, but in its real metaphysical significance. But we should consider where the beast ends and the man begins—the man, the one concern of nature. As long as anyone desires life as a pleasure in itself, he has not raised his eyes above the horizon of the beast; he only desires more consciously what the beast seeks by a blind impulse. It is so with us all, for the greater part of our lives. We do not shake off the beast but are beasts ourselves, suffering we know not what.

But there are moments when we do know; and then the clouds break, and we see how, with the rest of nature, we are straining toward the man, as if it were something that stood high above us. We look around and behind us and fear the sudden rush of light; the beasts are transfigured, and we are too. . . . There are moments when we all know that our most elaborate arrangements are only designed to give us refuge from our real task in life; we wish to hide our heads somewhere, as if our Argus-eyed conscience could not find us out. We are quick to give our hearts to the state or money-making, or social duties, or scientific work, in order to possess them no longer ourselves. We are more willing and instinctive slaves of the hard day's work than mere living requires because it seems to us more necessary not to be in a position to think. The hurry is universal because everyone is fleeing before himself; its concealment is just as universal as we wish to seem contented and hide our wretchedness from the keener eyes; and so there is a common need for a new carillon of words to hang in the temple of life and peal for its noisy festival. . . .

We understand this sometimes, as I say, and stand amazed at the whirl and the rush and the anxiety and all the dream that we call our life; we seem to fear the awakening, and our dreams also become vivid and restless as the awakening draws near. But we feel as well that we are too weak to long endure those intimate moments and that we are not the men to whom universal nature looks as her redeemers. It is something to be able to raise our heads but for a moment and see the stream in which we are sunk so deep. We cannot gain even this transitory moment of awakening by our own strength; we must be lifted up—and who are they that will uplift us?

The sincere men who have cast out the beast, the philosophers, artists and saints. Nature—which never leaps—has made her one leap in creating them; a leap of joy, as she feels herself for the first time at her goal, where she begins to see that she must learn not to have goals above her and that she has played the game of transition too long. The knowledge transfigures her, and there rests on her face the gentle weariness of evening that men call "beauty." Her words after this transfiguration are as a great light shed over existence; and the highest wish that mortals can reach is to listen continually to her voice with ears that hear. If a man think of all that Schopenhauer, for example, must have *heard* in his life, he may well say to himself: "The deaf ears, the feeble understanding and shrunken heart, everything that I call mine, how I despise them! Not to be able to fly but only to flutter one's wings! To look above one's self and have no power to rise! To know the road that leads to the wide vision of the philosopher and to reel back after a few steps! Were there but one day when the great wish might be fulfilled, how gladly would we pay for it with the rest of life! To rise as high as any thinker into the pure icy air of the mountain, where there are no mists and veils, and the inner constitution of things is shown in a stark and piercing clarity! Even by thinking of this the soul becomes infinitely alone; but were its wish fulfilled, did its glance once fall straight as a ray of light on the things below, were shame and anxiety and desire gone forever, one could find no words for its state then, for the mystic and tranquil emotion with which, like the soul of Schopenhauer, it would look down on the monstrous hieroglyphics of existence and the petrified doctrines of "becoming"; not as the brooding night, but as the red and glowing day that streams over the earth. And what a destiny it is only to know enough of the fixity and happiness of the philosopher to feel the complete unfixity and unhappiness of the false philosopher, 'who without hope lives in desire': to know one's self to be the fruit of a tree that is too much in the shade ever to ripen and to see a world of sunshine in front, where one may not go!"

There is enough sorrow here, to make such a man envious and spiteful: But he will turn aside, so that he will not destroy his soul by vain yearning; and will discover a new circle of duties.

I can now give an answer to the question of whether it is possible to approach the great ideal of Schopenhauer's man "by any ordinary activity of our own." In the first place, the new duties are certainly not those of a hermit; they imply rather a vast community, held together not by external forms but by a fundamental idea, namely that of *culture;* though only so far as it can put a single task before each of us—to bring the philosopher, the artist and the saint, within and without us, to the light, and to strive for the completion of nature. For nature needs the artist, as she needs the philosopher, for a metaphysical end, the explanation of herself, through which she may have a clear and sharp picture of what she only saw dimly in the troubled period of transition, and so may reach self-awareness. Goethe, in an arrogant yet profound phrase, showed how all nature's attempts only have value in so far as the artist interprets her stammering words, meets her halfway, and announces what she really means. "I have often said and will often repeat," he exclaims in one place, "that the *causa finalis* of natural and human activity is dramatic poetry. Otherwise, the stuff is of no use at all."

Finally, nature needs the saint. In him the ego has melted away, and the suffering of his life is practically no longer felt as an individual one, but as the spring of the deepest sympathy and intimacy with all living creatures. He sees the wonderful transformation that the comedy of "becoming" never reaches, the attainment at length of the high state of man after which all nature is striving, that she may be delivered from herself. Without doubt, we all stand in close relation to him, as well as to the philosopher and the artist. There are moments, sparks from the clear fire of love, in whose light we understand the word "I" no longer; there is something beyond our being that comes, for those moments, to this side of it; and this is why we long in our hearts for a bridge from here to there. In our ordinary state we can do nothing toward the production of the new redeemer, and so we hate ourselves in this state with a hatred that is the root of the pessimism which Schopenhauer had to teach again to our age, though it is as old as the aspiration for culture. Its root, not its flower; the foundation, not the summit; the beginning of the road, not the end: for we have to learn at some time to hate something else, more universal than our own personality with its wretched limitation, its change and its unrest—and this will be when we shall learn to love something else than we can love now. When we are ourselves received into that high order of philosophers, artists and saints, in this life or a reincarnation of it, a new object for our love and hate will also rise before us. As it is, we have our task and our circle of duties, our hates and our loves. For we know that culture requires us to prepare for the coming of the Schopenhauer man— and this is the "use" we are to make of him—we must know what obstacles there are and strike them from our path; in fact, wage unceasing war against everything that hindered our fulfilment and prevented us from becoming Schopenhauer's men.

VI

It is sometimes harder to agree to a thing than to recognize its truth; many will feel this when they consider the proposition—"Mankind must toil unceasingly to bring forth individual great men: this and nothing else is its task." One would like to apply to society and its ends a fact that holds universally in the animal and plant world; where progress depends only on the higher individual types, which are rarer yet more persistent, complex, and productive. But traditional notions of what the end of society is absolutely bar the way. We can easily understand how in the natural world, where one species passes at some point into a higher one, the aim of their evolution cannot lie in the high level attained by the mass of exemplari or in the exemplars that are most recently developed, but rather in what seem accidental beings produced here and there by favorable circumstances. It should be just as easy to understand that it is the duty of mankind to provide the circumstances favorable to the birth of great redemptive men, simply because mankind can become conscious of its goal. But there is always something to prevent them. They find their ultimate aim in the happiness of all, or the greatest number, or in the expansion of a great commonwealth. A man will very readily decide to sacrifice his life for the state; he will be much slower to respond if an individual, and not a state, ask for the sacrifice. It seems to be unreasonable that one man should exist for the sake of another: "Let it be rather for the sake of every other, or, at any rate, of as many as possible!" O righteous judge! As if it were more reasonable to let the majority decide a question of value and significance! For the problem is "in what way may your life, the individual life, retain the highest value and the deepest significance? And how may it least be squandered?" Only by your living for the good of the rarest and most valuable types, not for that of the major-

ity—who, taken as individuals, are the most worthless types. This way of thinking should be implanted and fostered in the mind of every young person; he should regard himself both as a failed product of nature's handiwork and a testimony to her grand aspirations. "She has done badly," he should say; "but I will do honor to her grand aspirations by helping so that she can do better."

With these thoughts he will enter the circle of culture, which is the child of every man's self-knowledge and dissatisfaction. He will approach and say aloud: "I see something above me, higher and more human than I. Let all help me to reach it as I will help all who know and suffer as I do, so that at last the man may arise who feels his knowledge and love, vision and power, to be complete and boundless, who in his completeness is one with nature, the educator and judge of existence." It is difficult to give anyone this courageous self-awareness because it is impossible to teach love. From love alone the soul gains, not only the clear vision that leads to self-contempt, but also the desire to go beyond itself and seek with all its power a higher self that is yet hidden and to strive upward to it with all its strength. And so he who rests his hope on a future great man receives his first "initiation into culture." The sign of this is shame or vexation at one's self, a hatred of one's own narrowness, a sympathy with the genius that ever raises its head again from our misty wastes, a feeling for all that is struggling into life, the conviction that nature its pressing towards man but repeatedly failing to achieve him, but still producing marvelous starts, forms, and projects, so that the men with whom we live are like the debris of some precious sculptures, which cry out, "Come and help us! Put us together for we long to become complete."

I called this internal condition the "first initiation into culture." I have now to describe the effects of the "second initiation," a task of greater difficulty. It is the passage from the inner life to the criticism of the outer life. The eye must be turned to find in the great world of movement the desire for culture that is known from the immediate experience of the individual; who must use his own strivings and aspirations as the alphabet to interpret those of humanity. He cannot rest here either, but must go higher. Culture demands from him not only that inner experience, not only the criticism of the outer world surrounding him, but action to crown them all, the fight for culture against the influences and conventions and institutions where he cannot find his own aim—the production of genius.

Anyone who can reach the second step will see how extremely rare and imperceptible the knowledge of that end is, though all men busy themselves with culture and expend vast labor in its service. He asks himself in amazement, "Is not such knowledge, after all, absolutely necessary? Can nature be said to attain her end, if men have a false idea about the reason for their own labor?" And anyone who thinks a great deal of nature's unconscious adaptation of means to ends will probably answer at once: "Yes, men may think and speak what they like about their ultimate end, but their blind instinct will tell them the right path." It requires some life experience to be able to contradict this: but he who is convinced of the real aim of culture—the production of true human beings and nothing else—let him consider that amid all the pageantry and ostentation of culture at the present time the conditions for his production are nothing but a continual "battle of the beasts": and he will see that there is great need for a conscious will to take the place of that blind instinct. . . .

Preface
from Human, All Too Human

2

When I found it necessary, I *invented* at one time the "free spirits," to whom this discouragingly encouraging book with the title *Human, All Too Human,* is dedicated. There are no such "free spirits" nor have there been such, but as already said, I then needed them for company to keep me cheerful in the midst of evils. . . . That such free spirits *will be possible* some day, that our Europe *will* have such bold and cheerful spirits among her children of tomorrow and the day after tomorrow, actually and bodily, and not merely, as in my case, as the shadows of a hermit's phantasmagoria—*I* should be the last to doubt that. Already I see them *coming,* slowly, slowly; and perhaps I am doing something to hasten their coming when I describe in advance under what auspices I *see* them originate and upon what paths I *see* them come.

3

One may suppose that a spirit in which the type "free spirit" is to become fully ripe and sweet, has had its decisive event in a *great emancipation,* and that it was all the more fettered previously and apparently bound forever to its corner and pillar. What is it that binds most strongly? What cords are almost unrendable? In people of a lofty and select type it will be their duties; the reverence which is suitable to youth, respect and tenderness for all that is time-honored and worthy, gratitude to the land which bore them, to the hand which led them, to the sanctuary where they learned to adore—their most exalted moments themselves will bind them most effectively, will lay upon them the most enduring obligations. For those who are so bound the great emancipation comes suddenly, like an earthquake; the young soul is all at once convulsed, unloosened, and extricated—it does not itself know what is happening. An impulsion and compulsion sway and conquer it like a command; a will and a wish awaken, to go forth on their course, anywhere, at any cost; a violent, dangerous curiosity about an undiscovered world flames and flares in every sense. "Better to die than live *here,*" says the imperious voice and seduction, and this "here," this "at home" is all that the soul has thus far loved! A sudden fear and suspicion of that which it loved, a flash of disdain for what was called its "duty," a rebellious, arbitrary, volcanically throbbing longing for travel, foreignness, estrangement, coldness, disenchantment, glaciation, a hatred of love, perhaps a sacrilegious clutch and look *backwards* to where it was once adored and loved, perhaps a glow of shame at what it was just doing, and at the same time a rejoicing *that* it was doing it, an intoxicated, internal, exulting thrill which betrays a triumph. A triumph? Over what? Over whom? An enigmatic, questionable, doubtful triumph, but the *first* triumph nevertheless—such evil and painful incidents belong to the history of the great emancipation. It is, at the same time, a disease which may destroy the man, this first outbreak of power and will to self-decision, self-valuation, this will to *free* will; and how much disease is manifested in the wild attempts and eccentricities by which the liberated and emancipated one now seeks to demonstrate his mastery over things! He roves about raging with unsatisfied longing; whatever he captures has to suffer for the dangerous tension of his pride; he tears to pieces whatever attracts him. With a malicious laugh he twirls around whatever he finds veiled or guarded by a sense of shame; he sees how these things look when turned upside down. It is a matter of arbitrariness with him, and pleasure in arbitrariness, if he now perhaps bestows his favor on what previously had a bad repute—if he inquisitively and temptingly haunts what is specially forbidden. In the background of his activities and wanderings—for he is restless and aimless in his course as in a desert—stands the note of interrogation of an increasingly dangerous curiosity. "Cannot *all* valuations be reversed? And is good perhaps evil? And God only an invention and artifice of the devil? Is everything, perhaps, radically false? And if we are the deceived, are we not also deceivers? *Must* we not also be deceivers?" Such thoughts lead and mislead him more and more, onward and away. Solitude encircles and engirdles him, always more threatening, more throttling, more heart-oppressing, that terrible goddess and *mater sæva cupidinum*,* but who knows nowadays what *solitude* is? . . .

6

. . . It may at last happen, under the sudden illuminations of still disturbed and changing health that the enigma of that great emancipation begins to reveal itself to the free, and ever freer, spirit—that enigma which had until now lain obscure, questionable, and almost intangible in his memory. If for a long time he scarcely dared to ask himself, "Why so apart? So alone? Denying everything that I revered? Denying reverence itself? Why this hatred, this suspicion, this severity toward my own virtues?"—he now dares and asks the questions aloud and already hears something like an answer to them—"You should become master over yourself and master also of your own virtues. Formerly *they* were your masters; but they are only entitled to be your tools among other tools. You should obtain power over your pro and con, and learn how to put them forth and withdraw them again in accordance with your higher purpose. You should learn how to take the proper perspective of every valuation—the shifting, distortion, and apparent teleology of the horizons and everything that belongs to

---

*Untamed mother of the passions.

perspective; also the amount of stupidity which opposite values involve, and all the intellectual loss with which every pro and every con has to be paid for. You should learn how much *necessary* injustice there is in every for and against; injustice as inseparable from life and life itself as *conditioned* by perspective and its injustice. Above all you should see clearly where the injustice is always greatest: namely, where life has developed at its most puny, narrow, needy, and most incipient and yet cannot help regarding *itself* as the purpose and standard of things, and for the sake of self-preservation, secretly, basely, and continuously wasting away and calling in question the higher, greater, and richer—you should see clearly the problem of gradation of rank, and how power and right and amplitude of perspective grow up together. You should—" But enough; the free spirit *knows* from now on which "thou shalt" he has obeyed and also what he *can* now *do*; what he only now *may do*. . . .

⌒ *Ennoblement through Degeneration*
from Human, All Too Human

History teaches that the past of a nation that is best preserved is the one in which most men have a sense of community in consequence of the similarity of their accustomed and indisputable principles: in consequence, therefore, of their common faith. Thus strength is afforded by good and thorough customs, thus is learned the subjection of the individual, and strenuousness of character becomes a birth gift and afterward is fostered as a habit. The danger to these communities founded on individuals of strong and similar character is that gradually increasing stupidity through transmission, which follows all stability like its shadow. It is on the more unrestricted, more uncertain and morally weaker individuals that depends the *intellectual progress* of such communities, it is they who attempt all that is new and manifold. Numbers of these perish on account of their weakness, without having achieved any especially visible effect. But generally, particularly when they have descendants, they flare up and from time to time inflict a wound on the stable element of the community. Precisely in this sore and weakened place the community is *inoculated* with something new; but its general strength must be great enough to absorb and assimilate this new thing into its blood. Deviating natures are of the utmost importance wherever there is to be progress. Every wholesale progress must be preceded by a partial weakening. The strongest natures *retain* the type, the weaker ones help it to *develop*. Something similar happens in the case of individuals; a deterioration, a mutilation, even a vice and, above all, a physical or moral loss is seldom without its advantage. For instance, a sickly man in the midst of a warlike and restless race will perhaps have more chance of being alone and thereby growing quieter and wiser, the one-eyed man will possess a stronger eye, the blind man will have a deeper inner sight and will certainly have a keener sense of hearing. In so far it appears to me that the famous struggle for existence is not the only point of view from which an explanation can be given of the progress or strengthening of an individual or a race. Rather must two different things converge: First, the increase of the stabilizing force through common beliefs and feelings; second, the possibility of achieving higher aims through the fact that there are deviating natures and, in consequence, partial weakening and wounding of the stabilizing force; it is precisely the weaker nature, as the more delicate and refined, that makes all progress at all possible. A people that is crumbling and weak in any one part, but as a whole still strong and healthy, is able to absorb the infection of what is new and incorporate it to its advantage. The task of education in a single individual is this: to plant him so firmly and surely that, as a whole, he can no longer be diverted from his path. Then, however, the educator must wound him or else make use of the wounds which fate inflicts, and when pain and need have then arisen, something new and noble can be inoculated into the wounded places. With regard to the state, Machiavelli says that "the form of government is of very small importance, although half-educated people think otherwise. The great aim of statehood should be duration, which outweighs all else, inasmuch as it is more valuable than liberty." It is only with securely founded and guaranteed duration that continual development and ennobling inoculation are at all possible. As a rule, however, authority, the

dangerous companion of all duration, will rise in opposition to this.

from The Joyful Wisdom

I

THE TEACHERS OF THE OBJECT OF EXISTENCE *

Whether I look with a benevolent or an evil eye upon men, I find them always at one problem, each and all of them: to do that which leads to the conservation of the human species. And certainly not out of any sentiment of love for this species, but simply because nothing in them is older, stronger, more inexorable and more unconquerable than that instinct because it is precisely *the essence* of our race and herd. Although we are accustomed easily enough, with our usual shortsightedness, to separate our neighbors precisely into useful and hurtful, into good and evil men, yet when we make a general calculation, and reflect longer on the whole question, we become distrustful of this defining and separating, and finally leave it alone. Even the most hurtful man is still perhaps, in respect to the conservation of the race, the most useful of all; for he conserves in himself, or by his effect on others, impulses without which mankind might long ago have languished or decayed. Hatred, delight in others' misfortune, greed and ambition, and whatever else is called evil, belong to the marvelous economy of the conservation of the race; to be sure a costly, lavish, and on the whole very foolish economy, which has, however, always preserved our race, *as is demonstrated to us.* I no longer know, my dear fellow man and neighbor, if you can at all live to the disadvantage of the race, and therefore, "unreasonably" and "badly"; that which could have injured the race has perhaps died out many millenniums ago, and now belongs to the things which are no longer possible even to God. Indulge your best or your worst desires, and above all, perish! In either case you are

―――――
*The original translation has been edited. Some of the alterations are based on the translation by Walter Kaufmann.

still probably the furtherer and benefactor of mankind in some way or other, and in that respect you may have your panegyrists—and similarly your mockers! But you will never find him who would be quite qualified to mock you as an individual, at your best, who could bring home to your conscience its limitless, buzzing and croaking wretchedness so as to be in accord with truth! To laugh at oneself as one would have to laugh in order to laugh *out of the whole truth*—to do this, the best have not always had enough of the sense of truth, and the most endowed have had far too little genius! There is perhaps still a future even for laughter! When the maxim, "The race is all, the individual is nothing," has incorporated itself in humanity, and when access stands open to everyone at all times to this ultimate emancipation and irresponsibility, perhaps then laughter will have united with wisdom, perhaps then there will be only "joyful wisdom." Meanwhile, it is quite otherwise, meanwhile the comedy of existence has not yet "become conscious" of itself, meanwhile it is still the period of tragedy, the period of morals and religions. What does the ever new appearing of founders of morals and religions, of instigators of struggles for moral valuations, of teachers of remorse of conscience and religious war, imply? What do these heroes on this stage imply? For they have been up to now the heroes of it; all else, though solely visible for the time being, and too close, has served only as preparation for these heroes, whether as machinery and coulisse, or in the role of confidants and valets. (The poets, for example, have always been the valets of some morality or other.) It is obvious that these tragedians also work in the interest of the *species,* though they may believe that they work in the interest of God and as emissaries of God. They also further the life of the species, *in that they further the belief in life.* "It is worthwhile to live," each of them calls out, "there is something of importance in this life; life has something behind it and under it; take care!" That impulse, which rules equally in the noblest and the ignoblest, the impulse to the conservation of the species, breaks forth from time to time as reason and passion of spirit; it has then a brilliant train of motives with it, and tries with all its power to make us forget that fundamentally it is just impulse, instinct, folly and baselessness. Life *should* be loved, *for . . .* ! Man *should* benefit himself and his neighbor, *for . . .* ! And whatever all these *shoulds* and

fors imply, and may imply in the future! In order that what necessarily and always happens by itself and without design, may then appear to be done by design and may appeal to men as reason and ultimate command, for that purpose the ethical instructor comes forward as the teacher of design in existence; for that purpose he devises a second and different existence, and by means of this new mechanism he lifts the old common existence off its old common hinges. No! He does not at all want us to *laugh* at existence, nor even at ourselves—nor at himself; to him an individual is always an individual, something first and last and immense, to him there are no species, no sums, no naughts. However foolish and fanatical his inventions and valuations may be, however much he may misunderstand the course of nature and deny its conditions—and all systems of ethics up to now have been foolish and against nature to such a degree that mankind would have been ruined by any one of them had it got the upper hand, at any rate, every time that "the hero" came upon the stage, something new was attained: The frightful counterpart of laughter, the profound convulsion of many individuals at the thought, "Yes, it is worthwhile to live! Yes, I am worthy to live!" Life, and you, and I, and all of us together became for a while *interesting* to ourselves once more. It is not to be denied that up until now laughter and reason and nature have *in the long run* had the upper hand over all the great teachers of design. In the end the short tragedy always passed over once more into the eternal comedy of existence; the "waves of innumerable laughters"—to use the expression of Aeschylus—must also in the end overcome the greatest of these tragedians. But with all this corrective laughter, human nature has on the whole been changed by the ever new appearance of those teachers of the design of existence; human nature has now an additional requirement, the very requirement of the ever new appearance of such teachers and doctrines of "design." Man has gradually become a visionary animal, who has to fulfil one more condition of existence than the other animals. Man *must* from time to time believe that he knows *why* he exists; his species cannot flourish without periodically trusting in life! Without the belief in *reason in life!* And always from time to time will the human race decree once again that "there is something which really may not be laughed at." And the most clairvoyant philanthropist will add that "not only laughing and joyful wisdom, but also the tragic with all its sublime irrationality, counts among the means and necessities for the conservation of the race!" And consequently! Consequently! Consequently! Do you understand me, oh, my brothers? Do you understand this new law of ebb and flow? We also shall have our time!

. . .

4

THAT WHICH PRESERVES THE SPECIES

The strongest and most evil spirits have up until now advanced mankind the most: they always rekindled the sleeping passions—all orderly arranged society lulls the passions to sleep—they always reawakened the sense of comparison, of contradiction, of delight in the new, the adventurous, the untried; they compelled men to set opinion against opinion, ideal plan against ideal plan. By means of arms, by upsetting boundary markers, by violations of piety most of all: but also by new religions and morals! The same kind of "wickedness" is in every teacher and preacher of the *new*—which makes a conqueror infamous, although it expresses itself more refinedly, and does not immediately set the muscles in motion (and just on that account does not make so infamous!). The new, however, is under all circumstances the *evil*, as that which wants to conquer, which tries to upset the old boundary markers and the old piety; only the old is the good! The good men of every age are those who go to the roots of the old thoughts and bear fruit with them, the agriculturists of the spirit. But every soil becomes finally exhausted, and the plowshare of evil must always come once more. There is at present a fundamentally erroneous theory of morals which is much celebrated, especially in England: according to it the judgments "good" and "evil" are the accumulation of the experiences of that which is "expedient" and "inexpedient"; according to this theory, that which is called good is conservative of the species, what is called evil, however, is detrimental to it. But in reality the evil impulses are in just as high a degree expedient, indispensable, and conserva-tive of the species as the good: only, their function is different.

. . .

26

WHAT IS LIVING?

Living is to continually eliminate from ourselves what wants to die; Living is to be cruel and inexorable towards all that becomes weak and old in ourselves and not only in ourselves. Living means, therefore, to be without piety toward the dying, the wretched and the old? To be continually a murderer? And yet old Moses said: "Thou shalt not kill!"

. . .

110

ORIGIN OF KNOWLEDGE

Throughout immense stretches of time the intellect produced nothing but errors; some of them proved to be useful and preservative of the species: He who fell in with them, or inherited them, waged the battle for himself and his offspring with better success. Those erroneous articles of faith which were successively transmitted by inheritance and have finally become almost the property and stock of the human species are, for example, the following: that there are enduring things, that there are equal things, that there are things, substances, and bodies, that a thing is what it appears, that our will is free, that what is good for me is also good absolutely. It was only very late that the deniers and doubters of such propositions came forward; it was only very late that truth made its appearance as the most impotent form of knowledge. It seemed as if it were impossible to get along with truth, our organism was adapted for the very opposite; all its higher functions, the perceptions of the senses, and in general every kind of sensation, cooperated with those primevally embodied, fundamental errors. Moreover, those propositions became the very standards of knowledge according to which the "true" and the "false" were determined throughout the whole domain of pure logic. The *strength* of conceptions does not, therefore, depend on their degree of truth, but on their antiquity, their embodiment, their character as conditions of life. Where life and knowledge seemed to conflict, there has never been serious contention; denial and doubt have there been regarded as madness. The exceptional thinkers like the Eleatics who, in spite of this, advanced and maintained the antitheses of the natural errors, believed that it was possible also *to live* these counterparts: it was they who devised the sage as the man of immutability, impersonality and universality of intuition, as one and all at the same time, with a special faculty for that reverse kind of knowledge; they were of the belief that their knowledge was at the same time the principle of *life*. To be able to affirm all this, however, they had to *deceive* themselves concerning their own condition; they had to attribute to themselves impersonality and unchanging permanence, they had to mistake the nature of the philosophic individual, deny the force of the impulses in cognition, and conceive of reason generally as an entirely free and self-originating activity; they kept their eyes shut to the fact that they also had reached their doctrines in contradiction to valid methods, or through their longing for repose or for exclusive possession or for domination. The subtler development of sincerity and of scepticism finally made these men impossible; their life also, and their judgments, turned out to be dependent on the primeval impulses and fundamental errors of all sentient beings. The subtler sincerity and scepticism arose wherever two antithetical maxims appeared to be *applicable* to life because both of them were compatible with the fundamental errors: where, therefore, there could be contention concerning a higher or lower degree of *utility* for life, and likewise where new maxims proved to be not necessarily useful, but at least not injurious, as expressions of an intellectual impulse to play a game that was like all games innocent and happy. The human brain was gradually filled with such judgments and convictions; and in this tangled skein arose ferment, strife, and lust for power. Not only utility and delight, but every kind of impulse took part in the struggle for "truths." The intellectual struggle became a business, an attraction, a calling, a duty, an honor: cognizing and striving for the true finally arranged themselves as needs among other needs. From that moment, not only belief and conviction, but also examination, denial, distrust, and contradiction became *forces;* all "evil" instincts were subordinated to knowledge, were placed in its service, and acquired the prestige of the permitted, the honored, the useful, and finally the appearance and innocence of the *good*. Knowledge, thus became a portion of life itself, and as life it became a continually growing power; until finally the cognitions and those primeval, fundamental errors clashed with each other, both as life, both as power, both in the same man. The thinker is now the being in whom the impulse to truth and those life-preserving errors wage their first conflict, now that the impulse to truth has also *proved* itself to be a life-preserving power. In comparison with the importance of this conflict everything else is indifferent; the final question concerning the conditions of life is here raised, and the first attempt is here made to answer it by experiment. How far is truth susceptible of embodiment? That is the question, that is the experiment.

· · ·

116

HERD INSTINCT

Wherever we meet with a morality we find a valuation and order of rank of the human impulses and activities. These valuations and orders of rank are always the expression of the needs of a community or herd: that which is in the first place to *its* advantage— and in the second place and third place—is also the authoritative standard for the worth of every individual. By morality the individual is taught to become a function of the herd and to ascribe to himself value only as a function. As the conditions for the maintenance of one community have been very different from those of another community, there have been very different moralities; and in relation to the future essential transformations of herds and communities, states and societies, one can prophesy that there will still be very divergent moralities. Morality is the herd instinct in the individual.

117

THE HERD'S REMORSE

In the longest and remotest ages of the human race, there was quite a different remorse from that of the present day. At present one only feels responsible for what one intends and for what one does, and we have our pride in ourselves. All our professors of jurisprudence start with this sentiment of individual independence and pleasure, as if the source of right had taken its rise here from the beginning. But throughout the longest period in the life of mankind, there was nothing more terrible to a person than to feel himself independent. To be alone, to feel independent, neither to obey nor to rule, to represent an individual—that was no pleasure to a person then, but a punishment; he was condemned "to be an individual." Freedom of thought was regarded as discomfort personified. While we feel law and regulation as constraint and loss, people formerly regarded egoism as a painful thing, and a veritable evil. For a person to be himself, to value himself according to his own measure and weight, that was then quite distasteful. The inclination to such a thing would have been regarded as madness, for all miseries and terrors were associated with being alone. At that time the "free will" had bad conscience in close proximity to it; and the less independently a person acted, the more the herd instinct, and not his personal character, expressed itself in his conduct, so much the more moral did he esteem himself. All that did injury to the herd, whether the individual had intended it or not, then caused him remorse and his neighbor likewise— indeed the whole herd! It is in this respect that we have most changed our mode of thinking.

118

BENEVOLENCE

Is it virtuous when a cell transforms itself into the function of a stronger cell? It must do so. And is it wicked when the stronger one assimilates the other? It must do so likewise; it is necessary for it has to have abundant indemnity and seeks to regenerate itself. One has therefore to distinguish the instinct of appropriation and the instinct of submission in benevolence, according as the stronger or the weaker feels benevolent. Gladness and desire are united in the stronger person, who wants to transform something to his function: gladness and desire-to-be-needed in the weaker person, who would like to become a function. The former case is essentially pity, a pleasant excitation of the instinct of appropriation at the sight of the weak. It is to be remembered, however, that "strong" and "weak" are relative conceptions.

. . .

125

THE MADMAN

Have you heard of the madman who on a bright morning lit a lantern and ran to the marketplace calling out unceasingly: "I seek God! I seek God!" As there were many people standing about who did not believe in God, he caused a great deal of amusement. "Why! Is he lost?" said one. "Has he strayed away like a child?" said another. "Or does he keep himself hidden? Is he afraid of us? Has he taken a sea voyage? Has he emigrated?" the people cried out laughingly, all in a hubbub. The insane man jumped into their midst and transfixed them with his glances. "Where is God gone?" he called out. "I will tell you! *We have killed him,* you and I! We are all his murderers! But how have we done it? How were we able to drink up the sea? Who gave us the sponge to wipe away the whole horizon? What did we do when we loosened this earth from its sun? How does it now move? How do we move? Away from all suns? Do we not dash on unceasingly? Backwards, sideways, forwards, in all directions? Is there still an above and below? Do we not stray, as through infinite nothingness? Does not empty space breathe upon us? Has it not become colder? Does not night come on continually, darker and darker? Shall we not have to light lanterns in the morning? Do we not hear the noise of the gravediggers who are burying God? Do we not smell the divine putrefaction? For even Gods putrefy! God is dead! God remains dead! And we have killed him! How shall we console ourselves, the most murderous of all murderers? The holiest and the mightiest that the world has ever possessed, has bled to death under our knife. Who will wipe the blood from us? With what water could we cleanse ourselves? What purifications, what sacred games shall we have to devise? Is not the magnitude of this deed too great for us? Shall we not ourselves have to become gods, merely to seem worthy of it? There never was a greater event, and on account of it, all who are born after us belong to a higher history than any other history before!" Here the madman was silent and looked again at his listeners; they also were silent and looked at him in surprise. At last he threw his lantern on the ground, so that it broke in pieces and was extinguished. "I come too early," he then said, "I am not yet at the right time. This prodigious event is still on its way, and is wandering. It has not yet reached men's ears. Lightning and thunder need time, the light of the stars needs time, deeds need time, even after they are done, to be seen and heard. This deed is as yet further from them than the furthest star—*and yet they have done it!*" It is further stated that the madman made his way into different churches on the same day, and there intoned his *Requiem aeternam deo.* When led out and called to account, he always gave the reply: "What are these churches now, if they are not the tombs and monuments of God?"

. . .

276

FOR THE NEW YEAR

I still live, I still think; I must still live, for I must still think. *Sum, ergo cogito: cogito, ergo sum.* Today everyone takes the liberty of expressing his wish and his favorite thought. Well, I also mean to tell what I have wished for myself today, and what thought first crossed my mind this year; a thought which ought to be the basis, the pledge, and the sweetening of all my future life! I want more and more to perceive the necessary characters in things as beautiful: I shall thus be one of those who beautify things. *Amor fati:* Let that be my love from now on! I do not want to wage war with the ugly. I do not want to accuse, I do not want even to accuse the accusers. *Looking aside,* let that be my sole negation! And all in all, to sum up: I wish to be at any time hereafter only a yes-sayer!

. . .

283

PIONEERS

I greet all the signs indicating that a more virile and warlike age is commencing, which will, above all, bring courage again into honor! For it has to prepare the way for a yet higher age, and gather the force which the latter will one day require—the age which will carry heroism into knowledge and *wage war* for the sake of ideas and their consequences. For that end many brave pioneers are now needed who, however, cannot originate out of nothing, and just as little out of the sand and slime of present-day civilization and the culture of great cities: human beings silent, soli-

tary, and resolute, who know how to be content and persistent in invisible activity: human beings who with innate disposition seek in all things that which is *to be overcome* in them: human beings to whom cheerfulness, patience, simplicity, and contempt of the great vanities belong just as much as do magnanimity in victory and indulgence to the trivial vanities of all the vanquished: human beings with an acute and independent judgment regarding all victors and concerning the part which chance has played in the winning of victory and fame: human beings with their own holidays, their own workdays, and their own periods of mourning; accustomed to command with perfect assurance and equally ready, if need be, to obey, proud in the one case as in the other, equally serving their own interests: human beings more imperiled, more productive, more happy! For believe me! The secret of realizing the largest productivity and the greatest enjoyment of existence is *to live dangerously*! Build your cities on the slope of Vesuvius! Send your ships into unexplored seas! Live in war with your equals and with yourselves! Be robbers and spoilers, you knowing ones, as long as you cannot be rulers and possessors! The time will soon pass when you can be satisfied to live like timorous deer concealed in the forests. The pursuit of knowledge will finally stretch out its hand for that which belongs to it: it means to *rule* and *possess,* and you with it!

. . .

290

ONE THING IS NEEDFUL

To "give style" to one's character, that is a grand and a rare art! He who surveys all that his nature presents in its strength and in its weakness, and then fashions it into an ingenious plan, until everything appears artistic and rational, and even the weaknesses enchant the eye—exercises that admirable art. Here there has been a great amount of second nature added, there a portion of first nature has been taken away: in both cases with long exercise and daily labor at the task. Here the ugly, which does not permit of being taken away, has been concealed, there it has been reinterpreted into the sublime. Much of the vague, which refuses to take form, has been reserved and utilized for the perspectives. It is meant to give a hint of the remote and immeasurable. In the end, when the work has been completed, it is revealed how it was the constraint of the same taste that organized and fashioned it in whole and in part: whether the taste was good or bad is of less importance than one thinks—it is sufficient that it was *a single taste*! It will be the strong imperious natures which experience their most refined joy in such constraint, in such confinement and perfection under their own law; the passion of their violent volition lessens at the sight of all disciplined nature, all conquered and ministering nature: even when they have palaces to build and gardens to lay out, it is not to their taste to allow nature to be free. It is the reverse with weak characters who have not power over themselves and *hate* the restriction of style. They feel that if this repugnant constraint were laid upon them, they would necessarily become demeaned under it: they become slaves as soon as they serve; they hate service. Such intellects—they may be intellects of the first rank—are always concerned with fashioning and interpreting themselves and their surroundings as *free* nature—wild, arbitrary, fantastic, disorderly and surprising—and it is well for them to do so because only in this manner can they please themselves! For one thing is needful: namely, that man should *attain* satisfaction with himself; be it but through this or that fable and artifice. It is only then that a man is tolerable to behold. He who is dissatisfied with himself is ever ready to avenge himself on that account. We others will be his victims, if only in having always to endure his ugliness. For the sight of the ugly makes one mean and sad.

· · ·

335

CHEERS FOR PHYSICS!

How many people are there who know how to observe? And among the few who do know, how many observe themselves? "Everyone is farthest from himself"; all the "triers of the reins" know that to their discomfort; and the saying, "Know thyself," in the mouth of a God and spoken to man, is almost a mockery. But that the case of self-observation is so desperate, is attested best of all by the manner in which *almost everybody* talks of the nature of a moral action, that prompt, willing, convinced, loquacious manner, with its look, its smile, and its pleasing eagerness! Everyone seems inclined to say to you: "Why, my dear friend, that is precisely *my* affair! You address yourself with your question to the one person who *is authorized* to answer, for I happen to be wiser with regard to this matter than in anything else. Therefore, when someone decides that *'this is right,'* when he accordingly concludes that *'it must therefore be done,'* and thereupon *does* what he has thus recognized as right and designated as necessary, then the nature of his action is *moral*!" But, my friend, you are talking to me about three actions instead of one: your deciding, for instance, that "this is right," is also an action, could one not judge either morally or immorally? *Why* do you regard this, and just this, as right? "Because my conscience tells me so; conscience never speaks immorally, indeed it determines in the first place what shall be moral!" But why do you *listen* to the voice of your conscience? And how far are you justified in regarding such a judgment as true and infallible? This *belief,* is there no further conscience for it? Do you know nothing of an intellectual conscience? A conscience behind your "conscience"? Your judgment, "this is right," has a previous history in your impulses, your likes and dislikes, your experiences and nonexperiences; "*How* has it originated?" you must ask, and afterward the further question: "*What* really impels me to pay attention to it?" You can listen to its command like a brave soldier who hears the command of his officer. Or like a woman who loves him who commands. Or like a flatterer and coward, afraid of the commander. Or like a blockhead who follows because he has nothing to say to the contrary. In short, you can pay attention to your conscience in a hundred different ways. But *that* you hear this or that judgment as the voice of conscience, consequently, *that* you feel a thing to be right, may have its cause in the fact that you have never thought about your nature, and have blindly accepted from your childhood what has been designated to you as *right,* or in the fact that up to now bread and honors have fallen to your share with what you call your duty: It is "right" to you, because it seems to be *your* "condition of existence" (that you, however, have a *right* to existence seems to you irrefutable!). The *intractability* of your moral judgment might still be just a proof of personal wretchedness or impersonality; your "moral force" might have its source in your obstinacy—or in your incapacity to perceive new ideals! And to be brief: If you had thought more acutely, observed more accurately, and had learned more, you would no longer under all circumstances call this and that your "duty" and your "conscience." The knowledge *how moral judgments have in general always originated* would make you tired of these pathetic words—as you have already grown tired of other pathetic words, for instance "sin," "salvation," and "redemption." And now, my friend, do not talk to me about the categorical imperative! That word tickles my ear, and I must laugh in spite of your presence and your seriousness. In this connection I recollect old Kant who, as a punishment for having *gained possession surreptitiously* of the "thing in itself"—also a very ludicrous affair!—was imposed upon by the categorical imperative and, with that in his heart, *strayed back again* to "God," the "soul," "freedom," and "immortality," like a fox which strays back into its cage. And it had been *his* strength and shrewdness which had *broken open* this cage! What? You admire the categorical imperative in you? This "persistency" of your so-called moral judgment? This absoluteness of the feeling that "as I think on this matter, so must everyone think"? Admire rather your *selfishness!* And the blindness, paltriness, and modesty of your selfishness! For it is selfishness to regard one's own judgment as universal law, and a blind, paltry and modest selfishness besides because it betrays that you have not yet discovered yourself, that you have not yet created for yourself any personal, quite personal ideal. For this could never be the ideal of another, to say nothing of every one! Anyone who still thinks that "each would have to act in this manner in this case," has not yet advanced half a dozen paces in self-knowledge, otherwise he would know that there neither are, nor can be, similar actions; that every action that has been done, has been done in an entirely unique and inimitable manner, and that it will be the same with regard to all future actions; that all precepts of conduct (and even the most esoteric and subtle precepts of all moralities up to the present), apply only to the coarse exterior; that by means of them, indeed, a semblance of equality can be attained, *but only a semblance;* that in outlook and retrospect *every* action is and remains an impenetrable affair; that our opinions of the "good," "noble," and "great" can never be proved by our actions because no action is cognizable; that our opinions, estimates, and tables of values are certainly among the most powerful levers in the mechanism of our actions; that in every single case, nevertheless, the law of their mechanism is untraceable. Let us *confine* ourselves, therefore, to the purification of our opinions and appreciations as well as to the *construction of new tables of value of our own:* we will, however, brood no longer over the "moral worth of our actions"! Yes, my friends! Regarding the whole moral chatter of people about one another, it is time to be disgusted with it! To sit in judgment morally ought to offend our taste! Let us leave this nonsense and this bad taste to those who have nothing else to do, except to drag the past a little further through time, and who live never themselves the present—consequently to the many, to the majority! We, however, *want to become who we are:* the new, the unique, the incomparable, making laws for ourselves and creating ourselves! And for this purpose we must become the best students and discoverers of all the laws and necessities in the world. We must be *physicists* in order to be *creators* in that sense, where before all appreciations and ideals have been based on *ignorance* of physics, or in *contradiction* to it. Therefore, three cheers for physics! And still louder cheers for that which *impels* us toward it—our honesty.

· · ·

341

THE HEAVIEST BURDEN

What if a demon crept after you into your loneliest loneliness some day or night, and said to you: "This life, as you live it at present, and have lived it, you must live it once more, and innumerable times again; and there will be nothing new in it, but every pain and every joy and every thought and every sigh, and all the unspeakably small and great in your life must come to you again, and all in the same series and sequence. And similarly, this spider and this moonlight among the trees, and similarly this moment, and I myself. The eternal hourglass of existence will always be turned once more, and you with it, you speck of dust!" Would you not throw yourself down and gnash your teeth, and curse the demon that so spoke? Or have you once experienced a tremendous moment in which you would answer him: "You are a God, and never did I hear anything so divine!" If that thought acquired power over you as you are, it would transform you, and perhaps crush you. The question with regard to all and everything: "Do you want this once more, and again for innumerable times?" would lie as the heaviest burden upon your activity! Or, how favorably inclined would you have to become to yourself and to life, so as *to long for nothing more ardently* than for this last eternal sanctioning and seal?

342

INCIPIT TRAGÆDIA

When Zarathustra was thirty years old, he left his home and the Lake of Urmi, and went into the mountains. There he enjoyed his spirit and his solitude and for ten years did not weary of it. But at last his heart changed, and rising one morning with the rosy dawn, he went before the sun and spoke to it: "You great star! What would be your happiness if you had not those for whom you shine! For ten years you have climbed here to my cave: you would have wearied of your light and of the journey, had it not been for me, my eagle, and my serpent. But we waited for you every morning, took from you your overflow, and blessed you for it. Behold! I am weary of my wisdom, like the bee that has gathered too much honey; I need outstretched hands to take it. I would rather bestow and distribute, until the wise have once more become joyous in their folly, and the poor happy in their riches. Therefore I must descend into the deep, as you do in the evening, when you go behind the sea and give light to the netherworld, you rich star! Like you I must *go down,* as men say, to whom I shall descend. Bless me then, tranquil eye, that can see even the greatest happiness without envy! Bless the cup that is about to overflow, that the water may flow golden out of it, and carry everywhere the reflection of your bliss! Behold! This cup is again going to empty itself, and Zarathustra is again going to be a man." Thus began Zarathustra's journey down.

343

WHAT OUR CHEERFULNESS SIGNIFIES

The most important of more recent events—that "God is dead," that the belief in the Christian God has become unworthy of belief—already begins to cast its first shadows over Europe. To the few at least whose eye, whose *suspecting* glance, is strong enough and subtle enough for this drama, some sun seems to have set, some old, profound confidence seems to have changed into doubt: our old world must seem to them daily more dark, distrustful, strange, and "old." Mainly, however, one may say that the event is far too great, too remote, too much beyond most people's power of apprehension, for one to suppose that so much as the report of it could have *reached* them; not to speak of many who already knew *what* had taken place, and what must now all collapse because this belief had been undermined, because so much was built upon it, so much rested on it and had become one with it: for example, our entire European morality. This lengthy, vast, and uninterrupted process of crumbling, destruction, ruin and calamity which is now imminent: who has realized it sufficiently today to have to stand up as the teacher and herald of such a tremendous logic of terror, as the prophet of a period of gloom and eclipse, the like of which has probably never taken place on earth before? . . . Even we, the born readers of riddles, who wait on the mountains, posted between today and tomorrow, and encompassed by their contradiction, we, the first and premature children of the coming century, into whose sight especially the shadows which must soon envelop Europe *should* already have come—how is it that even we, without genuine sympathy for this period of gloom, contemplate its advent without any *personal* solicitude or fear? Are we still, perhaps, too much under the *immediate effects* of the event—and are these effects, especially in regards to *ourselves,* perhaps the reverse of what was to be expected—not at all sad and depressing, but rather like a new and indescribable variety of light, happiness, relief, enlivenment, encouragement, and dawning day? . . . In fact, we philosophers and "free spirits" feel ourselves irradiated as by a new dawn by the report that the "old God is dead"; our hearts overflow with gratitude, astonishment, presentiment, and expectation. At last the horizon seems open once more, granting even that it is not bright; our ships can at last put out to sea in face of every danger; every hazard is again permitted to the discerner; the sea, *our* sea, again lies open before us; perhaps never before did such an "open sea" exist.

344

TO WHAT EXTENT EVEN WE ARE STILL PIOUS

It is said with good reason that convictions have no civic rights in the domain of science: it is only when a conviction voluntarily condescends to the modesty of hypothesis, a preliminary standpoint for experiment, or a regulative fiction, that its access to the realm of knowledge, and a certain value can be conceded, always, however, with the restriction that it must remain under police supervision, under the police of our distrust. Regarded more accurately, however, does not this imply that only when a conviction *ceases* to be a conviction can it obtain admission into science? Does not the discipline of the scientific spirit just commence when one no longer harbors any conviction? . . . It is probably so: only, it remains to be asked whether, *in order that this discipline may commence,* it is not necessary that there should already be a conviction, and in fact one so imperative and absolute, that it makes a sacrifice of all other convictions? One sees that science also rests on a belief: there is no science at all "without presuppositions." The question whether *truth* is necessary, must not merely be affirmed beforehand, but must be affirmed to such an extent that the principle, belief, or conviction finds expression, that "there is *nothing more necessary* than truth, and in comparison with it everything else has only secondary value." This absolute will to truth: what is it? Is it the will *not to allow ourselves to be deceived?* Is it the will *not to deceive?* For the will to truth could also be interpreted in this fashion, provided one included under the generalization, "I will not deceive," the special case, "I will not deceive myself." But why not deceive? Why not allow oneself to be deceived? Let it be noted that the reasons for the former eventuality belong to a category quite different from those for the latter: One does not want to be deceived oneself, under the supposition that it is injurious, dangerous, or fatal to be deceived—in this sense science would be a prolonged process of caution, foresight and utility; against which, however, one might reasonably make objections. What? Is not-wishing-to-be-deceived really less injurious, less dangerous, less fatal? What do you know of the character of existence in all its phases to be able to decide whether the greater advantage is on the side of

absolute distrust, or of absolute trustfulness? In case, however, of both being necessary, much trusting *and* much distrusting, where should science then derive the absolute belief, the conviction on which it rests, that truth is more important than anything else, even than every other conviction? This conviction could not have arisen if truth *and* untruth had both continually proved themselves to be useful: as is the case. Thus, the faith in science, which now undeniably exists, cannot have had its origin in such a utilitarian calculation, but rather *in spite of* the fact of the disutility and dangerousness of the "Will to truth," of "truth at all costs," being continually demonstrated. "At all costs." Alas, we understand that sufficiently well, after having sacrificed and slaughtered one belief after another at this altar! Consequently, "Will to truth" does *not* mean, "I will not allow myself to be deceived," but—there is no other alternative—"I will not deceive, not even myself." *And thus we have reached the realm of morality.* For, let one just ask oneself fairly: "Why don't you want to deceive?" especially if it should seem—and it does seem—as if life sought appearance, by which I mean, with a bias toward error, deceit, dissimulation, delusion, self-delusion; and when on the other hand it is a matter of fact that the great tendency of life has always manifested itself on the side of the most unscrupulous πολύτροποι.* Such an intention might perhaps, to express it mildly, be a piece of quixotism, a little enthusiastic craziness; it might also, however, be something worse; namely, a destructive principle, hostile to life. . . . "Will to Truth," might be a concealed Will to Death. Thus the question, Why is there science? leads back to the moral problem: *What in general is the purpose of morality,* if life, nature, and history are "nonmoral"? There is no doubt that the conscientious man in the daring and extreme sense in which he is presupposed by the belief in science, *affirms thereby a world other than* that of life, nature, and history; and in so far as he affirms this "other world," What? Must he not just in that deny its counterpart, this world, *our* world? . . . But what I have in mind will now be understood, that it is always a *metaphysical faith* on which our belief in science rests—and that

---

*Polytropoi; the term means versatile, wily, or well-traveled.

even we knowing ones of today, the godless and anti-metaphysical, still take *our* fire from the conflagration kindled by a belief a millennium old, the Christian belief, which was also the belief of Plato, that God is truth, that the truth is divine. . . . But what if this itself always becomes more untrustworthy, what if nothing any longer proves itself divine, except it be error, blindness, and falsehood; what if God himself turns out to be our most persistent lie?

·   ·   ·

354

THE "GENIUS OF THE SPECIES"

The problem of consciousness (or more correctly: of becoming conscious of something) meets us only when we begin to perceive in what measure we could dispense with it; and it is at the beginning of this perception that we are now placed by physiology and zoology (which have thus required two centuries to overtake the hint thrown out in advance by Leibniz). For we could in fact think, feel, will, and recollect; we could likewise "act" in every sense of the term, and nevertheless nothing of it all need necessarily "come into consciousness" (as one says metaphorically). The whole of life would be possible without its seeing itself as if in a mirror: as in fact even at present the far greater part of our life still goes on without this mirroring and even our thinking, feeling, volitional life as well, however painful this statement may sound to an older philosopher. *What* then is *the purpose* of consciousness generally, when it is mainly *superfluous?*— Now it seems to me, if you will hear my answer and its perhaps extravagant supposition, that the subtlety and strength of consciousness are always in proportion to the *capacity for communication* of a man (or an animal), the capacity for communication in its turn being in proportion to the *necessity for communication:* the latter not to be understood as if precisely the individual himself who is master in the art of communicating and making known his necessities would at the same time have to be most dependent upon others for his necessities. It seems to me, however, to be so, in relation to whole races and successions of generations; where necessity and need have long compelled men to communicate with their fellows and understand one another rapidly and subtly,

a surplus of the power and art of communication is at last acquired, as if it were a fortune which had gradually accumulated, and now waited for an heir to squander it extravagantly (the so-called artists are these heirs, in like manner the orators, preachers, and authors: all of them men who come at the end of a long succession, "late born" always, in the best sense of the word, and as has been said, *squanderers* by their very nature). Granted that this observation is correct, I may proceed further to the conjecture that *consciousness generally has only been developed under the pressure of the necessity for communication;* that from the first it has been necessary and useful only between human beings (especially between those commanding and those obeying), and has only developed in proportion to its utility. Consciousness is properly only a connecting network between human beings, it is only as such that it has had to develop; the recluse and wild-beast species of human beings would not have needed it. The very fact that our actions, thoughts, feelings and motions come within the range of our consciousness—at least a part of them—is the result of a terrible, prolonged "must" ruling man's destiny: as the most endangered animal he *needed* help and protection; he needed his fellows, he was obliged to express his distress, he had to know how to make himself understood—and for all this he needed "consciousness" first of all: he had to "know" himself what he lacked, to "know" how he felt, and to "know" what he thought. For, to repeat it once more, the human being, like every living creature, thinks unceasingly, but does not know it; the thinking which is becoming *conscious of itself* is only the smallest part thereof, we may say, the most superficial part, the worst part: For this conscious thinking alone *is done in words, that is to say, in the symbols for communication,* by means of which the origin of consciousness is revealed. In short, the development of speech and the development of consciousness (not of reason, but of reason becoming self-conscious) go hand in hand. Let it be further accepted that it is not only speech that serves as a bridge between humans, but also the looks, the pressure and the gestures; our becoming conscious of our sense impressions, our power of being able to fix them, and as if to locate them outside of ourselves, has increased in proportion as the necessity has increased for communicating them to *others* by means of signs. The sign-inventing man is at the same time the man who is always more acutely self-conscious; it is only as a social animal that man has learned to become conscious of himself; he is doing so still, and doing so more and more. As is obvious, my idea is that consciousness does not properly belong to the individual existence of man, but rather to the social and gregarious nature in him; that, as follows, it is only in relation to communal and gregarious utility that it is finely developed; and that consequently each of us, in spite of the best intention of *understanding* ourselves as individually as possible, and of "knowing ourselves," will always just call into consciousness not what is individual but average; that our thought itself is continuously as it were *outvoted* by the character of consciousness—by the imperious "genius of the species," and is translated back into the perspective of the herd. Fundamentally our actions are in an incomparable manner altogether personal, unique and absolutely individual—there is no doubt about it; but as soon as we translate them into consciousness, they *do not appear so any longer*. . . . This is the proper phenomenalism and perspectivism as I understand it: the nature of *animal consciousness* involves the notion that the world of which we can become conscious is only a superficial and symbolic world, a generalized and vulgarized world; that everything that becomes conscious *becomes* shallow, meager, relatively stupid just because of this—a generalization, a symbol, a characteristic of the herd; that with the evolving of consciousness there is always combined a great, radical perversion, falsification, superficialization, and generalization. Finally, the growing consciousness is a danger, and whoever lives among the most conscious Europeans knows that even it is a disease. As may be conjectured, it is not the antithesis of subject and object with which I am here concerned: I leave that distinction to the epistemologists who have remained entangled in the toils of grammar (popular metaphysics). It is still less the antithesis of "thing in itself" and phenomenon, for we do not "know" enough to be entitled even *to make such a distinction*. Indeed, we have not any organ at all for *knowing*, or for "truth": we "know" (or believe, or fancy) just as much as may be *of use* in the interest of the human herd, the species; and even what is here called "usefulness" is ultimately only a belief, a fancy, and perhaps precisely the most fatal stupidity by which we shall one day be ruined.

355

THE ORIGIN OF OUR CONCEPTION OF "KNOWLEDGE"

I take this explanation from the street. I heard one of the people saying that "he knew me," so I asked myself: What do the people really understand by knowledge? What do they want when they seek "knowledge"? Nothing more than that which is strange is to be traced back to something *familiar*. And we philosophers, have we really understood *anything more* by knowledge? The known, that is to say, what we are so accustomed to that we no longer marvel at it, the commonplace, any kind of rule to which we are habituated, all and everything in which we know ourselves to be at home: What? Is our need of knowing not just this need for the familiar? The will to discover in everything strange, unusual, or questionable, something which no longer disquiets us? Is it not possible that it should be the *instinct of fear* which enjoins upon us to know? Is it not possible that the rejoicing of the discerner should be just his rejoicing in the regained feeling of security? . . . One philosopher imagined the world "known" when he had traced it back to the "idea": Alas, was it not because the idea was so known, so familiar to him? Because he had so much less fear of the "idea"? Men of knowledge are so easily satisfied! Let us but look at their principles and at their solutions of the riddle of the world with this in mind! When they again find nothing in things, among things, or behind things that is not very well known to us, for example, our multiplication table, or our logic, or our willing and desiring, how happy they immediately are! For "what is familiar is understood": they are unanimous as to that. Even the most circumspect among them think that the familiar is at least *more easily knowable* than the strange; that, for example, it is methodically ordered to proceed outward from the "inner world," from "the facts of consciousness," because it is the world which is *more familiar to us*! Error of errors! The known is the accustomed, and the accustomed is the most difficult of all to "know," that is to say, to perceive as a problem, to perceive as strange, distant, "outside of us." . . . The great certainty of the natural sciences in comparison with psychology and the criticism of the elements of consciousness—*unnatural* sciences, as one might almost be entitled to call them—rests precisely on the fact that they take *what is strange* as their object: while it is almost like something contradictory and absurd *to wish* to take generally what is not strange as an object.

· · ·

370

WHAT IS ROMANTICISM?

It will be remembered perhaps, at least among my friends, that at first I assailed the modern world with some gross errors and exaggerations, but at any rate with *hope* in my heart. I recognized—who knows from what personal experiences—the philosophical pessimism of the nineteenth century as the symptom of a higher power of thought, a more daring courage and a more triumphant *plenitude* of life than had been characteristic of the eighteenth century, the age of Hume, Kant, Condillac, and the sensualists: so that the tragic view of things seemed to me the peculiar *luxury* of our culture, its most precious, noble, and dangerous mode of extravagance; but nevertheless, in view of its overflowing wealth, a *permissible* luxury. In the same way I interpreted for myself German music as the expression of a Dionysian power in the German soul: I thought I heard in it the earthquake by means of which a primeval force that had been imprisoned for ages was finally finding vent, indifferent as to whether all that usually calls itself culture was made to totter. It is obvious that I then misunderstood what constitutes the true character both of philosophical pessimism and of German music; namely, their *Romanticism.*

What is romanticism? Every art and every philosophy may be regarded as a healing and helping appliance in the service of growing, struggling life: they always presuppose suffering and sufferers. But there are two kinds of sufferers: On the one hand those that suffer from *overflowing vitality,* who need Dionysian art and require a tragic view of life and a tragic insight into life; and on the other hand those who suffer from *reduced vitality,* who seek repose, quietness, calm seas, and deliverance from themselves through art or knowledge, or else intoxication, spasm, bewilderment, and madness. All romanticism in art and knowledge responds to the twofold craving of the *latter.* To them Schopenhauer as well as Wagner responded (and responds), to name those most cele-brated and decided romanticists, who were then *misunderstood* by me (*not* however to their disadvantage, as may be reasonably conceded to me). The being richest in overflowing vitality, the Dionysian God and man, may not only allow himself the spectacle of the horrible and questionable, but even the fearful deed itself, and all the luxury of destruction, disorganization and negation. With him evil, senselessness and ugliness seem as if it were licensed, in consequence of the overflowing plenitude of procreative, fructifying power, which can convert every desert into a luxurious orchard. Conversely, the greatest sufferer, the man poorest in vitality, would have most need of mildness, peace and kindliness in thought and action: He would need, if possible, a God who is especially the God of the sick, a "Savior"; similarly he would have need of logic, the abstract intelligibility of existence—for logic soothes and gives confidence. In short, he would need a certain warm, fear-dispelling narrowness and imprisonment within optimistic horizons. In this manner I gradually began to understand Epicurus, the opposite of a Dionysian pessimist—in a similar manner also the "Christian," who in fact is only a type of Epicurean, and like him essentially a romanticist—and my vision has always become keener in tracing that most difficult and insidious of all forms of *backward inference,* in which most mistakes have been made, the inference from the work to its author, from the deed to its doer, from the ideal to him who *needs* it, from every mode of thinking and valuing to the imperative *want* behind it. In regard to all esthetic values I now avail myself of this radical distinction: I ask in every single case, "Has hunger or superabundance become creative here?" At the outset another distinction might seem to recommend itself more—it is far more conspicuous—namely, to have in view whether the desire for rigidity, for perpetuation, for *being* is the cause of the creating, or the desire for destruction, for change, for the new, for the future, for *becoming.* But when looked at more carefully, both these kinds of desire prove themselves ambiguous, and are explicable precisely according to the aforementioned, and as it seems to me, rightly preferred scheme. The desire for *destruction,* change and becoming, may be the expression of overflowing power, pregnant with futurity (my *terminus* for this is of course the word "Dionysian"); but it may also be the hatred of the ill-constituted, destitute and unfortunate, which destroys, and *must* destroy, because the enduring, yes, all that endures, in fact all being, excites and provokes it. To understand this emotion we have but to look closely at our anarchists. The will to *immortalize* requires equally a double interpretation. It may on the one hand proceed from gratitude and love: art of this origin will always be an art of apotheosis, perhaps dithyrambic, as with Rubens, mocking divinely, as with Hafiz, or clear and kindhearted as with Goethe, and spreading a Homeric brightness and glory over everything (in this case I speak of *Apollonian* art). It may also, however, be the tyrannical will of a sorely suffering, struggling or tortured being, who would like to stamp his most personal, individual and narrow characteristics, the very idiosyncrasy of his suffering, as an obligatory law and constraint on others; who takes revenge on all things, in that he imprints, enforces and brands *his* image, the image of *his* torture, upon them. The latter is *romantic pessimism* in its most extreme form, whether it be as Schopenhauerian philosophy of will, or as Wagnerian music: romantic pessimism, the last *great* event in the destiny of our civilization. (That there *may be* quite a different kind of pessimism, a classical pessimism—this presentiment and vision belongs to me, as something inseparable from me, as my *own* and my *quintessence;* only that the word "classical" is repugnant to my ears, it has become far too worn, too indefinite and indistinguishable. I call that pessimism of the future—for it is coming! I see it coming! *Dionysian* pessimism.)

. . .

374

OUR NEW "INFINITE"

How far the perspective character of existence extends, or whether it has any other character at all, whether an existence without explanation, without "sense" does not just become "nonsense," whether, on the other hand, all existence is not essentially engaged in *interpretation*—these questions, as is right and proper, cannot be determined even by the most diligent and severely conscientious analysis and self-examination of the intellect because in this analysis the human intellect cannot avoid seeing itself in its perspective forms and *only* in them. We cannot see around our corner: it is hopeless curiosity to want to know what other modes of intellect and perspective there *might* be: For example, whether any kind of

being could perceive time backwards, or alternately forwards and backwards (by which another direction of life and another conception of cause and effect would be given). But I think that we are today at least far from the ludicrous immodesty of decreeing from our nook that there *can* only be legitimate perspectives from that nook. The world, on the contrary, has once more become "infinite" to us: in so far we cannot dismiss the possibility that it *contains infinite interpretations.* Once more the great horror seizes us—but who would desire immediately to deify once more *this* monster of an unknown world in the old fashion? And perhaps worship *the* unknown thing as *the* "unknown person" in future? Ah! There are too many *ungodly* possibilities of interpretation comprised in this unknown, too much devilment, stupidity and folly of interpretation—our own human, all too human interpretation itself, which we know.

. . .

From Thus Spoke Zarathustra

ZARATHUSTRA'S PROLOGUE*

1

When Zarathustra was thirty years old, he left his home and the lake of his home and went into the mountains. There he enjoyed his spirit and his solitude and for ten years did not tire of it. But at last his heart changed, and rising one morning with the rosy dawn, he went before the sun, and spoke this to it:

You great star! What would your happiness be if you had no one to shine for!

For ten years you have climbed to my cave; you would have tired of your light and of the journey, had it not been for me, my eagle, and my serpent.

But we awaited you every morning, took from you your overflow, and blessed you for it.

Behold! I am weary of my wisdom, like the bee that has gathered too much honey; I need hands outstretched to take it.

I would like to bestow and distribute until the wise have once more become joyful in their folly, and the poor happy in their riches.

---

*The translation has been altered. Some of the changes were suggested by the translation by Walter Kaufmann.

Therefore must I descend into the deep: as you do in the evening, when you go behind the sea and give light also to the netherworld, you exuberant star!

Like you must I *go under,* as men say, to whom I shall descend.

Bless me, then, you tranquil eye that can behold even the greatest happiness without envy!

Bless the cup that is about to overflow, that the water may flow golden out of it and carry everywhere the reflection of your bliss!

Behold! This cup is again going to empty itself, and Zarathustra is again going to become a man.

Thus began Zarathustra's descent.

2

Zarathustra went down the mountain alone, no one meeting him. When he entered the forest, however, there suddenly stood before him an old man, who had left his holy cot to look for roots. And thus spoke the old man to Zarathustra:

"This wanderer is no stranger to me: many years ago he passed by. Zarathustra he was called; but he has changed.

Then you carried your ashes into the mountains: will you now carry your fire into the valleys? Do you not fear the incendiary's doom?

Yes, I recognize Zarathustra. Pure is his eye, and no loathing lurks about his mouth. He walks like a dancer, does he not?

Changed is Zarathustra; a child has Zarathustra become; an awakened one is Zarathustra: what will you do in the land of the sleepers?

As in the sea you have lived in solitude, and it has brought you forth. Alas, will you now go ashore? Alas, will you drag your own body?"

Zarathustra answered: "I love mankind."

"Why," said the saint, "did I go into the forest and the desert? Was it not because I loved men far too much?

Now I love God; men, I do not love. Man is a thing too imperfect for me. To love man would be fatal to me."

Zarathustra answered: "What, did I speak of love? I am bringing gifts to men."

"Give them nothing," said the saint. "Take rather part of their load and carry it along with them—that will be most agreeable to them: if only it be agreeable to you!

If, however, you wish to give them something, give them no more than alms, and let them beg for it!"

"No," replied Zarathustra, "I give no alms. I am not poor enough for that."

The saint laughed at Zarathustra, and spoke thus: "Then see to it that they accept your treasures! They are distrustful of anchorites and do not believe that we come with gifts.

The fall of our footsteps rings too hollow through their streets; just as at night, when they are in bed and hear a man going about long before sunrise, so they ask themselves about us: Where is the thief going?

Go not to men, but stay in the forest! Go rather to the animals! Why not be like me—a bear among bears, a bird among birds?"

"And what does the saint do in the forest?" asked Zarathustra.

The saint answered: "I make hymns and sing them; and in making hymns I laugh and weep and mumble: thus do I praise God.

With singing, weeping, laughing, and mumbling do I praise the God who is my God. But what do you bring us as a gift?"

When Zarathustra heard these words, he bowed to the saint and said: "What could I have to give you! Let me instead hurry away lest I take something away from you!" And thus they parted from one another, the old man and Zarathustra, laughing like schoolboys.

When Zarathustra was alone, however, he said to his heart: "Could it be possible! This old saint in the forest has not yet heard that *God is dead*!"

3

When Zarathustra arrived at the nearest town next to the forest, he found many people assembled in the marketplace for it had been announced that a tightrope walker would give a performance. And Zarathustra spoke thus to the people:

I teach you the Übermensch.* Man is something that is to be surpassed. What have you done to surpass man?

All beings thus far have created something beyond themselves: Do you want to be the ebb of that great

---

*This term has been translated in various ways, including as *superman* and *overman*.

tide, and even return to beasts rather than surpass man?

What is the ape to man? A laughingstock, a thing of shame. And just the same shall man be to the Übermensch: a laughingstock, a thing of shame.

You have made your way from the worm to man, and much within you is still worm. Once you were apes, and even now man is more of an ape than any of the apes.

Even the wisest among you is only a disharmony and hybrid of plant and phantom. But do I bid you to become phantoms or plants?

Behold, I teach you the Übermensch!

The Übermensch is the meaning of the earth. Let your will say: The Übermensch *shall be* the meaning of the earth!

I implore you, my brethren, *remain true to the earth,* and do not believe those who speak to you of supernatural hopes! They are poisoners, whether they know it or not.

Despisers of life are they, decaying ones and poisoned ones themselves, of whom the earth is weary: so away with them!

Once blasphemy against God was the greatest blasphemy; but God died, and with God died those blasphemers. To blaspheme the earth is now the worst sin, and to rate the heart of the unknowable higher than the meaning of the earth!

Once the soul looked contemptuously on the body, and then that contempt was the supreme thing: The soul wished the body meager, ghastly, and famished. Thus it thought to escape from the body and the earth.

Oh, that soul was itself meager, ghastly, and famished; and cruelty was the delight of that soul!

But you, my brothers, tell me: What does your body say about your soul? Is your soul not poverty and pollution and wretched self-complacency?

Indeed, a polluted stream is man. One must be a sea to receive a polluted stream without becoming impure.

Behold, I give you the Übermensch. He is that sea; in him can your great contempt be submerged.

What is the greatest thing you can experience? It is the hour of great contempt. The hour in which even your happiness becomes loathsome to you, as well as your reason and virtue.

The hour when you say: "What good is my happiness! It is poverty and pollution and wretched self-complacency. But my happiness should justify existence itself!"

The hour when you say: "What good is my reason! Does it long for knowledge as the lion for his food? It is poverty and pollution and wretched self-complacency!"

The hour when you say: "What good is my virtue! As it has not yet made me passionate. How weary I am of my good and my evil! It is all poverty and pollution and wretched self-complacency!"

The hour when you say: "What good is my justice! I do not see that I am flames and fuel. The just, however, are flames and fuel!"

The hour when we say: "What good is my pity! Is not pity the cross on which he is nailed who loves man? But my pity is not a crucifixion."

Have you ever spoken thus? Have you ever cried thus? Ah! If only I had heard you crying thus!

It is not your sin, it is your self-satisfaction that cries to heaven; your sparingness even in sin cries to heaven!

Where is the lightning to lick you with its tongue? Where is the frenzy with which you should be inoculated?

Behold, I give you the Übermensch. He is that lightning, he is that frenzy!

When Zarathustra had thus spoken, one of the people called out: "We have now heard enough of the tightrope walker; it is time now for us to see him!" And all the people laughed at Zarathustra. But the tightrope walker, who thought the words applied to him, began his performance.

4

Zarathustra, however, looked at the people and wondered. Then he spoke thus:

Man is a rope stretched between the animal and the Übermensch—a rope over an abyss.

A dangerous crossing, a dangerous wayfaring, a dangerous looking back, a dangerous trembling and halting.

What is great in man is that he is a bridge and not a goal. What is lovable in man is that he is an *over going* and a *going under.*

I love those who know not how to live except by going under, for they cross over.

I love the great despisers because they are the great adorers and arrows of longing for the other shore.

I love those who do not first seek a reason beyond the stars for going under and being sacrifices but sacrifice themselves to the earth that the earth of the Übermensch may later arrive.

I love him who lives in order to know and who seeks in order to know that the Übermensch may live from now on. Thus he wishes to go under.

I love him who labors and invents so that he may build the house for the Übermensch and may prepare for him earth, animal, and plant; for thus he wishes to go under.

I love him who loves his virtue for virtue is the will to go under, and an arrow of longing.

I love him who reserves no share of spirit for himself, but wants to be wholly the spirit of his virtue; thus he walks as spirit over the bridge.

I love him who makes his virtue his inclination and destiny; thus, for the sake of his virtue, he is willing to live on or live no more.

I love him who desires not too many virtues. One virtue is more virtue than two because it is more of a knot for one's destiny to cling to.

I love him whose soul is lavish, who wants no thanks and returns no thanks; for he always bestows and desires not to keep for himself.

I love him who is ashamed when the dice fall in his favor, and who then asks: "Am I a dishonest player?" for he is willing to perish.

I love him who scatters golden words before his deeds and always does more than he promises; for he wishes to go under.

I love him who justifies the future ones and redeems the past ones; for he is willing to perish through the present ones.

I love him who chastens his God because he loves his God; for he must perish through the wrath of his God.

I love him whose soul is deep even in the wounding, and may perish through a small matter; thus he goes willingly over the bridge.

I love him whose soul is so overfull that he forgets himself, and all things are in him; thus all things become his going under.

I love him who has a free spirit and a free heart, thus is his head only the bowels of his heart; his heart, however, causes him to go under.

I love all who are like heavy drops falling one by one out of the dark cloud that lowereth over man; they herald the coming of the lightning, and perish as heralds.

Behold, I am a herald of the lightning, and a heavy drop out of the cloud. The lightning, however, is the *Übermensch.*

5

When Zarathustra had spoken these words, he again looked at the people and was silent. "There they stand," he said to his heart, "There they laugh. They understand me not; I am not the mouth for these ears.

Must one first batter their ears that they may learn to hear with their eyes? Must one clatter like kettledrums and penitential preachers? Or do they only believe the stammerer?

They have something of which they are proud. What do they call it, that which makes them proud? Culture, they call it; it distinguishes them from the goatherds.

They dislike, therefore, to hear of 'contempt' of themselves. So I will appeal to their pride.

I will speak unto them of the most contemptible thing: that, however, is *the last man!*"

And thus spoke Zarathustra to the people:

It is time for man to set his goal. It is time for man to plant the seed of his highest hope.

His soil is still rich enough for it. But that soil will one day be poor and exhausted, and no lofty tree will any longer be able to grow on it.

Alas! There comes the time when man will no longer launch the arrow of his longing beyond man—and the string of his bow will have unlearned to whizz!

I tell you: one must still have chaos in oneself to give birth to a dancing star. I tell you: you still have chaos in you.

Alas! There comes the time when man will no longer give birth to a star. Alas! There comes the time of the most despicable man, who can no longer despise himself.

Behold! I show you *the last man.*

"What is love? What is creation? What is longing? What is a star?" so asks the last man and blinks.

The earth has then become small, and on it there hops the last man who makes everything small. His species is ineradicable like that of the flea; the last man lives longest.

"We have created happiness," say the last men, who then blink.

They have left the regions where it is hard to live for they need warmth. One still loves one's neighbor and rubs against him for one needs warmth.

They consider it sinful to become ill and suspicious: they walk warily. He is a fool who still stumbles over stones or men!

A little poison now and then; that makes pleasant dreams. And much poison at last for a pleasant death.

One still works, for work is a pastime. But one is careful lest the pastime should hurt one.

One no longer becomes poor or rich; both are too burdensome. Who still wants to rule? Who still wants to obey? Both are too burdensome.

No shepherd and one herd! Every one wants the same; every one is equal. He who has other sentiments goes voluntarily into the madhouse.

"Formerly all the world was insane," say the subtlest of them, who then blink.

They are clever and know all that has happened: so there is no end to their raillery. People still quarrel but are soon reconciled, otherwise it upsets their stomachs.

They have their little pleasures for the day and their little pleasures for the night, but they have a regard for health.

"We have discovered happiness," say the last men, who then blink.

And here ended the first discourse of Zarathustra, which is also called "The Prologue"; for at this point the shouting and mirth of the multitude interrupted him. "Give us this last man, O Zarathustra," they called out. "Make us into these last men! Then we will make a present of the Übermensch for you!" And all the people exulted and smacked their lips. Zarathustra, however, turned sad and said to his heart:

"They understand me not: I am not the mouth for these ears.

Too long, perhaps, have I lived in the mountains; too much have I listened to the brooks and trees. Now do I speak to them as to the goatherds.

Calm is my soul and clear like the mountains in the morning. But they think me cold and a mocker with terrible jests.

And now they look at me and laugh; and while they laugh they hate me too. There is ice in their laughter."

6

Then, however, something happened which made every mouth mute and every eye fixed. In the meantime, of course, the tightrope walker had commenced his performance. He had come out at a little door and was going along the rope which was stretched between two towers so that it hung above the marketplace and the people. When he was just midway across, the little door opened once more, and a gaudily-dressed fellow like a buffoon sprang out and went rapidly after the first one. "Go on, halt-foot," cried his frightful voice, "Go on, lazybones, interloper, sallow face! Lest I tickle you with my heel! What are you doing here between the towers? In the tower is the place for you; you should be locked up; to one better than yourself you block the way!" And with every word he came nearer and nearer the first one. When, however, he was but a step behind, there happened the frightful thing which made every mouth mute and every eye fixed: He uttered a yell like a devil and jumped over the other who was in his way. The latter, however, when he thus saw his rival triumph, lost at the same time his head and his footing on the rope; he threw his pole away and shot downward faster than it, like an eddy of arms and legs into the depth. The marketplace and the people were like the sea when the storm comes on: They all flew apart and in disorder, especially where the body was about to fall.

Zarathustra, however, remained standing, and just beside him fell the body, badly injured and disfigured, but not yet dead. After a while consciousness returned to the shattered man, and he saw Zarathustra kneeling beside him. "What are you doing there?" said he at last, "I knew long ago that the devil would trip me up. Now he drags me to hell. Will you stop him?"

"On mine honor, my friend," answered Zarathustra, "there is nothing of all that about which you speak. There is no devil and no hell. Your soul will be dead even sooner than your body. Fear, therefore, nothing any more!"

The man looked up distrustfully. "If you speak the truth," said he, "I lose nothing when I lose my life. I am not much more than an animal which has been taught to dance by blows and scanty fare."

"Not at all," said Zarathustra, "you have made danger your calling; in that there is nothing contemptible. Now you perish by your calling. Therefore, I will bury you with my own hands."

When Zarathustra had said this, the dying one did not reply further, but he moved his hand as if he sought the hand of Zarathustra in gratitude.

7

Meanwhile the evening came on, and the market-place became veiled in gloom. Then the people dispersed for even curiosity and terror become fatigued. Zarathustra, however, still sat beside the dead man on the ground absorbed in thought; so he forgot the time. But at last it became night, and a cold wind blew upon the lonely one. Then arose Zarathustra and said to his heart:

Indeed, a fine catch of fish has Zarathustra made today! Not a man has he caught, but a corpse.

Somber is human life and as yet without meaning: a buffoon may be fatal to it.

I want to teach men the meaning of their existence, which is the Übermensch, the lightning out of the dark cloud of man.

But I am still far from them, and my sense does not speak to their senses. To men I am still something between a fool and a corpse.

Gloomy is the night, gloomy are the ways of Zarathustra. Come, cold and stiff companion! I carry you to the place where I shall bury you with my own hands.

8

When Zarathustra had said this to his heart, he put the corpse upon his shoulders and set out on his way. He had not yet gone a hundred steps, when there stole a man up to him and whispered in his ear—and Behold! he that spoke was the buffoon from the tower. "Leave this town, O Zarathustra," said he, "there are too many here who hate you. The good and just hate you, and call you their enemy and despise you; the true believers hate you, and call you a danger to the multitude. It was your good fortune to be laughed at; and indeed you spoke like a buffoon. It was your good fortune to associate with the dead dog; by so humiliating yourself you have saved your life today. Depart, however, from this town, or tomorrow I shall jump over you, a living man over a dead one." And

when he had said this, the buffoon vanished; Zarathustra, however, went on through the dark streets.

At the gate of the town the gravediggers met him: they shone their torch on his face, and, recognizing Zarathustra, they sorely derided him. "Zarathustra is carrying away the dead dog: a fine thing that Zarathustra has become a gravedigger! For our hands are too cleanly for that roast. Will Zarathustra steal the bite from the devil? Well then, good luck to the repast! If only the devil is not a better thief than Zarathustra! He will steal them both, he will eat them both!" And they laughed among themselves, and put their heads together.

Zarathustra made no answer to that, but went on his way. When he had gone on for two hours, past forests and swamps, he had heard too much of the hungry howling of the wolves, and he himself became hungry. So he stopped at a lonely house in which a light was burning.

"Hunger attacks me," said Zarathustra, "like a robber. Among forests and swamps my hunger attacks me late in the night.

"My hunger is capricious. Often it comes to me only after a repast, and all day it has failed to come. Where has it been?"

And thereupon Zarathustra knocked at the door of the house. An old man appeared who carried a light and asked: "Who comes to me and my bad sleep?"

"A living man and a dead one," said Zarathustra. "Give me something to eat and drink. I forgot it during the day. He that feeds the hungry refreshes his own soul, so says wisdom."

The old man withdrew but came back immediately and offered Zarathustra bread and wine. "This is a bad area for the hungry," said he. "That is why I live here. Animal and man come to me, the anchorite. But ask your companion to eat and drink also; he is wearier than you." Zarathustra answered: "My companion is dead; I shall hardly be able to persuade him to eat." "That does not concern me," said the old man sullenly; "he that knocks at my door must take what I offer him. Eat, and leave!"

Afterwards, Zarathustra again went on for two hours, trusting to the path and the light of the stars; for he was an experienced nightwalker and liked to look into the face of all that slept. When the morning dawned, however, Zarathustra found himself in a thick forest, and no path was visible any longer. He then put the dead man in a hollow tree at his head—for he wanted to protect him from the wolves—and laid himself down on the ground and moss. And immediately he fell asleep, tired in body, but with a tranquil soul.

9

Long slept Zarathustra; and not only the rosy dawn passed over his head, but also the morning. At last, however, his eyes opened, and amazedly he gazed into the forest and the stillness, amazedly he gazed into himself. Then he arose quickly, like a seafarer who all at once saw the land; and he shouted for joy for he saw a new truth. And he spoke thus to his heart:

A light has dawned upon me: I need companions—living ones; not dead companions and corpses, which I carry with me where I will.

But I need living companions, who will follow me because they want to follow themselves where I want.

A light has dawned upon me. Not to the people is Zarathustra to speak, but to companions! Zarathustra shall not be the herd's shepherd and hound!

To allure many from the herd, for that purpose have I come. The people and the herd must be angry with me. A robber shall Zarathustra be called by the shepherds.

Shepherds, I say, but they call themselves the good and just. Shepherds, I say, but they call themselves the believers in the true faith.

Behold the good and just! Whom do they hate most? He who breaks up their tables of values, the breaker, the lawbreaker: he, however, is the creator.

Behold the believers of all beliefs! Whom do they hate most? Him who breaks up their tables of values, the breaker, the lawbreaker: he, however, is the creator.

Companions, the creator seeks, not corpses—and not herds or believers either. Fellow creators the creator seeks—those who engrave new values on new tables.

Companions, the creator seeks, and fellow reapers; for everything is ripe for the harvest with him. But he lacks the hundred sickles: so he plucks the ears of corn and is vexed.

The creator seeks companions who know how to whet their sickles. Destroyers, will they be called, and

despisers of good and evil. But they are the reapers and rejoicers.

Fellow creators, Zarathustra seeks; fellow reapers and fellow rejoicers; Zarathustra seeks: what has he to do with herds and herdsmen and corpses!

And you, my first companion, rest in peace! Well have I buried you in your hollow tree; well have I hid you from the wolves.

But I part from you; the time has arrived. Between rosy dawn and rosy dawn there came to me a new truth.

I am not to be a herdsman; I am not to be a grave-digger. No more will I discourse to the people; for the last time have I spoken to the dead.

With the creators, the reapers, and the rejoicers will I associate; the rainbow will I show them, and all the stairs to the Übermensch.

To the lone dwellers will I sing my song, and to the paired dwellers; and to him who still has ears for the unheard will I make the heart heavy with my happiness.

I make for my goal, I follow my course; over the loitering and tardy will I leap. Thus let my ongoing be their going under!

10

This had Zarathustra said to his heart when the sun stood at noon. Then he looked inquiringly aloft—for he heard above him the sharp call of a bird. And behold! An eagle swept through the air in wide circles and on it hung a serpent, not like a prey, but like a friend; for it kept itself coiled around the eagle's neck.

"They are my animals," said Zarathustra, and he rejoiced in his heart.

"The proudest animal under the sun, and the wisest animal under the sun; they have come out to reconnoiter.

They want to know whether Zarathustra still lives. Indeed do I still live?

More dangerous have I found it among men than among animals. Along dangerous paths Zarathustra goes. Let my animals lead me!"

When Zarathustra had said this, he remembered the words of the saint in the forest. Then he sighed and spoke thus to his heart:

"If only I were wiser! If only I were wise from the very heart, like my serpent!

But I am asking the impossible. Therefore do I ask my pride to go always with my wisdom!

And if my wisdom should some day forsake me:—Alas! It loves to fly away—may my pride then fly with my folly!"

Thus Zarathustra began to go under.

FIRST PART

The Three Metamorphoses

Three metamorphoses of the spirit do I describe to you: How the spirit becomes a camel, the camel a lion, and the lion at last a child.

Many heavy things are there for the spirit, the strong load-bearing spirit in which reverence dwells: for its strength demands the heavy and the difficult.

What is heavy? So asks the load-bearing spirit; then it kneels down like the camel and wants to be well laden.

What is the heaviest thing, heroes? asks the load-bearing spirit, that I may take it upon myself and rejoice in my strength.

Is it not this: To humiliate oneself in order to mortify one's pride? To exhibit one's folly in order to mock at one's wisdom?

Or is it this: To desert our cause when it celebrates its triumph? To ascend high mountains to tempt the tempter?

Or is it this: To feed on the acorns and grass of knowledge and for the sake of truth to suffer hunger of soul?

Or is it this: To be sick and dismiss comforters and make friends of the deaf, who never hear your requests?

Or is it this: To go into foul water when it is the water of truth and not repulse cold frogs and hot toads?

Or is it this: To love whose who despise us and give one's hand to the phantom that wants to frighten us?

All these heaviest things the load-bearing spirit takes upon itself: and like the camel, which, when laden, hastens into the desert, so hastens the spirit into its desert.

But in the loneliest desert occurs the second metamorphosis: Here the spirit becomes a lion bent on conquering its freedom and being master in its own desert.

Its last master it here seeks: Hostile will it be to him and to its last God; it will struggle with the great dragon for victory.

What is the great dragon which the spirit is no longer inclined to call lord and God? "Thou shalt," is the great dragon called. But the spirit of the lion says, "I will."

"Thou shalt," lies in its way, sparkling with gold—a scale-covered beast; and on every scale glitters a golden "Thou shalt!"

The values of a thousand years glitter on those scales, and thus speaks the mightiest of all dragons: "All the values of things glitter on me.

All values have already been created, and all created values do I represent. Indeed, there shall be no 'I will' any more." Thus speaks the dragon.

My brothers, where is there need of the lion in the spirit? Why does not the beast of burden suffice, which renounces and is reverent?

To create new values—that, even the lion cannot yet accomplish, but to create for itself freedom for new creating—that the lion can do.

To create for itself freedom, and to give a holy No even unto duty; for that, my brothers, there is need of the lion.

To assume the right to new values, that is the most formidable assumption for a reverent spirit. Truly, unto such a spirit it is preying, and the work of a beast of prey.

As its holiest, it once loved "Thou shalt"; now is it forced to find illusion and arbitrariness even in the holiest things, that it may capture freedom from its love. The lion is needed for this capture.

But tell me, my brothers, what the child can do, which even the lion could not do? Why must the preying lion still become a child?

Innocence is the child, and forgetfulness, a new beginning, a game, a self-rolling wheel, a first movement, a holy Yes.

For the game of creation, my brothers, is needed a holy Yes to life: *its own* will, the spirit now wills; *his own* world the world's outcast wins.

Three metamorphoses of the spirit have I described to you: how the spirit became a camel, the camel a lion, and the lion at last a child.

Thus spoke Zarathustra. And at that time he dwelled in the town which is called The Pied Cow.

The Teachers of Virtue

Zarathustra was told about a wise man whom people praised for his ability to speak well about sleep and virtue. Greatly was he honored and rewarded for it, and all the youths sat before his chair. To him went Zarathustra and sat among the youths before his chair. And thus spoke the wise man:

Be respectful and modest before sleep! That is the first thing! And keep out of the way of all who sleep badly and keep awake at night!

Even the thief is modest before sleep. He always steals softly through the night. Immodest, however, is the night watchman; immodestly he carries his horn.

No small art is it to sleep. It is necessary for that purpose to keep awake all day.

Ten times a day must you overcome yourself: that causes wholesome weariness and is opium to the soul.

Ten times must you reconcile again with yourself; for overcoming is bitterness, and badly sleep the unreconciled.

Ten truths must you find during the day; otherwise you will seek truth during the night, and your soul will remain hungry.

Ten times must you laugh during the day, and be cheerful; otherwise your stomach, the father of affliction, will disturb you in the night.

Few people know it, but one must have all the virtues in order to sleep well. Shall I bear false witness? Shall I commit adultery?

Shall I covet my neighbor's maidservant? All that would disturb good sleep. . . .

When Zarathustra heard the wise man thus speak, he laughed in his heart: for suddenly a light dawned upon him. And thus spoke he to his heart:

A fool seems this wise man with his forty thoughts: but I believe he knows well how to sleep.

Happy even is he who lives near this wise man! Such sleep is contagious—even through a thick wall it is contagious.

A magic resides even in his academic chair. And not in vain did the youths sit before the preacher of virtue.

His wisdom is to keep awake in order to sleep well. And indeed, if life had no sense, and had I to choose nonsense, this would be the most desirable nonsense for me also.

Now I know well what people sought formerly above all else when they sought teachers of virtue. Good sleep they sought for themselves, and opiate virtues to promote it!

To all those belauded sages of the academic chairs, wisdom was sleep without dreams. They knew no higher significance of life.

Even at present, to be sure, there are some like this preacher of virtue and not always so honorable; but their time is past. And not much longer do they stand; soon they will lie.

Blessed are those drowsy ones for they shall soon nod to sleep.

Thus spoke Zarathustra.

The Otherworldly

Once Zarathustra too cast his fancy beyond man, like all the otherworldly. The work of a suffering and tortured God did the world then seem to me.

The dream—and fiction—of a God, did the world then seem to me; colored vapors before the eyes of a divinely dissatisfied one.

Good and evil, and joy and woe, and I and you—colored vapors did they seem to me before creative eyes. The creator wished to look away from himself, and then he created the world.

Intoxicating joy is it for the sufferer to look away from his suffering and forget himself. Intoxicating joy and self-forgetting did the world once seem to me.

This world, the eternally imperfect, an eternal contradiction's image and imperfect image—an intoxicating joy to its imperfect creator—thus did the world once seem to me.

Thus, once did I also cast my fancy beyond man, like all the otherworldly. Beyond man, indeed?

Ah, my brothers, that God whom I created was human work and human madness, like all Gods!

Man was he, and only a poor fragment of man and ego. Out of my own ashes and glow it came unto me, that phantom. And indeed, it came not to me from the beyond!

What happened, my brothers? I surpassed myself, the suffering one; I carried my own ashes to the mountain; a brighter flame I contrived for myself. And behold! Thereupon the phantom *withdrew* from me!

To me the convalescent it would now be suffering and torment to believe in such phantoms: suffering it would now be to me, and humiliation. Thus speak I to the otherworldly.

It was suffering and impotence that created all otherworlds; and the short madness of happiness, which only the greatest sufferer experiences.

Weariness, which seeks to get to the ultimate with one leap, with a death leap; a poor ignorant weariness, unwilling even to will any longer: that created all Gods and otherworlds. . . .

A new will I teach men: To choose that path which man has followed blindly, and to affirm it—and no longer to slink aside from it, like the sick and perishing!

The sick and perishing—it was they who despised the body and the earth and invented the heavenly world and the redeeming drops of blood; but even those sweet and sad poisons they borrowed from the body and the earth!

From their misery they sought escape, and the stars were too remote for them. Then they sighed: "O that there were heavenly paths by which to steal into another existence and into happiness!" Then they contrived for themselves their side routes and bloody draughts!

Beyond the sphere of their body and this earth they now fancied themselves transported, these ungrateful ones. But to what did they owe the convulsion and rapture of their transport? To their body and this earth.

Gentle is Zarathustra to the sickly. Indeed, he is not indignant at their modes of consolation and ingratitude. May they become convalescents and overcomers and create higher bodies for themselves!

Neither is Zarathustra indignant at a convalescent who looks tenderly on his delusions, and at midnight steals around the grave of his God; but sickness and a sick body remain even in his tears.

Many sickly ones have there always been among those who muse and languish for God; violently they hate the discerning ones and the latest of virtues, which is honesty.

Backward they always gaze toward dark ages— then, indeed, were delusion and faith something different. Raving of the reason was likeness to God, and doubt was sin.

Too well do I know those godlike ones; they insist that we have faith in them; they insist that doubt is sin. Too well, also, do I know what they themselves most believe in.

Indeed, not in otherworlds and redeeming drops of blood; but in the body do they also believe most; and their own body is for them the thing-in-itself.

But it is a sickly thing to them, and gladly would they get out of their skin. Therefore they listen to the preachers of death and themselves preach otherworlds.

Listen rather, my brothers, to the voice of the healthy body; it is a more upright and pure voice.

More uprightly and purely speaks the healthy body, perfect and proportionately built; and it speaks of the meaning of the earth.

Thus spoke Zarathustra.

·   ·   ·

The Preachers of Death

There are preachers of death: and the earth is full of those to whom renunciation of life must be preached.

The earth is full of the superfluous; marred is life by the many too many. May they be lured out of this life by the "life eternal"!

"The yellow ones": so are called the preachers of death, or "the black ones." But I will show them to you in other colors besides.

There are the terrible ones who carry in themselves the beast of prey and have no choice except lust or self-laceration. And even their lust is self-laceration.

They have not yet become men, those terrible ones: may they preach renunciation of life and pass away themselves!

There are the spiritually consumptive ones. Hardly are they born when they begin to die, and to long for doctrines of lassitude and renunciation.

They would rather be dead, and we should approve of their wish! Let us beware of awakening those dead ones and of damaging those living coffins!

They meet an invalid, or an old man, or a corpse and immediately they say: "Life is refuted!"

But they only are refuted, and their eye, which sees only one aspect of existence.

Shrouded in thick melancholy, and eager for the little accidents that bring death; thus do they wait and clench their teeth.

Or else they grasp at sweetmeats and mock their childishness in that; they cling to their straw of life and mock at their still clinging to it.

Their wisdom speaks thus: "A fool, he who remains alive; but so far are we fools! And that is the most foolish thing in life!"

"Life is only suffering": so say others, and lie not. Then see to it that *you* cease! See to it that the life which is only suffering ceases!

And let this be the teaching of your virtue: "Thou shalt slay thyself! Thou shalt steal away!"

"Lust is sin," so say some who preach death: "Let us go apart and bear no children!"

"Giving birth is troublesome," say others: "Why still give birth? One bears only the unfortunate!" And they also are preachers of death.

"Pity is necessary," so says a third party. "Take what I have! Take what I am! That much less will life bind me!"

If they were completely full of pity, they would make their neighbors sick of life. To be wicked, that would be their true goodness.

But they want to be rid of life; what do they care if they bind others still faster with their chains and gifts!

And you also, to whom life is rough labor and disquiet, are you not very tired of life? Are you not very ripe for the sermon of death?

All you to whom rough labor is dear, and the rapid, new, and strange—you bear yourselves badly; your diligence is escape and the will to self-forgetfulness.

If you believed more in life, then would you devote yourselves less to the moment. But you lack the capacity to wait—or to be idle.

Everywhere resounds the voice of those who preach death; and the earth is full of those to whom death has to be preached.

Or "life eternal"; it is all the same to me—if only they pass away quickly!

Thus spoke Zarathustra.

The Way of the Creating One

Do you wish for solitude, my brother? Would you seek the way to yourself? Linger yet a little and listen to me.

"He who seeks may easily get lost himself. All isolation is wrong"; so say the herd. And long did you belong to the herd.

The voice of the herd will still echo in you. And when you say, "I have no longer a conscience in common with you," then will it be a complaint and an agony.

Behold, that agony itself did the common conscience produce; and the last gleam of that conscience still glows on your affliction.

But would you go the way of your affliction, which is the way to yourself? Then show me your right and your strength to do so!

Are you a new strength and a new right? A first motion? A self-rolling wheel? Can you also compel stars to revolve around you?

Alas! There is so much lusting for heights! There are so many convulsions of the ambitious! Show me that you are not lustful and ambitious!

Alas! There are so many great thoughts that do no more than a bellows: they inflate, and become emptier than ever.

Free, do you call yourself? Your ruling thought would I hear of, and not that you have escaped from a yoke.

Are you *entitled* to escape from a yoke? Many a man has cast away his final worth when he has cast away his servitude.

Free from what? What does that matter to Zarathustra! Clearly, however, should your eye show to me: free *for what*?

Can you give to yourself your evil and your good, and set up your will as a law over yourself? Can you be judge for yourself and avenger of your law?

Terrible is aloneness with the judge and avenger of one's own law. Thus is a star projected into the void, and into the icy breath of aloneness.

Today you still suffer from the multitude, you individual; today you still have your courage unabated, and your hopes.

But one day the solitude will make you weary; one day will your pride yield, and your courage quail. You will one day cry: "I am alone!"

One day that which appears high to you will be out of sight, and that which appears lowly will be all too visible; your sublimity itself will frighten you as a phantom. You will one day cry: "All is false!"

There are feelings which seek to slay the lonesome one; if they do not succeed, then they must themselves die! But are you capable of it—to be a murderer?

Have you ever known, my brother, the word "disdain"? And the anguish of your justice in being just to those that disdain you?

You force many to think differently about yourself; that they charge heavily against your account. You came close to them, and yet went past; for that they never forgive you.

You go beyond them: but the higher you rise, the smaller you seem to the eye of envy. Most hated of all, however, are those who fly.

"How could you be just to me!" you must say. "I choose your injustice as my allotted portion."

Injustice and filth cast they at the lonesome one: but, my brother, if you must be a star, you must shine for them none the less on that account!

And be on your guard against the good and just! They like to crucify those who devise their own virtue—they hate the lonesome ones.

Be on your guard, also, against holy simplicity! All that is not simple it considers unholy; likewise, it likes to play with the fire—of the fagot and stake.

And be on your guard, also, against the attacks of your love! Too readily does the recluse reach his hand to any one who meets him.

To many you may not give your hand, but only your paw; and I wish your paw also to have claws.

But the worst enemy you can come upon is always you yourself; you waylay yourself in caverns and forests.

Lonesome one, you go the way to yourself! And past yourself and your seven devils leading your way!

A heretic will you be to yourself, and a wizard and a soothsayer, and a fool, and a doubter, and a reprobate, and a villain.

Ready must you be to burn yourself in your own flame; how could you renew yourself if you have not first become ashes!

Lonesome one, you go the way of the creating one: a God will you create for yourself out of your seven devils!

Lonesome one, you go the way of the loving one: you love yourself, and on that account you despise yourself as only the loving ones despise.

To create, desires the loving one, because he despises! What does he know of love who has not been obliged to despise just what he loved!

With your love, go into your isolation, my brother, and with your creating; and only later will justice limp after you.

With my tears, go into your isolation, my brother. I love him who seeks to create beyond himself, and thus perishes.

Thus spoke Zarathustra.

The Bestowing Virtue

1

When Zarathustra had taken leave of the town to which his heart was attached, the name of which is "The Pied Cow," there followed him many people who called themselves his disciples and kept him company. Thus they came to a crossroad. Then Zarathustra told them that he now wanted to go alone; for he was fond of going alone. His disciples, however, presented him at his departure with a staff, on the golden handle of which a serpent twined around the sun. Zarathustra rejoiced on account of the staff and supported himself on it; then he spoke thus to his disciples:

Tell me: How did gold come to have the highest value? Because it is uncommon, and useless, and beaming, and soft in luster; it always gives of itself.

Only as image of the highest virtue did gold come to have the highest value. Goldlike, beams the glance of the bestower. Gold-luster makes peace between moon and sun.

Uncommon is the highest virtue, and unprofiting, beaming is it, and soft of luster; a gift-giving virtue is the highest virtue.

Indeed, I divine you well, my disciples; you strive like me for the bestowing virtue. What should you have in common with cats and wolves?

It is your thirst to become sacrifices and gifts yourselves: and therefore have you the thirst to accumulate all riches in your soul.

Insatiably strives your soul for treasures and jewels because your virtue is insatiable in desiring to bestow.

You constrain all things to flow toward you and into you so that they shall flow back again out of your fountain as the gifts of your love.

Indeed, an appropriator of all values must such bestowing love become; but healthy and holy, call I this selfishness.

Another selfishness is there, an all-too-poor and hungry kind, which would always steal—the selfishness of the sick, the sickly selfishness.

With the eye of the thief it looks upon all that is lustrous; with the craving of hunger it measures him who has abundance; and ever does it prowl around the tables of givers.

Sickness speaks in such craving and invisible degeneration; of a sickly body, speaks the larcenous craving of this selfishness.

Tell me, my brother, what do we think bad and worst of all? Is it not *degeneration*? And we always suspect degeneration when the bestowing soul is lacking.

Upward goes our course from species on to superspecies. But a horror to us is the degenerating sense, which says: "All for myself."

Upward soars our mind: thus is it an image of our body, an image of an elevation. Such images of elevations are the names of the virtues.

Thus goes the body through history, a becomer and fighter. And the spirit, what is it to the body? Its fights' and victories' herald, its companion and echo.

Similes, are all names of good and evil; they do not speak out, they only hint. A fool seeks knowledge from them!

Listen, my brothers, to every hour when your spirit would speak in images: there is the origin of your virtue.

Elevated is then your body and raised up; with its delight, it enraptures the spirit so that it becomes creator, and valuer, and lover, and everything's benefactor.

When your heart overflows broad and full like the river, a blessing and a danger to the lowlanders: there is the origin of your virtue.

When you are exalted above praise and blame, and your will would command all things, as a loving one's will: there is the origin of your virtue.

When you despise pleasant things, and the soft bed, and cannot rest far enough from the soft: there is the origin of your virtue.

When you are of one will, and when that change of every need is needful to you: there is the origin of your virtue.

Indeed, a new good and evil is it! Indeed, a new deep murmuring, and the voice of a new fountain!

Power is it, this new virtue; a ruling thought is it, and around it a subtle soul: a golden sun, with the serpent of knowledge around it.

2

Here paused Zarathustra awhile and looked lovingly on his disciples. Then he continued to speak thus—and his voice had changed:

Remain true to the earth, my brothers, with the power of your virtue! Let your bestowing love and your knowledge be devoted to be the meaning of the earth! Thus do I beseech you.

Let it not fly away from the earthly and beat against eternal walls with its wings! Ah, there has always been so much virtue that has flown away!

Lead, like me, the flown-away virtue back to the earth—yes, back to body and life; that it may give to the earth its meaning, a human meaning!

A hundred times has spirit as well as virtue flown away and blundered. Alas! In our body dwells still all this delusion and blundering: body and will has it there become.

A hundred times has spirit as well as virtue attempted and erred. Yes, man has been an attempt. Alas, much ignorance and error is embodied in us!

Not only the rationality of millenniums, also their madness breaks out in us. Dangerous is it to be an heir.

Still fight we step by step with the giant called chance, and until now over all mankind there has ruled only nonsense.

Let your spirit and your virtue be devoted to the sense of the earth, my brothers; let the value of everything be determined anew by you! Therefore you shall be fighters! Therefore you shall be creators!

Intelligently does the body purify itself; attempting with intelligence it exalts itself; to the discerners all impulses sanctify themselves; to the exalted the soul becomes joyful.

Physician, heal thyself: then will you also heal your patient. Let it be his best cure to see with his eyes him who makes himself whole.

A thousand paths are there which have never yet been trodden; a thousand forms of flourishing and hidden islands of life. Unexhausted and undiscovered is still man and man's world.

Awake and listen, you lonesome ones! From the future come winds with stealthy pinions, and to fine ears good tidings are proclaimed.

Lonesome ones of today, you seceding ones, you shall one day be a people: out of you who have chosen yourselves, shall a chosen people arise—and out of it the Übermensch.

Indeed, a place of healing shall the earth become! And already is a new odor diffused around it, a salvation-bringing odor—and a new hope!

3

When Zarathustra had spoken these words, he paused like one who had not said his last word; and long did he balance the staff doubtfully in his hand. At last he spoke thus—and his voice had changed:

I now go alone, my disciples! You also now go away, and alone! So will I have it.

Indeed, I advise you: Depart from me, and guard yourselves against Zarathustra! And better still, be ashamed of him! Perhaps he has deceived you.

The man of knowledge must be able not only to love his enemies, but also to hate his friends.

One repays a teacher badly if one remains merely a pupil. And why will you not pluck at my wreath?

You venerate me; but what if your veneration should someday collapse? Take heed lest a statue crush you!

You say, you believe in Zarathustra? But of what account is Zarathustra! You are my believers; but of what account are all believers!

You had not yet sought yourselves; then did you find me. So do all believers; therefore all faith is of so little account.

Now do I bid you to lose me and find yourselves; and only when you have all denied me will I return to you.

Indeed, with other eyes, my brothers, shall I then seek my lost ones; with another love shall I then love you.

And once again shall you have become friends with me and children of one hope; then will I be with you for the third time to celebrate the great noontide with you.

And it is the great noon, when man is in the middle of his course between animal and Übermensch, and celebrates his advance to the evening as his highest hope: for it is the advance to a new morning.

At such time will man going down bless himself, that he should be one who goes over; and the sun of his knowledge will be at noontide.

"Dead are all gods: now we want the Übermensch to live."—Let this be our final will at the great noontide!

Thus spoke Zarathustra.

SECOND PART

In the Happy Isles

The figs fall from the trees, they are good and sweet; and in falling the red skins of them break. A north wind am I to ripe figs.

Thus, like figs, do these doctrines fall for you, my friends: imbibe now their juice and their sweet substance! It is autumn all around, and clear sky, and afternoon.

Lo, what fullness is around us! And out of the midst of superabundance, it is delightful to look out upon distant seas.

Once did people say God, when they looked out upon distant seas; now, however, have I taught you to say, Übermensch.

God is a conjecture, but I do not wish your conjecturing to reach beyond your creating will.

Could you *create* a God? Then, I pray you, be silent about all Gods! But you could well create the Übermensch, or if you could not do so yourselves, my brothers, you could at least transform yourselves into fathers and forefathers of the Übermensch—and let that be your best creating!

God is a conjecture: but I should like your conjecturing restricted to the conceivable.

Could you *conceive* a God?—But your will to truth should mean that everything be transformed into the humanly conceivable, the humanly visible, the humanly sensible! Your own discernment shall you follow out to the end!

And what you have called the world shall but be created by you: your reason, your likeness, your will, your love, shall it itself become! And indeed, for your bliss, discerning ones!

And how would you endure life without that hope, you discerning ones? Neither into the inconceivable could you have been born, nor into the irrational.

But that I may reveal my heart entirely to you, my friends: *if* there were Gods, how could I endure it to be no God! *Therefore* there are no Gods.

Yes, I have drawn the conclusion; now, however, it draws me.

God is a conjecture. But who could drink all the bitterness of this conjecture without dying? Shall his faith be taken from the creating one and from the eagle his flights into eagle heights?

God is a thought—it makes all the straight crooked, and all that stands reel. What? Time would be gone, and all that is perishable would be but a lie?

To think this is giddiness and vertigo to human limbs, and even vomiting to the stomach; indeed, the reeling sickness do I call it, to conjecture such a thing. Evil do I call it and misanthropic: all that teaching about the one, and the plenum, and the unmoved, and the sufficient, and the imperishable!

All the imperishable—that's but a parable, and the poets lie too much.

But of time and of becoming shall the best parables speak: let them praise and justify all impermanence!

Creating—that is the great salvation from suffering and life's alleviation. But for the creator to appear, suffering itself is needed, and much transformation.

Yes, much bitter dying must there be in your life, creators! Thus are you advocates and justifiers of all perishableness.

For the creator himself to be the newborn child, he must also be willing to be the child bearer, and endure pains of the child bearer.

Truly, a hundred souls I have gone through on my way, and through a hundred cradles and the throes of birth. Many a farewell have I taken; I know the heartbreaking last hours.

But so it is willed by my creating will and destiny. Or, to tell you it more candidly: just such a fate wills my will.

All *feeling* suffers in me and is in prison; but my *willing* ever comes to me as my emancipator and comforter.

Willing emancipates: that is the true doctrine of will and emancipation—so teaches Zarathustra.

No longer willing, and no longer valuing, and no longer creating! Ah, that that great debility may ever be far from me!

And also in knowledge I feel only my will's delight in procreating and becoming; and if there be innocence in my knowledge, it is because there is will to procreation in it.

Away from God and Gods did this will lure me; what would there be to create if there were—Gods!

But to man does it ever impel me anew, my fervent creative will; thus is the hammer impelled to the stone.

Ah, within the stone slumbers an image, the image of my visions! Alas, that it should slumber in the hardest, ugliest stone!

Now my hammer rages ruthlessly against its prison. From the stone fly the fragments. What's that to me?

I will complete it; for a shadow came to me—the stillest and lightest of all things once came to me!

The beauty of the Übermensch came to me as a shadow. Alas, my brothers! Of what account now are the Gods to me!

Thus spoke Zarathustra.

THOSE WHO PITY

My friends, there has arisen a satire on your friend. Behold Zarathustra! Does he not walk among us as if among animals?"

But it is better said this way: "The discerning one walks among men *as* among animals."

To the discerning one man himself is the animal with red cheeks. How did that happen to him? Is it not because he had to be ashamed too often?

O my friends! Thus speaks the discerning one: Shame, shame, shame; that is the history of man!

And on that account does the noble one impose upon himself not to shame: shame he imposes on himself in the presence of all sufferers.

Truly, I like them not, the compassionate ones, whose bliss is in their pity. Their shame is inadequate.

If I must pity, I dislike it to be known; and if I do so, it is preferably at a distance.

Preferably also do I shroud my head, and flee, before being recognized; and thus do I bid you do, my friends!

May my destiny ever lead unafflicted ones like you across my path, and those with whom I *may* have hope and repast and honey in common!

Indeed, I have done this and that for the afflicted: but something better did I always seem to do when I had learned better joys.

Since humanity came into being, man has enjoyed himself too little; that alone, my brothers, is our original sin!

And when we learn better to enjoy ourselves, then do we learn best not to give pain to others, or to contrive pain.

Therefore do I wash the hand that has helped the sufferer; therefore do I wipe also my soul.

For in seeing the sufferer suffering was I ashamed on account of his shame; and in helping him, sorely did I wound his pride.

Great indebtedness does not make people grateful, but vengeful; and when a small kindness is not forgotten, it becomes a gnawing worm.

"Be shy in accepting! Distinguish by accepting!" Thus do I advise those who have nothing to bestow.

I, however, am a bestower: willingly do I give as a friend to friends. Strangers, however, and the poor, may pluck for themselves the fruit from my tree; thus does it cause less shame.

Beggars, however, one should entirely do away with! Indeed, it annoys one to give to them, and it annoys one not to give to them.

And likewise sinners and bad consciences! Believe me, my friends: the sting of conscience teaches one to sting. . . .

If, however, you have a suffering friend, then be a resting place for his suffering; like a hard bed, however, a camp bed. Thus will you serve him best.

And if a friend does you wrong, then say: "I forgive you what you have done unto me; that you have done it to *yourself*, however, how could I forgive that!"

Thus speaks all great love. It surpasses even forgiveness and pity.

One should hold fast one's heart, for when one lets it go, how quickly one's head runs away!

Ah, where in the world have there been greater follies than with those who pity? And what in the world has caused more suffering than the follies of those who pity?

Woe to all loving ones who have not an elevation which is above their pity!

Thus spoke the devil to me, once: "Even God has his hell: it is his love for man."

And lately, did I hear him say these words: "God is dead; of his pity for man has God died."

So be warned against pity: *from there* a heavy cloud will yet come to men! Indeed, I understand weather signs!

But heed also this word: All great love is above all its pity; for it seeks to create what is loved!

"Myself do I sacrifice to my love, *and my neighbor as myself*"; such is the language of all creators.

All creators, however, are hard.

Thus spoke Zarathustra.

The Priests

And one day Zarathustra made a sign to his disciples, and spoke these words to them:

"Here are priests; but although they are my enemies, pass them quietly and with sleeping swords!

Even among them there are heroes; many of them have suffered too much, so they want to make others suffer.

Bad enemies are they. Nothing is more revengeful than their humility. And readily does he soil himself who touches them.

But my blood is related to theirs; and I want to see my blood honored even in theirs."

And when they had passed, a pain attacked Zarathustra; but not long had he struggled with the pain, when he began to speak thus:

I feel compassion for those priests. I am also repulsed by them; but that is the smallest matter to me because I am among men.

But I suffer and have suffered with them; prisoners are they to me, and stigmatized ones. He whom they call Savior put them in fetters.

In fetters of false values and fatuous words! Oh, that some one would save them from their Savior!

On an isle they once thought they had landed, when the sea tossed them about; but behold, it was a slumbering monster!

False values and fatuous words; these are the worst monsters for mortals—long slumbers and waits the fate that is in them.

But at last it comes and awakens and devours whatever has built tabernacles upon it.

Oh, just look at those tabernacles which those priests have built themselves! Churches, they call their sweet-smelling caves!

Oh, that falsified light, that mustified air! Where the soul may not fly aloft to its height!

But so commands their belief: "Crawl up the stairs, you sinners!"

Indeed, I would rather see a shameless one than the distorted eyes of their shame and devotion!

Who created for themselves such caves and stairways of repentence? Was it not those who sought to conceal themselves and were ashamed under the clear sky?

And only when the clear sky looks again through ruined roofs and down upon grass and red poppies on ruined walls will I again turn my heart to the seats of this God.

They called God that which opposed and afflicted them; and indeed, there was much heroism in their worship!

And they knew not how to love their God otherwise than by nailing men to the cross!

As corpses they thought to live; in black draped they their corpses; even in their talk do I still feel the evil flavor of charnel houses.

And he who lives near them lives near black pools, in which the toad sings his song with sweet gravity.

Better songs would they have to sing, for me to believe in their Savior: more like saved ones would his disciples have to appear to me!

Naked, would I like to see them; for beauty alone should preach penitence. But whom would that disguised affliction convince!

Truly, their Saviors themselves came not from freedom and freedom's seventh heaven! Indeed, they themselves never trod the carpets of knowledge!

Of defects did the spirit of those Saviors consist; but into every defect had they put their illusion, their stopgap that they called God.

In their pity was their spirit drowned; and when they swelled and overswelled with pity, there always floated to the surface a great folly.

Eagerly and with shouts drove they their herd over their footbridge; as if there were but one footbridge to the future! Indeed, those shepherds also were still of the flock!

Small spirits and spacious souls had those shepherds: but, my brothers, what small domains have even the most spacious souls been before!

Characters of blood did they write on the way they went, and their folly taught that truth is proved by blood.

But blood is the very worst witness to truth; blood taints the purest teaching, and turns it into delusion and hatred of heart.

And when a person goes through fire for his teaching—what does that prove! It is more, indeed, when out of one's own fire comes one's own teaching!

Sultry heart and cold head; where these meet, there arises the blusterer, the "Savior."

Greater ones, verily, have there been, and higher-born ones, than those whom the people call Saviors, those rapturous blusterers!

And by still greater ones than any of the Saviors must you be saved, my brothers, if you would find the way to freedom!

Never yet has there been a Übermensch. Naked have I seen both of them, the greatest man and the smallest man. All too similar are they still to each other. Indeed, even the greatest found I—all too human!

Thus spoke Zarathustra.

The Virtuous

. . . You want to be paid besides, virtuous ones! You want rewards for virtue, and heaven for earth, and eternity for your today?

And now you upbraid me for teaching that there is no reward giver, nor paymaster? And indeed, I do not even teach that virtue is its own reward.

Alas! This is my sorrow: into the foundation of things have reward and punishment been insinuated—and now even into the foundation of your souls, virtuous ones!

But like the snout of the boar shall my word grub up the ground of your souls; a plowshare will I be called by you.

All the secrets of your heart shall be brought to light; and when you lie in the sun, uprooted and broken, then will also your falsehood be separated from your truth.

For this is your truth: you are *too pure* for the filth of the words: vengeance, punishment, recompense, retribution.

You love your virtue as a mother loves her child; but when did one hear of a mother wanting to be paid for her love?

It is your dearest self, your virtue. The ring's thirst is in you: to reach itself again struggles every ring, and turns itself.

And like the star that goes out, so is every work of your virtue: always its light is on its way and traveling—and when will it cease to be on its way?

Thus is the light of your virtue still on its way, even when its work is done. Be it forgotten and dead, still its ray of light lives and travels.

That your virtue is your self and not an outward thing, a skin, or a cloak: that is the truth from the basis of your souls, virtuous ones! . . .

That you might become weary of saying: "That an action is good is because it is unselfish."

Alas! My friends! That *your* very self be in your action, as the mother is in the child: let that be *your* formula of virtue! . . .

Thus spoke Zarathustra.

Self-Surpassing

"Will to truth" do you wisest call that which impels you and inspires your lust?

Will for the thinkableness of all being; thus do *I* call your will!

All being would you *make* thinkable; for you doubt with good reason whether it be already thinkable.

But it shall accommodate and bend itself to you! So wills your will. Smooth shall it become and subject to the spirit, as its mirror and reflection.

That is your entire will, you wisest ones, as a will to power; and even when you speak of good and evil, and of estimates of value.

You would still create a world before which you can kneel; such is your ultimate hope and ecstasy.

The ignorant, to be sure, the people—they are like a river on which a boat floats along; and in the boat sit the estimates of value, solemn and disguised.

Your will and your valuations have you put on the river of becoming; what the people consider good and evil, that betrays to me an ancient will to power.

It was you, you wisest ones, who put such guests in this boat and gave them pomp and proud names; you and your ruling will!

Onward the river now carries your boat: it *must* carry it. A small matter if the rough wave foams and angrily resists its keel!

It is not the river that is your danger and the end of your good and evil, you wisest ones; but that will itself, the will to power—the unexhausted, procreating will to live.

But that you may understand my gospel of good and evil, for that purpose will I tell you my gospel of life, and of the nature of all living things.

The living thing did I follow; I walked in the broadest and narrowest paths to learn its nature.

With a hundred-faced mirror did I catch its glance when its mouth was shut, so that its eye might speak to me. And its eye spoke to me.

But wherever I found living things, there I also heard the language of obedience. All living things are obeying things.

And this I heard secondly: Whatever cannot obey itself is commanded. Such is the nature of living things.

This, however, is the third thing which I heard: namely, that commanding is more difficult than obeying. And not only because the commander bears the burden of all obeyers and because this burden readily crushes him.

An experiment and a risk seemed all commanding to me; and whenever it commands, the living thing risks itself thereby.

Yes, even when it commands itself, then it must also atone for its commanding. Of its own law must it become the judge and avenger and victim.

How does this happen? so did I ask myself. What persuades the living thing to obey, and command, and even be obedient in commanding?

Listen now to my word, you wisest ones! Ask seriously whether I have crept into the heart of life itself and into the roots of its heart!

Wherever I found a living thing, there found I will to power; and even in the will of the servant found I the will to be master.

That the stronger the weaker shall serve—this is the conviction of him who would be master over a still weaker one. That delight alone he is unwilling to forego.

And as the lesser surrenders himself to the greater that he may have delight and power over the least of all, so even the greatest surrenders himself, and risks life, for the sake of power.

That is the surrender of the greatest: to run risk and danger, and play dice for death.

And where there is sacrifice and service and amorous glances, there also is the will to be master. By side streets does the weaker then slink into the fortress and into the heart of the mightier one—and there steals power.

And this secret spoke life herself unto me. "Behold," said she, "I am that *which must always surpass itself*.

To be sure, you call it will to procreation, or impulse toward a goal, toward the higher, remoter, more manifold; but all that is one and the same secret.

I would rather perish than disown this one thing; and indeed, where there is perishing and leaf falling, there does life sacrifice itself—for power!

That I have to be struggling, and becoming, and at purpose and cross-purpose—alas, he who divines my will, divines well also on what *crooked* paths it has to tread!

Whatever I create, and however much I love it, soon must I be adverse to it and to my love; so wills my will.

And even you, discerning one, are only a path and footstep of my will: indeed, my will to power walks on the heels of your will to truth!

He certainly did not hit the truth who shot at it the formula: 'Will to existence': that will does not exist!

For what is not, cannot will; that, however, which is in existence, how could it still strive for existence!

Only where there is life, is there also will; not, however, will to life, but, so I teach you, will to power!

Much is reckoned higher than life itself by the living one; but out of the very reckoning speaks the will to power!"

Thus did life once teach me; and through that, you wisest ones, do I solve for you the riddle of your hearts.

Indeed, I say to you: Good and evil which are everlasting do not exist! Of their own accord must they always surpass themselves anew.

With your values and formula of good and evil, you exercise power, you valuing ones; and that is your secret love, and the sparkling, trembling, and over-flowing of your souls.

But a stronger power and a new surpassing grows out of your values and breaks egg and eggshell.

And he who must be a creator in good and evil—indeed, he must first be a destroyer and break values in pieces.

Thus does the greatest evil pertain to the greatest good; that, however, is the creating good.

Let us *speak* of this, you wisest ones, even though it be bad. To be silent is worse; all suppressed truths become poisonous.

And let everything break up that can break up by our truths! Many a house is still to be built!

Thus spoke Zarathustra.

THIRD PART

The Vision and the Enigma

2

"Halt, dwarf!" said I. "Either I, or you! I, however, am the stronger of the two. You do not know my abysmal thought! *It* could you not endure!"

Then happened something that made me lighter; for the dwarf sprang from my shoulder, the prying sprite! And it squatted on a stone in front of me. There was however a gateway just where we halted.

"Look at this gateway, Dwarf!" I continued, "it has two faces. Two roads come together here. These has no one yet gone to the end of.

This long lane backward; it continues for an eter-nity. And that long lane ahead, that is another eternity.

They are antithetical to one another, these roads; they directly abut on one another; and it is here, at this gateway, that they come together. The name of the gateway is inscribed above: 'This Moment.'

But should one follow them further, and ever fur-ther and further on, do you think, dwarf, that these roads would be eternally antithetical?"

"Everything that is straight lies," murmured the dwarf contemptuously. "All truth is crooked; time it-self is a circle."

"You spirit of gravity!" said I wrathfully, "Do not take it too lightly! Or I shall let you squat where you squat, Haltfoot, and I carried you *high*!'

"Observe," continued I, "This moment! From the gateway, this moment, there runs a long eternal lane *backwards;* behind us lies an eternity.

Must not whatever *can* run have already run along that lane? Must not whatever *can* happen have already happened, resulted, and gone by?

And if everything has already existed, what do you think, dwarf, of this moment? Must not this gateway also have already existed?

And are not all things closely bound together in such ways that this moment draws behind it all that is to come? *Consequently* itself also?

For whatever *can* run its course *must* run it once more!

And this slow spider which creeps in the moon-light, and this moonlight itself, and you and I in this gateway, whispering together, whispering of eternal things, must we not all have already existed?

And must we not return and run in that other lane out before us, that long weird lane, must we not eter-nally return?"

Thus did I speak, and always more softly; for I was afraid of my own thoughts and the thoughts behind those. Then, suddenly did I hear a dog *howl* near me.

Had I ever heard a dog howl like that? My thoughts ran back. Yes! When I was a child, in my most distant childhood.

Then did I hear a dog howl like that. And saw it also, with hair bristling, its head upward, trembling in the stillest midnight, when even dogs believe in ghosts.

So that it inspired my pity. For just then went the full moon, silent as death, over the house; just then did it stand still, a glowing globe, at rest on the flat roof, as if on someone's property:

The dog had then been terrified; for dogs believe in thieves and ghosts. And when I again heard such howl-ing, I again took pity.

Where was now the dwarf? And the gateway? And the spider? And all the whispering? Had I dreamed? Had I awakened? Between rugged rocks did I suddenly stand alone, dreary in the dreariest moonlight.

But there lay a man! And there! The dog leaping, bristling, whining—now did it see me coming—then did it howl again, then did it *cry*. Had I ever heard a dog cry so for help?

And indeed, what I saw, the like had I never seen. A young shepherd did I see, writhing, choking, quiv-ering, with distorted countenance, and with a heavy black serpent hanging out of his mouth.

Had I ever seen so much loathing and pale horror on one countenance? He had perhaps gone to sleep? Then had the serpent crawled into his throat; there had it bitten itself fast.

My hand pulled at the serpent, and pulled, in vain! I failed to pull the serpent out of his throat. Then there cried out of me: "Bite! Bite! Its head off! Bite!" so came my cry out of me; my horror, my hatred, my loathing, my pity, all my good and my bad cried with one voice out of me.

You daring ones around me! You venturers and adventurers and whoever of you have embarked with cunning sails on unexplored seas! You who enjoy riddles!

Solve for me the riddle that I then beheld, interpret for me the vision of the lonesomest one!

For it was a vision and a foresight; *what* did I then behold in a parable? And *who* is it that must come some day?

Who is the shepherd into whose throat the serpent thus crawled? *Who* is the man into whose throat all the heaviest and blackest will thus crawl?

The shepherd however bit as my cry had admonished him; he bit with a strong bite! Far away did he spit the head of the serpent, and he sprang up.

No longer shepherd, no longer man; a transfigured being, a light-surrounded being that *laughed*! Never on earth laughed a man as *he* laughed!

O my brothers, I heard a laughter which was no human laughter, and now gnaws a thirst at me, a longing that is never allayed.

My longing for that laughter gnaws at me: oh, how can I still endure to live! And how could I bear to die now!

Thus spoke Zarathustra.

· · ·

The Bedwarfing Virtue

2

. . . I pass through this people and keep my eyes open; they have become *smaller,* and ever smaller— *the reason for that is their doctrine of happiness and virtue.*

For they are moderate also in virtue because they want contentment. With contentment, however, only moderate virtue is compatible. . . .

3

I pass through this people and let fall many words; but they know neither how to take nor how to retain them.

They wonder why I came not to revile venery and vice; and indeed, I came not to warn against pickpockets either!

They wonder why I am not ready to abet and whet their cleverness, as if they had not yet enough of wiseacres, whose voices grate on my ear like chalk!

And when I call out: "Curse all the cowardly devils in you, that like to whimper and fold their hands and pray." Then do they shout: "Zarathustra is godless."

And especially do their teachers of resignation shout this; but precisely in their ears do I love to cry: "Yes! I *am* Zarathustra, the godless!"

Those teachers of resignation! Wherever there is anything puny, or sickly, or scabby, there do they creep like lice; and only my disgust prevents me from crushing them.

Well! This is my sermon for *their* ears: I am Zarathustra the godless, who says: "Who is more godless than I, that I may enjoy his teaching?"

I am Zarathustra the godless: where do I find my equal? And all those are my equals who give themselves their own will, and divest themselves of all resignation.

I am Zarathustra the godless! I cook every chance in *my* pot. And only when it has been quite cooked do I welcome it as *my* food.

And indeed, many a chance came imperiously to me; but still more imperiously did my *will* speak to it, then did it lie imploringly upon its knees.

Imploring that it might find home and heart with me, and saying flatteringly: "See, O Zarathustra, how friend only comes to friend!"

But why do I talk, when no one has *my* ears! And so will I shout it out to all the winds.

You become ever smaller, you small people! You crumble away, you comfortable ones! You will yet perish.

By your many small virtues, by your many small abstentions, and by your many small resignations!

Too tender, too yielding; so is your soil! But for a tree to become *great*, it seeks to twine hard roots around hard rocks!

Also what you omit weaves at the web of all the human future; even your nothing is a cobweb, and a spider that lives on the blood of the future.

And when you receive, then is it like stealing, you small virtuous ones; but even among knaves *honor* says that "one shall only steal when one cannot rob."

"It gives itself," that is also a doctrine of resignation. But I say to you, you comfortable ones, that *it takes to itself* and will always take more and more from you!

Alas, that you would renounce all *half*-willing, and would decide for idleness as you decide for action!

Alas, that you understood my word: "Do whatever you will, but first be such as *can will*.

Love ever your neighbor as yourselves, but first be such as *love themselves*—

Such as love with great love, such as love with great contempt!" Thus spoke Zarathustra the godless.

But why do I talk, when no one has *my* ears? It is still an hour too early for me here.

My own forerunner am I among this people, my own cockcrow in dark lanes.

But *their* hour comes! And there comes also mine! Hourly do they become smaller, poorer, less fruitful. Poor herbs! Poor earth!

And *soon* shall they stand before me like dry grass and prairie, and indeed, weary of themselves, and panting for *fire* more than for water!

O blessed hour of the lightning! O mystery before noontide! Running fires will I one day make of them, and heralds with flaming tongues:

One day they shall proclaim with flaming tongues: It comes, it is nigh, *the great noontide*!

Thus spoke Zarathustra.

The Convalescent

. . .

2

. . . —"O Zarathustra," said then his animals, "for those who think like us, all things dance: they come and hold out the hand and laugh and flee and return.

Everything goes, everything returns; eternally rolls the wheel of existence. Everything dies, everything blossoms again; eternally runs on the year of existence.

Everything breaks, everything is integrated anew; eternally builds itself the same house of existence. All things separate, all things again greet one another; eternally true to itself remains the ring of existence.

Existence begins every moment, around every 'Here' rolls the ball 'There'. The middle is everywhere. Crooked is the path of eternity."

O ye wags and barrel organs! answered Zarathustra, and smiled once more, how well do you know what had to be fulfilled in seven days.

And how that monster crept into my throat and choked me! But I bit off its head and spat it away from me.

And you, you have made a lyre song out of it? Now, however, do I lie here, still exhausted with that biting and spitting away, still sick with my own salvation.

And you looked on at it all? O my animals, are even you cruel? Did you like to look at my great pain as men do? For man is the cruelest animal.

At tragedies, bullfights, and crucifixions has he always been happiest on earth; and when he invented his hell, behold, that was his heaven on earth.

When the great man cries, immediately runs the little man over there, and his tongue hangs out of his mouth with desire. He, however, calls it his "pity."

The little man, especially the poet, how passionately he accuses life in words! Listen to him, but do not fail to hear the delight which is in all accusation!

Such accusers of life, it is them that life overcomes with a wink. "You love me?" it says with insolence; "Wait a little, just yet I have no time for you."

Toward himself man is the cruelest animal; and in all who call themselves "sinners" and "bearers of the cross" and "penitents," do not overlook the voluptuousness in their complaints and accusations!

And I myself, do I thereby want to be man's accuser? Alas, my animals, this only have I learned thus far, that for man his most evil is necessary for his best.

That all that is most evil is the best *power,* and the hardest stone for the highest creator; and that man must become better *and* more evil.

My fortune is not in knowing that man is evil, but I cried, as no one has ever cried:

"Alas, that his worst evil is so very small! Alas, that his best is so very small!"

The great disgust with man, *this* strangled me and crept into my throat, and what the soothsayer had presaged: "All is alike, nothing is worthwhile, knowledge strangles."

A long twilight limped on before me, a sadness, fatally weary, intoxicated with death, which spoke with yawning mouth.

"Eternally he returns, the man of whom you are weary, the small man," so yawned my sadness and dragged its foot and could not go to sleep.

A cavern became the human earth to me; its breast caved in; everything living became to me human dust and bones and molding past.

My sighing sat on all human graves and could no longer arise; my sighing and questioning croaked and choked, and gnawed and nagged day and night.

"Alas, man returns eternally! The small man returns eternally!"

Naked had I once seen both of them, the greatest man and the smallest man. All too like one another, all too human, even the greatest man!

All too small, even the greatest man! That was my disgust at man! And the eternal return also of the smallest man! That was my disgust at all existence!

Alas, disgust! Disgust! Disgust! Thus spoke Zarathustra, and sighed and shuddered; for he remembered his sickness. Then did his animals prevent him from speaking further.

"Do not speak further, you convalescent!" so answered his animals, "but go out where the world waits for you like a garden.

Go out to the roses, the bees, and the flocks of doves! Especially, however, to the singing birds, to learn *singing* from them!

For singing is for the convalescent; the sound ones may talk. And when the sound also wants songs, it wants other songs than the convalescent."

"O you wags and barrel organs, do be silent!" answered Zarathustra and smiled at his animals. "How well you know what consolation I devised for myself in seven days!

That I have to sing once more, *that* consolation did I devise for myself, and *this* convalescence: would you also make another lyre song about that?"

"Do not talk further," answered his animals once more; "rather, you convalescent, prepare for yourself first a lyre, a new lyre!

For behold, O Zarathustra! For your new songs there are needed new lyres.

Sing and bubble over, O Zarathustra, heal your soul with new songs; that you may bear your great fate, which has not yet been anyone's fate!

For your animals know it well, O Zarathustra, who you are and must become. Behold, *you are the teacher of the eternal return,* that is now *your* fate!

That you must be the first to teach this teaching, how could this great fate not be your greatest danger and infirmity!

Behold, we know what you teach; that all things eternally return, and ourselves with them, and that we have already existed times without number, and all things with us.

You teach that there is a great year of becoming, a prodigy of a great year; it must, like an hourglass, always turn up anew, that it may anew run down and run out.

So that all those years are like one another in the greatest and also in the smallest, so that we ourselves, in every great year, are like ourselves in the greatest and also in the smallest.

And if you would now die, O Zarathustra, behold, we know also how you would then speak to yourself; but your animals beseech you not to die yet!

You would speak, and without trembling, buoyant with bliss, for a great weight and worry would be taken from you, patient one!

'Now do I die and disappear,' would you say, 'and in a moment I am nothing. Souls are as mortal as bodies.

But the plexus of causes returns in which I am intertwined; it will again create me! I myself pertain to the causes of the eternal return.

I come again with this sun, with this earth, with this eagle, with this serpent, *not* to a new life, or a better life, or a similar life:

I come again eternally to this identical and same life, in its greatest and its smallest, to teach again the eternal return of all things.

—To speak again the word of the great noon of earth and man, to announce again to man the Übermensch.

I have spoken my word. I break down by my word; so wills my eternal fate, as announcer do I perish!

The hour has now come when he who goes under blesses himself. Thus *ends* Zarathustra's going under.'"

When the animals had spoken these words they were silent and waited, so that Zarathustra might say something to them: but Zarathustra did not hear that they were silent. On the contrary, he lay quietly with closed eyes like a person sleeping, although he did not sleep; for he communed just then with his soul. The serpent, however, and the eagle, when they found him silent in such a way, respected the great stillness around him, and prudently retired.

· · ·

The Higher Man

1

When I came to men for the first time, then did I commit the anchorite folly, the great folly: I appeared in the marketplace.

And when I spoke to all, I spoke to none. In the evening, however, tightrope walkers were my companions, and corpses; and I myself almost a corpse.

With the new morning, however, there came to me a new truth; then did I learn to say: "Of what account to me are marketplace and people and their noise and long ears!"

You higher men, learn *this* from me: On the marketplace no one believes in higher men. But if you will speak there, very well! The people, however, blink: "We are all equal."

"You higher men," so blink the people, "there are no higher men; we are all equal. Man is man, before God, we are all equal!"

Before God! Now, however, this God has died. Before the people, however, we will not be equal. You higher men, away from the marketplace!

2

Before God! Now however this God has died! You higher men, this God was your greatest danger.

Only since he lay in the grave have you again arisen. Just now comes the great noontide, just now does the higher man become master!

Have you understood this word, O my brothers? You are frightened. Do your hearts turn giddy? Does the abyss here yawn for you? Does the hellhound here yelp at you?

Well! Take heart! you higher men! Now only travails the mountain of the human future. God has died. Now do *we* desire the Übermensch to live.

3

The most careful ask today: "How is man to be maintained?" Zarathustra however asks, as the first and only one: "How is man to be *surpassed*?"

The Übermensch, I have at heart; *that* is the first and only thing to me, and *not* man; not the neighbor, not the poorest, not the sorriest, not the best.

O my brothers, what I can love in man is that he is a going over and a going under. And also in you there is much that makes me love and hope.

In that you have despised, you higher men, that makes me hope. For the great despisers are the great reverers.

In that you have despaired, there is much to honor. For you have not learned to submit yourselves, you have not learned petty prudence.

For today have the petty people become master; they all preach submission and resignation and prudence and diligence and consideration and the long *et cetera* of petty virtues.

Whatever is effeminate, whatever originates from the servile type, and especially the plebian-mishmash; *that* wishes now to be master of all human destiny. O disgust! Disgust! Disgust!

That asks and asks and never tires: "How is man to maintain himself best, longest, most pleasantly?" In that are they the masters of today.

These masters of today—surpass them, O my brothers—these petty people; *they* are the Übermensch's greatest danger!

Surpass, you higher men, the petty virtues, petty prudence, the sand-grain considerateness, the anthill absurdness, the pitiable comfortableness, the "happiness of the greatest number"!

And rather despair than give in. And truly, I love you, because you know not today how to live, you higher men! For thus do *you* live best!

4

Have you courage, O my brothers? Are you stout hearted? *Not* the courage before witnesses, but anchorite and eagle courage, unwitnessed even by a God?

Cold souls, mules, the blind and the drunken, I do not call stout hearted. He has heart who knows fear, but *vanquishes* it; who sees the abyss, but with *pride*.

He who sees the abyss, but with eagle's eyes, he who with eagle's talons *grasps* the abyss; he has courage.

5

"Man is evil," so said to me for consolation, all the wisest ones. Alas, if only it were still true today! For evil is man's best strength.

"Man must become better and more evil," so do *I* teach. The worst evil is necessary for the Übermensch's best.

It may have been well for the preacher of the petty people to suffer and be burdened by men's sin. I, however, rejoice in great sin as my great *consolation*.

Such things, however, are not said for long ears. Every word, also, is not suited for every mouth. These are fine, far-away things; at them sheep's hoofs shall not grasp!

6

You higher men, do you think that I am here to put right what you have done wrong?

Or that I wished from now on to make snugger couches for you sufferers? Or show you restless, mis-wandering, misclimbing ones, new and easier foot-paths?

No! No! Three times No! Always more, always better ones of your type shall perish, for you shall always have it worse and harder. Thus only . . .

Thus only grows man up to the height where the lightning strikes and shatters him; high enough for the lightning!

Toward the few, the long, the remote goes my soul and my seeking; of what account to me are your many little, short miseries!

You do not yet suffer enough for me! For you suffer from yourselves, you have not yet suffered *from man*. You would lie if you spoke otherwise! None of you suffers from what *I* have suffered.

7

It is not enough for me that the lightning no longer does harm. I do not wish to conduct it away; it shall learn to work for *me*.

My wisdom has accumulated long like a cloud; it becomes stiller and darker. So does all wisdom that shall one day bear bolts of *lightning*.

To these men of today will I not be *light,* nor be called light. *Them* will I blind; lightning of my wisdom! Put out their eyes!

8

Do not will anything beyond your power: there is a bad falseness in those who will beyond their power.

Especially when they will great things! For they awaken distrust in great things, these subtle false coin-ers and stage players.

Until at last they are false toward themselves, squint-eyed, white cankers, glossed over with strong words, parade virtues and brilliant false deeds.

Take good care there, you higher men! For nothing is more precious to me, and rarer, than honesty.

Is this today not that of the people? The people however know not what is great and what is small, what is straight and what is honest. They are inno-cently crooked; they always lie.

. . .

15

The higher its type, the less frequently a thing suc-ceeds. You higher men here, have you not all been failures?

Be of good cheer; what does it matter? How much is still possible! Learn to laugh at yourselves, as you ought to laugh!

What wonder even that you have failed and only half-succeeded, you half-shattered ones! Does not man's *future* strive and struggle in you?

Man's furthest, profoundest, star-highest issues, his prodigious powers, do not all these froth against one another in your vessel?

What wonder that many a vessel shatters! Learn to laugh at yourselves, as you ought to laugh! You higher men, oh, how much is still possible!

And indeed, how much has already succeeded! How rich is this earth in small, good, perfect things, in well-constituted things!

Set around you small, good, perfect things, you higher men. Their golden maturity heals the heart. The perfect teaches one to hope.

16

What has until now been the greatest sin here on earth? Was it not the word of him who said: "Woe to them that laughs now!"

Did he himself find no cause for laughter on the earth? Then he sought badly. A child even finds cause for it.

He did not love sufficiently; otherwise would he also have loved us, the laughing ones! But he hated and mocked us; wailing and teeth gnashing did he promise us.

Must one then curse immediately, when one does not love? That seems to me in bad taste. Thus did he, however, this absolute one. He sprang from the people.

And he himself just did not love sufficiently; other-wise he would have raged less because people did not love him. All great love does not *want* love, it wants more.

Go out of the way of all such absolute ones! They are a poor sickly type, a mob type; they look at this life with ill will. They have an evil eye for this earth.

Go out of the way of all such absolute ones! They have heavy feet and sultry hearts; they do not know how to dance. How could the earth be light for such ones?

From Beyond Good and Evil*

FIRST CHAPTER

Prejudices of Philosophers

4

The falseness of an opinion is not for us any objection to it. It is here, perhaps, that our new language sounds strangest. The question is to what extent an opinion is life furthering, life preserving, species preserving, perhaps species rearing; and we are fundamentally inclined to maintain that the falsest opinions (to which the synthetic judgments *a priori* belong), are the most indispensable to us; that without a recognition of logical fictions, without a comparison of reality with the purely *imagined* world of the absolute and immutable, without a constant falsification of the world by means of numbers, man could not live— that the renunciation of false opinions would be a renunciation of life, a negation of life. *To recognize untruth as a condition of life:* that is certainly to impugn the traditional ideas of value in a dangerous manner, and a philosophy which ventures to do so, has by this alone placed itself beyond good and evil.

. . .

23

All psychology before has run aground on moral prejudices and timidities; it has not dared to descend into the depths. In so far as it is allowable to recognize in that which has before been written, evidence of that which has up to now been kept silent, it seems as if nobody had yet harbored the notion of psychology

as morphology and *the doctrine of the development of the will to power,* as I conceive of it. The power of moral prejudices has penetrated deeply into the most spiritual world, the world apparently most indifferent and unprejudiced, and has obviously operated in an injurious, obstructive, blinding, and distorting manner. A proper psychophysiology has to contend with unconscious antagonism in the heart of the investigator, it has "the heart" against it: even a doctrine of the reciprocal dependence of the "good" and the "bad" impulses, causes (as refined immorality) distress and aversion in a still strong and virile conscience—still more so, a doctrine of the derivation of all good impulses from bad ones. If, however, a person should regard even the emotions of hatred, envy, covetousness, and imperiousness as conditions of life, as factors which must be present, fundamentally and essentially, in the general economy of life (which must, therefore, be further developed if life is to be further developed), he will suffer from such a view of things as from seasickness. And yet, this hypothesis is far from being the strangest and most painful in this immense and almost new domain of dangerous knowledge; and there are in fact a hundred good reasons why every one should keep away from it who *can* do so! On the other hand, if one has once drifted here with one's ship, well! Very good! Now let us set our teeth firmly! Let us open our eyes and keep our hand fast on the helm! We sail away right *over* morality, we crash out, we destroy perhaps the remains of our own morality by daring to make our voyage—but what do *we* matter! Never yet did a *profounder* world of insight reveal itself to daring travelers and adventurers, and the psychologist who thus "makes a sacrifice"; it is *not* the *sacrifizio dell'intelletto,* on the contrary— will at least be entitled to demand in return that psychology shall once more be recognized as the queen of the sciences, for whose service and equipment the other sciences exist. For psychology is once more the path to the fundamental problems.

. . .

SECOND CHAPTER

The Free Spirit

32

Throughout the longest period of human history— call it the prehistoric period—the value or non-value

---

*The translation has been edited. Some of the changes were suggested by the translation of Walter Kaufmann.

of an action was inferred from its *consequences;* the action in itself was not taken into consideration, any more than its origin; but pretty much as in China at present, where the distinction or disgrace of a child reflects back on to its parents, the retro-operating power of success or failure was what induced men to think well or ill of an action. Let us call this period the *premoral* period of mankind; the imperative, "Know thyself" was then still unknown. In the last ten thousand years, on the other hand, on certain large portions of the earth, one has gradually got so far, that one no longer lets the consequences of an action, but its origin, decide with regard to its worth: A great achievement as a whole, an important refinement of vision and of standards, the unconscious effect of the rule of aristocratic values and of the belief in "origin," the mark of a period which may be designated in the narrower sense as the *moral* one: the first attempt at self-knowledge is thereby made. Instead of the consequences, the origin—what an inversion of perspective! And assuredly this is an inversion effected only after long struggle and wavering! To be sure, an ominous new superstition, a peculiar narrowness of interpretation, attained supremacy precisely there. The origin of an action was interpreted in the most definite sense possible, as origin out of an *intention;* people were agreed in the belief that the value of an action lay in the value of its intention. The intention as the sole origin and antecedent history of an action: under the influence of this prejudice, moral praise and blame have been bestowed, and men have judged and even philosophized almost up to the present day.

Is it not possible, however, that the necessity may now have arisen of again making up our minds with regard to the reversing and fundamental shifting of values, owing to a new self-consciousness and acuteness in man? Is it not possible that we may be standing on the threshold of a period which to begin with, would be distinguished negatively as *extra-moral:* nowadays when, at least among us immoralists, the suspicion arises that the decisive value of an action lies precisely in that which is *not intentional,* and that what is intentional in all that is seen, sensible, or "sensed" in it, belongs to its surface or skin—which, like every skin, betrays something, but *conceals* still more? In short, we believe that the intention is only a sign or symptom, which first requires interpretation—a sign, moreover, which has too many interpretations, and consequently hardly any meaning in itself alone: that morality, in the sense in which it has

been understood up to now, as intention-morality, has been a prejudice, perhaps a prematureness or preliminariness, probably something of the same rank as astrology and alchemy, but in any case something which must be surmounted. The surmounting of morality, in a certain sense even the self-surmounting of morality—let that be the name for the long secret labor which has been reserved for the most refined, the most honest, and also the most wicked consciences of today, as the living touchstones of the soul.

.   .   .

34

At whatever standpoint of philosophy one may place oneself nowadays, seen from every position, the *erroneousness* of the world in which we think we live is the surest and most certain thing our eyes can light upon: we find proof after proof of this, which would like to allure us into surmises concerning a deceptive principle in the "nature of things." However, whoever makes thinking itself, and consequently "the spirit," responsible for the falseness of the world—an honorable exit, which every conscious or unconscious *advocatus dei** avails himself of—whoever regards this world, including space, time, form, and movement, as falsely *inferred,* would have at least good reason in the end to become distrustful also of all thinking; has it not always been playing upon us the worst of tricks? And what guarantee would it give that it would not continue to do what it has always been doing? In all seriousness, the innocence of thinkers has something touching and inspires respect in it, which even nowadays permits them to wait upon consciousness with the request that it will give them *honest* answers: for example, whether it be "real" or not, and why it keeps the external world so resolutely at a distance, and other questions of the same description. The faith in "immediate certainties" is a *moral naiveté* which does honor to us philosophers; but we have now to cease being "*merely* moral" men! Apart from morality, such faith is a folly which does little honor to us! If in middle-class life an ever ready distrust is regarded as the sign of a "bad character," and consequently as imprudent, here among us, beyond the middle-class world and its yes's and no's, what

---

*God's advocate.

should prevent us being imprudent and saying: the philosopher has a *right* to "bad character," as the being who has up to now been most fooled on earth—he is now under *obligation* to distrustfulness, to the wickedest squinting out of every abyss of suspicion.

Forgive me the joke of this gloomy grimace and turn of expression; for I myself have long ago learned to think and estimate differently with regard to deceiving and being deceived, and I keep at least a couple of pokes in the ribs ready for the blind rage with which philosophers struggle against being deceived. Why *not*? It is nothing more than a moral prejudice that truth is worth more than appearance; it is, in fact, the worst proved supposition in the world. *So* much must be conceded: there could have been no life at all except upon the basis of perspective estimates and appearances; and if, with the virtuous enthusiasm and stupidity of many philosophers, one wished to do away altogether with the "world of appearance"—well, granted that *you* could do that—at least nothing of your "truth" would thereby remain! Indeed, what is it that forces us in general to the supposition that there is an essential opposition of "true" and "false"? Is it not enough to suppose degrees of apparentness, and lighter and darker shades and tones of appearance—different *valeurs*, as the painters say? Why might not the world *which concerns us*—be a fiction? And to any one who suggested, "But to a fiction belongs an originator?"—might it not be bluntly replied: *Why?* May not this "belong" also belong to the fiction? Is it not at length permitted to be a little ironical toward the subject, just as toward the predicate and object? Might not the philosopher elevate himself above faith in grammar? With all respect to governesses, is it not time that philosophy should renounce the faith of governesses?

. . . .

36

Supposing that nothing else is "given" as real but our world of desires and passions, that we cannot sink or rise to any other "reality" but that of our drives—for thinking is only a relation of these drives to one another—are we not permitted to make the attempt and to ask the question whether this which is "given" does not *suffice*, for the understanding even of the so-called mechanical (or "material") world? I do not mean as an illusion, an "appearance," a "representation" (in the Berkeleyan and Schopenhauerian sense),

but as possessing the same degree of reality as our emotions themselves—as a more primitive form of the world of emotions, in which everything still lies locked in a mighty unity, which afterwards branches off and develops itself in organic processes (naturally also, refined and weakened) as a kind of instinctive life in which all organic functions, including self-regulation, assimilation, nutrition, secretion, and metabolism, are still synthetically united with one another—as an antecedent *form* of life?

In the end, it is not only permitted to make this attempt, it is commanded by the conscience of *method*. Not to assume several kinds of causality, so long as the attempt to get along with a single one has not been pushed to its furthest extent (to absurdity, if I may be allowed to say so); that is a morality of method which one may not repudiate nowadays; it follows "from its definition," as mathematicians say. The question is ultimately whether we really recognize the will as *operating*, whether we believe in the causality of the will; if we do so—and fundamentally our belief *in this* is just our belief in causality itself—we *must* make the attempt to posit hypothetically the causality of the will as the only causality. "Will" can naturally only operate on "will"—and not on "matter" (not on "nerves," for instance). In short, the hypothesis must be hazarded, whether will does not operate on will wherever "effects" are recognized—and whether all mechanical action, inasmuch as a power operates in it, is not just the power of will, the effect of will. Suppose, finally, that we succeeded in explaining our entire instinctive life as the development and ramification of one fundamental form of will—namely, the will to power, as *my* thesis puts it; granted that all organic functions could be traced back to this will to power, and that the solution of the problem of generation and nutrition—it is one problem—could also be found in this: one would thus have acquired the rights to define *all* active force unequivocally as *will to power*. The world seen from within, the world defined and designated according to its "intelligible character"; it would simply be "will to power," and nothing else.

. . . .

39

Nobody will very readily regard a doctrine as true merely because it makes people happy or virtuous—except perhaps the amiable "idealists," who are enthusiastic about the good, true, and beautiful, and let all kinds of motley, coarse, and good-natured desiderata swim about confusedly in their pond. Happiness and virtue are no arguments. It is willingly forgotten, however, even on the part of thoughtful minds, that to make unhappy and to make evil are not counter-arguments. A thing could be *true*, although it would be in the highest degree injurious and dangerous; indeed, the fundamental constitution of existence might be such that a full knowledge of it would be fatal; so that the strength of a mind might be measured by the amount of "truth" it could endure, or to speak more plainly, by the extent to which it *required* truth attenuated, veiled, sweetened, damped, and falsified. But there is no doubt that for the discovery of certain *portions* of truth, the wicked and unfortunate are more favorably situated and have a greater likelihood of success; not to speak of the wicked who are happy—a species about whom moralists are silent. Perhaps severity and skill are more favorable conditions for the development of strong, independent spirits and philosophers than the gentle, refined, yielding good nature, and habit of taking things easily, which are prized, and rightly prized in a scholar. Presupposing always, to begin with, that the term "philosopher" be not confined to the philosopher who writes books, or even introduces *his* philosophy into books!

· · ·

42

A new order of philosophers is appearing; I shall venture to baptize them by a name not without danger. As far as I understand them, as far as they allow themselves to be understood—for it is their nature to *wish* to remain something of a puzzle—these philosophers of the future might rightly, perhaps also wrongly, claim to be designated as "*attempters*." This name itself is after all only an attempt, or if it be preferred, a temptation.

43

Will they be new friends of "truth," these coming philosophers? Very probably, for all philosophers have always loved their truths. But assuredly they will not be dogmatists. It must be contrary to their pride, and also contrary to their taste, that their truth should still be truth for every one—which has always been the secret wish and ultimate purpose of all dog-matic efforts. "My opinion is *my* opinion: another person has not easily a right to it"—such a philosopher of the future will say, perhaps. One must renounce the bad taste of wishing to agree with many people. "Good" is no longer good when one's neighbor mouths it. And how could there be a "common good"! The expression contradicts itself; that which can be common is always of small value. In the end things must be as they are and have always been—the great things remain for the great, the abysses for the profound, the delicacies and thrills for the refined, and to sum up, everything rare for the rare.

44

Need I say expressly after all this that they will be free, *very* free spirits, these philosophers of the future—as certainly also they will not be merely free spirits, but something more, higher, greater, and fundamentally different, which does not wish to be misunderstood and mistaken? But while I say this, I feel under *obligation* almost as much to them as to ourselves (we free spirits who are their heralds and forerunners), to sweep away from ourselves a stupid old prejudice and misunderstanding which, like a fog, has too long made the conception of "free spirit" obscure. In every country of Europe, and the same in America, there is at present something which makes an abuse of this name: a very narrow, prepossessed, enchained class of spirits, who desire almost the opposite of what our intentions and instincts prompt . . . What they would like to attain with all their strength, is the universal, green-meadow happiness of the herd, together with security, safety, comfort, and an easier life for everyone; their two most frequently chanted songs and doctrines are called "equality of rights" and "sympathy for all sufferers"—and suffering itself is looked upon by them as something which must be *done away with*. We opposite ones, however, who have opened our eye and conscience to the question how and where the plant "man" has always grown most vigorously, believe that this has always taken place under the opposite conditions, that for this end the dangerousness of his situation had to be increased enormously, his inventive faculty and dissembling power (his "spirit") had to develop into subtlety and daring under long oppression and compulsion, and his will to life had to be increased to the unconditioned will to power: we believe that severity, forcefulness, slavery, danger in the street and in the heart, secrecy, stoicism, tempter's art and devilry of every kind—that everything wicked, terrible, tyrannical, predatory, and serpentine in man, serves as well for the elevation of the human species as its opposite—we do not even say enough when we only say *this much;* and in any case we find ourselves here, both with our speech and our silence, at the *other* extreme of all modern ideology and herd desiderata, as their exact opposites perhaps?

· · ·

47

Wherever the religious neurosis has appeared on the earth so far, we find it connected with three dangerous dietary regimens: solitude, fasting, and sexual abstinence—but without it being possible to determine with certainty which is cause and which is effect, or *if* any relation at all of cause and effect exists there. This latter doubt is justified by the fact that one of the most regular symptoms among savage as well as among civilized peoples is the most sudden and excessive sensuality; which then with equal suddenness transforms into penitential paroxysms, world renunciation, and renunciation of will: both symptoms perhaps explainable as disguised epilepsy? But nowhere is it *more* obligatory to put aside interpretations; around no other type has there grown such a mass of absurdity and superstition, no other type seems to have been more interesting to men and even to philosophers—perhaps it is time to become just a little indifferent here, to learn caution, or better still, to look away, *to go away.*

Yet in the background of the most recent philosophy, that of Schopenhauer, we find almost as the "problem-in-itself," this terrible question mark of the religious crisis and awakening. How is the denial of will *possible?* How is the saint possible? That seems to have been the very question with which Schopenhauer made a start and became a philosopher. . . . If, however, one asks what has been so extremely interesting to men of all sorts in all ages, and even to philosophers, in the whole phenomenon of the saint, it is undoubtedly the appearance of the miraculous—namely, the immediate *succession of opposites,* of states of the soul that are judged morally in opposite ways: it was believed here to be self-evident that a "bad man" was all at once turned into a "saint," a good man. The existing psychology was wrecked at this point; is it not possible it may have happened principally because psychology had placed itself under the dominion of morals, because it *believed* in oppositions of moral values, and saw, read, and *interpreted* these oppositions into the text and facts of the case? What? "Miracle" only an error of interpretation? A lack of philology?

· · ·

49

That which is so astonishing in the religious life of the ancient Greeks is the irrestrainable stream of *gratitude* which it pours forth—it is a very superior kind of man who takes *such* an attitude towards nature and life.

Later on, when the rabble got the upper hand in Greece, *fear* became rampant also in religion; and Christianity was preparing itself.

· · ·

56

Whoever, like myself, prompted by some enigmatical desire, has long endeavored to go to the bottom of the question of pessimism and free it from the half-Christian, half-German narrowness and stupidity in which it has finally presented itself to this century; namely, in the form of Schopenhauer's philosophy; whoever, with an Asiatic and supra-Asiatic eye, has actually looked inside, and into the most world renouncing of all possible modes of thought—beyond good and evil, and no longer, like Buddha and Schopenhauer, under the dominion and delusion of morality—whoever has done this, has perhaps, without really desiring it, opened his eyes to behold the opposite ideal: the ideal of the most world approving, exuberant and alive man, who has not only come to terms with and learned to get along with that which was and is, but wishes to have it again as *it was and is,* for all eternity, insatiably calling out *da capo,* not only to himself, but to the whole spectacle and play; and not only to the play, but actually to him who requires the play—and makes it necessary because he always requires himself anew—and makes himself necessary.

What? And this would not be—*circulus vitiosus deus?**

---

*A divine vicious circle.

59

Whoever has seen deeply into the world has doubtless divined what wisdom there is in the fact that men are superficial. It is their preservative instinct which teaches them to be flighty, light, and false. Here and there one finds a passionate and exaggerated adoration of "pure forms" in philosophers as well as in artists: it is not to be doubted that whoever has *need* of the cult of the superficial to that extent, has at one time or another made an unlucky dive *beneath* it. Perhaps there is even an order of rank with respect to those burned children, the born artists who find the enjoyment of life only in trying to *falsify* its image (as if taking wearisome revenge on it). One might guess to what degree life has disgusted them, by the extent to which they wish to see its image falsified, attenuated, transcended, and deified; one might reckon the *homines religiosi* amongst the artists, as their *highest* rank. It is the profound, suspicious fear of an incurable pessimism that compels whole centuries to fasten their teeth into a religious interpretation of existence: The fear of the instinct which divines that truth might be attained *too soon,* before man has become strong enough, hard enough, artist enough.... Piety, the "life in God," regarded in this light, would appear as the most elaborate and ultimate product of the *fear* of truth, as artist adoration, and artist intoxication in presence of the most logical of all falsifications, as the will to the inversion of truth, to untruth at any price. Perhaps there has been up to now no more effective means of beautifying man than piety; by means of it man can become so artful, so superficial, so iridescent, and so gracious that his appearance no longer offends.

. . . .

FIFTH CHAPTER

The Natural History of Morals

186

The moral sentiment in Europe at present is perhaps as subtle, belated, diverse, sensitive, and refined, as the "science of morals" belonging to it is young, raw, awkward, and coarse fingered: an interesting contrast, which sometimes becomes incarnate and obvious in the very person of a moralist. Indeed, the expression, "science of morals" is, in respect to what is designated thereby, far too presumptuous and counter to *good* taste—which always prefers more modest expressions. One ought to acknowledge with the utmost fairness *what* is still necessary here for a long time to come, *what* is alone warranted at present: namely, the collection of material, the comprehensive survey and classification of an immense domain of delicate sentiments of worth, and distinctions of worth, which live, grow, propagate, and perish—and perhaps attempts to give a clear idea of the recurring and more common forms of these living crystallizations—as preparation for a *theory of types* of morality. To be sure, people have not up to now been so modest. All the philosophers, with a pedantic and ridiculous seriousness, demanded of themselves something very much higher, more pretentious, and ceremonious, when they concerned themselves with morality as a science: they wanted to provide a rational foundation for morality—and every philosopher up to now has believed that he has given it such a basis; morality itself, however, has been regarded as something "given." How far from their awkward pride was the seemingly insignificant problem—left in dust and decay—of a description of forms of morality, in spite of the fact that the finest hands and senses could hardly be subtle enough for it! It was precisely owing to moral philosophers knowing the moral facts imperfectly, in an arbitrary epitome, or an accidental abridgment—perhaps as the morality of their environment, their position, their church, their *Zeitgeist,* their climate and zone—it was precisely because they were badly instructed with regard to nations, eras, and past ages, and were by no means eager to know about these matters, that they did not even come in sight of the real problems of morals—problems which only disclose themselves by a comparison of *many* kinds of morality. In every "science of morals" up to this point, strange as it may sound, the problem of morality itself has been *omitted;* there has been no suspicion that there was anything problematic there! That which philosophers called "rationally justifying morality," and endeavored to provide has, when seen in a right light, proved merely a learned form of good *faith* in prevailing morality, a new means of its *expression,* consequently just a fact within the sphere of a definite morality, indeed, in its ultimate motive, a sort of denial that it is *permissible* for this morality to be called in question—and in any case the reverse of the testing, analyzing, doubting, and vivisecting of this very faith. Hear, for instance, with what innocence—almost worthy of honor—Schopenhauer represents his own task, and draw your conclusions concerning the scientific merit of a "science" whose latest master still talks like children and old wives: "The principle," he says (page 136 of the *Grundprobleme der Ethik**), "the axiom about the purport of which all moralists are *practically* agreed: *neminem læde, immo omnes quantum potes juva*†—is *really* the proposition which all moral teachers strive to establish, . . . the *real* basis of ethics which has been sought, like the philosopher's stone, for centuries."

The difficulty of establishing the proposition referred to may indeed be great—it is well known that Schopenhauer also was unsuccessful in his efforts; and whoever has thoroughly realized how absurdly false and sentimental this proposition is, in a world whose essence is will to power, may be reminded that Schopenhauer, although a pessimist, *actually*—played the flute . . . daily after dinner: one may read about the matter in his biography. A question by the way: a pessimist, a repudiator of God and of the world, who *stops* at morality—who assents to morality, and plays the flute to *læde-neminem* morals, what? Is that really—a pessimist?

187

Apart from the value of such assertions as "there is a categorical imperative in us," one can always ask: What does such an assertion indicate about him who makes it? There are systems of morals which are meant to justify their author in the eyes of other people; other systems of morals are meant to tranquilize him, and make him self-satisfied; with other systems he wants to crucify and humble himself; with others he wishes to take revenge; with others to conceal himself; with others to glorify himself and gain superiority and distinction;—this system of morals helps its author to forget, that system makes him, or something about him, forgotten; many a moralist would like to exercise power and arbitrary whims

over mankind; many another, perhaps Kant especially, gives us to understand by his morals that "what is estimable in me, is that I know how to obey—and with you it *shall* not be otherwise than with me!" In short, systems of morals are only a *sign language of the emotions*.

188

In contrast to *laisser-aller,** every system of morals is a sort of tyranny against "nature" and also against "reason"; that is, however, no objection, unless one should again decree by some system of morals, that all kinds of tyranny and unreasonableness are unlawful. What is essential and invaluable in every system of morals, is that it is a long constraint. In order to understand Stoicism, or Port-Royal, or Puritanism, one should remember the constraint under which every language has attained to strength and freedom—the metrical constraint, the tyranny of rhyme and rhythm. How much trouble have the poets and orators of every nation given themselves not excluding to some of the prose writers of today, in whose ear dwells an inexorable conscientiousness—"for the sake of a folly," as utilitarian bunglers say, and thereby deem themselves wise; "from submission to arbitrary laws," as the anarchists say, and thereby fancy themselves "free," even free spirited. The singular fact remains, however, that everything of the nature of freedom, elegance, boldness, dance, and masterly certainty, which exists or has existed, whether it be in thought itself, or in administration, or in speaking and persuading, in art just as in conduct, has only developed by means of the tyranny of such arbitrary law; and in all seriousness, it is not at all improbable that precisely this is "nature" and "natural"—and *not laisser-aller!* Every artist knows how different from the state of letting himself go, in his "most natural" condition, the free arranging, locating, disposing, and constructing in the moments of "inspiration," and how strictly and delicately he then obeys a thousand laws, which, by their very rigidness and precision, defy all formulation by means of ideas (even the most stable idea has, in comparison, something floating, manifold, and ambiguous in it). The essential thing "in heaven and in earth" is, apparently (to re-

---

*Pages 54–55 of Schopenhauer's *Basis of Morality*, translated by Arthur B. Bullock, M.A. (1903).
†Avoid harm; help as much as possible.

---

*Letting oneself go.

peat it once more), that there should be long-standing *obedience* in a single direction; there then results, and has always resulted in the long run, something which has made life worth living; for instance, virtue, art, music, dancing, reason, spirituality—anything whatever that is transfiguring, refined, foolish, or divine. The long bondage of the spirit, the distrustful constraint in the communicability of ideas, the discipline which the thinker imposed on himself to think in accordance with the rules of a church or a court, or conformable to Aristotelian premises, the persistent spiritual will to interpret everything that happened according to a Christian scheme, and in every occurrence to rediscover and justify the Christian God: all this violence, arbitrariness, severity, dreadfulness, and unreasonableness, has proved itself the disciplinary means whereby the European spirit has attained its strength, its remorseless curiosity and subtle mobility; granted also that much irrecoverable strength and spirit had to be stifled, suffocated, and spoiled in the process (for here, as everywhere, "nature" shows herself as she is, in all her extravagant and *indifferent* magnificence, which is shocking, but nevertheless noble). That for centuries European thinkers only thought in order to prove something—nowadays, on the contrary, we are suspicious of every thinker who "wishes to prove something"—that it was always settled beforehand what *was to be* the result of their strictest thinking, as it was perhaps in the Asiatic astrology of former times, or as it is still at the present day in the innocent, Christian-moral explanation of immediate personal events "for the glory of God," or "for the good of the soul": this tyranny, this arbitrariness, this severe and magnificent stupidity, has *educated* the spirit; slavery, both in the coarser and the finer sense, is apparently an indispensable means even of spiritual education and discipline. One may look at every system of morals in this light: it is "nature" which teaches to hate the *laisser-aller,* the too great freedom, and implants the need for limited horizons, for immediate duties—it teaches the *narrowing of perspectives,* and thus, in a certain sense, that stupidity is a condition of life and development. "You must obey someone, and for a long time; *otherwise* you will come to grief, and lose all respect for yourself"—this seems to me to be the moral imperative of nature, which is certainly neither "categorical," as old Kant wished (consequently the "otherwise"), nor does it address itself to the individual (what does nature care for the individual!), but to nations, races, ages, and

ranks, however, above all to the animal "man" generally, to *mankind.*

. . .

201

As long as the utility which determines moral estimates is only herd utility, as long as the preservation of the community is the only consideration, and the immoral is sought precisely and exclusively in what seems dangerous to the maintenance of the community, there can be no "morality of love for one's neighbor." Granted that even then there was a little constant exercise of consideration, sympathy, fairness, gentleness, and mutual assistance, granted that even in this condition of society all those instincts are already active that were later given the honorable name "virtues," and eventually almost coincide with the conception "morality": in that period they do not as yet belong to the domain of moral valuations— they are still *extra-moral.* An act of pity, for instance, is neither called good nor bad, moral nor immoral, in the best period of the Romans; and should it be praised, a sort of resentful disdain is compatible with this praise, even at the best, as soon as the sympathetic action is compared with one which contributes to the welfare of the whole, to the *res publica.* After all, "love of our neighbor" is always a secondary matter, partly conventional and arbitrarily manifest in relation to our *fear of our neighbor.* After the fabric of society seems on the whole established and secured against external dangers, it is this fear of our neighbor which again creates new perspectives of moral valuation. Certain strong and dangerous instincts, such as the love of enterprise, foolhardiness, vengefulness, astuteness, rapacity, and love of power, which up till then had not only to be honored from the point of view of general utility—under other names, of course, than those here given—but had to be fostered and cultivated (because they were perpetually required in the common danger against the common enemies), are now felt as doubly dangerous—when the outlets for them are lacking—and are gradually branded as immoral and given over to calumny. The contrary drives and inclinations now attain to moral honor; the herd instinct gradually draws its conclusions. How much or how little dangerousness to the community or to equality is contained in an opinion, a condition, an emotion, a disposition, or an endowment—that is now the moral perspective; here again fear is the mother of morals. It is by the loftiest and strongest drives, when they break out passionately and carry the individual far above and beyond the average, and the low level of the herd conscience, that the self-reliance of the community is destroyed; its faith in itself, its backbone, as it were, breaks; consequently these very drives will be most branded and defamed. The lofty independent spirituality, the will to stand alone, and even the cogent reason, are felt to be dangers; everything that elevates the individual above the herd, and is a source of fear to the neighbor, is from this time on called *evil*; the tolerant, unassuming, submissive, self-equalizing disposition, the *mediocrity* of desires, attains to moral distinction and honor. Finally, under very peaceful circumstances, there is always less opportunity and necessity for training the feelings to severity and rigor; and now every form of severity, even in justice, begins to disturb the conscience; a lofty and rigorous nobleness and self-responsibility almost offends, and awakens distrust, "the lamb," and still more "the sheep," wins respect. There is a point of diseased mellowness and effeminacy in the history of society, at which society itself sides with those who injure it, with *criminals* and does so, in fact, seriously and honestly. To punish, appears to it to be somehow unfair—it is then certain that the idea of "punishment" and "the obligation to punish" are painful and alarming to people. "Is it not sufficient if the criminal be rendered *harmless*? Why should we still punish? Punishment itself is terrible!"—with these questions herd morality, the morality of fear, draws its ultimate conclusion. If one could at all do away with danger, the cause of fear, one would have done away with this morality at the same time, it would no longer be necessary, it *would not consider itself* any longer necessary!

Whoever examines the conscience of the present-day European, will always elicit the same imperative from its thousand moral folds and hidden recesses, the imperative of the timidity of the herd: "We wish that some time or other there may be *nothing more to fear!*" Some time or other—the will and the way to this is nowadays called "progress" all over Europe.

202

Let us once say again what we have already said a hundred times, for people's ears nowadays are unwilling to hear such truths—*our* truths. We know well enough how offensively it sounds when any one plainly, and

without metaphor, counts man among the animals; but it will be charged against us almost as a *crime* that it is precisely in respect to men of "modern ideas" that we have constantly applied the terms "herd," "herd instincts," and such expressions. What is to be done about it? We cannot do otherwise, for it is precisely here that our new insight is. We have found that in all the principal moral judgments Europe has become unanimous, including likewise the countries where European influence prevails: in Europe people evidently *know* what Socrates thought he did not know, and what the famous serpent of old once promised to teach—they "know" today what is good and evil. It must then sound hard and be distasteful to the ear, when we continue to insist that that which here thinks it knows, that which here glorifies itself with praise and blame, and calls itself good, is the instinct of the herding human animal: the instinct which has come and is ever coming more and more to the front, to preponderance and supremacy over other instincts, according to the increasing physiological approximation and resemblance of which it is the symptom. *Morality in Europe at present is herding-animal morality*; and therefore, as we understand the matter, only one kind of human morality, beside which, before which, and after which many other moralities, and above all *higher* moralities, are or should be possible. Against such a "possibility," against such a "should be," however, this morality defends itself with all its strength; it says obstinately and inexorably: "I am morality itself and nothing else is morality!" Indeed, with the help of a religion which has humored and flattered the sublimest desires of the herding animal, things have reached such a point that we always find a more visible expression of this morality even in political and social arrangements: the *democratic* movement is the inheritance of the Christian movement. That its *tempo*, however, is much too slow and sleepy for the more impatient ones, for those who are sick and distracted by the herding instinct, is indicated by the increasingly furious howling, and always less disguised teeth gnashing of the anarchist dogs, who are now roving through the highways of European culture, apparently in opposition to the peacefully industrious democrats and Revolution ideologues, and still more so to the awkward philosophasters and fraternity visionaries who call themselves socialists and want a "free society"; but in reality at one with them all in their thorough and instinctive hostility to every form of society other than that of the *autonomous* herd (to the extent even of repudiating the notions "master" and "servant"—*ni dieu ni maître,** says a socialist formula); at one in their tenacious opposition to every special claim, every special right and privilege (this means ultimately opposition to *every* right, for when all are equal, no one needs "rights" any longer); at one in their distrust of punitive justice (as though it were a violation of the weak, a wrong to the *necessary* consequences of all former society); but equally at one in their religion of sympathy, in their compassion for all that feels, lives, and suffers (down to the very animals, up even to "God"—the extravagance of "sympathy for God" belongs to a democratic age); altogether at one in the cry and impatience of their sympathy, in their deadly hatred of suffering generally, in their almost feminine incapacity for witnessing it or *allowing* it; at one in their involuntary glooming and softening, under the spell of which Europe seems to be threatened with a new Buddhism; at one in their belief in the morality of shared pity, as though it were morality in itself, the climax, the *attained* climax of mankind, the sole hope of the future, the consolation of the present, the great discharge from all the obligations of the past; altogether one in their belief in the community as the *deliverer,* in the herd, and therefore in "themselves."

203

We, who hold a different belief—we, who regard the democratic movement, not only as a degenerating form of political organization, but as a form of degeneration, namely the diminution of humanity, making it mediocre and less valuable: where may *we* reach with our hopes? To *new philosophers*—there is no other alternative: in minds strong and original enough to initiate opposite estimates of value, to revalue and invert "eternal valuations"; in forerunners, in men of the future, who in the present shall fix the constraints and fasten the knots which will compel millenniums to take *new* paths. To teach man the future of humanity as his *will,* as depending on human will, and to make preparation for vast hazardous enterprises and collective attempts in rearing and educating, in order to put an end to the frightful rule of folly and chance which has always gone by the

name of "history" (the folly of the "greatest number" is only its last form)—for that purpose a new type of philosopher and commander will some time or other be needed, at the very idea of which everything that has existed in the way of occult, terrible, and benevolent beings might look pale and dwarfed. The image of such leaders hovers before *our* eyes: is it lawful for me to say it aloud, you free spirits? The conditions which one would partly have to create and partly utilize for their genesis; the presumptive methods and tests by virtue of which a soul should grow to such an elevation and power as to feel a *constraint* to these tasks; a revaluation of values, under the new pressure and hammer of which a conscience should be steeled and a heart transformed into brass, so as to bear the weight of such responsibility; and on the other hand the necessity for such leaders, the dreadful danger that they might be lacking, or miscarry and degenerate: these are *our* real anxieties and glooms, you know it well, you free spirits! These are the heavy distant thoughts and storms which sweep across the heaven of *our* life.

·   ·   ·

219

The practice of judging and condemning morally, is the favorite revenge of the spiritually shallow on those who are less so; it is also a kind of compensation for them being badly endowed by nature; and finally, it is an opportunity for acquiring spirit and *becoming* subtle: malice spiritualized. They are glad in their inmost heart that there is a standard according to which those who are overendowed with spiritual goods and privileges, are equal to them; they contend for the "equality of all before God," and almost *need* the belief in God for this purpose. It is among them that the most powerful antagonists of atheism are found. If any one were to say to them: "a lofty spirituality is beyond all comparison with the honesty and respectability of a merely moral man"—it would make them furious; I shall take care not to say so. I would rather flatter them with my theory that lofty spirituality itself exists only as the ultimate product of moral qualities; that it is a synthesis of all qualities attributed to the "merely moral" man, after they have been acquired singly through long training and practice, perhaps during a whole series of generations; that lofty spirituality is precisely the spiritualization of justice,

---

*Neither god nor master.

and the beneficent severity which knows that it is authorized to maintain *gradations of rank* in the world, even among things—and not only among men.

225

Whether it be hedonism, pessimism, utilitarianism, or eudemonism, all those modes of thinking which measure the worth of things according to *pleasure* and *pain,* that is, according to accompanying circumstances and secondary considerations, are plausible modes of thought and naivetés, which every one conscious of *creative* powers and an artist's conscience will look down upon with scorn, though not without pity. Pity for *you!*—To be sure, that is not pity as you understand it: it is not pity for social "distress," for "society" with its sick and misfortuned, for the hereditarily vicious and defective who litter the ground around us; still less is it pity for the grumbling, vexed, revolutionary slave classes who strive after power—they call it "freedom." *Our* pity is a loftier and far-sighted pity:—we see how *man* diminishes himself, how *you* diminish him! And there are moments when we view *your* pity with an indescribable anguish, when we resist it—when we regard your seriousness as more dangerous than any kind of levity. You want, if possible—and there is not a more foolish "if possible"—*to do away with suffering.* And we? It really seems that *we* would rather have it increased and made worse than it has ever been! Well being, as you understand it—is certainly no goal; it seems to us an *end;* a condition which at once renders man ludicrous and contemptible—and makes his destruction *desirable!* The discipline of suffering, of *great* suffering—don't you know that it is only *this* discipline that has produced all the elevations of humanity up to now? The tension of soul in misfortune which communicates to itself its energy, its shuddering in view of rack and ruin, its inventiveness and bravery in undergoing, enduring, interpreting, and exploiting misfortune, and whatever depth, mystery, disguise, spirit, artifice, or greatness has been bestowed upon the soul—has it not been bestowed through suffering, through the discipline of great suffering? In man *creature* and *creator* are united: in man there is not only matter, fragment, excess, clay, mire, folly, chaos; but there is also the creator, the sculptor, the hardness of the hammer, the divinity of the spectator, and the seventh day—don't you understand this contrast? And

that *your* pity for the "creature in man" applies to that which has to be fashioned, bruised, forged, stretched, roasted, annealed, refined—to that which must necessarily *suffer,* and *should* suffer? And *our* pity—don't you understand what our *reverse* pity applies to, when it resists your pity as the worst of all pampering and enervation?

So it is pity *against* pity! But to repeat it once more, there are higher problems than the problems of pleasure and pain and pity; and all systems of philosophy which deal only with these are naivetés.

226

We Immoralists—This world with which *we* are concerned, in which *we* fear and love, this almost invisible, inaudible world of delicate command and delicate obedience, a world of "almost" in every respect, captious, insidious, sharp, and tender—yes, it is well protected from clumsy spectators and familiar curiosity! We are woven into a strong net and garment of duties, and *cannot* disengage ourselves—precisely here, we are "men of duty," even we! Occasionally it is true we dance in our "chains" and between our "swords"; it is none the less true that more often we gnash our teeth under the circumstances, and are impatient at the secret hardship of our lot. But whatever we do, fools and appearances say of us: "These are men *without* duty," we always have fools and appearances against us!

227

Honesty, granting that it is the virtue from which we cannot rid ourselves, we free spirits—well, we will labor at it with all our malice and love, and not tire of "perfecting" ourselves in *our* virtue, which is the last one we have: may its splendor some day overspread like a gilded, blue, mocking twilight over this aging civilization with its dull gloomy seriousness! And if, nevertheless, our honesty should one day grow weary, and sigh, and stretch its limbs, and find us too hard, and would rather have it pleasanter, easier, and gentler, like an agreeable vice, let us remain *hard,* we last Stoics, and let us send to its help whatever devilry we have in us: our disgust at the clumsy and undefined, our *"nitimur in vetitum,"** our love of adventure, our

---

*We seek the forbidden.

sharpened and fastidious curiosity, our most subtle, disguised, spiritual will to power and universal conquest, which rambles and roves avidiously around all the realms of the future—let us go with all our "devils" to the help of our "God"!

. . .

229

In these later ages, which may be proud of their humanity, there still remains so much fear, so much *superstitious* fear, of the "cruel wild beast," the mastering of which constitutes the very pride of these more human ages—that even obvious truths, as if by the agreement of centuries, have long remained unuttered, because they have the appearance of helping the finally slain wild beast back to life again. I perhaps risk something when I allow such a truth to escape; let others capture it again and give it so much "milk of pious sentiment"[†] to drink, that it will lie down quiet and forgotten, in its old corner.

One ought to learn once again about cruelty, and open one's eyes; one ought at last to learn impatience, in order that such immodest gross errors—as, for instance, have been fostered by ancient and modern philosophers with regard to tragedy—may no longer wander about virtuously and boldly. Almost everything that we call "higher culture" is based upon the spiritualization and profundity of cruelty—this is my thesis; the "wild beast" has not been slain at all, it lives, it flourishes, it has only become—transfigured. That which constitutes the painful delight of tragedy is cruelty; that which operates agreeably in so-called tragic pity, and at the basis even of everything sublime, up to the highest and most delicate thrills of metaphysics, obtains its sweetness solely from the intermingled ingredient of cruelty. What the Roman enjoys in the arena, the Christian in the ecstasies of the cross, the Spaniard at the sight of the inquisitor's stake, or of the bullfight, the present-day Japanese who presses his way to the tragedy, the workman of the Parisian suburbs who has a nostalgia for bloody revolutions, the Wagnerian who, with suspended will, "undergoes" the performance of "Tristan and Isolde"—what all these enjoy, and strive with mysterious ardor to

----
[†] An expression from Schiller's *William Tell,* Act IV, Scene 3.

drink in, is the philter of the great Circe "cruelty." Here, to be sure, we must put aside entirely the blundering psychology of former times, which could only teach with regard to cruelty that it originated at the sight of the suffering of *others:* there is an abundant, superabundant enjoyment even in one's own suffering, in causing one's own suffering—and wherever man has allowed himself to be persuaded to self-denial in the *religious* sense, or to self-mutilation, as among the Phœnicians and ascetics, or in general, to desensualization, decarnalization, and contrition, to Puritanical repentance spasms, to vivisection of conscience and to Pascal-like *sacrifizio dell' intelletto,* he is secretly allured and impelled forwards by his cruelty, by the dangerous thrill of cruelty *towards himself.*

Finally, let us consider that even the seeker of knowledge operates as an artist and glorifier of cruelty, in that he compels his spirit to perceive *against* its own inclination, and often enough against the wishes of his heart: he forces it to say No, where he would like to affirm, love, and adore; indeed, every instance of taking a thing profoundly and fundamentally, is a violation, an intentional injuring of the fundamental will of the spirit, which instinctively aims at appearance and superficiality—even in every desire for knowledge there is a drop of cruelty.

. . .

NINTH CHAPTER

What Is Noble?

257

Every enhancement of the type "man," has always been the work of an aristocratic society—and so it will always be—a society believing in a long scale of gradations of rank and differences of worth among human beings, and requiring slavery in some form or other. Without the *pathos of distance,* such as grows out of the incarnated difference between strata, out of the constant outlooking and downlooking of the ruling caste on subordinates and instruments, and out of their equally constant practice of obeying and commanding, of keeping down and keeping at a distance—that other more mysterious pathos could never have arisen, the longing for an ever new widening of distance within the soul itself, the formation of ever higher, rarer, further, more extended, more comprehensive states, in sum, just the elevation of the type "man," the continued "self-surmounting of man," to use a moral formula in a supra-moral sense. To be sure, one must not resign oneself to any humanitarian illusions about the history of the origin of an aristocratic society (that is to say, of the preliminary condition for the enhancement of the type "man"): the truth is hard. Let us acknowledge unprejudicedly how every higher civilization has always *originated*! Men with a still natural nature, barbarians in every terrible sense of the word, men of prey, still in possession of unbroken strength of will and desire for power, threw themselves upon weaker, more moral, more peaceful races (perhaps trading or cattle-rearing communities), or upon old mellow civilizations in which the last vitality was flickering out in brilliant fireworks of spirit and depravity. At the commencement, the noble caste was always the barbarian caste: their superiority did not consist first of all in their physical, but in their psychical power—they were more *complete* men (which at every point also implies the same as "more complete beasts").

258

Corruption—as the indication that anarchy threatens to break out among the instincts, and that the foundation of the emotions, called "life," has been shaken—is something radically different according to the organization in which it manifests itself. When, for instance, an aristocracy like that of France at the beginning of the Revolution, flung away its privileges with sublime disgust and sacrificed itself to an excess of its moral sentiments, it was corruption: it was really only the closing act of the corruption which had existed for centuries, by virtue of which that aristocracy had abdicated step by step its lordly prerogatives and lowered itself to a *function* of royalty (in the end to nothing but its decoration and parade dress). The essential thing, however, in a good and healthy aristocracy is that it should *not* regard itself as a function either of the kingship or the commonwealth, but as the *significance* and highest justification of it—that it should therefore accept with a good conscience the sacrifice of a legion of individuals, who, *for its sake*, must be suppressed and reduced to incomplete men, to slaves and instruments. Its fundamental belief must be precisely that society is *not* allowed to exist for its own sake, but only as a foundation and scaffolding, by means of which a select class of beings may be able to elevate themselves to their higher duties, and in general to a higher *existence:* like those sun-seeking climbing plants in Java—they are called *Sipo Matador*—which encircle an oak so long and so often with their arms, until at last, high above it, but supported by it, they can unfold their tops in the open light, and exhibit their happiness.

259

To refrain mutually from injury, from violence, from exploitation, and put one's will on a par with that of others: this may result in a certain rough sense in good conduct among individuals when the necessary conditions are given (namely, the actual similarity of the individuals in amount of strength and degree of worth, and their co-relation within one organization). As soon, however, as one wished to take this principle more generally, and if possible even as *the fundamental principle of society*, it would immediately disclose what it really is—namely, a will to the *denial* of life, a principle of dissolution and decay. Here one must think profoundly to the very basis and resist all sentimental weakness: life itself is *essentially* appropriation, injury, conquest of the strange and weak, suppression, severity, obtrusion of one's own forms, incorporation, and at the least, putting it mildest, exploitation—but why should one for ever use precisely these words on which for ages a disparaging purpose has been stamped? Even the organization within which, as was previously supposed, the individuals treat each other as equal—it takes place in every healthy aristocracy—must itself, if it be a living and not a dying organization, do all that towards other bodies, which the individuals within it refrain from doing to each other: it will have to be the incarnated will to power, it will endeavor to grow, to gain ground, attract to itself and acquire ascendency—not owing to any morality or immorality, but because it *lives,* and because life *is* precisely will to power. On no point, however, is the ordinary consciousness of Europeans more unwilling to be corrected than on this matter; people now rave everywhere, even under the guise of science, about coming conditions of society in which "the exploiting character" is to be absent—that sounds to my ears as if they promised to invent a mode of life which should refrain from all organic functions. "Exploitation" does not belong to a depraved, or imperfect and primitive society: it belongs to the *nature* of the living being as a primary organic function; it is a consequence of the intrinsic will to power, which is precisely the will to live.

Granting that as a theory this is a novelty—as a reality it is the *fundamental fact* of all history: let us be so far honest with ourselves!

260

In a tour through the many finer and coarser moralities which have up to now prevailed or still prevail on the earth, I found certain traits recurring regularly together and connected with one another, until finally two primary types revealed themselves to me, and a radical distinction was brought to light. There is *master morality* and *slave morality*—I would at once add, however, that in all higher and mixed civilizations, there are also attempts at the reconciliation of the two moralities; but one finds still more often the confusion and mutual misunderstanding of them, indeed, sometimes their close juxtaposition—even in the same person, within one soul. The distinctions of moral values have either originated in a ruling caste —pleasantly conscious of being different from the ruled—or among the ruled class, the slaves and dependents of all sorts. In the first case, when it is the rulers who determine what is "good," it is the exalted, proud disposition which is regarded as the distinguishing feature and that which determines the order of rank. The noble type of human being separates from himself the beings in whom the opposite of this exalted, proud disposition displays itself: he despises them. Let it at once be noted that in this first kind of morality the antithesis "good" and "bad" means practically the same as "noble" and "despicable"; the antithesis "good" and "*evil*" is of a different origin. The cowardly, the timid, the insignificant, and those thinking merely of narrow utility are despised; moreover, also, the distrustful, with their constrained glances, the self-abasing, the dog-like kind of people who let themselves be abused, the mendicant flatterers, and above all the liars; it is a fundamental belief of all aristocrats that the common people are untruthful. "We truthful ones," the nobility in ancient Greece called themselves. It is obvious that everywhere the designations of moral value were at first applied to *people,* and were only derivatively and at a later period applied to *actions;* it is a gross mistake, therefore,

when historians of morals start with questions like, "Why have sympathetic actions been praised?" The noble type of man regards *himself* as determining values; he does not require to be approved of; he passes the judgment: "What is harmful to me is harmful in itself"; he knows that it is he himself only who confers honor on things; he is a *creator of values.* He honors whatever he recognizes in himself: such morality is self-glorification. In the foreground there is the feeling of plenitude, of power, which seeks to overflow, the happiness of high tension, the consciousness of a wealth which would give and bestow: the noble person also helps the unfortunate, but not—or scarcely—out of pity, but rather from an impulse generated by the superabundance of power. The noble person honors in himself the powerful one, him also who has power over himself, who knows how to speak and how to keep silence, who takes pleasure in subjecting himself to severity and hardness, and has reverence for all that is severe and hard. "Wotan placed a hard heart in my breast," says an old Scandinavian Saga: it is thus rightly expressed from the soul of a proud Viking. Such a type of man is even proud of *not* being made for sympathy; the hero of the Saga therefore adds warningly: "He who has not a hard heart when young, will never have one." The noble and brave who think thus are the furthest removed from the morality which sees precisely in pity, or in acting for the good of others, or in *désintéressement,* the characteristic of the moral; faith in oneself, pride in oneself, a radical enmity and irony towards "selflessness," belong as definitely to noble morality, as do a careless scorn and precaution in the presence of pity and the "warm heart."

It is the powerful who *know* how to honor, it is their art, their domain for invention. The profound reverence for age and for tradition—all law rests on this double reverence—the faith and prejudice in favor of ancestors and unfavorable to newcomers, is typical in the morality of the powerful; and if, reversely, men of "modern ideas" believe almost instinctively in "progress" and the "future," and are more and more lacking in respect for old age, the ignoble origin of these "ideas" has by this complacently betrayed itself. A morality of the ruling class, however, is more especially foreign and irritating to present-day taste in the sternness of its principle that one has duties only to one's equals; that one may act towards beings of a lower rank, towards all that is foreign, just as one pleases, or "as the heart desires," and in any case "beyond good and evil": it is here that pity and similar sentiments can have a place. The ability and obligation to exercise prolonged gratitude and prolonged revenge—both only within the circle of equals—artfulness in retaliation, *raffinement* of the idea in friendship, a certain necessity to have enemies (as outlets for the emotions of envy, quarrelsomeness, arrogance—in fact, in order to be a good *friend*): all these are typical characteristics of the noble morality, which, as has been pointed out, is not the morality of "modern ideas," and is therefore at present difficult to realize, and also to unearth and disclose. It is otherwise with the second type of morality, *slave morality*. Supposing that the abused, the oppressed, the suffering, the unfree, the weary, and those uncertain of themselves, should moralize, what will be the common element in their moral estimates? Probably a pessimistic suspicion with regard to the entire situation of man will find expression, perhaps a condemnation of man, together with his situation. The slave has an unfavorable eye for the virtues of the powerful; he has a skepticism and distrust, a *refinement* of distrust of everything "good" that is there honored—he would rather persuade himself that the very happiness there is not genuine. On the other hand, *those* qualities which serve to alleviate the existence of sufferers are brought into prominence and flooded with light; it is here that pity, the kind, helping hand, the warm heart, patience, diligence, humility, and friendliness attain to honor; for here these are the most useful qualities, and almost the only means of supporting the burden of existence. Slave morality is essentially the morality of utility. Here is the origin of the famous antithesis "good" and "*evil*": into the evil one are projected power and dangerousness, a certain dreadfulness, subtlety, and strength, which do not admit of being despised. According to slave morality, therefore, the "evil" man arouses fear; according to master morality, it is precisely the "good" man who arouses fear and seeks to arouse it, while the bad man is regarded as the despicable being. The contrast attains its maximum when, in accordance with the logical consequences of slave morality, a shade of disdain—it may be slight and well intentioned—at last attaches itself even to the "good" man of this morality; because, according to the servile mode of thought, the good man must in any case be the *safe* man: he is good natured, easily deceived, perhaps a little stupid, *un bonhomme.*

Everywhere that slave morality gains the ascendency, language shows a tendency to conjoin the significations of the words "good" and "stupid."

A last fundamental difference: the desire for *freedom*, the instinct for happiness and the refinements of the feeling of liberty belong as necessarily to slave morals and morality, as artifice and enthusiasm in reverence and devotion are the regular symptoms of an aristocratic mode of thinking and estimating. Hence we can understand without further detail why love *as passion*—it is our European speciality—must absolutely be of noble origin; as is well known, its invention is due to the Provençal troubadours, those brilliant ingenious men of the "*gai saber*," to whom Europe owes so much, and almost owes itself.

261

Vanity is one of the things which is perhaps most difficult for a noble individual to understand: he will be tempted to deny it, where another kind of human being thinks he sees it self-evidently. The problem for him is to represent to his mind beings who seek to arouse a good opinion of themselves which they themselves do not possess—and consequently also do not "deserve"—and who yet *believe* in this good opinion afterwards. This seems to him on the one hand such bad taste and so self-disrespectful, and on the other hand so grotesquely unreasonable, that he would like to consider vanity an exception and is doubtful about it in most cases when it is spoken of. . . .

262

A *species* originates, and a type becomes established and strong in the long struggle with essentially constant *unfavorable* conditions. On the other hand, it is known by the experience of breeders that species which receive superabundant nourishment, and in general a surplus of protection and care, immediately tend in the most marked way to develop variations, and are fertile in prodigies and monstrosities (also in monstrous vices). Now look at an aristocratic commonwealth, say an ancient Greek *polis*, or Venice, as a voluntary or involuntary contrivance for the purpose of *rearing* human beings; there are there men beside one another, thrown upon their own resources, who want to make their species prevail, chiefly because they *must* prevail, or else run the terrible danger of being exterminated. The favor, the superabundance, the protection are there lacking under which variations are fostered; the species needs itself as species, as something which, precisely by virtue of its hardness, its uniformity, and simplicity of structure, can in general prevail and make itself permanent in constant struggle with its neighbors, or with the oppressed who are rebellious or threatening rebellion. The most varied experience teaches it what are the qualities to which it principally owes the fact that it still exists, in spite of all Gods and men, and has up to now been victorious: these qualities it calls virtues, and these virtues alone it develops to maturity. It does so with severity, indeed it desires severity; every aristocratic morality is intolerant in the education of youth, in the control of women, in the marriage customs, in the relations of old and young, in the penal laws (which have an eye only for the degenerating): it counts intolerance itself among the virtues, under the name of "justice." A type with few, but very strong features, a species of severe, warlike, wisely silent, reserved and reticent men (and as such, with the most delicate sensibility for the charm and *nuances* of society) is thus established, unaffected by the vicissitudes of generations; the constant struggle with uniform *unfavorable* conditions is, as already remarked, the cause of a type becoming stable and hard. Finally, however, a happy state of things results, the enormous tension is relaxed; there are perhaps no more enemies among the neighboring peoples, and the means of life, even of the enjoyment of life, are present in superabundance. With one stroke the bond and constraint of the old discipline severs: it is no longer regarded as necessary, as a condition of existence—if it would continue, it can only do so as a form of *luxury,* as an archaizing *taste.* Variations, whether they be deviations (into the higher, finer, and rarer), or deteriorations and monstrosities, appear suddenly on the scene in the greatest exuberance and splendor; the individual dares to be individual and detach himself. At this turning point of history there manifest themselves, side by side, and often mixed and entangled together, a magnificent, varied, virgin-forestlike upgrowth and up striving, a kind of *tropical tempo* in the rivalry of growth, and an extraordinary decay and self-destruction, owing to the savagely opposing and seemingly exploding egoisms, which strive with one another "for sun and light," and can no longer assign any limit, restraint, or forbearance for themselves by means of the moral-

ity that has existed until then. It was this morality itself which piled up the strength so enormously, which bent the bow in so threatening a manner—it is now "out of date," it is outlived. The dangerous and disquieting point has been reached when the greater multifaceted, more comprehensive life *is lived beyond* the old morality; the "individual" stands out, and is obliged to have recourse to his own lawgiving, his own arts and artifices for self-preservation, self-elevation, and self-deliverance. Nothing but new "whys," nothing but new "hows," no common formulas any longer, misunderstanding and disregard in league with each other, decay, deterioration, and the loftiest desires frightfully entangled, the genius of the race overflowing from all the cornucopias of good and bad, a portentous simultaneousness of Spring and Autumn, full of new charms and mysteries peculiar to the fresh, still inexhausted, still unwearied corruption. Danger is again present, the mother of morality, great danger; this time shifted into the individual, into the neighbor and friend, into the street, into their own child, into their own heart, into all the most personal and secret recesses of their desires and volitions. What will the moral philosophers who appear at this time have to preach? They discover, these sharp onlookers and loafers, that the end is quickly approaching, that everything around them decays and produces decay, that nothing will endure until the day after tomorrow, except one species of man, the incurably *mediocre.* The mediocre alone have a prospect of continuing and propagating themselves— they will be the men of the future, the sole survivors; "Be like them! Become mediocre!" is now the only morality which has still a significance, which still obtains a hearing. But it is difficult to preach this morality of mediocrity! It can never avow what it is and what it desires! It has to talk of moderation and dignity and duty and brotherly love—it will have difficulty *in concealing its irony!*

· · ·

265

At the risk of displeasing innocent ears, I submit that egoism belongs to the essence of a noble soul, I mean the unalterable belief that to a being such as "we," other beings must naturally be in subjection, and have to sacrifice themselves. The noble soul accepts the fact of his egoism without question, and also without consciousness of harshness, constraint, or arbitrariness, but rather as something that may have its basis in the primary law of things: If he sought a designation for it he would say, "It is justice itself." He acknowledges under certain circumstances, which made him hesitate at first, that there are other equally privileged ones; as soon as he has settled this question of rank, he moves among those equals and equally privileged ones with the same assurance, as regards modesty and delicate respect, which he enjoys in intercourse with himself—in accordance with an innate heavenly mechanism which all the stars understand. It is an *additional* instance of his egoism, this artfulness and self-limitation in intercourse with his equals—every star is a similar egoist; he honors *himself* in them, and in the rights which he concedes to them, he has no doubt that the exchange of honors and rights, as the *essence* of all intercourse, belongs also to the natural condition of things. The noble soul gives as he takes, prompted by the passionate and sensitive instinct of requital, which is at the root of his nature. The notion of "grace" has, *inter pares,* neither significance nor good repute; there may be a sublime way of letting gifts light upon one from above and of drinking them thirstily like dewdrops; but for those arts and displays the noble soul has no aptitude. His egoism hinders him here: In general, he looks "aloft" unwillingly—he looks either *forward,* horizontally and deliberately, or downwards—*he knows that he is at a height.*

287

What is noble? What does the word "noble" still mean for us? How does the noble man betray himself, how is he recognized under this heavy overcast sky of the commencing plebeianism, by which everything is rendered opaque and leaden?

It is not his actions which establish his claim—actions are always ambiguous, always inscrutable; neither is it his "works." One finds today among artists and scholars plenty of those who betray by their works that a profound longing for nobleness impels them; but this very *need of* nobleness is radically different from the needs of the noble soul itself, and is in fact the eloquent and dangerous sign of the lack of it. It is not the works, but the *faith* which is here decisive and determines the order of rank—to employ once more an old religious formula with a new and deeper meaning—it is some fundamental certainty which a noble soul has about itself, something which is not to be sought, is not to be found, and perhaps, also, is not to be lost.

The noble soul has reverence for itself.

From *A Genealogy of Morals**

FOREWORD

6

The problem of the *value* of pity and morality of pity (I am an opponent of the shameful modern effeminacy of sentiment) seems, at first sight, to be something isolated—a single question mark; but he who will pause and *learn* to question here, will fare even as I have fared: a vast, new prospect reveals itself to him, a possibility seizes upon him like some giddiness; every kind of distrust, suspicion, fear springs up; the faith in morality, in all morality, is shaken, and finally, a new demand makes itself felt. Let us articulate this *new demand:* We stand in need of a criticism of moral values; *the value of these values is first of all itself to be put in question*—and to this end a knowledge is necessary of the conditions and circumstances from which they grew and under which they developed and shifted in meaning (morality as effect, as symptom, as mask, as tartuffism, as disease, as misunderstanding; but also, morality as cause, as remedy, as stimulant, as impediment, as poison), a knowledge which was until now not existent, no, not even desired. The *value* of these "values" was taken for granted, as a matter of fact, as being beyond all putting-in-question. Never until now was there the least doubt or hesitation, to set down "the good man" as of higher value than "the evil man"—of higher value in the sense of furtherance, utility, prosperity regarding *man* in general (the future of man included). What if the reverse were true? What if in the "good one" also a symptom of decline were contained, and a danger, a seduction, a poison, a narcotic by which the present might live at *the expense of the future?* Perhaps more

---

*The translation has been altered. Some of the changes were based on the translation by Walter Kaufmann.

comfortably, less dangerously, but also in humbler style, more meanly? . . . So that morality itself would be to blame, if the *highest power and splendor* of man—possible in itself—were never attained? And that, therefore, morality itself would be the danger of dangers? . . .

. . .

"Guilt," "Bad Conscience," and the Like

7

Formerly, when mankind did not as yet feel ashamed of its cruelty, life on earth was more cheerful than now that there exist pessimists. The darkening of the sky above man has always increased in the same ratio that man's shame *of man* kept growing. The weary, pessimistic look, the mistrust towards the riddle of life, the chilling No of the disgust with life—these are not the symptoms of the evilest periods of humanity. On the contrary, being swamp plants, they appear only when the swamp to which they belong has sprung into existence. By that I mean the sickly effeminacy and moralization, by means of which the animal "man" is taught to feel ashamed at last of all his instincts. On the road to become an "angel" (not to use an uglier word in this connection) man has reared for himself that spoiled stomach and "furred" tongue, which rendered obnoxious to him not only the pleasure and innocence of the animal, but made life itself of ill taste to him: so that at times he will stand before himself with shut nose and catalogue his own disagreeable features ("impure generation, nauseous alimentation in the womb, baseness of the matter from which man develops, fearful stench, secretion of saliva, urine and filth"). Now that "suffering" always is adduced as the first of the arguments *against* existence, and as the most serious interrogation mark of it, we do well to recall the times in which the reverse opinion prevailed, because the pleasure of *making* another suffer was held to be indispensable and constituted a most potent charm, a special seduction *to* life. . . .

. . .

. . . That which makes man revolt against suffering, is not suffering as such, but the senselessness of suffering: neither for the Christian, however, who interpreted into suffering a complete secret machinery of salvation, nor for the naive man of still earlier times, who contrived to interpret all suffering with a view to the spectator and the begetter of suffering, did this *senseless* suffering exist. In order to make it possible to banish from the world and honestly deny all hidden, undiscovered and unwitnessed suffering, man in those days was almost forced to invent gods and intermediary beings of every rank and degree, something, in short, also straying in secret abodes, seeing in the dark, and not very likely to let any interesting and painful exhibition escape its notice. By means of such inventions, life then performed the feat, which it has ever performed—the feat of self-vindication, of justifying its own "evils." At present other supporting inventions would seem to be necessary for this purpose (life for instance regarded as riddle, or life as epistemological problem). "All evils are justified, the sight of which edifies a god;" So ran in times of old the logic of feeling. And rightly considered, did it so run only in times of old? The gods conceived as the friends of *cruel* spectacles—oh, how far this primeval conception reaches over and into our European humanity! . . .

. . .

free will

. . . Might we not suppose, that this daring and fateful invention of the philosophers, made first for Europe, the invention of "free will," of absolute spontaneity of man regarding good and evil, was made with the express purpose of getting the right to the idea that the interest of the gods in man, and human virtue, *could never be exhausted*? On this earthly stage truly novel things—unheard of agitations, complications, catastrophes—must never be wanting; such was their idea. An entirely deterministically conceived world would have been predictable by the gods, and thereby, before long also boring—reason enough for these *friends of the gods,* the philosophers, not to impute to them such a deterministic world! All mankind of antiquity is full of delicate considerations for the "spectator"—being, as it was, an essentially public, an essentially ostentatious world to which happiness without feasts and spectacles was inconceivable.—And, once again, in grand *punishment* also, there is so much that is festival.

16

At this point of our inquiry a first provisional expression of my own hypothesis on the origin of "bad conscience" can hardly be avoided. It is not easy to make it intelligible and requires long and earnest attention and consideration. Bad conscience I take as the grave sickness which man had to fall into under the pressure of that most radical of all changes to which he was ever subjected—that change which he experienced when he found himself for ever locked within the walls of society and peace. Precisely as the sea animals must have felt, when forced to the alternative of either becoming land animals or of perishing, even so in the case of men, those semi-animals happily adapted to wildness, warring, roving and adventure. All at once their instincts were rendered worthless and "suspended." They were expected afterwards to go on their feet and to "carry themselves," whereas all along they had been carried by the water; a terrible heaviness lay upon them. For the execution of the simplest functions they found themselves too clumsy; for this new and strange world their old, reliable guides sufficed no longer—the unconsciously regulating and reliable instincts. They were reduced to the necessity of thinking, reasoning, calculating, of combining causes and effects (what misery!) to their consciousness—their meanest and least reliable organ! I believe that never before on earth did there exist a like feeling of misery, a similar state of leaden uncomfortableness. And, worse still, those old instincts had by no means ceased all at once to make their demands! Only it was difficult and rarely possible for man to comply with their claims. As a general rule they had to seek for new and, metaphorically speaking, subterranean gratifications. All instincts which do not discharge themselves outwards *turn inward*—this is what I call the *internalization* of man. It is only by this process that man developed that which later on is called his "soul." The entire inner world of man, being originally thin, as if it were stretched between two hides, expanded and extended, received depth, breadth and height, in the same measure as man's outward discharges were *checked*. Those terrible bulwarks by means of which a political organization guarded itself against the ancient instincts of freedom (punishments are first of all among these bulwarks) lead to the result that all those drives of wild, free and roving man turned inward *against man himself.* Enmity, cruelty, the pleasures of persecution, of surprise, of change, of destruction—imagine all these turning against the owners of such instincts: *this* is the origin of "bad conscience." Man who, from a lack of outer enemies and obstacles and because he found himself wedged into the unbearable straits and regularities of custom, impatiently tore, persecuted, gnawed at, maltreated himself; this captive animal grating against the bars of his cage while being "tamed," this creature deprived of, and pining for its home, the wild, he who was compelled to make out of himself an adventure, a torture chamber, an unsafe and dangerous wilderness—this fool, this homesick and despairing captive, became the inventor of "bad conscience." And with it, the greatest and most dismal morbidity was instituted from which mankind has not as yet recovered, the suffering of man *from man, from himself:* the consequence of a violent breaking with his past animal history, a leaping and plunging, so to speak, into other states and conditions of existence, a declaration of war against the old instincts, on which so far his strength, his pleasure and his terribleness had depended. Let us at once add that, on the other hand, with the fact of the existence upon earth of an animal soul antagonizing itself and turned against itself something so new, deep, unheard of, enigmatical, self-contradictory, *future-promising* was likewise given, that the aspect of the earth had undergone an essential change. And truly, divine spectators were necessary in order to appreciate the spectacle which was inaugurated, and of which the outcome can not as yet be imagined—a spectacle too fine, too wonderful, too paradoxical for its possibly being a mere meaningless and ludicrous sideshow upon some ridiculous star. Man ever since that time has counted *among* the oddest and most exciting haphazard throws practiced by the "great child" of Heraclitus, call it as you will, Zeus or chance. Man awakens for himself an interest, a suspense, a hope, almost a confidence that something important is about to happen, that something is in preparation, that man is not an end, but merely a way, an interact, a bridge, a great promise. . . .

17

Our hypothesis on the origin of bad conscience presupposes first of all that this change did not take place gradually, or spontaneously, and did not represent an organic ingrowing into new conditions, but rather a rupture, a leap, a compulsion, an unavoidable catastrophe which preempted all opposition, and even all resentment. Furthermore, that the fitting of a shapeless and undefined mass of people into a fixed form began with an act of violence and could *ipso facto* only be completed by a whole series of acts of violence—and hence, that the first "state" made its appearance in the form of a terrible tyranny, a violent and remorseless piece of machinery which kept grinding away till such a raw material—half men, half animals—was not only thoroughly kneaded and pliant, but also *shaped*. I made use of the word "state." It is plain on the face of it what it means—a pack of blond beasts of prey, a conqueror and master race, which, organized for war and possessing the power of organization, will unhesitatingly lay its terrible clutches upon some population perhaps vastly superior in numbers but as yet shapeless and roving. This is the origin of the "state" on earth; the fantastic theory which would have it begin by an "agreement," I should think, is done away with. He who can command, he who is a "master" by nature, he who in deed and gesture behaves violently—what has he to do with agreements! Such beings are not reckoned with; they come as fate will come, without reason, common sense, indulgence, pretext; they appear as a flash of lightning appears, too terrible, too sudden, too convincing, too "different" even to be hated. Their work is an instinctive creating of forms, impressing of forms—they are the most involuntary, most unconscious of all artists. Wherever they appear, something new will at once be created, a governmental structure which *lives,* in which the individual parts and functions are defined and coordinated, and in which nothing at all is tolerated unless first assigned a "meaning" in relation to the whole. They are innocent, in terms of the meaning of guilt, of responsibility, of regard—these born organizers; they are ruled by that terrible artist egotism which looks stern like bronze and knows itself to be justified to all eternity in its "work," as the mother knows herself justified in the child. "Bad conscience" has not grown among *them*—this much is self-evident—but it would never have grown at all *but for them,* that ill-shaped growth; it would be lacking altogether if, beneath the blows of their hammer and violence, an immense quantity of freedom had not disappeared from the world, or at any rate from visibility, and become latent. This *instinct for freedom,* suppressed, drawn back and imprisoned in consciousness and finally discharging and venting itself only inwards, against self: only this is the beginning of *bad conscience.*

. . .

21

The moralization of the concepts of guilt and duty, the pushing of them back into *bad* conscience, implies . . . an attempt to *reverse* the direction of the develop-ment described earlier, or, at least, to stay its progress. Now the very prospects of a final discharge of guilt *are asked,* once and for all, to be shut up in a pessimistic way; now the look *is asked* to shrink back and recoil disconsolately as though from some iron wall of impossibility; now those concepts "guilt" and "duty" *are asked* to turn backwards. Against *whom?* There is no question whatever: first of all against the "debtor," in whom bad conscience will now establish itself, eat into his flesh, extend, and polyp-like branch out into every depth and breadth until at last, in the conception of the irredeemableness of guilt, the idea of its unpayableness (*everlasting* punishment) is also conceived; but at last even against the "creditor," whether this be thought to be the *causa prima* of man, the beginning of mankind, its progenitor, who now will be burdened with a curse ("Adam," "original sin," "unfreedom of will"), or nature herself, from whose womb man takes his origin, and into which now the evil principle is projected ("diabolification of nature"), or existence in general which is declared as *worthless in itself* (nihilistic desertion of life, longing for nothingness, or a longing for one's antithesis, the state of being otherwise, Buddhism and kindred religions)—until all of a sudden, we find ourselves face to face with that paradoxical and frightful expedient which afforded at least temporary relief to tortured humanity, that master stroke of Christianity: God himself sacrificing himself for the guilt of man; God himself paying himself; God being alone able to redeem man from what has become irredeemable for man himself—the creditor sacrificing himself for his debtor, from *love* (would you believe it?), from love for his debtor! . . .

22

We shall have divined by this time the *real* and *inner* meaning of this entire phenomenon: that will to self-torture, that repressed cruelty of animal man who has become internalized, who is chased back into himself, who is caged in the "state" in order to be tamed, who invented bad conscience for the purpose of causing pain to himself after the *more natural* outlet of this will to cause pain had become obstructed—this man of bad conscience availed himself of religious presuppositions as a means of carrying his self-torture to an excess of frightful severity and cruelty. Guilt before God—this thought becomes his instrument of torture. In the concept of "God" he finds the ultimate antitheses of his own irredeemable animal instincts; by interpretation he transforms these animal instincts into guilt before God (as enmity, insurrection, rebellion against the "Lord," the "Father," the Progenitor, the Beginning of the world), he racks himself upon the antithesis "God" and "Devil"; he ejects from himself his denial of himself, of his nature, naturalness and actuality, in the form of a Yes, as something existing, bodily, real, as God, as the holy God, as God the judge, as God the hangman, as another world, as eternity, as everlasting torture, as hell, as immeasurableness of punishment and guilt.

. . .

24

I close with three question marks, as you will see. "Is here," some one will ask, "an ideal being erected, or an ideal being broken down?" But have you ever really asked yourselves sufficiently as to how dearly the erection of *all* ideals on earth was paid for? How much reality had to be slandered and misconceived for this purpose; how much falsehood sanctioned; how many consciences bothered; how much "God" sacrificed each time? In order that a sanctuary may be erected, a *sanctuary must be broken down:* this is the law—name me an instance in which it is violated! . . . We modern men, we are the heirs of the vivisection of conscience and self-torment of thousands of years. This has been our longest practice, perhaps our artist mastery or, in any case, our *raffinement,* our refined taste. For too long a time man regarded his natural inclinations with an "evil eye," so that in the end they became joined with "bad conscience." A reverse experiment is *in itself* possible—but who is strong enough for it?—who will join bad conscience with all *unnatural* inclinations, all those aspirations for another life, for all that is hostile to the senses, the drives, to nature, to animality; in one word, all the old ideals, which are, each and every one, ideals hostile to life and slandering the world? To whom today do we turn with *such* hopes and claims? . . . The *good* we should then have against us; and of course, also the indolent, the reconciled, the vain, the sentimental, the tired. . . . What offends more, what estranges more than to make others aware of the rigor and respect of our self-treatment! And, on the other hand, how obliging, how amiable all the world will show itself to us, as soon as we behave like all the world and "let ourselves go" like all the world! . . . For such a task requires a *different* kind of spirit than our age is likely to produce: spirits strengthened by wars and victories; to whom conquest, adventure, danger, even pain have become a need; for it an adjustment to thin, Alpine air, to winterly wanderings, to ice and mountains in every sense; no, even a kind of sublime maliciousness; an ultimate and most self-assured sprightliness of knowledge that is characteristic of great health: in brief, even this *great health* is requisite! . . . Is even this much possible today? . . . But at some time, and in a stronger time than this tottering and self-doubting age of ours, he *is* to come, the *redeeming* man of the great love and contempt, the creative spirit who, by his compelling power, is ever again driven away, from every corner and other world; whose loneliness is misunderstood by the people, as though it were a flight *from* reality, whereas it is but his absorption, immersion and penetration *into* reality, in order that when again he rises unto light, he may bring home with him the *redemption* of reality, its redemption from the curse which the old ideal has laid upon it. This man of the future who will redeem us from the old ideal, and also from that which *had to grow out of this ideal,* from great excess, from the will to nothingness, from nihilism; this bell stroke of noonday and the great decision which restores freedom to the will, which restores to the earth its goal, and to man his hope; this Antichrist and Antinihilist, this conqueror of God and of nothing—*he must come someday. . . .*

25

But what am I saying? Enough! Enough! At this point only one thing suits me—silence: unless otherwise I should infringe on what only one younger than I am, one more "futurous" than I am, one stronger than I am is free to do—on that which only *Zarathustra* has a right to do, *Zarathustra the godless. . . .*

WHAT DO ASCETIC IDEALS MEAN?

5

. . . What does it mean, when a genuine *philosopher* pays homage to the ascetic ideal, a really independent spirit like Schopenhauer, a man and knight with an iron look, who has the courage to be himself, the strength to stand alone, and disdains to wait for heralds and hints from above? . . .

. . .

7

. . . Let us, above all, not underestimate the fact that Schopenhauer—who actually treated sensuality (including the tool of sensuality, woman, this *instrumentum diaboli*) as his personal enemy—stood in *need* of enemies, to keep himself in good spirits; that he loved the grim-humored, terrifying black-green words; that he frowned for frowning's sake; from inclination; that he would have become sick, become *pessimist* (for pessimist he was not, much though he wished to be so), but for his enemies, but for Hegel, for woman, for sensuality, and the whole will to life, to persistence. Had Schopenhauer been a pessimist, he would not have persisted, to be sure; he would have run away. But his enemies held him fast; his enemies kept seducing him to existence; his anger, quite as in the case of the ancient cynics, constituted his comfort, his recreation, his reward, his *remedium* for disgust, his *happiness*. So much in regard to what is specifically personal in the case of Schopenhauer! But on the other hand his case presents also something typical—and now we come back to our problem. Undoubtedly there exists, as long as philosophers exist on earth, and wherever philosophers have existed (from India as far as England—to take the opposite poles of philosophical ability), a specific philosopher's irritation at and rancor against sensuality; Schopenhauer is, in fact, only the most eloquent and, if we have ears for such sounds, the most ravishing and rapturous outburst of it. In the same manner there exists a singular philosopher's prejudice toward and fondness for the whole ascetic ideal—against which fact it will hardly do for us to shut our eyes. Both things are, as I said, essential to the type. If either be lacking in a philosopher, then, we may be sure, he is always but a "so-called" philosopher. What does that *mean?* For this fact must first be interpreted: *in itself* it stands there, stupid to all eternity, like every "thing in itself". . . .

. . .

What, then, does the ascetic ideal mean in the case of a philosopher? My answer is—as long ago will have been anticipated—the aspect of the ascetic ideal draws

from the lips of the philosopher a smile because he recognizes in it the optimum conditions for the highest and keenest spirituality. In doing so, he does *not* negate "existence," but rather affirms *his own* existence and *only* his own existence, and this perhaps so much so that the impious wish is not far from him: *pereat mundus, fiat philosophia, fiat philosophus, fiam!*[*]

8

These philosophers, we see, are anything but unbiassed witnesses and judges as to the *value* of the ascetic ideal! They think *of themselves*—what does "the saint" concern them! In valuing the ascetic ideal, they think of that which is most indispensable to *them*: freedom from constraint, interference, noise, from tasks, duties, cares; they think of a clear head, of dancing, leaping, flying of thoughts; good air, thin, clear, free, dry mountain air, spiritualizing and lending wings to all animal being; peace in all surroundings; all dogs securely chained; no barking indicative of hostility or shaggy rancor; no gnawing worm of thwarted ambition; modest and obedient intestines, busy as mills, but far away; the heart distant, beyond, futurous, posthumous. All in all, the ascetic ideal suggests to them that cheerful asceticism of some deified and newly fledged animal which rises above life rather than resting in repose.

. . .

11

. . . The thought, around which the struggle turns, is the *valuation* of our life as pronounced by the ascetic priest. Life (together with that of which it forms part: "nature," "world," the entire sphere of becoming and of change) he juxtaposes with a completely different kind of existence which it excludes and opposes, *unless* it turns against itself, *denies itself*. In this case—the case of an ascetic life—life is regarded as a bridge leading to that other existence. The ascetic treats life as a wrong way which man had best retrace to the point from where it starts; or as an error which

------

[*]The world may perish, but let there be philosophy, philosopher, I!

can be, should be corrected by our deeds. For he *demands*, that one should follow him; he compels, wherever he can, *his* valuation of existence. What does that mean? A manner of valuation that eccentric is not marked down in the history of man as an exception and *curiosum*. It is one of the most common and enduring facts in existence. Read from some distant star, the high points of our earthly existence would perhaps lead the onlooker to infer that our earth is the essentially *ascetic planet*—a corner of malcontent, conceited and ugly creatures, unable to rid themselves of a deep chagrin at themselves, at the earth, at all life, and causing each other as much pain as possible, from the pleasure of causing pain— probably, their only pleasure. Let us but consider how regularly, how universally, how almost at any period, the ascetic priest makes his appearance; he does not belong, exclusively, to any one race; he flourishes anywhere; he grows out of all classes. It would be wrong to suppose that he fosters and propagates his manner of valuation by way of heredity. The contrary is the case: a deep instinct rather denies him propagation. It must be by a necessity of the first order that this kind of *life-inimical* species thrives and flourishes again and again—or perhaps it is in the interest of *life itself,* that this type of self-contradiction remains alive. For an ascetic life is a self-contradiction. Here a most extraordinary resentment prevails—the resentment of an insatiable instinct and will to power, that desires to become master—not merely over something in life but over life itself, over the deepest, strongest, and most fundamental conditions of life. Here an attempt is made to use power to block the sources of power. Here physiological thriving itself—especially its expression, beauty and joy —is viewed with dark and jealous eye; where a satisfaction is felt and *sought* in all abortive, degenerate growth, in pain, in mishap, in ugliness, in voluntary deprivation, in self-mortification, in self-castigation, in self-sacrificing. All this is paradoxical in the highest degree. We have before us a case of discord which *wills* to be discordant, which in this suffering *enjoys* itself and grows more and ever more self-confident and triumphant, in proportion to its own presupposition—its physiological vitality—*diminishes.* "Triumph in the very hour of ultimate agony," under this superlative symbol all battles of the ascetic ideal have always been fought. In this riddle of seduction, in this emblem of ecstasy and torture, it perceived its own

brightest light, its salvation, its final victory. *Crux, nux, lux,**—these three for it are one.

12

Assuming that this kind of incarnate will to contradiction and antinaturalness undertakes to *philosophize*—against what will it discharge its innermost arbitrariness? Against that which is felt to be most certainly true and real. It will seek out *error* even where the functional instinct of life posits truth unconditionally. It will for instance, in the manner of the ascetics of Vedânta philosophy, abase corporality to mere illusion, and also pain, multiplicity, the entire antithesis between the concepts of "subject" and "object." Errors, all errors! To refuse to believe in one's own *ego,* to deny one's own "reality"—what a triumph! Not over the senses merely, not over visible nature, no! A much higher kind of triumph, a violation and cruelty against *reason* itself; a voluptuousness that reaches its climax, when the ascetic self-contempt and self-scorn of reason decrees that *there is* a realm of truth and of being, but reason is *shut out* from it.

(By the way: even in the Kantian concept of the "intelligible character of things" a trace of this libidinous ascetic discord—which delights in setting reason against reason—still remains. For Kant, "intelligible character" shows already a kind of condition of things of which the intellect comprehends just this, that it is for the intellect *altogether incomprehensible.*) Let us finally—cognizers as we are—be not ungrateful to such resolute subversions of the ordinary perspectives and valuations that the spirit has, for all too long a time, as it would seem, criminally and futilely raged against itself! Thus to see and to *will* to see things in another manner forms a most excellent training and preparation of the intellect for its future "objectivity"—understanding the latter to be not an "uninterested contemplation" (which is a perverse absurdity), but as the ability to command and control one's pro and con so that one knows how to make use of the variety of perspectives and emotional interpretations for the advancement of knowledge. For, dear philosophers, let us from now on guard ourselves better against the dangerous, old fabling with con-

---

*Cross, bolt, light.

cepts which posited a "pure, will-less, painless, timeless knowing subject"; let us avoid the clutches of such contradictory concepts as "pure reason," "absolute spirituality," "knowledge as such." Here we must always conceive of an eye that cannot be conceived; an eye directed nowhere in particular; an eye whose active and interpretive powers (through which alone a looking at becomes a seeing something) are completely absent; *i.e.*, a perversity and misconcept of an eye is postulated. There is no other seeing but a perspective seeing; there is no other knowing but a perspective "knowing;" and the more emotions we allow to speak on a matter, the more eyes, the more different eyes, we place in our face, the more complete will be our "concept" of this matter, our "objectivity." But to eliminate the will altogether, to sever—provided this were possible—each and every emotion; what? Would not this mean to *castrate* the intellect? . . .

13

But back to the point. The kind of self-contradiction which seems to present itself in the ascetic, *i.e.*, "life *against* life" is—this much is clear on the face of it—physiologically (as well as psychologically) considered, sheer nonsense. It can be but a *seeming* contradiction; it can only be a kind of provisional expression, an interpretation, formula, accommodation, a psychological misunderstanding of a something the real nature of which could, for a long time, not be understood, not be described *as it really was*—a mere word crammed into an old *gap* in human knowledge. And, to state briefly the facts of the case: *the ascetic ideal is prompted by the self-protective and self-preservative instinct of degenerating life*—a life which struggles for existence and seeks to maintain itself by all means; it points to a partial physiological stagnation and exhaustion which the deepest remaining instincts of life incessantly seek to counteract with ever changing means and inventions. The ascetic ideal is such a means, and hence, precisely the reverse is the case from what the worshippers of this ideal believe—in it and through it, life struggles with and *against* death; the ascetic ideal is an artifice for the *preservation* of life. The fact that this ideal could, to the extent that history teaches us, sway and prevail over man, especially wherever the civilizing and taming of man was enforced, an important truth is expressed: the mor-

bidity of the type of man which prevailed until now, at least of tamed man; the physiological wrestling of man with death (more exactly stated: with disgust with life, with weariness, with the wish for the "end"). The ascetic priest is the incarnate wish for a state of being otherwise, being elsewhere; in fact, the greatest extreme of this wish, the hottest fervor and passion of this wish. But the very *power* of his wishing is the chain which binds him fast to life and makes him a tool for bringing about more favorable conditions, for being here and being a man. By this very power and by leading them instinctively as their shepherd, he holds fast to existence the entire herd of the misfashioned, the disappointed, the maltreated, the defective, all who suffer from themselves. I am already understood: this ascetic priest, this seeming enemy of life, this *denier*—this very man is among the great *conserving*, and *yes-creative* powers of life. . . .

. . .

15

. . . The ascetic priest must be taken as the predestined savior, herdsman and advocate of the sick herd; it is only by this that we understand his vast historic mission. *The sway over suffering* is his kingdom; to it his instinct leads him; in it he proves his own most distinctive art, his mastery, his kind of happiness. To understand the sick one and disinherited one and himself in them, he must be sick himself, he must be thoroughly related to them. But he must also be strong, more completely master of himself even than of others, undaunted, especially in his will to power, to be trusted and feared by the sick, to be their prop, resistance, crutch, constraint, taskmaster, tyrant, and god. He has to defend them, his herd. Against whom? Against the healthy, without doubt, and also against their envy of the sound; he must be the natural opponent *and despiser* of all health and might that are rude, impetuous, unbridled, brutal, relentless, and like a beast of prey. The priest is the first form of that *more* delicate animal which is quicker to despise than to hate. He will not be spared the necessity of waging war against the beasts of prey, a war of cunning (of "spirit") rather than of power, as is self-evident; to do that he will, under certain circumstances, be compelled to fashion of himself almost a new variety of the beast of prey, or, at least, to *signify* such a type,—

Übermensch mavid.

a new animal monstrosity in which the polar bear, the agile and calmly deliberative tiger and, last but not least, the fox seem to be fused into a unity that is fascinating and at the same time awe inspiring. If compelled by need, he may, with bearlike earnestness, gravity, sagacity, coldness, and superior craft, make his appearance among the other beasts of prey; as the herald and mouthpiece of more mysterious powers; resolved to scatter, wherever he can, the seed of mischief, discord and self-contradiction on this soil; and, only too sure of his power, to master *sufferers* at all times. He brings with him salves and balms, without doubt; but before applying the physician's leech he must inflict the wound. Then, in the very act of soothing the pain caused by the wound, *he will at the same time infect the wound.* For in this art he is master, this great sorcerer and tamer of beasts of prey in whose presence whatever is sound, of necessity becomes sick, and whatever is sick, tame. And truly, well enough he will defend his herd—this curious herdsman. He will also defend it against itself, against the meanness, knavery, malignity secretly smoldering within the herd; against whatever is owned by all the sick and sickly among themselves. He wages a cunning, hard and secret war against anarchy and self-dissolution, threatening at any moment to break out in the herd in which that most dangerous blasting and explosive power—*resentment*—keeps steadily accumulating. To discharge this powder in such a manner as not to blow up either the herd or the herdsman, this is his distinctive art, as also his highest usefulness. Were we to express the value of the priestly existence in the shortest formula, we should have to put it thus: the priest is the person who *changes the direction* of resentment. For every sufferer will instinctively seek for a cause of his suffering; more exactly, a doer; still more definitely a guilty agent susceptible of suffering; in short, anything living against which, under some pretence or other, he may discharge his emotions—either *in deed* or in effigy. For the discharge of emotions is the greatest attempt on the part of the sufferer to procure for himself alleviation—or rather, to bring about the *anesthetization* of his pain. It is his narcotic which he wants instinctively against pain of any kind. . . . "I suffer; for this some one must be to blame," so all sick sheep think. But their shepherd, the ascetic priest, says: "Exactly so, my sheep! Some one must be to blame for this. But you yourself are

this some one; you alone are to blame for this;—*you alone are to blame for yourself!*" . . . This is bold enough and false enough. But one thing, at least, is attained through it; as we have seen—the direction of resentment is *changed*.

Agree, No? Ho?

16

Now my readers will make out what the Aesculapian instincts of life have accomplished or, at least, have *tried* to accomplish through the ascetic priest, and for what purpose he has used, for the time being, the tyranny of such paradoxical and paralogical concepts as "guilt," "sin," "sinfulness," "perdition," "damnation" to render, in some measure, the sick *harmless;* to destroy the incurable through themselves; to redirect the resentment of the less diseased back to themselves, (*"One thing is needed"*); and to *make full use,* in this manner, of the bad instincts of all sufferers for the purpose of self-discipline, self-control and self-overcoming. . . .

.   .   .

28

The ascetic ideal apart, man, *animal* man, so far had no meaning. His existence on earth implied no goal. "Wherefore should man be at all?" This was a question without an answer. The will for man and earth was lacking. Every great human destiny was followed by the refrain of a still greater "in vain!" Precisely *this* is meant by the ascetic ideal: that something *was* lacking, that an immense *void* yawned round man. He was unable to justify, explain, affirm himself, he *suffered* from the problem of his significance. He suffered also in other respects; he was in the main a *sickly* animal. His problem was not suffering itself, however, but the lack of the answer to the cry of the question: "*Why* suffer?" Man, the animal bravest and best accustomed to pain, does *not* eschew suffering in itself: he *wills* to suffer; he even seeks for suffering, provided that he is shown a *significance,* a purpose for suffering. The senselessness of suffering, not suffering itself, was the curse which so far lay upon mankind. *And the ascetic ideal offered man a meaning.* It was so far the only meaning; any meaning is better than no meaning at all. The ascetic ideal was in every respect the *faute de mieux par excellence* which so far existed. In it suffering was interpreted; the immense void seemed to be filled out; the door closed to all suicidal nihilism. The interpretation—without doubt—brought with it new suffering, deeper, more internal, more poisonous, more life-undermining suffering; it brought all suffering under the perspective of *guilt*. . . . But, nevertheless, man was *saved* thereby; he had a *meaning;* he was henceforth no longer like a leaf in the wind; sport of nonsense, of "no-sense;" he could now will something; no matter for the present why, with what, and to what end he willed: *will itself was saved.* One cannot possibly hide from one's self *what* is ultimately expressed by all that willing, which has received its direction from the ascetic ideal. This hatred of what is human; still more, of what is animal; still more, of what is material; this horror of the senses, of reason itself; this fear of happiness and beauty; this longing to escape all appearance, change, becoming, death, desire, longing itself—all this implies (let us dare to comprehend it!) *a will to nothingness,* a horror of life, an insurrection against the most fundamental presuppositions of life; nevertheless, it is and remains a *will!* . . . And to say once more at the end what I have said at the outset: rather would man will *nothingness,* than *not* will. . . .

Selected Maxims
from Twilight of the Idols

4

"All truth is simple"—Is not this a double lie?

8

From the military school of life—That which does not kill me, makes me stronger.

12

If a man knows the purpose of his existence, then the manner of it can take care of itself. Man does not aspire to happiness; only the Englishman does that.

The Problem of Socrates
from Twilight of the Idols

1

In all ages the wisest have always agreed in their judgment of life: *it is no good.* At all times and places the same words have been on their lips; words full of doubt, full of melancholy, full of weariness of life, full of hostility to life. Even Socrates' dying words were: "To live means to be ill a long while: I owe a cock to the god Aesculapius." Even Socrates had had enough of it. What does that prove? What does it point to? Formerly people would have said (oh, it has been said, and loudly enough too; by our pessimists loudest of all!): "In any case there must be some truth in this! The *consensus sapientium** is a proof of truth." Shall we say the same today? *May* we do so? "In any case there must be some sickness here," we reply. These great sages of all periods should first be examined more closely! Is it possible that they were, everyone of them, a little shaky on their legs, effete, rocky, decadent? Does wisdom perhaps appear on earth after the manner of a raven attracted by a slight smell of carrion?

2

This irreverent belief that the great sages were decadent types, first occurred to me precisely in regard to that case in which both learned and vulgar prejudice was most opposed to my view. I recognized Socrates and Plato as symptoms of decline, as instruments in the disintegration of Hellas, as pseudo-Greek, as anti-Greek ("The Birth of Tragedy," 1872). That *consensus sapientium,* as I perceived ever more and more clearly, did not in the least prove that they were right in the matter on which they agreed. It proved rather that these sages themselves must have been alike in some physiological particular, because they assumed the same negative attitude towards life and were bound to assume that attitude. After all, judgments and valuations of life, whether for or against, cannot be true: their only value lies in the fact that they are symptoms; they can be considered only as symptoms—*per*

---

*Consensus among the wise.

se such judgments are nonsense. You must therefore attempt by all means to reach out and try to grasp this astonishingly subtle axiom, *that the value of life cannot be estimated*. A living man cannot do so, because he is a contending party, the very object in the dispute, and not a judge; neither can a dead man estimate it—for other reasons. For a philosopher to see a problem in the value of life, is almost an objection against him, a note of interrogation set against his wisdom—a lack of wisdom. What? Is it possible that all these great sages were not only decadents, but that they were not even wise? Let me however return to the problem of Socrates.

3

To judge from his origin, Socrates belonged to the lowest of the low: Socrates was rabble. You know, and you can still see it for yourself, how ugly he was. But ugliness, which in itself is an objection, was almost a refutation among the Greeks. Was Socrates really a Greek? Ugliness is not infrequently the expression of thwarted development, or of development arrested by crossbreeding. In other cases it appears as a decadent development. The anthropologists among the criminal specialists declare that the typical criminal is ugly: *monstrum in fronte, monstrum in animo.** But the criminal is a decadent. Was Socrates a typical criminal? At all events this would not clash with that famous physiognomist's judgment which was so repugnant to Socrates' friends. While on his way through Athens a certain foreigner who was no fool at judging by looks, told Socrates to his face that he was a monster, that his body harbored all the worst vices and passions. And Socrates replied simply: "You know me, sir!"

4

Not only are the acknowledged wildness and anarchy of Socrates' instincts indicative of decadence, but also that preponderance of the logical faculties and that malignity of the misshapen which was his special characteristic. Neither should we forget those aural delusions which were religiously interpreted as "the demon of Socrates." Everything in him is exaggerated, *buffo*, caricature, his nature is also full of concealment,

---

*Monstrosity in face and psyche.

of ulterior motives, and of underground currents. I try to understand the idiosyncrasy from which the Socratic equation—Reason = Virtue = Happiness—could have arisen: the weirdest equation ever seen, and one which was essentially opposed to all the instincts of the older Hellenes.

5

With Socrates Greek taste veers round in favor of dialectics: what actually occurs? In the first place a noble taste is vanquished; with dialectics the mob comes to the top. Before Socrates' time, dialectical manners were avoided in good society: they were regarded as bad manners, they were compromising. The young were cautioned against them. All such proffering of one's reasons was looked upon with suspicion. Honest things like honest men do not carry their reasons on their sleeve in such fashion. It is not good form to make a show of everything. That which needs to be proved cannot be worth much. Wherever authority still belongs to good usage, wherever one commands instead of giving reasons, the dialectician is regarded as a sort of clown. People laugh at him, they do not take him seriously. Socrates was a clown who succeeded in making people take him seriously: what then was happening?

6

One resorts to dialectics only when one has no other means to hand. People know that they excite suspicion with it and that it is not very convincing. Nothing is more easily dispelled than a dialectical effect: this is proved by the experience of every gathering in which discussions are held. It can be only the last defense of those who have no other weapons. One must require to extort one's right, otherwise one makes no use of it. That is why the Jews were dialecticians. Reynard the Fox was a dialectician. What? And was Socrates one as well?

7

Is the Socratic irony an expression of revolt, of mob resentment? Does Socrates, as a creature suffering under oppression, enjoy his innate ferocity in the knife thrusts of the syllogism? Does he wreak his revenge on the noblemen he fascinates? As a dialectician one has a merciless instrument to wield; one can play the tyrant with it: one compromises by conquering with it. The dialectician leaves it to his opponent to prove that he is no idiot: he infuriates, he likewise paralyzes. The dialectician cripples the intellect of his opponent. Can it be that dialectics was only a form of revenge in Socrates?

8

I have given you to understand in what way Socrates was able to repel: now it is all the more necessary to explain how he fascinated. One reason is that he discovered a new kind of *agon,* and that he was the first fencing master in the best circles in Athens. He fascinated by appealing to the combative instinct of the Greeks; he introduced a variation into the contests between men and youths. Socrates was also a great erotic.

9

But Socrates divined still more. He saw right through his noble Athenians; he perceived that his case, his peculiar case, was no exception even in his time. The same kind of degeneracy was silently preparing itself everywhere: ancient Athens was dying out. And Socrates understood that the whole world needed him: his means, his remedy, his special artifice for self-preservation. Everywhere the instincts were in a state of anarchy; everywhere people were within an ace of excess: the *monstrum in animo* was the general danger. "The instincts would play the tyrant; we must discover a countertyrant who is stronger than they." On the occasion when that physiognomist had unmasked Socrates, and had told him what he was, a crater full of evil desires, the great Master of Irony let fall one or two words more, which provide the key to his nature. "This is true," he said, "but I overcame them all." How did Socrates succeed in mastering himself? His case was at bottom only the extreme and most apparent example of a state of distress which was beginning to be general: that state in which no one was able to master himself and in which the instincts became mutually hostile. As the extreme example of this state, he fascinated—his terrifying ugliness made him conspicuous to every eye: What is

quite obvious is that he fascinated still more as a reply, as a solution, as an apparent cure of this case.

10

When a man finds it necessary, as Socrates did, to create a tyrant out of reason, there is no small danger that something else wishes to play the tyrant. Reason was then discovered as a savior; neither Socrates nor his "patients" were at liberty to be rational or not, as they pleased; at that time it was *de rigueur,* it had become a last shift. The fanaticism with which the whole of Greek thought plunges into reason, betrays a critical condition of things: men were in danger; there were only two alternatives: either perish or else be absurdly rational. The moral bias of Greek philosophy from Plato onward, is the outcome of a pathological condition, as is also its appreciation of dialectics. Reason = Virtue = Happiness, simply means: we must imitate Socrates, and confront the dark passions permanently with the light of day—the light of reason. We must at all costs be clever, precise, clear: all yielding to the instincts, to the unconscious, leads downward.

11

I have now explained how Socrates fascinated: he seemed to be a doctor, a Savior. Is it necessary to expose the errors which lay in his faith in "reason at any price"? It is a piece of self-deception on the part of philosophers and moralists to suppose that they can extricate themselves from degeneration by merely waging war upon it. They cannot thus extricate themselves: that which they choose as a means, as the road to salvation, is in itself again only an expression of degeneration—they only modify its mode of manifesting itself: they do not abolish it. Socrates was a misunderstanding. *The whole of the morality of improvement—that of Christianity as well—was a misunderstanding.* The most blinding light of day: reason at any price; life made clear, cold, cautious, conscious, without instincts, opposed to the instincts, was in itself only a disease, another kind of disease—and by no means a return to "virtue," to "health," and to happiness. To be obliged to fight the instincts—this is the formula of degeneration: as long as life is in the ascending line, happiness is the same as instinct.

12

Did he understand this himself, this most clever of self-deceivers? Did he confess this to himself in the end, in the wisdom of his courage before death? Socrates wished to die. Not Athens, but his own hand gave him the draught of hemlock; he drove Athens to the poisoned cup. "Socrates is not a physician," he whispered to himself, "death alone can be a physician here. . . . Socrates himself has only been ill a long while."

The "Improvers" of Mankind
from Twilight of the Idols

1

You are aware of my demand upon philosophers, that they should take up a stand beyond good and evil, that they should have the illusion of the moral judgment beneath them. This demand is the result of a point of view which I was the first to formulate: *that there are no such things as moral facts.* Moral judgment has this in common with the religious one, that it believes in realities which are not real. Morality is only an interpretation of certain phenomena: or, more strictly speaking, a misinterpretation of them. Moral judgment, like the religious one, belongs to a stage of ignorance in which even the concept of reality, the distinction between real and imagined things, is still lacking: so that truth, at such a stage, is applied to a host of things which today we call "imaginary." That is why the moral judgment must never be taken quite literally: as such it is sheer nonsense. As a sign code, however, it is invaluable: to one at least who knows, it reveals the most valuable facts concerning cultures and inner worlds, which did not know enough to "understand" themselves. Morality is merely a sign language, simply symptomatology: one must already know what it is all about in order to turn it to any use.

2

Let me give you one example, quite provisionally. In all ages there have been people who wished to "improve" mankind: this above all is what was called morality. But the most different tendencies are concealed beneath the same word. Both the taming of the beast man, and the rearing of a particular type of man, have been called "improvement": these zoological *termini,* alone, represent real things—real things of which the typical "improver," the priest, naturally knows nothing, and will know nothing. To call the taming of an animal "improving" it, sounds to our ears almost like a joke. He who knows what goes on in menageries, doubts very much whether an animal is improved in such places. It is certainly weakened, it is made less dangerous, and by means of the depressing influence of fear, pain, wounds, and hunger, it is converted into a sick animal. And the same holds good of the tamed man whom the priest has "improved." In the early years of the Middle Ages, during which the Church was most distinctly and above all a menagerie, the most beautiful examples of the "blond beast" were hunted down in all directions—the noble Germans, for instance, were "improved." But what did this "improved" German, who had been lured to the monastery look like after the process? He looked like a caricature of man, like an abortion: he had become a "sinner," he was caged up, he had been imprisoned behind a host of appalling notions. He now lay there sick, wretched, malevolent even toward himself: Full of hate for the instincts of life, full of suspicion in regard to all that is still strong and happy. In short a "Christian." In physiological terms: in a fight with an animal, the only way of making it weak may be to make it sick. The Church understood this: it ruined man, it made him weak, but it laid claim to having "improved" him.

. . .

Skirmishes of an Untimely Man
from Twilight of the Idols

10

What is the meaning of the antithetical concepts *Apollonian* and *Dionysian* which I have introduced into the vocabulary of esthetics, as representing two distinct modes of ecstasy? Apollonian ecstasy acts above all as a force stimulating the eye, so that it acquires the power of vision. The painter, the sculptor, the epic poet are essentially visionaries. In the Dionysian state, on the other hand, the whole system of passions is stimulated and intensified, so that it discharges itself by all the means of expression at once, and vents all its power of representation, of imitation, of transfiguration, of transformation, together with every kind of mimicry and histrionic display at the same time. The essential feature remains the facility in transforming, the inability to refrain from reaction (a similar state to that of certain hysterical patients, who at the slightest hint assume any role). It is impossible for the Dionysian artist not to understand any suggestion; no outward sign of emotion escapes him, he possesses the instinct of comprehension and of divination in the highest degree, just as he is capable of the most perfect art of communication. He enters into every skin, into every passion: he is continually changing himself. Music as we understand it today is likewise a general excitation and discharge of the emotions; but in spite of this, it is only the remnant of a much richer world of emotional expression, a mere residue of Dionysian histrionism. For music to be made possible as a special art, quite a number of senses, and particularly the muscular sense, had to be paralyzed (at least relatively: for all rhythm still appeals to our muscles to a certain extent), and thus man no longer imitates and represents physically everything he feels, as soon as he feels it. Nevertheless that is the normal Dionysian state, and in any case its primitive state. Music is the slowly attained specialization of this state at the cost of kindred capacities.

from The Antichrist

AN ATTEMPTED CRITICISM OF CHRISTIANITY

2

What is good? All that enhances the feeling of power, the will to power, and power itself. What is bad? All that proceeds from weakness. What is happiness? The feeling that power is *increasing*—that resistance has been overcome.

Not contentment, but more power; not peace, but war; not virtue, but efficiency* (virtue in the Renaissance sense, *virtù,* free from all moralic acid). The weak and the botched shall perish: first principle of our humanity. And they ought even to be helped to perish.

What is more harmful than any vice? Practical sympathy with all the botched and the weak—Christianity.

3

The problem I set in this work is not what will replace mankind in the order of living beings (Man is an *end*); but, what type of man must be *reared,* must be *willed,* as having the highest value, as being the most worthy of life and the surest guarantee of the future.

This more valuable type has appeared often enough already: but as a happy accident, as an exception, never as *willed.* He has rather been precisely the most feared. Hitherto he has been almost the terrible in itself; and from out the very fear he provoked there arose the will to rear the type which has now been reared, *attained:* the domestic animal, the gregarious animal, the sick human animal—the Christian.

. . .

5

We must not deck out and adorn Christianity: it has waged a deadly war upon this *higher* type of man, it has set a ban upon all the fundamental instincts of this type, and has distilled evil and the devil himself out of these instincts: the strong man as the typical pariah, the villain. Christianity has sided with everything weak, low, and botched; it has made an ideal out of *antagonism* against all the self-preservative instincts of strong life: it has corrupted even the reason of the strongest spirits, by teaching that the highest values of the spirit are sinful, misleading and full of temptations. The most lamentable example of this was the corruption of Pascal, who believed in the perversion of his reason through original sin, whereas it had only been perverted by his Christianity.

6

. . . I call an animal, a species, an individual corrupt, when it loses its instincts, when it selects and *prefers* that which is detrimental to it. A history of the "higher feelings," of "human ideals"—and it is not impossible that I shall have to write it—would almost

---

*The German "*Tüchtigkeit*" has a nobler ring than our word "efficiency."—TR.

explain why man is so corrupt. Life itself, to my mind, is nothing more nor less than the instinct of growth, of permanence, of accumulating forces, of power: where the will to power is lacking, degeneration sets in. My contention is that all the highest values of mankind *lack* this will,—that the values of decline and of *nihilism* are exercising the sovereign power under the cover of the holiest names.

7

Christianity is called the religion of *pity*. Pity is opposed to the tonic passions which enhance the energy of the feeling of life: its action is depressing. One loses power when he pities. By means of pity the drain on strength which suffering itself already introduces into the world is multiplied a thousandfold. Through pity, suffering itself becomes infectious; in certain circumstances it may lead to a total loss of life and vital energy, which is absurdly out of proportion to the magnitude of the cause (the case of the death of the Nazarene). This is the first standpoint; but there is a still more important one. Supposing one measures pity according to the value of the reactions it usually stimulates, its danger to life appears in a much more telling light. On the whole, pity thwarts the law of development which is the law of selection. It preserves that which is ripe for death, it fights in favor of the disinherited and the condemned of life; thanks to the multitude of abortions of all kinds which it maintains in life, it lends life itself a somber and questionable aspect. People have dared to call pity a virtue (in every *noble* ethic it is considered as a weakness); people went still further, they exalted it to *the* virtue, the root and origin of all virtues; but, of course, what must never be forgotten is the fact that this was done from the standpoint of a philosophy which was nihilistic, and on whose shield the device *the denial of life* was inscribed. Schopenhauer was right in this respect: by means of pity, life is denied and made *more worthy of denial*—pity is the *praxis* of nihilism. I repeat, this depressing and infectious instinct thwarts those instincts which aim at the preservation and enhancement of the value life: by *multiplying* misery quite as much as by preserving all that is miserable, it is the principal agent in promoting decadence—pity exhorts people to *nothingness!* But they do not say "*nothingness,*" they say "beyond," or "God," or "the true life"; or nirvana, or salvation, or blessedness, instead.

This innocent rhetoric, which belongs to the realm of the religio-moral idiosyncrasy, immediately appears to be *much less innocent* if one realizes what the tendency is that here tries to drape itself in the mantle of sublime expressions: this is the tendency of hostility to life. Schopenhauer was hostile to life: that is why he elevated pity to a virtue. . . .

8

It is necessary to state whom we regard as our antithesis: the theologians, and all those who have the blood of theologians in their veins—the whole of our philosophy. . . .

I unearthed the "arrogant" instinct of the theologian, wherever nowadays people feel themselves idealists,—wherever, thanks to superior antecedents, they claim the right to rise above reality and to regard it with suspicion. . . . Like the priest the idealist has every grandiloquent concept in his hand (and not only in his hand!), he wields them all with kindly contempt against the "understanding," the "senses," "honors," "decent living," "science"; he regards such things as *beneath* him, as detrimental and seductive forces, upon the face of which, "the spirit" moves in pure for-itselfness:—as if humility, chastity, poverty, in a word *holiness,* had not done incalculably more harm to life hitherto, than any sort of horror and vice. . . . Pure spirit is pure falsehood. . . . As long as the priest, the *professional* denier, calumniator and poisoner of life, is considered as the *highest* kind of man, there can be no answer to the question, what *is* truth? Truth has already been turned topsy-turvy, when the conscious advocate of nothingness and of denial passes as the representative of "truth."

9

It is upon this theological instinct that I wage war. I find traces of it everywhere. Whoever has the blood of theologians in his veins, stands from the start in a false and dishonest position to all things. The pathos which grows out of this state, is called *faith:* that is to say, to shut one's eyes once and for all, in order not to suffer at the sight of incurable falsity. People convert this faulty view of all things into a moral, a virtue, a thing of holiness. They endow their distorted vision with a good conscience—they claim that no *other* point of view is any longer of value, once theirs has been made sacrosanct with the names "God," "salvation," "eternity." I unearthed the instinct of the theologian everywhere: it is the most universal, and actually the most subterranean form of falsity on earth. . . .

. . .

18

The Christian concept of God—God as the deity of the sick, God as a spider, God as spirit—is one of the most corrupt concepts of God that has ever been attained on earth. Maybe it represents the low-water mark in the evolutionary ebb of the godlike type. God degenerated into the *contradiction of life,* instead of being its transfiguration and eternal Yes! With God war is declared on life, nature, and the will to live! God is the formula for every calumny of this world and for every lie concerning a beyond! In God, nothingness is deified, and the will to nothingness is declared holy!

. . .

43

When the center of gravity of life is laid, *not* in life, but in a beyond—*in nothingness*—life is utterly robbed of its balance. The great lie of personal immortality destroys all reason, everything that is natural in the instincts—everything in the instincts that is beneficent, that promotes life and that is a guarantee of the future, henceforward aroused suspicion. The very meaning of life is now construed as the effort to live in such a way that life no longer has any point. . . . Why show any public spirit? Why be grateful for one's origin and one's forebears? Why collaborate with one's fellows, and be confident? Why be concerned about the general weal or strive after it? . . . All these things are merely so many "temptations," so many deviations from the "straight path." "One thing only is necessary." . . . That everybody, as an "immortal soul," should have equal rank, that in the totality of beings, the "salvation" of each individual may lay claim to eternal importance, that insignificant bigots and three-quarter-lunatics may have the right to suppose that the laws of nature may be persistently *broken* on their account,—any such magnification of every kind of selfishness to infinity, to *insolence,* cannot be branded with sufficient contempt. And yet it is to this miserable flattery of personal vanity that

Christianity owes its *triumph;* by this means it lured all the bungled and the botched, all revolting and rebellious people, all abortions, the whole of the refuse and offal of humanity, over to its side. The "salvation of the soul"—in plain English: "the world revolves around me." . . . The poison of the doctrine "*equal* rights for all," has been dispensed with the greatest thoroughness by Christianity: Christianity, prompted by the most secret recesses of bad instincts, has waged a deadly war upon all feeling of reverence and distance between man and man—that is to say, the *prerequisite* of all elevation, of every growth in culture; out of the resentment of the masses it wrought its *principal weapons* against us, against everything noble, joyful, exalted on earth, against our happiness on earth. . . . To grant "immortality" to every Peter and Paul, was the greatest, the most vicious outrage upon *noble* humanity that has ever been perpetrated. And do not let us underestimate the fatal influence which, springing from Christianity, has insinuated itself even into politics! Nowadays no one has the courage of special rights, of rights of dominion, of a feeling of self-respect and of respect for his equals, of *pathos of distance.* Our politics are diseased with this lack of courage! The aristocratic attitude of mind has been most thoroughly undermined by the lie of the equality of souls; and if the belief in the "privilege of the greatest number" creates and will continue *to create revolutions;* it is Christianity, let there be no doubt about it, and Christian values, which convert every revolution into blood and crime! Christianity is the revolt of all things that crawl on their bellies against everything that is lofty: the gospel of the "lowly" lowers. . . .

Why I Am So Clever
from Ecce Homo

. . .

9

At this point I can no longer evade a direct answer to the question, *how one becomes what one is.* And in giving it, I shall have to touch upon that masterpiece in the art of self-preservation, which is *selfishness.* . . . Granting that one's task in life—the determination and the fate of one's task in life—greatly exceeds the average measure of such things, nothing more dangerous could be conceived than to confront one's self with this task. The fact that one becomes what one is, <u>presupposes that one has not the remotest suspicion of what one is.</u> From this standpoint even the blunders of one's life have their own meaning and value, the temporary deviations and aberrations, the moments of hesitation and of modesty, the earnestness wasted upon duties which lie outside the actual task. In these matters great wisdom, perhaps even the highest wisdom, comes into activity: in these circumstances, in which *nosce teipsum* * would be the sure road to ruin, forgetting one's self, misunderstanding one's self, belittling one's self, narrowing one's self, and making one's self mediocre, amount to reason itself. Expressed morally, to love one's neighbor and to live for others and for other things *may* be the means of protection employed to maintain the hardest kind of egoism. This is the exceptional case in which I, contrary to my principle and conviction, take the side of the altruistic instincts; for here they are concerned in subserving selfishness and self-discipline. The whole surface of consciousness—for consciousness *is* a surface—must be kept free from any one of the great imperatives. Beware even of every striking word, of every striking attitude! They are all so many risks which the instinct runs of "understanding itself" too soon. Meanwhile the organizing "idea," which is destined to become master, grows and continues to grow into the depths—it begins to command, it leads you slowly back from your deviations and aberrations, it prepares individual qualities and capacities, which one day will make themselves felt as indispensable to the whole of your task—step by step it cultivates all the serviceable faculties, before it ever whispers a word concerning the dominant task, the "goal," the "object," and the "meaning" of it all. Looked at from this standpoint my life is simply amazing. For the task of *transvaluing values,* more capacities were needful perhaps than could well be found side by side in one individual; and above all, antagonistic capacities which had to be free from the mutual strife and destruction which they involve. An order of rank among capacities; distance; the art of separating without creating hostility; to refrain from confounding things; to keep from reconciling things; to possess enormous multifariousness and yet to be the reverse of chaos—all this was the first condition, the long secret work, and the

_____
*Know yourself.

artistic mastery of my instinct. Its superior guardianship manifested itself with such exceeding strength, that not once did I ever dream of what was growing within me—until suddenly all my capacities were ripe, and one day burst forth in all the perfection of their highest bloom. I cannot remember ever having exerted myself, I can point to no trace of *struggle* in my life; I am the reverse of a heroic nature. To "will" something, to "strive" after something, to have an "aim" or a "desire" in my mind: I know none of these things from experience. Even at this moment I look out upon my future—a *broad* future!—as upon a calm sea: no sigh of longing makes a ripple on its surface. I have not the slightest wish that anything should be otherwise than it is: I myself would not be otherwise. . . . But in this matter I have always been the same. I have never had a desire. A man who, after his forty-fourth year, can say that he has never bothered himself about *honors, women,* or *money!* . . .

10

You may be wondering why I should actually have related all these trivial and, according to traditional accounts, insignificant details to you; such action can but tell against me, more particularly if I am fated to figure in great causes. To this I reply that these trivial matters—diet, locality, climate, and one's mode of recreation, the whole casuistry of self-love—are inconceivably more important than all that which has hitherto been held in high esteem. It is precisely in this quarter that we must begin to learn afresh. All those things which mankind has valued with such earnestness up until now are not even real; they are mere creations of fancy, or, more strictly speaking, *lies* born of the evil instincts of diseased and, in the deepest sense, noxious natures—all the concepts, "God," "soul," "virtue," "sin," "Beyond," "truth," "eternal life." . . . But the greatness of human nature, its "divinity," was sought for in them. . . . All questions of politics, of social order, of education, have been falsified, root and branch, owing to the fact that the most noxious men have been taken for great men, and that people were taught to despise the small things, or rather the fundamental things, of life. If I now choose to compare myself with those creatures who thus far have been honored as the first among men, the difference becomes obvious. I do not reckon the so-called "first" men even as human beings—for me they are the excrements of mankind, the products of disease and of the instinct of revenge: they are so many monsters laden with rottenness, so many hopeless incurables, who avenge themselves on life. . . . I wish to be the opposite of these people. It is my privilege to have the very sharpest discernment for every sign of healthy instincts. There is no such thing as a morbid trait in me; even in times of serious illness I have never grown morbid, and you might seek in vain for a trace of fanaticism in my nature. No one can point to any moment of my life in which I have assumed either an arrogant or a pathetic attitude. Pathetic attitudes are not in keeping with greatness; he who needs attitudes is false. . . . Beware of all picturesque men! Life was easy—in fact easiest—to me, in those periods when it exacted the heaviest duties from me. Whoever could have seen me during the seventy days of this autumn, when, without interruption, I did a host of things of the highest rank—things that no man can do nowadays—with a sense of responsibility for all the ages yet to come, would have noticed no sign of tension in my condition, but rather a state of overflowing freshness and good cheer. Never have I eaten with more pleasant sensations, never has my sleep been better. I know of no other manner of dealing with great tasks, than as *play*: this, as a sign of greatness, is an essential prerequisite. The slightest constraint, a somber mien, any hard accent in the voice—all these things are objections to a man, but how much more to his work! . . . One must not have nerves. . . . Even to *suffer* from solitude is an objection. The only thing I have always suffered from is "multitude."* At an absurdly tender age, in fact when I was seven years old, I already knew that no human speech would ever reach me: did any one ever see me sad on that account? At present I still possess the same affability towards everybody, I am even full of consideration for the lowest: in all this there is not an atom of haughtiness or of secret contempt. He whom I despise soon guesses that he is despised by me; the very fact of my existence is enough to rouse indignation in all those who have bad blood in their veins. My for-

mula for greatness in man is *amor fati*†: the fact that a man wishes nothing to be different, either in front of him or behind him, or for all eternity. Not merely bear the necessary, and on no account conceal it—all idealism is falsehood in the face of necessity—it must be *loved*. . . .

From The Will to Power

THE EPISTEMOLOGICAL STARTING POINT§

480

There are no such things as "mind," reason, thought, consciousness, soul, will, or truth: they all belong to fiction, and are useless. It is not a question of "subject and object," but of a particular species of animal which can prosper only by means of a certain *exactness*, or, better still, *regularity* of its perceptions (in order that experience may be cumulative). . . .

Knowledge works as an *instrument* of power. It is therefore obvious that it increases with each advance of power. . . .

The significance of "knowledge": in this case, as in the case of "good" or "beautiful," the concept must be regarded strictly and narrowly from an anthropocentric and biological standpoint. In order that a particular species may maintain and increase its power, its conception of reality must contain enough which is calculable and constant to allow of its formulating a scheme of conduct. *The utility of preservation*—and *not* some abstract or theoretical need to eschew deception—stands as the motive force behind the development of the organs of knowledge; . . . they evolve in such a way that their observations may suffice for our preservation. In other words, the *measure* of the desire for knowledge depends upon the extent to which the *will to power* grows in a certain species: a species gets a grasp of a given amount of reality, *in order to master it, in order to enlist that amount in its service.*

---

*The German words are, *Einsamkeit* and *Vielsamkeit*. The latter was coined by Nietzsche. The English word "multitude" should, therefore, be understood as signifying multifarious instincts and gifts.
†Love of fate.

---

§The translation has been edited. Some of the changes were suggested by the translation by Walter Kaufmann.

THE BELIEF IN THE "EGO." THE SUBJECT.

481

In opposition to positivism, which halts at phenomena and says, "These are only *facts* and nothing more," I would say: No, facts are precisely what is lacking, all that exists consists of *interpretations*. We cannot establish any fact "in itself": it may even be nonsense to desire to do such a thing. "Everything is *subjective*," you say: but that in itself is *interpretation*. The "subject" is nothing given, but something superimposed by fancy, something projected behind. Is it necessary to set an interpreter behind the interpretation already to hand? Even that would be posit, hypothesis.

To the extent to which knowledge has any sense at all, the world is knowable: But it may be interpreted *differently*, it has not one sense behind it, but hundreds of senses—"Perspectivism."

It is our needs that *interpret the world;* our drives and their impulses for and against. Every instinct is a sort of thirst for power; each has its perspective, which it would like to impose upon all the other drives as their norm.

482

Where our ignorance really begins, at that point from which we can see no further, we set a word; for instance, the word "I," the word "do," the word "suffer"—these may be the horizon of our knowledge, but they are not "truths."

483

Thought posits the ego; but up to the present everybody believed, like common people, that there was something unconditionally certain in "I think," and that this "I" was the given *cause* of the thinking, from which we understood all other causal reactions by analogy. However customary and indispensable this fiction may have become now, this fact proves nothing against the imaginary nature of its origin; it might be a life-preserving belief and *still* be *false*.

484

"Thinking occurs, therefore there is something that thinks": this is what Descartes' argument amounts to.

But this is tantamount to considering our belief in the notion "*substance*" as an *à priori* truth: that there must be something "that thinks" when we think, is merely a formulation of a grammatical custom which sets an agent to every action. In short, a metaphysico-logical postulate is already put forward here—and it is not merely *an ascertainment of fact.* . . . On Descartes' lines nothing absolutely certain is attained, but only the fact of a very powerful faith.

If the proposition be reduced to, "Thinking occurs, therefore there are thoughts," the result is mere tautology; and precisely the one factor which is in question, the "*reality* of thought," is not touched upon—so that, in this form, the "apparent character" of thought cannot be denied. What Descartes *wanted* to prove was, that thought not only had *apparent reality*, but absolute reality.

485

The concept *substance* is an outcome of the concept *subject*: and not conversely! If we surrender the concept soul, "the subject," the very conditions for the concept "substance" are lacking. *Degrees of Being* are obtained, but being is lost.

Criticism of "*reality*": what does a "*greater or lesser reality*" lead to, the gradation of being in which we believe?

The degree of our feeling of *life* and *power* (the logic and relationship of past life) presents us with the measure of "being," "reality," "nonappearance."

Subject: this is the term we apply to our belief in an *entity* underlying all the different moments of the most intense feeling of reality: we regard this belief as the effect of a cause—and we believe in our belief to such an extent that, on its account alone, we imagine "truth," "reality," "substantiality"—"Subject" is the fiction which would like to make us believe that several similar states were the effect of one substratum: but we it was who first *created* the "similarity" of these states; our adjusting them and our making them similar is the *fact—not* their similarity (on the contrary, this ought rather to be denied).

486

One would have to know what *being* is in order to be able to *decide* whether this or that is real (for instance, "the facts of consciousness"); it would also be necessary to know what *certainty* and *knowledge* are, and so forth.—But, as we do *not* know these things, a criticism of the faculty of knowledge is nonsensical: how is it possible for an instrument to criticize itself, when it is itself that exercises the critical faculty. It cannot even define itself!

487

Should not all philosophy ultimately disclose the first principles on which the reasoning processes depend? —that is to say, our *belief* in the "ego" as a substance, as the only reality according to which, we alone are able to ascribe reality to things? The oldest realism at length comes to light, simultaneously with man's recognition of the fact that his whole religious history is no more than a history of superstitions concerning the soul. *Here there is a barrier:* our very thinking involves that belief (with its distinctions—substance, accident, action, agent, etc.); to abandon it would mean to cease to be able to think.

But that a belief, however useful it may be for the preservation of a species, has nothing to do with the truth, may be seen from the fact that we *must* believe in time, space, and motion, without feeling ourselves compelled to regard them as absolute realities.

488

The psychological origin of our belief in reason—The ideas "reality," "Being," are derived from our *subject-feeling*.

"Subject," interpreted through ourselves so that the ego may pass as substance, as the cause of action, as the *agent*.

The metaphysico-logical postulates, the belief in substance, accident, attribute, etc. etc., draws its convincing character from our habit of regarding all our actions as the result of our will; so that the ego, as substance, does not vanish in the multiplicity of changes. *But there is no such thing as will.*

We have no categories which allow us to separate a "world as thing-in-itself," from "a world of appearance." All our *categories of reason* have a sensual origin: they are based on the empirical world. "The soul," "the ego"—the history of these concepts shows that here, also, the oldest distinction ("*spiritus*," "life") obtains. . . .

If there is nothing material, then there can be nothing immaterial. The concept no longer *means* anything.

No subject "atoms." The sphere of a subject *increasing* or *diminishing* unremittingly, the center of the system continually *displacing* itself; in the event of the system no longer being able to organize the appropriated mass, it divides into two. On the other hand, it is able, without destroying it, to transform a weaker subject into one of its own functionaries, and, to a certain extent, to form a new unity with it. Not a "substance," but rather something which in itself strives after greater strength; and which wishes to "preserve" itself only indirectly (it wishes to *surpass* itself).

489

Everything that reaches consciousness as a "unity" is already enormously complicated: we never have anything more than the *semblance of unity*.

The phenomenon of the *body* is the richer, more distinct, and more tangible phenomenon: it should be methodically drawn to the front, and no mention should be made of its ultimate significance.

490

The assumption of a *single subject* is perhaps not necessary; it may be equally permissible to assume a plurality of subjects, whose interaction and struggle underlies our thought and our consciousness in general. A sort of *aristocracy* of "cells" in which the ruling power is vested? Of course an aristocracy of equals, who are accustomed to ruling co-operatively and who understand how to command?

> *My hypothesis:* The subject as a plurality.
> Pain intellectual and dependent upon the judgment "harmful," projected.
> The effect always "unconscious": the inferred and imagined cause is projected, it *follows* the event.
> Pleasure is a form of pain.
> The only kind of power that exists is of the same nature as the power of will: a commanding of other subjects which thereupon alter themselves.

The unremitting transientness and volatility of the subject. "Mortal soul."
Number as perspective form.

491

The belief in the body is more fundamental than the belief in the soul; the latter arose from the unscientific observation of the agonies of the body. (Something which leaves it. The belief in the *truth of dreams*.)

492

The body and physiology the starting point: Why? We obtain a correct image of the nature of our subject unity, that is to say, as a number of regents at the head of a community (not as "souls" or as "life forces"), as also of the dependence of these regents upon their subjects, and upon the conditions of a hierarchy, and of the division of labor, as the means ensuring the existence of the part and the whole. We also obtain a correct image of the way in which the living entities continually come into being and expire, and we see how eternity cannot belong to the "subject"; we realize that the struggle finds expression in obeying as well as in commanding, and that a fluctuating definition of the limits of power is a factor of life. The comparative *ignorance* in which the ruler is kept, of the individual performances and even disturbances taking place in the community, also belong to the conditions under which government may be carried on. In short, we obtain a valuation even of *want-of-knowledge*, of seeing-things-generally-as-a-whole, of simplification, of falsification, and of perspective. What is most important, however, is, that we regard the ruler and his subjects as of the *same kind*, all feeling, willing, thinking—and that wherever we see or suspect movement in a body, we conclude that there is cooperative-subjective and invisible life. Movement as a symbol for the eye; it denotes that something has been felt, willed, thought.

The danger of directly questioning the subject *concerning* the subject, and all spiritual self-reflection consists in this, that it might be a necessary condition of its activity to interpret itself *erroneously*. That is why we appeal to the body and lay the evidence of sharpened senses aside; or we try and see whether the subjects themselves cannot enter into communication with us.

QUESTIONS FOR REFLECTION

1. Critically evaluate Schopenhauer's argument that death is not a misfortune:
   (a) We do not care about the fact that the matter out of which we are composed changes over time. We care only about "the form."
   (b) "If here we are always content to retain the form without lamenting the discarded matter, we must behave in the same way when in death the same thing happens . . . to the whole. . . ." What occurs in death is that we are replaced with other individuals.
   (c) So "it seems just as absurd to desire the continuance of our individuality, which is replaced by other individuals, as to desire the permanence of the matter of our body. . . ."

   Is it possible to accept Schopenhauer's argument and still affirm life?

2. Schopenhauer says that willing—constantly desiring more and more—is something we always do, and he thinks that it is pointless and makes us miserable:

   All *willing* springs from lack . . . and thus from suffering. Fulfillment brings this to an end; yet for one wish that is fulfilled there remain at least ten that are denied. Further, . . . demands and requests go on to infinity; fulfillment is short and meted out sparingly. But even the final satisfaction itself is only apparent; the wish fulfilled at once makes way for a new one; the former is a known delusion, the latter a delusion not as yet known. No attained object of willing can give a satisfaction that lasts. . . . Thus the subject of willing . . . is the eternally thirsting Tantalus. (*The World as Will and Representation,* I, sect. 38, p. 196)

   He goes on to conclude that our only hope is to bring willing to a stop:

   When, however, an external cause or inward disposition suddenly raises us out of the endless stream of willing . . . , [T]hen all at once the peace, always sought but always escaping us on that first path of willing, comes to us of its own accord, and all is well with us. It is the painless state, prized by Epicurus as the highest good . . .; for that moment we are delivered from the miserable pressure of the will. (ibid.)

Nietzsche, by contrast, reaches almost the diametrically opposed position; that the ideal life consists in the most intense willing, so that we are constantly replacing our ends with ever more demanding ones, constantly 'overcoming' ourselves and others.

Are the two positions compatible? Is one of the two positions more plausible than the other?

3. According to Schopenhauer, there are three basic motives of action: egoism or self-love, which moves us to seek our own advantage; malice or wickedness, which moves us to seek the disadvantage or harm of others; and compassion, which moves us to seek others' well-being. Concerning malice Schopenhauer writes:

… Much intense willing always entails much intense suffering. … From … inward torment, … there finally results even that delight at the suffering of another which has not sprung from egoism, but is disinterested; this is *wickedness* proper, and rises to the pitch of *cruelty*. For this the suffering of another is no longer a means of attaining the ends of his own will, but an end in itself … every privation is infinitely aggravated by the pleasure of others, and relieved by the knowledge that others also endure the same privation. … [The wicked person] tries to mitigate his own suffering by the sight of another's, and at the same time recognizes this as an expression of his power. (Vol. I, sect. 65, pp. 363–4)

And in "Human Nature," *Parerga*, pp. 284–288 of the Taylor edition, he writes:

To the boundless egoism of our nature there is joined more or less in every human breast a fund of hatred, anger, envy, rancour and malice. … [I]n the heart of every man there lies a wild beast which only waits for an opportunity … to inflict pain on others, or, if they stand in his way, to kill them. It is this which is the source of all the lust of war and battle. … It is [the result of] the will to live, which, more and more embittered by the constant sufferings of existence, seeks to alleviate its own torment by causing torment in others. But in this way a man gradually develops in himself real cruelty and malice.

In what ways does Schopenahuer's wicked person resemble Nietzsche's 'Übermensch'? Why does Nietzsche recommend that we aspire to the Übermensch? Should we become wicked in Schopenhauer's sense?

4. Nietzsche says that anyone who affirms existence just as it is would be happy to see it repeated over and over, forever. Is he correct? (If we affirm our existence, do we want it continued indefinitely or do we want it repeated indefinitely?) Why does he make this claim about eternal recurrence?

5. Recall that Kierkegaard says that Christian faith, properly understood, is not self-deceptive and is a way to avoid despair. How would Nietzsche reply? Would his response to Kierkegaard be correct?

6. What does Nietzsche mean by the term 'immoralist'? Critically evaluate Nietzsche's case for immoralism.

7. Read 351–390 of *Will to Power*. Is Nietzsche arguing that evil is desirable? Evaluate his argument.

8. What does Nietzsche mean by 'perspectivism'? Would Nietzsche say that any interpretation of the world is as defensible as any other? If not, what makes an interpretation more defensible than another? If, on the other hand, all interpretations are defensible, why is he so critical of various interpretations, such as religious interpretations?

FURTHER READINGS

Works by Nietzsche

The Birth of Tragedy from the Spirit of Music (1872). In *The Birth of Tragedy and The Case of Wagner*, Walter Kaufmann, trans. New York: Vintage Books, 1967.

Untimely Meditations (1873–1876). Translated by R. J. Hollingdale. Cambridge: Cambridge University Press, 1983.

Human, All-Too-Human: A Book for Free Spirits (1878–1880). Translated by R. J. Hollingdale. Cambridge: Cambridge University Press, 1986.

Daybreak: Thoughts on Moral Prejudices (1881). Translated by R. J. Hollingdale. Cambridge: Cambridge University Press, 1982.

The Gay Science (1882). Translated by Walter Kaufmann. New York: Vintage Books, 1974.

Thus Spoke Zarathustra: A Book for All and None (1883–1885). Translated by Walter Kaufmann. London: Penguin Books, 1954.

Beyond Good and Evil (1886). Translated by Walter Kaufmann. New York: Vintage Books, 1966.

Genealogy of Morals (1887). In *On the Genealogy of Morals and Ecce Homo,* translated by Walter Kaufmann. New York: Vintage Books, 1969.

The Antichrist: A Curse upon Christianity (1888). In *Twilight of the Idols and The Anti-Christ,* translated by R. J. Hollingdale. London: Penguin Books, 1968.

The Twilight of the Idols (1888). In *Twilight of the Idols and The Anti-Christ,* translated by R. J. Hollingdale. London: Penguin Books, 1968.

Ecce Homo (1888). In *On the Genealogy of Morals and Ecce Homo,* translated by Walter Kaufmann. New York: Vintage Books, 1969.

Nietzsche contra Wagner (1888). In *The Portable Nietzsche,* translated by Walter Kaufmann. New York: Viking Press, 1954.

The Will to Power (1906). Translated by Walter Kaufmann. New York: Viking Press, 1967.

Works on Nietzsche

Allison, David, ed. *The New Nietzsche.* Cambridge: MIT Press, 1985.

Ansell-Pearson, K. *An Introduction to Nietzsche as Political Thinker.* Cambridge: Cambridge University Press, 1994.

Berkowitz, Peter. *Nietzsche: The Ethics of an Immoralist.* Cambridge: Harvard University Press, 1995.

Higgins, Kathleen. *Nietzsche's Zarathustra.* Philadelphia: Temple University Press, 1987.

Nehamas, Alexander. *Nietzsche: Life as Literature.* Cambridge: Harvard University Press, 1985.

Kaufmann, Walter. *Nietzsche: Philosopher, Psychologist, Antichrist.* Princeton: Princeton University Press, 1974.

Richardson, John. *Nietzsche's System.* New York: Oxford University Press, 1996.

Rosset, Clement. *Joyful Cruelty: Toward a Philosophy of the Real.* New York: Oxford University Press, 1993.

Schacht, Richard. *Nietzsche.* London: Routledge & Kegan Paul, 1983.

Solomon, Robert. *Nietzsche: A Collection of Critical Essays.* Garden City, New York: Anchor Books, 1973.

Magnus, Bernd, and Higgins, Kathleen, eds. *The Cambridge Companion to Nietzsche.* Cambridge: Cambridge University Press, 1996.

CHAPTER 4

Martin Heidegger (1889–1976)

Hartin Heidegger was born in Messkirch, Germany. His family was Catholic and his early studies were designed to prepare him for the priesthood. He went so far as to become a Jesuit novice before he changed course and attended the University of Freiburg. There he studied theology and philosophy; there, too, he encountered the phenomenological philosophy of Edmund Husserl, which had a lasting impact on his development. After graduating, Heidegger lectured at Freiburg and served as assistant to Husserl. Heidegger went on to become a professor of philosophy at Marburg, where he befriended Rudolf Bultmann and Hannah Arendt. In 1927 he published *Being and Time* in a series edited by Husserl. A year later he was given the chair at Freiburg that Husserl had held since 1916. Five years later Heidegger became rector of the university and joined the National Socialist party. The depth of his involvement in Nazism is a matter of controversy to this day.

Like his predecessors Kierkegaard and Nietzsche, Heidegger thinks that various forces conspire to prevent us from taking stock of and affirming our existence. We may resist these forces and achieve a relatively lucid and compelling approach to our existence, but to do so requires that we first undertake an extensive investigation of human existence itself. This investigation will be primarily an ontological, or metaphysical study, approached using a methodology called phenomenology. Heidegger developed his phenomenological method under the influence of his teacher Husserl, who introduced phenomenology in his *Logical Investigations* (1900–1901), an excerpt from which is reproduced below, and developed it further in later work, a sketch of which appears in his "Paris Lectures," presented here. Heidegger provides a helpful introductory discussion of his own approach to understanding human existence in his essay "What is Metaphysics?", also reproduced below. The reader

might wish to read these essays before moving on to the more daunting selections from Heidegger's *Being and Time*.

HUSSERL AND HEIDEGGER ON PHENOMENOLOGY

Edmund Husserl (1859–1938) developed his phenomenological method largely in an attempt to clarify the nature of intentionality. Intentionality is what enables consciousness to be directed at or about the items that we contemplate. Heidegger inherited the project of clarifying intentionality from his teacher Franz Brentano (1838–1917). Brentano had claimed that each act of consciousness is directed at an object, but this view faced a difficulty: When people think about imaginary things, consciousness is not directed at anything real. Husserl introduced phenomenology as a way to study intentionality, and his first phenomenological investigations dealt with logic. These investigations were conducted in his two-volume *Logical Investigations* (1900 and 1901). In this early publication Husserl distinguishes between the linguistic expressions of logic on the one hand, and their "meaning-intention" on the other hand. He characterizes phenomenology as the description of the latter. Phenomenology "lays bare the 'sources' from which the basic concepts and ideal laws of pure logic 'flow'. . . ."[1] It gets us "back to the 'things themselves'," back to that which our expressions "really and truly stand for."[2] At the same time phenomenology is not an exercise in psychology. While Husserl had at one time believed that logical truths are empirically based generalizations about psychological facts, he rejected this doctrine of "psychologism" in his *Investigations*. Instead, phenomenologists grasp meanings-intentions through a form of direct intuition, and their task is to describe what they grasp thereby.

In later work, such as his *Ideas* (1913) and "Paris Lectures," which Husserl developed into the *Cartesian Meditations* (1931), Husserl's work took a more subjectivist turn. He accounted for intentionality by suggesting that consciousness constitutes the objects at which it is directed. Thus, when I experience a house, raw sensations are structured by consciousness so as to constitute a house, which is a whole that includes aspects not immediately in view, such as the inside and back of the house. Moreover, given exactly the same sensory input, different acts of consciousness might constitute different objects, as familiar ambiguous figures illustrate. Different people may structure the world differently, too, but the world each of us constitutes is a shared, intersubjectively available world. The world we experience is structured by consciousness through the agency of features that Husserl called *noema*. Husserl suggested that we may study these features by taking up a Cartesian stance in which we suspend belief in the reality of objects and focus on the aspects of consciousness that make it seem to us that there are objects of consciousness.

Heidegger says in "My Way to Phenomenology"[3] that he developed his own approach to phenomenology as a result of his attempt to understand Husserl's *Investigations* and not because he was influenced by later versions of Husserl's phenomenology. Indeed, Heidegger rejected the Cartesian approach Husserl developed in his later writings, which aimed at providing an indubitable foundation for knowledge. In section 7 of *Being and Time* Heidegger says "phenomenology is the science of the being of beings—ontology."[4] He assumes that being, the subject matter of phenomenology, is familiar because everyone has some grasp of what it is for something to be, but also that being is not straightforward to us and in any case not the sort of thing about which we may know with certainty. While normally it is partially hidden from us, the phenomenon can be coaxed into revealing itself more clearly. The way to coax being and particular beings into revealing themselves is to employ the very "way of access that genuinely belong to them."[5] The way of access, it turns out, is interpretation. Through interpretation, being reveals itself to itself, or is revealed to beings who are able to interpret. Hence, through interpretation the phenomenologist can coax being into opening itself up to investigation.

Because it is through interpretation that he hopes to coax being into revealing itself, Heidegger names his specific approach to phenomenology *hermeneutics*.

ONTOLOGY

Heidegger understands his account of human existence to be a contribution to ontology. Ontology, a branch of metaphysics, is the discipline that investigates what it is for things to exist. The number 1, a wrench, the property of redness, and a person can all be said to exist, but it is one thing to say that the number 1 exists, quite another to say some tool, such as a wrench, exists, and so on. Ontology attempts to clarify the different forms of existence; as Heidegger says, ontology is the study of the "*being of beings*." But Heidegger is most concerned with the sort of existence that is characteristic of people.

According to Heidegger, ontology is the key to understanding human being, but traditional philosophy has adopted a truncated view of what it is for an item to exist. Typically, philosophers think that an item's existence consists in its being a substance or an attribute (property) of a substance. Thus, philosophers tend to believe that people exist in the same sense as rocks: both are objects with various properties. But Heidegger attempts to show that this ontology is simplistic. He replaces the generic term "existence" with "being," and says that *being* is not equivalent to being "objectively present" (*vorhanden*) in the sense of being "thing-like," or "object-like." Human being is not primarily thing-like: "This being does not and never has the kind of being of what is merely objectively present within the world."[6] We can understand the human mode of being only if we avoid the common, simplistic understanding of being. Heidegger calls the human mode of being "existence." In Heidegger's usage, various things *are*, but existence is the human way of being.[7]

The human way of being is shaped by a distinctive project, for human being consists in engaging in the project of interpreting or disclosing all forms of being, starting with human being. Only that which operates with an understanding of what it is to exist can have the kind of being characteristic of human being. The human mode of being is more fundamental than other sorts of being, according to Heidegger. The being of other things is shaped by their participation in human existence, and all ontological classification is determined by human existence.

DA-SEIN AND THE "THEY"

In order to refer to the being of beings that reveal themselves to themselves through interpretation, Heidegger uses the German term 'Da-sein,' which means 'being there.' The term *there* in *being there* signals the fact that human being is not isolated; it is being-in-the-world. In speaking of 'being-in-the-world,' Heidegger draws attention to the fact that *Da-sein* always interprets existence as involving a world.[8] However, when Heidegger draws our attention to the fact that *Da-sein* is 'in the world,' he does not mean to say that *Da-sein* is physically contained in the world, as shoes might be in a box. Our relationship to our surroundings should not be thought of as one object spatially situated with respect to others. Rather, there are many kinds of being-in. As examples, Heidegger lists the following:

> to have to do with something, to produce, order and take care of something, to use something, to give something up and let it get lost, to undertake, to accomplish, to find out, to ask about, to observe, to speak about, to determine. . . . These ways of being-in have the kind of being of *taking care of.* . . .[9]

Surrounding us is an array of items that, individually and collectively, play various roles in and have significance in terms of our existence. What those items *are*, and their importance, is ultimately determined by the roles they play in our existence, and the "world" we are in is determined by the complex ways we interact with and use items to do things that accomplish purposes about which we are concerned.

Our comportment to most items is to regard them as "equipment" that is "ready," or "handy."[10] Equipment is defined in terms of an equipment nexus.[11] For example, ink is defined in terms of a nexus of writing equipment: Ink is the stuff used in pens in order to produce marks on paper, but by the same token pens are the things used to deliver ink to paper, and so on. This nexus, in turn, takes its shape because it serves all sorts of purposes in human existence, and ultimately the nexus and its elements are defined in terms of and have significance relative to the purposes

they serve. Even the work we do with equipment is itself encountered in terms of its useability. "As the what-for of the hammer, plane, and needle, the work to be produced has in its turn the kind of being of a useful thing. . . . The work that has been ordered exists in its turn only on the basis of its use and the referential context of beings discovered in that use."[12]

Da-sein not only involves operating with an interpretation of being there, it must also involve an interpreter of being there: being there cannot happen without an interpreter of being there. As Heidegger says, "The being whose analysis our task is, is always we ourselves. The being of this being is always *mine*."[13] But *Da-sein* does not refer to Cartesian egos or substances or subjects, nor does it designate consciousness or a particular stream of conscious. The I that is always associated with *Da-sein* has a capacity for interpretation that allows it to bind various phenomena, creating a unity with which the I at hand identifies.

We have said that human existence involves an interpreter and an interpretation. Now let us add that our interpretation of our existence is largely decisive. The qualifier "largely" is perhaps controversial. Often Heidegger appears to defend a radical and unqualified claim: To interpret ourselves a certain way, no matter what that interpretation may be, is to *be* that way. But he also says that we are "in the truth" when we avoid all evasions and allow existence to disclose itself.[14] Moreover, the radical claim that our interpretation of ourselves is always decisive does not sit well with his more fundamental claim that human existence just does involve various things (such as an interpreter, an interpretation, and worldliness) whether our interpretation of existence acknowledges these features or not. And Heidegger himself introduces a term to capture the sense in which existence just does involve certain features: "the factuality of the fact Dasein, as the way in which every Da-sein actually is, we call its *facticity*."[15] Hence, it seems best to attribute a somewhat less radical thesis to Heidegger; namely, that within certain limitations, our interpretation of our existence is decisive. Accordingly, if my understanding of existence differs substantially from yours, we might well exist in different senses, but your existence and mine will always share certain structural features, the main one being that it involves an interpretation that is largely decisive.

There will inevitably be a great deal of overlap in the way people interpret existence due to the fact that the basic interpretation of existence is shaped by and embodied in culture, and, at least initially, individuals are reared so that they end up operating with this dominant way of being. Even later in life people are subjected to and take part in idle talk that reinforces and perpetuates socially preferred attitudes, lifestyles, and social roles. People drift into a way of being, and to a great extent they are not even conscious of the mode of being within which they operate: A child may be trained to shake hands with others in certain circumstances but may be entirely unable to verbalize the conventions governing the institution of shaking hands. Even adults may be unaware of why this practice has taken the shape it has, and they may be influenced by it in ways they cannot articulate. A similar point holds generally of social practices: people differ in their ability to make these practices explicit.

The attitudes and lifestyles that are socially preferred and maintained go to define a point of view Heidegger calls "*das Man,*" meaning the "they," or "one" in section 27. A self occupies the point of view of the "they-self" when it inherits an indiscriminate understanding of "itself in terms of the 'world' taken care of." [16] The "they" comes to be our dominant perspective for several reasons. First, we indiscriminately inherit "their" existence and end up identifying with the "they." Unless we go out of our way to make discriminations that pick ourselves out as individuals, we will occupy the standpoint of the "they" and will live as "they" do. Second, we are all concerned about the ways in which we are related to others. We are concerned about our standing relative to others. But we find this fact about ourselves disquieting, and so we conceal it from ourselves, thus all the more firmly subjecting ourselves to the concern about relative standing. [17] Because of this concern, we are subservient to others:

> One belongs to the others oneself, and entrenches their power. "The others," whom one designates as such in order to cover over one's own essential belonging to them, are those who *are there* initially and for the most part in everyday being-with-one-another. The who is not this one and not that one, not oneself and not some and not the sum of them all. The "who" is the neuter, *the they.* [18]

Moreover, the "they" has its own "ways to be," such as creating and maintaining "averageness," which it does by deciding what is significant and prescribing

what people may do, "squashing" exceptionalness, controlling "every way in which the world and Dasein are interpreted," [19] and by obscuring these activities. Hence, the "they" is able to retain its own dominance over us, and we cooperate by refusing to notice.

INTERPRETIVE FREEDOM, ANGST, AND FLEEING

According to Heidegger, as I have said, an essential feature of human existence is that it involves an interpretation that is largely decisive. Hence, any particular interpretation must come to terms with this fact. But the idea that our existence is largely whatever we make it out to be causes us *Angst*—unfocused anxiety (as opposed to fear, which is focused upon a specific object)—for this idea presents us with the task of deciding what our existence shall be, and this decision is unlike any we are accustomed to making. Normally decisions are made (roughly) by taking for granted certain goals or values and some understanding of the situation at hand and then working out what will efficiently achieve those goals given the situation. But Heidegger's claim is that our interpretive freedom is not restricted by any goals or values or ways of understanding our situation. All goals, values, and ways of understanding our situation are part of the interpretation of existence we must choose. As many commentators point out, existence entails "interpretation all the way down." (When people explain Heidegger's view in this way, they are referring to an anecdote about a student who claimed that the world rested on a giant turtle. With some sarcasm the student's instructor asked the student what *that* turtle rests on, and the student said something like, "I know what you are trying to do, and it won't work; it's turtles all the way down!")

Thus, we must not only interpret our existence, we must also deal with the anxiety caused by the realization that we and our world have no fixed nature. But the socially preferred mode of existence of the "they" provides an alternative. It assuages anxiety by concealing the fact of our interpretive freedom. It fosters the idea that there is a fixed human nature, in which existence must take a certain shape. When we take up the point of view of the "they," we "flee" from our interpretive freedom. "They" respond to the self-interpretive nature of existence by misrepresenting existence. "They" make it tempting for us to "fall prey to" or "plunge into" the world and become "entangled," or absorbed in the world in a way that "mostly has the character of being lost in the publicness of the they."[20] "Falling prey" is tempting because entanglement is "tranquilizing."[21]

CONSCIENCE, GUILT, AND AUTHENTICITY

When we are lost in the they, our interpretive freedom is concealed from us, and we become alienated from, and indifferent to having, our own existence. Heidegger calls "this everyday indifference of Da-sein averageness," or "average everydayness."[22] Average everydayness confines us to an inauthentic form of existence, namely, "a distinctive kind of being-in-the-world which is completely taken in by the world and the *Mitda-sein* of the others in the they."[23] To exist authentically, we must self-consciously exercise our interpretive freedom so as to decide what shall constitute our existence. Heidegger suggests that despite the devices embedded in the everyday mode of existence that conceal interpretive freedom, we sense our freedom. Our awareness of our freedom is manifested in the form of "conscience," which calls us to authenticity.

Conscience calls our attention to our existential guilt. But our existential guilt is not a matter of our having violated moral duties. Our existential guilt stems from our inability to take full responsibility for our own existence. Individuals are responsible for themselves and their existence and so must take charge of and choose their existence, but something is always left out when individuals attempt to lay the ground for themselves. For all choosing is influenced by something else, and our choices are ultimately guided by the socially available way of being that we have taken over early in life. "The self, which as such has to lay the ground of itself, can never gain power over that ground, and yet it has to take over being the ground in existing."[24] Existential guilt is constituted by the fact that we are responsible for laying the ground for ourselves even though this responsibility extends to factors that we cannot fully grasp and that we cannot wholly choose.

But Heidegger adds[25] that when we shoulder our responsibility and own up to the existential guilt entailed by our inability to meet that responsibility fully, we choose ourselves and close ourselves off from the "they-self" and its idle chatter. We identify with, or "project" ourselves upon, our "being-guilty." According to Heidegger, our guilt becomes part of who we are, just as our sinfulness is part of who we are according to Kierkegaard. Heidegger uses the term "resoluteness" to refer to "the reticent projecting oneself upon one's ownmost being-guilty which is ready for Angst."[26] In living resolutely, we become individual selves with individual responsibility and guilt. This individuality does not entail indifference to the things and people around us; but it does prompt us to expect others to live resolutely. It prompts us to let those with whom we are involved be individuals too; we let them "'be' in their ownmost potentiality-of-being. . . ."[27]

DEATH, INDIVIDUALITY, AND TEMPORALITY

Interpretive freedom (which leaves existence with no settled nature) is not the only thing that causes *Da-sein* anxiety and that *Da-sein* consequently flees and covers over. Also troublesome is death. According to Heidegger, "being-toward-death belongs primordially and essentially to the being of Da-sein . . . ,"[28] and yet "being-toward-death is essentially Angst."[29] Heidegger's point is that while human existence is temporally extended into the past and into the future, it is bounded in the future by death, and hence we must work death into our plans and into the way we understand ourselves. Heidegger says that death is "not to be bypassed."[30] Not only is death inevitable and indeed possible at any time, but the fact of death cannot be ignored or interpreted away (although it can be denied or covered up in an inauthentic existence); it is part of our "facticity," or "thrownness." Presumably death is intractable to reinterpretation because no matter how it is interpreted death ends our capacity for projecting, planning, and interpreting. It ends "every way of existing."[31] Death presents us with "the possibility of the impossibility of existence in general."[32]

We react to the fact that we will die in much the same way that we react to the fact that we have no fixed nature: we view both as a failing, as a lack, as an encounter with nothingness. Both are unnerving, and in both cases we want to interpret away what we have discovered. But death, like our mostly unsettled nature, withstands all of our attempts to interpret it away.

Because it is difficult to accept the fact that our existence will come to an end, the socially preferred mode of existence conceals the fact of death. The "they" says: "People unknown to us 'die' daily and hourly. . . . One also dies at the end, but for now one is not involved."[33] We are led to think of death as something that the "they" encounters and indeed encounters without harm to itself, so that death is not a threat. "They" will also prompt one to say that one, too, will die in the end, but one is to understand this admission to imply that for now death does not concern one. "They" go further, and forbid anyone to think about death, stigmatizing those who do as cowardly. "The they does not permit the courage to have Angst about death."[34] We know that everyone is always anxious about death, however. The very phenomenon of "their" carefully cultivated indifference about death shows that even "they" are busy coping with their anxiety. Indeed, while "their" solicitude toward the dying is tranquilizing, "this tranquilization is not only for the 'dying person,' but just as much for 'those who are comforting him.'"[35]

When we evade our death by immersing ourselves in the "they," thinking like "they" do, and adopting one of "their" social roles, we lose ourselves in the "they." We lose sight of ourselves as separate individuals. In particular, we lose track of the fact that our death is "the ownmost nonrelational potentiality-of-being."[36] That is, it will be *you* who cease to exist, not the "they" or "their" social roles, and if you anticipate your death in an authentic way you will be pulled away from your relationships with others and from all being-alongside-things. "The nonrelational character of death understood in anticipation individualizes Da-sein down to itself."[37] An authentic anticipation of your death forces you to realize who you are, to free yourself from the "they-self" and pick out your individual identity. It makes you see that all along you have been an isolated individual and all along a particular death has been yours. These facts must be reflected in your existence if it is to be authentic. "[The nonrelational character of death] reveals the fact that any being-together-with what is taken care of and any being-with the others fails when one's ownmost potentiality-of-being is at stake. Da-sein can au-

thentically be itself only when it makes [being itself] possible of its own accord."[38] We may and indeed must care about the people and things around us, but we cannot regard them—or the "they-self"—as part of our individual identity.

An authentic being-toward-death does not mean brooding over death.[39] It means seeing our existence as a whole, and shaping our existence with the knowledge that (1) it is finite, and (2) it might be ended at any time. Given this knowledge we will not make plans that can be achieved only if we exist beyond a human lifespan, and we will make contingency plans such as taking out life insurance to protect our dependents in case we die unexpectedly. In this sense authentic being-toward-death avoids "clinging" to our existence and involves preparation for "giving it up."[40] Heidegger does not mean to say that we should cultivate indifference to dying. Indeed, the realization that our existence will end helps us to see that our existence is a matter of concern. The authentic response to losing our existence is anxiety, not indifference.

Anticipating our death prompts us to see ourselves in an authentic way. It prompts us to separate from the "they" and decide for ourselves what shall constitute our existence. Aware that our time is limited, we arrange our lives in an orderly way so that we can accomplish the goals we set ourselves in the time allotted us. We structure our lives into a unity that includes all of the stages of our finite lives, past, present, and future. The idea of time involved in this unity is called "temporality," and "*the primordial unity of the structure of care lies in temporality.*"[41] Moreover, we give a certain priority to the future stages of our lives, for we understand ourselves in terms of possibilities we project: "as projecting, understanding is the mode of being of Da-sein in which it *is* its possibilities as possibilities."[42] As Heidegger says, *Da-sein* "is always already 'beyond itself,' not as a way of behaving toward beings which it is not, but as being toward the potentiality-for-being which it itself is. This structure of being of the essential 'being concerned about' we formulate as the being-ahead-of-itself of Da-sein."[43] But if *Da-sein* is always ahead of itself, it is also true that *Da-sein* is behind itself as well. *Da-sein* is an unfolding whole that is future directed, temporally extended, but temporally limited. It does not exist simply in the moment, and it is not directionless. It considers its past as that which led up to its present, and it is constantly choosing among possibilities so as to bring into existence a future that is a suitable outcome of its past and present, a future that ends with death.

NOTES

1. Edmund Husserl, *Logical Investigations,* trans J. N. Findlay, 2 vols. (London: Routledge & Kegan Paul, 1970), 249.
2. Ibid, 252.
3. Available in Walter Kaufmann, ed., *Existentialism from Dostoevsky to Sartre* (New York: The New American Library, Inc., 1975).
4. References are to the standard German version of *Being and Time:* Martin Heidegger, *Sein und Zeit,* 7th edn. (Tubingen: Neomarius Verlag), 37.
5. Ibid., 37.
6. Ibid., 43.
7. Ibid., 42.
8. Ibid., 15–16.
9. Ibid., 56.
10. Ibid., sec. 15.
11. Ibid., 68.
12. Ibid., 70.
13. Ibid., 42.
14. Ibid., 297.
15. Ibid., 56.
16. Ibid., 321.
17. Ibid., 126.
18. Ibid., 126.
19. Ibid., 127.
20. Ibid., 175.
21. Ibid., 177.
22. Ibid., 43.
23. Ibid., 176.
24. Ibid., 284.
25. Ibid., 287.
26. Ibid., 297.
27. Ibid., 298.
28. Ibid., 252.
29. Ibid., 245.
30. Ibid., 251.
31. Ibid., 262.
32. Ibid., 262.
33. Ibid., 253.
34. Ibid., 254.
35. Ibid., 254.
36. Ibid., 251.
37. Ibid., 263.
38. Ibid., 263.
39. Ibid., 261.
40. Ibid., 264.
41. Ibid., 327.
42. Ibid., 145.
43. Ibid., 191–192.

PRECURSORS

EDMUND HUSSERL

Introduction

from Logical Investigations, Volume II

1. THE NECESSITY OF PHENOMENOLOGICAL INVESTIGATIONS AS A PRELIMINARY TO THE EPISTEMOLOGICAL CRITICISM AND CLARIFICATION OF PURE LOGIC

We are not here concerned with grammatical discussions, empirically conceived and related to some historically given language: we are concerned with discussions of a most general sort which cover the wider sphere of an objective *theory of knowledge* and, closely linked with this last, the *pure phenomenology of the experiences of thinking and knowing.* This phenomenology, like the more inclusive *pure phenomenology of experiences in general,* has, as its exclusive concern, experiences intuitively seizable and analysable in the pure generality of their essence, not experiences empirically perceived and treated as real facts, as experiences of human or animal experients in the phenomenal world that we posit as an empirical fact. This phenomenology must bring to pure expression, must *describe* in terms of their essential concepts and their governing formulae of essence, the essences which directly make themselves known in intuition, and the connections which have their roots purely in such essences. Each such statement of essence is an *a priori* statement in the highest sense of the word. This sphere we must explore in preparation for the epistemological criticism and clarification of pure logic: our investigations will therefore all move within it.

Pure phenomenology represents a field of neutral researches, in which several sciences have their roots. It is, on the one hand, an ancillary to *psychology* conceived as an *empirical science.* Proceeding in purely intuitive fashion, it analyses and describes in their essential generality—in the specific guise of a phenomenology of thought and knowledge—the experiences of presentation, judgement and knowledge, experiences which, treated as classes of real events in the natural context of zoological reality, receive a scientific probing at the hands of empirical psychology. Phenomenology, on the other hand, lays bare the 'sources' from which the basic concepts and ideal laws of *pure logic* 'flow', and back to which they must once more be traced, so as to give them all the 'clearness and distinctness' needed for an understanding, and for an epistemological critique, of pure logic. . . .

2. ELUCIDATION OF THE AIMS OF SUCH INVESTIGATIONS

All theoretical research, though by no means solely conducted in acts of verbal expression or complete statement, none the less terminates in such statement. Only in this form can truth, and in particular the truth of theory, become an abiding possession of science, a documented, ever available treasure for knowledge and advancing research. Whatever the connection of thought with speech may be, whether or not the appearance of our final judgements in the form of verbal pronouncements has a necessary grounding in essence, it is at least plain that judgements stemming from higher intellectual regions, and in particular from the regions of science, could barely arise without verbal expression.

The objects which pure logic seeks to examine are, in the first instance, therefore given to it in grammatical clothing. Or, more precisely, they come before us embedded in concrete mental states which further function either as the *meaning-intention* or *meaning-fulfilment* of certain verbal expressions—in the latter case intuitively illustrating, or intuitively providing evidence for, our meaning—and forming a *phenomenological unity* with such expressions.

In these complex phenomenological unities the logician must pick out the components that interest him, the characters of the acts, first of all, in which logical presentation, judgement and knowledge are consummated: he must pursue the descriptive analysis of such act-types to the extent that this helps the progress of his properly logical tasks. We cannot straightway leap, from the fact that theory 'realizes' itself in certain mental states, and has instances in them, to the seemingly obvious truth that such mental states must count as the primary object of our logical researches. The pure logician is not primarily or properly interested in the psychological judgement, the concrete mental phenomenon, but in the logical

judgement, the identical asserted meaning, which is one over against manifold, descriptively quite different, judgement-experiences.* There is naturally, in the singular experiences which correspond to this ideal unity, a certain pervasive common feature, but since the concern of the pure logician is not with the concrete instance, but with its corresponding Idea, its abstractly apprehended universal, he has, it would seem, no reason to leave the field of abstraction, nor to make concrete experiences the theme of his probing interest, instead of Ideas.

Even if phenomenological analysis of concrete thought-experiences does not fall within the true home-ground of pure logic, it none the less is indispensable to the advance of purely logical research. For all that is logical must be given in fully concrete fashion, if, as an object of research, it is to be made our own, and if we are to be able to bring to self-evidence the *à priori* laws which have their roots in it. What is logical is first given us in imperfect shape: the concept as a more or less wavering meaning, the law, built out of concepts, as a more or less wavering assertion. We do not therefore lack logical insights, but grasp the pure law with self-evidence, and see how it has its base in the pure forms of thought. Such self-evidence depends, however, on the verbal meanings which come alive in the actual passing of the judgement regarding the law. Unnoticed equivocation may permit the subsequent substitution of other concepts beneath our words, and an appeal on behalf of an altered propositional meaning may quite readily, but wrongly, be made on the self-evidence previously experienced. It is also possible, conversely, that a misinterpretation based on equivocation may distort the sense of the propositions of pure logic (perhaps turning them into empirical, psychological propositions), and may tempt us to abandon previously experienced self-evidence and the unique significance of all that belongs to pure logic.

It is not therefore enough that the Ideas of logic, and the pure laws set up with them, should be given in such a manner. Our great task is now *to bring the Ideas of logic, the logical concepts and laws, to epistemological clarity and definiteness.*

Here *phenomenological analysis* must begin. Logical concepts, as valid thought-unities, must have their origin in intuition: they must arise out of an ideational

---

*Cf. §11 of Investigation 1.

intuition founded on certain experiences, and must admit of indefinite reconfirmation, and of recognition of their self-identity, on the reperformance of such abstraction. Otherwise put: we can absolutely not rest content with 'mere words', i.e. with a merely symbolic understanding of 'words', such as we first have when we reflect on the sense of the laws for 'concepts', 'judgements', 'truths' etc. (together with their manifold specifications) which are set up in pure logic. Meanings inspired only by remote, confused, inauthentic intuitions—if by any intuitions at all— are not enough: we must go back to the 'things themselves'. We desire to render self-evident in fully-fledged intuitions that what is here given in actually performed abstractions is what the word-meanings in our expression of the law really and truly stand for....

. . .

The phenomenology of the logical experiences aims at giving us a sufficiently wide descriptive (though not empirically-psychological) understanding of these mental states and their indwelling sense, as will enable us to give fixed meanings to all the fundamental concepts of logic. Such meanings will be clarified both by going back to the analytically explored connections between meaning-intentions and meaning-fulfilments, and also by making their possible function in cognition intelligible and certain. They will be such meanings, in short, as the interest of pure logic itself requires, as well as the interest, above all, of epistemological insight into the essence of this discipline. Fundamental logical and noetic concepts have, up to this time, been quite imperfectly clarified: countless equivocations beset them, some so pernicious, so hard to track down, and to keep consistently separate, that they yield the main ground for the very backward state of pure logic and theory of knowledge....

. . .

Clarifying researches are especially needed to explain our by no means chance inclination to slip unwittingly from an objective to a psychological attitude, and to mix up two bodies of data distinguishable in principle however much they may be essentially related, and to be deceived by psychological misconstructions and misinterpretations of the objects of logic. Such clarifications can, by their nature, only be achieved within a phenomenological theory of the essences of our thought- and knowledge-experiences, with continuous regard to the things essentially meant

by, and so belonging to the latter (in the precise manners in which those things are *as such* 'shown forth', 'represented' etc.). Psychologism can only be radically overcome by a pure phenomenology, a science infinitely removed from psychology as the empirical science of the mental attributes and states of animal realities. In our sphere, too, the sphere of pure logic, such a phenomenology alone offers us all the necessary conditions for a finally satisfactory establishment of the totality of basic distinctions and insights. It alone frees us from the strong temptation, at first inevitable, since rooted in grounds of essence, to turn the logically objective into the psychological.

The above mentioned motives for phenomenological analysis have an obvious and essential connection with those which spring from *basic questions of epistemology.* For if these questions are taken in the *widest* generality, i.e. in the 'formal' generality which abstracts from all matter of knowledge—they form part of a range of questions involved in the full clarification of the Idea of pure logic. We have, on the one hand, the fact that all thought and knowledge have as their aim *objects* or *states of affairs,* which they putatively 'hit' in the sense that the 'intrinsic being' of these objects and states is supposedly shown forth, and made an identifiable item, in a multitude of actual or possible meanings, or acts of thought. We have, further, the fact that all thought is ensouled by a thought-form which is subject to ideal laws, laws circumscribing the objectivity or ideality of knowledge in general. These facts, I maintain, eternally provoke questions like: How are we to understand the fact that the intrinsic being of objectivity becomes 'presented', 'apprehended' in knowledge, and so ends up by becoming subjective? What does it mean to say that the object has 'intrinsic being', and is 'given' in knowledge? How can the ideality of the universal *qua* concept or law enter the flux of real mental states and become an epistemic possession of the thinking person?

. . .

EDMUND HUSSERL

The Paris Lectures

. . .

I am filled with joy at the opportunity to talk about the new phenomenology at this most venerable place of French learning, and for very special reasons. No philosopher of the past has affected the sense of phenomenology as decisively as René Descartes, France's greatest thinker. Phenomenology must honor him as its genuine patriarch. It must be said explicitly that the study of Descartes' *Meditations* has influenced directly the formation of the developing phenomenology and given it its present form, to such an extent that phenomenology might almost be called a new, a twentieth century, Cartesianism.

Under these circumstances I may have advance assurance of your interest, especially if I start with those themes in the *Meditationes de prima philosophia* which are timeless, and if through them I point out the transformations and new concepts which give birth to what is characteristic of the phenomenological method and its problems.

Every beginner in philosophy is familiar with the remarkable train of thought in the *Meditations.* Their goal, as we remember, is a complete reform of philosophy, including all the sciences, since the latter are merely dependent members of the one universal body of knowledge which is philosophy. Only through systematic unity can the sciences achieve genuine rationality, which, as they have developed so far, is missing. What is needed is a radical reconstruction which will *satisfy* the ideal of philosophy as being the *universal unity of knowledge* by means of a unitary and *absolutely rational foundation.* Descartes carries out the demand for reconstruction in terms of a subjectively oriented philosophy. This subjective turn is carried out in two steps.

First, anyone who seriously considers becoming a philosopher must once in his life withdraw into himself and then, from within attempt to destroy and rebuild all previous learning. Philosophy is the supremely personal affair of the one who philosophizes. It is the question of *his sapientia universalis,* the aspiration of *his* knowledge for the universal. In particular, the philosopher's quest is for truly scientific knowledge, knowledge for which he can assume—from the very beginning and in every subsequent step—complete responsibility by using *his* own absolutely self-evident justifications. I can become a genuine philosopher only by freely choosing to focus my life on this goal. Once I am thus committed and have accordingly chosen to begin with total poverty and destruction, my first problem is to discover an absolutely secure starting point and rules of procedure, when, in actual fact, I lack any support from the existing disciplines. Consequently, the Cartesian meditations must not be viewed as the private affair of the philosopher Descartes, but as the necessary prototype for the meditations of any beginning philosopher whatsoever.

When we now turn our attention to the content of the *Meditations,* a content which appears rather strange to us today, we notice immediately a *return to the philosophizing ego* in a second and deeper sense. It is the familiar and epoch-making return to the ego as subject of his pure *cogitationes.* It is the ego which, while it suspends all beliefs about the reality of the world on the grounds that these are not indubitable, discovers itself as the only apodictically certain being.

The ego is engaged, first of all, in philosophizing that is seriously solipsistic. He looks for apodictically certain and yet purely subjective procedures through which an objective external world can be deduced. Descartes does this in a well-known manner. He first infers both the existence and *veracitas* of God. Then, through their mediation, he deduces objective reality as a dualism of substances. In this way he reaches the objective ground of knowledge and the particular sciences themselves as well. All his inferences are based on immanent principles, *i.e.,* principles which are innate to the ego.

So much for Descartes. We now ask, is it really worthwhile to hunt critically for the eternal significance of these thoughts? Can these infuse life into our age?

. . . Descartes inaugurates a completely new type of philosophy. Philosophy, with its style now changed altogether, experiences a radical conversion from naive objectivism to *transcendental subjectivism.* This subjectivism strives toward a pure end-form through efforts that are constantly renewed yet always remain unsatisfactory. Might it not be that this continuing tendency has eternal significance? Perhaps it is a vast task assigned to us by history itself, invoking our collective cooperation.

The splintering of contemporary philosophy and its aimless activity make us pause. Must this situation not be traced back to the fact that the motivations from which Descartes' meditations emanate have lost their original vitality? Is it not true that the only fruitful renaissance is one which reawakens these meditations, not in order to accept them, but to reveal the profound truth in the radicalism of a return to the *ego cogito* with the eternal values that reside therein?

In any case, this is the path that led to transcendental phenomenology.

Let us now pursue this path together. In true Cartesian fashion, we will become philosophers meditating in a radical sense, with, of course, frequent and critical modifications of the older Cartesian meditations. What was merely germinal in them must be freely developed here.

We thus begin, everyone for himself and in himself, with the decision to disregard all our present knowledge. We do not give up Descartes' guiding goal of an absolute foundation for knowledge. At the beginning, however, to presuppose even the possibility of that goal would be prejudice. We are satisfied to discover the goal and nature of science by submerging ourselves in scientific activity. It is the spirit of science to count nothing as really scientific which cannot be fully justified by the evidence. In other words, science demands proof *by reference to the things and facts themselves, as these are given in actual experience and intuition.* Thus guided, we, the beginning philosophers, make it a rule to judge only by the evidence. Also, the evidence itself must be subjected to critical verification, and that on the basis, of course, of further available evidence. Since from the beginning we have disregarded the sciences, we operate within our pre-scientific life, which is likewise filled with immediate and mediate evidences. This, and nothing else, is first given to us.

Herein arises our first question. Can we find evidence that is both immediate and apodictic? Can we find evidence that is primitive, in the sense that it must by necessity precede all other evidence?

As we meditate on this question one thing does, in fact, emerge as both prior to all evidence and as apodictic. It is the existence of the world. All science refers to the world, and, before that, our ordinary life already makes reference to it. *That the being of the world precedes everything* is so *obvious* that no one thinks to articulate it in a sentence. Our experience of the world is continuous, incessant, and unquestionable. But is it true that this experiential evidence, even though taken for granted, is really apodictic and primary to all other evidence? We will have to deny both. Is it not the case that occasionally something manifests itself as a sensory illusion? Has not the coherent and unified totality of our experience been at times debased as a mere dream? We will ignore Descartes' attempt to prove that, notwithstanding the fact of its being constantly experienced, the world's nonbeing can be conceived. His proof is carried out by a much too superficial criticism of sensory experience. We will keep this much: experiential evidence that is to serve as radical foundation for knowledge needs, above all, a critique of its validity and range. It cannot be accepted as apodictic without question and qualification. Therefore, merely to disregard all knowledge and to treat the sciences as prejudices is not enough. Even the experience of the world as the true universal ground of knowledge becomes an unacceptably naive belief. We can no longer accept the reality of the world as a fact to be taken for granted. *It is a hypothesis that needs verification.*

Does there remain a ground of being? Do we still have a basis for all judgments and evidences, a basis on which a universal philosophy can rest apodictically? Is not "world" the name for the totality of all that is? Might it not turn out that the world is not the truly ultimate basis for judgment, but instead that its existence presupposes a prior ground of being?

Here, specifically following Descartes, we make the great shift which, when properly carried out, leads to *transcendental subjectivity.* This is the shift to the *ego cogito,* as the apodictically certain and *last basis for judgment* upon which all radical philosophy must be grounded.

Let us consider: as radically meditating philosophers we now have neither knowledge that is valid for us nor a world that exists for us. We can no longer say that the world is real—a belief that is natural enough in our ordinary experience—; instead, it merely makes a claim to reality. This skepticism also applies to other selves, so that we rightly should not speak communicatively, that is, in the plural. Other people and animals are, of course, given to me only through sensory experience. Since I have questioned the validity of the latter I cannot avail myself of it here. With the loss of other minds I lose, of course, all forms of sociability and culture. In short, the entire concrete world ceases to have reality for me and becomes instead mere appearance. However, whatever may be the veracity of the claim to being made by phenomena, whether they represent reality or appearance, phenomena in themselves cannot be disregarded as mere "nothing." On the contrary, it is precisely the phenomena themselves which, without exception, render possible for me the very existence of both reality and appearance. Again, I may freely abstain from entertaining any belief about experience—which I did. This simply means that I refuse to assert the reality of the world. Nonetheless, we must be careful to realize that this epistemological abstention is still what it is: it includes the whole stream of experienced life and all its particulars, the appearances of objects, other people, cultural situations, etc. Nothing changes, except that I no longer accept the world simply as real; I no longer judge regarding the distinction between reality and appearance. I must similarly abstain from any other of my opinions, judgments, and valuations about the world, since these likewise assume the reality of the world. But for these, as for other phenomena, epistemological abstention does not mean their disappearance, at least not as pure phenomena.

This ubiquitous detachment from any point of view regarding the objective world we term the *phenomenological epoché*. It is the methodology through which I come to understand myself as that ego and life of consciousness in which and through which the entire objective world exists for me, and is for me precisely as it is. Everything in the world, all spatio-temporal being, exists for me because I experience it, because I perceive it, remember it, think of it in any way, judge it, value it, desire it, etc. It is well known that Descartes designates all this by the term *cogito*. For me the world is nothing other than what I am aware of and what appears valid in such *cogitationes*. *The whole meaning and reality of the world rests exclusively on such cogitationes.* My entire worldly life takes its course within these. I cannot live, experience, think, value, and act in any world which is not in some sense in me, and derives its meaning and truth from me. If I place myself above that entire life and if I abstain from any commitment about reality, specifically one which accepts the world as existing, and if I view that life exclusively as consciousness *of* the world, then I reveal myself as the pure ego with its pure stream of *cogitationes*.

I certainly do not discover myself as one item among others in the world, since I have altogether suspended judgment about the world. I am not the ego of an individual man. I am the ego in whose stream of consciousness the world itself—including myself as an object in it, a man who exists in the world—first acquires meaning and reality.

We have reached a dangerous point. It seems simple indeed to understand the pure ego with its *cogitationes* by following Descartes. And yet it is as if we were on the brink of a precipice, where the ability to step calmly and surely decides between philosophic life and philosophic death. Descartes was thoroughly sincere in his desire to be radical and presuppositionless. However, we know through recent researches—particularly the fine and penetrating work of Messrs. Gilson and Koyré—that a great deal of Scholasticism is hidden in Descartes' meditations as unarticulated prejudice. But this is not all. We must above all avoid the prejudices, hardly noticed by us, which derive from our emphasis on the mathematically oriented natural sciences. These prejudices make it appear as if the phrase *ego cogito* refers to an apodictic and primitive axiom, one which, in conjunction with others to be derived from it, provides the foundation for a deductive and universal science, a science *ordine geometrico*. In relation to this we must under no circumstances take for granted that, with our apodictic and pure ego, we have salvaged a small corner of the world as the single indubitable fact about the world which can be utilized by the philosophizing ego. It is not true that all that now remains to be done is to infer the rest of the world through correct deductive procedures according to principles that are innate to the ego.

Unfortunately, Descartes commits this error, in the apparently insignificant yet fateful transformation of the ego to a *substantia cogitans,* to an independent human *animus,* which then becomes the point of departure for conclusions by means of the principle of causality. In short, this is the transformation which made Descartes the father of the rather absurd transcendental realism. We will keep aloof from all this if we remain true to radicalism in our self-examination and with it to the principle of pure intuition. We must regard nothing as veridical except the pure immediacy and givenness in the field of the *ego çogito* which the *epoché* has opened up to us. In other words, we must not make assertions about that which we do not ourselves *see*. In these matters Descartes was deficient. It so happens that he stands before the greatest of all discoveries—in a sense he has already made it—yet fails to see its true significance, that of transcendental subjectivity. He does not pass through the gateway that leads into genuine transcendental philosophy.

The independent *epoché* with regard to the nature of the world as it appears and is real to me—that is, "real" to the previous and natural point of view—discloses the greatest and most magnificent of all facts: I and my life remain—in my sense of reality—

untouched by whichever way we decide the issue of whether the world is or is not. To say, in my natural existence, "I am, I think, I live," means that I am one human being among others in the world, that I am related to nature through my physical body, and that in this body my *cogitationes,* perceptions, memories, judgments, etc. are incorporated as psycho-physical facts. Conceived in this way, I, we, humans, and animals are subject-matter for the objective sciences, that is, for biology, anthropology, and zoology, and also for psychology. The life of the psyche, which is the subject-matter of all psychology, is understood only as the psychic life in the world. The methodology of a purified Cartesianism demands of me, the one who philosophizes, the phenomenological *epoché.* This *epoché* eliminates as worldly facts from my field of judgment both the reality of the objective world in general and the sciences of the world. *Consequently, for me there exists no "I" and there are no psychic actions,* that is, psychic phenomena in the psychological sense.* To myself I do not exist as a human being, <nor> do my *cogitationes* exist as components of a psycho-physical world. But through all this I have discovered my true self. I have discovered that I alone am the pure ego, with pure existence and pure capacities (for example, the obvious capacity to abstain from judging). Through this ego alone does *the being of the world,* and, for that matter, any being whatsoever, make sense *to me* and has possible validity. The world —whose conceivable non-being does not extinguish my pure being but rather presupposes it—is termed *transcendent,* whereas my pure being or my pure ego is termed *transcendental.* Through the phenomenological *epoché* the natural human ego, specifically my own, is reduced to the transcendental ego. This is the meaning of the phenomenological reduction.

Further steps are needed so that what has been developed up to this point can be adequately applied. What is the philosophic use of the transcendental ego? To be sure, for me, the one who philosophizes, it obviously precedes, in an epistemological sense, all objective reality. In a way, it is the basis for all objective knowledge, be it good or bad. But does the fact that the transcendental ego precedes and presupposes all

objective knowledge mean also that it is an epistemological ground in the ordinary sense? The thought is tempting. All realistic theories are guilty of it. But the temptation to look in the transcendental subjectivity for premises guaranteeing the existence of the subjective world evanesces once we realize that all arguments, considered in themselves, exist already in transcendental subjectivity itself. Furthermore, all proofs for the world have their criteria set in the world just as it is given and justified in experience. However, these considerations must not be construed as a rejection of the great Cartesian idea that the ultimate basis for objective science and the reality of the objective world is to be sought in transcendental subjectivity. Otherwise—our criticisms aside—we would not be true to Descartes' method of meditation. However, the Cartesian discovery of the ego may perhaps open up a *new concept of foundation, namely, a transcendental foundation.*

In point of fact, instead of using the *ego cogito* merely as an apodictic proposition and as an absolutely primitive premise, we notice that the phenomenological *epoché* has uncovered for us (or for me, the one who philosophizes), through the apodictic *I am,* a new kind and an endless sphere of being. This is the sphere of a new kind of experience: transcendental experience. And herewith also arises the possibility of both transcendental epistemology and transcendental science.

A most extraordinary epistemological situation is disclosed here. The phenomenological *epoché* reduces me to my transcendental and pure ego. I am, thus, at least *prima facie,* in a certain sense *solus ipse,* but not in the ordinary sense, in which one might say that a man survived a universal holocaust in a world which itself remained unaffected. Once I have banished from my sphere of judgments the world, as one which receives its being from me and within me, then I, as the transcendental ego which is prior to the world, am *the sole source and object capable of judgement* [das einzig urteilsmäßig Setzbare und Gesetzte]. And now I am supposed to develop an unheard-of and unique science, since it is one that is created exclusively by and inside my transcendental subjectivity! Furthermore, this science is meant to apply, at least at the outset, to my transcendental subjectivity alone. It thus becomes a transcendental-solipsistic science. It is therefore not the *ego cogito,* but a science about the ego—a pure

---

*As a rule, "*Leistungen*" is here translated as "acts," and "*Akte*" as "actions." (Tr.).

egology—which becomes the ultimate foundation of philosophy in the Cartesian sense of a universal science, and which must provide at least the cornerstone for its absolute foundation. In actual fact this science exists already as the lowest transcendental phenomenology. And I mean the lowest, not the fully developed phenomenology, because to the latter, of course, belongs the further development from transcendental solipsism to transcendental intersubjectivity.

To make all this intelligible it is first necessary to do what was neglected by Descartes, namely, to describe the endless field of the ego's transcendental experience itself. His own experience, as is well known, and especially when he judged it to be apodictic, plays a role in the philosophy of Descartes. But he neglected to describe the ego in the full concretion of its transcendental being and life, nor did he regard it as an unlimited work-project to be pursued systematically. It is an insight central to a philosopher that, by introducing the transcendental reduction, he can reflect truthfully on his *cogitationes* and on their pure phenomenological content. In this way he can uncover all aspects of his transcendental being with respect to both his transcendental-temporal life and also his capabilities. We are clearly dealing with a train of thought parallel to what the world-centered psychologist calls inner experience or experience of the self.

One thing of the greatest, even decisive, importance remains. One cannot lightly dismiss the fact—even Descartes has so remarked on occasion—that the *epoché* changes nothing in the world. All experience is still his experience, all consciousness, still his consciousness. The expression *ego cogito* must be expanded by one term. Every *cogito* contains a meaning: its *cogitatum*. The experience of a house, as I experience it, and ignoring theories of perception, is precisely an experience of this and only this house, a house which appears in such-and-such a way, and has certain specific determinations when seen from the side, from near-by, and from afar. Similarly, a clear or a vague recollection is the recollection of a vaguely or clearly apprehended house. Even the most erroneous judgment means a judgment about such-and-such factual content, and so on. *The essence of consciousness, in which I live as my own self, is the so-called intentionality.* Consciousness is always consciousness of something. The nature of consciousness includes, as modes of being, presentations, probabilities, and

non-being, and also the modes of appearance, goodness, and value, etc. Phenomenological experience as reflection must avoid any interpretative constructions. Its descriptions must reflect accurately the concrete contents of experience, precisely as these are experienced.

To interpret consciousness as a complex of sense data and then to bring forth gestalt-like qualities [*Gestaltqualitäten*] out of these—which are subsequently equated with the totality—is a sensualist invention. This interpretation is a basic error even from the worldly and psychological perspective, and much more so from the transcendental point of view. It is true that in the process of phenomenological analyses sense data do occur, and something is, in fact, disclosed about them. But what phenomenological analysis fails to find as primary is the "perception of an external world." The honest description of the unadulterated data of experience must disclose what appears first of all, *i.e.*, the *cogito*. For example, we must describe closely the perception of a house in terms of what it means as object and its modes of appearing. The same applies to all forms of consciousness. . . .

When phenomenology examines objects of consciousness—regardless of what kind, whether real or ideal—it deals with these exclusively as objects of the immediate consciousness. The description—which attempts to grasp the concrete and rich phenomena of the *cogitationes*—must constantly glance back from the side of the object to the side of consciousness and pursue the general existing connections. . . .

. . .

. . . The object of perception, considered phenomenologically, does not appear as a real thing either in perception or in the streaming perspectives that are unified through synthesis, or in any other manifold of experience. Two appearances which, because of a synthesis, present themselves to me as appearances of the same thing are nonetheless really separate, and because of this separation they possess no datum in common; at the most, they have only related and similar traits. The hexahedron which one sees as one and the same is one and the same in intentionality. What appears as spatial reality, when examined as it is given in variegated perception, is identical in an ideational sense, that is, it is identical in intention; this identity is immanent in the modes of consciousness, in the acts of the ego, not as a real datum, but in the sense that it means an object. *The same* hexahedron may thus appear to me in a variety of recollections, expectations, or distinct or vacuous conceptions as intentionally the same; also, it can be the identical substratum for predications, valuations, etc. This identity always resides in consciousness proper and is apprehended through synthesis. *It follows that the stream of consciousness is permeated by the fact that consciousness relates itself to objects* [Gegenständlichkeit]. This relation is an essential characteristic of every act of consciousness. It is the ability to pass over—through synthesis—from perennially new and greatly disparate forms of consciousness to an awareness of their unity.

In this connection it is evident that the ego contains no individual isolated *cogito.* This is the case to such an extent that it is finally shown that all of existence—with its fluctuations, its Heraclitean flux—is one universal synthetic unity. It is because of this unity that we can say, not only that the transcendental ego exists, but that it exists for itself. The transcendental ego is a concrete unity that can be synoptically apprehended. It lives individualized in steadily new types of consciousness, yet it constantly objectifies itself as unitary through the form of immanent time.

This is not all. *Potentiality* in existence is just as important as *actuality,* and potentiality is not empty possibility. Every *cogito*—for instance, an external perception, a recollection, etc.—carries in itself a potentiality immanent to it and capable of being disclosed. It is a potentiality for possible experiences referring to the same intentional object, experiences which the ego can actualize. In each *cogito* we find, using phenomenological terminology, *horizons,* and in various senses. Perception occurs and sketches a horizon of expectations, which is a horizon of intentionality. The horizon anticipates the future as it might be perceived, that is to say, it points to coming series of perceptions. Each series, in turn, carries potentialities with it, such as the fact that I can look in one direction rather than another, and can redirect the run of my perceptions. Each recollection leads me to a long chain of possible recollections ending in the now; and at each point of immanent time it refers me to other present events that might be disclosed; and so on.

All these are intentional structures, and are governed by the laws of synthesis. I can question every intentional event, which means that I can penetrate and display its horizons. In doing this I disclose, on the one hand, potentialities of my existence, and on the other I clarify the intended meaning of objective reference.

Intentional analysis is thus something altogether different from analysis in the ordinary sense. The life of consciousness is neither a mere aggregate of data, nor a heap of psychic atoms, or a whole composed of elements united through gestalt-like qualities [Gestaltqualitäten]. This is true also of pure introspective psychology, as a parallel to transcendental phenomenology. *Intentional analysis is the disclosure of the actualities and potentialities in which objects constitute themselves as perceptual units.* Furthermore, all perceptual analysis takes place in the transition from real events to the intentional horizons suggested by them.

This late insight prescribes to phenomenological analysis and description an altogether new methodology. It is a methodology which goes into action whenever objects and meanings, questions about being, questions about possibilities, questions of origin, and questions of right are to be considered seriously. Every intentional analysis reaches beyond the immediately and actually [reell] given events of the immanent sphere, and in such a way that the analysis discloses potentialities—which are now given actually [reell] and whose horizons have been sketched—and brings out manifold aspects of new experiences in which are made manifest what earlier was meant only implicitly and in this way was already present intentionally. When I see a hexahedron I say, in reality and in truth I see it only from one side. It is nonetheless evident that what I now experience is in reality more. The perception includes a non-sensory belief through which the visible side can be understood to be a mere side in the first place. But how does this belief, that there is more, disclose itself? How does it become obvious that I mean more? It occurs through the transition to a synthetic sequence of possible perceptions, perceptions I would have—as indeed I can—were I to walk around the object. Phenomenology always explains meanings, that is, intentionality, by producing these sense-fulfilling syntheses. The tremendous task placed on description is to expound the universal structure of transcendental consciousness in its reference to and creation of meanings.

. . .

An object exists for me; that is to say, it has reality for me in consciousness. But this reality is reality for me only as long as I believe that I can confirm it. By this I mean that I must be able to provide usable procedures, that is, procedures which run through automatically, and other evidences, which lead me then to the object itself and through which I realize the object as being *truly there*. The same holds when my awareness of the object is a matter of experience, that is, when my awareness tells me that the object itself is already there, that the object itself is seen. This act of seeing, in turn, points to further seeing, that is, it points to the possibility of confirmation. Finally, it points to the fact that what has already once been realized as being can nonetheless be restored, again and again, to its previous condition of progressive confirmation.

Think about the tremendous importance of this remark, considering that we are on an egological foundation. We can see, from this ultimate point of view, that existence and essence have for us, in reality and truth, no other meaning than that of possible confirmation. Furthermore, these confirmation-procedures and their accessibility belong to me as transcendental subjectivity and make sense only as such.

True being, therefore, whether real or ideal, *has significance only as a particular correlate of my own intentionality,* actual or potential. Of course, this is not true of an isolated *cogito.* For example, the being of a real thing is not the mere *cogito* of an isolated perception that I now have. But the perception and its intentionally given object call to my attention, by virtue of the presumed horizon, an endless and open system of *possible* perceptions, perceptions which are not invented but which are motivated from within my intentional existence, and which can lose their presumed validity only when conflicting experience eliminates it. These possible perceptions are necessarily presupposed as *my* possibilities, ones which I can bring about—provided I am not hindered—by approaching the object, looking around it, etc.

Needless to say, the foregoing has been stated very crudely. Extremely far-reaching and complex intentional analyses are needed in order to explain the structure of these possibilities as they relate to the specific horizons belonging to every individual class of objects, and to clarify therewith the meaning of actual being. At the outset only one fact is evident and guides me, namely, that I accept as being only that which presents itself to me as being, and that all conceivable justification of it lies within my own self and is determined in my immediate and mediate intentionality, in which any other meaning of being is also to be determined. . . .

WORKS BY MARTIN HEIDEGGER

What Is Metaphysics?

"What is metaphysics?" The question leads one to expect a discussion about metaphysics. Such is not our intention. Instead, we shall discuss a definite metaphysical question, thus, as it will appear, landing ourselves straight into metaphysics. Only in this way can we make it really possible for metaphysics to speak for itself.

Our project begins with the presentation of a metaphysical question, then goes on to its development and ends with its answer.

THE PRESENTATION OF A METAPHYSICAL QUESTION

Seen from the point of view of sound common sense, Philosophy, according to Hegel, is the "world stood on its head." Hence the peculiar nature of our task calls for some preliminary definition. This arises out of the dual nature of metaphysical questioning.

Firstly, every metaphysical question always covers the whole range of metaphysical problems. In every case it is itself the whole. Secondly, every metaphysical question can only be put in such a way that the questioner as such is by his very questioning involved in the question.

From this we derive the following pointer: metaphysical questioning has to be put as a whole and has always to be based on the essential situation of existence, which puts the question. We question here and *science.*

now, on our own account. Our existence—a community of scientists, teachers and students—is ruled by science. What essential things are happening to us in the foundations of our existence, now that science has become our passion?

The fields of the sciences lie far apart. Their methodologies are fundamentally different. This disrupted multiplicity of disciplines is today only held together by the technical organisation of the Universities and their faculties, and maintained as a unit of meaning by the practical aims of those faculties. As against this, however, the root of the sciences in their essential ground has atrophied.

And yet—insofar as we follow their most specific intentions—in all the sciences we are related to what-is. Precisely from the point of view of the sciences no field takes precedence over another, neither Nature over History nor vice versa. No one methodology is superior to another. Mathematical knowledge is no stricter than philological or historical knowledge. It has merely the characteristic of "exactness," which is not to be identified with strictness. To demand exactitude of history would be to offend against the idea of the kind of strictness that pertains to the humanistic sciences. The world-relationship which runs through all the sciences as such constrains them to seek what-is *in itself*, with a view to rendering it, according to its quiddity (*Wasgehalt*) and its modality (*Seinsart*), an object of investigation and basic definition. What the sciences accomplish, ideally speaking, is an approximation to the essential nature of all things.

This distinct world-relationship to what-is in itself is sustained and guided by a freely chosen attitude on the part of our human existence. It is true that the pre-scientific and extra-scientific activities of man also relate to what-is. But the distinction of science lies in the fact that, in an altogether specific manner, it and it alone explicitly allows the object itself the first and last word. In this objectivity of questioning, definition and proof there is a certain limited submission to what-is, so that this may reveal itself. This submissive attitude taken up by scientific theory becomes the basis of a possibility: the possibility of science acquiring a leadership of its own, albeit limited, in the whole field of human existence. The world-relationship of science and the attitude of man responsible for it can, of course, only be fully understood when we see and understand what is going on in the world-relationship so maintained. Man—one entity (*Seiendes*) among others—"pursues" science. In this "pursuit" what is happening is nothing less than the irruption of a particular entity called "Man" into the whole of what-is, in such a way that in and through this irruption what-is manifests itself *as* and *how* it is. The manner in which the revelatory irruption occurs is the chief thing that helps what-is to become what it is.

This triple process of world-relationship, attitude, and irruption—a radical unity—introduces something of the inspiring simplicity and intensity of *Da-sein* into scientific existence. If we now explicitly take possession of scientific *Da-sein* as clarified by us, we must necessarily say:

That to which the world-relationship refers is what-is—and nothing else.

That by which every attitude is moulded is what-is—and nothing more.

That with which scientific exposition effects its "irruption" is what-is—and beyond that, nothing.

But is it not remarkable that precisely at that point where scientific man makes sure of his surest possession he should speak of something else? What is to be investigated is what-is—and nothing else; only what-is—and nothing more; simply and solely what-is—and beyond that, nothing.

But what about this "nothing"? Is it only an accident that we speak like that quite naturally? Is it only a manner of speaking—and nothing more?

But why worry about this Nothing? "Nothing" is absolutely rejected by science and abandoned as null and void (*das Nichtige*). But if we abandon Nothing in this way are we not, by that act, really admitting it? Can we, though, speak of an admission when we admit Nothing? But perhaps this sort of cross-talk is already degenerating into an empty wrangling about words.

Science, on the other hand, has to assert its soberness and seriousness afresh and declare that it is concerned solely with what-is. Nothing—how can it be for science anything other than a horror and a phantasm? If science is right then one thing stands firm: science wishes to know nothing of Nothing. Such is after all the strictly scientific approach to Nothing. We know it by wishing to know nothing of Nothing.

Science wishes to know nothing of Nothing. Even so the fact remains that at the very point where science tries to put its own essence in words it invokes the aid of Nothing. It has recourse to the very thing it rejects. What sort of schizophrenia is this?

A consideration of our momentary existence as one ruled by science has landed us in the thick of an argument. In the course of this argument a question has already presented itself. The question only requires putting specifically: What about Nothing?

THE DEVELOPMENT OF THE QUESTION

The development of our enquiry into Nothing is bound to lead us to a position where either the answer will prove possible or the impossibility of an answer will become evident. "Nothing" is admitted. Science, by adopting an attitude of superior indifference, abandons it as that which "is not."

All the same we shall endeavour to enquire into Nothing. What is Nothing? Even the initial approach to this question shows us something out of the ordinary. So questioning, we postulate Nothing as something that somehow or other "is"—as an entity (*Seiendes*). But it is nothing of the sort. The question as to the what and wherefore of Nothing turns the thing questioned into its opposite. The question deprives itself of its own object.

Accordingly, every answer to this question is impossible from the start. For it necessarily moves in the form that Nothing "is" this, that or the other. Question and answer are equally nonsensical in themselves where Nothing is concerned.

Hence even the rejection by science is superfluous. The commonly cited basic rule of all thinking—the proposition that contradiction must be avoided—and common "logic" rule out the question. For thinking, which is essentially always thinking about something, would, in thinking of Nothing, be forced to act against its own nature.

Because we continually meet with failure as soon as we try to turn Nothing into a subject, our enquiry into Nothing is already at an end—always assuming, of course, that in this enquiry "logic" is the highest court of appeal, that reason is the means and thinking the way to an original comprehension of Nothing and its possible revelation.

But, it may be asked, can the law of "logic" be assailed? Is not reason indeed the master in this enquiry into Nothing? It is in fact only with reason's help that we can define Nothing in the first place and postulate it as a problem—though a problem that consumes only itself. For Nothing is the negation (*Verneinung*) of the totality of what-is: that which is absolutely not. But at this point we bring Nothing into the higher category of the Negative (*Nichthaftes*) and therefore of what is negated. But according to the overriding and unassailable teachings of "logic" negation is a specific act of reason. How, then, in our enquiry into Nothing and into the very possibility of holding such an enquiry can we dismiss reason? Yet is it so sure just what we are postulating? Does the Not (*das Nicht*), the state of being negated (*die Verneintheit*) and hence negation itself (*Verneinung*), in fact represent that higher category under which Nothing takes its place as a special kind of thing negated? Does Nothing "exist" only because the Not, i.e. negation exists? Or is it the other way about? Does negation and the Not exist only because Nothing exists? This has not been decided—indeed, it has not even been explicitly asked. We assert: "Nothing" is more original than the Not and negation.

If this thesis is correct then the very possibility of negation as an act of reason, and consequently reason itself, are somehow dependent on Nothing. How, then, can reason attempt to decide this issue? May not the apparent nonsensicality of the question and answer where Nothing is concerned only rest, perhaps, on the blind obstinacy of the roving intellect?

If, however, we refuse to be led astray by the formal impossibility of an enquiry into Nothing and still continue to enquire in the face of it, we must at least satisfy what remains the fundamental pre-requisite for the full pursuit of any enquiry. If Nothing as such is still to be enquired into, it follows that it must be "given" in advance. We must be able to encounter it.

Where shall we seek Nothing? Where shall we find Nothing? In order to find something must we not know beforehand that it is there? Indeed we must! First and foremost we can only look if we have presupposed the presence of a thing to be looked for. But here the thing we are looking for is Nothing. Is there after all a seeking without pre-supposition, a seeking complemented by a pure finding?

However that may be, we do know "Nothing" if only as a term we bandy about every day. This ordinary hackneyed Nothing, so completely taken for granted and rolling off our tongue so casually—we can even give an off-hand "definition" of it:

Nothing is the complete negation of the totality of what-is.

Does not this characteristic of Nothing point, after all, in the direction from which alone it may meet us?

The totality of what-is must be given beforehand so as to succumb as such to the negation from which Nothing is then bound to emerge.

But, even apart from the questionableness of this relationship between negation and Nothing, how are we, as finite beings, to render the whole of what-is in its totality accessible *in itself*—let alone to ourselves? We can, at a pinch, think of the whole of what-is as an "idea" and then negate what we have thus imagined in our thoughts and "think" it negated. In this way we arrive at the formal concept of an imaginary Nothing, but never Nothing itself. But Nothing is nothing, and between the imaginary and the "authentic" (*eigentlich*) Nothing no difference can obtain, if Nothing represents complete lack of differentiation. But the "authentic" Nothing—is this not once again that latent and nonsensical idea of a Nothing that "is"? Once again and for the last time rational objections have tried to hold up our search, whose legitimacy can only be attested by a searching experience of Nothing.

As certainly as we shall never comprehend absolutely the totality of what-is, it is equally certain that we find ourselves placed in the midst of what-is and that this is somehow revealed in totality. Ultimately there is an essential difference between comprehending the totality of what-is and finding ourselves in the midst of what-is-in-totality. The former is absolutely impossible. The latter is going on in existence all the time.

Naturally enough it looks as if, in our everyday activities, we were always holding on to this or that actuality (*Seiendes*), as if we were lost in this or that region of what-is. However fragmentary the daily round may appear it still maintains what-is, in however shadowy a fashion, within the unity of a "whole." Even when, or rather, precisely when we are not absorbed in things or in our own selves, this "wholeness" comes over us—for example, in real boredom. Real boredom is still far off when this book or that play, this activity or that stretch of idleness merely bores us. Real boredom comes when "one is bored." This profound boredom, drifting hither and thither in the abysses of existence like a mute fog, draws all things, all men and oneself along with them, together in a

queer kind of indifference. This boredom reveals what-is in totality.

There is another possibility of such revelation, and this is in the joy we feel in the presence of the being—not merely the person—of someone we love.

Because of these moods in which, as we say, we "are" this or that (i.e. bored, happy, etc.) we find ourselves (*befinden uns*) in the midst of what-is-in-totality, wholly pervaded by it. The affective state in which we find ourselves not only discloses, according to the mood we are in, what-is in totality, but this disclosure is at the same time far from being a mere chance occurrence and is the ground-phenomenon of our *Da-sein*.

Our "feelings," as we call them, are not just the fleeting concomitant of our mental or volitional behaviour, nor are they simply the cause and occasion of such behaviour, nor yet a state that is merely "there" and in which we come to some kind of understanding with ourselves.

Yet, at the very moment when our moods thus bring us face to face with what-is-in-totality they hide the Nothing we are seeking. We are now less than ever of the opinion that mere negation of what-is-in-totality as revealed by these moods of ours can in fact lead us to Nothing. This could only happen in the first place in a mood so peculiarly revelatory in its import as to reveal Nothing itself.

Does there ever occur in human existence a mood of this kind, through which we are brought face to face with Nothing itself?

This may and actually does occur, albeit rather seldom and for moments only, in the key-mood of dread (*Angst*). By "dread" we do not mean "anxiety" (*Aengstlichkeit*), which is common enough and is akin to nervousness (*Furchtsamkeit*)—a mood that comes over us only too easily. Dread differs absolutely from fear (*Furcht*). We are always *afraid* of this or that definite thing, which threatens us in this or that definite way. "Fear of" is generally "fear about" something. Since fear has this characteristic limitation—"of" and "about"—the man who is afraid, the nervous man, is always bound by the thing he is afraid of or by the state in which he finds himself. In his efforts to save himself from this "something" he becomes uncertain in relation to other things; in fact, he "loses his bearings" generally.

In dread no such confusion can occur. It would be truer to say that dread is pervaded by a peculiar kind of peace. And although dread is always "dread of," it is not dread of this or that. "Dread of" is always a dreadful feeling "about"—but not about this or that. The indefiniteness of *what* we dread is not just lack of definition: it represents the essential impossibility of defining the "what." The indefiniteness is brought out in an illustration familiar to everybody.

In dread, as we say, "one feels something uncanny."[1] What is this "something" (*es*) and this "one"? We are unable to say what gives "one" that uncanny feeling. "One" just feels it generally (*im Ganzen*). All things, and we with them, sink into a sort of indifference. But not in the sense that everything simply disappears; rather, in the very act of drawing away from us everything turns towards us. This withdrawal of what-is-in-totality, which then crowds round us in dread, this is what oppresses us. There is nothing to hold on to. The only thing that remains and overwhelms us whilst what-is slips away, is this "nothing."

Dread reveals Nothing.

In dread we are "in suspense" (*wir schweben*). Or, to put it more precisely, dread holds us in suspense because it makes what-is-in-totality slip away from us. Hence we too, as existents in the midst of what-is, slip away from ourselves along with it. For this reason it is not "you" or "I" that has the uncanny feeling, but "one." In the trepidation of this suspense where there is nothing to hold on to, pure *Da-sein* is all that remains.

Dread strikes us dumb. Because what-is-in-totality slips away and thus forces Nothing to the fore, all affirmation (lit. "Is"-saying: "*Ist*"-*Sagen*) fails in the face of it. The fact that when we are caught in the uncanniness of dread we often try to break the empty silence by words spoken at random, only proves the presence of Nothing. We ourselves confirm that dread reveals Nothing—when we have got over our dread. In the lucid vision which supervenes while yet the experience is fresh in our memory we must needs say that what we were afraid of was "actually" (*eigentlich:* also "authentic") Nothing. And indeed Nothing itself, Nothing as such, was there.

With this key-mood of dread, therefore, we have reached that event in our *Da-sein* which reveals Nothing, and which must therefore be the starting-point of our enquiry.

What about Nothing?

THE ANSWER TO THE QUESTION

The answer which alone is important for our purpose has already been found if we take care to ensure that we really do keep to the problem of Nothing. This necessitates changing man into his *Da-sein*—a change always occasioned in us by dread—so that we may apprehend Nothing as and how it reveals itself in dread. At the same time we have finally to dismiss those characteristics of Nothing which have not emerged as a result of our enquiry.

"Nothing" is revealed in dread, but not as something that "is." Neither can it be taken as an object. Dread is not an apprehension of Nothing. All the same, Nothing is revealed in and through dread, yet not, again, in the sense that Nothing appears as if detached and apart from what-is-in-totality when we have that "uncanny" feeling. We would say rather: in dread Nothing functions as if *at one with* what-is-in-totality. What do we mean by "at one with"?

In dread what-is-in-totality becomes untenable (*hinfällig*). How? What-is is not annihilated (*vernichtet*) by dread, so as to leave Nothing over. How could it, seeing that dread finds itself completely powerless in face of what-is-in-totality! What rather happens is that Nothing shows itself as essentially belonging to what-is while this is slipping away in totality.

In dread there is no annihilation of the whole of what-is in itself; but equally we cannot negate what-is-in-totality in order to reach Nothing. Apart from the fact that the explicitness of a negative statement is foreign to the nature of dread as such, we would always come too late with any such negation intended to demonstrate Nothing. For Nothing is anterior to it. As we said, Nothing is "at one with" what-is as this slips away in totality.

In dread there is a retreat from something, though it is not so much a flight as a spell-bound (*gebannt*) peace. This "retreat from" has its source in Nothing. The latter does not attract: its nature is to repel. This "repelling from itself" is essentially an "expelling into": a conscious gradual relegation to the vanishing what-is-in-totality (*das entgleitenlassende Verweisen auf das versinkende Seiende im Ganzen*). And this total relegation to the vanishing what-is-in-totality—such being the form in which Nothing crowds round us in dread—is the essence of Nothing: nihilation.[2] Nihilation is neither an annihilation (*Vernichtung*) of what-is, nor does it spring from negation (*Verneinung*). Nihilation cannot be reckoned in terms of annihilation or negation at all. Nothing "nihilates" (*nichtet*) of itself.

Nihilation is not a fortuitous event; but, understood as the relegation to the vanishing what-is-in-totality, it reveals the latter in all its till now undisclosed strangeness as the pure "Other"—contrasted with Nothing.

Only in the clear night of dread's Nothingness is what-is as such revealed in all its original overtness (*Offenheit*): that it "is" and is not Nothing. This verbal appendix "and not Nothing" is, however, not an *a posteriori* explanation but an *à priori* which alone makes possible any revelation of what-is. The essence of Nothing as original nihilation lies in this: that it alone brings *Da-sein* face to face with what-is as such.

Only on the basis of the original manifestness of Nothing can our human *Da-sein* advance towards and enter into what-is. But insofar as *Da-sein* naturally relates to what-is, as that which it is not and which itself is, Da-sein *qua Da-sein* always proceeds from Nothing as manifest.[3]

Da-sein means *being projected into* Nothing (*Hineingehaltenheit in das Nichts*).

Projecting into Nothing, *Da-sein* is already beyond what-is-in-totality. This "being beyond" (*Hinaussein*) what-is we call Transcendence. Were *Da-sein* not, in its essential basis, transcendent, that is to say, were it not projected from the start into Nothing, it could never relate to what-is, hence could have no self-relationship.

Without the original manifest character of Nothing there is no self-hood and no freedom.

Here we have the answer to our question about Nothing. Nothing is neither an object nor anything that "is" at all. Nothing occurs neither by itself nor "apart from" what-is, as a sort of adjunct. Nothing is that which makes the revelation of what-is as such possible for our human existence. Nothing not merely provides the conceptual opposite of what-is but is also an original part of essence (*Wesen*). It is in the Being (*Sein*) of what-is that the nihilation of Nothing (*das Nichten des Nichts*) occurs.

But now we must voice a suspicion which has been withheld far too long already. If it is only through "projecting into Nothing" that our *Da-sein* relates to what-is, in other words, has any existence, and if Nothing is only made manifest originally in dread,

should we not have to be in a continual suspense of dread in order to exist at all? Have we not, however, ourselves admitted that this original dread is a rare thing? But above all, we all exist and are related to actualities which we ourselves are not and which we ourselves are—without this dread. Is not this dread, therefore, an arbitrary invention and the Nothing attributed to it an exaggeration?

Yet what do we mean when we say that this original dread only occurs in rare moments? Nothing but this: that as far as we are concerned and, indeed, generally speaking, Nothing is always distorted out of its original state. By what? By the fact that in one way or another we completely lose ourselves in what-is. The more we turn to what-is in our dealings the less we allow it to slip away, and the more we turn aside from Nothing. But all the more certainly do we thrust ourselves into the open superficies of existence.

And yet this perpetual if ambiguous aversion from Nothing accords, within certain limits, with the essential meaning of Nothing. It—Nothing in the sense of nihilation—relegates us to what-is. Nothing "nihilates" unceasingly, without our really knowing what is happening—at least, not with our everyday knowledge.

What could provide more telling evidence of the perpetual, far-reaching and yet ever-dissimulated overtness of Nothing in our existence, than negation? This is supposed to belong to the very nature of human thought. But negation cannot by any stretch of imagination produce the Not out of itself as a means of distinguishing and contrasting given things, thrusting this Not between them, as it were. How indeed could negation produce the Not out of itself, seeing that it can only negate when something is there to be negated? But how can a thing that is or ought to be negated be seen as something negative (*nichthaft*) unless all thinking as such is on the look-out for the Not? But the Not can only manifest itself when its source—the nihilation of Nothing and hence Nothing itself—is drawn out of concealment. The Not does not come into being through negation, but negation is based on the Not, which derives from the nihilation of Nothing. Nor is negation only a mode of nihilating behaviour, i.e. behaviour based *à priori* on the nihilation of Nothing.

Herewith we have proved the above thesis in all essentials: Nothing is the source of negation, not the other way about. If this breaks the sovereignty of reason in the field of enquiry into Nothing and Being, then the fate of the rule of "logic" in philosophy is also decided. The very idea of "logic" disintegrates in the vortex of a more original questioning.

However often and however variously negation—whether explicit or not—permeates all thinking, it cannot *of itself* be a completely valid witness to the manifestation of Nothing as an essential part of *Da-sein*. For negation cannot be cited either as the sole or even the chief mode of nihilation, with which, because of the nihilation of Nothing, *Da-sein* is saturated. More abysmal than the mere propriety of rational negation is the harshness of opposition and the violence of loathing. More responsible the pain of refusal and the mercilessness of an interdict. More oppressive the bitterness of renunciation.

These possible modes of nihilating behaviour, through which our *Da-sein* endures, even if it does not master, the fact of our being thrown upon the world[4] are not modes of negation merely. That does not prevent them from expressing themselves in and through negation. Indeed, it is only then that the empty expanse of negation is really revealed. The permeation of *Da-sein* by nihilating modes of behavior points to the perpetual, ever-dissimulated manifestness of Nothing, which only dread reveals in all its originality. Here, of course, we have the reason why original dread is generally repressed in *Da-sein*. Dread is there, but sleeping. All *Da-sein* quivers with its breathing: the pulsation is slightest in beings that are timorous, and is imperceptible in the "Yea, yea!" and "Nay, nay!" of busy people; it is readiest in the reserved, and surest of all in the courageous. But this last pulsation only occurs for the sake of that for which it expends itself, so as to safeguard the supreme greatness of *Da-sein*.

The dread felt by the courageous cannot be contrasted with the joy or even the comfortable enjoyment of a peaceable life. It stands—on the hither side of all such contrasts—in secret union with the serenity and gentleness of creative longing.

Original dread can be awakened in *Da-sein* at any time. It need not be awakened by any unusual occurrence. Its action corresponds in depth to the shallowness of its possible cause. It is always on the brink, yet only seldom does it take the leap and drag us with it into the state of suspense.

Because our *Da-sein* projects into Nothing on this basis of hidden dread, man becomes the "stand-in" (*Platzhalter*) for Nothing. So finite are we that we cannot, of our own resolution and will, bring ourselves originally face to face with Nothing. So bottomlessly does finalisation (*Verendlichung*) dig into existence that our freedom's peculiar and profoundest finality fails.

This projection into Nothing on the basis of hidden dread is the overcoming of what-is-in-totality: Transcendence.

Our enquiry into Nothing will, we said, lead us straight to metaphysics. The name "metaphysics" derives from the Greek τὰ μετὰ τὰ φυσικὰ. This quaint title was later interpreted as characterising the sort of enquiry which goes μετὰ—trans, beyond—what-is as such.

Metaphysics is an enquiry over and above what-is, with a view to winning it back again as such and in totality for our understanding.

In our quest for Nothing there is similar "going beyond" what-is, conceived as what-is-in-totality. It therefore turns out to be a "metaphysical" question. We said in the beginning that such questioning had a double characteristic: every metaphysical question at once embraces the whole of metaphysics, and in every question the being (*Da-sein*) that questions is himself caught up in the question.

To what extent does the question about Nothing span and pervade the whole of metaphysics?

Since ancient times metaphysics has expressed itself on the subject of Nothing in the highly ambiguous proposition: *ex nihilo nihil fit*—nothing comes from nothing. Even though the proposition as argued never made Nothing itself the real problem, it nevertheless brought out very explicitly, from the prevailing notions about Nothing, the over-riding fundamental concept of what-is.

Classical metaphysics conceives Nothing as signifying Not-being (*Nichtseiendes*), that is to say, unformed matter which is powerless to form itself into "being"[5] and cannot therefore present an appearance (εἶδος). What has "being" is the self-creating product (*Gebilde*) which presents itself as such in an image (*Bild*), i.e. something seen (*Anblick*). The origin, law and limits of this ontological concept are discussed as little as Nothing itself.

Christian dogma, on the other hand, denies the truth of the proposition *ex nihilo nihil fit* and gives a twist to the meaning of Nothing, so that it now comes to mean the absolute absence of all "being"[6] outside

God: *ex nihilo fit—ens creatum:* the created being is made out of nothing. "Nothing" is now the conceptual opposite of what truly and authentically (*eigentlich*) "is"; it becomes the *summum ens,* God as *ens increatum.* Here, too, the interpretation of Nothing points to the fundamental concept of what-is. Metaphysical discussion of what-is, however, moves on the same plane as the enquiry into Nothing. In both cases the questions concerning Being (*Sein*) and Nothing as such remain unasked. Hence we need not be worried by the difficulty that if God creates "out of nothing" he above all must be able to relate himself to Nothing. But if God is God he cannot know Nothing, assuming that the "Absolute" excludes from itself all nullity (*Nichtigkeit*).

This crude historical reminder shows Nothing as the conceptual opposite of what truly and authentically "is," i.e. as the negation of it. But once Nothing is somehow made a problem this contrast not only undergoes clearer definition but also arouses the true and authentic metaphysical question regarding the Being of what-is. Nothing ceases to be the vague opposite of what-is: it now reveals itself as integral to the Being of what-is.

"Pure Being and pure Nothing are thus one and the same." This proposition of Hegel's ("The Science of Logic," I, WW III, p. 74) is correct. Being and Nothing hang together, but not because the two things—from the point of view of the Hegelian concept of thought—are one in their indefiniteness and immediateness, but because Being itself is finite in essence and is only revealed in the Transcendence of *Da-sein* as projected into Nothing.

If indeed the question of Being as such is the all-embracing question of metaphysics, then the question of Nothing proves to be such as to span the whole metaphysical field. But at the same time the question of Nothing pervades the whole of metaphysics only because it forces us to face the problem of the origin of negation, that is to say, forces a decision about the legitimacy of the rule of "logic" in metaphysics.

The old proposition *ex nihilo nihil fit* will then acquire a different meaning, and one appropriate to the problem of Being itself, so as to run: *ex nihilo omne ens qua ens fit:* every being, so far as it is a being, is made out of nothing. Only in the Nothingness of *Da-sein* can what-is-in-totality—and this in accordance with its peculiar possibilities, i.e. in a finite manner—come to itself. To what extent, then, has

the enquiry into Nothing, if indeed it be a metaphysical one, included our own questing *Da-sein?*

Our *Da-sein* as experienced here and now is, we said, ruled by science. If our *Da-sein,* so ruled, is put into this question concerning Nothing, then it follows that it must itself have been put in question by this question.

The simplicity and intensity of scientific *Da-sein* consist in this: that it relates in a special manner to what-is and to this alone. Science would like to abandon Nothing with a superior gesture. But now, in this question of Nothing, it becomes evident that scientific *Da-sein* is only possible when projected into Nothing at the outset. Science can only come to terms with itself when it does not abandon Nothing. The alleged soberness and superiority of science becomes ridiculous if it fails to take Nothing seriously. Only because Nothing is obvious can science turn what-is into an object of investigation. Only when science proceeds from metaphysics can it conquer its essential task ever afresh, which consists not in the accumulation and classification of knowledge but in the perpetual discovery of the whole realm of truth, whether of Nature or of History.

Only because Nothing is revealed in the very basis of our *Da-sein* is it possible for the utter strangeness of what-is to dawn on us. Only when the strangeness of what-is forces itself upon us does it awaken and invite our wonder. Only because of wonder, that is to say, the revelation of Nothing, does the "Why?" spring to our lips. Only because this "Why?" is possible as such can we seek for reasons and proofs in a definite way. Only because we can ask and prove are we fated to become enquirers in this life.

The enquiry into Nothing puts us, the enquirers, ourselves in question. It is a metaphysical one.

Man's *Da-sein* can only relate to what-is by projecting into Nothing. Going beyond what-is is of the essence of *Da-sein.* But this "going beyond" is metaphysics itself. That is why metaphysics belongs to the nature of man. It is neither a department of scholastic philosophy nor a field of chance ideas. Metaphysics is the ground-phenomenon of *Da-sein.* It is *Da-sein* itself. Because the truth of metaphysics is so unfathomable there is always the lurking danger of profoundest error. Hence no scientific discipline can hope to equal the seriousness of metaphysics. Philosophy can never be measured with the yard-stick of the idea of science.

Once the question we have developed as to the nature of Nothing is really asked by and among our own selves, then we are not bringing in metaphysics from the outside. Nor are we simply "transporting" ourselves into it. It is completely out of our power to transport ourselves into metaphysics because, in so far as we exist, we are already there. φύσει γὰρ, ὦ φίλε, ἔνεστί τις φιλοσοφία τῇ τον ἀνδρὸς διανίᾳ (Plato: Phaedrus 279a). While man exists there will be philosophising of some sort. Philosophy, as we call it, is the setting in motion of metaphysics; and in metaphysics philosophy comes to itself and sets about its explicit tasks. Philosophy is only set in motion by leaping with all its being, as only it can, into the ground-possibilities of being as a whole. For this leap the following things are of crucial importance: firstly, leaving room for what-is-in-totality; secondly, letting oneself go into Nothing, that is to say, freeing oneself from the idols we all have and to which we are wont to go cringing; lastly, letting this "suspense" range where it will, so that it may continually swing back again to the ground-question of metaphysics, which is wrested from Nothing itself:

Why is there any Being at all—why not far rather Nothing?

POSTSCRIPT

Metaphysics is the word before which, however abstract and near to thinking it be, most of us flee as from one smitten with the plague.*

The question "What is Metaphysics?" remains a question. For those who persevere with this question the following postscript is more of a foreword. The question "What is Metaphysics?" asks a question that goes beyond metaphysics. It arises from a way of thinking which has already entered into the overcoming of metaphysics. It is of the essence of such transitions that they are, within certain limits, compelled to speak the language of that which they help to overcome. The particular circumstances in which our enquiry into the nature of metaphysics is held should not lead us to the erroneous opinion that this question is bound to make the sciences its starting-point. Modern science, with its completely different ways of conceiving and establishing what-is, has penetrated to that basic feature of truth according to which everything that "is" is characterised by the will to will, as the prototype of which—"the will to power"—all appearance began. "Will," conceived as the basic feature of the "is-ness" (*Seiendheit*) of what-is, is the equation of what-is with the Real, in such a way that the reality of the Real becomes invested with the sovereign power to effect a general objectivisation. Modern science neither serves the purpose originally entrusted to it, nor does it seek truth in itself. As a method of objectivising what-is by calculation it is a condition, imposed by the will to will, through which the will to will secures its own sovereignty. But because all objectivisation of what-is ends in the provision and safeguarding of what-is and thus provides itself with the possibility of further advance, the objectivisation gets stuck in what-is and regards this as nothing less than Being (*Sein*). Every relationship to what-is thus bears witness to a knowledge of Being, but at the same time to its own inability by and of itself to authenticate the truth of this knowledge. This truth is merely the truth about what-is. Metaphysics is the history of this truth. It tells us what what-is is by conceptualising the "is-ness" of what-is. In the is-ness of what-is metaphysics thinks the thought of Being, but without being able to reflect on the truth of Being with its particular mode of thought. Metaphysics moves everywhere in the realm of the truth of Being, which truth remains the unknown and unfathomable ground. But supposing that not merely what-is comes from Being but that, in a manner still more original, Being itself reposes in its truth and that the truth of Being is a function of the Being of truth, then we must necessarily ask what metaphysics is in its own ground. Such a question must think metaphysically and, at the same time, think in terms of the ground of metaphysics, i.e. no longer metaphysically. All such questions must remain equivocal in an essential sense.

Any attempt to follow the train of thought of the preceding lecture is bound, therefore, to meet with obstacles. That is good. It will make our questioning more genuine. All questions that do justice to the subject are themselves bridges to their own answering. Essential answers are always but the last step in our questioning. The last step, however, cannot be taken without the long series of first and next steps. The

---

*Hegel (1770–1831), Works XVII, p. 400.

essential answer gathers its motive power from the inwardness (*Inständigkeit*) of the asking and is only the beginning of a responsibility where the asking arises with renewed originality. Hence even the most genuine question is never stilled by the answer found.

The obstacles to following the thought of the lecture are of two kinds. The first arise from the enigmas which lurk in this region of thought. The others come from the inability and often the reluctance to think. In the region of cerebral enquiry even fleeting intimations can sometimes help, although real help only comes from those that have been carefully thought out. Gross errors may also bear fruit, flung out, perhaps, in the heat of blind controversy. Only, reflection must take everything back again in the calm mood of patient meditation.

The chief misgivings and misconceptions to which the lecture gives rise may be grouped under three heads. It is said that:

1. The lecture makes "Nothing" the sole subject of metaphysics. But since Nothing is simply the nugatory (*das Nichtige*), this kind of thinking leads to the idea that everything is nothing, so that it is not worth while either to live or to die. A "Philosophy of Nothing" is the last word in "Nihilism."

2. The lecture raises an isolated and, what is more, a morbid mood, namely dread, to the status of the one key-mood. But since dread is the psychic state of nervous people and cowards, this kind of thinking devalues the stout-hearted attitude of the courageous. A "Philosophy of Dread" paralyses the will to act.

3. The lecture declares itself against "logic." But since reason contains the criteria for all calculation and classification, this kind of thinking delivers all judgements regarding the truth up to a chance mood. A "Philosophy of Pure Feeling" imperils "exact" thinking and the certainty of action.

The right attitude to these propositions will emerge from a renewed consideration of the lecture. It may show whether Nothing, which governs the whole nature of dread, can be exhausted by an empty negation of what-is, or whether that which never and nowhere "is" discloses itself as that which differs from everything that "is," i.e. what we call "Being." No matter where and however deeply science investigates what-is it will never find Being. All it encounters, always, is what-is, because its explanatory purpose makes it insist at the outset on what-is. But Being is

not an existing quality of what-is, nor, unlike what-is, can Being be conceived and established objectively. This, the purely "Other" than everything that "is," is that-which-is-not (*das Nicht-Seinde*). Yet this "Nothing" functions as Being. It would be premature to stop thinking at this point and adopt the facile explanation that Nothing is merely the nugatory, equating it with the non-existent (*das Wesenlose*). Instead of giving way to such precipitate and empty ingenuity and abandoning Nothing in all its mysterious multiplicity of meanings, we should rather equip ourselves and make ready for one thing only: to experience in Nothing the vastness of that which gives every being the warrant to be. That is Being itself. Without Being, whose unfathomable and unmanifest essence is vouchsafed us by Nothing in essential dread, everything that "is" would remain in Beinglessness (*Sein-losigkeit*). But this too, in its turn, is not a nugatory Nothing, assuming that it is of the truth of Being that Being may be without what-is, but never what-is without Being.

An experience of Being as sometimes "other" than everything that "is" comes to us in dread, provided that we do not, from dread of dread, i.e. in sheer timidity, shut our ears to the soundless voice which attunes us to the horrors of the abyss. Naturally if, in this matter of essential dread, we depart at will from the train of thought of the lecture; if we detach dread conceived as the mood occasioned by that voice from its relationship to Nothing, then dread is left over as an isolated "feeling" which we can analyse and contrast with other feelings in the well-known assortment of psychological stock-types. Using the simple distinction between "upper" and "lower" as a clue we can then group the various "moods" into classes: those which are exalting and those which are lowering. But this zealous quest for "types" and "counter-types" of "feelings," for the varieties and sub-varieties of these "types," will never get us anywhere. It will always be impossible for the anthropological study of man to follow the mental track of the lecture, since the latter, though paying attention to the voice of Being, thinks beyond it into the attunement occasioned by this voice—an attunement which takes possession of the essential man so that he may come to experience Being in Nothing.

Readiness for dread is to say "Yes!" to the inwardness of things, to fulfil the highest demand which alone touches man to the quick. Man alone of all beings, when addressed by the voice of Being, experiences the marvel of all marvels: that what-is *is*. Therefore the being that is called in its very essence to the truth of Being is always attuned in an essential sense. The clear courage for essential dread guarantees that most mysterious of all possibilities: the experience of Being. For hard by essential dread, in the terror of the abyss, there dwells awe (*Scheu*). Awe clears and enfolds that region of human being within which man endures, as at home, in the enduring.

Dread of dread, on the other hand, may stray so far as to mistake the simple relationships obtaining in the essence of dread. What would all courage avail did it not find continual hold in the experience of essential dread? To the degree that we degrade this essential dread and the relationship cleared within it for Man to Being, we demean the essence of courage. Courage can endure Nothing: it knows, in the abyss of terror, the all-but untrodden region of Being, that "clearing" whence everything that "is" returns into *what* is and is able to be. Our lecture neither puts forward a "Philosophy of Dread" nor seeks to give the false impression of being an "heroic" philosophy. Its sole thought is that thing which has dawned on Western thinking from the beginning as the one thing that has to be thought—Being. But Being is not a product of thinking. It is more likely that essential thinking is an occurrence of Being.

For this reason the scarcely formulated question now forces itself on us as to whether this kind of thinking conforms to the law of its truth when it only follows the thinking whose forms and rules constitute "logic." Why do we put this word in inverted commas? In order to indicate that "logic" is only *one* exposition of the nature of thinking, and one which, as its name shows, is based on the experience of Being as attained in Greek thought. The animus against "logic"—the logical degeneration of which can be seen in "logistics," derives from the knowledge of that thinking which has its source not in the observation of the objectivity of what-is, but in the experience of the truth of Being. "Exact" thinking is never the strictest thinking, if the essence of strictness lies in the strenuousness with which knowledge keeps in touch with the essential features of what-is. "Exact" thinking merely binds itself to the calculation of what-is and ministers to this alone.

All calculation makes the calculable "come out" in the sum so as to use the sum for the next count. Nothing counts for calculation save what can be calculated. Any particular thing is only what it "adds up to," and any count ensures the further progress of the counting. This process is continually using up numbers and is itself a continual self-consumption. The "coming out" of the calculation with the help of what-is counts as the explanation of the latter's Being. Calculation uses everything that "is" as units of computation, in advance, and, in the computation, uses up its stock of units. This consumption of what-is reveals the consuming nature of calculation. Only because number can be multiplied indefinitely—and this regardless of whether it goes in the direction of the great or the small—is it possible for the consuming nature of calculation to hide behind its "products" and give calculative thought the appearance of "productivity"—whereas it is of the prime essence of calculation, and not merely in its results, to assert what-is only in the form of something that can be arranged and used up. Calculative thought places itself under compulsion to master everything in the logical terms of its procedure. It has no notion that in calculation everything calculable is already a whole before it starts working out its sums and products, a whole whose unity naturally belongs to the incalculable which, with its mystery, ever eludes the clutches of calculation. That which, however, is always and everywhere closed at the outset to the demands of calculation and, despite that, is always closer to man in its enigmatic unknowableness than anything that "is," than anything he may arrange and plan, this can sometimes put the essential man in touch with a thinking whose truth no "logic" can grasp. The thinking whose thoughts not only do not calculate but are absolutely determined by what is "other" than what-is, might be called essential thinking. Instead of counting *on* what-is *with* what-is, it expends itself in Being for the truth of Being. This thinking answers to the demands of Being in that man surrenders his historical being to the simple, sole necessity whose constraints do not so much necessitate as create the need (*Not*) which is consummated in the freedom of sacrifice. The need is: to preserve the truth of Being no matter what may happen to man and everything that "is." Freed from all constraint, because born of the abyss of freedom, this sacrifice is the expense of our human being for the preservation of the truth of Being in respect of what-is. In sacrifice there is expressed that hidden *thanking* which alone does homage to the grace wherewith Being has endowed the nature of man, in order that he may take over in his relationship to Being the guardianship of Being. Original thanking is the echo of Being's favour wherein it clears a space for itself and causes the unique occurrence: that what-is is. This echo is man's answer to the Word of the soundless voice of Being. The speechless answer of his thanking through sacrifice is the source of the human word, which is the prime cause of language as the enunciation of the Word in words. Were there not an occasional thanking in the heart of historical man he could never attain the thinking—assuming that there must be thinking (*Denken*) in all doubt (*Bedenken*) and memory (*Andenken*)—which originally thinks the thought of Being. But how else could humanity attain to original thanking unless Being's favour preserved for man, through his open relationship to this favour, the splendid poverty in which the freedom of sacrifice hides its own treasure? Sacrifice is a valediction to everything that "is" on the road to the preservation of the favour of Being. Sacrifice can be made ready and can be served by doing and working in the midst of what-is, but never consummated there. Its consummation comes from the inwardness out of which historical man by his actions—essential thinking is also an act—dedicates the *Da-sein* he has won for himself to the preservation of the dignity of Being. This inwardness is the calm that allows nothing to assail man's hidden readiness for the valedictory nature of all sacrifice. Sacrifice is rooted in the nature of the event through which Being claims man for the truth of Being. Therefore it is that sacrifice brooks no calculation, for calculation always miscalculates sacrifice in terms of the expedient and the inexpedient, no matter whether the aims are set high or low. Such calculation distorts the nature of sacrifice. The search for a purpose dulls the clarity of the awe, the spirit of sacrifice ready prepared for dread, which takes upon itself kinship with the imperishable.

The thought of Being seeks no hold in what-is. Essential thinking looks to the slow signs of the incalculable and sees in this the unforeseeable coming of the ineluctable. Such thinking is mindful of the truth of Being and thus helps the Being of truth to make a place for itself in man's history. This help effects no results because it has no need of effect. Essential thinking helps as the simple inwardness of existence, insofar as this inwardness, although unable to exercise such thinking or only having theoretical knowledge of it, kindles its own kind.

Obedient to the voice of Being, thought seeks the Word through which the truth of Being may be expressed. Only when the language of historical man is born of the Word does it ring true. But if it does ring true, then the testimony of the soundless voice of hidden springs lures it ever on. The thought of Being guards the Word and fulfils its function in such guardianship, namely care for the use of language. Out of long-guarded speechlessness and the careful clarification of the field thus cleared, comes the utterance of the thinker. Of like origin is the naming of the poet. But since like is only like insofar as difference allows, and since poetry and thinking are most purely alike in their care of the word, the two things are at the same time at opposite poles in their essence. The thinker utters Being. The poet names what is holy.

We may know something about the relations between philosophy and poetry, but we know nothing of the dialogue between poet and thinker, who "dwell near to one another on mountains farthest apart."[7]

One of the essential theatres of speechlessness is dread in the sense of the terror into which the abyss of Nothing plunges us. Nothing conceived as the pure "Other" than what-is, is the veil of Being. In Being all that comes to pass in what-is is perfected from everlasting.

The last poem of the last poet of the dawn-period of Greece—Sophocles' "Oedipus in Colonos"—closes with words that hark back far beyond our ken to the hidden history of these people and marks their entry into the unknown truth of Being:

> ἀλλ' ἀποπαύετε μηδ' ἐπὶ πλείω
> θρῆνον ἐγείρετε.
> πάντων γὰρ ἔχει τάδε κῦρος.

> But cease now, and nevermore
> Lift up the lament:
> For all this is determined.

NOTES

1. *ist es einem unheimlich.* Literally, "it is uncanny to one."
2. *Nichtung.* The word "nihilation" has been coined in the hope of conveying Heidegger's meaning. His thought, which is also expressed in the verb *nichten* at the end of this paragraph and elsewhere, is very difficult to reproduce in the negative terms of its German formulation. *Nichtung* is a causative process, and *nichten* a causative and intransitive verb. Ordi-

narily we would express the process in positive terms and would speak, for instance, of the "becoming" of Nothing or the "de-becoming" of something, as would be clear in a term like *Nichtswerdung* or the *Entwerdung* of Meister Eckhart.

3. Cf. "Tao Te Ching" XL: for though all creatures under heaven are the products of Being, Being itself is the product of Not-being. Trans.

4. *Geworfenheit.* Literally "thrownness." M. Corbin, in his French version of this essay, renders the term by *déréliction.* The underlying thought would appear to be that in *Da-sein* we are "thrown there" and left derelict, like a thing cast up by the waves on the seashore.

5. Here *Seiendes* has been translated by "being," with the proviso that it be understood as "being" in simple contrast to "not-being." Heidegger's *Sein* is always rendered as "Being" with a capital B.

6. See note 5.

7. Hölderlin, "Patmos."

The Preparatory Fundamental Analysis of Da-sein

from Being and Time

I   THE EXPOSITION OF THE TASK OF A PREPARATORY ANALYSIS OF DA-SEIN

9.   The Theme of the Analytic of Da-sein

The being whose analysis our task is, is always we* ourselves.† The being of this being is always *mine.* In the being of this being it is related to its being,‡ As the being of this being, it is entrusted to its own being. It is being§ about which this being is concerned. From this characteristic of Da-sein two things follow:

1. The "essence" of this being lies in its to be.** The whatness (*essentia*) of this being must be understood in terms of its being (*existentia*) insofar as one can speak of it at all. Here the ontological task is precisely to show that when we choose the word exis-

tence for the being of this being, this term does not and cannot have the ontological meaning of the traditional expression of *existentia.* Ontologically, *existentia* means *objective presence* [*Vorhandenheit*], a kind of being which is essentially inappropriate to characterize the being which has the character of Da-sein. We can avoid confusion by always using the interpretive expression *objective presence* [*Vorhandenheit*] for the term *existentia,* and by attributing existence as a determination of being only to Da-sein.

The "essence" of Da-sein lies in its existence. The characteristics to be found in this being are thus not objectively present "attributes" of an objectively present being which has such and such an "outward appearance," but rather possible ways for it to be, and only this. The thatness of this being is primarily being. Thus the term "Da-sein" which we use to designate this being does not express its what, as in the case of table, house, tree, but being.††

2. The being which this being is concerned about in its being is always my own. Thus, Da-sein is never to be understood ontologically as a case and instance of a genus of beings as objectively present. To something objectively present its being is a matter of "indifference," more precisely, it "is" in such a way that its being can neither be indifferent nor non-indifferent to it. In accordance with the character of *always-being-my-own-being* [*Jemeinigkeit*], when we speak of Da-sein, we must always use the *personal* pronoun along with whatever we say: "I am," "You are."‡‡

Da-sein is my own, to be always in this or that way. It has somehow always already decided in which way Da-sein is always my own. The being which is concerned in its being about its being is related to its being as its truest possibility. Da-sein *is* always its possibility. It does not "have" that possibility only as a mere attribute of something objectively present. And because Da-sein is always essentially its possibility, it *can* "choose" itself in its being, it can win itself, it can lose itself, or it can never and only "apparently" win itself. It can only have lost itself and it can only have not yet gained itself because it is essentially possible as authentic, that is, it belongs to itself. The two kinds of being of *authenticity* and *inauthenticity*—these expressions are terminologically chosen in the strictest

---

*always "I"

†Some footnotes have been omitted—ed.

‡But this is historical being-in-the-world.

§Which one? To be the There and thus to perdure being as such.

**that it "has" to be; definition.

---

††The Being "of" the There, "of": *genitivus objectivus.*

‡‡That is, in each case my own means being appropriated.

sense of the word—are based on the fact that Da-sein is in general determined by always being-mine. But the inauthenticity of Da-sein does not signify a "lesser" being or a "lower" degree of being. Rather, inauthenticity can determine Da-sein even in its fullest concretion, when it is busy, excited, interested, and capable of pleasure.

The two characteristics of Da-sein sketched out—on the one hand, the priority of "*existentia*" over *essentia,* and then, always-being-mine—already show that an analytic of this being is confronted with a unique phenomenal region. This being does not and never has the kind of being of what is merely objectively present within the world. Thus, it is also not to be thematically found in the manner of coming across something objectively present. The correct presentation of it is so little a matter of course that its determination itself constitutes an essential part of the ontological analytic of this being. The possibility of understanding the being of this being stands and falls with the secure accomplishment of the correct presentation of this being. No matter how provisional the analysis may be, it always demands the securing of the correct beginning.

As a being, Da-sein always defines itself in terms of a possibility which it *is* and somehow understands in its being. That is the formal meaning of the constitution of the existence of Da-sein. But for the *ontological* interpretation of this being, this means that the problematic of its being* is to be developed out of the existentiality of its existence. However, this cannot mean that Da-sein is to be construed in terms of a concrete possible idea of existence. At the beginning of the analysis, Da-sein is precisely not to be interpreted in the differentiation of a particular existence; rather, to be uncovered in the indifferent way in which it is initially and for the most part. This indifference of the everydayness of Da-sein is *not nothing*; but rather, a positive phenomenal characteristic. All existing is how it is out of this kind of being, and back into it. We call this everyday indifference of Da-sein *averageness.*

. . .

But the average everydayness of Da-sein must not be understood as a mere "aspect." In it, too, and even in

the mode of inauthenticity, the structure of existentiality lies *à priori.* In it, too, Da-sein is concerned with a particular mode of its being to which it is related in the way of average everydayness, if only in the way of fleeing *from* it and of forgetting *it.*

. . .

II BEING-IN-THE-WORLD IN GENERAL AS THE FUNDAMENTAL CONSTITUTION OF DA-SEIN

12. A Preliminary Sketch of Being-in-the-World in Terms of the Orientation toward Being-in as Such

In the preparatory discussions (section 9) we already profiled characteristics of being which are to provide us with a steady light for our further investigation, but which at the same time receive their structural concretion in this investigation. Da-sein is a being which is related understandingly in its being toward that being. In saying this we are calling attention to the formal concept of existence. Da-sein exists. Furthermore, Da-sein is the being which I myself always am. Mineness belongs to existing Da-sein as the condition of the possibility of authenticity and inauthenticity. Da-sein exists always in one of these modes, or else in the modal indifference to them.

These determinations of being of Da-sein, however, must now be seen and understood *à priori* as grounded upon that constitution of being which we call *being-in-the-world.* The correct point of departure of the analytic of Da-sein consists in the interpretation of this constitution.

The compound expression "being-in-the-world" indicates, in the very way we have coined it, that it stands for a *unified* phenomenon. This primary datum must be seen as a whole. But while being-in-the-world cannot be broken up into components that may be pieced together, this does not prevent it from having several constitutive structural factors. The phenomenal fact indicated by this expression actually gives us a threefold perspective. If we pursue it while keeping the whole phenomenon in mind from the outset we have the following:

1. "*In-the-world*": In relation to this factor, we have the task of questioning the ontological structure

---

*better: of its understanding of being

of "world" and of defining the idea of *worldliness* as such (cf. chapter 3 of this division).

2. The *being* which always is in the way of being-in-the-world. In it we are looking for what we are questioning when we ask about the "who?". In our phenomenological demonstration we should be able to determine who is in the mode of average everydayness of Da-sein (cf. chapter 4 of this division).

3. *Being in* as such: The ontological constitution of in-ness itself is to be analyzed (cf. chapter 5 of this division). Any analysis of one of these constitutive factors involves the analysis of the others; that is, each time seeing the whole phenomenon. It is true that being-in-the-world is an *à priori* necessary constitution of Da-sein, but it is not at all sufficient to fully determine Da-sein's being. Before we thematically analyze the three phenomena indicated individually, we shall attempt to orient ourselves toward a characteristic of the third of these constitutive factors.

What does *being-in* mean? Initially, we supplement the expression being-in with the phrase "in the world," and are inclined to understand this being-in as "being-in something." With this term, the kind of being of a being is named which is "in" something else, as water is "in" the glass, the dress is "in" the closet. By this "in" we mean the relation of being that two beings extended "in" space have to each other with regard to their location in that space. Water and glass, dress and closet, are both "in" space "at" a location in the same way. This relation of being can be expanded; that is, the bench in the lecture hall, the lecture hall in the university, the university in the city, and so on until: the bench in "world space." These beings whose being "in" one another can be determined in this way all have the same kind of being—that of being objectively present—as things occurring "within" the world. The objective presence "in" something objectively present, the being objectively present together with something having the same kind of being in the sense of a definite location relationship are ontological characteristics which we call *categorial.* They belong to beings whose kind of being is unlike Da-sein.

In contrast, being-in designates a constitution of being of Dasein, and is an *existential.* But we cannot understand by this the objective presence of a material thing (the human body) "in" a being objectively present. Nor does the term being-in designate a spatial "in one another" of two things objectively present, any more than the word "in" primordially means a spatial relation of this kind. "In" stems from *innan-,* to live, *habitare,* to dwell. "*An*" means I am used to, familiar with, I take care of something. It has the meaning of *colo* in the sense of *habito* and *diligo.* We characterized this being to whom being-in belongs in this meaning as the being which I myself always am. The expression "*bin*" is connected with "*bei.*" "*Ich bin*" (I am) means I dwell, I stay near . . . the world as something familiar in such and such a way. Being* as the infinitive of "I am": that is, understood as an existential, means to dwell near . . . , to be familiar with. . . . *Being-in is thus the formal existential expression of the being of Da-sein*† which has the essential constitution of being-in the world. . . .

With its facticity, the being-in-the-world of Da-sein is already dispersed in definite ways of being-in, perhaps even split up. The multiplicity of these kinds of being-in can be indicated by the following examples: to have to do with something, to produce, order and take care of something, to use something, to give something up and let it get lost, to undertake, to accomplish, to find out, to ask about, to observe, to speak about, to determine. . . . These ways of being-in have the kind of being of *taking care of* which we shall characterize in greater detail. The *deficient* modes of omitting, neglecting, renouncing, resting, are also ways of taking care of something, in which the possibilities of taking care are kept to a "bare minimum." The term "taking care" has initially its prescientific meaning and can imply: carrying something out, settling something, "to straighten it out." The expression could also mean to take care of something in the sense of "getting it for oneself." Furthermore, we use the expression also in a characteristic turn of phrase: I will see to it or take care that the enterprise fails. Here "to take care" amounts to apprehensiveness. In contrast to these prescientific ontic meanings, the expression "taking care" is used in this inquiry as an ontological term (an existential) to designate the being of a possible being-in-the-world. We do not choose this term because Da-sein is initially economical and "practical" to a large extent, but because the being of Da-sein itself is to be made visible as *care.*

---

* "To be" is also the infinitive of the "is": a being is.
† But not of being in general and not at all of being itself—absolutely.

Again, this expression is to be understood as an onto-logical structure concept (compare chapter 6 of this division). The expression has nothing to do with "distress," "melancholy," or "the cares of life" which can be found ontically in every Da-sein. These—like their opposites, "carefreeness" and "gaiety"—are ontically possible only because Dasein, *ontologically* understood, is care. Because being-in-the-world belongs essentially to Da-sein, its being toward the world is essentially taking care.

. . .

III   THE WORLDLINESS OF THE WORLD

14.   The Idea of the Worldliness of the World in General

First of all, being-in-the-world is to be made visible with regard to the structural factor "world." The accomplishment of this task appears to be easy and so trivial that we still believe we may avoid it. What can it mean, to describe "the world" as a phenomenon? It means letting what shows itself in the "beings" within the world be seen. Thus, the first step is to enumerate the things which are "in" the world: houses, trees, people, mountains, stars. We can *describe* the "out-ward appearance" of these beings and *tell of* the events occurring with them. But that is obviously a pre-phenomenological "business" which cannot be phenomenologically relevant at all. The description gets stuck in beings. It is ontic. But we are, after all, seeking being. We formally defined "phenomenon" in the phenomenological sense as that which shows itself as being and the structure of being.

Thus, to describe the "world" phenomenologically means to show and determine the being of beings objectively present in the world conceptually and cat-egorially. Beings within the world are things, natural things and "valuable" things. Their thingliness be-comes a problem. And since the thingliness of the lat-ter is based upon natural thingliness, the being of nat-ural things, nature as such, is the primary theme. The character of being of natural things, of substances, which is the basis of everything, is substantiality. What constitutes its ontological meaning? Now we have given our investigation an unequivocal direction.

But are we asking ontologically about the "world"? The problematic characterized is undoubtedly onto-logical. But even if it succeeds in the purest explica-tion of the being of nature, in comparison with the fundamental statements made by the mathematical natural sciences about this being, this ontology never gets at the phenomenon of the "world." Nature is it-self a being which is encountered within the world and is discoverable on various paths and stages.

Should we accordingly keep to the beings with which Da-sein initially and for the most part dwells, to "valuable" things? Do not these things "really" show the world in which we live? Perhaps they do in fact show something like "world" more penetratingly. But these things are, after all, also beings "within" the world.

Neither the ontic description of innerworldly beings nor the ontological interpretation of the being of these beings gets as such at the phenomenon of "world." In both kinds of access to "objective being," "world" is already "presupposed" in various ways.

Can "world" ultimately not be addressed as a deter-mination of the beings mentioned at all? But, after all, we do say that these beings are innerworldly. Is "world" indeed a character of being of Da-sein? And then does every Da-sein "initially" have its own world? Doesn't "world" thus become something "subjec-tive"? Then how is a "common" world still possible "in" which we, after all, *are*? If we pose the question of "world," *which* world is meant? Neither this nor that world, but rather the *worldliness of world in general.* How can we encounter this phenomenon?

"Worldliness" is an ontological concept and desig-nates the structure of a constitutive factor of being-in-the-world. But we have come to know being-in-the-world as an existential determination of Da-sein. Accordingly, worldliness is itself an existential. When we inquire ontologically about the "world," we by no means abandon the thematic field of the analytic of Da-sein. "World" is ontologically not a determina-tion of *those* beings which Da-sein essentially is *not*, but rather a characteristic of Da-sein itself. This does not preclude the fact that the path of the investigation of the phenomenon of "world" must be taken by way of innerworldly beings and their being. The task of a phenomenological "description" of the world is so far from obvious that its adequate determination already requires essential ontological clarification.

The multiplicity of meanings of the word "world" is striking now that we have discussed it and made frequent application of it. Unraveling this multiplicity can point toward the phenomena intended in their various meanings and their connection.

1. World is used as an ontic concept and signifies the totality of beings which can be objectively present within the world.

2. World functions as an ontological term and signifies the being of those beings named in 1. Indeed, "world" can name the region which embraces a multiplicity of beings. For example, when we speak of the "world" of the mathematician, we mean the region of all possible mathematical objects.

3. Again, world can be understood in an ontic sense, but not as beings essentially unlike Da-sein that can be encountered within the world; but, rather, as that "*in which*" a factical Da-sein "lives." Here world has a pre-ontological, existentiell meaning. There are various possibilities here: world can mean the "public" world of the we or one's "own" and nearest (in the home) surrounding world.

4. Finally, world designates the ontological and existential concept of *worldliness*. Worldliness itself can be modified into the respective structural totality of particular "worlds," and contains *à priori* of worldliness in general. We shall reserve the expression world as a term for the meaning established in 3. If we use it at times in the first meaning, we shall put it in quotation marks.

Thus, terminologically "worldly" means a kind of being of Da-sein, never a kind of being of something objectively present "in" the world. We shall call the latter something belonging* to the world, or innerworldly.

. . .

15. The Being of Beings Encountered in the Surrounding World

The phenomenological exhibition of the being of beings encountered nearest to us can be accomplished under the guidance of the everyday being-in-the-world, which we also call *association in* the world *with* inner-worldly beings. Associations are already dispersed in manifold ways of taking care of things. However, as we showed, the nearest kind of associa-

tion is not mere perceptual cognition, but, rather, a handling, using, and taking care of things which has its own kind of "knowledge." Our phenomenological question is initially concerned with the being of those beings encountered when taking care of something. A methodical remark is necessary to secure the kind of seeing required here.

In the disclosure and explication of being, beings are always our preliminary and accompanying theme. The real theme is being. What shows itself in taking care of things in the surrounding world constitutes the pre-thematic being in the domain of our analysis. This being is not the object of a theoretical "world"-cognition; it is what is used, produced, and so on. As a being thus encountered, it comes pre-thematically into view for a "knowing" which, as a phenomenological knowing, primarily looks toward being and on the basis of this thematization of being thematizes actual beings as well. Thus, this phenomenological interpretation is not a cognition of existent qualities of beings; but, rather, a determination of the structure of their being. But as an investigation of being it independently and explicitly brings about the understanding of being which always already belongs to Da-sein and is "alive" in every association with beings. Phenomenologically pre-thematic beings, what is used and produced, become accessible when we put ourselves in the place of taking care of things in the world. Strictly speaking, to talk of putting ourselves in the place of taking care is misleading. We do not first need to put ourselves in the place of this way of being in associating with and taking care of things. Everyday Da-sein always already *is* in this way; for example, in opening the door, I use the doorknob. Gaining phenomenological access to the beings thus encountered consists rather in rejecting the interpretational tendencies crowding and accompanying us which cover over the phenomenon of "taking care" of things in general, and thus even more so beings *as* they are encountered of their own accord *in* taking care. These insidious mistakes become clear when we ask: Which beings are to be our preliminary theme and established as a pre-phenomenal basis?

We answer: things. But perhaps we have already missed the pre-phenomenal basis we are looking for with this self-evident answer. For an unexpressed anticipatory ontological characterization is contained in addressing beings as "things" (*res*). An analysis which starts with such beings and goes on to inquire about

---

*It is just Da-sein that *obeys and listens to the world* (*welthörig*).

being comes up with thingliness and reality. Onto-logical explication thus finds, as it proceeds, charac-teristics of being such as substantiality, materiality, extendedness, side-by-sideness. . . . But the beings encountered and taken care of are also pre-ontologi-cally hidden at first in this being. When one desig-nates things as the beings that are "initially given" one goes astray ontologically, although one means some-thing else ontically. What one really means remains indefinite. Or else one characterizes these "things" as "valuable." What does value mean ontologically? How is this "having" value and being involved with value to be understood categorially? Apart from the obscu-rity of this structure of having value, is the phenome-nal character of being of what is encountered and taken care of in association thus attained?

The Greeks had an appropriate term for "things": *pragmata,* that is, that with which one has to do in tak-ing care of things in association (*praxis*). But the spe-cifically "pragmatic" character of the *pragmata* is just what was left in obscurity and "initially" determined as "mere things."* We shall call the beings encoun-tered in taking care *useful things.* In association we find things for writing, things for sewing, things for working, driving, measuring. We must elucidate the kind of being of useful things. This can be done fol-lowing the guideline of the previous definition of what makes useful thing a useful thing: usable material.

Strictly speaking, there "is" no such thing as *a* use-ful thing. There always belongs to the being of a use-ful thing a totality of useful things in which this useful thing can be what it is. A useful thing is essentially "something in order to . . .". The different kinds of "in order to" such as serviceability, helpfulness, usa-bility, handiness, constitute a totality of useful things. The structure of "in order to" contains a *reference* of something to something. Only in the following analy-ses can the phenomenon indicated by this word be made visible in its ontological genesis. At this time, our task is to bring a multiplicity of references phenome-nally into view. In accordance with their character of being usable material, useful things always are *in terms of* their belonging to other useful things: writing ma-terials, pen, ink, paper, desk blotter, table, lamp, fur-niture, windows, doors, room. These "things" never

show themselves initially by themselves, in order then to fill out a room as a sum of real things. What we encounter as nearest to us, although we do not grasp it thematically, is the room, not as what is "between the four walls" in a geometrical, spatial sense, but rather as material for living. On the basis of the latter we find "accommodations," and in accommodations the ac-tual "individual" useful thing. A totality of useful things is always already discovered *before* the individ-ual useful thing.

Association geared to useful things which show themselves genuinely only in this association, that is, hammering with the hammer, neither *grasps* these beings thematically as occurring things nor does it even know of using or the structure of useful things as such. Hammering does not just have a knowledge of the useful character of the hammer; rather, it has appropriated this useful thing in the most adequate way possible. When we take care of things, we are sub-ordinate to the in-order-to constitutive for the actual useful thing in our association with it. The less we just stare at the thing called hammer, the more actively we use it, the more original our relation to it becomes and the more undisguisedly it is encountered as what it is, as a useful thing. The act of hammering itself dis-covers the specific "handiness" of the hammer. We shall call the useful thing's kind of being in which it reveals itself by itself *handiness.* It is only because use-ful things have *this* "being-in-themselves," and do not merely occur, that they are handy in the broadest sense and are at our disposal. No matter how keenly we just *look at* the "outward appearance" of things constituted in one way or another, we cannot dis-cover handiness. When we just look at things "theo-retically," we lack an understanding of handiness. But association which makes use of things is not blind, it has its own way of seeing which guides our operations and gives them their specific thingly quality. Our association with useful things is subordinate to the manifold of references of the "in-order-to." The kind of seeing of this accommodation to things is called *circumspection.*

"Practical" behavior is not "atheoretical" in the sense of a lack of seeing, and the difference between it and theoretical behavior lies not only in the fact that on the one hand we observe and on the other we *act,* and that action must apply theoretical cognition if it is not to remain blind. Rather, observation is a kind of taking care just as primordially as action has *its own* kind of seeing. Theoretical behavior is just look-

---

*Why? *eidos-morphē-hylē,* after all, come from *technē,* thus from an "artistic" interpretation ! if *morphē* is not interpreted as *eidos,* idea.

ing, noncircumspectly. Because it is noncircumspect, looking is not without rules; its canon takes shape in *method.*

Handiness is not grasped theoretically at all, nor is it itself initially a theme for circumspection. What is peculiar to what is initially at hand is that it withdraws, so to speak, in its character of handiness in order to be really handy. What everyday association is initially busy with is not tools themselves, but the work. What is to be produced in each case is what is primarily taken care of and is thus also what is at hand. The work bears the totality of references in which useful things are encountered.

As the *what-for* of the hammer, plane, and needle, the work to be produced has in its turn the kind of being of a useful thing. The shoe to be produced is for wearing (footgear), the clock is made for telling time. The work which we primarily encounter when we deal with things and take care of them—what we are at work with—always already lets us encounter the what-for of *its* usability in the usability which essentially belongs to it. The work that has been ordered exists in its turn only on the basis of its use and the referential context of beings discovered in that use.

But the work to be produced is not just useful for . . . ; production itself is always a using *of* something for something. A reference to "materials" is contained in the work at the same time. The work is dependent upon leather, thread, nails, and similar things. Leather in its turn is produced from hides. These hides are taken from animals which were bred and raised by others. We also find animals in the world which were not bred and raised and even when they have been raised these beings produce themselves in a certain sense. Thus beings are accessible in the surrounding world which in themselves do not need to be produced and are always already at hand. Hammer, tongs, nails in themselves refer to—they consist of—steel, iron, metal, stone, wood. "Nature" is also discovered in the use of useful things, "nature" in the light of products of nature.

But nature must not be understood here as what is merely objectively present, nor as the *power of nature.* The forest is a forest of timber, the mountain a quarry of rock, the river is water power, the wind is wind "in the sails." As the "surrounding world" is discovered, "nature" thus discovered is encountered along with it. We can abstract from nature's kind of being as handiness; we can discover and define it in its pure objective presence. But in this kind of discovery of nature, nature as what "stirs and strives," what overcomes us, entrances us as landscape, remains hidden. The botanist's plants are not the flowers of the hedgerow, the river's "source" ascertained by the geographer is not the "source in the ground."

The work produced refers not only to the what-for of its usability and the whereof of which it consists. The simple conditions of craft contain a reference to the wearer and user at the same time. The work is cut to his figure; he "is" there as the work emerges. This constitutive reference is by no means lacking when wares are produced by the dozen; it is only undefined, pointing to the random and the average. Thus not only beings which are at hand are encountered in the work but also beings with the kind of being of Da-sein for whom what is produced becomes handy in its taking care. Here the world is encountered in which wearers and users live, a world which is at the same time our world. The work taken care of in each case is not only at hand in the domestic world of the workshop, but rather in the *public world.* Along with the public world, the *surrounding world of nature* is discovered and accessible to everyone. In taking care of things, nature is discovered as having some definite direction on paths, streets, bridges, and buildings. A covered railroad platform takes bad weather into account, public lighting systems take darkness into account, the specific change of the presence and absence of daylight, the "position of the sun." Clocks take into account a specific constellation in the world system. When we look at the clock, we tacitly use the "position of the sun" according to which the official astronomical regulation of time is carried out. The surrounding world of nature is also at hand in the usage of clock equipment which is at first inconspicuously at hand. Our absorption in taking care of things in the work world nearest to us has the function of discovering; depending upon the way we are absorbed, innerworldly beings that are brought along together with their constitutive references are discoverable in varying degrees of explicitness and with a varying attentive penetration.

The kind of being of these beings is "handiness" (*Zuhandenheit*). But it must not be understood as a mere characteristic of interpretation,* as if such "aspects" were discursively forced upon "beings" which we initially encounter, as if an initially objectively

---

*But only as a characteristic of being encountered.

present world-stuff were "subjectively colored" in this way. Such an interpretation overlooks the fact that in that case beings would have to be understood beforehand and discovered as purely objectively present, and would thus have priority and take the lead in the order of discovering and appropriating association with the "world." But this already goes against the ontological meaning of the cognition which we showed to be a *founded* mode of being-in-the-world. To expose what is merely objectively present, cognition must first penetrate *beyond* things at hand being taken care of. *Handiness is the ontological categorial definition of beings as they are "in themselves."* But "there are" handy things, after all, only on the basis of what is objectively present. Admitting this thesis, does it then follow that handiness is ontologically founded in objective presence?

. . .

IV   BEING-IN-THE-WORLD AS BEING-WITH AND BEING A SELF: THE "THEY"

The analysis of the worldliness of the world continually brought the whole phenomenon of being-in-the-world into view without thereby delimiting all of its constitutive factors with the same phenomenal clarity as the phenomenon of world itself. The ontological interpretation of the world which discussed innerworldly things at hand came first not only because Da-sein in its everydayness is in a world in general and remains a constant theme with regard to that world, but because it relates itself to the world in a predominant mode of being. Initially and for the most part, Da-sein is taken in by its world. This mode of being, being absorbed in the world, and thus being-in which underlies it, essentially determine the phenomenon which we shall now pursue with the question: *Who* is it who is in the everydayness of Da-sein? All of the structures of being of Da-sein, thus also the phenomenon that answers to this question of who, are modes of its being. Their ontological characteristic is an existential one. Thus, we need to pose the question correctly and outline the procedure for bringing to view a broader phenomenal domain of the everydayness of Da-sein. By investigating in the direction of the phenomenon which allows us to answer the question of the who, we are led to structures of Da-sein which are equiprimordial with being-in-the-world:

being-with and *Mitda-sein.* In this kind of being, the mode of everyday being a self is grounded whose explication makes visible what we might call the "subject" of everydayness, the *they.* This chapter on the "who" of average Da-sein thus has the following structure: (1) The approach to the existential question of the who of Da-sein (section 25). (2) The *Mitda-sein* of the others and everyday being-with (section 26). (3) Everyday being a self and the they (section 27).

25.   The Approach to the Existential Question of the Who of Da-sein

The answer to the question of who this being actually is (Da-sein) seems to have already been given with the formal indication of the basic characteristics of Da-sein (cf. section 9). Da-sein is a being which I myself am, its being is in each case mine. This determination *indicates* an *ontological* constitution, but no more than that. At the same time, it contains an *ontic* indication, albeit an undifferentiated one, that an I is always this being, and not others. The who is answered in terms of the I itself, the "subject," the "self." The who is what maintains itself in the changes throughout its modes of behavior and experiences as something identical and is, thus, related to this multiplicity. Ontologically, we understand it as what is always already and constantly objectively present in a closed region and for that region, as that which lies at its basis in an eminent sense, as the *subjectum.* As something self-same in manifold otherness, this subject has the character of the *self.* Even if one rejects a substantial soul, the thingliness of consciousness and the objectivity of the person, ontologically one still posits something whose being retains the meaning of objective presence, whether explicitly or not. Substantiality is the ontological clue for the determination of beings in terms of whom the question of the who is answered. Da-sein is tacitly conceived in advance as objective presence. In any case, the indeterminacy of its being always implies this meaning of being. However, objective presence is the mode of being of beings unlike Da-sein.

The ontic obviousness of the statement that it is I who is in each case Da-sein must not mislead us into supposing that the way for an ontological interpretation of what is thus "given" has been unmistakably prescribed. It is even questionable whether the ontic content of the above statement reaches the phenomenal content of everyday Da-sein. It could be the case that the who of everyday Da-sein is precisely *not* I myself.

Even when we manage to gain ontic and ontological statements, if the phenomenal demonstration in terms of the mode of being of beings is to retain priority over the most obvious and usual answers and the problems arising from these, the phenomenological interpretation of Da-sein must be protected from a distortion of the problematic with regard to the question to be raised now.

But does it not go against the rules of a sound method when the approach to a problematic does not stick to the evident data of the thematic realm? And what is less dubious than the givenness of the I? And (for the purpose of working this givenness out in a primordial way) does it not direct us to abstract from everything else that is "given," not only from an existing "world," but also from the being of the other "I"'s? Perhaps what gives this kind of giving, this simple, formal, reflective perception of the I, is indeed evident. This insight even opens access to an independent phenomenological problematic which has its fundamental significance in the framework known as "formal phenomenology of consciousness."

In the present context of an existential analytic of factical Da-sein, the question arises whether the way of the giving of the I which we mentioned discloses Da-sein in its everydayness, if it discloses it at all. Is it then *à priori* self-evident that the access to Da-sein must be simple perceiving reflection of the I of acts? What if this kind of "self-giving" of Da-sein were to lead our existential analytic astray and do so in a way grounded in the being of Da-sein itself? Perhaps when Da-sein addresses itself in the way which is nearest to itself, it always says it is I, and finally says this most loudly when it is "not" this being. What if the fact that Da-sein is so constituted that it is in each case mine, were the reason for the fact that Da-sein *is,* initially and for the most part, *not itself*? What if, with the approach mentioned above, the existential analytic fell into the trap, so to speak, of starting with the givenness of the I for Da-sein itself and its obvious self-interpretation? What if it should turn out that the ontological horizon for the determination of what is accessible in simple giving should remain fundamentally undetermined? We can probably always correctly say ontically of this being that "I" am it. However, the ontological analytic which makes use of

such statements must have fundamental reservations about them. The "I" must be understood only in the sense of a noncommittal *formal indication* of something which perhaps reveals itself in the actual phenomenal context of being as that being's "opposite." Then "not I" by no means signifies something like a being which is essentially lacking "I-hood," but means a definite mode of being of the "I" itself; for example, having lost itself.*

But even the positive interpretation of Da-sein that has been given up to now already forbids a point of departure from the formal givenness of the I if the intention is to find a phenomenally adequate answer to the question of value. The clarification of being-in-the-world showed that a mere subject without a world "is" not initially and is also never given. And, thus, an isolated I without the others is in the end just as far from being given initially. But if the "others" *are* always already *there with us* in being-in-the-world, ascertaining this phenomenally, too, must not mislead us into thinking that the *ontological* structure of what is thus "given" is self-evident and not in need of an investigation. The task is to make this *Mitda-sein* of the nearest everydayness phenomenally visible and to interpret it in an ontologically adequate way.

Just as the ontic, self-evident character of being-in-itself of inner-worldly beings misleads us to the conviction of the ontological self-evident character of the meaning of this being and makes us overlook the phenomenon of world, the ontic, self-evident character that Da-sein is always my own also harbors the possibility that the ontological problematic indigenous to it might be led astray. *Initially* the who of Da-sein is not only a problem *ontologically,* it also remains concealed *ontically.*

But, then, is the existential analytical answer to the question of the who without any clues at all? By no means. To be sure, of the formal indications of the constitution of being of Da-sein given above (sections 9 and 12), it is not so much the one which we discussed which is functional, but rather, the one according to which the "essence" of Da-sein is grounded in its existence. *If the "I" is an essential determination of Da-sein, it must be interpreted existentially.* The question of the who can then be answered only by a phenomenal demonstration of a definite kind of

---

*Or else genuine selfhood as opposed to miserable egotism.

being of Da-sein. If Da-sein is always only its self *in existing,* the constancy of the self as well as its possible "inconstancy" require an existential-ontological kind of questioning as the only adequate access to the problematic.

But if the self is conceived "only" as a way of the being of this being, then that seems tantamount to volatizing the true "core" of Da-sein. But such fears are nourished by the incorrect preconception that the being in question really has, after all, the kind of being of something objectively present, even if one avoids attributing to it the massive element of a corporeal thing. However, the "*substance*" of human being is not the spirit as the synthesis of body and soul, but *existence.*

26. The *Mitda-sein* of the Others and Everyday Being-with

The answer to the question of the who of everyday Da-sein is to be won through the analysis of *the* kind of being in which Da-sein, initially and for the most part, lives. Our investigation takes its orientation from being-in-the-world. This fundamental constitution of Da-sein determines every mode of its being. If we justifiably stated that all other structural factors of being-in-the-world already came into view by means of the previous explication of the world, the answer to the question of the who must also be prepared by that explication.

The "description" of the surrounding world nearest to us, for example, the work-world of the handworker, showed that together with the useful things found in work, others are "also encountered" for whom the "work" is to be done. In the kind of being of these things at hand, that is, in their relevance, there lies an essential reference to possible wearers for whom they should be "cut to the figure." Similarly, the producer or "supplier" is encountered in the material used as one who "serves" well or badly. The field, for example, along which we walk "outside" shows itself as belonging to such and such a person who keeps it in good order, the book which we use is bought at such and such a place, given by such and such a person, and so on. The boat anchored at the shore refers in its being-in-itself to an acquaintance who undertakes his voyages with it, but as a "boat strange to us," it also points to others. The others who are "encountered" in the context of useful things in

the surrounding world at hand are not somehow added on in thought to an initially merely objectively present thing, but these "things" are encountered from the world in which they are at hand for the others. This world is always already from the outset my own. In our previous analysis, the scope of what is encountered in the world was initially narrowed down to useful things at hand, or nature objectively present, thus to beings of a character unlike Da-sein. This restriction was not only necessary for the purpose of simplifying the explication; but, above all, because the kind of being of the existence of the others encountered within the surrounding world is distinct from handiness and objective presence. The world of Da-sein thus frees beings which are not only completely different from tools and things, but which themselves in accordance with their kind of being as *Da-sein* are themselves "in" the world as being-in-the-world in which they are at the same time encountered. These beings are neither objectively present nor at hand, but they *are like* the very Da-sein which frees them—*they are there, too, and there with it.* So, if one wanted to identify the world in general with innerworldly beings, one would have to say the "world" is also Da-sein.

But the characteristic of encountering the *others* is, after all, oriented toward one's *own* Da-sein. Does not it, too, start with the distinction and isolation of the "I," so that a transition from this isolated subject to the others must then be sought? In order to avoid this misunderstanding, we must observe in what sense we are talking about "the others." "The others" does not mean everybody else but me—those from whom the I distinguishes itself. They are, rather, those from whom one mostly does *not* distinguish oneself, those among whom one is, too. This being-there-too with them does not have the ontological character of being objectively present "with" them within a world. The "with" is of the character of Da-sein, the "also" means the sameness of being as circumspect, heedful being-in-the-world. "With" and "also" are to be understood *existentially,* not categorially. On the basis of this *like-with* being-in-the-world, the world is always already the one that I share with the others. The world of Da-sein is a *with-world.* Being-in is *being-with* others. The innerworldly being-in-itself of others is *Mitda-sein.*

The others are not encountered by grasping and previously discriminating one's own subject, initially objectively present, from other subjects also present.

They are not encountered by first looking at oneself and then ascertaining the opposite pole of a distinction. They are encountered from the *world* in which Da-sein, heedful and circumspect, essentially dwells. As opposed to the theoretically concocted "explanations" of the objective presence of others which easily urge themselves upon us, we must hold fast to the phenomenal fact which we have indicated of their being encountered in the *surrounding world*. This nearest and elemental way of Da-sein of being encountered in the world goes so far that even one's *own* Da-sein *initially* becomes "discoverable" by *looking away* from its "experiences" and the "center of its actions" or by not yet "seeing" them all. Da-sein initially finds "itself" in *what* it does, needs, expects, has charge of, in the things at hand which it initially *takes care of* in the surrounding world.

. . .

The disclosedness of the *Mitda-sein* of others which belongs to being-with means that the understanding of others already lies in the understanding of being of Da-sein because its being is being-with. This understanding, like all understanding, is not a knowledge derived from cognition, but a primordially existential kind of being which first makes knowledge and cognition possible. Knowing oneself is grounded in primordially understanding being-with. It operates initially in accordance with the nearest kind of being of being-together-in-the-world in the understanding knowledge of what Da-sein circumspectly finds and takes care of with the others. Concernful taking care of things is understood in terms of what is taken care of and with an understanding of them. Thus the other is initially disclosed in the taking care of concern.

But because concern, initially and for the most part, dwells in the deficient or at least indifferent modes—in the indifference of passing-one-another-by—a nearest and essential knowing oneself is in need of a getting-to-know-oneself. And when even knowing oneself loses itself in aloofness, concealing oneself and misrepresenting oneself, being-with-one-another requires special ways in order to come near to the others or to "see through them."

. . .

Our analysis has shown that being-with is an existential constituent of being-in-the-world. *Mitda-sein* has proved to be a manner of being which beings encountered within the world have as their own. In that Da-sein *is* at all, it has the kind of being of being-with-one-another. Being-with-one-another cannot be understood as a summative result of the occurrence of several "subjects." Encountering a number of "subjects" itself is possible only by treating the others encountered in their *Mitda-sein* merely as "numerals." This number is discovered only by a definite being with and toward one another. "Inconsiderate" being-with "reckons" with others without seriously "counting on them" or even wishing "to have anything to do" with them.

One's own Da-sein, like the *Mitda-sein* of others, is encountered, initially and for the most part, in terms of the world-together in the surrounding world taken care of. In being absorbed in the world of taking care of things, that is, at the same time in being-with toward others, Da-sein is not itself. *Who* is it, then, who has taken over being as everyday being-with-one-another?

27. Everyday Being One's Self and the They

The *ontologically* relevant result of the foregoing analysis of being-with is the insight that the "subject character" of one's own Da-sein and of the others is to be defined existentially, that is, in terms of certain ways to be. In what is taken care of in the surrounding world, the others are encountered as what they are; they *are* what they do.

In taking care of the things which one has taken hold of, for, and against others, there is constant care as to the way one differs from them, whether this difference is to be equalized, whether one's own Da-sein has lagged behind others and wants to catch up in relation to them, whether Da-sein in its priority over others is intent on suppressing them. Being-with-one-another is, unknown to itself, disquieted by the care about this distance. Existentially expressed, being-with-one-another has the character of *distantiality*. The more inconspicuous this kind of being is to everyday Da-sein itself, all the more stubbornly and primordially does it work itself out.

But this distantiality which belongs to being-with is such that, as everyday being-with-one-another, Da-sein stands in *subservience* to the others. It itself *is* not; the others have taken its being away from it. The everyday possibilities of being of Da-sein are at the disposal of the whims of the others. These others are not *definite* others. On the contrary, any other can represent them. What is decisive is only the inconspicuous domination by others that Da-sein as being-with has already taken over unawares. One belongs to the others oneself, and entrenches their power. "The others," whom one designates as such in order to cover over one's own essential belonging to them, are those who *are there* initially and for the most part in everyday being-with-one-another. The who is not this one and not that one, not oneself and not some and not the sum of them all. The "who" is the neuter, *the they.*

We have shown earlier how the public "surrounding world" is always already at hand and taken care of in the surrounding world nearest to us. In utilizing public transportation, in the use of information services such as the newspaper, every other is like the next. This being-with-one-another dissolves one's own Da-sein completely into the kind of being of "the others" in such a way that the others, as distinguishable and explicit, disappear more and more. In this inconspicuousness and unascertainability, the they unfolds its true dictatorship. We enjoy ourselves and have fun the way *they* enjoy themselves. We read, see, and judge literature and art the way *they* see and judge. But we also withdraw from the "great mass" the way *they* withdraw, we find "shocking" what *they* find shocking. The they, which is nothing definite and which all are, though not as a sum, prescribes the kind of being of everydayness.

The they has its own ways to be. The tendency of being-with which we called distantiality is based on the fact that being-with-one-another as such creates *averageness.* It is an existential character of the they. In its being, the they is essentially concerned with averageness. Thus, the they maintains itself factically in the averageness of what is proper, what is allowed, and what is not. Of what is granted success and what is not. This averageness, which prescribes what can and may be ventured, watches over every exception which thrusts itself to the fore. Every priority is noiselessly squashed. Overnight, everything primordial is flattened down as something long since known. Everything gained by a struggle becomes something to be manipulated. Every mystery loses its power. The care of averageness reveals, in turn, an essential tendency of Da-sein, which we call the *levelling down* of all possibilities of being.

Distantiality, averageness, and levelling down, as ways of being of the they, constitute what we know as "publicness." Publicness initially controls every way in which the world and Da-sein are interpreted, and it is always right, not because of an eminent and primary relation of being to "things," not because it has an explicitly appropriate transparency of Da-sein at its disposal, but because it does not get to "the heart of the matter," because it is insensitive to every difference of level and genuineness. Publicness obscures everything, and then claims that what has been thus covered over is what is familiar and accessible to everybody.

The they is everywhere, but in such a way that it has always already stolen away when Da-sein presses for a decision. However, because the they presents every judgment and decision as its own, it takes the responsibility of Da-sein away from it. The they can, as it were, manage to have "them" constantly invoking it. It can most easily be responsible for everything because no one has to vouch for anything. The they always "did it," and yet it can be said that "no one" did it. In the everydayness of Da-sein, most things happen in such a way that we must say "no one did it."

Thus, the they *disburdens* Da-sein in its everydayness. Not only that; by disburdening it of its being, the they accommodates Da-sein in its tendency to take things easily and make them easy. And since the they constantly accommodates Da-sein, it retains and entrenches its stubborn dominance.

Everyone is the other, and no one is himself. The *they,* which supplies the answer to the *who* of everyday Da-sein, is the *nobody* to whom every Da-sein has always already surrendered itself, in its being-among-one-another.

In these characteristics of being which we have discussed—everyday being-among-one-another, distantiality, averageness, levelling down, publicness, disburdening of one's being, and accommodation—lies the initial "constancy" of Da-sein. This constancy pertains not to the enduring objective presence of something, but to the kind of being of Da-sein as being-with. Existing in the modes we have mentioned, the self of one's own Da-sein and the self of the other have neither found nor lost themselves. One is in the manner of dependency and inauthenticity. This way of being does not signify a lessening of the facticity of Da-sein, just as the they as the nobody is not nothing. On the contrary, in this kind of being Da-sein is an *ens realissimum,* if by "reality" we understand a being that is like Da-sein.

Of course, the they is as little objectively present as Da-sein itself. The more openly the they behaves, the more slippery and hidden it is, but the less is it nothing at all. To the unprejudiced ontic-ontological "eye," it reveals itself as the "most real subject" of everydayness. And if it is not accessible like an objectively present stone, that is not in the least decisive about its kind of being. One may neither decree prematurely that this they is "really" nothing, nor profess the opinion that the phenomenon has been interpreted ontologically if one "explains" it as the result of the objective presence of several subjects which one has put together in hindsight. On the contrary, the elaboration of the concepts of being must be guided by these indubitable phenomena.

Nor is the they something like a "universal subject" which hovers over a plurality of subjects. One could understand it this way only if the being of "subjects" is understood as something unlike Da-sein, and if these are regarded as factually objectively present cases of an existing genus. With this approach, the only possibility ontologically is to understand everything which is not a case of this sort in the sense of genus and species. The they is not the genus of an individual Da-sein, nor can it be found in this being as an abiding characteristic. That traditional logic also fails in the face of these phenomena, cannot surprise us if we consider that it has its foundation in an ontology of objective presence—an ontology which is still rough at that. Thus, it fundamentally cannot be made more flexible no matter how many improvements and expansions might be made. These reforms of logic, oriented toward the "humanistic sciences," only increase the ontological confusion.

The they is an existential and belongs as a primordial phenomenon to the positive constitution of Da-sein. It itself has, in turn, various possibilities of concretion in accordance with Da-sein. The extent to which its dominance becomes penetrating and explicit may change historically.

The self of everyday Da-sein is the *they-self* which we distinguish from the *authentic self,* the self which has explicitly grasped itself. As the they-self, Da-sein is *dispersed* in the they and must first find itself. This dispersion characterizes the "subject" of the kind of being which we know as heedful absorption in the world nearest encountered. If *Da-sein* is familiar with itself as the they-self, this also means that the they prescribes the nearest interpretation of the world and of being-in-the-world. The they itself, for the sake of which Da-sein is every day, articulates the referential context of significance. The world of Da-sein frees the beings encountered for a totality of relevance which is familiar to the they in the limits which are established with the averageness of the they. *Initially,* factical Da-sein is in the with-world, discovered in an average way. *Initially,* "I" "am" not in the sense of my own self, but I am the others in the mode of the they. In terms of the they, and as the they, I am initially "given" to "myself." Initially, Da-sein is the they and for the most part it remains so. If Da-sein explicitly discovers the world and brings it near, if it discloses its authentic being to itself, this discovering of "world" and disclosing of Da-sein always comes about by clearing away coverings and obscurities, by breaking up the disguises with which Da-sein cuts itself off from itself.

With this interpretation of being-with and being one's self in the they, the question of the who in the everydayness of being-with-one-another is answered. These considerations have at the same time given us a concrete understanding of the basic constitution of Da-sein. Being-in-the-world became visible in its everydayness and averageness.

Everyday Da-sein derives the pre-ontological interpretation of its being from the nearest kind of being of the they. The ontological interpretation initially follows this tendency of interpretation, it understands Da-sein in terms of the world and finds it there as an innerworldly being. Not only this; the "nearest" ontology of Da-sein takes the meaning of being on the basis of which these existing "subjects" are understood also in terms of the "world." But since the phenomenon of world itself is passed over in this absorption in the world, it is replaced by objective presence in the world, by things. The being of beings, which *is there, too,* is understood as objective presence. Thus, by showing the positive phenomenon of nearest, everyday being-in-the-world, we have made possible an insight into the root of missing the ontological interpretation of this constitution of being. It itself, in its everyday kind of being, is what initially misses itself and covers itself over.

If the being of everyday being-with-one-another, which seems ontologically to approach pure objective presence, is really fundamentally different from that kind of presence, still less can the being of the authentic self be understood as objective presence. *Authentic being one's self* is not based on an exceptional state of the subject, a state detached from the they, *but is an existentiell modification of the they as an essential existential.*

But, then, the sameness of the authentically existing self is separated ontologically by a gap from the identity of the I maintaining itself in the multiplicity of its "experiences."

V   BEING-IN AS SUCH

28.   The Task of a Thematic Analysis of Being-in

What we have set forth so far needs to be supplemented in many ways with respect to a full elaboration of the existential *à priori* of philosophical anthropology. But this is not the aim of our investigation. *Its aim is that of fundamental ontology.* If we thus inquire into being-in thematically, we cannot be willing to nullify the primordiality of the phenomenon by deriving it from others, that is, by an inappropriate analysis in the sense of dissolving it. But the fact that we cannot derive something primordial does not exclude a multiplicity of characteristics of being constitutive for it. If these characteristics show themselves, they are existentially equiprimordial. . . .

In which direction must we look for the phenomenal characteristics of being-in as such? We get the answer to this question by recalling what we were charged with keeping in view phenomenologically when we pointed out this phenomenon: being-in in contradistinction to the objectively present insideness of something objectively present "in" an other; being-in not as an attribute of an objectively present subject effected or even initiated by the objective presence of the "world"; rather, being-in essentially as the kind of being of this being itself. . . .

The being which is essentially constituted by being-in-the-world *is* itself always its "there." According to the familiar meaning of the word, "there" points to "here" and "over there." The "here" of an "I-here" is always understood in terms of an "over there" at hand in the sense of being toward it which de-distances, is directional, and takes care. The existential spatiality of Da-sein which determines its "place" for it in this

way is itself based upon being-in-the-world. The over there is the determinateness of something encountered within the *world*. "Here" and "over there" are possible only in a "there," that is, when there is a being which has disclosed spatiality as the being of the there. This being bears in its ownmost being the character of not being closed. The expression "there" means this essential disclosedness. Through disclosedness this being (Da-sein) is "there" for itself together with the Da-sein of the world.

When we talk in an ontically figurative way about the *lumen naturale* in human being, we mean nothing other than the existential-ontological structure of this being, the fact that it *is* in the mode of being its there. To say that it is "illuminated" means that it is cleared * in itself *as* being-in-the-world, not by another being, but in such a way that it *is* itself the clearing.† Only for a being thus existentially do objectively present things become accessible in the light or concealed in darkness. By its very nature, Da-sein brings its there along with it. If it lacks its there, it is not only factically not of this nature, but not at all a being. *Da-sein is its disclosure.*‡

We must set forth the constitution of this being. But since the nature of this being is existence, the existential statement that "*Da-sein is its disclosure*" means at the same time that the being about which these beings are concerned in their being is to be their "there." In addition to characterizing the primary constitution of the being of disclosure, we must, in accordance with the character of our analysis, interpret the kind of being in which this being is its there in an *everyday way*.

THE EXISTENTIAL CONSTITUTION OF THE THERE

29.   Da-sein as Attunement

What we indicate *ontologically* with the term *attunement* is *ontically* what is most familiar and an everyday kind of thing: mood, being in a mood. Prior to all

---

Aletheia—openness—clearing, light, shining.
†But not produced.
‡Da-sein exists, and it alone. Thus existence is standing out and perduring the openness of the there: Ek-sistence.

psychology of moods, a field which, moreover, still lies fallow, we must see this phenomenon as a fundamental existential and outline its structure.

Both the undisturbed equanimity and the inhibited discontent of everyday heedfulness, the way we slide over from one to another or slip into bad moods, are by no means nothing ontologically although these phenomena remain unnoticed as what is supposedly the most indifferent and fleeting in Da-sein. The fact that moods can be spoiled and change only means that Da-sein is always already in a mood.

mood - angst.

In being in a mood, Da-sein is always already disclosed in accordance with its mood as *that* being to which Da-sein was delivered over in its being as the being which it, existing, has to be. Disclosed does not, as such, mean to be known. Just in the most indifferent and harmless everydayness the being of Da-sein can burst forth as the naked "that it is and has to be." The pure "that it is" shows itself, the whence and whither remain obscure. The fact that Da-sein normally does not "give in" to such everyday moods, that is, does not pursue what they disclose and does not allow itself to confront what has been disclosed, is no evidence *against* the phenomenal fact of the mood-like disclosure of the being of the there in its that, but is rather evidence for it. For the most part Da-sein evades the being that is disclosed in moods in an *ontic* and existentiell way. *Ontologically* and existentially this means that in that to which such a mood pays no attention Da-sein is unveiled in its being delivered over to the there. In the evasion itself the there *is* something disclosed.

We shall call this character of being of Da-sein which is veiled in its whence and whither, but in itself all the more openly disclosed, this "that it is," the *thrownness* of this being into its there; it is thrown in such a way that it is the there as being-in-the-world. The expression thrownness is meant to suggest the *facticity of its being delivered over*. The "that it is and has to be" disclosed in the attunement of Da-sein is not the "that" which expresses ontologically and categorially the factuality belonging to objective presence; The latter is accessible only when we ascertain it by looking at it. Rather, the that disclosed in attunement must be understood as an existential attribute of *that* being which is in the mode of being-in-the-

world. *Facticity is not the factuality of the* factum brutum *of something objectively present, but is a characteristic of the being of Da-sein taken on in existence, although initially thrust aside*. The that of facticity is never to be found by looking.

· · ·

Attunement is far removed from anything like finding a psychical condition. Far from having the character of an apprehension which first turns itself around and then turns back, all immanent reflection can find "experiences" only because the there is already disclosed in attunement. "Mere mood" discloses the there more primordially, but it also *closes* it *off* more stubbornly than any *not*-perceiving.

Bad moods show this. In bad moods, Da-sein becomes blind to itself, the surrounding world of heedfulness is veiled, the circumspection of taking care is led astray. Attunement is so far from being reflected upon that it precisely assails Da-sein in the unreflected falling prey to the "world" of its heedfulness. Mood assails. It comes neither from "without" nor from "within," but rises from being-in-the-world itself as a mode of that being. But thus by negatively contrasting attunement with the reflective apprehension of the "inner," we arrive at a positive insight into its character of disclosure. *Mood has always already disclosed being-in-the-world as a whole and first makes possible directing oneself toward something*. Being attuned is not initially related to something psychical, it is itself not an inner condition which then in some mysterious way reaches out and leaves its mark on things and persons. This is the *second* essential characteristic of attunement. It is a fundamental existential mode of being of the *equiprimordial disclosedness* of world, being-there-with, and existence because this disclosure itself is essentially being-in-the-world.

Besides these two essential determinations of attunement just explicated, the disclosure of thrownness and the actual disclosure of the whole of being-in-the-world, we must notice a *third* which above all contributes to a more penetrating understanding of the worldliness of the world. We said earlier that the world already disclosed lets inner-worldly things be encountered. This prior disclosedness of the world which belongs to being-in is also constituted by attunement. Letting something be encountered is primarily *circumspective*, not just a sensation or staring out at something. Letting things be encountered in a circumspect heedful way has—we can see this now more precisely in terms of attunement—the character of being affected or moved. But being affected by the unserviceable, resistant, and threatening character of things at hand is ontologically possible only because being-in as such is existentially determined beforehand in such a way that what it encounters in the world can *matter* to it in this way. This mattering to it is grounded in attunement, and as attunement it has disclosed the world, for example, as something by which it can be threatened. Only something which is the attunement of fearing, or fearlessness, can discover things at hand in the surrounding world as being threatening. The moodedness of attunement constitutes existentially the openness to world of Da-sein.

. . .

30.   Fear as a Mode of Attunement

That *before which* we are afraid, the "fearsome," is always something encountered within the world, either with the kind of being of something at hand or something objectively present or *Mitda-sein.* We do not intend to report ontically about things which often and for the most part can be "fearsome," but to determine phenomenally what is fearsome in its fearsome character. What is it that belongs to the fearsome as such which is encountered in fearing? What is feared has the character of being threatening. . . .

Fearing itself frees what we have characterized as threatening in a way which lets us be concerned with it. It is not that we initially ascertain a future evil (*malum futurum*) and then are afraid of it. But neither does fearing first confirm something approaching us, but rather discovers it beforehand in its fearsomeness. And then fear, in being afraid, can "clarify" what is fearsome by explicitly looking at it. Circumspection sees what is fearsome because it is in the attunement of fear. As a dormant possibility of attuned being-in-the-world, fearing, "fearfulness" has already disclosed the world with regard to the fact that something like a fearful thing can draw near to us from this fearfulness. The ability to draw near is itself freed by the essential, existential spatiality of being-in-the-world.

The *about which* fear is afraid is the fearful being itself, Da-sein. Only a being which is concerned in its being about that being can be afraid. Fearing discloses this being in its jeopardization, in its being left to itself. Although in varying degrees of explicitness, fear always reveals Da-sein in the being of its there. When we are afraid for house and home, this is not a counter-example for the above determination of what it is we are fearful about. For as being-in-the-world, Da-sein is always a heedful being-with. Initially and for the most part, Da-sein *is* in terms of *what* it takes care of. The jeopardization of that is a threat to being with. Fear predominantly discloses Da-sein in a privative way. It bewilders us and makes us "lose our heads." At the same time, fear closes off our jeopardized being in by letting us see it so that when fear has subsided Da-sein has to first find its way about again.

Fear about as being afraid of always equiprimordially discloses, whether privatively or positively, innerworldly beings in their possibility of being threatening and being-in with regard to its being threatened. Fear is a mode of attunement.

. . .

31.   Da-sein as Understanding

Attunement is *one* of the existential structures in which the being of the "there" dwells. Equiprimordially with it, *understanding* constitutes this being. Attunement always has its understanding, even if only by suppressing it. Understanding is always attuned. If we interpret understanding as a fundamental existential,* we see that this phenomenon is conceived as a fundamental mode of the *being* of Da-sein. In contrast, "understanding" in the sense of one possible kind of cognition among others, let us say distinguished from "explanation," must be interpreted along with that as an existential derivative of the primary understanding which constitutes the being of the there in general.

Our previous inquiry already encountered this primordial understanding, but without explicitly taking it up in the theme under consideration. The statement that Da-sein, existing, is its there means: World is "there"; its *Da-sein* is being-in. Being-in is "there" as that for the sake of which Da-sein is. Existing being-in-the-world as such is disclosed in the for-

---

*Fundamentally and ontologically, that is, from the relation of the truth of being.

the-sake-of-which, and we called this disclosedness understanding. In understanding the for-the-sake-of-which, the significance grounded therein is also disclosed. The disclosure of understanding, as that of the for-the-sake-of-which and of significance, is equiprimordially concerned with complete being-in-the-world. Significance is that for which world as such is disclosed. The statement that the for-the-sake-of-which and significance are disclosed in Da-sein means that Da-sein is a being which, as being-in-the-world, is concerned about itself.

Speaking ontically, we sometimes use the expression "to understand something" to mean "being able to handle a thing," "being up to it," "being able to do something." In understanding as an existential, the thing we are able to do is not a what, but being as existing. The mode of being of Da-sein as a potentiality of being lies existentially in understanding. Da-sein is not something objectively present which then has as an addition the ability to do something, but is rather primarily being-possible. Da-sein is always what it can be and how it is its possibility. The essential possibility of Da-sein concerns the ways of taking care of the "world" which we characterized, of concern for others and, always already present in all of this, the potentiality of being itself, for its own sake. The being-possible, which Da-sein always is existentially, is also distinguished from empty, logical possibility and from the contingency of something objectively present, where this or that can "happen" to it. As a modal category of objective presence, possibility means what is *not yet* real and *not always* necessary. It characterizes what is *only* possible. Ontologically, it is less than reality and necessity. In contrast, possibility as an existential is the most primordial and the ultimate positive ontological determination of Da-sein; as is the case with existentiality, it can initially be prepared for solely as a problem. Understanding as a potentiality of being disclosive offers the phenomenal ground to see it at all.

As an existential, possibility does not refer to a free-floating potentiality of being in the sense of the "liberty of indifference" (*libertas indifferentiae*). As essentially attuned, Da-sein has always already got itself into definite possibilities. As a potentiality for being which it *is,* it has let some go by; it constantly adopts the possibilities of its being, grasps them, and goes astray. But this means that Da-sein is a being-possible

entrusted to itself, *thrown possibility* throughout. Da-sein is the possibility of being free *for* its ownmost potentiality of being. Being-possible is transparent for it in various possible ways and degrees.

Understanding is the being of such a potentiality of being which is never still outstanding as something not yet objectively present, but as something essentially never objectively present, *is* together with the being of Da-sein in the sense of existence. Da-sein is in the way that it actually understands or has not understood to be in this or that way. As this understanding, it "knows" *what* is going on, that is, what its potentiality of being is. This "knowing" does not first come from an immanent self-perception, but belongs to the being of the there which is essentially understanding. And only *because* Da-sein, in understanding is its there, *can* it go astray and fail to recognize itself. And since understanding is attuned and attunement is existentially surrendered to thrownness, Da-sein has always already gone astray and failed to recognize itself. In its potentiality of being, it is thus delivered over to the possibility of first finding itself again in its possibilities.

Understanding is the existential being of the ownmost potentiality of being of Da-sein in such a way that this being discloses in itself what its very being is about. The structure of this existential must be grasped more precisely.

As disclosing, understanding always concerns the whole fundamental constitution of being-in-the-world. As a potentiality of being, being-in is always a potentiality of being-in-the-world. Not only is the world, qua world, disclosed in its possible significance, but innerworldly beings themselves are freed, these beings are freed for *their own* possibilities. What is at hand is discovered as such in its service*ability,* us*ability,* detriment*ality.* The totality of relevance reveals itself as the categorial whole of a *possibility* of the connection of things at hand. But the "unity," too, of manifold objective presence, nature, is discoverable only on the basis of the disclosedness of one of its *possibilities.* Is it a matter of chance that the question of the *being* of nature aims at the "conditions of its *possibility*?" On what is this questioning based? It cannot omit the question: *Why* are beings unlike Da-sein understood in their being if they are disclosed in terms of the conditions of their possibility? Kant presupposed something like this, perhaps correctly so. But this presupposition itself cannot be left without demonstrating how it is justified.

Why does understanding always penetrate into possibilities according to all the essential dimensions of what can be disclosed to it? Because understanding in itself has the existential structure which we call *project*. It projects the being of Da-sein upon its for-the-sake-of-which just as primordially as upon significance as the worldliness of its actual world. The project character of understanding constitutes being-in-the-world with regard to the disclosedness of its there as the there of a potentiality of being. Project is the existential constitution of being in the realm of factical potentiality of being. And, as thrown, Da-sein is thrown into the mode of being of projecting. Projecting has nothing to do with being related to a plan thought out, according to which Da-sein arranges its being, but, as Da-sein, it has always already projected itself and is, as long as it is, projecting. As long as it is, Da-sein always has understood and will understand itself in terms of possibilities. Furthermore, the project character of understanding means that understanding does not thematically grasp that upon which it projects, the possibilities themselves. Such a grasp precisely takes its character of possibility away from what is projected, it degrades it to the level of a given, intended content, whereas in projecting project throws possibility before itself as possibility, and as such lets it *be*. As projecting, understanding is the mode of being of Da-sein in which it *is* its possibilities as possibilities.

Because of the kind of being which is constituted by the existential of projecting, Da-sein is constantly "more" than it actually is, if one wanted to and if one could register it as something objectively present in its content of being. But it is nevermore than it factically is because its potentiality of being belongs essentially to its facticity. But, as being-possible, Da-sein is also never less. It is existentially that which it is *not yet* in its potentiality of being. And only because the being of the there gets its constitution through understanding and its character of project, only because it *is* what it becomes or does not become, can it say understandingly to itself: "become what you are!"*

. . .

---

*But who are "you"? The one who lets *go*—and *becomes.*

THE EVERYDAY BEING OF THE THERE AND THE FALLING PREY OF DA-SEIN

In returning to the existential structures of the disclosedness of being-in-the-world, our interpretation has in a way lost sight of the everydayness of Da-sein. The analysis must again regain this phenomenal horizon that was our thematic point of departure. Now the question arises: What are the existential characteristics of the disclosedness of being-in-the-world, to the extent that the latter, as something everyday, maintains itself in the mode of being of the they? Is a specific attunement, a special understanding, discourse, and interpretation appropriate to the they? The answer to this question becomes all the more urgent when we remember that Da-sein initially and for the most part is immersed in the they and mastered by it. Is not Da-sein, as thrown being-in-the-world, initially thrown into the publicness of the they? And what else does this publicness mean than the specific disclosedness of the they?

If understanding must be conceived primarily as the potentiality-for-being of Da-sein, we shall be able to gather from an analysis of the understanding and interpretation belonging to the they which possibilities of its being Da-sein as the they has disclosed and appropriated to itself. These possibilities themselves, however, reveal an essential tendency of being of everydayness. And everydayness must finally, when explicated in an ontologically sufficient way, unveil a primordial mode of being of Da-sein in such a way that from it the phenomenon of thrownness which we have pointed out can be exhibited in its existential concreteness.

What is initially required is to make visible the disclosedness of the they, that is, the everyday mode of being of discourse, sight, and interpretation, in specific phenomena. With regard to these, the remark may not be superfluous that our interpretation has a purely ontological intention and is far removed from any moralizing critique of everyday Da-sein and from the aspirations of a "philosophy of culture."

38. Falling Prey and Thrownness

Idle talk, curiosity, and ambiguity characterize the way in which Da-sein is its "there," the disclosedness of being-in-the-world, in an everyday way. As existential determinations, these characteristics are not objectively present in Da-sein; they constitute its being. In them and in the connectedness of their being, a basic kind of the being of everydayness reveals itself, which we call the *entanglement* of Da-sein.

This term, which does not express any negative value judgment, means that Da-sein is initially and for the most part *together with* the "world" that it takes care of. This absorption in . . . mostly has the character of being lost in the publicness of the they. As an authentic potentiality for being a self, Da-sein has initially always already fallen away from itself and fallen prey to the "world." Falling prey to the "world" means being absorbed in being-with-one-another as it is guided by idle talk, curiosity, and ambiguity. What we called the inauthenticity of Da-sein may now be defined more precisely through the interpretation of falling prey. But inauthentic and unauthentic by no means signify "not really," as if Da-sein utterly lost its being in this kind of being. Inauthenticity does not mean anything like no-longer-being-in-the-world, but rather it constitutes precisely a distinctive kind of being-in-the-world which is completely taken in by the world and the *Mitda-sein* of the others in the they. Not-being-its-self functions as a *positive* possibility of beings which are absorbed in a world, essentially taking care of that world. This *nonbeing* must be conceived as the kind of being of Da-sein nearest to it and in which it mostly maintains itself.

Thus neither must the entanglement of Da-sein be interpreted as a "fall" from a purer and higher "primordial condition." Not only do we not have any experience of this ontically, but also no possibilities and guidelines of interpretation ontologically.

As factical being-in-the-world, Da-sein, falling prey, has already fallen *away from itself;* and it has not fallen prey to some being which it first runs into in the course of its being, or perhaps does not, but it has fallen prey to the *world* which itself belongs to its being. Falling prey is an existential determination of Da-sein itself, and says nothing about Da-sein as something objectively present, or about objectively present relations to beings from which it is "derived" or to beings with which it has subsequently gotten into a *commercium.*

The ontological-existential structure of falling prey would also be misunderstood if we wanted to attribute to it the meaning of a bad and deplorable

ontic quality which could perhaps be removed in the advanced stages of human culture.

Neither in our first reference to being-in-the-world as the fundamental constitution of Da-sein nor in our characterization of its constitutive structural factors, did we go beyond an analysis of the *constitution* of this kind of being, and note its character as a phenomenon. It is true that the possible basic kinds of being-in, taking care and concern, were described. But we did not discuss the question of the everyday kind of being of these ways of being. It also became evident that being-in is quite different from a confrontation which merely observes and acts, that is, the concurrent objective presence of a subject and an object. Still, it must have seemed that being-in-the-world functions as a rigid framework within which the possible relations of Da-sein to its world occur, without the "framework" itself being touched upon in its kind of being. But this supposed "framework" itself belongs to the kind of being of Da-sein. An *existential mode* of being-in-the-world is documented in the phenomenon of falling prey.

Idle talk discloses to Da-sein a being toward its world, to others and to itself—a being in which these are understood, but in a mode of groundless floating. Curiosity discloses each and every thing, but in such a way that being-in is everywhere and nowhere. Ambiguity conceals nothing from the understanding of Da-sein, but only in order to suppress being-in-the-world in this uprooted everywhere and nowhere.

With the ontological clarification of the kind of being of everyday being-in-the-world discernible in these phenomena, we first gain an existentially adequate determination of the fundamental constitution of Da-sein. What structure does the "movement" of falling prey show?

Idle talk and the public interpretedness contained in it are constituted in being-with-one-another. Idle talk is not objectively present for itself within the world, as a product detached from being-with-one-another. Nor can it be volatilized to mean something "universal" which, since it essentially belongs to no one, "really" is nothing and "actually" only occurs in individual Da-sein that speaks. Idle talk is the kind of being of being-with-one-another itself, and does not first originate through certain conditions which influence Da-sein "from the outside." But when Da-sein itself presents itself with the possibility in idle talk and public interpretedness of losing itself in the they, of falling prey to groundlessness, that means that Da-sein prepares for itself the constant temptation of falling prey. Being-in-the-world is in itself *tempting*.

Having already become a temptation for itself in this way, the way in which things have been publicly interpreted holds fast to Da-sein in its falling prey. Idle talk and ambiguity, having-seen-everything and having-understood-everything, develop the supposition that the disclosedness of Da-sein thus available and prevalent could guarantee to Da-sein the certainty, genuineness, and fullness of all the possibilities of its being. In the self-certainty and decisiveness of the they, it gets spread abroad increasingly that there is no need of authentic, attuned understanding. The supposition of the they that one is leading and sustaining a full and genuine "life" brings a *tranquillization* to Da-sein, for which everything is in "the best order" and for whom all doors are open. Entangled being-in-the-world, tempting itself, is at the same time *tranquillizing*.

This tranquillization in inauthentic being, however, does not seduce one into stagnation and inactivity, but drives one to uninhibited "busyness." Being entangled in the "world" does not somehow come to rest. Tempting tranquillization aggravates entanglement. With special regard to the interpretation of Da-sein, the opinion may now arise that understanding the most foreign cultures and "synthesizing" them with our own may lead to the thorough and first genuine enlightenment of Da-sein about itself. Versatile curiosity and restlessly knowing it all masquerade as a universal understanding of Da-sein. But fundamentally it remains undetermined and unasked *what* is then really to be understood; nor has it been understood that understanding itself is a potentiality for being which must become *free* solely in one's *ownmost* Da-sein. When Da-sein, tranquillized and "understanding" everything, thus compares itself with everything, it drifts toward an alienation in which its ownmost potentiality for being-in-the-world is concealed. Entangled being-in-the-world is not only tempting and tranquillizing, it is at the same time *alienating*.

However, alienation cannot mean that Da-sein is factically torn away from itself. On the contrary, this alienation drives Da-sein into a kind of being intent upon the most exaggerated "self-dissection" which tries out all kinds of possibilities of interpretation, with the result that the "characterologies" and "typol-

ogies" which it points out are themselves too numerous to grasp. Yet this alienation, which *closes off* to Da-sein its authenticity and possibility, even if only that of genuinely getting stranded, still does not surrender it to beings which it itself is not, but forces it into its inauthenticity, into a possible kind of being of *itself*. The tempting and tranquillizing alienation of falling prey has its own kind of movement with the consequence that Da-sein gets *entangled* in itself.

The phenomena pointed out of temptation, tranquillizing, alienation, and self-entangling (entanglement) characterize the specific kind of being of falling prey. We call this kind of "movement" of Da-sein in its own being the *plunge*. Da-sein plunges out of itself into itself, into the groundlessness and nothingness of inauthentic everydayness. But this plunge remains concealed from it by the way things have been publicly interpreted so that it is interpreted as "getting ahead" and "living concretely."

The kind of movement of plunging into and within the groundlessness of inauthentic being in the they constantly tears understanding away from projecting authentic possibilities, and into the tranquillized supposition of possessing or attaining everything. Since the understanding is thus constantly torn away from authenticity and into the they (although always with a sham of authenticity), the movement of falling prey is characterized by *eddying*.

Not only does falling prey determine being-in-the-world existentially; at the same time the eddy reveals the character of throwing and movement of thrownness which can force itself upon Da-sein in its attunement. Not only is thrownness not a "finished fact," it is also not a self-contained fact. The facticity of Da-sein is such that Da-sein, *as long as* it is what it is, remains in the throw and is sucked into the eddy of the they's inauthenticity. Thrownness, in which facticity can be seen phenomenally, belongs to Da-sein, which is concerned in its being about that being. Da-sein exists factically.

But now that falling prey has been exhibited, have we not set forth a phenomenon which directly speaks *against* the definition in which the formal idea of existence was indicated? Can Da-sein be conceived as a being whose being is concerned *with* potentiality for being if this being *has lost itself* precisely in its everydayness and "lives" *away from itself* in falling prey? Falling prey to the world is, however, phenomenal "evidence" *against* the existentiality of Da-sein only if Da-sein is posited as an isolated I-subject, as a self-point from which it moves away. Then the world is an object. Falling prey to the world is then reinterpreted ontologically as objective presence in the manner of innerworldly beings. However, if we hold on to the being of Da-sein in the constitution indicated of *being-in-the-world,* it becomes evident that falling prey *as the kind of being of this being-in* rather represents the most elemental proof *for* the existentiality of Da-sein. In falling prey, nothing other than our potentiality for being-in-the-world is the issue, even if in the mode of inauthenticity. Da-sein *can* fall prey *only* because it is concerned with understanding, attuned being-in-the-world. On the other hand, *authentic* existence is nothing which hovers over entangled everydayness, but is existentially only a modified grasp of everydayness.

Nor does the phenomenon of falling prey give something like a "night view" of Da-sein, a property occurring ontically which might serve to round out the harmless aspect of this being. Falling prey reveals an *essential,* ontological structure of Da-sein itself. Far from determining its nocturnal side, it constitutes all of its days in their everydayness.

Our existential, ontological interpretation thus does not make any ontic statement about the "corruption of human nature," not because the necessary evidence is lacking but because its problematic is *prior to* any statement about corruption or incorruption. Falling prey is an ontological concept of motion. Ontically, we have not decided whether human being is "drowned in sin," in the *status corruptionis,* or whether he walks in the *status integritatis* or finds himself in an interim stage, the *status gratiae.* But faith and "worldview," when they state such and such a thing and when they speak about Da-sein as being-in-the-world, must come back to the existential structures set forth, provided that their statements at the same time claim to be *conceptually* comprehensible.

The leading question of this chapter pursued the being of the there. Its theme was the ontological constitution of the disclosedness essentially belonging to Da-sein. The being of disclosedness is constituted in attunement, understanding, and discourse. Its everyday mode of being is characterized by idle talk, curiosity, and ambiguity. These show the kind of movement of falling prey with the essential characteristics of temptation, tranquillization, alienation, and entanglement.

But with this analysis the totality of the existential constitution of Da-sein has been laid bare in its main features and the phenomenal basis has been obtained for a "comprehensive" interpretation of the being of Da-sein as care.

· · ·

VI. CARE AS THE BEING OF DA-SEIN

40. The Fundamental Attunement of *Angst* as an Eminent Disclosedness of Da-sein

One possibility of being of Da-sein is to give ontic "information" about itself as a being. Such information is possible only in the disclosedness belonging to Da-sein which is based on attunement and understanding. To what extent is *Angst* a distinctive attunement? How is Da-sein brought before itself in it through its own being so that phenomenologically the being disclosed in *Angst* is defined as such in its being, or adequate preparations can be made for doing so?

With the intention of penetrating to the being of the totality of the structural whole, we shall take our point of departure from the concrete analysis of entanglement carried out in the last chapter. The absorption of Da-sein in the they and in the "world" taken care of reveals something like a *flight* of Da-sein from itself as an authentic potentiality for being itself. This phenomenon of the flight of Da-sein *from itself* and its authenticity seems, however, to be least appropriate to serve as a phenomenal foundation for the following inquiry. In this flight, Da-sein precisely does not bring itself before itself. In accordance with its ownmost trait of entanglement, this turning away leads *away from* Da-sein. But in investigating such phenomena, our inquiry must guard against conflating ontic-existentiell characteristics with ontological-existential interpretation, and must not overlook the positive, phenomenal foundations provided for this interpretation by such a characterization.

· · ·

That for which *Angst* is anxious is not a *definite* kind of being and possibility of Da-sein. The threat itself is, after all, indefinite and thus cannot penetrate threateningly to this or that factically concrete potentiality of being. What *Angst* is anxious for is being-in-the-world itself. In *Angst,* the things at hand in the surrounding world sink away, and so do innerworldly beings in general. The "world" can offer nothing more, nor can the *Mitda-sein* of others. Thus *Angst* takes away from Da-sein the possibility of understanding itself, falling prey, in terms of the "world" and the public way of being interpreted. It throws Da-sein back upon that for which it is anxious, its authentic potentiality-for-being-in-the-world. *Angst* individuates Da-sein to its ownmost being-in-the-world which, as understanding, projects itself essentially upon possibilities. Thus along with that for which it is anxious, *Angst* discloses Da-sein as *being-possible,* and indeed as what can be individualized in individuation of its own accord.

Angst reveals in Da-sein its *being toward* its ownmost potentiality of being, that is, *being free for* the freedom of choosing and grasping itself. *Angst* brings Da-sein *before its being free for . . .* (*propensio in*), the authenticity of its being as possibility which it always already is. But at the same time, it is this being to which Da-sein as being-in-the-world is entrusted.

That *about which Angst* is anxious reveals itself as that *for which* it is anxious: being-in-the-world. The identity of that about which and that for which one has *Angst* extends even to anxiousness itself. For as attunement, anxiousness is a fundamental mode of being-in-the-world. *The existential identity of disclosing and what is disclosed so that in what is disclosed the world is disclosed as world, as being-in, individualized, pure, thrown potentiality for being, makes it clear that with the phenomenon of* Angst *a distinctive kind of attunement has become the theme of our interpretation. Angst* individualizes and thus discloses Da-sein as "*solus ipse.*" This existential "solipsism," however, is so far from transposing an isolated subject-thing into the harmless vacuum of a worldless occurrence that it brings Da-sein in an extreme sense precisely before its world as world, and thus itself before itself as being-in-the-world.

Again, everyday discourse and the everyday interpretation of Da-sein furnish the most unbiased evidence that *Angst* as a basic attunement is disclosive in this way. We said earlier that attunement reveals "how one is." In *Angst* one has an "*uncanny*" feeling. Here the peculiar indefiniteness of that which Da-sein finds itself involved in with *Angst* initially finds expression: the nothing and nowhere. But uncanniness means at the same time not-being-at-home.

. . .

Da-sein and Temporality, *from* Being and Time

I   THE POSSIBLE BEING-A-WHOLE OF DA-SEIN AND BEING-TOWARD-DEATH

50.   A Preliminary Sketch of the Existential and Ontological Structure of Death

From our considerations of something outstanding, end, and totality there has resulted the necessity of interpreting the phenomenon of death as being-toward-the-end in terms of the fundamental constitution of Da-sein. Only in this way can it become clear how a wholeness constituted by being-toward-the-end is possible in Da-sein itself, in accordance with its structure of being. We have seen that care is the fundamental constitution of Da-sein. The ontological significance of this expression was expressed in the "definition": being-ahead-of-itself-already-being-in (the world) as being-together-with beings encountered (within the world). Thus the fundamental characteristics of the being of Da-sein are expressed: in being-ahead-of-itself, existence, in already-being-in . . . , facticity, in being-together-with . . . , falling prey. Provided that death belongs to the being of Da-sein in an eminent sense, it (or being-toward-the-end) must be able to be defined in terms of these characteristics.

. . .

Death is a possibility of being that Da-sein always has to take upon itself. With death, Da-sein stands before itself in its ownmost potentiality-of-being. In this possibility, Da-sein is concerned about its being-in-the-world absolutely. Its death is the possibility of no-longer-being-able-to-be-there. When Da-sein is imminent to itself as this possibility, it is *completely* thrown back upon its ownmost potentiality-of-being. Thus imminent to itself, all relations to other Da-sein are dissolved in it. This nonrelational ownmost possibility is at the same time the most extreme one. As a potentiality of being, Da-sein is unable to bypass the possibility of death. Death is the possibility of the absolute impossibility of Da-sein. Thus *death* reveals itself as the *ownmost nonrelational possibility not to be bypassed.* As such, it is *an eminent* imminence. Its existential possibility is grounded in the fact that

Da-sein is essentially disclosed to itself, in the way of being-ahead-of-itself. This structural factor of care has its most primordial concretion in being-toward-death. Being-toward-the-end becomes phenomenally clearer as being toward the eminent possibility of Da-sein which we have characterized.

The ownmost nonrelational possibility not to be bypassed is not created by Da-sein subsequently and occasionally in the course of its being. Rather, when Da-sein exists, it is already *thrown* into this possibility. Initially and for the most part, Da-sein does not have any explicit or even theoretical knowledge of the fact that it is delivered over to its death, and that death thus belongs to being-in-the-world. Thrownness into death reveals itself to it more primordially and penetratingly in the attunement of *Angst*. *Angst* in the face of death is *Angst* "in the face of" the ownmost non-relational potentiality-of-being not to be bypassed. What *Angst* is about is being-in-the-world itself. What *Angst* is about is the potentiality-of-being of Da-sein absolutely. *Angst* about death must not be confused with a fear of one's demise. It is not an arbitrary and chance "weak" mood of the individual, but, as a fundamental attunement of Da-sein, the disclosedness of the fact that Da-sein exists as thrown being-*toward*-its-end. Thus the existential concept of dying is clarified as thrown being toward the ownmost nonrelational potentiality-of-being not to be bypassed. Precision is gained by distinguishing this from pure disappearance, and also from merely perishing, and finally from the "experience" of a demise.

. . .

51. Being-toward-Death and the Everydayness of Da-sein

The exposition of everyday, average being-toward-death was oriented toward the structures of everydayness developed earlier. In being-toward-death, Da-sein is related *to itself* as an eminent potentiality-of-being. But the self of everydayness is the they which is constituted in public interpretedness which expresses itself in idle talk. Thus, idle talk must make manifest in what way everyday Da-sein interprets its being-toward-death. Understanding, which is also always attuned, that is, mooded, always forms the basis of this interpretation. Thus we must ask how the attuned understanding lying in the idle talk of the they has disclosed being-toward-death. How is the they related in an understanding way to its ownmost non-

relational possibility not-to-be-bypassed of Da-sein? What attunement discloses to the they that it has been delivered over to death, and in what way?

The publicness of everyday being-with-one-another "knows" death as a constantly occurring event, as a "case of death." Someone or another "dies," be it a neighbor or a stranger. People unknown to us "die" daily and hourly. "Death" is encountered as a familiar event occurring within the world. As such, it remains in the inconspicuousness characteristic of everyday encounters. The they has also already secured an interpretation for this event. The "fleeting" talk about this which is either expressed or else mostly kept back says: One also dies at the end, but for now one is not involved.

The analysis of "one dies" reveals unambiguously the kind of being of everyday being toward death. In such talk, death is understood as an indeterminate something which first has to show up from somewhere, but which right now is *not yet objectively present* for oneself, and is thus no threat. "One dies" spreads the opinion that death, so to speak, strikes the they. The public interpretation of Da-sein says that "one dies" because in this way everybody can convince him/herself that in no case is it I myself, for this one is *no one*. "Dying" is levelled down to an event which does concern Da-sein, but which belongs to no one in particular. If idle talk is always ambiguous, so is this way of talking about death. Dying, which is essentially and irreplaceably mine, is distorted into a publicly occurring event which the they encounters. Characteristic talk speaks about death as a constantly occurring "case." It treats it as something always already "real," and veils its character of possibility and concomitantly the two factors belonging to it, that it is nonrelational and cannot-be-bypassed. With such ambiguity, Da-sein puts itself in the position of losing itself in the they with regard to an eminent potentiality-of-being that belongs to its own self. The they justifies and aggravates the *temptation* of covering over for itself its ownmost being-toward-death.

The evasion of death which covers over, dominates everydayness so stubbornly that, in being-with-one-another, the "neighbors" often try to convince the "dying person" that he will escape death and soon return again to the tranquillized everydayness of his world taken care of. This "concern" has the intention of thus "comforting" the "dying person." It wants to bring him back to Da-sein by helping him to veil completely his ownmost nonrelational possibility.

Thus, the they makes sure of a *constant tranquilliza-tion about death*. But, basically, this tranquillization is not only for the "dying person," but just as much for "those who are comforting him." And even in the case of a demise, publicness is still not to be disturbed and made uneasy by the event in the carefreeness it has made sure of. Indeed, the dying of others is seen often as a social inconvenience, if not a downright tactlessness, from which publicness should be spared.

But along with this tranquillization, which keeps Da-sein away from its death, the they at the same time justifies itself and makes itself respectable by silently ordering the way in which *one* is supposed to behave toward death in general. Even "thinking about death" is regarded publicly as cowardly fear, a sign of insecu-rity on the part of Da-sein and a dark flight from the world. *The they does not permit the courage to have* Angst *about death*. The dominance of the public inter-pretedness of the they has already decided what at-tunement is to determine our stance toward death. In *Angst* about death, Da-sein is brought before itself as delivered over to its possibility not-to-be-bypassed. The they is careful to distort this *Angst* into the fear of a future event. Angst, made ambiguous as fear, is, moreover, taken as a weakness which no self-assured Da-sein is permitted to know. What is "proper" ac-cording to the silent decree of the they is the indiffer-ent calm as to the "fact" that one dies. The cultivation of such a "superior" indifference *estranges* Da-sein from its ownmost nonrelational potentiality-of-being.

Temptation, tranquillization, and estrangement, however, characterize the kind of being of *falling prey*. Entangled, everyday being-toward-death is a con-stant *flight from death*. Being *toward* the end has the mode of *evading that end*—reinterpreting it, under-standing it inauthentically, and veiling it. Factically one's own Da-sein is always already dying, that is, it is in a being-toward-its-end. And it conceals this fact from itself by reinterpreting death as a case of death occurring every day with others, a case which always assures us still more clearly that "one oneself" is still "alive." But in the entangled flight *from* death, the everydayness of Da-sein bears witness to the fact that the they itself is always already determined *as being toward death*, even when it is not explicitly engaged in "thinking about death." *Even in average everydayness, Da-sein is constantly concerned with its ownmost non-relational potentiality-of-being not-to-be-bypassed, if*

only in the mode of taking care of things in a mode of untroubled indifference toward *the most extreme possi-bility of its existence.*

The exposition of everyday being-toward-death, however, gives us at the same time a directive to attempt to secure a complete existential concept of being-toward-the-end, by a more penetrating inter-pretation in which entangled being-toward-death is taken as an evasion *of death. That from which* one flees has been made visible in a phenomenally adequate way. We should now be able to project phenomeno-logically how evasive Da-sein itself understands its death.

52. Everyday Being-toward-Death and the Complete Existential Concept of Death

They say that it is certain that "death" comes. *They* say it and overlook the fact that, in order to be able to be certain of death, Da-sein itself must always be certain of its ownmost nonrelational potentiality-of-being not-to-be-bypassed. They say that death is certain, and thus entrench in Da-sein the illusion that it is *itself* certain of its own death. And what is the ground of everyday being-certain? Evidently it is not just mutual persuasion. Yet one experiences daily the "dy-ing" of others. Death is an undeniable "fact of expe-rience."

The way in which everyday being-toward-death understands the certainty thus grounded, betrays it-self when it tries to "think" about death, even when it does so with critical foresight—that is to say, in an appropriate way. So far as one knows, all human be-ings "die." Death is probable to the highest degree for every human being, yet it is not "unconditionally" cer-tain. Strictly speaking, "only" an *empirical* certainty may be attributed to death. Such certainty falls short of the highest certainty, the apodictical one, which we attain in certain areas of theoretical knowledge.

In this "critical" determination of the certainty of death and its imminence, what is manifested in the first instance is, once again, the failure to recognize the kind of being of Da-sein and the being-toward-death belonging to it, a failure characteristic of every-dayness. *The fact that demise, as an event that occurs, is "only" empirically certain, in no way decides about the certainty of death.* Cases of death may be the facti-cal occasion for the fact that Da-sein initially notices death at all. But, remaining within the empirical certainty which we characterized, Da-sein cannot become certain at all of death as it "is." Although in the publicness of the they Da-sein seemingly "talks" only of this "empirical" certainty of death, *basically* it does *not* keep exclusively and primarily to those cases of death that merely occur. *Evading its death,* everyday being-toward-the-end is indeed certain of death in another way than it itself would like to realize in purely theoretical considerations. For the most part, everydayness veils this from itself "in another way." It does not dare to become transparent to itself in this way. We have already characterized the everyday attunement that consists in an air of superiority with regard to the certain "fact" of death—a superiority that is "anxiously" concerned while seemingly free of *Angst.* In this attunement, everydayness acknowledges a "higher" certainty than the merely empirical one. One *knows* about the certainty of death, and yet "*is*" not really certain about it. The entangled everydayness of Da-sein knows about the certainty of death, and yet avoids *being*-certain. But in the light of what it evades, this evasion bears witness phenomenally to the fact that death must be grasped as the ownmost nonrelational, *certain* possibility not-to-be-bypassed.

One says that death certainly comes, but not right away. With this "but . . . ," the they denies that death is certain. "Not right away" is not a purely negative statement, but a self-interpretation of the they with which it refers itself to what is initially accessible to Da-sein to take care of. Everydayness penetrates to the urgency of taking care of things, and divests itself of the fetters of a weary, "inactive thinking about death." Death is postponed to "sometime later," by relying on the so-called "general opinion." Thus the they covers over what is peculiar to the certainty of death, *that it is possible in every moment.* Together with the certainty of death goes the *indefiniteness* of its when. Everyday being-toward-death evades this indefiniteness by making it something definite. But this procedure cannot mean calculating when the demise is due to arrive. Da-sein rather flees from such definiteness. Everyday taking care of things makes definite for itself the indefiniteness of certain death by interposing before it those manageable urgencies and possibilities of the everyday matters nearest to us.

But covering over this indefiniteness also covers over certainty. Thus the ownmost character of the possibility of death gets covered over: a possibility that

is certain, and yet indefinite, that is, possible at any moment.

Now that we have completed our interpretation of the everyday talk of the they about death and the way death enters Da-sein, we have been led to the characteristics of certainty and indefiniteness. The full existential and ontological concept of death can now be defined as follows: *As the end of Da-sein, death is the ownmost nonrelational, certain, and, as such, indefinite and not to be bypassed possibility of Da-sein.* As the end of Da-sein, *death is* in this being-*toward*-its-end. . . .

53. Existential Project of an Authentic Being-toward-Death

Da-sein is constituted by disclosedness, that is, by attuned understanding. *Authentic* being-toward-death can*not evade* its ownmost nonrelational possibility or *cover* it *over* in this flight and *reinterpret* it for the common sense of the they. The existential project of an authentic being-toward-death must thus set forth the factors of such a being which are constitutive for it as an understanding of death—in the sense of being toward this possibility without fleeing it or covering it over. . . .

Evidently being-toward-death, which is now in question, cannot have the character of being out for something and taking care of it with a view toward its actualization. For one thing, death as something possible is not a possible thing at hand or objectively present, but a possibility-of-being of *Da-sein.* Then, however, taking care of the actualization of what is thus possible would have to mean bringing about one's own demise. Thus Da-sein would precisely deprive itself of the very ground for an existing being-toward-death.

Thus if being-toward-death is not meant as an "actualization" of death, neither can it mean to dwell near the end in its possibility. This kind of behavior would amount to "thinking about death," thinking about this possibility, how and when it might be actualized. Brooding over death does not completely take away from it its character of possibility. It is always brooded over as something coming, but we weaken it by calculating how to have it at our disposal. As something possible, death is supposed to show as little as possible of its possibility. On the contrary, if being-toward-death has to disclose understandingly the possibility which we have characterized as *such,* then in such being-toward-death this possibility must not be weakened, it must be understood *as possibility,* cultivated *as possibility,* and *endured as possibility* in our relation to it.

. . .

But being toward this possibility, as being-toward-death, should relate itself to that *death* so that it reveals itself, in this being and for it, *as possibility.* Terminologically, we shall formulate this being toward possibility as *anticipation of this possibility.* But does not this mode of behavior contain an approach to the possible, and does not its actualization emerge with its nearness? In this kind of coming near, however, one does not tend toward making something real available and taking care of it, but as one comes nearer understandingly, the possibility of the possible only becomes "greater." *The nearest nearness of being-toward-death as possibility is as far removed as possible from anything real.* The more clearly this possibility is understood, the more purely does understanding penetrate to it *as the possibility of the impossibility of existence in general.* As possibility, death gives Da-sein nothing to "be actualized" and nothing which it itself could *be* as something real. It is the possibility of the impossibility of every mode of behavior toward . . . , of every way of existing. In running ahead to this possibility, it becomes "greater and greater," that is, it reveals itself as something which knows no measure at all, no more or less, but means the possibility of the measureless impossibility of existence. Essentially, this possibility offers no support for becoming intent on something, for "spelling out" the real thing that is possible and so forgetting its possibility. As anticipation of possibility, being-toward-death first *makes* this possibility *possible* and sets it free as possibility.

Being-toward-death is the anticipation of a potentiality-of-being of *that* being whose kind of being is anticipation itself. In the anticipatory revealing of this potentiality-of-being, Da-sein discloses itself to itself with regard to its most extreme possibility. But to project oneself upon one's ownmost potentiality of being means to be able to understand oneself in the being of the being thus revealed: to exist. Anticipation shows itself as the possibility of understanding one's *ownmost* and extreme potentiality-of-being, that is, as the possibility of *authentic existence.* Its ontological constitution must be made visible by setting forth the con-

crete structure of anticipation of death. How is the phenomenal definition of this structure to be accomplished? Evidently by defining the characteristics of anticipatory disclosure which must belong to it so that it can become the pure understanding of the ownmost nonrelational possibility not-to-be-bypassed which is certain and, as such, indefinite. We must remember that understanding does not primarily mean staring at a meaning, but understanding oneself in the potentiality-of-being that reveals itself in the project.

Death is the *ownmost* possibility of Da-sein. Being toward it discloses to Da-sein its *ownmost* potentiality-of-being in which it is concerned about the being of Da-sein absolutely. Here the fact can become evident to Da-sein that in the eminent possibility of itself it is torn away from the they, that is, anticipation can always already have torn itself away from the they. The understanding of this "ability," however, first reveals its factical lostness in the everydayness of the they-self.

The ownmost possibility is *nonrelational.* Anticipation lets Da-sein understand that it has to take over solely from itself the potentiality-of-being in which it is concerned absolutely about its ownmost being. Death does not just "belong" in an undifferentiated way to one's own Da-sein, but it *lays claim* on it as something *individual.* The nonrelational character of death understood in anticipation individualizes Da-sein down to itself. This individualizing is a way in which the "there" is disclosed for existence. It reveals the fact that any being-together-with what is taken care of and any being-with the others fails when one's ownmost potentiality-of-being is at stake. Da-sein can *authentically* be *itself* only when it makes that possible of its own accord. But if taking care of things and being concerned fail us, this does not, however, mean at all that these modes of Da-sein have been cut off from its authentic being a self. As essential structures of the constitution of Da-sein they also belong to the condition of the possibility of existence in general. Da-sein is authentically itself only if it projects itself, *as* being-together-with things taken care of and concernful being-with . . . , primarily upon its ownmost potentiality-of-being, rather than upon the possibility of the they-self. Anticipation of its nonrelational possibility forces the being that anticipates into the possibility of taking over its ownmost being of its own accord.

The ownmost nonrelational possibility is *not to be bypassed*. Being toward this possibility lets Da-sein understand that the most extreme possibility of existence is imminent, that of giving itself up. But anticipation does not evade the impossibility of bypassing death, as does inauthentic being-toward-death, but *frees* itself *for* it. Becoming free *for* one's own death in anticipation frees one from one's lostness in chance possibilities urging themselves upon us, so that the factual possibilities lying before the possibility not-to-be-bypassed can first be authentically understood and chosen. Anticipation discloses to existence that its extreme inmost possibility lies in giving itself up and thus shatters all one's clinging to whatever existence one has reached. In anticipation, Da-sein guards itself against falling back behind itself, or behind the potentiality-for-being that it has understood. It guards against "becoming too old for its victories" (Nietzsche). Free for its ownmost possibilities, that are determined by the *end,* and so understood as *finite,* Da-sein prevents the danger that it may, by its own finite understanding of existence, fail to recognize that it is getting overtaken by the existence-possibilities of others, or that it may misinterpret these possibilities, thus divesting itself of its ownmost factical existence. As the nonrelational possibility, death individualizes, but only, as the possibility not-to-be-bypassed, in order to make Da-sein as being-with understand the potentialities-of-being of the others. Because anticipation of the possibility not-to-be-bypassed also disclosed all the possibilities lying before it, this anticipation includes the possibility of taking the *whole* of Da-sein in advance in an existentiell way, that is, the possibility of existing as a *whole potentiality-of-being.*

What is characteristic about authentic, existentially projected being-toward-death can be summarized as follows: *Anticipation reveals to Da-sein its lostness in the they-self, and brings it face to face with the possibility to be itself, primarily unsupported by concern taking care of things, but to be itself in passionate anxious **freedom toward death** which is free of the illusions of the they, factical, and certain of itself.*

All relations, belonging to being-toward-death, to the complete content of the most extreme possibility of Da-sein, constitute an anticipation that they com-bine in revealing, unfolding, and holding fast, as that which makes this possibility possible. The existential project in which anticipation has been delimited, has made visible the *ontological* possibility of an existentiell, authentic being-toward-death. But with this, the possibility then appears of an authentic potentiality-for-being-a-whole—*but only as an ontological possibility.*

· · ·

II   THE ATTESTATION OF DA-SEIN OF AN AUTHENTIC POTENTIALITY-OF-BEING, AND RESOLUTENESS

60.   The Existential Structure of the Authentic Potentiality-of-Being Attested in Conscience

We shall call the eminent, authentic disclosedness attested in Da-sein itself by its conscience—the *reticent projecting oneself upon one's ownmost being-guilty which is ready for* Angst—*resoluteness.*

Resoluteness is an eminent mode of the disclosedness of Da-sein. But in an earlier passage disclosedness was interpreted existentially as *primordial truth.* This is not primarily a quality of "judgment" or of any particular mode of behavior at all, but an essential constituent of being-in-the-world as such. Truth must be understood as a fundamental existential. Our ontological clarification of the statement that "Da-sein is in the truth" has pointed to the primordial disclosedness of this being as the *truth of existence;* and for its delineation we have referred to the analysis of the authenticity of Da-sein.

· · ·

… Now, in resoluteness the most primordial truth of Da-sein has been reached, because it is *authentic.* The disclosedness of the there discloses equiprimordially the whole of being-in-the-world—the world, being-in, and the self that is this being as "I am." With the disclosedness of world, innerworldly beings have always already been discovered. The discoveredness of things at hand and objectively present is grounded in the discoveredness of the world; for if the actual totality of relevance of things at hand is to be freed, this requires a pre-understanding of significance. In understanding significance, Da-sein, taking care of things, is circumspectly referred to the things at hand encountered. The understanding of significance as the disclosedness of the actual world is again grounded in the understanding of the for-the-sake-of-which, to which discovering of the totality of relevance goes back. In seeking shelter, sustenance, and livelihood, we do so for-the-sake-of the constant possibilities of Da-sein that are near to it; upon these, this being which is concerned about its being has always already projected itself. Thrown into its "there," Da-sein is always factically dependent on a definite "world"— its "world." At the same time those nearest factical projects are guided by the *lostness* in the they taking care of things. This lostness can be summoned by one's own Da-sein, the summons can be understood in the mode of resoluteness. But *authentic* disclosedness then modifies equiprimordially the discoveredness of "world" grounded in it and the disclosedness of being-with with others. The "world" at hand does not become different as far as "content," the circle of the others is not exchanged for a new one, and yet the being toward things at hand which understands and takes care of things, and the concerned being-with with the others is now defined in terms of their ownmost potentiality-of-being-a-self.

As *authentic being a self,* resoluteness does not detach Da-sein from its world, nor does it isolate it as free floating ego. How could it, if resoluteness as authentic disclosedness is, after all, nothing other than *authentically being-in-the-world*? Resoluteness brings the self right into its being together with things at hand, actually taking care of them, and pushes it toward concerned being-with with the others.

In the light of the for-the-sake-of-which of the potentiality-of-being which it has chosen, resolute Da-sein frees itself for its world. The resoluteness toward itself first brings Da-sein to the possibility of letting the others who are with it "be" in their ownmost potentiality-of-being, and also discloses that potentiality in concern which leaps ahead and frees. Resolute Da-sein can become the "conscience" of others. It is from the authentic being a self of resoluteness that authentic being-with-one-another first arises, not from ambiguous and jealous stipulations and talkative fraternizing in the they and in what they wants to undertake.

In accordance with its ontological essence, resoluteness always belongs to a factical Da-sein. The essence of this being is its existence. Resoluteness "exists" only as a resolution that projects itself understandingly. But to what does Da-sein resolve itself in resoluteness? On what is it to resolve? *Only* the resolution itself can answer this. It would be a complete misunderstanding of the phenomenon of resoluteness if one were to believe that it is simply a matter of receptively taking up possibilities presented and suggested. *Resolution is precisely the disclosive projection and determination of the actual factical possibility.* The *indefiniteness* that characterizes every factically projected potentiality-of-being of Da-sein *belongs* necessarily to resoluteness. Resoluteness is certain of itself only in a resolution. But the *existentiell indefiniteness* of resoluteness never makes itself definite except in a resolution; it nevertheless has its *existential definiteness.*

What one resolves upon in resoluteness is prefigured ontologically in the existentiality of Da-sein in general as a potentiality-of-being in the mode of heedful concern. But, as care, Da-sein is determined by facticity and falling prey. Disclosed in its "there," it stays equiprimordially in truth and in untruth. This "really" is true in particular for resoluteness as authentic truth. Thus resoluteness appropriates untruth authentically. Da-sein is always already in irresoluteness, and perhaps will be soon again. The term irresoluteness merely expresses the phenomenon that was interpreted as being at the mercy of the dominant interpretedness of the they. As the they-self, Da-sein is "lived" by the commonsense ambiguity of publicness in which no one resolves, but which has always already made its decision. Resoluteness means letting oneself be summoned out of one's lostness in the they. The irresoluteness of the they nevertheless remains in dominance, but it cannot attack resolute existence. As the counter-concept to existentially understood resoluteness, irresoluteness does not mean an ontic, psychical quality in the sense of being burdened with inhibitions. Even resolutions are dependent upon the they and its world. Understanding this is one of the things that resolution discloses, in that resoluteness first gives to Da-sein its authentic transparency. In resoluteness, Da-sein is concerned with its ownmost potentiality-of-being that, as thrown, can project itself only upon definite, factical possibilities.

.   .   .

III   THE AUTHENTIC POTENTIALITY-FOR-BEING-A-WHOLE OF DA-SEIN

62.   The Existentielly Authentic Potentiality-for-Being-a-Whole of Da-sein as Anticipatory Resoluteness

Resoluteness was characterized as the reticent self-projecting upon one's ownmost being-guilty, and as demanding *Angst* of oneself. Being-guilty belongs to Da-sein and means: null *being* the ground of a nullity. The "guilty" that belongs to the being of Da-sein admits neither of increase nor decrease. It lies *before* all quantification, if the latter has any meaning at all. Being essentially guilty, Da-sein is not just guilty *occasionally* and *other times not*. Wanting-to-have-a-conscience resolves itself for this being-guilty. The intrinsic sense of resoluteness is to project upon itself this being-guilty that Da-sein is *as long as it is.* Taking over this "guilt" existentielly in resoluteness occurs authentically only if resoluteness in its disclosing of Da-sein has become so transparent that it understands being-guilty *as something constant.* But this understanding is made possible only in such a way that Da-sein discloses to itself its potentiality-of-being "up to its end." The *being*-at-an-end of Da-sein, however, means existentially being-*toward*-the-end. Resoluteness becomes authentically what it can be as *being-toward-the-end-that-understands,* that is, an anticipation of death. Resoluteness does not simply "have" a connection with anticipation as something other than itself. *It harbours in itself authentic being-toward-death as the possible existentiell modality of its own authenticity.* We want now to clarify this "connection" phenomenally.

Resoluteness means: letting oneself be called forth to one's ownmost *being*-guilty. Being-*guilty* belongs to the being of Da-sein itself, which we defined primarily as potentiality-of-being. The statement that Da-sein "is" constantly guilty can only mean that it always maintains itself in this being either as authentic or inauthentic existence. *Being*-guilty is not just a lasting quality of something constantly objectively present, but the *existentiell possibility* of *being* authentically or inauthentically guilty. "Guilty" *is* always only in the actual factical potentiality-of-being. Thus, being-guilty must be conceived as a potentiality-for-being-guilty, because it belongs to the *being* of Da-

sein. Resoluteness projects itself upon this potentiality-of-being, that is, understands itself in it. Thus, this understanding stays in a primordial possibility of Da-sein. It stays *in it authentically* when resoluteness is primordially what it tends to be. But we revealed the primordial being of Da-sein toward its potentiality-of-being as being-toward-death, that is, toward the eminent possibility of Da-sein which we characterized. Anticipation disclosed this possibility as possibility. Thus, resoluteness becomes a primordial being toward the ownmost potentiality-of-being of Da-sein only *as anticipatory.* Resoluteness understands the "can" of its potentiality-for-being-guilty only when it "qualifies" itself as being-toward-death.

Resolutely, Da-sein takes over authentically in its existence the fact that it *is* the null ground of its nullity. We conceived of death existentially as what we characterized as the possibility of the *im*possibility of existence, that is, as the absolute nothingness of Da-sein. Death is not pieced on to Da-sein as its "end," but, as care, Da-sein is the thrown (that is, null) ground of its death. The nothingness primordially dominant in the being of Da-sein is revealed to it in authentic being-toward-death. Anticipation makes being-guilty evident only on the basis of the *whole* being of Da-sein. Care contains death and guilt equiprimordially. Only anticipatory resoluteness understands the potentiality-for-being-guilty *authentically and wholly,* that is, *primordially.*

. . .

With the phenomenon of resoluteness we were led to the primordial *truth* of existence. Resolute, Da-sein is revealed to itself in its actual factical potentiality-of-being in such a way that it itself *is* this revealing and being revealed. To any truth, there belongs a corresponding holding-for-true. The explicit appropriation of what is disclosed or discovered is *being*-certain. The primordial truth of existence requires an equiprimordial being-certain in which one holds oneself in what resoluteness discloses. It *gives* itself the actual factical situation and *brings* itself into that situation. The situation cannot be calculated in advance and pregiven like something objectively present waiting to be grasped. It is disclosed only in a free act of resolve that has not been determined beforehand, but is open to the possibility of such determination. *What, then, does the certainty belonging to such resoluteness mean?* This certainty must hold itself in what is disclosed in resolution. But this means that it simply cannot become *rigid* about the situation, but must understand that the resolution must be *kept* free and *open* for the actual factical possibility in accordance with its own meaning as a disclosure. The certainty of the resolution means *keeping oneself free for* the possibility of *taking it back,* a possibility that is always factically necessary. This holding-for-true in resoluteness (as the truth of existence), however, by no means lets us fall back into irresoluteness. On the contrary, this holding-for-true, as a resolute holding oneself free for taking back, is the *authentic resoluteness to retrieve itself.* But thus one's very lostness in irresoluteness is existentielly undermined. The holding-for-true that belongs to resoluteness tends, in accordance with its meaning, toward *constantly* keeping itself free, that is, to keep itself free for the *whole* potentiality-of-being of Da-sein. This constant certainty is guaranteed to resoluteness only in such a way that it relates to that possibility of which it can *be* absolutely certain. In its death, Da-sein must absolutely "take itself back." Constantly certain of this, that is, *anticipating,* resoluteness gains its authentic and whole certainty.

But Da-sein is equiprimordially in untruth. Anticipatory resoluteness at the same time gives Da-sein the primordial certainty of its being closed off. In anticipatory resoluteness, Da-sein *holds* itself open for its constant lostness in the irresoluteness of the they—a lostness which is possible from the very ground of its own being. As a constant possibility of Da-sein, irresoluteness is *also certain.* Resoluteness, transparent to itself, understands that the *indefiniteness* of its potentiality-of-being is always determined only in a resolution with regard to the actual situation. It knows about the indefiniteness that prevails in a being that exists. But this knowledge must itself arise from an authentic disclosure if it is to correspond to authentic resoluteness. Although it always becomes certain in resolution, the *indefiniteness* of one's own potentiality-of-being, however, always reveals itself *completely* only in being-toward-death. Anticipation brings Da-sein face to face with a possibility that is constantly certain and yet remains indefinite at every moment as to when this possibility becomes impossibility. Anticipation makes evident the fact that this being has been thrown into the indefiniteness of its "borderline situation," when, resolved upon the latter, Da-sein gains its authentic potentiality-of-being-a-whole. . . .

Anticipatory resoluteness is not a way out fabricated for the purpose of "overcoming" death, but it is rather the understanding that follows the call of conscience and that frees for death the possibility of *gaining power over* the *existence* of Da-sein and of basically dispersing every fugitive self-covering-over. Nor does wanting to have a conscience, which we defined as being-toward-death, mean a detachment in which one flees from the world, but brings one without illusions to the resoluteness of "acting." Nor does anticipatory resoluteness stem from "idealistic" expectations soaring above existence and its possibilities; but arises from the sober understanding of the basic factical possibilities of Da-sein. Together with the sober *Angst* that brings us before our individualized potentiality-of-being, goes the unshakable joy in this possibility. In it Da-sein becomes free of the entertaining "incidentals" that busy curiosity provides for itself, primarily in terms of the events of the world.

. . .

QUESTIONS FOR REFLECTION

1. In what ways does Heidegger's notion of existential guilt resemble Kierkegaard's notion of sin?
2. Compare and contrast the modes of existence discussed by Kierkegaard with the modes of existence discussed by Heidegger.
3. What does Heidegger mean by existential guilt? Why does he use the morally loaded term "guilt" to mark our inability wholly to ground ourselves? Do you agree with his claim that we cannot wholly ground ourselves? If so, does your admission make you feel guilty in some sense?
4. Like Heidegger, Nietzsche thinks that human nature is in a certain sense unsettled. But does Nietzsche think that our unsettled nature is cause for anxiety? If not, can you explain the discrepancy in the ways these two philosophers react to our unsettled nature?
5. Clarify, and critically discuss, Heidegger's claim that "As projecting, understanding is the mode of being of Da-sein in which it *is* its possibilities as possibilities." How does this point tie in with the idea that we become what we are? Does Heidegger mean to say that I am everything I will be-

come or everything that I might become? Can it be that I am both a philosopher and not a philosopher, both a generous person and a selfish person?

6. Why does Heidegger think that death, properly understood, shows that the identities of other people are not part of our identities? Is he correct? Given death, what is left to our identities in his view?

7. Critically assess Heidegger's view of "truth." Does he accept Nietzsche's perspectivism?

8. Critically assess the following argument: Heidegger's view that our interpretations of human existence are largely decisive is absurd. For in his view I could interpret myself as a book (say), and my interpretation would be decisive. Yet patently I am not a book.

9. What does Heidegger mean when he condemns certain forms of existence (such as interpreting ourselves as the "they-self") as inauthentic? Is that condemnation consistent with his view that our interpretations of human existence are largely decisive?

10. Why does Heidegger resist the approach to phenomenology taken by Husserl in the years after Husserl published his *Investigations*? (Husserl's approach is discussed in "The Paris Lectures.")

11. Is Merleau-Ponty correct when he says, in the Preface to his *Phenomenology of Perception* (Chapter 6), that "the whole of *Being and Time* springs from an indication given by Husserl and amounts to no more than an explicit account of . . . the 'Lebenswelt' which Husserl, towards the end of his life, identified as the central theme of phenomenology. . . ."? 'Lebenswelt,' or 'lifeworld,' is Husserl's term for the intersubjectively available world in which people live and engage in projects; he discusses it in *The Crisis of European Sciences and Transcendental Phenomenology* (1936), Evanston, Ill.: Northwestern University Press, 1970.

FURTHER READINGS

Works by Husserl

Logical Investigations. 2 vols. (1900–1901). Translated by J. N. Findlay. London: Routledge & Kegan Paul, 1970.
Ideas. 3 vols. (1913). Vol. 1, translated by F. Kersten. The Hague: Nijhoff, 1982. Vol. 2, translated by R. Rojce-wicz and A. Schuwer. Dordrecht: Kluwer, 1989. Vol. 3, translated by T. E. Klein and W. E. Pohl. Dordrecht: Kluwer, 1980.
Cartesian Meditations (1931). Translated by D. Cairns. The Hague: Nijhoff, 1960.
The Crisis of European Sciences and Transcendental Phenomenology (1936). Translated by D. Carr, Evanston, Ill.: Northwestern University Press, 1970.

Works on Husserl

Bell, D. *Husserl, The Arguments of the Philosophers*. London: Routledge, 1990.
Dreyfus, Hubert. *Husserl, Intentionality and Cognitive Science*. Cambridge: MIT Press, 1982.
Smith, B., and D. Woodruff Smith, eds. *The Cambridge Companion to Husserl*. Cambridge: Cambridge University Press, 1995.
Sokolowski, R., ed. *Edmund Husserl and the Phenomenological Tradition*. Washington, D.C.: Catholic University of America Press, 1988.

Works by Heidegger

Being and Time (1927). Translated by John Macquarrie and Edward Robinson. New York: Harper & Row, 1962. And translated by Joan Stambaugh. New York: State University of New York Press, 1996.
The End of Philosophy (1936–1946). Translated by J. Stambaugh. New York: Harper & Row, 1973.
Introduction to Metaphysics (1953). Translated by Ralph Manheim. New Haven: Yale University Press, 1959.
The Question of Being (1955). Translated by W. Kluback, and J. T. Wilde. New York: Twayne Publishers, 1959.
What Is Called Thinking? (1956). Translated by F. D. Wieck and J. G. Gray. New York: Harper & Row, 1969.
What Is a Thing? (1967). Translated by W. B. Barton, Jr., and Vera Deutsch. Chicago: Henry Regnery, 1968.
Basic Writings. Edited by David Krell. New York: Harper & Row, 1977.
The Question Concerning Technology and Other Essays. Edited and translated by W. Lovitt. New York: Harper & Row, 1977.

Works on Heidegger

Dreyfus, Hubert. *Being-in-the-World: A Commentary on Heidegger's Being and Time, Division I*. Cambridge: MIT Press, 1991.
Dreyfus, Hubert, and H. Hall, eds. *Heidegger: A Critical Reader*. Oxford: Oxford University Press, 1992.
Gelven, Michael. *A Commentary on Heidegger's "Being and Time"*. New York: Harper & Row, 1970.

Guignon, Charles. *The Cambridge Companion to Heidegger.* Cambridge: Cambridge University Press, 1993.

Inwood, Michael. *Heidegger.* Oxford: Oxford University Press, 1997.

Kisiel, Theodore. *The Genesis of Heidegger's Being and Time.* Berkeley: University of California Press, 1993.

Mulhall, Stephen. *Heidegger and Being and Time.* London: Routledge, 1996.

Mulhall, Stephen. *Routledge Philosophy Guidebook to Heidegger and Being and Time.* London: Routledge, 1996.

Olafson, Frederick. *Heidegger and the Philosophy of Mind.* New Haven: Yale University Press, 1987.

Pöggeler, Otto. *Martin Heidegger's Path of Thinking.* Atlantic Highlands, NJ: Humanities Press, 1987.

Richardson, John. *Existential Epistemology: A Heideggerian Critique of the Cartesian Project.* Oxford: Oxford University Press, 1986.

Richardson, William. *Heidegger: Through Phenomenology to Thought.* The Hague: Nijhoff, 1963.

Steiner, George. *Martin Heidegger.* Harmondsworth: Penguin Books, 1978.

CHAPTER 5

Jean-Paul Sartre (1905–1980)

Jean-Paul Sartre was born in Paris and educated at the Ecole Normale Supérieure, which was affiliated with the Sorbonne. During his student years he began a lifelong relationship with the writer Simone de Beauvoir; it was to her that he dedicated his book *Being and Nothingness,* using for her the nickname "Castor," or beaver, signifying her industriousness. During the Second World War Sartre served in the French Army until he was captured by the Germans. When he was released, he continued to be active in the French resistance to the German occupation, and he wrote his magnum opus, *Being and Nothingness* (1943). During this time he also contributed to a clandestine paper called *Combat,* edited by his friend Albert Camus. He continued his literary career after the war, founding an influential magazine called *Les Temps Modernes,* and was eventually awarded the Nobel prize for literature (which he declined for political reasons). In his day he was a highly acclaimed literary figure and the leading proponent of existentialism. He was influential in the political sphere as well, having expended a great deal of effort during the latter part of his career on working out an acceptable version of Marxism. His attitude towards Marxism remained ambivalent, but at one point he was so thoroughly immersed in Marxism that he declared existentialism to be a mere ideology.

Sartre's literary contributions include the novel *Nausea,* "The Wall" and other short stories, and plays such as *No Exit.** In his early philosophical work, comprising *The Transcendence of the Ego* (1936), *The Emotions: Outline of a Theory* (1939), and *The Psychology of Imagination* (1940), he offered phenomenological accounts of consciousness, a notable element

of which is the argument, as against Husserl, that the ego or self is not a transcendental being but rather a construction of consciousness. *Being and Nothingness* develops Sartre's ontological theory of human being. He offered an influential characterization of existentialism and restated some of his central ideas about human being in *Existentialism is a Humanism* (1946), which therefore can serve as a useful introduction to *Being and Nothingness.*

EXISTENTIALISM

In *Existentialism is a Humanism,* Sartre offers an influential definition of existentialism: It is the doctrine that we exist before we have an essence or definitive attributes. This doctrine is easily misinterpreted if too much emphasis is placed on the term "essence," because in Sartre's view very little is actually essential to human beings. They are free to define themselves as they wish and permanently free to change that definition. Nonetheless, the doctrine is a helpful account of Sartre's brand of existentialism because it calls to mind four theses that Sartre associates with existentialism.

1. Human beings were not created to serve a pre-existing purpose. We are unlike tools such as scissors, whose essence or definitive purpose does in fact precede their existence. Human beings might be alive for some time before they adopt a purpose for themselves. Of course, one might think that God created people for some purpose. But Sartre denies the existence of God.
2. In large measure people are self-creating. As Sartre clarifies in his other writings, the self is a construction of the individual consciousness.

---

*A selection from Sartre's literary contributions can be found in Chapter 7—ed.

259

3. The individual consciousness is not causally determined to construct a particular identity or pursue particular ends; it freely chooses its identity and projects and even its emotions. Neither the individual's circumstances nor a pre-existing purpose or human nature force the individual to be a particular self or to pursue particular ends, and this would be true even if God existed, as Sartre dramatizes in his play *The Flies*:

> *Zeus:* Impudent spawn! So I am not your king? Who, then, made you?
> *Orestes:* You. But you blundered; you should not have made me free.
> *Zeus:* I gave you freedom so that you might serve me.
> *Orestes:* Perhaps. But now it has turned against its giver. . . . I *am* my freedom. No sooner had you created me than I ceased to be yours.[1]

4. Values are subjective. Something is valuable because I choose to value it, rather than the other way around. My values will result from my choice of a fundamental project by which I am engaged in the world and which constitutes the center of my identity. There are no objective values upon which to base the (continuously renewed) decision to be the self I am.

PHENOMENOLOGY

Sartre begins *Being and Nothingness* with a discussion of his phenomenological approach to human being. Like Heidegger (and Hegel), Sartre thought that a proper phenomenological method could overcome troublesome forms of dualism that are the inevitable outcome of traditional epistemological approaches. Especially troublesome is the chasm between the mental and the physical. This chasm was deeply entrenched in Western philosophy by Descartes.

According to Cartesian dualism, both minds (or souls) and the physical things of the world are object-like. Minds and physical things are substances in that neither is dependent upon the other for its existence. Moreover, mental substances interact with physical substances—otherwise minds could not perceive other things or control the body (itself a physical

thing). However, the form of interaction between mental and physical things is unintelligible to us because mental substances do not have physical attributes (such as mass and location) that would seem to be necessary if they are to alter the physical world.

Sartre's (neutral monistic) idea is to start with phenomena, or appearances, that are not initially presumed to be mental or physical and on that basis to reach conclusions about what is mental and what is physical. At this initial stage we must be especially careful to avoid the presumption that the phenomena constitute a veil of ideas that separate the "inner" and the "outer," the subject and the object; the phenomena do not constitute a "superficial covering which hides from sight the true nature of the object." Instead, "the being of an existent is exactly what it appears. . . . The phenomenon can be studied and described as such, for it is absolutely indicative of itself. . . . The appearance does not hide the essence, it reveals it; it *is* the essence."[2]

Sartre wishes to avoid traditional forms of dualism by avoiding the suggestion that the appearances are sense data. He also wants to avoid smuggling in the idealist thesis that to be is to be perceived or the realist view that to be is to be a physical object (or a physical property).

CONSCIOUSNESS, BEING FOR-ITSELF, AND BEING IN-ITSELF

However, Sartre's philosophy does not banish all forms of dualism. As he realizes, his account of being builds on a sharp dualism between (1) consciousness itself and (2) what consciousness is conscious of—the objects of consciousness, or that to which consciousness refers. The objects of consciousness disclose themselves in a relatively familiar way: we are conscious of them. But how is consciousness disclosed to us? Well, in being conscious of an object such as a wine bottle, we are *aware of our consciousness* of that object. But this awareness is implicit in our consciousness of the bottle. Our awareness of our consciousness of the bottle is not separate from our consciousness of the bottle. Sartre is especially concerned to avoid saying that our consciousness of a bottle entails our consciousness of our consciousness of the bottle, for then being conscious of the bottle would also entail being conscious of our consciousness of the bottle, as well as being conscious of all *that,* and so on, which seems impossible. In fact, this regress of consciousness can never get started, according to Sartre, for consciousness itself can never be its own object; it always separates itself from its objects.

Consciousness, then, cannot be disclosed to us as its own object. But according to Sartre this means that it must be disclosed to us in contrast to its object. Let me try to make Sartre's idea clearer. Our grasp of something, say A, might be constituted entirely by the idea that it is not something else, say B. This presupposes that we have a positive conception of B, and our grasp of A consists in the fact that *A is not B.* Things we apprehend in this contrastive way Sartre calls *negativities.* Sartre thinks that negativities are a part of the world as it presents itself to us. He also thinks that negativities could not exist if there were no human beings to think of ways the world might be if it were not as it is. For example, *the absence of Pierre from the café* is a negativity that I might discover but only if I were expecting to find Pierre in a café and failed to find him. In such a case I grasp a part of the world by contrasting it against my positive conception of Pierre's presence in the café. I grasp *Pierre's absence from the café:* As Sartre says, "I myself expected to see Pierre, and my expectation has caused the absence of Pierre to happen as a real event concerning this café."

According to Sartre, it is in this contrastive way that we grasp the being of consciousness. We start with our positive conception of the being of an object. This type of being is called *being in-itself.* Sartre says that being in-itself "is what it is," but he adds a more helpful characterization: the in-itself "*has to be* what it is."[3] Sartre's idea is that an in-itself is not free; to be presented as an object of consciousness is to be presented as a mere thing, a thing that is part of the causal order.

In terms of our positive conception of being in-itself we form our conception of the being of consciousness, which Sartre calls being *for*-itself. Being for-itself is being that is not being in-itself. Consciousness, unlike its object, is free, and is conceived as outside of the causal order. But the freedom of consciousness is tantamount to its lacking any definite shape. Its being is that of a for-itself, and, as Sartre says in several places, "the being of the *for-itself* is defined . . .

as being what it is not and not being what it is."[4] What this paradoxical definition means is that the for-itself *may* be what it is not and *need not be* what it is. To exist as a for-itself is to be without a fixed identity; it is to be capable of changing from one identity to another. It is to be (largely) self-defining.

CONSCIOUSNESS AND THE SELF

In order to elaborate upon the relationship between consciousness and identity, Sartre distinguishes between pre-reflective (or nonthetic or nonpositional) consciousness on the one hand and reflective consciousness on the other. To grasp the distinction Sartre has in mind, notice that sometimes we do not explicitly spell out for ourselves the activities we are engaged in although we are *conscious* of those activities. This form of consciousness Sartre calls *pre-reflective* consciousness. Your reading the first sentence of this paragraph may be a good example of an act that is pre-reflective, for although you were certainly aware of reading the sentence, you probably did not explicitly spell out for yourself what you were doing. Contrast your reading the sentence just before this one, which literally spelled out your act of reading the first sentence in the paragraph, and which therefore prompted *reflective consciousness.* You cannot be reflectively aware of reading a sentence unless you are pre-reflectively aware of doing so, but pre-reflective consciousness is possible without reflective consciousness. You read the first sentence in this paragraph and you were aware of what you were doing, yet you did not spell out to yourself "I am reading this sentence."

According to Sartre, consciousness is not the same thing as the self or ego; in fact, the self is *constructed* by reflective consciousness. But in constructing the self, consciousness must decide how to situate the self with respect to the two modes of being, the in-itself and the for-itself, which he describes as incommensurable: the in-itself and the for-itself are "absolutely separated regions of being" that are "without communication."[5] Sartre stresses that consciousness is capable of constructing the self in any number of ways, but he also suggests that an accurate view (a) portrays the self as continuous with consciousness and (b) reflects the nature of consciousness as a for-itself.

FREEDOM AND ANGUISH

Insofar as our being is that of a for-itself, we are free. But we experience our freedom as anguish, according to Sartre. The anguish resulting from our freedom takes several forms. One form of anguish is a consequence of the fact that nothing determines that an individual consciousness will construct and identify with a given self rather than some other possible self. Our choice of identity is not causally determined. Hence, nothing determines that an individual consciousness will not abandon the self it has constructed and replace it with another. Nothing an individual consciousness does now can guarantee that the identity it embraces today will be the identity it embraces tomorrow. Sartre expresses this point in a paradoxical way: "I *am* not the self which I will be."[6] A more straightforward way to put his point is to say that an individual consciousness may always replace the identity it has chosen. His point is that whether I choose as an individual consciousness to retain a particular identity over time is always up to me; if I remain the same self, I do so only by a continuously renewed decision.

This discovery causes me anguish (more exactly: "anguish in the face of the future") because I care about my continued existence; I would really like to persist as the very same person indefinitely, and hence, I would like to ensure right now that I will do so. But ensuring my continuation would require that I do something now that will deprive the individual consciousness that will animate my body tomorrow of the freedom to construct a new identity, and that is something I cannot do. I cannot eliminate my freedom. Sartre adds that anguish in the face of the past is possible, too, as when a gambler wishes to abandon his identity as a gambler, but discovers that there is no decision that he can make now to deprive himself of the freedom later to renew his identity as a gambler.

Another form of anguish Sartre calls *ethical anguish*. We are completely free to decide for ourselves what is valuable, according to Sartre, and this decision cannot be based on an appeal to the objective facts about what is valuable, for according to Sartre there are no such objective facts: "Value derives its being from its exigency and not its exigency from its being." That is, as Schopenhauer suggested, I do not decide to value things because they are valuable in themselves; rather, something is valuable to me because I decide to value it. Therefore, "nothing, absolutely nothing, justifies me in adopting this or that particular value, this or that particular scale of values," and "as a being by whom values exist, I am unjustifiable."[7] Ethical anguish results when I recognize my groundlessness as a creator of value and my permanent freedom to replace those values with others.

FLIGHT AND BAD FAITH

The typical response to anguish is flight, according to Sartre. We attempt to flee or deny the freedom that causes us anguish. The main way people conceal their freedom from themselves is by adopting *psychological determinism,* the view that human nature is responsible for what we do. By adopting psychological determinism, we attempt to reduce ourselves to "never being anything but what we are";[8] that is, we convince ourselves that we cannot help but retain our identity, which is to think of ourselves as no more than an in-itself. The fictional story we tell ourselves, according to Sartre, calls to mind some of the views of the Dutch philosopher Benedict Spinoza (1632–1677). The story is that the self is my essence and "an act is free when it exactly reflects my essence. It is a matter of envisaging the self as a little God which inhabits me and which possesses my freedom as a metaphysical virtue."[9]

The attitude by which I try to hide something from myself Sartre calls *mauvaise foi,* which is literally translated as "bad faith" (it is sometimes translated as self-deception). Thus, when we flee our freedom and our anguish, we are in "bad faith." Sartre thinks that "people can *live* in bad faith," but he also thinks that bad faith is difficult to comprehend. He characterizes it as "evanescent," "metastable," and "precarious."[10] Bad faith is difficult to understand because we can hide something from ourselves only if we know what we are hiding; we must know the truth in order to conceal it from ourselves. Consciousness is entirely translucent to itself; because it must be aware of something in order to launch the project of concealing it, the project cannot succeed. In particular, we can never fully succeed in hiding our anguish from ourselves because we must acknowledge that we are in anguish in order to hide our anguish from ourselves. According to Sartre, "I flee in order not to know, but I can not avoid knowing that I am fleeing; and the flight from anguish is only a mode of becoming conscious of anguish."[11]

Even though he says that bad faith is something "we can neither reject nor comprehend,"[12] Sartre does offer illuminating descriptions of some patterns of bad faith. Principally, people vacillate between seeing themselves as what Sartre calls a "facticity" and as a "transcendence." That is, people vacillate between seeing themselves as an in-itself or as a for-itself. Such vacillation allows us to disarm unwelcome truths, such as "I am cowardly" or "my values are baseless," by alternating between two positions whenever it suits us: (1) saying that the repugnant claim would be true of us only insofar as we had a given nature when in fact we are free to transcend our nature, or (2) saying that the repugnant claim would be true of us only insofar as we were free to transcend when in fact we have a fixed nature. Thus, to disarm "I am cowardly," I would adopt (1), but to disarm "my values are baseless," I would switch to (2).

A second device is to vacillate between our own self-conception and the conception of us held by other people. If I have managed to con people into thinking that I am humble, I might assess my character in light of their view rather than in light of my own opinion that I am better than anyone else. But I will switch to my own self-conception when others (falsely!) believe that my character is unsavory. A third device is to chop our selves into different person stages and identify with some of these at one time, and with others at other times.

The project of bad faith gives us powerful grounds to leave the question of our identity up in the air. If the question were finally resolved, we could not continue to deceive ourselves through caginess about how to see ourselves. Finally deciding who we are is also made difficult by something else. According to Sartre, sincerity, "the antithesis of self-deception," is problematic because sincerity seems to require "that a man be for himself only what he is," which appears to entail identifying ourselves entirely as an in-itself. But that suggests that sincerity is itself a form of self-deception.

THE OTHER

According to Sartre, I can be aware of my own existence only if other people, other conscious beings, exist, for self-awareness involves awareness of a public dimension of the self. There is a "primary relation between my consciousness and the Other's" by which "the Other must be given to me directly as a subject although in connection with me...."[13] To illustrate his point, Sartre uses the example of shame. Shame reveals something about my self, but "I am ashamed of myself *as I appear* to the Other.... I recognize that I *am* as the Other sees me."[14]

Much like Hegel before him, Sartre suggests that there is a permanent tension between the way we see ourselves and the way others see us. Under examination by another, we are objects deprived of our transcendence or freedom. But the same is true of them when we examine them: "While I seek to enslave the Other, the Other seeks to enslave me."[15] To resolve the tension, therefore, we would have to submit to the perspective by which we are objects for others, or else we would have to impose upon others the perspective by which they are objects for us. Neither perspective can win out, because our freedom precludes our being objects for others, and their freedom precludes their being objects for us. However, Sartre is able to use his account of the struggle over objectification to illuminate various aspects of human psychology such as love, sexual desire, masochism, and sadism.

EXISTENTIAL PSYCHOANALYSIS

In the last part of *Being and Nothingness* Sartre sketches the approach to psychoanalysis that his account of human being favors. In his view the proper foundation for a psychological explanation of someone's personality is the identity freely chosen by that person. One's identity will involve a fundamental project, a "project of being," by which one is engaged in the world, and it will not only establish one's values, it will give a meaning to one's behavior, a meaning that transcends that behavior and renders it intelligible. Sartre likens the freely chosen identity to something Spinoza calls an "intelligible character," but Sartre says that "the distinguishing characteristic of the intelligible choice . . . is that it can exist only as the transcendent meaning of each concrete, empirical choice."

Sartre also returns to his theme that the conscious individual must come to terms with both the in-itself and the for-itself when constructing the self. The ideal self would partake of both forms of being. We would like to remain free (the for-itself component of our ideal), but simultaneously we would like the fact that we remain who we are to be a matter of absolute necessity (the in-itself component of our ideal). Because God has precisely this ideal self, Sartre says "to be man means to reach toward being God." [16]

NOTES

1. Jean-Paul Sartre, *No Exit and Three Other Plays,* trans. S. Gilbert (New York: Vintage Books, 1946), 120.
2. Jean-Paul Sartre, Introduction to *Being and Nothingness,* trans. Hazel Barnes (New York: Washington Square Press, 1966), 5.
3. Sartre, *Being and Nothingness,* 28.
4. Ibid., 28.
5. Ibid., 26.
6. Ibid., 68.
7. Ibid., 76.
8. Ibid., 79.
9. Ibid., 81.
10. Ibid., 90.
11. Ibid., 83.
12. Ibid., 90.
13. Ibid., 341.
14. Ibid., 302.
15. Ibid., 475.
16. Ibid., 724.

WORKS BY JEAN-PAUL SARTRE

Existentialism and Humanism

My purpose here is to offer a defence of existentialism against several reproaches that have been laid against it.

First, it has been reproached as an invitation to people to dwell in quietism of despair. For if every way

to a solution is barred, one would have to regard any action in this world as entirely ineffective, and one would arrive finally at a contemplative philosophy. Moreover, since contemplation is a luxury, this would be only another bourgeois philosophy. This is, especially, the reproach made by the Communists.

From another quarter we are reproached for having underlined all that is ignominious in the human situation, for depicting what is mean, sordid or base to the neglect of certain things that possess charm and beauty and belong to the brighter side of human nature: for example, according to the Catholic critic, Mlle. Mercier, we forget how an infant smiles. Both from this side and from the other we are also reproached for leaving out of account the solidarity of mankind and considering man in isolation. And this, say the Communists, is because we base our doctrine upon pure subjectivity—upon the Cartesian "I think": which is the moment in which solitary man attains to himself; a position from which it is impossible to regain solidarity with other men who exist outside of the self. The *ego* cannot reach them through the *cogito.*

From the Christian side, we are reproached as people who deny the reality and seriousness of human affairs. For since we ignore the commandments of God and all values prescribed as eternal, nothing remains but what is strictly voluntary. Everyone can do what he likes, and will be incapable, from such a point of view, of condemning either the point of view or the action of anyone else.

It is to these various reproaches that I shall endeavour to reply to-day; that is why I have entitled this brief exposition "Existentialism and Humanism." Many may be surprised at the mention of humanism in this connection, but we shall try to see in what sense we understand it. In any case, we can begin by saying that existentialism, in our sense of the word, is a doctrine that does render human life possible; a doctrine, also, which affirms that every truth and every action imply both an environment and a human subjectivity. The essential charge laid against us is, of course, that of over-emphasis upon the evil side of human life. I have lately been told of a lady who, whenever she lets slip a vulgar expression in a moment of nervousness, excuses herself by exclaiming, "I believe I am becoming an existentialist." So it appears that ugliness is being identified with existentialism. That is why some people say we are "naturalistic," and if we are, it is strange to see how much we scandalise and horrify them, for no one seems to be much frightened or humiliated nowadays by what is properly called naturalism. Those who can quite well keep down a novel by Zola such as *La Terre* are sickened as soon as they read an existentialist novel. Those who appeal to the wisdom of the people—which is a sad wisdom—find ours sadder still. And yet, what could be more disillusioned than such sayings as "Charity begins at home" or "Promote a rogue and he'll sue you for damage, knock him down and he'll do you homage"? * We all know how many common sayings can be quoted to this effect, and they all mean much the same—that you must not oppose the powers-that-be; that you must not fight against superior force; must not meddle in matters that are above your station. Or that any action not in accordance with some tradition is mere romanticism; or that any undertaking which has not the support of proven experience is foredoomed to frustration; and that since experience has shown men to be invariably inclined to evil, there must be firm rules to restrain them, otherwise we shall have anarchy. It is, however, the people who are forever mouthing these dismal proverbs and, whenever they are told of some more or less repulsive action, say "How like human nature!"—it is these very people, always harping upon realism, who complain that existentialism is too gloomy a view of things. Indeed their excessive protests make me suspect that what is annoying them is not so much our pessimism, but, much more likely, our optimism. For at bottom, what is alarming in the doctrine that I am about to try to explain to you is—is it not?—that it confronts man with a possibility of choice. To verify this, let us review the whole question upon the strictly philosophic level. What, then, is this that we call existentialism?

Most of those who are making use of this word would be highly confused if required to explain its meaning. For since it has become fashionable, people cheerfully declare that this musician or that painter is "existentialist." A columnist in *Clartés* signs himself "The Existentialist," and, indeed, the word is now so loosely applied to so many things that it no longer means anything at all. It would appear that, for the

lack of any novel doctrine such as that of surrealism, all those who are eager to join in the latest scandal or movement now seize upon this philosophy in which, however, they can find nothing to their purpose. For in truth this is of all teachings the least scandalous and the most austere: it is intended strictly for technicians and philosophers. All the same, it can easily be defined.

The question is only complicated because there are two kinds of existentialists. There are, on the one hand, the Christians, amongst whom I shall name Jaspers and Gabriel Marcel, both professed Catholics; and on the other the existential atheists, amongst whom we must place Heidegger as well as the French existentialists and myself. What they have in common is simply the fact that they believe that *existence* comes before *essence*—or, if you will, that we must begin from the subjective. What exactly do we mean by that?

If one considers an article of manufacture—as, for example, a book or a paper-knife—one sees that it has been made by an artisan who had a conception of it; and he has paid attention, equally, to the conception of a paper-knife and to the pre-existent technique of production which is a part of that conception and is, at bottom, a formula. Thus the paper-knife is at the same time an article producible in a certain manner and one which, on the other hand, serves a definite purpose, for one cannot suppose that a man would produce a paper-knife without knowing what it was for. Let us say, then, of the paper-knife that its essence—that is to say the sum of the formulae and the qualities which made its production and its definition possible—precedes its existence. The presence of such-and-such a paper-knife or book is thus determined before my eyes. Here, then, we are viewing the world from a technical standpoint, and we can say that production precedes existence.

When we think of God as the creator, we are thinking of him, most of the time, as a supernal artisan. Whatever doctrine we may be considering, whether it be a doctrine like that of Descartes, or of Leibnitz himself, we always imply that the will follows, more or less, from the understanding or at least accompanies it, so that when God creates he knows precisely what he is creating. Thus, the conception of man in the mind of God is comparable to that of the paper-knife in the mind of the artisan: God makes man according to a procedure and a conception, exactly as the arti-

Handwritten margin notes: Paper, Knife, Letter opener

Handwritten note: Essence: what defines you.

san manufactures a paper-knife, following a definition and a formula. Thus each individual man is the realisation of a certain conception which dwells in the divine understanding. In the philosophic atheism of the eighteenth century, the notion of God is suppressed, but not, for all that, the idea that essence is prior to existence; something of that idea we still find everywhere, in Diderot, in Voltaire and even in Kant. Man possesses a human nature; that "human nature," which is the conception of human being, is found in every man; which means that each man is a particular example of an universal conception, the conception of Man. In Kant, this universality goes so far that the wild man of the woods, man in the state of nature and the bourgeois are all contained in the same definition and have the same fundamental qualities. Here again, the essence of man precedes that historic existence which we confront in experience.

Atheistic existentialism, of which I am a representative, declares with greater consistency that if God does not exist there is at least one being whose existence comes before its essence, a being which exists before it can be defined by any conception of it. That being is man or, as Heidegger has it, the human reality. What do we mean by saying that existence precedes essence? We mean that man first of all exists, encounters himself, surges up in the world—and defines himself afterwards. If man as the existentialist sees him is not definable, it is because to begin with he is nothing. He will not be anything until later, and then he will be what he makes of himself. Thus, there is no human nature, because there is no God to have a conception of it. Man simply is. Not that he is simply what he conceives himself to be, but he is what he wills, and as he conceives himself after already existing—as he wills to be after that leap towards existence. Man is nothing else but that which he makes of himself. That is the first principle of existentialism. And this is what people call its "subjectivity," using the word as a reproach against us. But what do we mean to say by this, but that man is of a greater dignity than a stone or a table? For we mean to say that man primarily exists—that man is, before all else, something which propels itself towards a future and is aware that it is doing so. Man is, indeed, a project which possesses a subjective life, instead of being a kind of moss, or a fungus or a cauliflower. Before that projection of the self nothing exists; not even in the heaven of intel-

ligence: man will only attain existence when he is what he purposes to be. Not, however, what he may wish to be. For what we usually understand by wishing or willing is a conscious decision taken—much more often than not—after we have made ourselves what we are. I may wish to join a party, to write a book or to marry—but in such a case what is usually called my will is probably a manifestation of a prior and more spontaneous decision. If, however, it is true that existence is prior to essence, man is responsible for what he is. Thus, the first effect of existentialism is that it puts every man in possession of himself as he is, and places the entire responsibility for his existence squarely upon his own shoulders. And, when we say that man is responsible for himself, we do not mean that he is responsible only for his own individuality, but that he is responsible for all men. The word "subjectivism" is to be understood in two senses, and our adversaries play upon only one of them. Subjectivism means, on the one hand, the freedom of the individual subject and, on the other, that man cannot pass beyond human subjectivity. It is the latter which is the deeper meaning of existentialism. When we say that man chooses himself, we do mean that every one of us must choose himself; but by that we also mean that in choosing for himself he chooses for all men. For in effect, of all the actions a man may take in order to create himself as he wills to be, there is not one which is not creative, at the same time, of an image of man such as he believes he ought to be. To choose between this or that is at the same time to affirm the value of that which is chosen; for we are unable ever to choose the worse. What we choose is always the better; and nothing can be better for us unless it is better for all. If, moreover, existence precedes essence and we will to exist at the same time as we fashion our image, that image is valid for all and for the entire epoch in which we find ourselves. Our responsibility is thus much greater than we had supposed, for it concerns mankind as a whole. If I am a worker, for instance, I may choose to join a Christian rather than a Communist trade union. And if, by that membership, I choose to signify that resignation is, after all, the attitude that best becomes a man, that man's kingdom is not upon this earth, I do not commit myself alone to that view. Resignation is my will for everyone, and my action is, in consequence, a commitment on behalf of all mankind. Or if, to take a more personal case, I decide to marry and to have children, even though this decision proceeds simply from my situation, from my passion or my desire, I am thereby committing not only myself, but humanity as a whole, to the practice of monogamy. I am thus responsible for myself and for all men, and I am creating a certain image of man as I would have him to be. In fashioning myself I fashion man.

This may enable us to understand what is meant by such terms—perhaps a little grandiloquent—as anguish, abandonment and despair. As you will soon see, it is very simple. First, what do we mean by anguish? The existentialist frankly states that man is in anguish. His meaning is as follows—When a man commits himself to anything, fully realising that he is not only choosing what he will be, but is thereby at the same time a legislator deciding for the whole of mankind—in such a moment a man cannot escape from the sense of complete and profound responsibility. There are many, indeed, who show no such anxiety. But we affirm that they are merely disguising their anguish or are in flight from it. Certainly, many people think that in what they are doing they commit no one but themselves to anything: and if you ask them, "What would happen if everyone did so?" they shrug their shoulders and reply, "Everyone does not do so." But in truth, one ought always to ask oneself what would happen if everyone did as one is doing; nor can one escape from that disturbing thought except by a kind of self-deception. The man who lies in self-excuse, by saying "Everyone will not do it" must be ill at ease in his conscience, for the act of lying implies the universal value which it denies. By its very disguise his anguish reveals itself. This is the anguish that Kierkegaard called "the anguish of Abraham." You know the story: An angel commanded Abraham to sacrifice his son: and obedience was obligatory, if it really was an angel who had appeared and said, "Thou, Abraham, shalt sacrifice thy son." But anyone in such a case would wonder, first, whether it was indeed an angel and secondly, whether I am really Abraham. Where are the proofs? A certain mad woman who suffered from hallucinations said that people were telephoning to her, and giving her orders. The doctor asked, "But who is it that speaks to you?" She replied: "He says it is God." And what, indeed, could prove to her that it was God? If an angel appears to me, what is the proof that it is an angel; or, if I hear voices, who can prove that they proceed from heaven and not from hell, or from my own subconsciousness or some pathological condition? Who can prove that they are really addressed to me?

Who, then, can prove that I am the proper person to impose, by my own choice, my conception of man upon mankind? I shall never find any proof whatever; there will be no sign to convince me of it. If a voice speaks to me, it is still I myself who must decide whether the voice is or is not that of an angel. If I regard a certain course of action as good, it is only I who choose to say that it is good and not bad. There is nothing to show that I am Abraham: nevertheless I also am obliged at every instant to perform actions which are examples. Everything happens to every man as though the whole human race had its eyes fixed upon what he is doing and regulated its conduct accordingly. So every man ought to say, "Am I really a man who has the right to act in such a manner that humanity regulates itself by what I do." If a man does not say that, he is dissembling his anguish. Clearly, the anguish with which we are concerned here is not one that could lead to quietism or inaction. It is anguish pure and simple, of the kind well known to all those who have borne responsibilities. When, for instance, a military leader takes upon himself the responsibility for an attack and sends a number of men to their death, he chooses to do it and at bottom he alone chooses. No doubt he acts under a higher command, but its orders, which are more general, require interpretation by him and upon that interpretation depends the life of ten, fourteen or twenty men. In making the decision, he cannot but feel a certain anguish. All leaders know that anguish. It does not prevent their acting, on the contrary it is the very condition of their action, for the action presupposes that there is a plurality of possibilities, and in choosing one of these, they realise that it has value only because it is chosen. Now it is anguish of that kind which existentialism describes, and moreover, as we shall see, makes explicit through direct responsibility towards other men who are concerned. Far from being a screen which could separate us from action, it is a condition of action itself.

And when we speak of "abandonment"—a favourite word of Heidegger—we only mean to say that God does not exist, and that it is necessary to draw the consequences of his absence right to the end. The existentialist is strongly opposed to a certain type of secular moralism which seeks to suppress God at the least possible expense. Towards 1880, when the French professors endeavoured to formulate a secular morality, they said something like this:—God is a useless and costly hypothesis, so we will do without it. However, if we are to have morality, a society and a law-abiding world, it is essential that certain values should be taken seriously; they must have an *à priori* existence ascribed to them. It must be considered obligatory *à priori* to be honest, not to lie, not to beat one's wife, to bring up children and so forth; so we are going to do a little work on this subject, which will enable us to show that these values exist all the same, inscribed in an intelligible heaven although, of course, there is no God. In other words—and this is, I believe, the purport of all that we in France call radicalism—nothing will be changed if God does not exist; we shall re-discover the same norms of honesty, progress and humanity, and we shall have disposed of God as an out-of-date hypothesis which will die away quietly of itself. The existentialist, on the contrary, finds it extremely embarrassing that God does not exist, for there disappears with Him all possibility of finding values in an intelligible heaven. There can no longer be any good *à priori*, since there is no infinite and perfect consciousness to think it. It is nowhere written that "the good" exists, that one must be honest or must not lie, since we are now upon the plane where there are only men. Dostoievsky once wrote "If God did not exist, everything would be permitted"; and that, for existentialism, is the starting point. Everything is indeed permitted if God does not exist, and man is in consequence forlorn, for he cannot find anything to depend upon either within or outside himself. He discovers forthwith, that he is without excuse. For if indeed existence precedes essence, one will never be able to explain one's action by reference to a given and specific human nature; in other words, there is no determinism—man is free, man *is* freedom. Nor, on the other hand, if God does not exist, are we provided with any values or commands that could legitimise our behaviour. Thus we have neither behind us, nor before us in a luminous realm of values, any means of justification or excuse. We are left alone, without excuse. That is what I mean when I say that man is condemned to be free. Condemned, because he did not create himself, yet is nevertheless at liberty, and from the moment that he is thrown into this

world he is responsible for everything he does. The existentialist does not believe in the power of passion. He will never regard a grand passion as a destructive torrent upon which a man is swept into certain actions as by fate, and which, therefore, is an excuse for them. He thinks that man is responsible for his passion. Neither will an existentialist think that a man can find help through some sign being vouchsafed upon earth for his orientation: for he thinks that the man himself interprets the sign as he chooses. He thinks that every man, without any support or help whatever, is condemned at every instant to invent man. As Ponge has written in a very fine article, "Man is the future of man." That is exactly true. Only, if one took this to mean that the future is laid up in Heaven, that God knows what it is, it would be false, for then it would no longer even be a future. If, however, it means that, whatever man may now appear to be, there is a future to be fashioned, a virgin future that awaits him—then it is a true saying. But in the present one is forsaken.

As an example by which you may the better understand this state of abandonment, I will refer to the case of a pupil of mine, who sought me out in the following circumstances. His father was quarrelling with his mother and was also inclined to be a "collaborator"; his elder brother had been killed in the German offensive of 1940 and this young man, with a sentiment somewhat primitive but generous, burned to avenge him. His mother was living alone with him, deeply afflicted by the semitreason of his father and by the death of her eldest son, and her one consolation was in this young man. But he, at this moment, had the choice between going to England to join the Free French Forces or of staying near his mother and helping her to live. He fully realised that this woman lived only for him and that his disappearance—or perhaps his death—would plunge her into despair. He also realised that, concretely and in fact, every action he performed on his mother's behalf would be sure of effect in the sense of aiding her to live, whereas anything he did in order to go and fight would be an ambiguous action which might vanish like water into sand and serve no purpose. For instance, to set out for England he would have to wait indefinitely in a Spanish camp on the way through Spain; or, on arriving in England or in Algiers he might be put into an office to fill up forms. Consequently, he found himself confronted by two very different modes of action;

God's existence.

the one concrete, immediate, but directed towards only one individual; and the other an action addressed to an end infinitely greater, a national collectivity, but for that very reason ambiguous—and it might be frustrated on the way. At the same time, he was hesitating between two kinds of morality; on the one side the morality of sympathy, of personal devotion and, on the other side, a morality of wider scope but of more debatable validity. He had to choose between those two. What could help him to choose? Could the Christian doctrine? No. Christian doctrine says: Act with charity, love your neighbour, deny yourself for others, choose the way which is hardest, and so forth. But which is the harder road? To whom does one owe the more brotherly love, the patriot or the mother? Which is the more useful aim, the general one of fighting in and for the whole community, or the precise aim of helping one particular person to live? Who can give an answer to that *à priori*? No one. Nor is it given in any ethical scripture. The Kantian ethic says, Never regard another as a means, but always as an end. Very well; if I remain with my mother, I shall be regarding her as the end and not as a means: but by the same token I am in danger of treating as means those who are fighting on my behalf; and the converse is also true, that if I go to the aid of the combatants I shall be treating them as the end at the risk of treating my mother as a means.

If values are uncertain, if they are still too abstract to determine the particular, concrete case under consideration, nothing remains but to trust in our instincts. That is what this young man tried to do; and when I saw him he said, "In the end, it is feeling that counts; the direction in which it is really pushing me is the one I ought to choose. If I feel that I love my mother enough to sacrifice everything else for her—my will to be avenged, all my longings for action and adventure—then I stay with her. If, on the contrary, I feel that my love for her is not enough, I go." But how does one estimate the strength of a feeling? The value of his feeling for his mother was determined precisely by the fact that he was standing by her. I may say that I love a certain friend enough to sacrifice such or such a sum of money for him, but I cannot prove that unless I have done it. I may say, "I love my mother enough to remain with her," if actually I have remained with her. I can only estimate the strength of this affection if I have performed an action by which it is defined and ratified. But if I then appeal to this affection to

justify my action, I find myself drawn into a vicious circle.

Moreover, as Gide has very well said, a sentiment which is play-acting and one which is vital are two things that are hardly distinguishable one from another. To decide that I love my mother by staying beside her, and to play a comedy the upshot of which is that I do so—these are nearly the same thing. In other words, feeling is formed by the deeds that one does; therefore I cannot consult it as a guide to action. And that is to say that I can neither seek within myself for an authentic impulse to action, nor can I expect, from some ethic, formulae that will enable me to act. You may say that the youth did, at least, go to a professor to ask for advice. But if you seek counsel—from a priest, for example—you have selected that priest; and at bottom you already knew, more or less, what he would advise. In other words, to choose an adviser is nevertheless to commit oneself by that choice. If you are a Christian, you will say, Consult a priest; but there are collaborationists, priests who are resisters and priests who wait for the tide to turn: which will you choose? Had this young man chosen a priest of the resistance, or one of the collaboration, he would have decided beforehand the kind of advice he was to receive. Similarly, in coming to me, he knew what advice I should give him, and I had but one reply to make. You are free, therefore choose—that is to say, invent. No rule of general morality can show you what you ought to do: no signs are vouchsafed in this world. The Catholics will reply, "Oh, but they are!" Very well; still, it is I myself, in every case, who have to interpret the signs. Whilst I was imprisoned, I made the acquaintance of a somewhat remarkable man, a Jesuit, who had become a member of that order in the following manner. In his life he had suffered a succession of rather severe setbacks. His father had died when he was a child, leaving him in poverty, and he had been awarded a free scholarship in a religious institution, where he had been made continually to feel that he was accepted for charity's sake, and, in consequence, he had been denied several of those distinctions and honours which gratify children. Later, about the age of eighteen, he came to grief in a sentimental affair; and finally, at twenty-two—this was a trifle in itself, but it was the last drop that overflowed his cup—he failed in his military examination. This young man, then, could regard himself as a total failure: it was a sign—but a sign of what? He might have taken refuge in bitterness or despair. But he took it—very cleverly for him—as a sign that he was not intended for secular successes, and that only the attainments of religion, those of sanctity and of faith, were accessible to him. He interpreted his record as a message from God, and became a member of the Order. Who can doubt but that this decision as to the meaning of the sign was his, and his alone? One could have drawn quite different conclusions from such a series of reverses—as, for example, that he had better become a carpenter or a revolutionary. For the decipherment of the sign, however, he bears the entire responsibility. That is what "abandonment" implies, that we ourselves decide our being. And with this abandonment goes anguish.

As for "despair," the meaning of this expression is extremely simple. It merely means that we limit ourselves to a reliance upon that which is within our wills, or within the sum of the probabilities which render our action feasible. Whenever one wills anything, there are always these elements of probability. If I am counting upon a visit from a friend, who may be coming by train or by tram, I presuppose that the train will arrive at the appointed time, or that the tram will not be derailed. I remain in the realm of possibilities; but one does not rely upon any possibilities beyond those that are strictly concerned in one's action. Beyond the point at which the possibilities under consideration cease to affect my action, I ought to disinterest myself. For there is no God and no prevenient design, which can adapt the world and all its possibilities to my will. When Descartes said, "Conquer yourself rather than the world," what he meant was, at bottom, the same—that we should act without hope.

Marxists, to whom I have said this, have answered: "Your action is limited, obviously, by your death; but you can rely upon the help of others. That is, you can count both upon what the others are doing to help you elsewhere, as in China and in Russia, and upon what they will do later, after your death, to take up your action and carry it forward to its final accomplishment which will be the revolution. Moreover you must rely upon this; not to do so is immoral." To this I rejoin, first, that I shall always count upon my comrades-in-arms in the struggle, in so far as they are committed, as I am, to a definite, common cause; and in the unity of a party or a group which I can more or less control—that is, in which I am enrolled as a militant and

whose movements at every moment are known to me. In that respect, to rely upon the unity and the will of the party is exactly like my reckoning that the train will run to time or that the tram will not be derailed. But I cannot count upon men whom I do not know, I cannot base my confidence upon human goodness or upon man's interest in the good of society, seeing that man is free and that there is no human nature which I can take as foundational. I do know not whither the Russian revolution will lead. I can admire it and take it as an example in so far as it is evident, to-day, that the proletariat plays a part in Russia which it has attained in no other nation. But I cannot affirm that this will necessarily lead to the triumph of the proletariat: I must confine myself to what I can see. Nor can I be sure that comrades-in-arms will take up my work after my death and carry it to the maximum perfection, seeing that those men are free agents and will freely decide, to-morrow, what man is then to be. To-morrow, after my death, some men may decide to establish Fascism, and the others may be so cowardly or so slack as to let them do so. It so, Fascism will then be the truth of man, and so much the worse for us. In reality, things will be such as men have decided they shall be. Does that mean that I should abandon myself to quietism? No. First I ought to commit myself and then act my commitment, according to the time-honoured formula that "one need not hope in order to undertake one's work." Nor does this mean that I should not belong to a party, but only that I should be without illusion and that I should do what I can. For instance, if I ask myself "Will the social ideal as such, ever become a reality?" I cannot tell, I only know that whatever may be in my power to make it so, I shall do; beyond that, I can count upon nothing.

Quietism is the attitude of people who say, "let others do what I cannot do." The doctrine I am presenting before you is precisely the opposite of this, since it declares that there is no reality except in action. It goes further, indeed, and adds, "Man is nothing else but what he purposes, he exists only in so far as he realises himself, he is therefore nothing else but the sum of his actions, nothing else but what his life is." Hence we can well understand why some people are horrified by our teaching. For many have but one resource to sustain them in their misery, and that is to think, "Circumstances have been against me, I was worthy to be something much better than I have been. I admit I have never had a great love or a great friendship; but that is because I never met a man or a woman who were worthy of it; if I have not written any very good books, it is because I had not the leisure to do so; or, if I have had no children to whom I could devote myself it is because I did not find the man I could have lived with. So there remains within me a wide range of abilities, inclinations and potentialities, unused but perfectly viable, which endow me with a worthiness that could never be inferred from the mere history of my actions." But in reality and for the existentialist, there is no love apart from the deeds of love; no potentiality of love other than that which is manifested in loving; there is no genius other than that which is expressed in works of art. The genius of Proust is the totality of the works of Proust; the genius of Racine is the series of his tragedies, outside of which there is nothing. Why should we attribute to Racine the capacity to write yet another tragedy when that is precisely what he did not write? In life, a man commits himself, draws his own portrait and there is nothing but that portrait. No doubt this thought may seem comfortless to one who has not made a success of his life. On the other hand, it puts everyone in a position to understand that reality alone is reliable; that dreams, expectations and hopes serve to define a man only as deceptive dreams, abortive hopes, expectations unfulfilled; that is to say, they define him negatively, not positively. Nevertheless, when one says, "You are nothing else but what you live," it does not imply that an artist is to be judged solely by his works of art, for a thousand other things contribute no less to his definition as a man. What we mean to say is that a man is no other than a series of undertakings, that he is the sum, the organisation, the set of relations that constitute these undertakings.

In the light of all this, what people reproach us with is not, after all, our pessimism, but the sternness of our optimism. If people condemn our works of fiction, in which we describe characters that are base, weak, cowardly and sometimes even frankly evil, it is not only because those characters are base, weak, cowardly or evil. For suppose that, like Zola, we showed that the behaviour of these characters was caused by their heredity, or by the action of their environment upon them, or by determining factors, psychic or organic. People would be reassured, they would say, "You see, that is what we are like, no one can do anything about it." But the existentialist, when he portrays a coward, shows him as responsible for his cowardice. He is not like that on account of a cowardly heart or lungs or cerebrum, he has not become like that through his physiological organism; he is like that because he has made himself into a coward by his actions. There is no such thing as a cowardly temperament. There are nervous temperaments; there is what is called impoverished blood, and there are also rich temperaments. But the man whose blood is poor is not a coward for all that, for what produces cowardice is the act of giving up or giving way; and a temperament is not an action. A coward is defined by the deed that he has done. What people feel obscurely, and with horror, is that the coward as we present him is guilty of being a coward. What people would prefer would be to be born either a coward or a hero. One of the charges most often laid against the *Chemins de la Liberté* is something like this—"But, after all, these people being so base, how can you make them into heroes?" That objection is really rather comic, for it implies that people are born heroes: and that is, at bottom, what such people would like to think. If you are born cowards, you can be quite content, you can do nothing about it and you will be cowards all your lives whatever you do; and if you are born heroes you can again be quite content; you will be heroes all your lives, eating and drinking heroically. Whereas the existentialist says that the coward makes himself cowardly, the hero makes himself heroic; and that there is always a possibility for the coward to give up cowardice and for the hero to stop being a hero. What counts is the total commitment, and it is not by a particular case or particular action that you are committed altogether.

We have now, I think, dealt with a certain number of the reproaches against existentialism. You have seen that it cannot be regarded as a philosophy of quietism since it defines man by his action; nor as a pessimistic description of man, for no doctrine is more optimistic, the destiny of man is placed within himself. Nor is it an attempt to discourage man from action since it tells him that there is no hope except in his action, and that the one thing which permits him to have life is the deed. Upon this level therefore, what we are considering is an ethic of action and self-commitment. However, we are still reproached, upon these few data, for confining man within his individual subjectivity. There again people badly misunderstand us.

Our point of departure is, indeed, the subjectivity of the individual, and that for strictly philosophic reasons. It is not because we are bourgeois, but because we seek to base our teaching upon the truth, and not upon a collection of fine theories, full of hope but lacking real foundations. And at the point of departure there cannot be any other truth than this, *I think, therefore I am,* which is the absolute truth of consciousness as it attains to itself. Every theory which begins with man, outside of this moment of self-attainment, is a theory which thereby suppresses the truth, for outside of the Cartesian *cogito,* all objects are no more than probable, and any doctrine of probabilities which is not attached to a truth will crumble into nothing. In order to define the probable one must possess the true. Before there can be any truth whatever, then, there must be an absolute truth, and there is such a truth which is simple, easily attained and within the reach of everybody; it consists in one's immediate sense of one's self.

In the second place, this theory alone is compatible with the dignity of man, it is the only one which does not make man into an object. All kinds of materialism lead one to treat every man including oneself as an object—that is, as a set of pre-determined reactions, in no way different from the patterns of qualities and phenomena which constitute a table, or a chair or a stone. Our aim is precisely to establish the human kingdom as a pattern of values in distinction from the material world. But the subjectivity which we thus postulate as the standard of truth is no narrowly individual subjectivism, for as we have demonstrated, it is not only one's own self that one discovers in the *cogito,* but those of others too. Contrary to the philosophy of Descartes, contrary to that of Kant, when we say "I think" we are attaining to ourselves in the presence of the other, and we are just as certain of the other as we are of ourselves. Thus the man who discovers himself directly in the *cogito* also discovers all the others, and discovers them as the condition of his own existence. He recognises that he cannot be anything (in the sense in which one says one is spiritual, or that one is wicked or jealous) unless others recognise him as such. I cannot obtain any truth whatsoever about myself, except through the mediation of another. The other is indispensable to my existence, and equally so to any knowledge I can have of myself. Under these conditions, the intimate discovery of myself is at the same time the revelation of the other as a freedom which confronts mine, and which cannot think or will without doing so either for or against me. Thus, at once, we find ourselves in a world which

is, let us say, that of "inter-subjectivity." It is in this world that man has to decide what he is and what others are.

Furthermore, although it is impossible to find in each and every man a universal essence that can be called human nature, there is nevertheless a human universality of *condition.* It is not by chance that the thinkers of to-day are so much more ready to speak of the condition than of the nature of man. By his condition they understand, with more or less clarity, all the *limitations* which à priori define man's fundamental situation in the universe. His historical situations are variable: man may be born a slave in a pagan society, or may be a feudal baron, or a proletarian. But what never vary are the necessities of being in the world, of having to labour and to die there. These limitations are neither subjective nor objective, or rather there is both a subjective and an objective aspect of them. Objective, because we meet with them everywhere and they are everywhere recognisable: and subjective because they are *lived* and are nothing if man does not live them—if, that is to say, he does not freely determine himself and his existence in relation to them. And, diverse though man's purposes may be, at least none of them is wholly foreign to me, since every human purpose presents itself as an attempt either to surpass these limitations, or to widen them, or else to deny or to accommodate oneself to them. Consequently every purpose, however individual it may be, is of universal value. Every purpose, even that of a Chinese, an Indian or a Negro, can be understood by a European. To say it can be understood, means that the European of 1945 may be striving out of a certain situation towards the same limitations in the same way, and that he may re-conceive in himself the purpose of the Chinese, of the Indian or the African. In every purpose there is universality, in this sense that every purpose is comprehensible to every man. Not that this or that purpose defines man for ever, but that it may be entertained again and again. There is always some way of understanding an idiot, a child, a primitive man or a foreigner if one has sufficient information. In this sense we may say that there is a human universality, but it is not something given; it is being perpetually made. I make this universality in choosing myself; I also make it by understanding the purpose of any other man, of whatever epoch. This absoluteness of the act of choice does not alter the relativity of each epoch.

What is at the very heart and centre of existential-ism, is the absolute character of the free commit-ment, by which every man realises himself in realising a type of humanity—a commitment always under-standable, to no matter whom in no matter what epoch—and its bearing upon the relativity of the cul-tural pattern which may result from such absolute commitment. One must observe equally the relativity of Cartesianism and the absolute character of the Cartesian commitment. In this sense you may say, if you like, that every one of us makes the absolute by breathing, by eating, by sleeping or by behaving in any fashion whatsoever. There is no difference between free being—being as self-committal, as existence choosing its essence—and absolute being. And there is no difference whatever between being as an abso-lute, temporarily localised—that is, localised in his-tory—and universally intelligible being.

This does not completely refute the charge of sub-jectivism. Indeed that objection appears in several other forms, of which the first is as follows. People say to us, "Then it does not matter what you do," and they say this in various ways. First they tax us with anarchy; then they say, "You cannot judge others, for there is no reason for preferring one purpose to an-other"; finally, they may say, "Everything being merely voluntary in this choice of yours, you give away with one hand what you pretend to gain with the other." These three are not very serious objections. As to the first, to say that it matters not what you choose is not correct. In one sense choice is possible, but what is not possible is not to choose. I can always choose, but I must know that if I do not choose, that is still a choice. This, although it may appear merely formal, is of great importance as a limit to fantasy and caprice. For, when I confront a real situation—for example, that I am a sexual being, able to have relations with a being of the other sex and able to have children—I am obliged to choose my attitude to it, and in every re-spect I bear the responsibility of the choice which, in committing myself, also commits the whole of hu-manity. Even if my choice is determined by no *a pri-ori* value whatever, it can have nothing to do with ca-price: and if anyone thinks that this is only Gide's theory of the *acte gratuit* over again, he has failed to see the enormous difference between this theory and that of Gide. Gide does not know what a situation is, his "act" is one of pure caprice. In our view, on the contrary, man finds himself in an organised situation

in which he is himself involved: his choice involves mankind in its entirety, and he cannot avoid choos-ing. Either he must remain single, or he must marry without having children, or he must marry and have children. In any case, and whichever he may choose, it is impossible for him, in respect of this situation, not to take complete responsibility. Doubtless he chooses without reference to any pre-established values, but it is unjust to tax him with caprice. Rather let us say that the moral choice is comparable to the construction of a work of art.

But here I must at once digress to make it quite clear that we are not propounding an aesthetic moral-ity, for our adversaries are disingenuous enough to reproach us even with that. I mention the work of art only by way of comparison. That being understood, does anyone reproach an artist when he paints a pic-ture for not following rules established *à priori*? Does one ever ask what is the picture that he ought to paint? As everyone knows, there is no pre-defined picture for him to make; the artist applies himself to the com-position of a picture, and the picture that ought to be made is precisely that which he will have made. As everyone knows, there are no aesthetic values *à priori*, but there are values which will appear in due course in the coherence of the picture, in the relation between the will to create and the finished work. No one can tell what the painting of to-morrow will be like; one cannot judge a painting until it is done. What has that to do with morality? We are in the same creative situ-ation. We never speak of a work of art as irrespon-sible; when we are discussing a canvas by Picasso, we understand very well that the composition became what it is at the time when he was painting it, and that his works are part and parcel of his entire life.

It is the same upon the plane of morality. There is this in common between art and morality, that in both we have to do with creation and invention. We cannot decide *à priori* what it is that should be done. I think it was made sufficiently clear to you in the case of that student who came to see me, that to whatever ethical system he might appeal, the Kantian or any other, he could find no sort of guidance whatever; he was obliged to invent the law for himself. Certainly we cannot say that this man, in choosing to remain with his mother—that is, in taking sentiment, per-sonal devotion and concrete charity as his moral foun-dations—would be making an irresponsible choice, nor could we do so if he preferred the sacrifice of going away to England. Man makes himself; he is not found ready-made; he makes himself by the choice of his morality, and he cannot but choose a morality, such is the pressure of circumstances upon him. We define man only in relation to his commitments; it is therefore absurd to reproach us for irresponsibility in our choice.

In the second place, people say to us, "You are unable to judge others." This is true in one sense and false in another. It is true in this sense, that whenever a man chooses his purpose and his commitment in all clearness and in all sincerity, whatever that purpose may be it is impossible to prefer another for him. It is true in the sense that we do not believe in progress. Progress implies amelioration; but man is always the same, facing a situation which is always changing, and choice remains always a choice in the situation. The moral problem has not changed since the time when it was a choice between slavery and anti-slavery—from the time of the war of Secession, for example, until the present moment when one chooses between the M.R.P.* and the Communists.

We can judge, nevertheless, for, as I have said, one chooses in view of others, and in view of others one chooses himself. One can judge, first—and perhaps this is not a judgment of value, but it is a logical judgment—that in certain cases choice is founded upon an error, and in others upon the truth. One can judge a man by saying that he deceives himself. Since we have defined the situation of man as one of free choice, without excuse and without help, any man who takes refuge behind the excuse of his passions, or by inventing some deterministic doctrine, is a self-deceiver. One may object: "But why should he not choose to deceive himself?" I reply that it is not for me to judge him morally, but I define his self-deception as an error. Here one cannot avoid pronouncing a judgment of truth. The self-deception is evidently a falsehood, because it is a dissimulation of man's complete liberty of commitment. Upon this same level, I say that it is also a self-deception if I choose to declare that certain values are incumbent upon me; I am in contradiction with myself if I will these values and at the same time say that they impose themselves upon me. If anyone says to me, "And what if I wish to deceive myself?" I answer, "There is no reason why

you should not, but I declare that you are doing so, and that the attitude of strict consistency alone is that of good faith. Furthermore, I can pronounce a moral judgment. For I declare that freedom, in respect of concrete circumstances, can have no other end and aim but itself; and when once a man has seen that values depend upon himself, in that state of forsakenness he can will only one thing, and that is freedom as the foundation of all values. That does not mean that he wills it in the abstract: it simply means that the actions of men of good faith have, as their ultimate significance, the quest of freedom itself as such. A man who belongs to some communist or revolutionary society wills certain concrete ends, which imply the will to freedom, but that freedom is willed in community. We will freedom for freedom's sake, and in and through particular circumstances. And in thus willing freedom, we discover that it depends entirely upon the freedom of others and that the freedom of others depends upon our own. Obviously, freedom as the definition of a man does not depend upon others, but as soon as there is a commitment, I am obliged to will the liberty of others at the same time as mine. I cannot make liberty my aim unless I make that of others equally my aim. Consequently, when I recognise, as entirely authentic, that man is a being whose existence precedes his essence, and that he is a free being who cannot, in any circumstances, but will his freedom, at the same time I realise that I cannot not will the freedom of others. Thus, in the name of that will to freedom which is implied in freedom itself, I can form judgments upon those who seek to hide from themselves the wholly voluntary nature of their existence and its complete freedom. Those who hide from this total freedom, in a guise of solemnity or with deterministic excuses, I shall call cowards. Others, who try to show that their existence is necessary, when it is merely an accident of the appearance of the human race on earth,—I shall call scum. But neither cowards nor scum can be identified except upon the plane of strict authenticity. Thus, although the content of morality is variable, a certain form of this morality is universal. Kant declared that freedom is a will both to itself and to the freedom of others. Agreed: but he thinks that the formal and the universal suffice for the constitution of a morality. We think, on the contrary, that principles that are too abstract break down when we come to defining action. To take once again the case of that student; by what authority, in the name of what golden rule of morality, do

---

*Mouvement Républicain Populaire.

you think he could have decided, in perfect peace of mind, either to abandon his mother or to remain with her? There are no means of judging. The content is always concrete, and therefore unpredictable; it has always to be invented. The one thing that counts, is to know whether the invention is made in the name of freedom.

Let us, for example, examine the two following cases, and you will see how far they are similar in spite of their difference. Let us take *The Mill on the Floss*. We find here a certain young woman, Maggie Tulliver, who is an incarnation of the value of passion and is aware of it. She is in love with a young man, Stephen, who is engaged to another, an insignificant young woman. This Maggie Tulliver, instead of heedlessly seeking her own happiness, chooses in the name of human solidarity to sacrifice herself and to give up the man she loves. On the other hand, La Sanseverina in Stendhal's *Chartreuse de Parme* believing that it is passion which endows man with his real value, would have declared that a grand passion justifies its sacrifices, and must be preferred to the banality of such conjugal love as would unite Stephen to the little goose he was engaged to marry. It is the latter that she would have chosen to sacrifice in realising her own happiness, and, as Stendhal shows, she would also sacrifice herself upon the plane of passion if life made that demand upon her. Here we are facing two clearly opposed moralities; but I claim that they are equivalent, seeing that in both cases the overruling aim is freedom. You can imagine two attitudes exactly similar in effect, in that one girl might prefer, in resignation, to give up her lover whilst the other preferred, in fulfilment of sexual desire, to ignore the prior engagement of the man she loved; and, externally, these two cases might appear the same as the two we have just cited, while being in fact entirely different. The attitude of La Sanseverina is much nearer to that of Maggie Tulliver than to one of careless greed. Thus, you see, the second objection is at once true and false. One can choose anything, but only if it is upon the plane of free commitment.

The third objection, stated by saying, "You take with one hand what you give with the other," means, at bottom, "your values are not serious, since you choose them yourselves." To that I can only say that I am very sorry that it should be so; but if I have excluded God the Father, there must be somebody to invent values. We have to take things as they are. And moreover, to say that we invent values means neither more nor less than this; that there is no sense in life *à priori*. Life is nothing until it is lived; but it is yours to make sense of, and the value of it is nothing else but the sense that you choose. Therefore, you can see that there is a possibility of creating a human community. I have been reproached for suggesting that existentialism is a form of humanism: people have said to me, "But you have written in your *Nauseé* that the humanists are wrong, you have even ridiculed a certain type of humanism, why do you now go back upon that?" In reality, the word humanism has two very different meanings. One may understand by humanism a theory which upholds man as the end-in-itself and as the supreme value. Humanism in this sense appears, for instance, in Cocteau's story *Round the World in 80 Hours*, in which one of the characters declares, because he is flying over mountains in an aeroplane, "Man is magnificent!" This signifies that although I, personally, have not built aeroplanes I have the benefit of those particular inventions and that I personally, being a man, can consider myself responsible for, and honoured by, achievements that are peculiar to some men. It is to assume that we can ascribe value to man according to the most distinguished deeds of certain men. That kind of humanism is absurd, for only the dog or the horse would be in a position to pronounce a general judgment upon man and declare that he is magnificent, which they have never been such fools as to do—at least, not as far as I know. But neither is it admissible that a man should pronounce judgment upon Man. Existentialism dispenses with any judgment of this sort: an existentialist will never take man as the end, since man is still to be determined. And we have no right to believe that humanity is something to which we could set up a cult, after the manner of Auguste Comte. The cult of humanity ends in Comtian humanism, shut-in upon itself, and—this must be said—in Fascism. We do not want a humanism like that.

But there is another sense of the word, of which the fundamental meaning is this: Man is all the time outside of himself: it is in projecting and losing himself beyond himself that he makes man to exist; and, on the other hand, it is by pursuing transcendent aims that he himself is able to exist. Since man is thus self-surpassing, and can grasp objects only in relation to his self-surpassing, he is himself the heart and centre of his transcendence. There is no other universe except the human universe, the universe of human subjectivity. This relation of transcendence as constitutive of man (not in the sense that God is transcendent, but in the sense of self-surpassing) with subjectivity (in such a sense that man is not shut up in himself but forever present in a human universe)—it is this that we call existential humanism. This is humanism, because we remind man that there is no legislator but himself; that he himself, thus abandoned, must decide for himself; also because we show that it is not by turning back upon himself, but always by seeking, beyond himself, an aim which is one of liberation or of some particular realisation, that man can realise himself as truly human.

You can see from these few reflections that nothing could be more unjust than the objections people raise against us. Existentialism is nothing else but an attempt to draw the full conclusions from a consistently atheistic position. Its intention is not in the least that of plunging men into despair. And if by despair one means—as the Christians do—any attitude of unbelief, the despair of the existentialists is something different. Existentialism is not atheist in the sense that it would exhaust itself in demonstrations of the nonexistence of God. It declares, rather, that even if God existed that would make no difference from its point of view. Not that we believe God does exist, but we think that the real problem is not that of His existence; what man needs is to find himself again and to understand that nothing can save him from himself, not even a valid proof of the existence of God. In this sense existentialism is optimistic, it is a doctrine of action, and it is only by self-deception, by confusing their own despair with ours that Christians can describe us as without hope.

⟨ *The Phenomenon* ⟩
from Being and Nothingness

Modern thought has realized considerable progress by reducing the existent to the series of appearances which manifest it.* Its aim was to overcome a certain number of dualisms which have embarrassed philosophy and to replace them by the monism of the phenomenon. Has the attempt been successful?

———

*Footnotes omitted—ed.

In the first place we certainly thus get rid of that dualism which in the existent opposes interior to exterior. There is no longer an exterior for the existent if one means by that a superficial covering which hides from sight the true nature of the object. And this true nature in turn, if it is to be the secret reality of the thing, which one can have a presentiment of or which one can suppose but can never reach because it is the "interior" of the object under consideration—this nature no longer exists. The appearances which manifest the existent are neither interior nor exterior; they are all equal, they all refer to other appearances, and none of them is privileged. Force, for example, is not a metaphysical conatus of an unknown kind which hides behind its effects (accelerations, deviations, *etc.*); it is the totality of these effects. Similarly an electric current does not have a secret reverse side; it is nothing but the totality of the physical-chemical actions which manifest it (electrolysis, the incandescence of a carbon filament, the displacement of the needle of a galvanometer, *etc.*). No one of these actions alone is sufficient to reveal it. But no action indicates anything which is *behind itself*; it indicates only itself and the total series.

The obvious conclusion is that the dualism of being and appearance is no longer entitled to any legal status within philosophy. The appearance refers to the total series of appearances and not to a hidden reality which would drain to itself all the *being* of the existent. And the appearance for its part is not an inconsistent manifestation of this being. To the extent that men had believed in noumenal realities, they have presented appearance as a pure negative. It was "that which is not being"; it had no other being than that of illusion and error. But even this being was borrowed, it was itself a pretense, and philosophers met with the greatest difficulty in maintaining cohesion and existence in the appearance so that it should not itself be reabsorbed in the depth of non-phenomenal being. But if we once get away from what Nietzsche called "the illusion of worlds-behind-the-scene," and if we no longer believe in the being-behind-the-appearance, then the appearance becomes full positivity; its essence is an "appearing" which is no longer opposed to being but on the contrary is the measure of it. For the being of an existent is exactly what it *appears*. Thus we arrive at the idea of the *phenomenon* such as we can find, for example, in the "phenomenology" of Husserl or of Heidegger—the phenomenon or the relative-absolute. Relative the phenomenon remains, for "to appear" supposes in essence somebody to whom to appear. But it . . . does not point over its shoulder to a true being which would be, for it, absolute. What it is, it is absolutely, for it reveals itself as it is. The phenomenon can be studied and described as such, for it is *absolutely indicative of itself.*

The duality of potency and act falls by the same stroke. The act is everything. Behind the act there is neither potency . . . nor virtue. We shall refuse, for example, to understand by "genius"—in the sense in which we say that Proust "had genius" or that he "was" a genius—a particular capacity to produce certain works, which was not exhausted exactly in producing them. The genius of Proust is neither the work considered in isolation nor the subjective ability to produce it; it is the work considered as the totality of the manifestations of the person.

That is why we can equally well reject the dualism of appearance and essence. The appearance does not hide the essence, it reveals it; it *is* the essence. The essence of an existent is no longer a property sunk in the cavity of this existent; it is the manifest law which presides over the succession of its appearances, it is the principle of the series. To the nominalism of Poincaré, defining a physical reality (an electric current, for example) as the *sum* of its various manifestations, Duhem rightly opposed his own theory, which makes of the concept the *synthetic unity* of these manifestations. To be sure phenomenology is anything but a nominalism. But essence, as the principle of the series, is definitely only the concatenation of appearances; that is, itself an appearance. This explains how it is possible to have an intuition of *essences* (the *Wesenschau* of Husserl, for example). The phenomenal being manifests itself; it manifests its essence as well as its existence, and it is nothing but the well connected series of its manifestations. . . .

. . .

The Question
from Being and Nothingness

. . .

It is enough now to open our eyes and question ingenuously this totality which is man-in-the-world.

It is by the description of this totality that we shall be able to reply to these two questions: (1) What is the synthetic relation which we call being-in-the-world? (2) What must man and the world be in order for a relation between them to be possible? In truth, the two questions are interdependent, and we can not hope to reply to them separately. But each type of human conduct, being the conduct of man in the world, can release for us simultaneously man, the world, and the relation which unites them, only on condition that we envisage these forms of conduct as realities objectively apprehensible and not as subjective affects which disclose themselves only in the face of reflection.

We shall not limit ourselves to the study of a single pattern of conduct. We shall try on the contrary to describe several and, proceeding from one kind of conduct to another, attempt to penetrate into the profound meaning of the relation "man-world." But first of all we should choose a single pattern which can serve us as a guiding thread in our inquiry.

Now this very inquiry furnishes us with the desired conduct; this man that *I am*—if I apprehend him such as he is at this moment in the world, I establish that he stands before being in an attitude of interrogation. At the very moment when I ask, "Is there any conduct which can reveal to me the relation of man with the world?" I pose a question. This question I can consider objectively, for it matters little whether the questioner is myself or the reader who reads my work and who is questioning along with me. But on the other hand, the question is not simply the objective totality of the words printed on this page; it is indifferent to the symbols which express it. In a word, it is a human attitude filled with meaning. What does this attitude reveal to us?

In every question we stand before a being which we are questioning. Every question presupposes a being who questions and a being which is questioned. This is not the original relation of man to being-in-itself, but rather it stands within the limitations of this relation and takes it for granted. On the other hand, this being which we question, we question *about* something. That *about which* I question the being participates in the transcendence of being. I question being about its ways of being or about its being. From this point of view the question is a kind of expectation; I expect a reply from the being questioned. That is, on the basis of a preinterrogative familiarity with being, I expect from this being a revelation of its being or of its way of being. The reply will be a "yes" or a "no." It is the existence of these two equally objective and contradictory possibilities which on principle distinguishes the question from affirmation or negation. There are questions which on the surface do not permit a negative reply—like, for example, the one which we put earlier, "What does this attitude reveal to us?" But actually we see that it is always possible with questions of this type to reply, "Nothing" or "Nobody" or "Never." Thus at the moment when I ask, "Is there any conduct which can reveal to me the relation of man with the world?" I admit *on principle* the possibility of a negative reply such as, "No, such a conduct does not exist." This means that we admit to being faced with the transcendent fact of the nonexistence of such conduct.

One will perhaps be tempted not to believe in the objective existence of a non-being; one will say that in this case the fact simply refers me to my subjectivity; I would learn from the transcendent being that the conduct sought is a pure fiction. But in the first place, to call this conduct a pure fiction is to disguise the negation without removing it. "To be pure fiction" is equivalent here to "to be only a fiction." Consequently to destroy the reality of the negation is to cause the reality of the reply to disappear. This reply, in fact, is the very being which gives it to me; that is, reveals the negation to me. There exists then for the questioner the permanent objective possibility of a negative reply. In relation to this possibility the questioner, by the very fact that he is questioning, posits himself as in a state of indetermination; he *does not know* whether the reply will be affirmative or negative. Thus the question is a bridge set up between two non-beings: the non-being of knowing in man, the possibility of non-being of being in transcendent being. Finally the question implies the existence of a truth. By the very question the questioner affirms that he expects an objective reply, such that we can say of it, "It is thus and not otherwise." In a word the truth, as differentiated from being, introduces a third non-being as determining the question—the non-being of limitation. This triple non-being conditions every question and in particular the metaphysical question, which is *our* question.

We set out upon our pursuit of being, and it seemed to us that the series of our questions had led us to the heart of being. But behold, at the moment when we thought we were arriving at the goal, a glance cast on the question itself has revealed to us suddenly that we are encompassed with nothingness. The permanent possibility of non-being, outside us and within, conditions our questions about being. Furthermore it is non-being which is going to limit the reply. What being *will be* must of necessity arise on the basis of what *it is not.* Whatever being is, it will allow this formulation: "Being is *that* and outside of that, *nothing.*"

Thus a new component of the real has just appeared to us—non-being. Our problem is thereby complicated, for we may no longer limit our inquiry to the relations of the human being to being in-itself, but must include also the relations of being with non-being and the relations of human non-being with transcendent-being. But let us consider further.

Negations
from Being and Nothingness

Someone will object that being-in-itself can not furnish negative replies. Did not we ourselves say that it was beyond affirmation as beyond negation? Furthermore ordinary experience reduced to itself does not seem to disclose any non-being to us. I think that there are fifteen hundred francs in my wallet, and I find only thirteen hundred; that does not mean, someone will tell us, that experience had discovered for me the non-being of fifteen hundred francs but simply that I have counted thirteen hundred-franc notes. Negation proper (we are told) is unthinkable; it could appear only on the level of an act of judgment by which I should establish a comparison between the result anticipated and the result obtained. Thus negation would be simply a quality of judgment and the expectation of the questioner would be an expectation of the judgment-response. As for Nothingness, this would derive its origin from negative judgments; it would be a concept establishing the transcendent unity of all these judgments, a propositional function of the type, "X is not."

.   .   .

It is evident that non-being always appears within the limits of a human expectation. It is because I expect to find fifteen hundred francs that I find *only* thirteen hundred. It is because a physicist *expects* a certain verification of his hypothesis that nature can tell him no. It would be in vain to deny that negation appears on the original basis of a relation of man to the world. The world does not disclose its non-beings to one who has not first posited them as possibilities. But is this to say that these non-beings are to be reduced to pure subjectivity? . . . We think not.

First it is not true that negation is only a quality of judgment. The question is formulated by an interrogative judgment, but it is not itself a judgment; it is a pre-judicative attitude. I can question by a look, by a gesture. In posing a question I stand facing being in a certain way and this relation to being is a relation of being; the judgment is only one optional expression of it. At the same time it is not necessarily a person whom the questioner questions about being; this conception of the question by making of it an intersubjective phenomenon, detaches it from the being to which it adheres and leaves it in the air as pure modality of dialogue. On the contrary, we must consider the question in dialogue to be only a particular species of the genus "question"; the being in question is not necessarily a thinking being. If my car breaks down, it is the *carburetor,* the *spark plugs, etc.,* that I question. If my watch stops, I can question the watchmaker about the cause of the stopping, but it is the various mechanisms of the watch that the watchmaker will in turn question. What I expect from the carburetor, what the watchmaker expects from the works of the watch, is not a judgment; it is a disclosure of being on the basis of which we can make a judgment. And if I *expect* a disclosure of being, I am prepared at the same time for the eventuality of a disclosure of a non-being. If I question the carburetor, it is because I consider it possible that "there is nothing there" in the carburetor. Thus my question by its nature envelops a certain pre-judicative comprehension of non-being; it is in itself a relation of being with non-being, on the basis of the original transcendence; that is, in a relation of being with being.

Moreover if the proper nature of the question is obscured by the fact that questions are frequently put by one man to other men, it should be pointed out here that there are numerous non-judicative conducts which present this immediate comprehension of non-being on the basis of being—in its original purity. If, for example, we consider *destruction,* we must recognize that it is an *activity* which doubtless could utilize judgment as an instrument but which can not be defined as uniquely or even primarily judicative. "De-

struction" presents the same structure as "the question." In a sense, certainly, man is the only being by whom a destruction can be accomplished. A geological plication, a storm do not destroy—or at least they do not destroy *directly;* they merely modify the distribution of masses of beings. There is no *less* after the storm than before. There is *something else.* Even this expression is improper, for to posit otherness there must be a witness who can retain the past in some manner and compare it to the present in the form of *no longer.* In the absence of this witness, there is being before as after the storm—that is all. If a cyclone can bring about the death of certain living beings, this death will be destruction only if it is experienced as such. In order for destruction to exist, there must be first a relation of man to being—*i.e.,* a transcendence; and within the limits of this relation, it is necessary that man apprehend one being as destructible. This supposes a limiting cutting into being by a being, which, as we saw in connection with truth, is already a process of nihilation. The being under consideration is *that* and outside of that *nothing.* The gunner who has been assigned an objective carefully points his gun in a certain direction *excluding* all others. But even this would still be nothing unless the being of the gunner's objective is revealed as *fragile.* And what is fragility if not a certain probability of non-being for a given being under determined circumstances. A being is fragile if it carries in its being a definite possibility of non-being. But once again it is through man that fragility comes into being, for the individualizing limitation which we mentioned earlier is the condition of fragility; *one* being is fragile and not *all* being, for the latter is beyond all possible destruction.

. . .

But if we wish to decide with certainty, we need only to consider an example of a negative judgment and to ask ourselves whether it causes non-being to appear at the heart of being or merely limits itself to determining a prior revelation. I have an appointment with Pierre at four o'clock. I arrive at the café a quarter of an hour late. Pierre is always punctual. Will he have waited for me? I look at the room, the patrons, and I say, "He is not here." Is there an intuition of Pierre's absence, or does negation indeed enter in only with judgment? At first sight it seems absurd to speak here of intuition since to be exact there could not be an intuition of *nothing* and since the absence of Pierre is this nothing. Popular consciousness, however, bears witness to this intuition. Do we not say, for example, "I suddenly saw that he was not there." Is this just a matter of misplacing the negation? Let us look a little closer.

It is certain that the café by itself with its patrons, its tables, its booths, its mirrors, its light, its smoky atmosphere, and the sounds of voices, rattling saucers, and footsteps which fill it—the café is a fullness of being. And all the intuitions of detail which I can have are filled by these odors, these sounds, these colors, all phenomena which have a transphenomenal being. Similarly Pierre's actual presence in a place which I do not know is also a plenitude of being. We seem to have found fullness everywhere. But we must observe that in perception there is always the construction of a figure on a ground. No one object, no group of objects is especially designed to be organized as specifically either ground or figure; all depends on the direction of my attention. When I enter this café to search for Pierre, there is formed a synthetic organization of all the objects in the café, on the ground of which Pierre is given as about to appear. This organization of the café as the ground is an original nihilation. Each element of the setting, a person, a table, a chair, attempts to isolate itself, to lift itself upon the ground constituted by the totality of the other objects, only to fall back once more into the undifferentiation of this ground; it melts into the ground. For the ground is that which is seen only in addition, that which is the object of a purely marginal attention. Thus the original nihilation of all the figures which appear and are swallowed up in the total neutrality of a *ground* is the necessary condition for the appearance of the principle figure, which is here the person of Pierre. This nihilation is given to my intuition; I am witness to the successive disappearance of all the objects which I look at—in particular of the faces, which detain me for an instant (Could this be Pierre?) and which as quickly decompose precisely because they "are not" the face of Pierre. Nevertheless if I should finally discover Pierre, my intuition would be filled by a solid element, I should be suddenly arrested by his face and the whole café would organize itself around him as a discrete presence.

But now Pierre is not here. This does not mean that I discover his absence in some precise spot in the establishment. In fact Pierre is absent from the *whole* café; his absence fixes the café in its evanescence; the café remains *ground;* it persists in offering itself as an undifferentiated totality to my only marginal attention; it slips into the background; it pursues its nihilation. Only it makes itself ground for a determined figure; it carries the figure everywhere in front of it, presents the figure everywhere to me. This figure which slips constantly between my look and the solid, real objects of the café is precisely a perpetual disappearance; it is Pierre raising himself as nothingness on the ground of the nihilation of the café. So that what is offered to intuition is a flickering of nothingness; it is the nothingness of the ground, the nihilation of which summons and demands the appearance of the figure, and it is the figure—the nothingness which slips as a *nothing* to the surface of the ground. It serves as foundation for the judgment—"Pierre is not here." It is in fact the intuitive apprehension of a double nihilation. To be sure Pierre's absence supposes an original relation between me and this café; there is an infinity of people who are without any relation with this café for want of a real expectation which establishes their absence. But, to be exact, I myself expected to see Pierre, and my expectation has caused the absence of Pierre *to happen* as a real event concerning this café. It is an objective fact at present that I have *discovered* this absence, and it presents itself as a synthetic relation between Pierre and the setting in which I am looking for him. Pierre absent haunts this café and is the condition of its self-nihilating organization as ground. By contrast, judgments which I can make subsequently to amuse myself, such as, "Wellington is not in this café, Paul Valéry is no longer here, *etc.*"— these have a purely abstract meaning; they are pure applications of the principle of negation without real or efficacious foundation, and they never succeed in establishing a *real* relation between the café and Wellington or Valéry. Here the relation "is not" is merely *thought.* This example is sufficient to show that nonbeing does not come to things by a negative judgment; it is the negative judgment, on the contrary, which is conditioned and supported by non-being.

. . .

But where does nothingness come from? If it is the original condition of the questioning attitude and more generally of all philosophical or scientific inquiry, what is the original relation of the human being to nothingness? What is the original nihilating conduct?

The Origin of Nothingness
from Being and Nothingness

It would be well at this point to cast a glance backward and to measure the road already covered.* We raised first the question of being. Then examining this very question conceived as a type of human conduct, we questioned this in turn. We next had to recognize that no question could be asked, in particular not that of being, if negation did not exist. But this negation itself when inspected more closely referred us back to Nothingness as its origin and foundation. In order for negation to exist in the world and in order that we may consequently raise questions concerning Being, it is necessary that in some way Nothingness be given. We perceived then that Nothingness can be conceived neither *outside of* being, nor as a complementary, abstract notion, nor as an infinite milieu where being is suspended. Nothingness must be given at the heart of Being, in order for us to be able to apprehend that particular type of realities which we have called *négatités*. But this intra-mundane Nothingness can not be produced by Being-in-itself; the notion of Being as full positivity does not contain Nothingness as one of its structures. We can not even say that Being excludes it. Being lacks all relation with it. Hence the question which is put to us now with a particular urgency: if Nothingness can be conceived neither outside of Being, nor in terms of Being, and if on the other hand, since it is non-being, it can not derive from itself the necessary force to "nihilate itself," *where does Nothingness come from?*

If we wish to pursue the problem further, we must first recognize that we can not grant to nothingness the property of "nihilating itself." For although the expression "to nihilate itself" is thought of as removing from nothingness the last semblance of being, we must recognize that only *Being* can nihilate itself; however it comes about, in order to nihilate itself, it must

be. But Nothingness *is not.* If we can speak of it, it is only because it possesses an appearance of being, a borrowed being, as we have noted above. Nothingness is not, Nothingness "is made-to-be," Nothingness does not nihilate itself; Nothingness "is nihilated." It follows therefore that there must exist a Being (this can not be the In-itself) of which the property is to nihilate Nothingness, to support it in its being, to sustain it perpetually in its very existence, *a being by which nothingness comes to things.* But how can this Being be related to Nothingness so that through it Nothingness comes to things? We must observe first that the being postulated can not be passive in relation to Nothingness, can not receive it; Nothingness could not *come* to this being except through another Being—which would be an infinite regress. But on the other hand, the Being by which Nothingness comes to the world can not *produce* Nothingness while remaining indifferent to that production—like the Stoic cause which produces its effect without being itself changed. It would be inconceivable that a Being which is full positivity should maintain and create outside itself a Nothingness or transcendent being, for there would be nothing in Being by which Being could surpass itself toward Non-Being. The Being by which Nothingness arrives in the world must nihilate Nothingness in its Being, and even so it still runs the risk of establishing Nothingness as a transcendent in the very heart of immanence unless it nihilates Nothingness in its being *in connection with its own being.* The Being by which Nothingness arrives in the world is a being such that in its Being, the Nothingness of its Being is in question. *The being by which Nothingness comes to the world must be its own Nothingness.* By this we must understand not a nihilating act, which would require in turn a foundation in Being, but an ontological characteristic of the Being required. It remains to learn in what delicate, exquisite region of Being we shall encounter that Being which is its own Nothingness.

We shall be helped in our inquiry by a more complete examination of the conduct which served us as a point of departure. We must return to the question. We have seen, it may be recalled, that every question in essence posits the possibility of a negative reply. In a question we question a being about its being or its way of being. This way of being or this being is veiled; there always remains the possibility that it may unveil itself as a Nothingness. But from the very fact that we

---

*Footnotes omitted—ed.

presume that an Existent can always be revealed as *nothing,* every question supposes that we realize a nihilating withdrawal in relation to the given, which becomes a simple *presentation,* fluctuating between being and Nothingness.

It is essential therefore that the questioner have the permanent possibility of dissociating himself from the causal series which constitutes being and which can produce only being. If we admitted that the question is determined in the questioner by universal determinism, the question would thereby become unintelligible and even inconceivable. A real cause, in fact, produces a real effect and the caused being is wholly engaged by the cause in positivity; to the extent that its being depends on the cause, it can not have within itself the tiniest germ of nothingness. Thus in so far as the questioner must be able to effect in relation to the questioned a kind of nihilating withdrawal, he is not subject to the causal order of the world; he detaches himself from Being. This means that by a double movement of nihilation he nihilates the thing questioned in relation to himself by placing it in a *neutral* state, between being and non-being—and that he nihilates himself in relation to the thing questioned by wrenching himself from being in order to be able to bring out of himself the possibility of a non-being. Thus in posing a question, a certain negative element is introduced into the world. We see nothingness making the world iridescent, casting a shimmer over things. But at the same time the question emanates from a questioner who, in order to motivate himself in his being as one who questions, disengages himself from being. This disengagement is then by definition a human process. Man presents himself at least in this instance as a being who causes Nothingness to arise in the world, inasmuch as he himself is affected with non-being to this end.

These remarks may serve as guiding thread as we examine the *négatités* of which we spoke earlier. There is no doubt at all that these are transcendent realities; distance, for example, is imposed on us as something which we have to take into account, which must be cleared with effort. However these realities are of a very peculiar nature; they will indicate immediately an essential relation of human reality to the world. They derive their origin from an act, an expectation, or a project of the human being; they all indicate an aspect of being as it appears to the human being who is engaged in the world. The relations of man in the world, which the *négatités* indicate, have nothing in common with the relations *a posteriori* which are brought out by empirical activity. We are no longer dealing with those relations of *instrumentality* by which, according to Heidegger, objects in the world disclose themselves to "human reality." Every *négatité* appears rather as one of the essential conditions of this relation of instrumentality. In order for the totality of being to order itself around us as instruments, in order for it to parcel itself into differentiated complexes which refer one to another and which can *be used,* it is necessary that negation rise up not as a thing among other things but as the rubric of a category which presides over the arrangement and the redistribution of great masses of being in things. Thus the rise of man in the midst of the being which "invests" him causes a world to be discovered. But the essential and primordial moment of this rise is the negation. Thus we have reached the first goal of this study. Man is the being through whom nothingness comes to the world. But this question immediately provokes another: What must man be in his being in order that through him nothingness may come to being?

Being can generate only being and if man is inclosed in this process of generation, only being will come out of him. If we are to assume that man is able to question this process—*i.e.,* to make it the object of interrogation—he must be able to hold it up to view as a totality. He must be able to put himself *outside of* being and by the same stroke weaken the structure of the being of being. Yet it is not given to "human reality" to annihilate even provisionally the mass of being which it posits before itself. Man's *relation* with being is that he can modify it. For man to put a particular existent out of circuit is to put himself out of circuit in relation to that existent. In this case he is not subject to it; he is out of reach; it can not act on him, for he has retired *beyond a nothingness.* Descartes following the Stoics has given a name to this possibility which human reality has to secrete a nothingness which isolates it—it is *freedom.* But freedom here is only a name. If we wish to penetrate further into the question, we must not be content with this reply and we ought to ask now, What is human freedom if through it nothingness comes into the world?

· · · ·

What we call freedom is impossible to distinguish from the *being* of "human reality." Man does not exist *first* in order to be free *subsequently;* there is no difference between the being of man and his *being-free.* This is not the time to make a frontal attack on a question which can be treated exhaustively only in the light of a rigorous elucidation of the human being. Here we are dealing with freedom in connection with the problem of nothingness and only to the extent that it conditions the appearance of nothingness.

What first appears evident is that human reality can detach itself from the world—in questioning, in systematic doubt, in sceptical doubt, in the ἐποχή, etc.—only if by nature it has the possibility of self-detachment. This was seen by Descartes, who is establishing doubt on freedom when he claims for us the possibility of suspending our judgments. Alain's position is similar. It is also in this sense that Hegel asserts the freedom of the mind to the degree that mind is mediation—*i.e.,* the Negative. Furthermore it is one of the trends of contemporary philosophy to see in human consciousness a sort of escape from the self; such is the meaning of the transcendence of Heidegger. The intentionality of Husserl and of Brentano has also to a large extent the characteristic of a detachment from self. But we are not yet in a position to consider freedom as an inner structure of consciousness. We lack for the moment both instruments and technique to permit us to succeed in that enterprise. What interests us at present is a temporal operation since questioning is, like doubt, a kind of behavior; it assumes that the human being reposes first in the depths of being and then detaches himself from it by a nihilating withdrawal. Thus we are envisaging the condition of the nihilation as a relation to the self in the heart of a temporal process. We wish simply to show that by identifying consciousness with a causal sequence indefinitely continued, one transmutes it into a plenitude of being and thereby causes it to return into the unlimited totality of being—as is well illustrated by the futility of the efforts to dissociate psychological determinism from universal determinism and to constitute it as a separate series.

The room of someone absent, the books of which he turned the pages, the objects which he touched are in themselves only *books, objects, i.e.,* full actualities. The very traces which he has left can be deciphered as traces of him only within a situation where he has been already posited as absent. The dog-eared book with the well-read pages is not by itself a book of which Pierre has turned the pages, of which he no longer turns the pages. If we consider it as the present, transcendent motivation of my perception or even as the synthetic flux, regulated by my sensible impressions, then it is merely a volume with turned down, worn pages; it can refer only to itself or to present objects, to the lamp which illuminates it, to the table which holds it. It would be useless to invoke an association by contiguity as Plato does in the *Phaedo,* where he makes the image of the absent one appear on the margin of the perception of the lyre or of the cithara which he has touched. This image, if we consider it in itself and in the spirit of classical theories, is a definite plenitude; it is a concrete and positive psychic fact. Consequently we must of necessity pass on it a doubly negative judgment: subjectively, to signify that the image *is not* a perception; objectively, to deny that the Pierre of whom I form the image *is here* at this moment.

This is the famous problem of the characteristics of the true image, which has concerned so many psychologists from Taine to Spaier. Association, we see, does not solve the problem; it pushes it back to the level of reflection. But in every way it demands a negation; that is, at the very least a nihilating withdrawal of consciousness in relation to the image apprehended as subjective phenomenon, in order to posit it precisely as being only a subjective phenomenon.

Now I have attempted to show elsewhere that if we posit the image *first* as a renascent perception, it is radically impossible to distinguish it *subsequently* from actual perceptions. The image must enclose in its very structure a nihilating thesis. It constitutes itself qua image while positing its object as existing *elsewhere* or *not existing.* It carries within it a double negation; first it is the nihilation of the world (since the world is not offering the imagined object as an actual object of perception), secondly the nihilation of the object of the image (it is posited as not actual), and finally by the same stroke it is the nihilation of itself (since it is not a concrete, full psychic process). In explaining how I apprehend the absence of Pierre in the room, it would be useless to invoke those famous "empty intentions" of Husserl, which are in great part constitutive of perception. Among the various perceptive intentions, indeed, there are relations of *motivation* (but motivation is not causation), and among these intentions, some are full (*i.e.,* filled with what they aim at) and others empty. But precisely because the matter which should fill the empty intentions *does not exist,* it can not be this which motivates them in their structure. And since the other intentions are full, neither can they motivate the empty intentions inasmuch as the latter are empty. Moreover these intentions are of psychic nature and it would be an error to envisage them in the mode of things; that is, as recipients which would first be given, which according to circumstances could be emptied or filled, and which would be by nature indifferent to their state of being empty or filled. It seems that Husserl has not always escaped the materialist illusion. To be empty an intention must be conscious of itself as empty and precisely as empty *of* the exact matter at which it aims. An empty intention constitutes itself as empty to the exact extent that it posits its matter as non-existing or absent. In short an empty intention is a consciousness of negation which transcends itself toward an object which it posits as absent or non-existent.

Thus whatever may be the explanation which we give of it, Pierre's absence, in order to be established or realized, requires a negative moment by which consciousness, in the absence of all prior determination, constitutes itself as a negation. If in terms of my perceptions of the room, I conceive of the former inhabitant who is no longer in the room, I am of necessity forced to produce an act of thought which no prior state can determine nor motivate, in short to effect in myself a break with being. And in so far as I continually use *négatités* to isolate and determine existents—*i.e.,* to think them—the succession of my "states of consciousness" is a perceptual separation of effect from cause, since every nihilating process must derive its source only from itself. Inasmuch as my present state would be a prolongation of my prior state, every opening by which negation could slip through would be completely blocked. Every psychic process of nihilation implies then a cleavage between the immediate psychic past and the present. This cleavage is precisely nothingness. At least, someone will say, there remains the possibility of successive implication between the nihilating processes. My establishment of Pierre's absence could still be determinant for my regret at not seeing him; you have not excluded the possibility of a determinism of nihilations. But aside from the fact that the original nihilation of the series must necessarily be disconnected

from the prior positive processes, what can be the meaning of the motivation of nothingness by nothingness? A being indeed can *nihilate itself* perpetually, but to the extent that it nihilates itself, it foregoes being the origin of another phenomenon, even of a second nihilation.

It remains to explain what this separation is, this disengaging of consciousness which conditions every negation. If we consider the prior consciousness envisaged as motivation we see suddenly and evidently that *nothing* has just slipped in between that state and the present state. There has been no break in continuity within the flux of the temporal development, for that would force us to return to the inadmissible concept of the infinite divisibility of time and of the temporal point or instant as the limit of the division. Neither has there been an abrupt interpolation of an opaque element to separate prior from subsequent in the way that a knife blade cuts a piece of fruit in two. Nor is there a *weakening* of the motivating force of the prior consciousness; it remains what it is, it does not lose anything of its urgency. What separates prior from subsequent is exactly *nothing.* This nothing is absolutely impassable, just because it is nothing; for in every obstacle to be cleared there is something positive which gives itself as about to be cleared. The prior consciousness is always *there* (though with the modification of "pastness"). It constantly maintains a relation of interpretation with the present consciousness, but on the basis of this existential relation it is put out of the game, out of the circuit, between parentheses—exactly as in the eyes of one practicing the phenomenological ἐποχή, the world both is within him and outside of him.

Thus the condition on which human reality can deny all or part of the world is that human reality carry nothingness within itself as the *nothing* which separates its present from all its past. But this is still not all, for the *nothing* envisaged would not yet have the sense of nothingness; a suspension of being which would remain unnamed, which would not be consciousness of suspending being would come from outside consciousness and by reintroducing opacity into the heart of this absolute lucidity, would have the effect of cutting it in two. Furthermore this nothing would by no means be negative. Nothingness, as we have seen above, is the ground of the negation because it conceals the negation within itself, because it is the negation as being. It is necessary then that conscious being constitute itself in relation to its past as separated from this past by a nothingness. It must necessarily be conscious of this cleavage in being, but not as a phenomenon which it experiences, rather as a structure of consciousness which it is. Freedom is the human being putting his past out of play by secreting his own nothingness. Let us understand indeed that this original necessity of being its own nothingness does not belong to consciousness intermittently and on the occasion of particular negations. This does not happen just at a particular moment in psychic life when negative or interrogative attitudes appear; consciousness continually experiences itself as the nihilation of its past being.

But someone doubtless will believe that he can use against us here an objection which we have frequently raised ourselves: if the nihilating consciousness exists only as consciousness of nihilation, we ought to be able to define and describe a constant mode of consciousness, present *qua* consciousness, which would be consciousness of nihilation. Does this consciousness exist? Behold, a new question has been raised here: if freedom is the being of consciousness, consciousness ought to exist as consciousness of freedom. What form does this consciousness of freedom assume? In freedom the human being *is* his own past (as also his own future) in the form of nihilation. If our analysis has not led us astray, there ought to exist for the human being, in so far as he is conscious of being, a certain mode of standing opposite his past and his future, as being both this past and this future and as not being them. We shall be able to furnish an immediate reply to this question; it is in anguish that man gets the consciousness of his freedom, or if you prefer, anguish is the mode of being of freedom as consciousness of being; it is in anguish that freedom is, in its being, in question for itself.

Kierkegaard describing anguish in the face of what one lacks characterizes it as anguish in the face of freedom. But Heidegger, whom we know to have been greatly influenced by Kierkegaard,* considers anguish instead as the apprehension of nothingness. These two descriptions of anguish do not appear to us contradictory; on the contrary the one implies the other.

_____

* J. Wahl: *Etudes Kierkegaardiennes,* Kierkegaard et Heidegger.

First we must acknowledge that Kierkegaard is right; anguish is distinguished from fear in that fear is fear of beings in the world whereas anguish is anguish before myself. Vertigo is anguish to the extent that I am afraid not of falling over the precipice, but of throwing myself over. A situation provokes fear if there is a possibility of my life being changed from without; my being provokes anguish to the extent that I distrust myself and my own reactions in that situation. The artillery preparation which precedes the attack can provoke fear in the soldier who undergoes the bombardment, but anguish is born in him when he tries to foresee the conduct with which he will face the bombardment, when he asks himself if he is going to be able to "hold up." Similarly the recruit who reports for active duty at the beginning of the war can in some instances be afraid of death, but more often he is "afraid of being afraid"; that is, he is filled with anguish before himself. Most of the time dangerous or threatening situations present themselves in facets; they will be apprehended through a feeling of fear or of anguish according to whether we envisage the situation as acting on the man or the man as acting on the situation. The man who has just received a hard blow—for example, losing a great part of his wealth in a crash—can have the fear of threatening poverty. He will experience anguish a moment later when nervously wringing his hands (a symbolic reaction to the action which is imposed but which remains still wholly undetermined), he exclaims to himself: "What am I going do? But what am I going to do?" In this sense fear and anguish are exclusive of one another since fear is unreflective apprehension of the transcendent and anguish is reflective apprehension of the self; the one is born in the destruction of the other. The normal process in the case which I have just cited is a constant transition from the one to the other. But there exist also situations where anguish appears pure; that is, without ever being preceded or followed by fear. If, for example, I have been raised to a new dignity and charged with a delicate and flattering mission, I can feel anguish at the thought that I will not be capable perhaps of fulfilling it, and yet I will not have the least fear in the world of the consequences of my possible failure.

What is the meaning of anguish in the various examples which I have just given? Let us take up again the example of vertigo. Vertigo announces itself through fear; I am on a narrow path—without a guard rail—which goes along a precipice. The precipice presents itself to me as *to be avoided;* it represents a danger of death. At the same time I conceive of a certain number of causes, originating in universal determinism, which can transform that threat of death into reality: I can slip on a stone and fall into the abyss; the crumbling earth of the path can give way under my steps. Through these various anticipations, I am given to myself as a thing; I am passive in relation to these possibilities; they come to me from without; in so far as I am also an object in the world, subject to gravitation; they are *my* possibilities. At this moment *fear* appears, which in terms of the situation is the apprehension of myself as a destructible transcendent in the midst of transcendents, as an object which does not contain in itself the origin of its future disappearance. My reaction will be of the reflective order; I will pay attention to the stones in the road; I will keep myself as far as possible from the edge of the path. I realize myself as pushing away the threatening situation with all my strength, and I project before myself a certain number of future conducts destined to keep the threats of the world at a distance from me. These conducts are *my* possibilities. I escape fear by the very fact that I am placing myself on a plane where *my own* possibilities are substituted for the transcendent probabilities where human action had no place.

But these conducts, precisely because they are *my* possibilities, do not appear to me as determined by foreign causes. Not only is it not strictly certain that they will be effective; in particular it is not strictly certain that they will be adopted, for they do not have existence sufficient in itself. We could say, varying the expression of Berkeley, that their "being is a sustained-being" and that their "possibility of being is only an ought-to-be-sustained." Due to this fact their possibility has as a necessary condition the possibility of negative conduct (*not* to pay attention to the stones in the road, to run, to think of something else) and the possibility of the opposite conduct (to throw myself over the precipice). The possibility which I make *my* concrete possibility can appear as my possibility only by raising itself on the basis of the totality of the logical possibilities which the situation allows. But these rejected possibilities in turn have no other being than their "sustained being"; it is I who sustain them in being, and inversely their present non-being is an "ought-not-to-be-sustained." No external cause will remove them. I alone am the permanent source of

their non-being, I engage myself in them; in order to cause *my* possibility to appear, I posit the other possibilities so as to nihilate them. This would not produce anguish if I could apprehend myself in my relations with these possibles as a cause producing its effects. In this case the effect defined as my possibility *would be strictly* determined. But then it would cease to be *possible;* it would become simply "about-to-happen." If then I wished to avoid anguish and vertigo, it would be enough if I were to consider the motives (instinct of self-preservation, prior fear, *etc.*), which make me reject the situation envisaged, as *determining* my prior activity in the same way that the presence at a determined point of one given mass determines the courses followed by other masses; it would be necessary, in other words, that I apprehend in myself a strict psychological determinism. But I am in anguish precisely because any conduct on my part is only *possible,* and this means that while constituting a totality of motives *for* pushing away that situation, I at the same moment apprehend these motives as not sufficiently effective. At the very moment when I apprehend my being as *horror* of the precipice, I am conscious of that horror as *not determinant* in relation to my possible conduct. In one sense that horror calls for prudent conduct, and it is in itself a pre-outline of that conduct; in another sense, it posits the final developments of that conduct only as possible, precisely because I do not apprehend it as the *cause* of these final developments but as need, appeal, *etc.*

Now as we have seen, consciousness of being is the being of consciousness. There is no question here of a contemplation which I could make after the event, of a horror already constituted; it is the very being of horror to appear to itself as "not being the cause" of the conduct it calls for. In short, to avoid fear, which reveals to me a transcendent future strictly determined, I take refuge in reflection, but the latter has only an undetermined future to offer. This means that in establishing a certain conduct as a possibility and precisely because it is *my* possibility, I am aware that *nothing* can compel me to adopt that conduct. Yet I am indeed already there in the future; it is for the sake of that being which I will be there at the turning of the path that I now exert all my strength, and in this sense there is already a relation between my future being and my present being. But a nothingness has slipped into the heart of this relation; I *am* not the self which I will be. First I am not that self because time separates me from it. Secondly, I am not that self because what I am is not the foundation of what I will be. Finally I am not that self because no actual existent can determine strictly what I am going to be. Yet as I am already what I will be (otherwise I would not be interested in any one being more than another), *I am the self which I will be, in the mode of not being it.* It is through my horror that I am carried toward the future, and the horror nihilates itself in that it constitutes the future as possible. Anguish is precisely my consciousness of being my own future, in the mode of not-being. To be exact, the nihilation of horror as a *motive,* which has the effect of reinforcing horror as a *state,* has as its positive counterpart the appearance of other forms of conduct (in particular that which consists in throwing myself over the precipice) as *my* possible *possibilities.* If *nothing* compels me to save my life, *nothing* prevents me from precipitating myself into the abyss. The decisive conduct will emanate from a self which I am not yet. Thus the self which I am depends on the self which I am not yet to the exact extent that the self which I am not yet does not depend on the self which I am. Vertigo appears as the apprehension of this dependence. I approach the precipice, and my scrutiny is searching for myself in my very depths. In terms of this moment, I play with my possibilities. My eyes, running over the abyss from top to bottom, imitate the possible fall and realize it symbolically; at the same time suicide, from the fact that it becomes a *possibility* possible for *me,* now causes to appear possible motives for adopting it (suicide would cause anguish to cease). Fortunately these motives in their turn, from the sole fact that they are motives of a possibility, present themselves as ineffective, as non-determinant; they can no more *produce* the suicide than my horror of the fall can *determine me* to avoid it. It is this counteranguish which generally puts an end to anguish by transmuting it into indecision. Indecision in its turn calls for decision. I abruptly put myself at a distance from the edge of the precipice and resume my way.

The example which we have just analyzed has shown us what we could call "anguish in the face of the future." There exists another: anguish in the face of the past. It is that of the gambler who has freely and sincerely decided not to gamble anymore and who, when he approaches the gaming table, suddenly sees all his resolutions melt away. This phenomenon has often been described as if the sight of the gaming table reawakened in us a tendency which entered into conflict with our former resolution and ended by drawing us in spite of this. Aside from the fact that such a description is done in materialistic terms and peoples the mind with opposing forces (there is, for example, the moralists' famous "struggle of reason with the passions"), it does not account for the facts. In reality—the letters of Dostoevsky bear witness to this—there is nothing in us which resembles an inner *debate* as if we had to weigh motives and incentives before deciding. The earlier resolution of "not playing anymore" is always *there,* and in the majority of cases the gambler when in the presence of the gaming table, turns toward it as if to ask it for help; for he does not wish to play, or rather having taken his resolution the day before, he thinks of himself still as not wishing to play anymore; he believes in the effectiveness of this resolution. But what he apprehends then in anguish is precisely the total inefficacy of the past resolution. It is there doubtless but fixed, ineffectual, surpassed by the very fact that I am conscious *of* it. The resolution is still *me* to the extent that I realize constantly my identity with myself across the temporal flux, but it is no longer *me*—due to the fact that it has become an object *for* my consciousness. I am not subject to it, it fails in the mission which I have given it. The resolution is there still, I *am* it in the mode of not-being. What the gambler apprehends at this instant is again the permanent rupture in determinism; it is nothingness which separates him from himself; I should have liked so much not to gamble anymore; yesterday I even had a synthetic apprehension of the situation (threatening ruin, disappointment of my relatives) as *forbidding me* to play. It seemed to me that I had established a *real barrier* between gambling and myself, and now I suddenly perceive that my former understanding of the situation is no more than a memory of an idea, a memory of a feeling. In order for it to come to my aid once more, I must remake it *ex nihilo* and freely. The not-gambling is only one of my possibilities, as the fact of gambling is another of them, neither more nor less. *I must rediscover* the fear of financial ruin or of disappointing my family, *etc.,* I must re-create it as experienced fear. It stands behind me like a boneless phantom. It depends on me alone to lend it flesh. I am alone and naked before temptation as I was the day before. After having patiently built up barriers and walls, after enclosing myself in the magic circle of a resolution, I perceive with anguish that *nothing* prevents me from gambling. The anguish is *me* since by the very fact of taking my position in existence as consciousness of being, I make myself *not to be* the past of good resolutions *which I am.*

. . .

Now at each instant we are thrust into the world and engaged there. This means that we act before positing our possibilities and that these possibilities which are disclosed as realized or in process of being realized refer to meanings which necessitate special acts in order to be put into question. The alarm which rings in the morning refers to the possibility of my going to work, which is *my* possibility. But to apprehend the summons of the alarm as a summons is to get up. Therefore the very act of getting up is reassuring, for it eludes the question, "Is work *my* possibility?" Consequently it does not put me in a position to apprehend the possibility of quietism, of refusing to work, and finally the possibility of refusing the world and the possibility of death. In short, to the extent that I apprehend the meaning of the ringing, I am already up at its summons; this apprehension guarantees me against the anguished intuition that it is I who confer on the alarm clock its exigency—I and I alone.

In the same way, what we might call everyday morality is exclusive of ethical anguish. There is ethical anguish when I consider myself in my original relation to values. Values in actuality are demands which lay claim to a foundation. But this foundation can in no way be *being,* for every value which would base its ideal nature on its being would thereby cease even to be a value and would realize the heteronomy of my will. Value derives its being from its exigency and not its exigency from its being. It does not deliver itself to a contemplative intuition which would apprehend it as *being* value and thereby would remove from it its right over my freedom. On the contrary, it can be revealed only to an active freedom which makes it exist as value by the sole fact of recognizing it as such. It follows that my freedom is the unique foundation of values and that *nothing,* absolutely nothing, justifies me in adopting this or that particular value, this or that particular scale of values. As a being by whom values exist, I am unjustifiable. My freedom is anguished at being the foundation of values while itself without foundation. It is anguished in addition because values, due to the fact that they are essentially revealed to a freedom, can not disclose themselves

without being at the same time "put into question," for the possibility of overturning the scale of values appears complementarily as *my* possibility. It is anguish before values which is the recognition of the ideality of values.

Ordinarily, however, my attitude with respect to values is eminently reassuring. In fact I am engaged in a world of values. The anguished apperception of values as sustained in being by my freedom is a secondary and mediated phenomenon. The immediate is the world with its urgency; and in this world where I engage myself, my acts cause values to spring up like partridges. My indignation has given to me the negative value "baseness," my admiration has given the positive value "grandeur." Above all my obedience to a multitude of tabus, which is real, reveals these tabus to me as existing in fact. The bourgeois who call themselves "respectable citizens" do not become respectable as the result of contemplating moral values. Rather from the moment of their arising in the world they are thrown into a pattern of behavior the meaning of which is respectability. Thus respectability acquires a being; it is not put into question. Values are sown on my path as thousands of little real demands, like the signs which order us to keep off the grass.

Thus in what we shall call the world of the immediate, which delivers itself to our unreflective consciousness, we do not first appear to ourselves, to be thrown subsequently into enterprises. Our being is immediately "in situation"; that is, it arises in enterprises and knows itself first in so far as it is reflected in those enterprises. We discover ourselves then in a world peopled with demands, in the heart of projects "in the course of realization." I write. I am going to smoke. I have an appointment this evening with Pierre. I must not forget to reply to Simon. I do not have the right to conceal the truth any longer from Claude. All these trivial passive expectations of the real, all these commonplace, everyday values, derive their meaning from an original projection of myself which stands as my choice of myself in the world. But to be exact, this projection of myself toward an original possibility, which causes the existence of values, appeals, expectations, and in general a world, appears to me only beyond the world as the meaning and the abstract, logical signification of my enterprises. For the rest, there exist concretely alarm clocks, signboards, tax forms, policemen, so many guard rails against anguish. But as soon as the enterprise is held at a distance from me, as soon as I am referred to myself because I must await myself in the future, then I discover myself suddenly as the one who gives its meaning to the alarm clock, the one who by a signboard forbids himself to walk on a flower bed or on the lawn, the one from whom the boss's order borrows its urgency, the one who decides the interest of the book which he is writing, the one finally who makes the values exist in order to determine his action by their demands. I emerge alone and in anguish confronting the unique and original project which constitutes my being; all the barriers, all the guard rails collapse, nihilated by the consciousness of my freedom. I do not have nor can I have recourse to any value against the fact that it is I who sustain values in being. Nothing can ensure me against myself, cut off from the world and from my essence by this nothingness which I *am*. I have to realize the meaning of the world and of my essence; I make my decision concerning them—without justification and without excuse.

Anguish then is the reflective apprehension of freedom by itself. In this sense it is mediation, for although it is immediate consciousness of itself, it arises from the negation of the appeals of the world. It appears at the moment that I disengage myself from the world where I had been engaged—in order to apprehend myself as a consciousness which possesses a pre-ontological comprehension of its essence and a pre-judicative sense of its possibilities. Anguish is opposed to the mind of the serious man who apprehends values in terms of the world and who resides in the reassuring, materialistic substantiation of values. In the serious mood I define myself in terms of the object by pushing aside *à priori* as impossible all enterprises in which I am not engaged at the moment; the meaning which my freedom has given to the world, I apprehend as coming from the world and constituting my obligations. In anguish I apprehend myself at once as totally free and as not being able to derive the meaning of the world except as coming from myself.

We should not however conclude that being brought on to the reflective place and envisaging one's distant or immediate possibilities suffice to apprehend oneself in *pure* anguish. In each instance of reflection anguish is born as a structure of the reflective consciousness in so far as the latter considers consciousness as an object of reflection: but it still remains possible for me to maintain various types of conduct with respect to my own anguish—in particular, patterns of flight. Everything takes place, in fact, as if our essential and immediate behavior with respect to anguish is flight. Psychological determinism, before being a theoretical conception, is first an attitude of excuse, or if you prefer, the basis of all attitudes of excuse. It is reflective conduct with respect to anguish; it asserts that there are within us antagonistic forces whose type of existence is comparable to that of things. It attempts to fill the void which encircles us, to re-establish the links between past and present, between present and future. It provides us with a *nature* productive of our acts, and these very acts it makes transcendent; it assigns to them a foundation in something other than themselves by endowing them with an inertia and externality eminently reassuring because they constitute a permanent game of *excuses*. Psychological determinism denies that transcendence of human reality which makes it emerge in anguish beyond its own essence. At the same time by reducing us to *never being anything but what we are,* it reintroduces in us the absolute positivity of being-in-itself and thereby reinstates us at the heart of being.

.   .   .

... [F]light before anguish is not only an effort at distraction before the future; it attempts also to disarm the past of its threat. What I attempt to flee here is my very transcendence in so far as it sustains and surpasses my essence. I assert that I *am* my essence in the mode of being of the in-itself. At the same time I always refuse to consider that essence as being historically constituted and as implying my action as a circle implies its properties. I apprehend it, or at least I try to apprehend it as the original beginning of my possible, and I do not admit at all that it has in itself a beginning. I assert then that an act is free when it exactly reflects my essence. However, this freedom which would disturb me if it were freedom before myself, I attempt to bring back to the heart of my essence— *i.e.,* of my self. It is a matter of envisaging the self as a little God which inhabits me and which possesses my freedom as a metaphysical virtue. It would be no longer my being which would be free qua being but my Self which would be free in the heart of my consciousness. It is a fiction eminently reassuring since freedom has been driven down into the heart of an opaque being; to the extent that my essence is not translucency, that it is transcendent in immanence, freedom would become one of its properties. In short, it is a matter of apprehending my freedom in my self as the freedom of another. We see the principal themes of this fiction: My self becomes the origin of its acts as the other of his, by virtue of a personality already constituted. To be sure, he (the self) lives and transforms himself; we will admit even that each of his acts can contribute to transforming him. But these harmonious, continued transformations are conceived on a biological order. They resemble those which I can establish in my friend Pierre when I see him after a separation. Bergson expressly satisfied these demands for reassurance when he conceived his theory of the profound self which endures and organizes itself, which is constantly contemporary with the consciousness which I have of it and which can not be surpassed by consciousness, which is found at the origin of my acts not as a cataclysmic power but as a father begets his children, in such a way that the act without following from the essence as a strict consequence, without even being foreseeable, enters into a reassuring relation with it, a family resemblance. The act goes farther than the self but along the same road; it preserves, to be sure, a certain irreducibility, but we recognize ourselves in it, and we find ourselves in it as a father can recognize himself and find himself in the son who continues his work. Thus by a projection of freedom—which we apprehend in ourselves—into a psychic object which is the self. Bergson has contributed to disguise our anguish, but it is at the expense of consciousness itself. What he has established and described in this manner is not our freedom as it appears to itself; *it is the freedom of the Other.*

Such then is the totality of processes by which we try to hide anguish from ourselves; we apprehend our particular possible by avoiding considering all other possibles, which we make the possibles of an undifferentiated Other. The chosen possible we do not wish to see as sustained in being by a pure nihilating freedom, and so we attempt to apprehend it as engendered by an object already constituted, which is no other than our self, envisaged and described as if it were another person. We should like to preserve from the original intuition what it reveals to us as our independence and our responsibility but we tone down all the original nihilation in it; moreover we are always ready to take refuge in a belief in determinism if this freedom weighs upon us or if we need an excuse. Thus we flee from anguish by attempting to

apprehend ourselves from without as an Other or as *a thing.* What we are accustomed to call a revelation of the inner sense or an original intuition of our freedom contains nothing original; it is an already constructed process, expressly designed to hide from ourselves anguish, the veritable "immediate given" of our freedom.

Do these various constructions succeed in stifling or hiding our anguish? It is certain that we can not overcome anguish, for we *are* anguish. As for veiling it, aside from the fact that the very nature of consciousness and its translucency forbid us to take the expression literally, we must note the particular type of behavior which it indicates. We can hide an external object because it exists independently of us. For the same reason we can turn our look or our attention away from it—that is, very simply, fix our eyes on some other object; henceforth each reality—mine and that of the object—resumes its own life, and the accidental relation which united consciousness to the thing disappears without thereby altering either existence. But if I *am* what I wish to veil, the question takes on quite another aspect. I can in fact wish "not to see" a certain aspect of my being only if I am acquainted with the aspect which I do not wish to see. This means that in my being I must indicate this aspect in order to be able to turn myself away from it; better yet, I must think of it constantly in order to take care not to think of it. In this connection it must be understood not only that I must of necessity perpetually carry within me what I wish to flee but also that I must aim at the object of my flight in order to flee it. This means that anguish, the intentional aim of anguish, and a flight from anguish toward reassuring myths must all be given in the unity of the same consciousness. In a word, I flee in order not to know, but I can not avoid knowing that I am fleeing; and the flight from anguish is only a mode of becoming conscious of anguish. Thus anguish, properly speaking, can be neither hidden nor avoided.

Yet to flee anguish and to be anguish can not be exactly the same thing. If I am my anguish in order to flee it, that presupposes that I can decenter myself in relation to what I am, that I can be anguish in the form of "not-being it," that I can dispose of a nihilating power at the heart of anguish itself. This nihilating power nihilates anguish in so far as I flee it and nihilates itself in so far as *I am anguish in order to flee it.* This attitude is what we call *bad faith.* There is then no question of expelling anguish from consciousness nor of constituting it in an unconscious psychic phenomenon; very simply I can make myself guilty of bad faith while apprehending the anguish which I am, and this bad faith, intended to fill up the nothingness which I *am* in my relation to myself, precisely implies the nothingness which it suppresses.

. . .

Bad Faith and Falsehood
from Being and Nothingness

The human being is not only the being by whom *négatités* are disclosed in the world; he is also the one who can take negative attitudes with respect to himself. In our Introduction we defined consciousness as "a being such that in its being, its being is in question in so far as this being implies a being other than itself." But now that we have examined the meaning of "the question," we can at present also write the formula thus: "Consciousness is a being, the nature of which is to be conscious of the nothingness of its being." In a prohibition or a veto, for example, the human being denies a future transcendence. But this negation is not explicative. My consciousness is not restricted to *envisioning* a *négatité*. It constitutes itself in its own flesh as the nihilation of a possibility which another human reality projects as *its* possibility. For that reason it must arise in the world as a *No;* it is as a No that the slave first apprehends the master, or that the prisoner who is trying to escape sees the guard who is watching him. There are even men (*e.g.,* caretakers, overseers, gaolers), whose social reality is uniquely that of the No, who will live and die, having forever been only a No upon the earth. Others, so as to make the No a part of their very subjectivity, establish their human personality as a perpetual negation. This is the meaning and function of what Scheler calls "the man of resentment"—in reality, the No. But there exist more subtle behaviors, the description of which will lead us further into the inwardness of consciousness. Irony is one of these. In irony a man annihilates what he posits within one and the same act; he leads us to believe in order not to be believed; he affirms to deny and denies to affirm; he creates a positive object but it has no being other than its nothingness. Thus attitudes of negation toward the self permit us to raise a new question: What are we to say is the being of man who has the possibility of denying himself? But it is out of the question to discuss the attitude of "self-negation" in its universality. The kinds of behavior which can be ranked under this heading are too diverse; we risk retaining only the abstract form of them. It is best to choose and to examine one determined attitude which is essential to human reality and which is such that consciousness instead of directing its negation outward turns it toward itself. This attitude, it seems to me, is *bad faith* (*mauvaise foi*).

Frequently this is denied with falsehood. We say indifferently of a person that he shows signs of bad faith or that he lies to himself. We shall willingly grant that bad faith is a lie to oneself, on condition that we distinguish the lie to oneself from lying in general. Lying is a negative attitude, we will agree to that. But this negation does not bear on consciousness itself; it aims only at the transcendent. The essence of the lie implies in fact that the liar actually is in complete possession of the truth which he is hiding. A man does not lie about what he is ignorant of; he does not lie when he spreads an error of which he himself is the dupe; he does not lie when he is mistaken. The ideal description of the liar would be a cynical consciousness, affirming truth within himself, denying it in his words, and denying that negation as such. Now this doubly negative attitude rests on the transcendent; the fact expressed is transcendent since it does not exist, and the original negation rests on a *truth;* that is, on a particular type of transcendence. As for the inner negation which I effect correlatively with the affirmation for myself of the truth, this rests on *words;* that is, on an event in the world. Furthermore the inner disposition of the liar is positive; it could be the object of an affirmative judgment. The liar intends to deceive and he does not seek to hide this intention from himself nor to disguise the translucency of consciousness; on the contrary, he has recourse to it when there is a question of deciding secondary behavior. It explicitly exercises a regulatory control over all attitudes. As for his flaunted intention of telling the truth ("I'd never want to deceive you! This is true! I swear it!")—all this, of course, is the object of an inner negation, but also it is not recognized by the liar as *his* intention. It is played, imitated, it is the intention of the character which he plays in the eyes of his questioner, but this character, precisely because he *does not exist,* is a transcendent. Thus the lie does not put into the play the inner structure of present consciousness; all the negations which constitute it bear on objects which by this fact are removed from consciousness. The lie then does not require special ontological foundation, and the explanations which the existence of negation in general requires are valid without change in the case of deceit. Of course we have described the ideal lie: doubtless it happens often enough that the liar is more or less the victim of his lie, that he half persuades himself of it. But these common, popular forms of the lie are also degenerate aspects of it; they represent intermediaries between falsehood and bad faith. The lie is a behavior of transcendence.

The lie is also a normal phenomenon of what Heidegger calls the *"mit-sein."** It presupposes my existence, the existence of the *Other,* my existence *for* the Other, and the existence of the Other *for* me. Thus there is no difficulty in holding that the liar must make the project of the lie in entire clarity and that he must possess a complete comprehension of the lie and of the truth which he is altering. It is sufficient that an over-all opacity hide his intentions from the *Other;* it is sufficient that the Other can take the lie for truth. By the lie consciousness affirms that it exists by nature as *hidden from the Other;* it utilizes for its own profit the ontological duality of myself and myself in the eyes of the Other.

The situation can not be the same for bad faith if this, as we have said, is indeed a lie to oneself. To be sure, the one who practices bad faith is hiding a displeasing truth or presenting as truth a pleasing untruth. Bad faith then has in appearance the structure of falsehood. Only what changes everything is the fact that in bad faith it is from myself that I am hiding the truth. Thus the duality of the deceiver and the deceived does not exist here. Bad faith on the contrary implies in essence the unity of a *single* consciousness. This does not mean that it can not be conditioned by the *mit-sein* like all other phenomena of human reality, but the *mit-sein* can call forth bad faith only by presenting itself as *a situation* which bad faith permits surpassing; bad faith does not come from outside to human reality. One does not undergo his bad faith; one is not infected with it; it is not a *state.* But consciousness affects itself with bad faith. There must be

an original intention and a project of bad faith; this project implies a comprehension of bad faith as such and a pre-reflective apprehension (of) consciousness as affecting itself with bad faith. It follows first that the one to whom the lie is told and the one who lies are one and the same person, which means that I must know in my capacity as deceiver the truth which is hidden from me in my capacity as the one deceived. Better yet I must know the truth very exactly *in order* to conceal it more carefully—and this not at two different moments, which at a pinch would allow us to reestablish a semblance of duality—but in the unitary structure of a single project. How then can the lie subsist if the duality which conditions it is suppressed?

To this difficulty is added another which is derived from the total translucency of consciousness. That which affects itself with bad faith must be conscious (of) its bad faith since the being of consciousness is consciousness of being. It appears then that I must be in good faith, at least to the extent that I am conscious of my bad faith. But then this whole psychic system is annihilated. We must agree in fact that if I deliberately and cynically attempt to lie to myself, I fail completely in this undertaking; the lie falls back and collapses beneath my look: it is ruined *from behind* by the very consciousness of lying to myself which pitilessly constitutes itself well within my project as its very condition. We have here an *evanescent* phenomenon which exists only in and through its own differentiation. To be sure, these phenomena are frequent and we shall see that there is in fact an "evanescence" of bad faith, which, it is evident, vacillates continually between good faith and cynicism: Even though the existence of bad faith is very precarious, and though it belongs to the kind of psychic structures which we might call *metastable,†* it presents nonetheless an autonomous and durable form. It can even be the normal aspect of life for a very great number of people. A person can *live* in bad faith, which does not mean that he does not have abrupt awakenings to cynicism or to good faith, but which implies a constant and particular style of life. Our embarrassment then appears extreme since we can neither reject nor comprehend bad faith.

· · ·

---

*Tr. A "being-with" others in the world.

† Tr. Sartre's own word, meaning subject to sudden changes or transitions.

Patterns of Bad Faith
from Being and Nothingness

If we wish to get out of this difficulty, we should examine more closely the patterns of bad faith and attempt a description of them.* This description will permit us perhaps to fix more exactly the conditions for the possibility of bad faith; that is, to reply to the question we raised at the outset: "What must be the being of man if he is to be capable of bad faith?"

Take the example of a woman who has consented to go out with a particular man for the first time. She knows very well the intentions which the man who is speaking to her cherishes regarding her. She knows also that it will be necessary sooner or later for her to make a decision. But she does not want to realize the urgency; she concerns herself only with what is respectful and discreet in the attitude of her companion. She does not apprehend this conduct as an attempt to achieve what we call "the first approach"; that is, she does not want to see possibilities of temporal development which his conduct presents. She restricts this behavior to what is in the present; she does not wish to read in the phrases which he addresses to her anything other than their explicit meaning. If he says to her, "I find you so attractive!" she disarms this phrase of its sexual background; she attaches to the conversation and to the behavior of the speaker, the immediate meanings, which she imagines as objective qualities. The man who is speaking to her appears to her sincere and respectful as the table is round or square, as the wall coloring is blue or gray. The qualities thus attached to the person she is listening to are in this way fixed in a permanence like that of things, which is no other than the projection of the strict present of the qualities into the temporal flux. This is because she does not quite know what she wants. She is profoundly aware of the desire which she inspires, but the desire cruel and naked would humiliate and horrify her. Yet she would find no charm in a respect which would be only respect. In order to satisfy her, there must be a feeling which is addressed wholly to her *personality*—i.e., to her full freedom—and which would be a recognition of her freedom. But at the

same time this feeling must be wholly desire; that is, it must address itself to her body as object. This time then she refuses to apprehend the desire for what it is; she does not even give it a name; she recognizes it only to the extent that it transcends itself toward admiration, esteem, respect and that it is wholly absorbed in the more refined forms which it produces, to the extent of no longer figuring anymore as a sort of warmth and density. But then suppose he takes her hand. This act of her companion risks changing the situation by calling for an immediate decision. To leave the hand there is to consent in herself to flirt, to engage herself. To withdraw it is to break the troubled and unstable harmony which gives the hour its charm. The aim is to postpone the moment of decision as long as possible. We know what happens next; the young woman leaves her hand there, but she *does not notice* that she is leaving it. She does not notice because it happens by chance that she is at this moment all intellect. She draws her companion up to the most lofty regions of sentimental speculation; she speaks of Life, of her life, she shows herself in her essential aspect—a personality, a consciousness. And during this time the divorce of the body from the soul is accomplished; the hand rests inert between the warm hands of her companion—neither consenting nor resisting—a thing.

We shall say that this woman is in bad faith. But we see immediately that she uses various procedures in order to maintain herself in this bad faith. She has disarmed the actions of her companion by reducing them to being only what they are; that is, to existing in the mode of the in itself. But she permits herself to enjoy his desire, to the extent that she will apprehend it as not being what it is, will recognize its transcendence. Finally while sensing profoundly the presence of her own body—to the point of being aroused, perhaps—she realizes herself as *not being* her own body, and she contemplates it as though from above as a passive object to which events can *happen* but which can neither provoke them nor avoid them because all its possibilities are outside of it. What unity do we find in these various aspects of bad faith? It is a certain art of forming contradictory concepts which unite in themselves both an idea and the negation of that idea. The basic concept which is thus engendered utilizes the double property of the human being, who is at once a *facticity and a transcendence.* These two aspects of human reality are and ought to be capable of a valid coordination. But bad faith does not wish either to

---

*Some footnotes have been omitted—ed.

coordinate them or to surmount them in a synthesis. Bad faith seeks to affirm their identity while preserving their differences. It must affirm facticity as *being* transcendence and transcendence as *being* facticity, in such a way that at the instant when a person apprehends the one, he can find himself abruptly faced with the other.

We can find the prototype of formulae of bad faith in certain famous expressions which have been rightly conceived to produce their whole effect in a spirit of bad faith. Take for example the title of a work by Jacques Chardonne, *Love Is Much More than Love.* We see here how unity is established between *present* love in its facticity—"the contact of two skins," sensuality, egoism, Proust's mechanism of jealousy, Adler's battle of the *sexes, etc.*—and love as transcendence—Mauriac's "river of fire," the longing for the infinite, Plato's *eros,* Lawrence's deep cosmic intuition, *etc.* Here we leave facticity to find ourselves suddenly beyond the present and the factual condition of man, beyond the psychological, in the heart of metaphysics. On the other hand, the title of a play by Sarment, *I Am Too Great for Myself,* which also presents characters in bad faith, throws us first into full transcendence in order suddenly to imprison us within the narrow limits of our factual essence. We will discover this structure again in the famous sentence: "He has become what he was" or in its no less famous opposite: "Eternity at last changes each man into himself." It is well understood that these various formulae have only the appearance of bad faith; they have been conceived in this paradoxical form explicitly to shock the mind and discountenance it by an enigma. But it is precisely this appearance which is of concern to us. What counts here is that the formulae do not constitute new, solidly structured ideas; on the contrary, they are formed so as to remain in perpetual disintegration and so that we may slide at any time from naturalistic present to transcendence and *vice versa.*

We can see the use which bad faith can make of these judgments which all aim at establishing that I am not what I am. If I were only what I *am,* I could, for example, seriously consider an adverse criticism which someone makes of me, question myself scrupulously, and perhaps be compelled to recognize the truth in it. But thanks to transcendence, I am not subject to all that I am. I do not even have to discuss the justice of the reproach. As Suzanne says to Figaro, "To

prove that I am right would be to recognize that I can be wrong." I am on a plane where no reproach can touch me since what I really am is my transcendence. I flee from myself, I escape myself, I leave my tattered garment in the hands of the fault-finder. But the ambiguity necessary for bad faith comes from the fact that I affirm here that I *am* my transcendence in the mode of being of a thing. It is only thus, in fact, that I can feel that I escape all reproaches. It is in the sense that our young woman purifies the desire of anything humiliating by being willing to consider it only as pure transcendence, which she avoids even naming. But inversely "I Am Too Great for Myself," while showing our transcendence changed into facticity, is the source of an infinity of excuses for our failures or our weaknesses. Similarly the young coquette maintains transcendence to the extent that the respect, the esteem manifested by the actions of her admirer are already on the plane of the transcendent. But she arrests this transcendence, she glues it down with all the facticity of the present; respect is nothing other than respect, it is an arrested surpassing which no longer surpasses itself toward anything.

But although this *metastable* concept of "transcendence-facticity" is one of the most basic instruments of bad faith, it is not the only one of its kind. We can equally well use another kind of duplicity derived from human reality which we will express roughly by saying that its being-for-itself implies complementarily a being-for-others. Upon any one of my conducts it is always possible to converge two looks, mine and that of the Other. The conduct will not present exactly the same structure in each case. But as we shall see later, as each look perceives it, there is between these two aspects of my being, no difference between appearance and being—as if I were to my self the truth of myself and as if the Other possessed only a deformed image of me. The equal dignity of being, possessed by my being-for-others and by my being-for-myself, permits a perpetually disintegrating synthesis and a perpetual game of escape from the for-itself to the for-others and from the for-others to the for-itself. We have seen also the use which our young lady made of our being-in-the-midst-of-the-world—*i.e.,* of our inert presence as a passive object among other objects—in order to relieve herself suddenly from the functions of her being-in-the world—that is, from the being which causes there to be a world by projecting itself beyond the world toward its own possibilities. Let us note finally the confusing syntheses which play on the nihilating ambiguity of these temporal ekstases, affirming at once that I am what I have been (the man who deliberately *arrests himself* at one period in his life and refuses to take into consideration the later changes) and that I am not what I have been (the man who in the face of reproaches or rancor dissociates himself from his past by insisting on his freedom and on his perpetual re-creation). In all these concepts, which have only a transitive role in the reasoning and which are eliminated from the conclusion (like the imaginaries in the computations of physicists), we find again the same structure. We have to deal with human reality as a being which is what it is not and which is not what it is.

But what exactly is necessary in order for these concepts of disintegration to be able to receive even a pretence of existence, in order for them to be able to appear for an instant to consciousness, even in a process of evanescence? A quick examination of the idea of sincerity, the antithesis of bad faith, will be very instructive in this connection. Actually sincerity presents itself as a demand and consequently is not a *state*. Now what is the ideal to be attained in this case? It is necessary that a man be *for himself* only what he *is*. But is this not precisely the definition of the in-itself—or if you prefer—the principle of identity? To posit as an ideal the being of things, is this not to assert by the same stroke that this being does not belong to human reality and that the principle of identity, far from being a universal axiom universally applied, is only a synthetic principle enjoying a merely regional universality? Thus in order that the concepts of bad faith can put us under illusion at least for an instant, in order that the candor of "pure hearts" (*cf.* Gide, Kessel) can have validity for human reality as an ideal, the principle of identity must not represent a constitutive principle of human reality and human reality must not be necessarily what it is but must be able to be what it is not. What does this mean?

If man is what he is, bad faith is forever impossible and candor ceases to be his ideal and becomes instead his being. But is man what he is? And more generally, how can he *be* what he is when he exists as consciousness of being? If candor or sincerity is a universal value, it is evident that the maxim "one must be what one is" does not serve solely as a regulating principle for judgments and concepts by which I express what I am. It posits not merely an ideal of knowing but an ideal of *being;* it proposes for us an absolute equivalence of being with itself as a prototype of being. In this sense it is necessary that we *make ourselves* what we are. But what *are we* then if we have the constant obligation to make ourselves what we are, if our mode of being is having the obligation to be what we are?

Let us consider this waiter in the café. His movement is quick and forward, a little too precise, a little too rapid. He comes toward the patrons with a step a little too quick. He bends forward a little too eagerly; his voice, his eyes express an interest a little too solicitous for the order of the customer. Finally there he returns, trying to imitate in his walk the inflexible stiffness of some kind of automaton while carrying his tray with the recklessness of a tight-rope-walker by putting it in a perpetually unstable, perpetually broken equilibrium which he perpetually re-establishes by a light movement of the arm and hand. All his behavior seems to us a game. He applies himself to chaining his movements as if they were mechanisms, the one regulating the other; his gestures and even his voice seem to be mechanisms; he gives himself the quickness and pitiless rapidity of things. He is playing, he is amusing himself. But what is he playing? We need not watch long before we can explain it: he is playing at *being* a waiter in a café. There is nothing there to surprise us. The game is a kind of marking out and investigation. The child plays with his body in order to explore it, to take inventory of it; the waiter in the café plays with his condition in order to *realize* it. This obligation is not different from that which is imposed on all tradesmen. Their condition is wholly one of ceremony. The public demands of them that they realize it as a ceremony; there is the dance of the grocer, of the tailor, of the auctioneer, by which they endeavor to persuade their clientele that they are nothing but a grocer, an auctioneer, a tailor. A grocer who dreams is offensive to the buyer, because such a grocer is not wholly a grocer. Society demands that he limit himself to his function as a grocer, just as the soldier at attention makes himself into a soldier-thing with a direct regard which does not see at all, which is no longer meant to see, since it is the rule and not the interest of the moment which determines the point he must fix his eyes on (the sight "fixed at ten paces"). There are indeed many precautions to imprison a man in what he is, as if we lived in perpetual fear that he might escape from it, that he might break away and suddenly elude his condition.

In a parallel situation, from within, the waiter in the café can not be immediately a café waiter in the sense that this inkwell *is* an inkwell, or the glass is a glass. It is by no means that he can not form reflective judgments or concepts concerning his condition. He knows well what it "means": the obligation of getting up at five o'clock, of sweeping the floor of the shop before the restaurant opens, of starting the coffee pot going, *etc.* He knows the rights which it allows: the right to the tips, the right to belong to a union, *etc.* But all these concepts, all these judgments refer to the transcendent. It is a matter of abstract possibilities, of rights and duties conferred on a "person possessing rights." And it is precisely this person *who I have to be* (if I am the waiter in question) and who I am not. It is not that I do not wish to be this person or that I want this person to be different. But rather there is no common measure between his being and mine. It is a "representation" for others and for myself, which means that I can be he only in *representation*. But if I represent myself as him, I am not he; I am separated from him as the object from the subject, separated *by nothing,* but this nothing isolates me from him. I can not be he, I can only play *at being* him; that is, imagine to myself that I am he. And thereby I affect him with nothingness. In vain do I fulfill the functions of a café waiter. I can be he only in the neutralized mode, as the actor is Hamlet, by mechanically making the *typical gestures* of my state and by aiming at myself as an imaginary café waiter through those gestures taken as an "analogue." * What I attempt to realize is a being-in-itself of the café waiter, as if it were not just in my power to confer their value and their urgency upon my duties and the rights of my position, as if it were not my free choice to get up each morning at five o'clock or to remain in bed, even though it meant getting fired. As if from the very fact that I sustain this role in existence I did not transcend it on every side, as if I did not constitute myself as one *beyond* my condition. Yet there is no doubt that I *am* in a sense a café waiter—otherwise could I not just as well call myself a diplomat or a reporter? But if I am one, this can not be in the mode of being in-itself. I am a waiter in the mode of *being what I am not.*

Furthermore we are dealing with more than mere social positions; I am never any one of my attitudes, any one of my actions. The good speaker is the one who *plays* at speaking, because he can not *be speaking.* The attentive pupil who wishes to *be* attentive, his eyes riveted on the teacher, his ears wide open, so exhausts himself in playing the attentive role that he ends up by no longer hearing anything. Perpetually absent to my body, to my acts, I am despite myself that "divine absence" of which Valéry speaks. I can not say either that I *am* here or that I *am* not here, in the sense that we say "that box of matches *is* on the table"; this would be to confuse my "being-in-the-world" with a "being-in-the-midst-of-the-world." Nor that I *am* standing, nor that I *am* seated: this would be to confuse my body with the idiosyncratic totality of which it is only one of the structures. On all sides I escape being and yet—I am.

But take a mode of being which concerns only myself: I am sad. One might think that surely I am the sadness in the mode of being what I am. What is the sadness, however, if not the intentional unity which comes to reassemble and animate the totality of my conduct? It is the meaning of this dull look with which I view the world, of my bowed shoulders, of my lowered head, of the listlessness in my whole body. But at the very moment when I adopt each of these attitudes, do I not know that I shall not be able to hold on to it? Let a stranger suddenly appear and I will lift up my head, I will assume a lively cheerfulness. What will remain of my sadness except that I obligingly promise it an appointment for later after the departure of the visitor? Moreover is not this sadness itself a *conduct?* Is it not consciousness which affects itself with sadness as a magical recourse against a situation too urgent? † And in this case even, should we not say that being sad means first to make oneself sad? That may be, someone will say, but after all doesn't giving oneself the being of sadness mean to *receive* this being? It makes no difference from where I receive it. The fact is that a consciousness which affects itself with sadness is sad precisely for this reason. But it is difficult to comprehend the nature of

---

*L'Imaginaire, psychologie phénoménologique de l'imagination. Paris: Gallimard. 1940. [The Psychology of Imagination. Philosophical Library. 1948.]

† Esquisse d'une théorie des émotions. Paris: Hermann. 1939. In English: The Emotions: Outline of a Theory. Philosophical Library. 1948.

consciousness; the being-sad is not a ready-made being which I give to myself as I can give this book to my friend. I do not possess the property of *affecting myself with being*. If I make myself sad, I must continue to make myself sad from beginning to end. I can not treat my sadness as an impulse finally achieved and put it on file without re-creating it, nor can I carry it in the manner of an inert body which continues its movement after the initial shock. There is no inertia in consciousness. If I make myself sad, it is because I *am* not sad—the being of the sadness escapes me by and in the very act by which I affect myself with it. The being-in-itself of sadness perpetually haunts my consciousness (of) being sad, but it is as a value which I can not realize; it stands as a regulative meaning of my sadness, not as its constitutive modality.

Someone may say that my consciousness at least *is*, whatever may be the object or the state of which it makes itself consciousness. But how do we distinguish my consciousness (of) being sad from sadness? Is it not all one? It is true in a way that my consciousness *is*, if one means by this that for another it is a part of the totality of being on which judgments can be brought to bear. But it should be noted, as Husserl clearly understood, that my consciousness appears originally to the Other as an absence. It is the object always present as the *meaning* of all my attitudes and all my conduct—and always absent, for it gives itself to the intuition of another as a perpetual question—still better, as a perpetual freedom. When Pierre looks at me, I know of course that he is looking at me. His eyes, things in the world, are fixed on my body, a thing in the world—that is the objective fact of which I can say: it *is*. But it is also a fact *in the world*. The meaning of this look is not a fact in the world, and this is what makes me uncomfortable. Although I make smiles, promises, threats, nothing can get hold of the approbation, the free judgment which I seek; I know that it is always beyond. I sense it in my very attitude, which is no longer like that of the worker toward the things he uses as instruments. My reactions, to the extent that I project myself toward the Other, are no longer for myself but are rather mere *presentations;* they await being constituted as graceful or uncouth, sincere or insincere, *etc.,* by an apprehension which is always beyond my efforts to provoke, an apprehension which will be provoked by my efforts only if of itself it lends them force (that is, only in so far as it causes itself to be provoked from the outside), *which*

is its own mediator with the transcendent. Thus the objective fact of the being-in-itself of the Other's consciousness is posited in order to disappear in negativity and in freedom: the Other's consciousness is as not-being; its being-in-itself "here and now" is not-to-be. *The Other's consciousness is what it is not.*

Furthermore the being of my own consciousness does not appear to me as the consciousness of the Other. It *is* because it makes itself, since its being is consciousness of being. But this means that making sustains being; consciousness has to be its own being, it is never sustained by being; it sustains being in the heart of subjectivity, which means once again that it is inhabited by being but that it is not being: *consciousness is not what it is.*

Under these conditions what can be the significance of the ideal of sincerity except as a task impossible to achieve, of which the very meaning is in contradiction with the structure of my consciousness. To be sincere, we said, is to be what one is. That supposes that I am not originally what I am. But here naturally Kant's "You ought, therefore you can" is implicitly understood. I can *become* sincere; this is what my duty and my effort to achieve sincerity imply. But we definitely establish that the original structure of "not being what one is" renders impossible in advance all movement toward being in itself or "being what one is." And this impossibility is not hidden from consciousness; on the contrary, it is the very stuff of consciousness; it is the embarrassing constraint which we constantly experience; it is our very incapacity to recognize ourselves, to constitute ourselves as being what we are. It is this necessity which means that, as soon as we posit ourselves as a certain being, by a legitimate judgment, based on inner experience or correctly deduced from *à priori* or empirical premises, then by that very positing we surpass this being—and that not toward another being but toward emptiness, toward *nothing*.

How then can we blame another for not being sincere or rejoice in our own sincerity since this sincerity appears to us at the same time to be impossible? How can we in conversation, in confession, in introspection, even attempt sincerity since the effort will by its very nature be doomed to failure and since at the very time when we announce it we have a prejudicative comprehension of its futility? In introspection I try to determine exactly what I am, to make up my mind to be my true self without delay—even though it means consequently to set about searching for ways to change myself. But what does this mean if not that I am constituting myself as a thing? Shall I determine the ensemble of purposes and motivations which have pushed me to do this or that action? But this is already to postulate a causal determinism which constitutes the flow of my states of consciousness as a succession of physical states. Shall I uncover in myself "drives," even though it be to affirm them in shame? But is this not deliberately to forget that these drives are realized with my consent, that they are not forces of nature but that I lend them their efficacy by a perpetually renewed decision concerning their value? Shall I pass judgment on my character, on my nature? Is this not to veil from myself at that moment what I know only too well, that I thus judge a past to which by definition my present is not subject? The proof of this is that the same man who in sincerity posits that he is what in actuality he was, is indignant at the reproach of another and tries to disarm it by asserting that he can no longer be what he was. We are readily astonished and upset when the penalties of the court affect a man who in his new freedom *is no longer* the guilty person he was. But at the same time we require of this man that he recognize himself as *being* this guilty one. What then is sincerity except precisely a phenomenon of bad faith? Have we not shown indeed that in bad faith human reality is constituted as a being which is what it is not and which is not what it is?

Let us take an example: A homosexual frequently has an intolerable feeling of guilt, and his whole existence is determined in relation to this feeling. One will readily foresee that he is in bad faith. In fact it frequently happens that this man, while recognizing his homosexual inclination, while avowing each and every particular misdeed which he has committed, refuses with all his strength to consider himself "*a paederast.*" His case is always "different," peculiar; there enters into it something of a game, of chance, of bad luck; the mistakes are all in the past; they are explained by a certain conception of the beautiful which women can not satisfy; we should see in them the results of a restless search, rather than the manifestations of a deeply rooted tendency, *etc., etc.* Here is assuredly a man in bad faith who borders on the comic since, acknowledging all the facts which are imputed to him, he refuses to draw from them the conclusion which they impose. His friend, who is his most severe critic, becomes irritated with this duplicity. The critic

asks only one thing—and perhaps then he will show himself indulgent: that the guilty one recognize himself as guilty, that the homosexual declare frankly—whether humbly or boastfully matters little—"I am a paederast." We ask here: Who is in bad faith? The homosexual or the champion of sincerity?

The homosexual recognizes his faults, but he struggles with all his strength against the crushing view that his mistakes constitute for him a *destiny*. He does not wish to let himself be considered as a thing. He has an obscure but strong feeling that a homosexual is not a homosexual as this table is a table or as this red-haired man is red-haired. It seems to him that he has escaped from each mistake as soon as he has posited it and recognized it; he even feels that the psychic duration by itself cleanses him from each misdeed, constitutes for him an undetermined future, causes him to be born anew. Is he wrong? Does he not recognize in himself the peculiar, irreducible character of human reality? His attitude includes then an undeniable comprehension of truth. But at the same time he needs this perpetual rebirth, this constant escape in order to live; he must constantly put himself beyond reach in order to avoid the terrible judgment of collectivity. Thus he plays on the word *being*. He would be right actually if he understood the phrase "I am not a paederast" in the sense of "I am not what I am." That is, if he declared to himself, "To the extent that a pattern of conduct is defined as the conduct of a paederast and to the extent that I have adopted this conduct, I am a paederast. But to the extent that human reality can not be finally defined by patterns of conduct, I am not one." But instead he slides surreptitiously toward a different connotation of the word "being." He understands "not being" in the sense of "not-being-in-itself." He lays claim to "not being a paederast" in the sense in which this table *is not* an inkwell. He is in bad faith.

But the champion of sincerity is not ignorant of the transcendence of human reality, and he knows how at need to appeal to it for his own advantage. He makes use of it even and brings it up in the present argument. Does he not wish, first in the name of sincerity, then of freedom, that the homosexual reflect on himself and acknowledge himself as a homosexual? Does he not let the other understand that such a confession will win indulgence for him? What does this mean if not that the man who will acknowledge himself as a homosexual will no longer be *the same* as the homosexual whom he acknowledges being and that he will escape into the region of freedom and of good will? The critic asks the man then to be what he is in order no longer to be what he is. It is the profound meaning of the saying, "A sin confessed is half pardoned." The critic demands of the guilty one that he constitute himself as a thing, precisely in order no longer to treat him as a thing. And this contradiction is constitutive of the demand of sincerity. Who can not see how offensive to the Other and how reassuring for me is a statement such as, "He's just a paederast," which removes a disturbing freedom from a trait and which aims at henceforth constituting all the acts of the Other as consequences following strictly from his essence. That is actually what the critic is demanding of his victim — that he constitute himself as a thing, that he should entrust his freedom to his friend as a fief, in order that the friend should return it to him subsequently — like a suzerain to his vassal. The champion of sincerity is in bad faith to the degree that in order to reassure himself, he pretends to judge, to the extent that he demands that freedom as freedom constitute itself as a thing. We have here only one episode in that battle to the death of consciousnesses which Hegel calls "the relation of the master and the slave." A person appeals to another and demands that in the name of his nature as consciousness he should radically destroy himself as consciousness, but while making this appeal he leads the other to hope for a rebirth beyond this destruction.

Very well, someone will say, but our man is abusing sincerity, playing one side against the other. We should not look for sincerity in the relation of the *mit-sein* but rather where it is pure — in the relations of a person with himself. But who can not see that objective sincerity is constituted in the same way? Who can not see that the sincere man constitutes himself as a thing in order to escape the condition of a thing by the same act of sincerity? The man who confesses that he is evil has exchanged his disturbing "freedom-for-evil" for an inanimate character of evil; he *is* evil, he clings to himself, he is what he is. But by the same stroke, he escapes from that *thing*, since it is he who contemplates it, since it depends on him to maintain it under his glance or to let it collapse in an infinity of particular acts. He derives a *merit* from his sincerity, and the deserving man is not the evil man as he is evil but he is beyond his evilness. At the same time the evil is disarmed since it is nothing, save on the plane of

determinism, and since in confessing it, I posit my freedom in respect to it; my future is virgin; everything is allowed to me.

Thus the essential structure of sincerity does not differ from that of bad faith since the sincere man constitutes himself as what he is *in order not to be it*. This explains the truth recognized by all that one can fall into bad faith through being sincere. As Valéry pointed out, this is the case with Stendhal. Total, constant sincerity as a constant effort to adhere to oneself is by nature a constant effort to dissociate oneself from oneself. A person frees himself from himself by the very act by which he makes himself an object for himself. To draw up a perpetual inventory of what one is means constantly to redeny oneself and to take refuge in a sphere where one is no longer anything but a pure, free regard. The goal of bad faith, as we said, is to put oneself out of reach; it is an escape. Now we see that we must use the same terms to define sincerity. What does this mean?

In the final analysis the goal of sincerity and the goal of bad faith are not so different. To be sure there is a sincerity which bears on the past and which does not concern us here; I am sincere if I confess *having had* this pleasure or that intention. We shall see that if this sincerity is possible, it is because in his fall into the past, the being of man is constituted as a being-in-itself. But here our concern is only with the sincerity which aims at itself in present immanence. What is its goal? To bring me to confess to myself what I am in order that I may finally coincide with my being; in a word, to cause myself to be, in the mode of the in-itself, what I am in the mode of "not being what I am." Its assumption is that fundamentally I am already, in the mode of the in-itself, what I have to be. Thus we find at the base of sincerity a continual game of mirror and reflection, a perpetual passage from the being which is what it is to the being which is not what it is and inversely from the being which is not what it is to the being which is what it is. And what is the goal of bad faith? To cause me to be what I am, in the mode of "not being what one is," or not to be what I am in the mode of "being what one is." We find here the same game of mirrors. In fact in order for me to have an intention of sincerity, I must at the outset simultaneously be and not be what I am. Sincerity does not assign to me a mode of being or a particular quality, but in relation to that quality it aims at making me pass from one mode of being to another mode of being.

This second mode of being, the ideal of sincerity, I am prevented by nature from attaining; and at the very moment when I struggle to attain it, I have a vague prejudicative comprehension that I shall not attain it. But all the same, in order for me to be able to conceive an intention in bad faith, I must have such a nature that within my being I escape from my being. If I were sad or cowardly in the way in which this inkwell is an inkwell, the possibility of bad faith could not even be conceived. Not only should I be unable to escape from my being; I could not even imagine that I could escape from it. But if bad faith is possible by virtue of a simple project, it is because so far as my being is concerned, there is no difference between being and non-being if I am cut off from my project.

Bad faith is possible only because sincerity is conscious of missing its goal inevitably, due to its very nature. I can try to apprehend myself as *"not being cowardly,"* when I *am* so, only on condition that the "being cowardly" is itself "in question" at the very moment when it exists, on condition that it is itself *one* question, that at the very moment when I wish to apprehend it, it escapes me on all sides and annihilates itself. The condition under which I can attempt an effort in bad faith is that in one sense, I *am not* this coward which I do not wish to be. But if I *were not* cowardly in the simple mode of not-being-what-one-is-not, I would be "in good faith" by declaring that I am not cowardly. Thus this inapprehensible coward is evanescent; in order for me not to be cowardly, I must in some way also be cowardly. That does not mean that I must be "a little" cowardly, in the sense that "a little" signifies "to a certain degree cowardly—and not cowardly to a certain degree." No. I must at once both be and not be totally and in all respects a coward. Thus in this case bad faith requires that I should not be what I am; that is, that there be an imponderable difference separating being from non-being in the mode of being of human reality.

But bad faith is not restricted to denying the qualities which I possess, to not seeing the being which I am. It attempts also to constitute myself as being what I am not. It apprehends me positively as courageous when I am not so. And that is possible, once again, only if I am what I am not; that is, if non-being in me does not have being even as non-being. Of course necessarily I *am not* courageous; otherwise bad faith would not be *bad* faith. But in addition my effort in bad faith must include the ontological comprehension that even in my usual being what I *am*, I am not it really and that there is no such difference between the being of "being-sad," for example—which I *am* in the mode of not being what I am—and the "non-being" of not-being-courageous which I wish to hide from myself. Moreover it is particularly requisite that the very negation of being should be itself the object of a perpetual nihilation, that the very meaning of "non-being" be perpetually in question in human reality. If I *were not* courageous in the way in which this inkwell is not a table; that is, if I were isolated in my cowardice, propped firmly against it, incapable of putting it in relation to its opposite, if I were not capable of *determining* myself as cowardly—that is, to deny courage to myself and thereby to escape my cowardice in very moment that I posit it—if it were not on principle *impossible* for me to coincide with my *not-being-courageous* as well as with my being-courageous—then any project of bad faith would be prohibited me. Thus in order for bad faith to be possible, sincerity itself must be in bad faith. The condition of the possibility for bad faith is that human reality, in its most immediate being, in the intra-structure of the pre-reflective *cogito,* must be what it is not and not be what it is.

The "Faith" of Bad Faith
from Being and Nothingness

We have indicated for the moment only those conditions which render bad faith conceivable, the structures of being which permit us to form concepts of bad faith. We can not limit ourselves to these considerations; we have not yet distinguished bad faith from falsehood. The two-faced concepts which we have described would without a doubt be utilized by a liar to discountenance his questioner, although their two-faced quality being established on the being of man and not on some empirical circumstance, can and ought to be evident to all. The true problem of bad faith stems evidently from the fact that bad faith is *faith.* It can not be either a cynical lie or certainty—if certainty is the intuitive possession of the object. But if we take belief as meaning the adherence of being to its object when the object is not given or is given indistinctly, then bad faith is belief; and the essential problem of bad faith is a problem of belief.

How can we believe by bad faith in the concepts which we forge expressly to persuade ourselves? We must note in fact that the project of bad faith must be itself in bad faith. I am not only in bad faith at the end of my effort when I have constructed my two-faced concepts and when I have persuaded myself. In truth, I have not persuaded myself; to the extent that I could be so persuaded, I have always been so. And at the very moment when I was disposed to put myself in bad faith, I of necessity was in bad faith with respect to this same disposition. For me to have represented it to myself as bad faith would have been cynicism; to believe it sincerely innocent would have been in good faith. The decision to be in bad faith does not dare to speak its name; it believes itself and does not believe itself in bad faith; it believes itself and does not believe itself in good faith. It is this which, from the upsurge of bad faith, determines the later attitude and, as it were, the *Weltanschauung* of bad faith.

Bad faith does not hold the norms and criteria of truth as they are accepted by the critical thought of good faith. What it decides first, in fact, is the nature of truth. With bad faith a truth appears, a method of thinking, a type of being which is like that of objects; the ontological characteristic of the world of bad faith with which the subject suddenly surrounds himself is this: that here being is what it is not, and is not what it is. Consequently a peculiar type of evidence appears: *non-persuasive* evidence. Bad faith apprehends evidence but it is resigned in advance to not being fulfilled by this evidence, to not being persuaded and transformed into good faith. It makes itself humble and modest; it is not ignorant, it says, that faith is decision and that after each intuition, it must decide and *will what it is.* Thus bad faith in its primitive project and in its coming into the world decides on the exact nature of its requirements. It stands forth in the firm resolution *not to demand too much,* to count itself satisfied when it is barely persuaded, to force itself in decisions to adhere to uncertain truths. This original project of bad faith is a decision in bad faith on the nature of faith. Let us understand clearly that there is no question of a reflective, voluntary decision, but of a spontaneous determination of our being. One *puts oneself* in bad faith as one goes to sleep and one is in bad faith as one dreams. Once this mode of being has been realized, it is as difficult to get out of it as to wake oneself up; bad faith is a type of being in the world, like waking or dreaming, which by itself tends to perpetuate itself, although its structure is of the *metastable* type. But bad faith is conscious of its structure, and it has taken precautions by deciding that the metastable structure is the structure of being and that non-persuasion is the structure of all convictions. It follows that if bad faith is faith and if it includes in its original project its own negation (it determines itself to be not quite convinced in order to convince itself that I am what I am not), then to start with, a faith which wishes itself to be not quite convinced must be possible. What are the conditions for the possibility of such a faith?

I believe that my friend Pierre feels friendship for me. I believe it *in good faith.* I believe it but I do not have for it any self-evident intuition, for the nature of the object does not lend itself to intuition. I *believe it;* that is, I allow myself to give in to all impulses to trust it; I decide to believe in it, and to maintain myself in this decision; I conduct myself, finally, as if I were certain of it—and all this in the synthetic unity of one and the same attitude. This which I define as good faith is what Hegel would call the *immediate.* It is simple faith. Hegel would demonstrate at once that the immediate calls for mediation and that belief, by becoming *belief for itself,* passes to the state of non-belief. If I *believe* that my friend Pierre likes me, this means that his friendship appears to me as the meaning of all his acts. Belief is a particular consciousness of *the meaning* of Pierre's acts. But if I know that I believe, the belief appears to me as pure subjective determination without external correlative. This is what makes the very word "to believe" a term utilized indifferently to indicate the unwavering firmness of belief ("My God, I believe in you") and its character as disarmed and strictly subjective ("Is Pierre my friend? I do not know; I believe so"). But the nature of consciousness is such that in it the mediate and the immediate are one and the same being. To believe is to know that one believes, and to know that one believes is no longer to believe. Thus to believe is not to believe any longer because that is only to believe—this in the unity of one and the same non-thetic self-consciousness. To be sure, we have here forced the description of the phenomenon by designating it with the word *to know;* non-thetic consciousness is not to *know.* But it is in its very translucency at the origin of all knowing. Thus the non-thetic consciousness (of) believing is destructive of belief. But at the same time the very law of the pre-reflective *cogito* implies that the being of believing ought to be the consciousness of believing.

Thus belief is a being which questions its own being, which can realize itself only in its destruction, which can manifest itself to itself only by denying itself. It is a being for which to be is to appear and to appear is to deny itself. To believe is not-to-believe. We see the reason for it; the being of consciousness is to exist by itself, then to make itself be and thereby to pass beyond itself. In this sense consciousness is perpetually escaping itself, belief becomes non-belief, the immediate becomes mediation, the absolute becomes relative, and the relative becomes absolute. The ideal of good faith (to believe what one believes) is, like that of sincerity (to be what one is), an ideal of being-in-itself. Every belief is a belief that falls short; one never wholly believes what one believes. Consequently the primitive project of bad faith is only the utilization of this self-destruction of the fact of consciousness. If every belief in good faith is an impossible belief, then there is a place for every impossible belief. My inability to *believe* that I am courageous will not discourage me since every belief involves not quite believing. I shall define this impossible belief as my belief. To be sure, I shall not be able to hide from myself that I believe in order not to believe and that I do not believe *in order to* believe. But the subtle, total annihilation of bad faith by itself can not surprise me; it exists at the basis of all faith. What is it then? At the moment when I wish to believe myself courageous I *know* that I am a coward. And this certainly would come to destroy my belief. But *first, I am* not any more courageous than cowardly, if we are to understand this in the mode of being of the in-itself. In the second place, I do not *know* that I am courageous: such a view of myself can be accompanied only by *belief,* for it surpasses pure reflective certitude. In the third place, it is very true that bad faith does not succeed in believing what it wishes to believe. But it is precisely as the acceptance of not believing what it believes that it is bad faith. Good faith wishes to flee the "not-believing-what-one-believes" by finding refuge in being. Bad faith flees being by taking refuge in "not-believing-what-one-believes." It has disarmed all beliefs in advance—those which it would like to take hold of and, by the same stroke, the others, those which it wishes to flee. In *willing* this self-destruction of belief, from which science escapes by searching for evidence, it ruins the beliefs which are opposed to it, which reveal themselves as *being only* belief. Thus we can better understand the original phenomenon of bad faith.

In bad faith there is no cynical lie nor knowing preparation for deceitful concepts. But the first act of bad faith is to flee what it can not flee, to flee what it

is. The very project of flight reveals to bad faith an inner disintegration in the heart of being, and it is this disintegration which bad faith wishes to be. In truth, the two immediate attitudes which we can take in the face of our being are conditioned by the very nature of this being and its immediate relation with the in-itself. Good faith seeks to flee the inner disintegration of my being in the direction of the in-itself which it should be and is not. Bad faith seeks to flee the in-itself by means of the inner disintegration of my being. But it denies this very disintegration as it denies that it is itself bad faith. Bad faith seeks by means of "not-being-what-one-is" to escape from the in-itself which I am not in the mode of being what one is not. It denies itself as bad faith and aims at the in-itself which I am not in the mode of "not-being-what-one-is-not." * If bad faith is possible, it is because it is an immediate, permanent threat to every project of the human being; it is because consciousness conceals in its being a permanent risk of bad faith. The origin of this risk is the fact that the nature of consciousness simultaneously is to be what it is not and not to be what it is. In the light of these remarks we can now approach the ontological study of consciousness, not as the totality of the human being, but as the instantaneous nucleus of this being.

The Problem
from Being and Nothingness

We have described human reality from the standpoint of negating conduct and from the standpoint of the *cogito*. Following this lead we have discovered that human reality is-for-itself. Is this *all* that it is? Without going outside our attitude of reflective description, we can encounter modes of consciousness which seem, even while themselves remaining strictly in for-

---

*If it is indifferent whether one is in good or in bad faith, because bad faith reapprehends good faith and slides to the very origin of the project of good faith, that does not mean that we can not radically escape bad faith. But this supposes a self-recovery of being which was previously corrupted. This self-recovery we shall call authenticity, the description of which has no place here.

itself, to point to a radically different type of ontological structure. This ontological structure is *mine;* it is in relation to myself as subject that I am concerned about myself, and yet this concern (for-myself) reveals to me a being which is *my* being without being-for-me.

Consider for example shame. Here we are dealing with a mode of consciousness which has a structure identical with all those which we have previously described. It is a non-positional self-consciousness, conscious (of) itself as shame; as such, it is an example of what the Germans call *Erlebnis,* and it is accessible to reflection. In addition its structure is intentional; it is a shameful apprehension *of* something and this something is *me.* I am ashamed of what I *am.* Shame therefore realizes an intimate relation of myself to myself. Through shame I have discovered an aspect of *my* being. Yet although certain complex forms derived from shame can appear on the reflective plane, shame is not originally a phenomenon of reflection. In fact no matter what results one can obtain in solitude by the religious *practice* of shame, it is in its primary structure shame *before somebody.* I have just made an awkward or vulgar gesture. This gesture clings to me; I neither judge it nor blame it. I simply live it. I realize it in the mode of for-itself. But now suddenly I raise my head. Somebody was there and has seen me. Suddenly I realize the vulgarity of my gesture, and I am ashamed. It is certain that my shame is not reflective, for the presence of another in my consciousness, even as a catalyst, is incompatible with the reflective attitude; in the field of my reflection I can never meet with anything but the consciousness which is mine. But the Other is the indispensable mediator between myself and me. I am ashamed of myself *as I appear* to the Other.

By the mere appearance of the Other, I am put in the position of passing judgment on myself as on an object, for it is as an object that I appear to the Other. Yet this object which has appeared to the Other is not an empty image in the mind of another. Such an image, in fact, would be imputable wholly to the Other and so could not "touch" me. I could feel irritation, or anger before it as before a bad portrait of myself which gives to my expression an ugliness or baseness which I do not have, but I could not be touched to the quick. Shame is by nature *recognition.* I recognize that I *am* as the Other sees me. There is however no question of a comparison between what I am for myself and what I am for the Other as if I found in myself, in the mode of being of the For-itself, an equivalent of what I am for the Other. In the first place this comparison is not encountered in us as the result of a concrete psychic operation. Shame is an immediate shudder which runs through me from head to foot without any discursive preparation. In addition the comparison is impossible; I am unable to bring about any relation between what I am in the intimacy of the For-Itself, without distance, without recoil, without perspective, and this unjustifiable being-in-itself which I am for the Other. There is no standard here, no table of correlation. Moreover the very notion of *vulgarity* implies an inter-monad relation. Nobody can be vulgar all alone!

Thus the Other has not only revealed to me what I was; he has established me in a new type of being which can support new qualifications. This being was not in me potentially before the appearance of the Other, for it could not have found any place in the For-itself. Even if some power had been pleased to endow me with a body wholly constituted before it should be for-others, still my vulgarity and my awkwardness could not lodge there potentially; for they are meanings and as such they surpass the body and at the same time refer to a witness capable of understanding them and to the totality of my human reality. But this new being which appears *for* the other does not reside *in* the Other; I am responsible for it as is shown very well by the education system which consists in making children ashamed of what they are.

Thus shame is shame *of oneself before the Other;* these two structures are inseparable. But at the same time I need the Other in order to realize fully all the structures of my being. The For-itself refers to the For-others. Therefore if we wish to grasp in its totality the relation of man's being to being-in-itself, we can not be satisfied with the descriptions outlined in the earlier chapters of this work. We must answer two far more formidable questions: first that of the existence of the Other, then that of the relation of my *being* to the being of the Other.

The Look
from Being and Nothingness

This woman whom I see coming toward me, this man who is passing by in the street, this beggar whom I hear calling before my window, all are for me *objects*— of that there is no doubt. Thus it is true that at least one of the modalities of the Other's presence to me is *object-ness*. But we have seen that if this relation of object-ness is the fundamental relation between the Other and myself, then the Other's existence remains purely conjectural. Now it is not only conjectural but *probable* that this voice which I hear is that of a man and not a song on a phonograph; it is infinitely *probable* that the passerby whom I see is a man and not a perfected robot. This means that without going beyond the limits of probability and indeed because of this very probability, my apprehension of the Other as an object essentially refers me to a fundamental apprehension of the Other in which he will not be revealed to me as an object but as a "presence in person." In short, if the Other is to be a probable object and not a dream of an object, then his object-ness must of necessity refer not to an original solitude beyond my reach, but to a fundamental connection in which the Other is manifested in some way other than through the knowledge which I have of him. The classical theories are right in considering that every perceived human organism *refers* to something and that this to which it refers is the foundation and guarantee of its probability. Their mistake lies in believing that this reference indicates a separate existence, a consciousness which would be behind its perceptible manifestations. . . . The problem of Others has generally been treated as if the primary relation by which the Other is discovered is object-ness; that is, as if the Other were first revealed—directly or indirectly—to our perception. But since this perception by its very nature *refers* to something other than to itself and since it can refer neither to an infinite series of appearances of the same type—as in idealism the perception of the table or of the chair does— nor to an isolated entity located on principle outside my reach, its essence must be to refer to a primary relation between my consciousness and the Other's. This relation, in which the Other must be given to me directly as a subject although in connection with me, is the fundamental relation, the very type of my being-for-others.

Nevertheless the reference here cannot be to any mystic or ineffable experience. It is in the reality of everyday life that the Other appears to us, and his probability refers to everyday reality. The problem is precisely this: there is in everyday reality an original

relation to the Other which can be constantly pointed to and which consequently can be revealed to me outside all reference to a religious or mystic unknowable. In order to understand it I must question more exactly this ordinary appearance of the Other in the field of my perception; since this appearance refers to that fundamental relation, the appearance must be capable of revealing to us, at least as a reality aimed at, the relation to which it refers.

I am in a public park. Not far away there is a lawn and along the edge of that lawn there are benches. A man passes by those benches. I see this man; I apprehend him as an object and at the same time as a man. What does this signify? What do I mean when I assert that this object *is a man?*

If I were to think of him as being only a puppet, I should apply to him the categories which I ordinarily use to group temporal-spatial "things." That is, I should apprehend him as being "beside" the benches, two yards and twenty inches from the lawn, as exercising a certain pressure on the ground, *etc.* His relation with other objects would be of the purely additive type; this means that I could have him disappear without the relations of the other objects around him being perceptibly *changed.* In short, no new relation would appear *through him* between those things in my universe: grouped and synthesized *from my point of view* into instrumental complexes, they would *from his* disintegrate into multiplicities of indifferent relations. Perceiving him as a *man,* on the other hand, is not to apprehend an additive between the chair and him; it is to register an organization *without distance* of the things in my universe around that privileged object. To be sure, the lawn remains two yards and twenty inches away from him, but it is also *as a lawn* bound to him in a relation which at once both transcends distance and contains it. Instead of the two terms of the distance being indifferent, interchangeable, and in a reciprocal relation, the distance *is unfolded starting from* the man whom I see and *extending up to* the lawn as the synthetic upsurge of a univocal relation. We are dealing with a relation which is without *parts,* given at one stroke, inside of which there unfolds a spatiality which is not *my* spatiality; for instead of a grouping *toward me* of the objects, there is now an orientation *which flees from me.*

Of course this relation without distance and without parts is in no way that original relation of the Other to me which I am seeking. In the first place, it concerns only the man and the things in the world. In addition it is still an object of knowledge; I shall express it, for example, by saying that this man sees the lawn, or that in spite of the prohibiting sign he is preparing to walk on the grass, *etc.* Finally it still retains a pure character of probability: First, it is *probable* that this object is a man. Second, even granted that he is a man, it remains only probable that he sees the lawn at the moment that I perceive him; it is possible that he is dreaming of some project without exactly being aware of what is around him, or that he is blind, *etc., etc.* Nevertheless this new relation of the object-man to the object-lawn has a particular character; it is simultaneously given to me as a whole, since it is there in the world as an object which I can know (it is, in fact, an objective relation which I express by saying: Pierre has glanced at this watch, Jean has looked out the window, *etc.*), and at the same time it entirely escapes me. To the extent that the man-as-object is the fundamental term of this relation, to the extent that the relation *reaches toward him,* it escapes me. I can not put myself at the center of it. The distance which unfolds between the lawn and the man across the synthetic upsurge of this primary relation is a negation of the distance which I establish—as a pure type of external negation—between these two objects. The distance appears as a pure *disintegration* of the relations which I apprehend between the objects of my universe. It is not I who realize this disintegration; it appears to me as a relation which I aim at emptily across the distances which I originally established between things. It stands as a background of things, a background which on principle escapes me and which is conferred on them from without. Thus the appearance among the objects of *my* universe of an element of disintegration in that universe is what I mean by the appearance of a man in my universe.

The Other is first the permanent flight of things toward a goal which I apprehend as an object at a certain distance from me but which escapes me inasmuch as it unfolds about itself its own distances. Moreover this disintegration grows by degrees; if there exists between the lawn and the Other a relation which is without distance and which creates distance, then there exists necessarily a relation between the Other and the statue which stands on a pedestal *in the middle of* the lawn, and a relation between the Other and the big chestnut trees which border the walk; there is a total space which is grouped around the Other,

and this space is made *with my space;* there is a regrouping in which I take part but which escapes me, a regrouping of all the objects which people my universe. This regrouping does not stop there. The grass is something qualified; it is *this* green grass which exists for the Other; in this sense the very quality of the object, its deep, raw green is in direct relation to this man. This green turns toward the Other a face which escapes me. I apprehend the relation of the green to the Other as an objective relation, but I can not apprehend the green *as* it appears to the Other. Thus suddenly an object has appeared which has stolen the world from me. Everything is in place; everything still exists for me; but everything is traversed by an invisible flight and fixed in the direction of a new object. The appearance of the Other in the world corresponds therefore to a fixed sliding of the whole universe, to a decentralization of the world which undermines the centralization which I am simultaneously effecting.

But *the Other* is still an object *for me.* He belongs to *my distances;* the man is there, twenty paces from me, he is turning his back on me. As such he is again two yards, twenty inches from the lawn, six yards from the statue; hence the disintegration of my universe is contained within the limits of this same universe; we are not dealing here with a flight of the world toward nothingness or outside itself. Rather it appears that the world has a kind of drain hole in the middle of its being and that it is perpetually flowing off through this hole. The universe, the flow, and the drain hole are all once again recovered, reapprehended, and fixed as an object. All this is there *for me* as a partial structure of the world, even though the total disintegration of the universe is involved. Moreover these disintegrations may often be contained within more narrow limits. There, for example, is a man who is reading while he walks. The disintegration of the universe which he represents is purely virtual: he has ears which do not hear, eyes which see nothing except his book. Between his book and him I apprehend an undeniable relation without distance of the same type as that which earlier connected the walker with the grass. But this time the form has closed in on itself. There is a full object for me to grasp. In the midst of the world I can say "man-reading" as I could say "cold stone," "fine rain." I apprehend a closed "Gestalt" in which the *reading* forms the essential quality; for the rest, it remains blind and mute, lets itself be known and perceived as a pure and simple temporal-spatial thing, and seems to be related to the rest of the world by a purely indifferent externality. The quality "man-reading" as the relation of the man to the book is simply a little particular crack in my universe. At the heart of this solid, visible form he makes himself a particular emptying. The form is massive only in appearance; its peculiar meaning is to be—in the midst of my universe, at ten paces from me, at the heart of that massivity—a closely consolidated and localized flight.

None of this enables us to leave the level on which the Other is an *object*. At most we are dealing with a particular type of objectivity akin to that which Husserl designated by the term *absence* without, however, his noting that the Other is defined not as the absence of a consciousness in relation to the body which I see but by the absence of the world which I perceive, an absence discovered at the very heart of my perception of this world. On this level the Other is an object in the world, an object which can be defined by the world. But this relation of flight and of absence on the part of the world in relation to me is only probable. If it is this which defines the objectivity of the Other, then to what original presence of the Other does it refer? At present we can give this answer: if the Other-as-object is defined in connection with the world as the object which sees what I see, then my fundamental connection with the Other-as-subject must be able to be referred back to my permanent possibility of *being seen* by the Other. It is in and through the revelation of my being-as-object for the Other that I must be able to apprehend the presence of his being-as-subject. For just as the Other is a probable object for me-as-subject, so I can discover myself in the process of becoming a probable object for only a certain subject. This revelation can not derive from the fact that *my universe is an object for the Other-as-object,* as if the Other's look after having wandered over the lawn and the surrounding objects came following a definite path to place itself on me. I have observed that I can not be an object for an object. A radical conversion of the Other is necessary if he is to escape objectivity. Therefore I can not consider the look which the Other directs on me as one of the possible manifestations of his objective being; the Other can not look at *me* as he looks at the grass. Furthermore my objectivity can not itself derive *for me* from the objectivity of the world since I am precisely the one by whom *there is a* world; that is, the one who on principle can not be an object for himself.

Thus this relation which I call "being-seen-by-another," far from being merely one of the relations signified by the word *man,* represents an irreducible fact which can not be deduced either from the essence of the Other-as-object, or from my being-as-subject. On the contrary, if the concept of the Other-as-object is to have any meaning, this can be only as the result of the conversion and the degradation of that original relation. In a word, my apprehension of the Other in the world as *probably being* a man refers to my permanent possibility of *being-seen-by-him;* that is, to the permanent possibility that a subject who sees me may be substituted for the object seen by me. "Being-seen-by-the-Other" is the *truth* of "seeing-the-Other." Thus the notion of the Other can not under any circumstances aim at a solitary, extra-mundane consciousness which I can not even think. The man is defined by his relation to the world and by his relation to myself. He is that object in the world which determines an internal flow of the universe, an internal hemorrhage. He is the subject who is revealed to me in that flight of myself toward objectivation. But the original relation of myself to the Other is not only an absent truth aimed at across the concrete presence of an object in my universe; it is also a concrete, daily relation which at each instant I experience. At each instant the Other *is looking at me.* It is easy therefore for us to attempt with concrete examples to describe this fundamental connection which must form the basis of any theory concerning the Other. If the Other is on principle the *one who looks at me,* then we must be able to explain the meaning of the Other's look.

. . .

Let us imagine that moved by jealousy, curiosity, or vice I have just glued my ear to the door and looked through a keyhole. I am alone and on the level of a non-thetic self-consciousness. This means first of all that there is no self to inhabit my consciousness, nothing therefore to which I can refer my acts in order to qualify them. They are in no way *known; I am my acts* and hence they carry in themselves their whole justification. I am a pure consciousness *of* things, and things, caught up in the circuit of my selfness, offer to me their potentialities as the proof of my non-thetic consciousness (of) my own possibilities. This means that behind that door a spectacle is presented as "to be seen," a conversation as "to be heard." The door, the keyhole are at once both instruments and obstacles; they are presented as "to be handled with care"; the keyhole is given as "to be looked through close by and a little to one side," *etc.* Hence from this moment "I do what I have to do." No transcending view comes to confer upon my acts the character of a *given* on which a judgment can be brought to bear. My consciousness sticks to my acts, it *is* my acts; and my acts are commanded only by the ends to be attained and by the instruments to be employed. My attitude, for example, has no "outside"; it is a pure process of relating the instrument (the keyhole) to the end to be attained (the spectacle to be seen), a pure mode of losing myself in the world, of causing myself to be drunk in by things as ink is by a blotter in order that an instrumental-complex oriented toward an end may be synthetically detached on the ground of the world. The order is the reverse of causal order. It is the end to be attained which organizes all the moments which precede it. The end justifies the means; the means do not exist for themselves and outside the end.

Moreover the ensemble exists only in relation to a free project of my possibilities. Jealousy, as the possibility which I *am,* organizes this instrumental complex by transcending it toward itself. But I *am* this jealousy; I do not *know* it. If I contemplated it instead of making it, then only the worldly complex in instrumentality could teach it to me. This ensemble in the world with its double and inverted determination (there is a spectacle to be seen behind the door only because I am jealous, but my jealousy is nothing except the simple objective fact that *there is* a sight *to be seen* behind the door)—this we shall *situation.* This situation reflects to me at once both my facticity and my freedom; on the occasion of a certain objective structure of the world which surrounds me, it refers my freedom to me in the form of tasks to be freely done. There is no constraint here since my freedom eats into my possibles and since correlatively the potentialities of the world indicate and offer only themselves. Moreover I can not truly define myself as *being* in a situation: first because I am not a positional consciousness of myself; second because I am my own nothingness. In this sense—and since I am what I am not and since I am not what I am—I can not even define myself as truly *being* in the process of listening at doors. I escape this provisional definition of myself by means of all my transcendence. There as we have seen is the origin of bad faith. Thus not only am I unable to *know* myself, but my very being escapes—although I *am* that very escape from my being—and I am absolutely nothing. There is nothing *there* but a pure nothingness encircling a certain objective ensemble and throwing it into relief outlined upon the world, but this ensemble is a real system, a disposition of means in view of an end.

But all of a sudden I hear footsteps in the hall. Someone is looking at me! What does this mean? It means that I am suddenly affected in my being and that essential modifications appear in my structure—modifications which I can apprehend and fix conceptually by means of the reflective *cogito.*

First of all, I now exist as *myself* for my unreflective consciousness. It is this irruption of the self which has been most often described: I see *myself* because *somebody* sees me—as it is usually expressed. This way of putting it is not wholly exact. But let us look more carefully. So long as we considered the for-itself in its isolation, we were able to maintain that the unreflective consciousness can not be inhabited by a self; the self was given in the form of an object and only for the reflective consciousness. But here the self comes to haunt the unreflective consciousness. Now the unreflective consciousness is a consciousness *of* the world. Therefore for the unreflective consciousness the self exists on the level of objects in the world; this role which devolved only on the reflective consciousness—the making-present of the self—belongs now to the unreflective consciousness. Only the reflective consciousness has the self directly for an object. The unreflective consciousness does not apprehend the *person* directly or as *its* object; the person is presented to consciousness *in so far as the person is an object for the Other.* This means that all of a sudden I am conscious of myself as escaping myself, not in that I am the foundation of my own nothingness but in that I have my foundation outside myself. I am for myself only as I am a pure reference to the Other.

Nevertheless we must not conclude here that the object is the Other and that the *Ego* present to my consciousness is a secondary structure or a meaning of the Other-as-object; the Other is not an object here and can not be an object, as we have shown, unless by the same stroke *my* self ceases to be an object-for-the-Other and vanishes. Thus I do not aim at the Other as an object nor at my *Ego* as an object for myself; I do not even direct an empty intention toward that *Ego* as toward an object presently out of my reach. In fact it is separated from me by a nothingness which I can not fill since I apprehend it *as not being for me* and since on principle it exists for the *Other*. Therefore I do not aim at it as if it could someday be given me but on the contrary in so far as it on principle flees from me and will never belong to me. Nevertheless I *am that Ego;* I do not reject it as a strange image, but it is present to me as a self which I *am* without *knowing* it; for I discover it in shame and, in other instances, in pride. It is shame or pride which reveals to me the Other's look and myself at the end of that look. It is the shame or pride which makes me *live,* not *know* the situation of being looked at.

Now, shame, as we noted at the beginning of this chapter, is shame of *self;* it is the *recognition* of the fact that I *am* indeed that object which the Other is looking at and judging. I can be ashamed only as my freedom escapes me in order to become a *given* object. Thus originally the bond between my unreflective consciousness and my *Ego,* which is being looked at, is a bond not of knowing but of being. Beyond any knowledge which I can have, I am this self which another knows. And this self which I am—this I am in a world which the Other has made alien to me, for the Other's look embraces my being and correlatively the walls, the door, the keyhole. All these instrumental-things, in the midst of which I am, now turn toward the Other a face which on principle escapes me. Thus I am my *Ego* for the Other in the midst of a world which flows toward the Other. Earlier we were able to call this internal hemorrhage the flow of *my* world toward the Other-as-object. This was because the flow of blood was trapped and localized by the very fact that I fixed as an object in my world that Other toward which this world was bleeding. Thus not a drop of blood was lost; all was recovered, surrounded, localized although in a being which I could not penetrate. Here on the contrary the flight is without limit; it is lost externally; the world flows out of the world and I flow outside myself. The Other's look makes me be beyond my being in this world and puts me in the midst of the world which is at once *this world* and beyond this world. What sort of relations can I enter into with this being which I am and which shame reveals to me?

In the first place there is a relation of being. I *am* this being. I do not for an instant think of denying it; my shame is a confession. I shall be able later to use bad faith so as to hide it from myself, but bad faith is also a confession since it is an effort to flee the being which I am. But I am this being, neither in the mode of "having to be" nor in that of "was"; I do not found it in its being; I can not produce it directly. But neither is it the indirect, strict effect of my acts as when my shadow on the ground or my reflection in the mirror is moved in correlation with the gestures which I make. This being which I am preserves a certain indetermination, a certain unpredictability. And these new characteristics do not come only from the fact that I can not *know* the Other; they stem also and especially from the fact that the Other is free. Or to be exact and to reverse the terms, the Other's freedom is revealed to me across the uneasy indetermination of the being which I am for him. Thus this being is not my possible; it is not always in question at the heart of my freedom. On the contrary, it is the limit of my freedom, its "backstage" in the sense that we speak of "behind the scenes." It is given to me as a burden which I carry without ever being able to turn back to know it, without even being able to realize its weight. If it is comparable to my shadow, it is like a shadow which is projected on a moving and unpredictable material such that no table of reference can be provided for calculating the distortions resulting from these movements. Yet we still have to do with *my* being and not with an image of my being. We are dealing with my being as it is written in and by the Other's freedom. Everything takes place as if I had a dimension of being from which I was separated by a radical nothingness; and this nothingness is the Other's freedom. The Other has to make my being-for-him *be* in so far as he has to be his being. Thus each of my free conducts engages me in a new environment where the very stuff of my being is the unpredictable freedom of another. Yet by my very shame I claim as mine that freedom of another. I affirm a profound unity of consciousness, not that harmony of monads which has sometimes been taken as a guarantee of objectivity but a unity of being; for I accept and wish that others should confer upon me a being which I recognize.

Shame reveals to me that I *am* this being, not in the mode of "was" or of "having to be" but *in-itself.* When I am alone, I can not realize my "being-seated"; at most it can be said that I simultaneously both am it and am not it. But in order for me to be what I am, it suffices merely that the Other look at me. It is not for myself, to be sure; I myself shall never succeed at realizing this being-seated which I grasp in the Other's look. I shall remain forever a consciousness. But it is for the Other. Once more the nihilating escape of the for-itself is fixed, once more the in-itself closes in upon the for-itself. But once more this metamorphosis is effected *at a distance*. For the Other *I am seated* as this inkwell *is on* the table; for the Other, *I am leaning over* the keyhole as this tree *is bent* by the wind. Thus for the Other I have stripped myself of transcendence. This is because my transcendence becomes for whoever makes himself a witness of it (*i.e.*, determines himself *as not being* my transcendence) a purely established transcendence, a given-transcendence; that is, it acquires a nature by the sole fact that the *Other* confers on it an outside. This is accomplished, not by any distortion or by a refraction which the Other would impose on my transcendence through his categories, but by his very being. If there is an Other, whatever or whoever he may be, whatever may be his relations with me, and without his acting upon me in any way except by the pure upsurge of his being—then I have an outside, I have a *nature*. My original fall is the existence of the Other. Shame—like pride—is the apprehension of myself as a nature although that very nature escapes me and is unknowable as such. Strictly speaking, it is not that I perceive myself losing my freedom in order to become a *thing*, but my nature is—over there, outside my lived freedom—as a given attribute of this being which I am for the Other.

· · ·

First Attitude Toward Others: Love, Language, Masochism
from Being and Nothingness

Everything which may be said of me in my relations with the Other applies to him as well. While I attempt to free myself from the hold of the Other, the Other is trying to free himself from mine; while I seek to enslave the Other, the Other seeks to enslave me. We are by no means dealing with unilateral relations with an object-in-itself, but with reciprocal and moving relations. The following descriptions of concrete behavior must therefore be envisaged within the perspective of *conflict*. Conflict is the original meaning of being-for-others.

If we start with the first revelation of the Other as a *look*, we must recognize that we experience our inapprehensible being-for-others in the form of a *possession*. I am possessed by the Other; the Other's look fashions my body in its nakedness, causes it to be born, sculptures it, produces it as it *is*, sees it as I shall never see it. The Other holds a secret—the secret of what I am. He makes me be and thereby he possesses me, and this possession is nothing other than the consciousness of possessing me. I in the recognition of my object-state have proof that he has this consciousness. By virtue of consciousness the Other is for me simultaneously the one who has stolen my being from me and the one who causes "there to be" a being which is my being. Thus I have a comprehension of this ontological structure: I am responsible for my being-for-others, but I am not the foundation of it. It appears to me therefore in the form of a contingent given for which I am nevertheless responsible; the Other founds my being in so far as this being is in the form of the "there is." But he is not responsible for my being although he founds it in complete freedom—in and by means of his free transcendence. Thus to the extent that I am revealed to myself as responsible for my being, I *lay claim to* this being which I am; that is, I wish to recover it, or, more exactly, I am the project of the recovery of my being. I want to stretch out my hand and grab hold of this being which is presented to me as *my being* but at a distance—like the dinner of Tantalus; I want to found it by my very freedom. For if in one sense my being-as-object is an unbearable contingency and the pure "possession" of myself by another, still in another sense this being stands as the indication of what I should be obliged to recover and found in order to be the foundation of myself. But this is conceivable only if I assimilate the Other's freedom. Thus my project of recovering myself is fundamentally a project of absorbing the Other.

Nevertheless this project must leave the Other's nature intact. Two consequences result: (1) I do not thereby cease to assert the Other—that is, to deny concerning myself that I am the Other. Since the Other is the foundation of my being, he could not be dissolved in me without my being-for-others disappearing. Therefore if I project the realization of unity for the Other, this means that I project my assimilation of the Other's Otherness as my own possibility. In fact the problem for me is to make myself be by acquiring the possibility of taking the Other's point of view on myself. It is not a matter of acquiring a pure, abstract faculty of knowledge. It is not the pure *category* of the Other which I project appropriating to myself. This category is not conceived nor even conceivable. But on the occasion of concrete experience with the Other, an experience suffered and realized, it is this concrete Other as an absolute reality whom in his otherness I wish to incorporate into myself. (2) The Other whom I wish to assimilate is by no means the Other-as-object. Or, if you prefer, my project of incorporating the Other in no way corresponds to a recapturing of my for-itself as myself and to a surpassing of the Other's transcendence toward my own possibilities. For me it is not a question of obliterating my object-state by making an object of the Other, which would amount to *releasing* myself from my being-for-others. Quite the contrary, I want to assimilate the Other as the Other-looking-at-me, and this project of assimilation includes an augmented recognition of my being-looked-at. In short, in order to maintain before me the Other's freedom which is looking at me, I identify myself totally with my being-looked-at. And since my being-as-object is the only possible relation between me and the Other, it is this being-as-object which alone can serve me as an instrument to effect my assimilation of the *other freedom*.

Thus as a reaction to the failure of the third ekstasis, the for-itself wishes to be identified with the Other's freedom as founding its own being-in-itself. To be other to oneself—the ideal always aimed at concretely in the form of being *this Other* to oneself—is the primary value of my relations with the Other. This means that my being-for-others is haunted by the indication of an absolute-being which would be itself as other and other as itself and which, by freely giving to itself its being-itself as other and its being-other as itself, would be the very being of the ontological proof— that is, God. This ideal can not be realized without my surmounting the original contingency of my relations to the Other; that is, by overcoming the fact that there is no relation of internal negativity between the negation by which the Other is made other than I and the negation by which I am made other than the Other. We have seen that this contingency is insurmountable; it is the *fact* of my relations with the Other, just as my

body is the *fact* of my being-in-the-world. Unity with the Other is therefore *in fact* unrealizable. It is also unrealizable *in theory,* for the assimilation of the for-itself and the Other in a single transcendence would necessarily involve the disappearance of the characteristic of otherness in the Other. Thus the condition on which I project the identification of myself with the Other is that I persist in denying that I am the Other. Finally this project of unification is the source of *conflict* since while I experience myself as an object for the Other and while I project assimilating him in and by means of this experience, the Other apprehends me as an object in the midst of the world and does not project identifying me with himself. It would therefore be necessary—since being-for-others includes a double internal negation—to act upon the internal negation by which the Other transcends my transcendence and makes me exist for the Other; that is, *to act upon the Other's freedom.*

This unrealizable ideal which haunts my project of myself in the presence of the Other is not to be identified with love in so far as love is an enterprise; *i.e.,* an organic ensemble of projects toward my own possibilities. But it is the ideal of love, its motivation and its end, its unique value. Love as the primitive relation to the Other is the ensemble of the projects by which I aim at realizing this value.

·   ·   ·

Second Attitude Toward Others: *Indifference, Desire, Hate, Sadism* *from* Being and Nothingness

The failure of the first attitude toward the Other can be the occasion for my assuming the second. But of course neither of the two is really first; each of them is a fundamental reaction to being-for-others as an original situation. It can happen therefore that due to the very impossibility of my identifying myself with the Other's consciousness through the intermediacy of my object-ness for him, I am led to turn deliberately toward the Other and *look* at him. In this case to look at the Other's look is to posit oneself in one's own freedom and to attempt on the ground of this freedom to confront the Other's freedom. The meaning of the conflict thus sought would be to bring out into the open the struggle of two freedoms confronted as freedoms. But this intention must be immediately disappointed, for by the sole fact that I assert myself in my freedom confronting the Other, I make the Other a transcendence-transcended—that is, an object. It is the story of that failure which we are about to investigate. We can grasp its general pattern. I direct my look upon the Other who is looking at me. But a look can not be looked at. As soon as I look in the direction of the look it disappears, and I no longer see anything but eyes. At this instant the Other becomes a being which I possess and which recognizes my freedom. It seems that my goal has been achieved since I possess the being who has the key to my object-state and since I can cause him to make proof of my freedom in a thousand different ways. But in reality the whole structure has collapsed, for the being which remains within my hands is an Other-as-object. As such he has lost the key to my being-as-object, and he possesses a pure and simple image of me which is nothing but one of its objective affects and which no longer touches me. If he experiences the effects of my freedom, if I can act upon his being in a thousand different ways and transcend his possibilities with all my possibilities, this is only in so far as he is an object in the world and as such is outside the state of recognizing my freedom. My disappointment is complete since I seek to appropriate the Other's freedom and perceive suddenly that I can act upon the Other only in so far as this freedom has collapsed beneath my look. This disappointment will be the result of my further attempts to seek again for the Other's freedom across the object which he is for me and to find privileged attitudes or conduct which would appropriate this freedom across a total appropriation of the Other's body. These attempts, as one may suspect, are on principle doomed to failure.

.   .   .

My original attempt to get hold of the Other's free subjectivity through his objectivity-for-me is *sexual desire*. Perhaps it will come as a surprise to see a phenomenon which is usually classified among "psycho-physiological reactions" now mentioned on the level of primary attitudes which manifest our original mode of realizing Being-for-Others. For the majority of psychologists indeed, desire, as a fact of consciousness, is in strict correlation with the nature of our sexual organs, and it is only in connection with an elaborate study of these that sexual desire can be understood. But since the differentiated structure of the body (mammalian, viviparous, *etc.*) and consequently the particular sexual structure (uterus, Fallopian tubes, ovaries, *etc.*) are in the domain of absolute contingency and in no way derive from the ontology of "consciousness" or of the *Dasein,* it seems that the same must be true for sexual desire. Just as the sex organs are a contingent and particular formation of our body, so the desire which corresponds to them would be a contingent modality of our psychic life; that is, it would be described only on the level of an empirical psychology based on biology. This is indicated sufficiently by the term *sex instinct,* which is reserved for desire and all the psychic structures which refer to it. The term "instinct" always in fact qualifies contingent formations of psychic life which have the double character of being co-extensive with all the duration of this life— or in any case of not deriving from our "history"— and of nevertheless not being such that they can not be deduced as belonging to the very essence of the psychic. This is why existential philosophies have not believed it necessary to concern themselves with sexuality. Heidegger, in particular, does not make the slightest allusion to it in his existential analytic with the result that his *Dasein* appears to us as asexual. Of course one may consider that it is contingent for "human reality" to be specified as "masculine" or "feminine"; of course one may say that the problem of sexual differentiation has nothing to do with that of *Existence (Existenz)* since man and woman equally exist.

These reasons are not wholly convincing. That sexual differentiation lies within the domain of facticity we accept without reservation. But does this mean that the For-itself is sexual "accidentally," by the pure contingency of having this particular body? Can we admit that this tremendous matter of the sexual life comes as a kind of addition to the human condition? Yet it appears at first glance that desire and its opposite, sexual repulsion, are fundamental structures of being-for-others. It is evident that if sexuality derives its origin from *sex* as a physiological and contingent determination of man, it can not be indispensable to the being of the For-Others. But do we not have the right to ask whether the problem is not perchance of the same order as that which we encountered apropos of sensations and sense organs? Man, it is said, is a sexual being because he possesses a sex. And if the reverse were true? If sex were only the instrument and, so to speak, the *image* of a fundamental sexuality? If man possessed a sex only because he is originally and fundamentally a sexual being as a being who exists in the world in relation with other men? Infantile sexuality precedes the physiological maturation of the sex organs. Men who have become eunuchs do not thereby cease to feel desire. Nor do many old men. The fact of being able to *make use of* a sex organ fit to fertilize and to procure enjoyment represents only one phase and one aspect of our sexual life. There is one mode of sexuality "with the possibility of satisfaction," and the developed sex represents and makes concrete this possibility. But there are other modes of sexuality of the type which can not get satisfaction, and if we take these modes into account we are forced to recognize that sexuality appears with birth and disappears only with death. Moreover neither the tumescence of the penis nor any other physiological phenomenon can ever explain or provoke sexual desire—no more than the vaso-constriction or the dilation of the pupils (or the simple consciousness of these physiological modifications) will be able to explain or to provoke fear. In one case as in the other although the body plays an important role, we must—in order to understand it—refer to being-in-the-world and to being-for-others. I desire a human being, not an insect or a mollusk, and I desire him (or her) as he is and as I am in situation in the world and as he is an Other for me and as I am an Other for him.

The fundamental problem of sexuality can therefore be formulated thus: is sexuality a contingent accident bound to our physiological nature, or is it a necessary structure of being-for-itself-for-others? From the sole fact that the question can be posited in these terms, we see that we must go back to ontology to decide it. Moreover ontology can decide this question only by determining and fixing the meaning of sexual existence for-the-Other. To have sex means . . . to exist sexually for an Other who exists sexually for me. And it must be well understood that at first this Other is not necessarily *for me*—nor I for him—a *heterosexual* existent but only a being who has sex. Considered from the point of view of the For-itself, this apprehension of the Other's sexuality could not be the pure disinterested contemplation of his primary or secondary sexual characteristics. *My first* apprehension of the Other as having sex does not come when I conclude from the distribution of his hair, from the coarseness of his hands, the sound of his voice, his strength that he is of the masculine sex. We are dealing there with derived conclusions which refer to an original state. The first apprehension of the Other's sexuality in so far as it is lived and suffered can be only *desire;* it is by desiring the Other (or by discovering myself as incapable of desiring him) or by apprehending his desire for me that I discover his being-sexed. Desire reveals to me simultaneously *my* being-sexed and *his* being-sexed, *my* body as sex and *his* body. Here therefore in order to decide the nature and ontological position of sex we are referred to the study of desire. What therefore is desire?

And first, desire *of what?*

We must abandon straight off the idea that desire is the desire of pleasure or the desire for the cessation of a pain. For we can not see how the subject could get out of this state of immanence so as to "attach" his desire to an object. Every subjectivist and immanentist theory will fail to explain how we desire a particular woman and not simply our sexual satisfaction. It is best therefore to define desire by its transcendent object. Nevertheless it would be wholly inaccurate to say that desire is a desire for "physical possession" of the desired object—if by "possess" we mean here "to make love to." Of course the sexual act for a moment frees us from desire, and in certain cases it can be posited explicitly as the hoped-for issue of the desire—when desire, for example, is painful and fatiguing. But in this case it is necessary that the desire itself be the object which is posited as "to be overcome," and this can be accomplished only by means of a reflective consciousness. But desire by itself is non-reflective; therefore it could never posit itself as an object to be overcome. Only a roué represents his desire to himself, treats it as an object, excites it, "turns it off," varies the means of assuaging it, *etc.* . . .

But what is the object of desire? Shall we say that desire is the desire of a *body?* In one sense this can not be denied. But we must take care to understand this correctly. To be sure it is the body which disturbs us: an arm or a half-exposed breast or perhaps a leg. But we must realize at the start that we desire the arm or the uncovered breast only on the ground of the presence of the whole body as an organic totality. The body itself as totality may be hidden. I may see only a bare arm. But the body is there. It is from the standpoint of the body that I apprehend the arm as an arm. The body is as much present, as adherent to the arm which I see as the designs of the rug, which are hidden by the feet of the table, are present and adherent to those designs which I see. And my desire is not mistaken; it is addressed not to a sum of physiological elements but to a total form—better yet, to a form *in situation.* . . . A living body as an organic totality in situation with consciousness at the horizon: such is the object to which desire *is addressed.* What does desire wish from this object? We can not determine this until we have answered a preliminary question: *Who* is the one who desires?

The answer is clear. *I am* the one who desires, and desire is a particular mode of my subjectivity. Desire is consciousness since it can *be* only as a non-positional consciousness of itself. Nevertheless we need not hold that the desiring consciousness differs from the cognitive consciousness, for example, only in the nature of its object. For the For-itself, to choose itself as desire is not to produce a desire while remaining indifferent and unchanged—as the Stoic cause produces its effect. The For-itself puts itself on a certain plane of existence which is not the same, for example, as that of a For-itself which chooses itself as a metaphysical being. Every consciousness, as we have seen, supports a certain relation with its own facticity. But this relation can vary from one mode of consciousness to another. The facticity of a pain-consciousness, for example, is a facticity discovered in a perpetual flight. The case is not the same for the facticity of desire. The man who desires *exists* his body in a particular mode and thereby places himself on a particular level of existence. In fact everyone will agree that desire is not only *longing,* a clear and translucent *longing* which directs itself through our body toward a certain object. Desire is defined as *trouble.* The notion of "trouble" can help us better to determine the nature of desire. We contrast troubled water with transparent water, a troubled look with a clear look. Troubled water remains water; it preserves the fluidity and the essential characteristics of water; but its translucency is "troubled" by an inapprehensible presence which makes one with it, which is everywhere and nowhere and which is given as a clogging of the water by itself. To be sure, we can explain the troubled quality by the presence of fine solid particles suspended in the liquid, but this explanation is that of the *scientist.* Our original apprehension of the troubled water is given us as changed by the presence of an invisible *something* which is not itself distinguished and which is manifested as a pure factual resistance. If the desiring consciousness is *troubled,* it is because it is analogous to the troubled water.

To make this analogy precise, we should compare sexual desire with another form of desire—for example, with hunger. Hunger, like sexual desire, supposes a certain state of the body, defined here as the impoverishment of the blood, abundant salivary secretion, contractions of the tunica, *etc.* These various phenomena are described and classified from the point of view of the Other. For the For-itself they are manifested as pure facticity. But this facticity *does not compromise* the nature of the For-itself, for the For-itself immediately flees it toward its possibles; that is, toward a certain state of satisfied-hunger which, as we have pointed out in Part Two,* is the In-itself-for-itself of hunger. Thus hunger is a pure surpassing of corporal facticity; and to the extent that the For-itself becomes conscious of this facticity in a non-thetic form, the For-itself becomes conscious of it as a surpassed facticity. The body here is indeed the *past, the passed-beyond.* In sexual desire, to be sure, we can find that structure common to all appetites—a state of the body. The Other can note various physiological modifications (the erection of the penis, the turgescence of the nipples of the breasts, changes in the circulatory system, rise in temperature, *etc.*). The desiring consciousness exists this facticity; it is *in terms of this facticity*—we could even say *through* it—that the desired body appears as desirable. Nevertheless if we limited ourselves to this description, sexual desire would appear as a *distinct and clear desire,* comparable to the desire of eating and drinking. It would be a pure flight from facticity toward other possibles. Now everyone is aware that there is a great abyss between sexual desire and other appetites. We all know the famous saying; "Make love to a pretty woman when you want her just as you would drink a glass of cold water when you are thirsty." We know also how unsatisfactory and even shocking this statement is to the mind. This is because when we do desire a woman, we do not keep ourselves wholly outside the desire; the desire *compromises* me; I am the accomplice of my desire. Or rather the desire has fallen wholly into complicity with the body. Let any man consult his own

---

*From Part Two: Being-for-Itself in *Being and Nothingness*—ed.

experience; he knows how consciousness is clogged, so to speak, by sexual desire; it seems that one is invaded by facticity, that one ceases to flee it and that one slides toward a *passive* consent to the desire. At other moments it seems that facticity invades consciousness in its very flight and renders consciousness opaque to itself. It is like a yeasty tumescence of *fact*.

The expressions which we use to designate desire sufficiently show its specificity. We say that it *takes hold of you,* that it *overwhelms you,* that it *paralyzes you.* Can one imagine employing the same words to designate hunger? Can one think of a hunger which "would overwhelm" one? Strictly speaking, this would be meaningful only when applied to impressions of emptiness. But, on the contrary, even the feeblest desire is already overwhelming. One can not hold it at a distance as one can with hunger and "think of something else" while keeping desire as an undifferentiated tonality of non-thetic consciousness which would be desire and which would serve as a sign of the body-as-ground. But *desire is consent to desire.* The heavy, fainting consciousness slides toward a languor comparable to sleep. Everyone has been able to observe the appearance of desire in another. Suddenly the man who desires becomes a heavy tranquillity which is frightening, his eyes are fixed and appear half-closed, his movements are stamped with a heavy and sticky sweetness; many seem to be falling asleep. And when one "struggles against desire," it is precisely this languor which one resists. If one succeeds in resisting it, the desire before disappearing will become wholly distinct and clear, like hunger. And then there will be "an awakening." One will feel that one is lucid but with heavy head and beating heart. Naturally all these descriptions are inexact; they show rather the way in which we interpret desire. However they indicate the primary fact of desire: in desire consciousness chooses to exist its facticity on another plane. It no longer flees it; it attempts to subordinate itself to its own contingency—as it apprehends another body—*i.e.,* another contingency—as desirable. In this sense desire is not only the revelation of the Other's body but the revelation of my own body. And this, not in so far as this body *is an instrument* or a *point of view,* but in so far as it is pure facticity; that is, a simple contingent form of the necessity of my contingency. I *feel* my skin and my muscles and my breath, and I feel them not in order to transcend them

toward something as in emotion or appetite but as a living and inert datum, not simply as the pliable and discrete instrument of my action upon the world but as a *passion* by which I am engaged in the world and in danger in the world. The For-itself *is not* this contingency; it continues to exist but it experiences the vertigo of its own body. Or, if you prefer, this vertigo is precisely its way of existing its body. The non-thetic consciousness allows itself to go over to the body, *wishes to be* the body and to be only body. In desire the body, instead of being only the contingency which the For-itself flees toward possibles which are peculiar to it, becomes at the same time the most immediate possible of the For-itself. Desire is not only the desire of the Other's body; it is—within the unity of a single act—the non-thetically lived project of being swallowed up in the body. Thus the final state of sexual desire can be swooning as the final stage of consent to the body. It is in this sense that desire can be called the desire of one body for another body. It is in fact an appetite directed *toward* the Other's body, and it is lived as the vertigo of the For-itself before its own body. The being which desires is consciousness *making itself body.*

But granted that desire is a consciousness which makes itself body in order to appropriate the Other's body apprehended as an organic totality in situation with consciousness on the horizon—what then is the meaning of desire? That is, why does consciousness make itself body—or vainly attempt to do so—and what does it expect from the object of its desire? The answer is easy if we realize that in desire I make myself flesh *in the presence of the Other in order to appropriate* the Other's flesh. This means that it is not merely a question of my grasping the Other's shoulders or thighs or of my drawing a body over against me; it is necessary as well for me to apprehend them with this particular instrument which is the body as it produces a clogging of consciousness. In this sense when I grasp these shoulders, it can be said not only that my body is a means for touching the shoulders but that the Other's shoulders are a means for my discovering my body as the fascinating revelation of facticity—that is, as flesh. Thus desire is the desire to appropriate a body as this appropriation reveals to me my body as flesh. But this body which I wish to appropriate, I wish to appropriate as *flesh.* Now at first the Other's body is not flesh for me; it appears as a synthetic form in action. As we have seen, we can not perceive the Other's body as pure flesh; that is, in the form of an isolated object maintaining external relations with other *thises*. The Other's body is as originally a body in situation; flesh, on the contrary, appears as the *pure contingency of presence*. Ordinarily it is hidden by cosmetics, clothing, *etc.;* in particular it is hidden by *movements*. Nothing is less "in the flesh" than a dancer even though she is nude. Desire is an attempt to strip the body of its movements as of its clothing and to make it exist as pure flesh; it is an attempt to *incarnate* the Other's body.

It is in this sense that the caress is an appropriation of the Other's body. It is evident that if caresses were only a stroking or brushing of the surface, there could be no relation between them and the powerful desire which they claim to fulfill; they would remain on the surface like looks and could not *appropriate* the Other for me. We know well the deceptiveness of that famous expression, "The contact of two epidermises." The caress does not want simple *contact;* it seems that man alone can reduce the caress to a contact, and then he loses its unique meaning. This is because the caress is not a simple stroking; it is a *shaping*. In caressing the Other I cause her * flesh to be born beneath my caress, under my fingers. The caress is the ensemble of those rituals which *incarnate* the Other. But, someone will object, was the Other not already incarnated? To be precise, *no*. The Other's flesh did not exist explicitly for me since I grasped the Other's body in situation; neither did it exist for her since she transcended it toward her possibilities and toward the object. The caress causes the Other to be born as flesh for me and for herself. And by flesh we do not mean a *part* of the body such as the dermis, the connective tissues or, specifically, epidermis; neither need we assume that the body will be "at rest" or dozing although often it is thus that its flesh is best revealed. But the caress reveals the flesh by stripping the body of its action, by cutting it off from the possibilities which surround it; the caress is designed to uncover the web of inertia beneath the action—i.e., the pure "being-

there"—which sustains it. For example, by *clasping* the Other's hand and *caressing* it, I discover underneath the act of *clasping,* which this hand is *at first,* an extension of flesh and bone which can be grasped; and similarly my look caresses when it discovers underneath this leaping which is at first the dancer's legs, the curved extension of the thighs. Thus the caress is in no way distinct from the desire: to caress with the eyes and to desire are one and the same. *Desire is expressed by the caress as thought is by language.* The caress reveals the Other's flesh as flesh to myself *and to the Other.* But it reveals this flesh in a very special way. To take hold of the Other reveals to her her inertia and her passivity as a transcendence-transcended; but this is not to caress her. In the caress it is not only my body as a synthetic form in action which caresses the Other; it is my body as flesh which causes the Other's flesh to be born. The caress is designed to cause the Other's body to be born, through pleasure, for the Other— and for myself—as a *touched* passivity in such a way that my body is made flesh in order to touch the Other's body with its own passivity; that is, by caressing itself with the Other's body rather than by caressing her. This is why amorous gestures have a language which could almost be said to be studied; it is not a question so much of taking hold of a part of the Other's body as of placing one's own body against the Other's body. Not so much to push or to touch in the active sense but to place against. It seems that I lift my own arm as an inanimate object and that I *place* it against the flank of the desired woman, that my fingers which I run over her arm are inert at the end of my hand. Thus the revelation of the Other's flesh is made through my own flesh; in desire and in the caress which expresses desire, I incarnate myself in order to realize the incarnation of the Other. The caress by *realizing* the Other's incarnation reveals to me my own incarnation; that is, I make myself flesh in order to impel the Other to realize *for-herself* and *for me* her own flesh, and my caresses cause my flesh to be born for me in so far as it is for the Other *flesh causing her to be born as flesh.* I make her enjoy my flesh through her flesh in order to compel her to feel herself flesh. And so possession truly appears as a *double reciprocal incarnation.* Thus in desire there is an attempt at the incarnation of consciousness (this is what we called earlier the clogging of consciousness, a troubled consciousness, *etc.*) in order to realize the incarnation of the Other.

---

*Tr. The pronouns in French are masculine because they refer to *autrut* (the Other) which may stand for either man or woman but which, grammatically, is masculine. The feminine sounds more natural in English.

. . . *Why* does consciousness nihilate itself in the form of desire?

. . .In the primordial reaction to the Other's look I constitute myself as a look. But if I look at his look in order to defend myself against the Other's freedom and to transcend it as freedom, then both the freedom and the look of the Other collapse. I see eyes; I see a being-in-the-midst-of-the-world. Henceforth the Other escapes me. I should like to act upon his freedom, to appropriate it, or at least, to make the Other's freedom recognize my freedom. But this freedom is death; it is no longer absolutely *in the world* in which I encounter the Other-as-object, for his characteristic is to be transcendent to the world. To be sure, I can *grasp* the Other, grab hold of him, knock him down. I can, providing I have the power, compel him to perform this or that act, to say certain words. But everything happens as if I wished to get hold of a man who runs away and leaves only his coat in my hands. It is the coat, it is the outer shell which I possess. I shall never get hold of more than a body, a psychic object in the midst of the world. And although all the acts of this body can be interpreted in terms of freedom, I have completely lost the key to this interpretation; I can act only upon a facticity. If I have preserved my awareness of a transcendent freedom in the Other, this awareness provokes me to no purpose by indicating a reality which is on principle beyond my reach and by revealing to me every instant the fact that I *am missing* it, that everything which I do is done "blindly" and takes on a meaning elsewhere in a sphere of existence from which I am on principle excluded. I can make the Other beg for mercy or ask my pardon, but I shall always be ignorant of what this submission means for and in the Other's freedom.

Moreover at the same time my *awareness* is altered; I lose the exact comprehension of *being-looked-at,* which is, as we know, the only way in which I can make proof of the Other's freedom. Thus I am engaged in an enterprise the meaning of which I have forgotten. I am dismayed confronting this Other as I see him and touch him but am at a loss as to what to do with him. It is exactly as if I had preserved the vague memory of a certain *Beyond* which is beyond what I see and what I touch, a Beyond concerning which I know that this is precisely what I want to appropriate. It is now that I *make myself desire.* Desire is an attitude aiming at enchantment. Since I can grasp the Other

only in his objective facticity, the problem is to ensnare his freedom within this facticity. It is necessary that he be "caught" in it as the cream is caught up by a person skimming milk. So the Other's For-itself must come to play on the surface of his body, and be extended all through his body; and by touching this body I should finally touch the Other's free subjectivity. This is the true meaning of the word *possession.* It is certain that I want to *possess* the Other's body, but I want to possess it in so far as it is itself a "possessed"; that is, in so far as the Other's consciousness is identified with his body. Such is the impossible ideal of desire: to possess the Other's transcendence as pure transcendence and at the same time as *body,* to reduce the Other to his simple *facticity* because he is then in the midst of my world but to bring it about that this facticity is a perpetual appresentation of his nihilating transcendence.

But in truth the Other's facticity (his pure being-there) can not be given to my intuition without a profound modification of my own unique being. In so far as I surpass my personal facticity toward my own possibilities, so far as I exist my facticity in an impulse of flight, I surpass as well not only the Other's facticity but also the pure *existence of things.* In my very upsurge I cause them to emerge in instrumental existence; their pure and simple being is hidden by the complexity of indicative references which constitute their *manageability* and their *instrumentality.* To pick up a fountain pen is already to surpass my being-there toward the possibility of writing, but it is also to surpass the pen as a simple existent toward its potentiality and once again to surpass this potentiality toward certain future existents which are the "words-about-to-be-formed" and finally the "book-about-to-be-written." This is why the being of existents is ordinarily veiled by their function. The same is true for the being of the Other. If the Other appears to me as a servant, as an employee, as a civil servant, or simply as the passerby whom I must avoid or as this voice which is speaking in the next room and which I try to *understand* (or on the other hand, which I want to forget because it "keeps me from sleeping"), it is not only the Other's extra-mundane transcendence which escapes me but also his "being-there" as a pure contingent existence in the midst of the world. This is because it is exactly in so far as I treat him as a servant, or as an office clerk, that I surpass his potentialities (transcendence-transcended, dead-possibilities) by the very project by which I surpass and nihilate my own facticity. If I want to return to his simple presence and taste it *as presence,* it is necessary for me to reduce myself to my own presence. Every surpassing of my being-there is in fact a surpassing of the Other's being-there. And if the world is around me as the situation which I surpass toward myself, then I apprehend the Other in terms of *his situation;* that is, already as a center of reference.

Of course the desired Other must also be apprehended in situation: I desire a woman *in the world,* standing *near a table,* lying naked *on a bed,* or seated *at my side.* But if the desire flows back from the situation upon the being who is in situation, it is in order to dissolve the situation and to corrode the Other's relations in the world. The movement of desire which goes from the surrounding "environment" to the desired person is an isolating movement which destroys the environment and cuts off the person in question in order to effect the emergence of his pure facticity. But this is possible only if each object which refers me to the person is fixed in its pure contingency at the same time that it indicates him to me; consequently this return movement to the Other's being is a movement of return to myself as pure being-there. I destroy my possibilities in order to destroy those of the world and to constitute the world as a "world of desire"; that is, as a destructured world which has lost its meaning, a world in which things jut out like fragments of pure matter, like brute qualities. Since the For-itself is a choice, this is possible only if I project myself toward a new possibility: that of being "absorbed by my body as ink is by a blotter," that of being reduced to my pure being-there. This project, inasmuch as it is not simply conceived and thematically posited but rather lived—that is, inasmuch as its realization is not distinct from its conception—is "disturbance" or "trouble." Indeed we must not understand the preceding descriptions as meaning that I deliberately put myself in a state of disturbance with the purpose of rediscovering the Other's pure "being-there." Desire is a lived project which does not suppose any preliminary deliberation but which includes within itself its meaning and its interpretation. As soon as I throw myself toward the Other's facticity, as soon as I wish to push aside his acts and his functions so as to touch him in his flesh,

I incarnate myself, for I can neither wish nor even conceive of the incarnation of the Other except in and by means of my own incarnation. Even the empty outline of a desire (as when one absentmindedly "undresses a woman with one's look") is an empty outline of troubled disturbance, for I desire only with my trouble, and I disrobe the Other only by disrobing myself; I foreshadow and outline the Other's flesh only by outlining my own flesh.

But my *incarnation* is not only the preliminary condition of the appearance of the Other as flesh *to my eyes.* My goal is to cause him to be incarnated as flesh in *his own eyes.* It is necessary that I drag him onto the level of pure facticity; he must be reduced for himself to being only flesh. Thus I shall be reassured as to the permanent possibilities of a transcendence which can at any instant transcend me on all sides. This transcendence *will be no more than this;* it will remain enclosed within the limits of an object; in addition and because of this very fact, I shall be able to touch it, feel it, possess it. Thus the other meaning of my incarnation— that is, of my troubled disturbance—is that it is a magical language. I make myself flesh so as to fascinate the Other by my nakedness and to provoke in her the desire for my flesh—exactly because this desire will be nothing else in the Other but an incarnation similar to mine. Thus desire is an invitation to desire. It is my flesh alone which knows how to find the road to the Other's flesh and I lay my flesh next to her flesh so as to awaken her to the meaning of flesh. In the caress when I slowly lay my inert hand against the Other's flank, I am making that flank feel my flesh, and this can be achieved only if it renders itself inert. The shiver of pleasure which it feels is precisely the awakening of its consciousness as flesh. If I extend my hand, remove it, or clasp it, then it becomes again body in action; but by the same stroke I make my hand disappear as flesh. To let it run indifferently over the length of her body, to reduce my hand to a soft brushing almost stripped of meaning, to a pure existence, to a pure matter slightly silky, slightly satiny, slightly rough—this is to give up for oneself being the one who establishes references and unfolds distances; it is to be made pure mucous membrane. At this moment the communion of desire is realized; each consciousness by incarnating itself has realized the incarnation of the other; each one's disturbance has caused disturbance to be born in the Other and is thereby so much enriched. By each caress I experience my own flesh and the Other's flesh through my flesh, and I am conscious that this flesh which I feel and appropriate through my flesh is flesh-realized-by-the Other. It is not by chance that desire while aiming at the body as a whole attains it especially through masses of flesh which are very little differentiated, grossly nerveless, hardly capable of spontaneous movement, through breasts, buttocks, thighs, stomach: these form a sort of image of pure facticity. This is why also the true caress is the contact of two bodies in their mostly fleshy parts, the contact of stomachs and breasts; the caressing hand is too delicate, too much like a per- fected instrument. But the full pressing together of the flesh of two people against one another is the true goal of desire.

Nevertheless desire is itself doomed to failure. As we have seen, coitus, which ordinarily terminates de- sire, is not its essential goal. To be sure, several ele- ments of our sexual structure are the necessary expres- sion of the nature of desire, in particular the erection of the penis and the clitoris. This is nothing else in fact but the affirmation of the flesh by the flesh. Therefore it is absolutely necessary that it should not be accom- plished *voluntarily;* that is, that we can not use it as an instrument but that we are dealing with a biological and autonomous phenomenon whose autonomous and involuntary expression accompanies and signifies the submerging of consciousness in the body. It must be clearly understood that no fine, prehensile organ provided with striated muscles can be a sex organ, a *sex.* If sex were to appear as an organ, it could be only one manifestation of the vegetative life. But contin- gency reappears if we consider that *there are* sexes and *particular* sexes. Consider especially the penetration of the female by the male. This does, to be sure, con- form to that radical incarnation which desire wishes to be. (We may in fact observe the organic passivity of sex in coitus. It is the whole body which advances and withdraws, which *carries* sex forward or withdraws it. Hands help to introduce the penis; the penis itself ap- pears as an instrument which one manages, which one makes penetrate, which one withdraws, which one uti- lizes. And similarly the opening and the lubrication of the vagina can not be obtained voluntarily.) Yet coitus remains a perfectly contingent modality of our sexual life. It is as much a pure contingency as sexual pleasure proper. In truth the ensnarement of con- sciousness in the body normally has its own peculiar

result—that is, a sort of particular ecstasy in which consciousness is no more than consciousness (of) the body and consequently a reflective consciousness *of* corporeality. Pleasure in fact—like too keen a pain— motivates the appearance of reflective consciousness which is *"attention to pleasure."*

But pleasure is the death and the failure of desire. It is the death of desire because it is not only its ful- fillment but its limit and its end. This, moreover, is only an organic contingency: it *happens that* the in- carnation is manifested by erection and that the erec- tion ceases with ejaculation. But in addition pleasure closes the sluice to desire because it motivates the appearance of a reflective consciousness *of* pleasure, whose object becomes a reflective enjoyment; that is, it is *attention to the incarnation of the For-itself which is reflected-on* and by the same token it is forgetful of the Other's incarnation. Here we are no longer within the province of contingency. Of course it remains con- tingent that the passage to the fascinated reflection should be effected on the occasion of that particular mode of incarnation which is pleasure (although there are numerous cases of passage to the reflective without the intervention of pleasure), but there is a permanent danger for desire in so far as it is an at- tempt at incarnation. This is because consciousness by incarnating itself loses sight of the Other's incar- nation, and its own incarnation absorbs it to the point of becoming the ultimate goal. In this case the plea- sure of caressing is transformed into the pleasure of being caressed; what the For-itself demands is to feel within it its own body expanding to the point of nau- sea. Immediately there is a rupture of contact and desire misses its goal. It happens very often that this failure of desire motivates a passage to masochism; that is, consciousness apprehending itself in its factic- ity demands to be apprehended and transcended as body-for-the-Other by means of the Other's con- sciousness. In this case the Other-as-object collapses, the Other-as-look appears, and my consciousness is a consciousness swooning in its flesh beneath the Oth- er's look.

Yet conversely desire stands at the origin of its own failure inasmuch as it is a desire of *taking* and of *appro- priating.* It is not enough merely that troubled distur- bance should effect the Other's incarnation; desire is the desire to appropriate this incarnated conscious- ness. Therefore desire is naturally continued not by *caresses* but by acts of taking and of penetration. The caress has for its goal only to impregnate the Other's body with consciousness and freedom. Now it is necessary to take this saturated body, to seize it, to enter into it. But by the very fact that I now attempt to seize the Other's body, to pull it toward me, to grab hold of it, to bite it, my own body ceases to be flesh and becomes again the synthetic instrument *which I am*. And by the same token the *Other* ceases to be an incarnation; she becomes once more an instrument in the midst of the world which I apprehend in terms of its situation. Her consciousness, which played on the surface of her flesh and which I tried to *taste* with my flesh,* disappears under my sight; she remains no more than an *object* with object-images inside her. At the same time my disturbance disappears. This does not mean that I cease to desire but that desire has lost its matter; it has become *abstract;* it is a desire to handle and to take. I insist on taking the Other's body but my very insistence makes my incarnation disappear. At present I surpass my body anew toward my own possibilities (here the possibility of taking), and similarly the Other's body which is surpassed toward its potentialities falls from the level of *flesh* to the level of pure object. This situation brings about the rupture of that reciprocity of incarnation which was precisely the unique goal of desire. The Other may remain troubled; she may remain flesh *for herself,* and I can understand it. But it is a flesh which I no longer apprehend through my flesh, a flesh which is no longer anything but the *property* of an Other-as-object and not the incarnation of an Other-as-consciousness. Thus I *am body* (a synthetic totality in situation) confronting a *flesh*. I find myself in almost the same situation as that from which I tried to escape by means of desire; that is, I try to use the object-Other so as to make her deliver her transcendence, and precisely because she is *all* object she escapes me with *all* her transcendence. Once again I have even lost the precise comprehension of what I seek and yet I am engaged in the search. I take and discover myself in the process of taking, but what I take in my hands is *something else* than what I wanted to take. I feel this and I suffer from it but without being capable of saying what I wanted to take; for along with my troubled distur-

bance the very comprehension of my desire escapes me. I am like a sleepwalker who wakens to find himself in the process of gripping the edge of the bed while he can not recall the nightmare which provoked his gesture. It is this situation which is at the origin of *sadism*.

. . .

Existential Psychoanalysis from Being and Nothingness

If it is true that human reality—as we have attempted to establish—identifies and defines itself by the ends which it pursues, then a study and classification of these ends becomes indispensable. In the preceding chapter we have considered the For-itself only from the point of view of its free project, which is the impulse by which it thrusts itself toward its end. We should now question this end itself, for it *forms a part* of absolute subjectivity and is, in fact, its transcendent, objective limit. This is what empirical psychology has hinted at by admitting that a particular man is defined by his desires. Here, however, we must be on our guard against two errors. First, the empirical psychologist, while defining man by his desires, remains the victim of the illusion of substance. He views desire as being *in* man by virtue of being "contained" by his consciousness, and he believes that the meaning of the desire is inherent in the desire itself. Thus he avoids everything which could evoke the idea of transcendence. But if I desire a house or a glass of water or a woman's body, how could this body, this glass, this piece of property reside in my desire, and how can my desire be anything but the consciousness of these objects as desirable? Let us beware then of considering these desires as little psychic entities dwelling in consciousness; they are consciousness itself in its original projective, transcendent structure, for consciousness is on principle consciousness *of* something.

The other error, which fundamentally is closely connected with the first, consists in considering psychological research as terminated as soon as the investigator has reached the concrete ensemble of empirical desires. Thus a man would be defined by the bundle of drives or tendencies which empirical observation could establish. Naturally the psychologist will not always limit himself to making up the *sum* of these

---

*Doña Prouhèze (*Soulier de Satin, 11ᵉ journée*): "*Il ne connaitra pas le goût que j'ai.*" (He will not know the taste which I have.)

tendencies; he will want to bring to light their relationship, their agreements and harmonies; he will try to present the ensemble of desires as a synthetic organization in which each desire acts on the others and influences them. A critic, for example, wishing to explain the "psychology" of Flaubert, will write that he "appeared in his early youth to know as his normal state, a continual exaltation resulting from the twofold feeling of his grandiose ambition and his invincible power.... The effervescence of his young blood was *then* turned into literary passion as happens about the eighteenth year in precocious souls who find in the energy of style or the intensities of fiction some way of escaping from the need of violent action or of intense feeling, which torments them." *

In this passage there is an effort to reduce the complex personality of an adolescent to a few basic desires, as the chemist reduces compound bodies to merely a combination of simple bodies. The primitive givens will be grandiose ambition, the need of violent action and of intense feeling; these elements, when they enter into combination, produce a permanent exaltation. Then—as Bourget remarks in a few words which we have not quoted—this exaltation, nourished by numerous well-chosen readings, is going to seek to delude itself by self-expression in fictions which will appease it symbolically and channel it. There in outline is the genesis of a literary "temperament."

Now in the first place such a psychological *analysis* proceeds from the postulate that an individual fact is produced by the intersection of abstract, universal laws. The fact to be explained—which is here the literary disposition of the young Flaubert—is resolved into a combination of *typical,* abstract desires such as we meet in "the average adolescent." What is concrete here is only their combination; in themselves they are only possible patterns. The abstract then is by hypothesis prior to the concrete, and the concrete is only an organization of abstract qualities; the individual is only the intersection of universal schemata. But—aside from the logical absurdity of such a postulate—we see clearly in the example chosen, that it simply fails to explain what makes the individuality of the project under consideration. The fact that "the need

to feel intensely," a universal pattern, is disguised and channeled into becoming the need to write—this is not the *explanation* of the "calling" of Flaubert; on the contrary, it is what must be explained. Doubtless one could invoke a thousand circumstances, known to us and unknown, which have shaped this need to feel into the need to act. But this is to give up at the start all attempt to explain and refers the question to the undiscoverable.[†] In addition this method rejects the pure individual who has been banished from the pure subjectivity of Flaubert into the external circumstances of his life. Finally, Flaubert's correspondence proves that long before the "crisis of adolescence," from his earliest childhood, he was tormented by the need to write.

At each stage in the description just quoted, we meet with a hiatus. Why did ambition and the feeling of his power produce in Flaubert *exaltation* rather than tranquil waiting or gloomy impatience? Why did this exaltation express itself specifically in the need to act violently and feel intensely? Or rather why does this need make a sudden appearance by spontaneous generation at the end of the paragraph? And why does this need instead of seeking to appease itself in acts of violence, by amorous adventures, or in debauch, choose precisely to satisfy itself symbolically? And why does Flaubert turn to writing rather than to painting or music for this symbolic satisfaction; he could just as well not resort to the artistic field at all (there is also mysticism, for example). "I could have been a great actor," wrote Flaubert somewhere. Why did he not try to be one? In a word, we have understood nothing; we have seen a succession of accidental happenings, of desire springing forth fully armed, one from the other, with no possibility for us to grasp their genesis. The *transitions,* the becomings, the transformations, have been carefully veiled from us, and we have been limited to putting order into the succession by invoking empirically established but literally unintelligible sequences (the need to act preceding in the adolescent the need to write).

. . .

---

*Paul Bourget. *Essai de Psychologie contemperaine: G. Flaubert.*

[†] Since Flaubert's adolescence, so far as we can know it, offers us nothing specific in this connection, we must suppose the action of imponderable facts which on principle escape the critic.

But most important of all, these "psychological" explanations refer us ultimately to inexplicable original givens. These are the simple bodies of psychology. We are told, for example, that Flaubert had a "grandiose ambition" and all of the previously quoted description depends on this original ambition. So far so good. But this ambition is an irreducible fact which by no means satisfies the mind. The irreducibility here has no justification other than refusal to push the analysis further. . . . In one sense Flaubert's ambition is a fact with all a fact's contingency—and it is true that it is impossible to advance beyond that fact—but in another sense *it makes itself*, and our satisfaction is a guarantee to us that we may able to grasp beyond this ambition something more, something like a radical decision which, without ceasing to be contingent, would be the veritable psychic irreducible.

What we are demanding then—and what nobody ever attempts to give us—is a *veritable* irreducible; that is, an irreducible of which the irreducibility would be self-evident, which would not be presented as the postulate of the psychologist and the result of his refusal or his incapacity to go further, but which when established would produce in us an accompanying feeling of satisfaction. This demand on our part does not come from that ceaseless pursuit of a cause, that infinite regress which has often been described as constitutive of rational research and which consequently— far from being exclusively associated with psychological investigation—may be found in all disciplines and in all problems. This is not the childish quest of a "because," which allows no further "why?" It is on the contrary a demand based on a pre-ontological comprehension of human reality and on the related refusal to consider man as capable of being analyzed and reduced to original givens, to determined desires (or "drives"), supported by the subject as properties by an object. Even if we were to consider him as such, it would be necessary to choose: either *Flaubert*, the man, whom we can love or detest, blame or praise, who represents for us *the Other,* who directly attacks our being by the very fact that he has existed, would be originally a substratum unqualified by these desires, that is, a sort of indeterminate clay which would have to receive them passively; or he would be reduced to the simple bundle of these irreducible drives or tendencies. In either case the *man* disappears; we can no longer find "the one" to *whom* this or that

experience has *happened;* either in looking for the *person,* we encounter a useless, contradictory metaphysical substance—or else the being whom we seek vanishes in a dust of phenomena bound together by external connections. But what each one of us requires in his very effort to comprehend another is that he should never have to resort to this idea of substance which is inhuman because it is well this side of the human. Finally the fact is that the being considered does not crumble into dust, and one can discover in him that unity—for which substance was only a caricature—which must be a unity of responsibility, a unity agreeable or hateful, blamable and praiseworthy, in short *personal.* This unity, which is the being of the man under consideration, is a *free unification,* and this unification can not come *after* a diversity which it unifies.

. . .

The problem poses itself in approximately these terms: If we admit that the person is a totality, we can not hope to reconstruct him by an addition or by an organization of the diverse tendencies which we have empirically discovered in him. On the contrary, in each inclination, in each tendency the person expresses himself completely, although from a different angle, a little as Spinoza's substance expresses itself completely in each of its attributes. But if this is so, we should discover in each tendency, in each attitude of the subject, a meaning which transcends it. A jealousy of a particular date in which a subject historicizes himself in relation to a certain woman, signifies for the one who knows how to interpret it, the total relation to the world by which the subject constitutes himself as a self. In other words this *empirical* attitude is by itself the expression of the "choice of an intelligible character." There is no mystery about this. We no longer have to do with an intelligible pattern which can be present in our thought only, while we apprehend and conceptualize the unique pattern of the subject's empirical existence. If the empirical attitude signifies the choice of the intelligible character, it is because it is itself this choice. Indeed the distinguishing characteristic of the intelligible choice, as we shall see later, is that it can exist as internal limits of a lack of being which can exist only as the transcendent meaning of each concrete, empirical choice. It is by no means first effected in some unconscious or on the noumenal level to be *subsequently* expressed in a particular observable attitude; there is not even an *ontological* pre-eminence over the empirical choice, but it is on principle that which must always detach itself from the empirical choice as its *beyond* and the infinity of its transcendence. Thus if I am rowing on the river, I am nothing—either here or in any other world—save this concrete project of rowing. But this project itself, inasmuch as it is the totality of my being, expresses my original choice in particular circumstances; it is nothing other than the choice of myself as a totality in these circumstances. That is why a special method must aim at detaching the fundamental meaning which the project admits and which can be only the individual secret of the subject's being-in-the-world. It is then rather by a *comparison* of the various empirical drives of a subject that we try to discover and disengage the fundamental project which is common to them all—and not by a simple summation or reconstruction of these tendencies; each drive or tendency is the entire person.

There is naturally an infinity of possible projects as there is an infinity of possible human beings. Nevertheless, if we are to recognize certain common characteristics among them and if we are going to attempt to classify them in larger categories, it is best first to undertake individual investigations in the cases which we can study more easily. In our research, we will be guided by this principle: to stop only in the presence of evident irreducibility; that is, never to believe that we have reached the initial project until the projected end appears as *the very being* of the subject under consideration. This is why we can stop at those classifications of "authentic project" and "unauthentic project of the self" which Heidegger wishes to establish. In addition to the fact that such a classification, in spite of its author's intent, is tainted with an ethical concern shown by its very terminology, it is based on the attitude of the subject toward his own death. Now if death causes anguish, and if consequently we can either flee the anguish or throw ourselves resolutely into it, it is a truism to say that this is because we wish to hold on to life. Consequently anguish before death and resolute decision or flight into unauthenticity can not be considered as fundamental projects of our being. On the contrary, they can be understood only on the foundation of an original project of *living;* that is, on an original choice of our being. It is right then in each

case to pass beyond the results of Heidegger's interpretation toward a still more fundamental project.

This fundamental project must not of course refer to any other and should be conceived by itself. It can be concerned neither with death nor life nor any particular characteristic of the human condition; the original project of a for-itself *can aim only at its being.* The project of being or desire of being or drive toward being does not originate in a physiological differentiation or in an empirical contingency; in fact it is not distinguished from the being of the for-itself. The for-itself is a being such that in its being, its being is in question in the form of a project of being. To the for-itself *being* means to make known to oneself what one is by means of a possibility appearing as a value. Possibility and value belong to the being of the for-itself. The for-itself is defined ontologically as a *lack of being,* and possibility belongs to the for-itself as that which it lacks, in the same way that value haunts the for-itself as the totality of being which is lacking. What we have expressed in Part Two in terms of lack can be just as well expressed in terms of *freedom.* The for-itself chooses because it is lack; freedom is really synonymous with lack. Freedom is the concrete mode of being of the lack of being. Ontologically then it amounts to the same thing to say that value and possibility exist as internal limits of a lack of being which can exist only as a lack of being—or that the upsurge of freedom determines its possibility and thereby circumscribes *its* value.

Thus we can advance no further but have encountered the self-evident irreducible when we have reached the *project of being;* for obviously it is impossible to advance further than *being,* and there is no difference between the project of being, possibility, value, on the one hand, and *being,* on the other. Fundamentally man is *the desire to be,* and the existence of this desire is not to be established by an empirical induction; it is the result of an *à priori* description of the being of the for-itself, since desire is a lack and since the for-itself is the being which is to itself its own lack of being. The original project which is expressed in each of our empirically observable tendencies is then the *project of being;* or, if you prefer, each empirical tendency exists with the original project of being, in a relation of expression and symbolic satisfaction just as conscious drives, with Freud, exist in relation to the complex and to the original libido. Moreover the desire to be by no means exists *first* in order to cause itself to be expressed subsequently by desires *a posteriori*. There is nothing outside of the symbolic expression which it finds in concrete desires. There is not first a single desire of being, then a thousand particular feelings, but the desire to be exists and manifests itself only in and through jealousy, greed, love of art, cowardice, courage, and a thousand contingent, empirical expressions which always cause human reality to appear to us only as *manifested* by *a particular man,* by a specific person.

As for the being which is the object of this desire, we know *à priori* what this is. The for-itself is the being which is to itself its own lack of being. The being which the for-itself lacks is the in-itself. The for-itself arises as the nihilation of the in-itself and this nihilation is defined as the project toward the in-itself. Between the nihilated in-itself and the projected in-itself the for-itself is nothingness. Thus the end and the goal of the nihilation which I am is the in-itself. Thus human reality is the desire of being-in-itself. But the in-itself which it desires can not be pure contingent, absurd in-itself, comparable at every point to that which it encounters and which it nihilates. The nihilation, as we have seen, is in fact like a revolt of the in-itself, which nihilates itself against its contingency. To say that the for-itself lives its facticity, as we have seen in the chapter concerning the body, amounts to saying that the nihilation is the vain effort of a being to found its own being and that it is the withdrawal to found being which provokes the minute displacement by which nothingness enters into being. The being which forms the object of the desire of the for-itself is then an in-itself which would be to itself its own foundation; that is, which would be to its facticity in the same relation as the for-itself is to its motivations. In addition the for-itself, being the negation of the in-itself, could not desire the pure and simple return to the in-itself. Here as with Hegel, the negation of the negation can not bring us back to our point of departure. Quite the contrary, what the for-itself demands of the in-itself is precisely the totality detotalized—"In-itself nihilated in for-itself." In other words the for-itself projects *being as for-itself,* a being which is what it is. It is as being which is what it is not, and which is not what it is, that the for-itself projects being what it is. It is as consciousness that it wishes to have the impermeability and infinite density of the in-itself. It is as the nihilation of the in-

itself and a perpetual evasion of contingency and of facticity that it wishes to be its own foundation. This is why the possible is projected in general as what the for-itself lacks in order to become in-itself-for-itself. The fundamental value which presides over this project is exactly the in-itself-for-itself; that is, the ideal of a consciousness which would be the foundation of its own being-in-itself by the pure consciousness which it would have of itself. It is this ideal which can be called God. Thus the best way to conceive of the fundamental project of human reality is to say that man is the being whose project is to be God. Whatever may be the myths and rites of the religion considered, God is first "sensible to the heart" of man as the one who identifies and defines him in his ultimate and fundamental project. If man possesses a pre-ontological comprehension of the being of God, it is not the great wonders of nature nor the power of society which have conferred it upon him. God, value and supreme end of transcendence, represents the permanent limit in terms of which man makes known to himself what he is. To be man means to reach toward being God. Or if you prefer, man fundamentally is the desire to be God.

· · ·

QUESTIONS FOR REFLECTION

1. One might argue that for Descartes, a mental substance is simply a substance that is not physical. Is this Sartre's view as well? In what ways does Sartre's account improve upon Descartes'?

2. Critically assess the following criticism: Sartre's contrastive analysis of consciousness is largely unhelpful because picking out some things that consciousness is not does not reveal very much about consciousness. If I do not know what "bicycle" means, it is not helpful to me to be told that a bicycle is not toffee.

3. In "Existential Psychoanalysis" Sartre criticizes Heidegger for not explaining flight from death on the basis of something more fundamental, namely, "an original project of living." How penetrating is Sartre's criticism? How might Heidegger respond? (Would Heidegger *deny* that the flight from death presupposes "an original project of living"? Might not culture's original project have been altered

partly in response to the threat of death long before an individual takes it on?)

4. Sartre also says in "Existential Psychoanalysis" that "the for-itself chooses because it is lack" and that "man is *the desire to be*." To what extent is Sartre saying what Schopenhauer does when the latter characterizes "the will" as "lack" and then identifies the self with "the will to live"?

5. Is there a reason a person desires to be, according to Sartre? Do we desire to be because we have adopted a project by which we are engaged in the world? Do we adopt a project because we desire to be? (Recall that Sartre says in "Existential Psycho-analysis" that "there is not first a single desire of being, then a thousand particular feelings. . . .")

6. Sartre speaks of flight from anguish where Hei-degger speaks of flight from anxiety. Is Sartre's for-mulation preferable to Heidegger's? If so, why?

7. Sartre speaks of bad faith where Heidegger speaks of inauthenticity. Do the two notions function the same way? Is one an improvement over the other?

FURTHER READINGS

Works by Sartre

The Transcendence of the Ego (1936). Translated by For-rest Williams and Robert Kirkpatrick. New York: Far-rar, Straus and Giroux, 1957.

Nausea (1938). Translated by Lloyd Alexander. New York: New Directions Publishing Corporation, 1964.

No Exit (1945) and *The Flies* (1943). Translated as *No Exit and Three Other Plays* by Stuart Gilbert. New York: Vintage Books, 1946.

The Emotions: Outline of a Theory (1939). Translated by Philip Mairet. London: Methuen, 1962.

The Psychology of Imagination (1940). New York: Citadel Press, 1991.

Being and Nothingness (1943). Translated by Hazel Barnes. New York: Washington Square Press, 1966.

Existentialism is a Humanism (1946). Translated by Philip Mairet. New York: Haskell House Publishers, 1948.

Critique of Dialectical Reason. Vol. 1: *Theory of Practical Ensembles.* Translated by Alan Sheridan Smith. London: New Left Books, 1976.

Works on Sartre

Barnes, Hazel. *Sartre.* Philadelphia: J. B. Lippincott, 1973.

Blackham, H. J. *Six Existentialist Thinkers.* London: Routledge & Kegan Paul, 1952.

Cooper, David. *Existentialism: A Reconstruction.* Oxford: Oxford University Press, 1990.

Dobson, A. *Jean-Paul Sartre and the Politics of Reason.* Cambridge: Cambridge University Press, 1993.

Fell, J. *Heidegger and Sartre.* New York: Columbia University Press, 1979.

Fingarette, Herbert. *Self-Deception.* London: Routledge & Kegan Paul, 1969.

Grene, Marjorie. *Sartre.* New York: New Viewpoints, 1973.

Hayman, Ronald. *Sartre: A Biography.* New York: Carroll & Graf Publishers, 1987.

Howells, C., ed. *The Cambridge Companion to Sartre.* Cambridge: Cambridge University Press, 1992.

Macquarrie, John. *Existentialism.* Harmondsworth: Penguin Books, 1972.

McCullock, Gregory. *Using Sartre: An Analytical Introduction to Early Sartrean Themes.* London: Routledge & Kegan Paul, 1994.

Olafson, Frederick. *Principles and Persons.* Baltimore, Md.: Johns Hopkins University Press, 1967.

Warnock, Mary. *Existentialism.* Oxford: Oxford University Press, 1970.

Wilcocks, R., ed. *Critical Essays on Jean-Paul Sartre.* Boston: G. K. Hall, 1988.

CHAPTER 6

Further Twentieth-Century Existential Thought

In this chapter we consider several influential contributions by twentieth-century writers associated with existentialism: Miguel de Unamuno, Gabriel Marcel, Karl Jaspers, Simone de Beauvoir, Albert Camus, Maurice Merleau-Ponty, Martin Buber, and Paul Tillich. Three of these writers—de Beauvoir, Camus, and Merleau-Ponty—were close friends and colleagues of Sartre. Like Sartre, they develop atheistic existentialist philosophies and are influenced primarily by Kant, Hegel, Nietzsche, Husserl, and Heidegger. The other five writers—Unamuno, Jaspers, Marcel, Buber, and Tillich—use existentialist ideas in support of different religious views. Each of these five is influenced by Kant, Hegel, and Kierkegaard. Some of the five influenced the others as well. Of the five, the writer whose work shows the greatest affinity to Kierkegaard's is Unamuno. Unamuno shared Kierkegaard's distaste for Hegelianism and developed an irrationalist defense of faith that owed much to the Danish writer. Marcel was drawn to Hegel at least as much as he was drawn to Kierkegaard and resisted the latter's irrationalism. Buber's work aligns with that of Marcel in important ways. In particular, each suggested that we have access to a personal God. But this idea that God is a person is denied flatly by the last of our writers, Tillich, who offers a suggestion that is very much in the spirit of Hegel: Each person may participate in God who is the ground of all being.

Each of the selections presented here is prefaced by a brief introduction to the author and his work.

MIGUEL DE UNAMUNO (1864–1936)

Don Miguel de Unamuno y Jugo de Larraza was born in the city of Bilbao, a Basque town. He studied philosophy and classics at the University of Madrid, then took a position as Professor of Greek at the University of Salamanca. Unamuno was proud of his Basque heritage and was politically radical to the point of being expelled for attacking totalitarianism. For a few years he served on a government post of the Spanish republic but remained independent-minded and was placed under house arrest in Salamanca in 1936, where he stayed for about a year until he died.

In his book *Tragic Sense of Life* (1913), Unamuno suggests that if death ends our existence, then our lives are valueless. Consequently, he maintains that the whole point of philosophy is to decide whether there is a way to achieve immortality. As for why Unamuno thinks that death undermines the value of life, his answer is found near the beginning of "The Hunger for Immortality": "Nothing is real that is not eternal."[1] In his view, only what is eternal has value; so only an eternal life has value.

Unamuno suggests that what people desire above all else is that they will forever remain in conscious existence with their identities intact. He thinks that this desire is an extension of the preservation instinct that makes us seek to remain alive; hence, he thinks the desire is perfectly healthy. This emphasis on the importance of individual survival leads him to follow Kierkegaard in rejecting the practical (Epicurean, stoical) advice that we accept our mortality and cultivate equanimity in the face of death:

> The manly attitude, they say, is to resign oneself to fate; since we are not immortal, do not let us want to be so; let us submit ourselves to reason. . . . No! I do not submit to reason, and I

---

[1] Miguel de Unamuno, *Tragic Sense of Life,* trans. J. E. Crawford Flitch (New York: Dover Publications, 1954), 39.

rebel against it, and I persist in creating by the energy of faith my immortalizing God. . . .[2]

Unamuno's emphasis on *personal* survival also prompts him to reject the sentiments expressed in the *Upanishads,* ancient mystical texts that have a central place in Hindu thought. The *Upanishads* suggest that the self is in some sense one with the world, so that our individuality is illusory. But Unamuno rejected this view.

> No, my longing is not to be submerged in the vast All, . . . or in God; not to be possessed by God, but to possess Him, to become myself God, yet without ceasing to be I myself, I who am now speaking to you. Tricks of monism avail us nothing; we crave the substance and not the shadow of immortality.[3]

Unamuno believed that the only hope for achieving immortality is through the aid of the Christian God. Indeed, the promise of immortality is the essence of all religion, according to Unamuno: "all religion has sprung historically from . . . the cult of immortality."[4] He adds in "The Practical Problem" that it is a "human God" we are dealing with—"that is the only kind of God we are able to conceive"—so no one need worry if he is "unable to believe in Him with his head" for "it is not in his head but in his heart that the wicked man says that there is no God, which is equivalent to saying that he wishes that there may not be a God."[5] Instead, Unamuno says, echoing Kierkegaard, "if the attainment of eternal happiness could be bound up with any particular belief, it would be with the belief in the possibility of its realization."[6] Indeed, according to Unamuno, it is enough that we *desire* eternal happiness.

In view of the fact that we depend on God for securing what we most desire (immortality), Unamuno proposes as a principle for our behavior the following:

> If it is nothingness that awaits us, let us make an injustice of it; let us fight against destiny, even though without hope of victory; let us fight against it quixotically. . . . Our greatest endeavor must be to make ourselves irreplaceable; to make the . . . fact that each one of us is unique and irreplaceable, that no one else can fill the gap that will be left when we die, a practical truth.[7]

Thus, the attempt to excel takes on a religious significance for Unamuno.

The Hunger of Immortality
from Tragic Sense of Life

. . . It is impossible for us, in effect, to conceive of ourselves as not existing, and no effort is capable of enabling consciousness to realize absolute unconsciousness, its own annihilation. Try, reader, to imagine to yourself, when you are wide awake, the condition of your soul when you are in a deep sleep; try to fill your consciousness with the representation of no-consciousness, and you will see the impossibility of it. The effort to comprehend it causes the most tormenting dizziness. We cannot conceive ourselves as not existing.

The visible universe, the universe that is created by the instinct of self-preservation, becomes all too narrow for me. It is like a cramped cell, against the bars of which my soul beats its wings in vain. Its lack of air stifles me. More, more, and always more! I want to be myself, and yet without ceasing to be myself to be others as well, to merge myself into the totality of things visible and invisible, to extend myself into the illimitable of space and to prolong myself into the infinite of time. Not to be all and for ever is as if not to be—at least, let me be my whole self, and be so for ever and ever. And to be the whole of myself is to be everybody else. Either all or nothing!

All or nothing! And what other meaning can the Shakespearean "To be or not to be" have, or that passage in *Coriolanus* where it is said of Marcius "He wants nothing of a good but eternity"? Eternity, eternity!—that is the supreme desire! The thirst of eternity is what is called love among men, and whosoever

---

[2] Ibid., 50.
[3] Ibid., 47.
[4] Ibid., 40.
[5] Ibid., 266.
[6] Ibid., 267.

---

[7] Ibid., 268–269.

loves another wishes to eternalize himself in him. Nothing is real that is not eternal. . . .

Everything passes! Such is the refrain of those who have drunk, lips to the spring, of the fountain of life, of those who have tasted of the fruit of the tree of the knowledge of good and evil.

To be, to be for ever, to be without ending! thirst of being, thirst of being more! hunger of God! thirst of love eternalizing and eternal! to be for ever! to be God!

"Ye shall be as gods!" we are told in Genesis that the serpent said to the first pair of lovers (Gen. iii. 5). "If in this life only we have hope in Christ, we are of all men most miserable," wrote the Apostle (I Cor. xv. 19); and all religion has sprung historically from the cult of the dead—that is to say, from the cult of immortality. . . .

This cult, not of death but of immortality, originates and preserves religions. In the midst of the delirium of destruction, Robespierre induced the Convention to declare the existence of the Supreme Being and "the consolatory principle of the immortality of the soul," the Incorruptible being dismayed at the idea of having himself one day to turn to corruption. . . .

If at the death of the body which sustains me, and which I call mine to distinguish it from the self that is I, my consciousness returns to the absolute unconsciousness from which it sprang, and if a like fate befalls all my brothers in humanity, then is our toil-worn human race nothing but a fatidical procession of phantoms, going from nothingness to nothingness, and humanitarianism the most inhuman thing known.

And the remedy is not that suggested in the quatrain that runs—

> Cada vez que considero
> que me tengo de morir,
> tiendo la capa en el suelo
> y no me harto de dormir.*

No! The remedy is to consider our mortal destiny without flinching, to fasten our gaze upon the gaze of the Sphinx, for it is thus that the malevolence of its spell is discharmed.

---

* Each time that I consider that it is my lot to die, I spread my cloak upon the ground and am never surfeited with sleeping.

If we all die utterly, wherefore does everything exist? Wherefore? It is the Wherefore of the Sphinx; it is the Wherefore that corrodes the marrow of the soul; it is the begetter of that anguish which gives us the love of hope. . . .

And I must confess, painful though the confession be, that in the days of the simple faith of my childhood, descriptions of the tortures of hell, however terrible, never made me tremble, for I always felt that nothingness was much more terrifying. He who suffers lives, and he who lives suffering, even though over the portal of his abode is written "Abandon all hope!" loves and hopes. It is better to live in pain than to cease to be in peace. The truth is that I could not believe in this atrocity of Hell, of an eternity of punishment, nor did I see any more real hell than nothingness and the prospect of it. And I continue in the belief that if we all believed in our salvation from nothingness we should all be better.

What is this *joie de vivre* that they talk about nowadays? Our hunger for God, our thirst of immortality, of survival, will always stifle in us this pitiful enjoyment of the life that passes and abides not. It is the frenzied love of life, the love that would have life to be unending, that most often urges us to long for death. "If it is true that I am to die utterly," we say to ourselves, "then once I am annihilated the world has ended so far as I am concerned—it is finished. Why, then, should it not end forthwith, so that no new consciousnesses, doomed to suffer the tormenting illusion of a transient and apparential existence, may come into being? If, the illusion of living being shattered, living for the mere sake of living or for the sake of others who are likewise doomed to die, does not satisfy the soul, what is the good of living? Our best remedy is death." And thus it is that we chant the praises of the never-ending rest because of our dread of it, and speak of liberating death.

·　·　·

The greater part of those who seek death at their own hand are moved thereto by love; it is the supreme longing for life, for more life, the longing to prolong and perpetuate life, that urges them to death, once they are persuaded of the vanity of this longing.

The problem is tragic and eternal, and the more we seek to escape from it, the more it thrusts itself upon us. Four-and-twenty centuries ago, in his dialogue on the immortality of the soul, the serene Plato—but was he serene?—spoke of the uncertainty of our dream of being immortal and of the *risk* that the dream might be vain, and from his own soul there escaped this profound cry—Glorious is the risk!—καλὸς γὰρ ὁ κίνδυνος, glorious is the risk that we are able to run of our souls never dying—a sentence that was the germ of Pascal's famous argument of the wager.

Faced with this risk, I am presented with arguments designed to eliminate it, arguments demonstrating the absurdity of the belief in the immortality of the soul; but these arguments fail to make any impression upon me, for they are reasons and nothing more than reasons, and it is not with reasons that the heart is appeased. I do not want to die—no; I neither want to die nor do I want to want to die; I want to live for ever and ever and ever. I want this "I" to live—this poor "I" that I am and that I feel myself to be here and now, and therefore the problem of the duration of my soul, of my own soul, tortures me.

I am the centre of my universe, the centre of the universe, and in my supreme anguish I cry with Michelet, "Mon moi, ils m'arrachent mon moi!" What is a man profited if he shall gain the whole world and lose his own soul? (Matt. xvi. 26). Egoism, you say? There is nothing more universal than the individual, for what is the property of each is the property of all. Each man is worth more than the whole of humanity, nor will it do to sacrifice each to all save in so far as all sacrifice themselves to each. That which we call egoism is the principle of psychic gravity, the necessary postulate. "Love thy neighbour as thyself," we are told, the presupposition being that each man loves himself; and it is not said "Love thyself." And, nevertheless, we do not know how to love ourselves.

Put aside the persistence of your own self and ponder what they tell you. Sacrifice yourself to your children! And sacrifice yourself to them because they are yours, part and prolongation of yourself, and they in their turn will sacrifice themselves to their children, and these children to theirs, and so it will go on without end, a sterile sacrifice by which nobody profits. I came into the world to create my self, and what is to become of all our selves? Live for the True, the Good, the Beautiful! We shall see presently the supreme vanity and the supreme insincerity of this hypocritical attitude.

"That art thou!" they tell me with the Upanishads. And I answer: Yes, I am that, if that is I and all is mine, and mine the totality of things. As mine I love the All, and I love my neighbour because he lives in me and is part of my consciousness, because he is like me, because he is mine.

Oh, to prolong this blissful moment, to sleep, to eternalize oneself in it! Here and now, in this discreet and diffused light, in this lake of quietude, the storm of the heart appeased and stilled the echoes of the world! Insatiable desire now sleeps and does not even dream; use and wont, blessed use and wont, are the rule of my eternity; my disillusions have died with my memories, and with my hopes my fears.

And they come seeking to deceive us with a deceit of deceits, telling us that nothing is lost, that everything is transformed, shifts and changes, that not the least particle of matter is annihilated, not the least impulse of energy is lost, and there are some who pretend to console us with this! Futile consolation! It is not my matter or my energy that is the cause of my disquiet, for they are not mine if I myself am not mine—that is, if I am not eternal. No, my longing is not to be submerged in the vast All, in an infinite and eternal Matter or Energy, or in God; not to be possessed by God, but to possess Him, to become myself God, yet without ceasing to be I myself, I who am now speaking to you. Tricks of monism avail us nothing; we crave the substance and not the shadow of immortality.

Materialism, you say? Materialism? Without doubt; but either our spirit is likewise some kind of matter or it is nothing. I dread the idea of having to tear myself away from my flesh; I dread still more the idea of having to tear myself away from everything sensible and material, from all substance. Yes, perhaps this merits the name of materialism; and if I grapple myself to God with all my powers and all my senses, it is that He may carry me in His arms beyond death, looking into these eyes of mine with the light of His heaven when the light of earth is dimming in them for ever. Self-illusion? Talk not to me of illusion—let me live!

They also call this pride—"stinking pride" Leopardi called it—and they ask us who are we, vile earthworms, to pretend to immortality; in virtue of what? wherefore? by what right? "In virtue of what?" you ask; and I reply, In virtue of what do we now live? "Wherefore?"—and wherefore do we now exist? "By what right?"—and by what right are we? To exist is just as gratuitous as to go on existing for ever. Do not let us talk of merit or of right or of the wherefore of our longing, which is an end in itself, or we shall lose our reason in a vortex of absurdities. I do not claim any right or merit; it is only a necessity; I need it in order to live.

And you, who are you? you ask me; and I reply with Obermann, "For the universe, nothing; for myself, everything!" Pride? Is it pride to want to be immortal? Unhappy men that we are! 'Tis a tragic fate, without a doubt, to have to base the affirmation of immortality upon the insecure and slippery foundation of the desire for immortality; but to condemn this desire on the ground that we believe it to have been proved to be unattainable, without undertaking the proof, is merely supine. I am dreaming . . . ? Let me dream, if this dream is my life. Do not awaken me from it. I believe in the immortal origin of this yearning for immortality, which is the very substance of my soul. But do I really believe in it . . . ? And wherefore do you want to be immortal? you ask me, wherefore? Frankly, I do not understand the question, for it is to ask the reason of the reason, the end of the end, the principle of the principle.

.   .   .

[S]ensible men, those who do not intend to let themselves be deceived, keep on dinning into our ears the refrain that it is no use giving way to folly and kicking against the pricks, for what cannot be is impossible. The manly attitude, they say, is to resign oneself to fate; since we are not immortal, do not let us want to be so; let us submit ourselves to reason without tormenting ourselves about what is irremediable, and so making life more gloomy and miserable. This obsession, they add, is a disease. Disease, madness, reason . . . the everlasting refrain! Very well then— No! I do not submit to reason, and I rebel against it, and I persist in creating by the energy of faith my immortalizing God, and in forcing by my will the stars out of their courses, for if we had faith as a grain of mustard seed we should say to that mountain, "Remove hence," and it would remove, and nothing would be impossible to us (Matt. xvii. 20).

There you have that "thief of energies," as he* so obtusely called Christ who sought to wed nihilism with the struggle for existence, and he talks to you about courage. His heart craved the eternal All while his head convinced him of nothingness, and, desperate and mad to defend himself from himself, he cursed

_____
* Nietzsche.

that which he most loved. Because he could not be Christ, he blasphemed against Christ. Bursting with his own self, he wished himself unending and dreamed his theory of eternal recurrence, a sorry counterfeit of immortality, and, full of pity for himself, he abominated all pity. And there are some who say that his is the philosophy of strong men! No, it is not. My health and my strength urge me to perpetuate myself. His is the doctrine of weaklings who aspire to be strong, but not of the strong who are strong. Only the feeble resign themselves to final death and substitute some other desire for the longing for personal immortality. In the strong the zeal for perpetuity overrides the doubt of realizing it, and their superabundance of life overflows upon the other side of death.

.   .   .

Unhappy, I know well, are these confessions; but from the depth of unhappiness springs new life, and only by draining the lees of spiritual sorrow can we at last taste the honey that lies at the bottom of the cup of life. Anguish leads us to consolation.

.   .   .

The Practical Problem
from Tragic Sense of Life

.   .   .

What is our heart's truth, anti-rational though it be? The immortality of the human soul, the truth of the persistence of our consciousness without any termination whatsoever, the truth of the human finality of the Universe. And what is its moral proof? We may formulate it thus: Act so that in your own judgement and in the judgement of others you may merit eternity, act so that you may become irreplaceable, act so that you may not merit death. Or perhaps thus: Act as if you were to die to-morrow, but to die in order to survive and be eternalized. The end of morality is to give personal, human finality to the Universe; to discover the finality that belongs to it—if indeed it has any finality—and to discover it by acting.

More than a century ago, in 1804, in Letter XC of that series that constitutes the immense monody of his *Obermann,* Sénancour wrote the words which I have put at the head of this chapter—and of all the spiritual descendants of the patriarchal Rousseau, Sénancour was the most profound and the most intense; of all the men of heart and feeling that France has produced, not excluding Pascal, he was the most tragic. "Man is perishable. That may be; but let us perish resisting, and if it is nothingness that awaits us, do not let us so act that it shall be a just fate." Change this sentence from its negative to the positive form—"And if it is nothingness that awaits us, let us so act that it shall be an unjust fate"—and you get the firmest basis of action for the man who cannot or will not be a dogmatist.

That which is irreligious and demoniacal, that which incapacitates us for action and leaves us without any ideal defence against our evil tendencies, is the pessimism that Goethe puts into the mouth of Mephistopheles when he makes him say, "All that has achieved existence deserves to be destroyed" (*denn alles was ensteht ist wert dass es zugrunde geht*). This is the pessimism which we men call evil, and not that other pessimism that consists in lamenting what it fears to be true and struggling against this fear— namely, that everything is doomed to annihilation in the end. Mephistopheles asserts that everything that exists deserves to be destroyed, annihilated, but not that everything will be destroyed or annihilated; and we assert that everything that exists deserves to be exalted and eternalized, even though no such fate is in store for it. The moral attitude is the reverse of this.

Yes, everything deserves to be eternalized, absolutely everything, even evil itself, for that which we call evil would lose its evilness in being eternalized, because it would lose its temporal nature. For the essence of evil consists in its temporal nature, in its not applying itself to any ultimate and permanent end.

· · ·

It must be admitted that there exists in truth no more solid foundation for morality than the foundation of the Catholic ethic. The end of man is eternal happiness, which consists in the vision and enjoyment of God *in sæcula sæculorum*. Where it errs, however, is in the choice of the means conducive to this end; for to make the attainment of eternal happiness dependent upon believing or not believing in the Procession of the Holy Ghost from the Father and the Son and not from the Father alone, or in the Divinity of Jesus, or in the theory of the Hypostatic Union, or even in the existence of God, is, as a moment's reflection will show, nothing less than monstrous. A human God—and that is the only kind of God we are able to conceive—would never reject him who was unable to believe in Him with his head, and it is not in his head but in his heart that the wicked man says that there is no God, which is equivalent to saying that he wishes that there may not be a God. If any belief could be bound up with the attainment of eternal happiness it would be the belief in this happiness itself and in the possibility of it.

And what shall we say of that other proposition of the king of pedants, to the effect that we have not come into the world to be happy but to fulfil our duty (*Wir sind nicht auf der Welt, um glücklich zu sein, sondern um unsere Schuldigkeit zu tun*)? If we are in the world *for* something (*um etwas*), whence can this *for* be derived but from the very essence of our own will, which asks for happiness and not duty as the ultimate end? And if it is sought to attribute some other value to this *for*, an objective value, as some Sadducean pedant would say, then it must be recognized that the objective reality, that which would remain even though humanity should disappear, is as indifferent to our duty as to our happiness, is as little concerned with our morality as with our felicity. I am not aware that Jupiter, Uranus, or Sirius would allow their course to be affected by the fact that we are or are not fulfilling our duty any more than by the fact that we are or are not happy.

Such considerations must appear to these pedants to be characterized by a ridiculous vulgarity and a dilettante superficiality. (The intellectual world is divided into two classes—dilettanti on the one hand, and pedants on the other.) What choice, then, have we? The modern man is he who resigns himself to the truth and is content to be ignorant of the synthesis of culture—witness what Windelband says on this head in his study of the fate of Hölderlin (*Praeludien*, i.). Yes, these men of culture are resigned, but there remain a few poor savages like ourselves for whom resignation is impossible. We do not resign ourselves to the idea of having one day to disappear, and the criticism of the great Pedant does not console us.

The quintessence of common sense was expressed by Galileo Galilei when he said: "Some perhaps will say that the bitterest pain is the loss of life, but I say that there are others more bitter; for whosoever is deprived of life is deprived at the same time of the power to lament, not only this, but any other loss whatsoever."

Whether Galileo was conscious or not of the humour of this sentence I do not know, but it is a tragic humour.

But, to turn back, I repeat that if the attainment of eternal happiness could be bound up with any particular belief, it would be with the belief in the possibility of its realization. And yet, strictly speaking, not even with this. The reasonable man says in his head, "There is no other life after this," but only the wicked says it in his heart. But since the wicked man is possibly only a man who has been driven to despair, will a human God condemn him because of his despair? His despair alone is misfortune enough.

But in any event let us adopt the Calderónian formula in *La Vida es Sueño:*

> *Que estoy soñando y que quiero*
> *obrar hacer bien, pues no se pierde*
> *el hacer bien aun en sueños**

But are good deeds really not lost? Did Calderón know? And he added:

> *Acudamos a lo eterno*
> *que es la fama vividora*
> *donde ni duermen las dichas*
> *no las grandezas reposan.*†

Is it really so? Did Calderón know?

Calderón had faith, robust Catholic faith; but for him who lacks faith, for him who cannot believe in what Don Pedro Calderón de la Barca believed, there always remains the attitude of *Obermann.*

If it is nothingness that awaits us, let us make an injustice of it; let us fight against destiny, even though without hope of victory; let us fight against it quixotically.

And not only do we fight against destiny in longing for what is irrational, but in acting in such a way that we make ourselves irreplaceable, in impressing our seal and mark upon others, in acting upon our neighbours in order to dominate them, in giving our-selves to them in order that we may eternalize ourselves so far as we can.

Our greatest endeavour must be to make ourselves irreplaceable, to make the theoretical fact—if this expression does not involve a contradiction in terms—the fact that each one of us is unique and irreplaceable, that no one else can fill the gap that will be left when we die, a practical truth.

For in fact each man is unique and irreplaceable; there cannot be any other I; each one of us—our soul, that is, not our life—is worth the whole Universe. I say the spirit and not the life, for the ridiculously exaggerated value which those attach to human life who, not really believing in the spirit—that is to say, in their personal immortality—tirade against war and the death penalty, for example, is a value which they attach to it precisely because they do not really believe in the spirit of which life is the servant. For life is of use only in so far as it serves its lord and master, spirit, and if the master perishes with the servant, neither the one nor the other is of any great value.

And to act in such a way as to make our annihilation an injustice, in such a way as to make our brothers, our sons, and our brothers' sons, and their sons' sons, feel that we ought not to have died, is something that is within the reach of all.

The essence of the doctrine of the Christian redemption is in the fact that he who suffered agony and death was the unique man—that is, Man, the Son of Man, or the Son of God; that he, because he was sinless, did not deserve to have died; and that this propitiatory divine victim died in order that he might rise again and that he might raise us up from the dead, in order that he might deliver us from death by applying his merits to us and showing us the way of life. And the Christ who gave himself for his brothers in humanity with an absolute self-abnegation is the pattern for our action to shape itself on.

All of us, each one of us, can and ought to determine to give as much of himself as he possibly can—nay, to give more than he can, to exceed himself, to go beyond himself, to make himself irreplaceable, to give himself to others in order that he may receive himself back again from them. And each one in his own civil calling or office. The word office, *officium,* means obligation, debt, but in the concrete, and that is what it always ought to mean in practice. We ought not so much to try to seek that particular calling which we think most fitting and suitable for ourselves, as to

---

* Act II., Scene 4: "I am dreaming and I wish to act rightly, for good deeds are not lost, though they be wrought in dreams."

† Act III., Scene 10: "Let us aim at the eternal, the glory that does not wane, where bliss slumbers not and where greatness does not repose."

make a calling of that employment in which chance, Providence, or our own will has placed us.

· · ·

GABRIEL MARCEL (1889–1973)

Gabriel Marcel was born in Paris. During the Second World War he worked for the Red Cross locating missing persons. Marcel was a playwright as well as a Catholic philosopher. His main works were *Metaphysical Journal* (1927) and *Being and Having* (1935).

Marcel draws attention to elusive ways in which our possessions affect our identity. On the one hand, we seem to assume that we are distinct from something when we speak of possessing it. We confront the possession as something that is not us. On the other hand, when we truly possess something, we seem to assimilate it into our identities. In some cases we might even be tempted to say that a possession displaces our identity. Of nothing does this fact seem truer than our own bodies. As Marcel says, "I seem . . . to be annihilating myself in this attachment, by sinking myself in this body to which I cling. It seems that my body literally devours me, and it is the same with all the other possessions which are somehow attached or hung upon my body." Alluding to Hegel's dialectic of the master and the slave, Marcel describes in *Being and Having* how possessing can turn into being possessed: "Having as such seems to have a tendency to destroy and lose itself in the very thing it began by possessing, but which now absorbs the master who thought he controlled it."[8]

Our situation becomes even more mysterious when we attempt to grasp reality as a whole by describing it for ourselves. In characterizing reality, we attempt to possess it, and face the tension between being assimilated by it and assimilating it. On the one hand:

Characterisation implies a certain setting of myself in front of the other, and . . . a sort of radical banishment or cutting-off of me from it.

I bring about this banishment, by myself implicitly coming to a halt, separating myself, and treating myself . . . as a thing bounded by its outlines.[9]

Yet on the other hand:

. . . as we raise ourselves towards Reality, . . . we find that it cannot be compared with an object placed before us on which we can take bearings: and we find, too, that we are ourselves actually changed in the process.[10]

Marcel finally speaks of something he calls *Absolute Being* that is completely beyond understanding. To put ourselves in touch with Being, is to enter "a sphere which transcends all possible possession," which is reached in worship.

Outlines of a Phenomenology of Having*
from Being and Having

The first point I want to make this evening is that the ideas which I am about to put before you are in my opinion nuclear ideas. They contain the germ of a whole philosophy. I will confine myself to the mere adumbration of a great part of it; for if it is sound, others will probably be in a position to elaborate its various branches in forms which I cannot imagine in detail. It is also possible that some of these tracks, whose general direction I hope to indicate, may turn out to lead nowhere.

I think I should tell you, first of all, how it was that I came to ask myself questions about Having. The general consideration was grafted, as it were, on to inquiries which were more particular and concrete, and I think it is essential to begin by referring to them. I apologise for having to quote from myself, but it will be the simplest way of sharing with you the interests which occasioned these researches, otherwise they must seem to you hopelessly abstract.

---

[8] Gabriel Marcel, *Being and Having,* trans. Katharine Farrer (New York: Harper Torchbooks, 1949), 164.

[9] Ibid., 168.
[10] Ibid., 169.
*Paper delivered to the Lyons Philosophical Society in November, 1933.

In the *Journal Métaphysique* I had already begun to state the following problem, which seems at first to be of a purely psychological order. How, I asked, is it possible to identify a feeling which we have for the first time? Experience shows that such an identification is often extremely difficult. (Love may appear in such disconcerting shapes as to prevent those who feel it from suspecting its real nature.) I observed that an identification of this sort can be realised in proportion as the feeling can be compared with something I *have,* in the sense that I *have* a cold or the measles. In that case, it can be limited, defined and intellectualised. So far as this can be done, I can form some idea of it and compare it with the previous notion I may have had about this feeling in general. (I am, of course, just giving you a skeleton at present, but never mind.) On the other hand, I went on to say, in proportion as my feeling cannot be isolated, and so distinguished, I am less sure of being able to recognise it. But is there not really a sort of emotional woof running across the warp of the feeling I *have?* and is it not consubstantial with what I *am,* and that to such a degree that I cannot really set it before myself and so form a conception of it? This is how I got my first glimpse of something which, though it was not a clear-cut distinction, was at least a sort of scale of subtle differences, an imperceptible shading-off from a feeling I have to a feeling I am. Hence this note written on March 16th, 1933:

'Everything really comes down to the distinction between what we have and what we are. But it is extraordinarily hard to express this in conceptual terms, though it must be possible to do so. What we *have* obviously presents an appearance of externality to ourselves. But it is not an absolute externality. In principle, what we *have* are things (or what can be compared to things, precisely in so far as this comparison is possible). I can only *have,* in the strict sense of the word, something whose existence is, up to a certain point, independent of me. In other words, what I have is added to me; and the fact that it is possessed by me is added to the other properties, qualities, etc., belonging to the thing I have. I only have what I can in some manner and within certain limits dispose of; in other words, in so far as I can be considered as a force, a being endowed with powers. We can only transmit what we have.'

From this point I went on to consider the extremely difficult question of whether there was anything in reality which we cannot transmit and in what manner it could be thought of.

Here, then, is one approach, but it is not the only one. I cannot, for instance, concentrate my attention on what is properly called *my* body—as distinct from the body-as-object considered by physiologists—without coming once more upon this almost impenetrable notion of having. And yet, can I, with real accuracy, say that my body is something which I have? In the first place, can my body as such be called a thing? If I treat it as a thing, what is this 'I' which so treats it? 'In the last analysis,' I wrote in the *Journal Métaphysique* (p. 252), 'we end up with the formula: My body is (an object), I am—nothing. Idealism has one further resource: it can declare that I am the act which posits the objective reality of my body. But is not this a mere sleight-of-hand? I fear so. The difference between this sort of idealism and pure materialism amounts almost to nothing.' But we can go much deeper than this. In particular, we can show the consequences of such a mode of representation or imagination for our attitude towards death or suicide.

Surely killing ourselves is disposing of our bodies (or lives) as though they are something we *have,* as though they are things. And surely this is an implicit admission that we belong to ourselves? But almost unfathomable perplexities then assail us: what is the self? What is this mysterious relation between the self and ourself? It is surely clear that the relation is quite a different thing for the man who refuses to kill himself, because he does not recognise a right to do so, since he does not belong to himself. Beneath this apparently negligible difference of formulae, may we not perceive a kind of gulf which we cannot fill in, and can only explore a step at a time?

I limit myself to these two pointers. There may be others, and we shall notice them as they arise, or at least some of them.

It now becomes necessary to make an analysis. I must warn you that this analysis will not be a *reduction.* On the contrary; it will show us that we are here in the presence of a datum which is opaque and of which we may even be unable to take full possession. But the recognition of an *irreducible* is already an extremely important step in philosophy, and it may even effect a kind of change in the consciousness which makes it.

We cannot, in fact, conceive of this irreducible without also conceiving of a Beyond, in which it is never resolved; and I think that the double existence of an irreducible and the Beyond goes far towards an exact definition of man's metaphysical condition.

We should first notice that the philosophers seem to have always shown a sort of implicit mistrust towards the notion of having (I say 'notion', but we must ask whether this is a suitable expression, and I really think it is not). It almost looks as if the philosophers had on the whole turned away from having, as if it were an impure idea, essentially incapable of being made precise.

The essential ambiguity of having should certainly be underlined from the very beginning. But I think that we cannot, at present, exempt ourselves from going on to the enquiry I am suggesting today. I was prosecuting this enquiry when I first came across Herr Gunter Stern's book *Ueber das Haben* (published at Bonn by Cohen, 1928). I will content myself with quoting these few lines:

'We have a body. We have. . . . In ordinary talk we are perfectly clear about what we mean by this. And yet nobody has thought of turning his attention upon what, in common parlance, is intended by the word "have"; no one has attended to it as a complex of relations, and asked himself in what having consists, simply as having.'

Herr Stern rightly observes that when I say 'I have a body', I do not only mean 'I am conscious of my body': but neither do I mean 'something exists which can be called my body'. It seems that there must be a middle term, a third kingdom. Herr Stern then plunges into an analysis steeped in Husserl's terminology. I will not follow him there, especially as I know (for he has told me so himself) that the results of his enquiry have now ceased to satisfy him. It is now the time, I think, to proceed to the most direct explanation we can manage; and we must take care not to have recourse to the language of German phenomenologists, which is so often untranslatable.

It may be asked why, in these circumstances, I have myself made use of the term *phenomenology*.

I reply that the non-psychological character of such an enquiry as this must be emphasised as strongly as possible; for it really concerns the content of the thoughts which it is trying to bring out, so that they may expand in the light of reflection.

I should like to start with the clearest examples I can, where having is plainly in its strongest and most exact sense. There are other cases where this sense (or perhaps we should more properly call it this emphasis) is weakened almost to vanishing point. Such limiting cases can and should be practically neglected (having headaches, for instance, having need, etc.— the absence of the article is a revealing sign here). In cases of the first type, however, that is, in significant cases, it seems that we are right to distinguish two kinds, so long as we do not forget afterwards to ask ourselves about the relations between them. Having-as-possession can itself develop varieties that are very different, and arranged, as it were, in a hierarchy. But the possessive index is as clearly marked when I say, 'I have a bicycle,' as it is when I assert, 'I have my own views on that,' or even when I say (and this takes us in a slightly different direction), 'I have time to do so-and-so.' We will provisionally set aside having-as-implication. In all having-as-possession there does seem to be a certain content. That is too definite a word. Call it a certain *quid* relating to a certain *qui* who is treated as a centre of inherence or apprehension. I purposely abstain from the use of the word subject, because of the special meanings, whether logical or epistemological, which it connotes: whereas it is our task—and difficult for this very reason—to try to blaze a trail for ourselves across territory outside the realms either of logic or of the theory of knowledge.

Notice that the *qui* is from the first taken as in some degree transcendent to the *quid*. By transcendent I just mean that there is a difference of level or degree between the two of them, but I make no attempt to pronounce on the nature of that difference. It is as clear when I say, 'I have a bicycle,' or 'Paul has a bicycle', as when I say 'James has very original ideas about that'.

This is all perfectly simple. The position becomes more complicated when we observe that any assertion about having seems to be somehow built on the model of a kind of prototypical statement, where the *qui* is no other than *myself*. It looks as if having is only felt in its full force, and given its full weight, when it is within 'I have'. If a 'you have' or a 'he has' is possible, it is only possible in virtue of a kind of transference, and such a transference cannot be made without losing something in the process.

This can be made somewhat clearer if we think of the relation which plainly joins possession to power, at any rate where the possession is actual and literal. Power is something which I experience by exercising it or by resisting it—after all, it comes to the same thing.

I should be told here that having is often apt to reduce itself to the fact of containing. But even if we admit that this is so, the important point must still be made, that the containing itself cannot be defined in purely spatial terms. It seems to me always to imply the idea of a potentiality. To contain is to enclose; but to enclose is to prevent, to resist, and to oppose the tendency of the content towards spreading, spilling out, and escaping.

And so I think that the objection, if it is one, turns, on a closer examination, against the man who makes it.

At the heart of having, then, we can discern a kind of *suppressed* dynamic, and suppression is certainly the key-word here. It is this which lights up what I call the transcendence of the *qui*. It is significant that the relation embodied in having is, grammatically, found to be intransitive. The verb 'to have' is only used in the passive in exceptional and specialised ways. It is as though we saw passing before us a kind of irreversible progress from the *qui* towards the *quid*. Let me add that we are not here concerned with a mere step taken by the subject reflecting upon having. No, the progress seems to be carried out by the *qui* itself: it seems to be within the *qui*. Here we must pause for a moment, as we are drawing close to the central point.

We can only express ourselves in terms of *having* when we are moving on a level where, in whatever manner and whatever degree of transposition, the contrast between within and without retains a meaning.

This is completely applicable to having-as-implication, of which it is now time to say a few words. It is really perfectly clear that when I say, 'Such-and-such a body has such-and-such a property,' the property appears to me to be inside, or, as it were, rooted in the inside, of the body which it characterises. I observe, on the other hand, that we cannot think of implication without also thinking of force, however obscure the notion may be. I think that we cannot avoid representing the property or character as defining a certain efficacy, a certain essential energy.

But we are not at the end of our investigations.

Reflection will, in fact, now bring before our eyes the existence of a kind of dialectic of internality. *To have* can certainly mean, and even chiefly mean, *to have for one's-self*, to keep for one's-self, to hide. The most interesting and typical example is *having a secret*. But we come back at once to what I said about content. This secret is only a secret because I keep it; but also and at the same time, it is only a secret because I could reveal it. The possibility of betrayal or discov-

ery is inherent in it, and contributes to its definition as a secret. This is not a unique case; it can be verified whenever we are confronted with having in the strongest sense of the word.

The characteristic of a possession is being shewable. There is a strict parallel between having drawings by X in one's portfolios, which can be shewn to this or that visitor, and having ideas or opinion on this or that question.

This act of shewing may take place or unfold before another or before one's-self. The curious thing is that analysis will reveal to us that this difference is devoid of meaning. In so far as I shew my own views to myself, I myself become someone else. That, I suppose, is the metaphysical basis for the possibility of expression. I can only express myself in so far as I can become someone else to myself.

And now we see the transition take place from the first formula to the second one: we can only express ourselves in terms of having, when we are moving on a level implying reference to another taken as another. There is no contradiction between this formula and my remarks just now on 'I have'. The statement 'I have' can only be made over against *another* which is felt to be other.

In so far as I conceive myself as having in myself, or more exactly, as mine, certain characteristics, certain trappings, I consider myself from the point of view of another—but I do not separate myself from this other except after having first implicitly identified myself with him. When I say, for instance, 'I have my own opinion about that,' I imply, 'My opinion is not everybody's; but I can only exclude or reject everybody's opinion if I have first, by a momentary fiction, assimilated it and made it mine.

Having, therefore, is not found in the scale of purely interior relations, far from it. It would there be meaningless. It is found, rather, in a scale where externality and internality can no longer be really separated, any more than height and depth of musical tone. And here, I think, it is the tension between them that is important.

We must now return to having-as-possession in its strict sense. Take the simplest case, possession of any object whatever, say a picture. From one point of view we should say that this object is exterior to its possessor. It is spatially distinct from him, and their destinies are also different. And yet this is only a superficial view. The stronger the emphasis placed on having and possession, the less permissible is it to harp upon this externality. It is absolutely certain that there is a link between the *qui* and the *quid,* and that this link is not simply an external conjunction. But in so far as this *quid* is a thing, and consequently subject to the changes and chances proper to things, it may be lost or destroyed. So it becomes, or is in danger of becoming, the centre of a kind of whirlpool of fears and anxieties, thus expressing exactly the tension which is an essential part of the order of having.

It may be said that I can easily be indifferent to the fate of this or that object in my possession. But in that case, I should say that the possession is only nominal, or again, residual.

It is, on the other hand, very important to notice that having already exists, in a most profound sense, in desire or in covetousness. To desire is in a manner to have without having. That is why there is a kind of suffering or burning which is an essential part of desire. It is really the expression of a sort of contradiction; it expresses the friction inseparable from an untenable position. There is also an absolute balance between covetousness and the pain I feel at the idea that I am going to lose what I have, what I thought I had, and what I have no longer. But if this is so, then it seems (a point we had noticed before) that having in some way depends upon time. Here again we shall find ourselves confronted with a kind of mysterious polarity.

There is certainly a two-fold permanency in having: there is the permanency of the *qui,* and the permanency of the *quid.* But this permanency is, of its very nature, threatened. It is willed, or at least wished, and it slips from our grasp. The threat is the hold exerted by the other *qua* other, the other which may be the world itself, and before which I so painfully feel that I am I. I hug to myself this thing which may be torn from me, and I desperately try to incorporate it in myself, to form myself and it into a single and indissoluble complex. A desperate, hopeless struggle.

This brings us back to the body, and corporeity. The primary object with which I identify myself, but which still eludes me, is my own body. We may well think that we are here at the very heart of the mystery, in the very deepest recesses of having. The body is the typical possession. Or is it?

Before pursuing this further, let us return once more to having-as-implication. In this, the characteristics to which I have been drawing attention seem to

disappear. Let us go right to one extreme end of the ladder which links up abstract and concrete, and consider the statement, 'A certain geometrical figure has a certain property'. I confess that I cannot, without recourse to pure sophistry, find in this anything at all like that tension between external and internal, that polarity of the same and the other. It is therefore a proper question whether, in taking Having into the very heart of essences—for what I have just said of the geometrical figure seems to me to cover also the living body or species exhibiting certain characteristics—we are not making a sort of unconscious transference which is in the last analysis unjustifiable. That point I will not press, at any rate not now, for it seems to me of secondary interest. But I think that the setting-up of my body as the typical possession marks an essential stage in metaphysical thought.

Having as such is essentially something that *affects* the *qui.* It is never reduced, except in a completely abstract and ideal way, to something of which the *qui* can have the disposal. Always there is a sort of boomerang action, and nowhere is this clearer than in the case of my body, or of an instrument which is an extension of it, or which multiplies its powers. Perhaps this has some analogy with the dialectic of the master and the slave as Hegel has defined it in *The Phenomenology of the Mind.* This dialectic has its spring in the tension without which *real having* does not and cannot exist.

The point we are discussing now lies at the very heart of the world of every day, the world of daily experience with its dangers, its anxieties, and its techniques. At the heart of experience, but also at the heart of the unintelligible. For the fact must be faced, that this tension, this fateful double action, may at any moment turn our lives into a kind of incomprehensible and intolerable slavery.

Before going further, let us once again sum up the position in which we stand.

Normally, or (if you prefer it) usually, I find myself confronted with things: and some of these things have a relationship with me which is at once peculiar and mysterious. These things are not *only external*: it is as though there were a connecting corridor between them and me; they reach me, one might say, underground. In exact proportion as I am attached to these things, they are seen to exercise a power over me which my attachment confers upon them, and which grows as the attachment grows. There is one particular thing which really stands first among them, or which enjoys an absolute priority, in this respect, over them—my body. The tyranny it exercises over me depends, by no means completely, but to a considerable degree, upon the attachment I have for it. But—and this is the most paradoxical feature of the situation—I seem, in the last resort, to be annihilating myself in this attachment, by sinking myself in this body to which I cling. It seems that my body literally devours me, and it is the same with all the other possessions which are somehow attached or hung upon my body. So that in the last analysis—and this is a new point of view—Having as such seems to have a tendency to destroy and lose itself in the very thing it began by possessing, but which now absorbs the master who thought he controlled it. It seems that it is of the very nature of my body, or of my instruments in so far as I treat them as possessions, that they should tend to blot me out, although it is I who possess them.

But if I think again, I shall see that this kind of dialectic is only possible if it starts from an act of desertion which makes it possible. And this observation at once opens up the way to a whole new region.

And yet, what difficulties we find! What an array of possible objections! In particular, could it not be said, 'In so far as you treat the instrument as pure instrument, it has no power over you. You control it yourself and it does not react upon you.' This is perfectly true. But there is a division or interval, hardly measurable by thought, between having something, and controlling or using it: and the danger we are speaking of lies just in this division or interval. Spengler, in the very remarkable book he has just published on *The Decisive Years* and the state of the world today, somewhere notices the distinction that I am getting at here. In speaking of investments or shares in companies, he emphasises the difference between pure having (*das blosse Haben*), and the responsible work of direction which falls to the head of the undertaking. Elsewhere he insists upon the contrast between money, treated as an abstract, in the mass (*Wertmenge*), and real property (*Besitz*), in a piece of land, for example. There is something in this to throw indirect light upon the difficult piece of thinking which I am now trying to explain. 'Our possessions eat us up,' I said just now: and it is truer of us, strangely enough, when we are in a state of inertia in face of objects which are themselves inert, but false when we are more vitally and actively bound up with something serving as the immediate subject-matter of a personal creative act, a subject-matter perpetually renewed. (It may be the garden of the keen gardener, the farm of a farmer, the violin of a musician, or the laboratory of a scientist.) In all these cases, we may say, having tends, not to be destroyed, but to be sublimated and changed into being.

Wherever there is pure creation, having as such is transcended or etherialised within the creative act: the duality of possessor and possessed is lost in a living reality. This demands the most concrete illustration we can think of, and not mere examples taken from the category of material possessions. I am thinking in particular of such pseudo-possessions as *my ideas and opinions.* In this case, the word 'have' takes on a meaning which is at once positive and threatening. The more I treat my own ideas, or even my convictions, as something *belonging* to me—and so as something I am proud of (unconsciously perhaps) as I might be proud of my greenhouse or my stables—the more surely will these ideas and opinions tend, by their very inertia (or my inertia towards them, which comes to the same thing) to exercise a tyrannical power over me; that is the principle of fanaticism in all its shapes. What happens in the case of the fanatic, and in other cases too, it seems, is a sort of unjustified alienation of the subject—the use of the term is unavoidable here—in face of the thing, whatever it may be. That, in my opinion, is the difference between the ideologist, on the one hand, and the thinker or artist on the other. The ideologist is one of the most dangerous of all human types, because he is unconsciously enslaved to a part of himself which has mortified, and this slavery is bound to manifest itself outwardly as tyranny. There, by the way, may be seen a connexion which deserves serious and separate examination. The thinker, on the other hand, is continually on guard against this alienation, this possible fossilising of his thought. He lives in a continual state of creativity, and the whole of his thought is always being called in question from one minute to the next.

This throws light, I think, on what I have left to say. The man who remains on the plane of having (or of desire) is *centred,* either on himself or on another treated as another; the result is the same in either case, so far as the tension or polarity goes which I was emphasising just now. This point needs a much more detailed development than I can give it at present. The notion of the self, and of one's-self, should really be firmly seized upon. We should then realise that, contrary to the belief of many idealists, particularly the philosophers of consciousness, the *self* is always a thickening, a sclerosis, and perhaps—who knows?— a sort of apparently spiritualised expression (an expression *of* an expression) of the body, not taken in the objective sense but in the sense of *my* body in as far as it is mine, in so far as my body is something I have. Desire is at the same time auto-centric and hetero-centric; we might say that it appears to itself to be hetero-centric when it is really auto-centric, but its appearing so is itself a fact. But we know very well that it is possible to transcend the level of the self and the other; it is transcended both in love and in charity. Love moves on a ground which is neither that of the self, nor that of the other *qua* other; I call it the Thou. I should think a more philosophical designation would be better, if it could be found; but at the same time I do think that abstract terms here might betray us, and land us once more in the region of the *other*, the *He*.

Love, in so far as distinct from desire or as opposed to desire, love treated as the subordination of the self to a superior reality, a reality at my deepest level more truly me than I am myself—love as the breaking of the tension between the self and the other, appears to me to be what one might call the essential ontological datum. I think, and will say so by the way, that the science of ontology will not get out of the scholastic rut until it takes full cognisance of the fact that love comes first.

Along these lines, I think, we can see what is to be understood by the uncharacterisable. I said that, underlying our mental picture of things, as subjects possessing predicates or characteristics, there must be a transference. It seems plain to me that the distinction between the thing and its characteristics cannot have any metaphysical bearing: it is, shall we say, purely phenomenal. Notice, too, that characteristics can only be asserted in an order which admits of the use of the word 'also'. The characteristic is picked out from others; but at the same time, we cannot say that the thing is a collection of characteristics. Characteristics cannot be juxtaposed, and we do not juxtapose them except in so far as we ignore their specifying function and treat them as units or homogeneous entities; but that is a fiction which does not bear examination. I can, strictly speaking, treat an apple, a bullet, a key, and a ball of string as objects of the same nature, and

as a sum of units. But it is quite different with the smell of a flower and its colour, or the consistency, flavour and digestibility of a dish. In so far, then, as characterisation consists in enumerating properties, placing one beside the other, it is an absolutely external proceeding; it misleads us, and never, in any circumstances, gives us the least opportunity of reaching the heart of that reality which we are trying to characterise. But, speaking philosophically, the really important point to recognise is that characterisation implies a certain setting of myself in front of the other, and (if I may say so) a sort of radical banishment or cutting-off of me from it. I myself bring about this banishment, by myself implicitly coming to a *halt*, separating myself, and treating myself (though I probably am not conscious of so doing) as a thing bounded by its outlines. It is only in relation to this implicitly limited *thing* that I can place whatever I am trying to characterise.

It is plain that the will to characterise implies, in the man who is exerting it, a belief at once sincere and illusory that he can make abstraction from himself *qua* himself. The Leibnizian idea of *characteristica universalis* shows us how far this *pretention* can go. But I am inclined to think that we forget how untenable, metaphysically speaking, is the position of a thought which believes that it can place itself over against things in order to grasp them. It can certainly develop a system of taking its bearings by things, a system of increasing and even infinite complexity: but its aim is to let the essence of things go.

To say that reality is perhaps uncharacterisable is certainly to make an ambiguous and apparently contradictory pronouncement, and we must be careful not to interpret it in a way which conforms with the principles of present-day agnosticism. This means:— If I adopt that attitude to Reality, which all efforts to characterise it would presuppose, I at once cease to apprehend it *qua* Reality: it slips away from my eyes, leaving me face to face with no more than its ghost. I am deceived by the inevitable coherence of this ghost, and so sink into self-satisfaction and pride, when in fact I ought rather to be attacked by doubts of the soundness of my undertaking.

Characterisation is a certain kind of possession, or claim to possession, of that which cannot be possessed. It is the construction of a little abstract effigy, a *model* as English physicists call it, of a reality which will not lend itself to these tricks, these deceptive pretences, except in the most superficial way. Reality will only play this game with us in so far as we cut ourselves off from it, and consequently are guilty of self-desertion.

I think, therefore, that as we raise ourselves towards Reality, and approach it more nearly, we find that it cannot be compared with an object placed before us on which we can take bearings: and we find, too, that we are ourselves actually changed in the process. If, as I believe, there is an ascending scale of dialectic, in a sense not so essentially different as one might suppose from the Platonic doctrine, then this dialectic is two-fold, and relates not only to reality but also to the being who apprehends it. I cannot, at this time, go into the nature of such a dialectic. I will be content to point out that such a philosophy would give a totally new direction to the doctrine, for example, of the Divine Attributes. I confess that, to myself at any rate, the attributes of God are exactly what certain post-Kantians have called *Grentzbegriff.* If Being is more uncharacterisable (i.e. more unpossessable and more transcendent in every way) in proportion as it has more Being, then the attributes can do no more than express and translate, in terms that are completely inadequate, the fact that Absolute Being is as a whole rebellious to descriptions which will never fit anything but what has less Being. They will only fit an object before which we can place ourselves, reducing ourselves, to some extent, to its measure, and reducing it to ours. God can only be given to me as Absolute Presence in worship; any idea I form of Him is only an abstract expression or intellectualisation of the Presence. I must never fail to remember this, when I try to handle such thoughts; otherwise the thoughts will suffer distortion in my sacrilegious hands.

And so we come at last to what is for me the essential distinction—the central point of my essay on *The Ontological Mystery,* to be published in a few days—the distinction between problem and mystery, already presupposed in the paper you have just heard.

I venture to read now a passage from a paper delivered last year to the Marseilles Philosophical Society. It will appear in a few days from now as the appendix to a play, *le Monde Cassé.**

'In turning my attention to what one usually thinks of as ontological problems, such as Does Being exist?

What is Being? etc., I came to observe that I cannot think about these problems without seeing a new gulf open beneath my feet, namely, This I, I who ask questions about being, can I be sure that I exist? What qualifications have I for pursuing these inquiries? If I do not exist, how can I hope to bring them to a conclusion? Even admitting that I do exist, how can I be assured that I do? In spite of the thought which comes first into my head, I do not think that Descartes' *cogito* can be of any help to us here. The *cogito,* as I have written elsewhere, is at the mere threshold of validity; the subject of the *cogito* is the epistemological subject. Cartesianism implies a severance, which may be fatal anyhow, between intellect and life; its result is a depreciation of the one, and an exaltation of the other, both arbitrary. There is here an inevitable rhythm only too familiar to us, for which we are bound to find an explanation. It would certainly not be proper to deny the legitimacy of making distinctions of order within the unity of a living subject, who *thinks* and strives to *think of himself.* But the ontological problem can only arise beyond such distinctions, and for the living being grasped in his full unity and vitality.

This leads us to ask what conditions are involved in the idea of working out a problem. Wherever a problem is found, I am working upon data placed before me; but at the same time, the general state of affairs authorises me to carry on as if I had no need to trouble myself with this Me who is at work: he is here simply presupposed. It is, as we have just seen, quite a different matter when the inquiry is about Being. Here the ontological status of the questioner becomes of the highest importance. Could it be said, then, that I am involving myself in an infinite regress? No, for by the very act of so conceiving the regress, I am placing myself above it. I am recognising that the whole reflexive process remains within a certain assertion which I *am*—rather than *which I pronounce*—an assertion of which I am the place, and not the subject. Thereby we advance into the realm of the metaproblematic, that is, of mystery. A mystery is a problem which encroaches upon its own data and invades them, and so is transcended *qua* problem.'

We cannot now go on to make further developments, indispensible though they are. I will limit myself to one example in order to give definiteness to my conceptions, and that shall be the mystery of evil.

I am naturally inclined to consider evil as a disorder which I look into; I try to make out its causes, the

*Published by Desclée de Brouwer.

reason for its existence, and even its hidden ends. How is it that this machine is so defective in its functioning? Or is this apparent defect due to a defect, not apparent but real, in my own vision, a kind of spiritual presbyopia or astigmatism? If so, the real disorder would lie in myself, and yet would remain objective in relation to the mental censorship which unmasked it. But evil simply recognised, or even contemplated, ceases to be evil *suffered,* in fact I think it simply ceases to be evil. I only really grasp it as evil in proportion as it touches me; that is, where I am involved in it in the sense that one is involved in business. This being involved is fundamental, and I can only discount it by an act of the mind, legitimate in some cases, but fictional, and which I must not allow to deceive me.

Traditional philosophy has tended to reduce the mystery of evil to the problem of evil. That is why, when it touches realities of this kind—evil, love and death—it so often gives the impression of being a game, or a kind of intellectual sleight-of-hand. The more idealist the philosophy, the more strong the impression; for the thinking subject is then more deeply intoxicated with an emancipation which is in fact deceptive.

I ought now (though there is hardly time) to go over the whole of the first part of my paper, and try to shew how light can be thrown upon it by these distinctions. It seems clear to me that the realm of having is identical with the realm of the problematic—and at the same time, of course, with the realm where technics can be used. The metaproblematic is in fact metatechnical. Every technic presupposes a group of previously made abstractions which are the condition of its working; it is powerless where full-blooded Being is in question. This point might be drawn out in several directions. At the root of having, as also at the root of the problem or the technic, there lies a certain specialisation or specification of the self, and this is connected with that partial alienation of the self which I mentioned earlier. And this brings us to the examination of a distinction which, to me, seems extremely important and with which I will end this already overloaded lecture—I mean the distinction between autonomy and freedom.

It is essential to note that autonomy is above all the negation of a heteronomy presupposed and rejected. 'I want to run my own life'—that is the radical formula of autonomy. It is here that we can see that ten-

sion between the Same and the Other, which is the very pulse of the world of having. We should further recognise, I think, that autonomy bears on any realm which admits of administration, however conceived. It in fact implies the idea of a certain sphere of activity, and can be more closely defined when this sphere can be closely circumscribed in space and time. Anything in the nature of interests, whatever the interests are, can be treated with relative ease as a sphere or district with fixed boundaries. And further, I can, to a great extent, treat my own life as capable of being administered by another or by myself (myself here meaning the not-other). I can administer anything which admits the comparison, however indirect, with a fortune or possession. But it is quite different when the category of having can no longer be applied, for then I can no longer talk of administration in any sense, and so cannot speak of autonomy. Take, for example, the realm of literary or artistic talents. To a certain extent a talent may be administered, when its possessor has taken the measure of it, when his talent resides in him as a possession. But for genius, properly so-called, the idea of such administration is a complete contradiction; for it is of the essence of genius to be always outrunning itself and spilling over in all directions. A man *is* a genius, but *has* talent (the expression 'to *have* genius' is literally meaningless). I really think that the idea of autonomy, whatever we may have thought of it, is bound up with a kind of reduction or particularisation of the subject. The more I enter into the whole of an activity with the whole of myself, the less legitimate it is to say that I am autonomous. In this sense, the philosopher is less autonomous than the scientist, and the scientist less autonomous than the technician. The man who is most autonomous is, in a certain sense, most fully involved. Only this non-autonomy of the philosopher or the great artist is not heteronomy any more than love is hetero-centricity. It is rooted in Being, at a point either short of self or beyond self, and in a sphere which transcends all possible possession; the sphere, indeed, which I reach in contemplation or worship. And, in my view, this means that such non-autonomy is very freedom.

It is not our business here even to outline a theory of freedom, if only because we should have to begin by asking whether the idea of a theory of freedom did not imply contradiction. Here I will point out just one thing: the self-evident truth that in the scale of sanctity and of artistic creation, where freedom glows with its fullest light, it is never autonomy. For the saint and the artist alike, autocentricity and the self are entirely swallowed up in love. We might perhaps seize this opportunity to show that most of the defects of Kant's philosophy are essentially bound up with the fact that he had no suspicion of all this; he never saw that the self can and should be transcended without there being any need for heteronomy to replace autonomy in consequence.

I must come to a conclusion, and this is not easy. I will simply return to my preliminary formula. I said then that we should end by the recognition of an irreducible, but that we should also find something beyond this irreducible; and I said that such a duality seemed to me part of the very nature of man's metaphysical condition. What is this irreducible? I do not think that we can, properly speaking, define it, but we can in some measure locate it. It is the ontological deficiency proper to the creature, or at least to the fallen creature. This deficiency is essentially a kind of inertia, but apt to turn into a sort of negative activity, and it cannot be eliminated. On the contrary, our first task is to recognise it. It makes possible a certain number of autonomous and subordinate disciplines; each of them certainly representing danger to the unity of the creature in so far as it tends to absorb it, but each also having its own worth, and partial justification. And therefore it is also necessary that these activities and autonomous functions should be balanced and harmonised by the central activities. In these, man is recalled into the presence of mystery, that mystery which is the foundation of his very being, and apart from which he is nothingness: the grand mystery of religion, art and metaphysic.

KARL JASPERS (1883–1969)*

As he writes in "On My Philosophy," Karl Jaspers "was born in Oldenburg, a son of Karl Jaspers, the former sheriff and later bank director, and his wife Henriette, née Tantzen," and "passed a well-guarded childhood in the company of [his] brothers and sisters, either in the country with [his] grandparents or at the seaside, sheltered by loved and revered par-

ents, led by the authority of [his] father, brought up with a regard for truth and loyalty, for achievement and reliability, yet without church religion. . . ." Jaspers studied law and medicine, receiving his M.D. from the University of Heidelberg. He worked as a psychiatrist before teaching philosophy at the University of Heidelberg. His main philosophical work was *Philosophy* (1932) whose three volumes explore the nature of the real self or *Existenz*. When the National Socialists took control of Germany, his ideas were suppressed. Partly as a result of his treatment by the Nazis, Jaspers devoted his post-war work to such topics as political philosophy and the philosophy of religion.

"The Search for Being" is from the first chapter of volume 1 of *Philosophy,* while "Existenz" is from volume 2. In these excerpts Jaspers distinguishes between "objective being," or the being of objects, and "subjective being," or the being of subjects. In turn, he distinguishes these two kinds of being from a third called "being-in-itself." To conceive of being-in-itself, we must conceive of an item "the way it is independently of its being an object for a subject."[11] Roughly speaking, it is the mode of being possessed by that which Kant called "things-in-themselves." Of these three kinds of being Jaspers says that "None of them is being pure and simple, and none can do without the other; each one is a being within being. The whole eludes us."[12]

I exist in the first way—objectively—insofar as I am a particular object for consciousness—insofar as "I am this body, this individual." I exist in the second way—subjectively—insofar as I am consciousness itself. As a subject (as consciousness), I am "essentially identical with every other subject."[13] I am "the subject whose objects are the things of reality and general validity."[14] To mark my subjective existence, Jaspers says that I am *consciousness at large.* But I also have an additional form of being that cannot be reduced to subjective or objective being, according to Jaspers. This additional form

---

* In Walter Kaufmann's *Existentialism from Dostoevsky to Sartre* (Cleveland: Meridian Books, 1956).

[11] Karl Jaspers, *Philosophy,* trans. E. B. Ashton (Chicago: University of Chicago Press, 1969), 47.
[12] Ibid., 48.
[13] Ibid., 54.
[14] Ibid., 55.

reflects my freedom and potentiality. "As possible Existenz, I am a being related to its potential and, as such, nonexistent for any consciousness at large. To conceive the meaning of possible Existenz is to break through the circle of all modes of objective and subjective being."[15]

Self-realization as Existenz, in which we express our autonomy, requires our being in communication with others engaged in the same form of self-realization. Moreover, as Existenz we may relate to "true being," to something outside Existenz that Jaspers calls "transcendence" or God.[16]

The Search for Being
from Philosophy

GENERAL, FORMAL CONCEPTS OF BEING: OBJECTIVE BEING, SUBJECTIVE BEING, BEING-IN-ITSELF

To think of being is to make it a distinct being. If we ask what being is, we have many answers to choose from: empirical reality in space and time; dead and living matter; persons and things; tools and material; ideas that apply to reality; cogent constructions of ideal objects, as in mathematics; contents of the imagination—in a word, objectiveness. Whatever being I find in my situation is to me an object.

I am different. I do not confront myself as I confront things. I am the questioner; I know that I do the asking and that those modes of objective being are offered to me as replies. Whichever way I turn, trying to make an object of myself, there is always the "I" for which my self becomes an object. There remains a being that is I.

Objective being and *subjective being* are the two modes that strike us first of all, as most different in essence. Objects include persons, of course, who are their own subjects just as I can be their object—and I, as I exist, can even become my own object. But there

[15] Ibid., 55.
[16] Ibid., 63.

remains a point where the objective and subjective I are one, despite the dichotomy.

The being of things is unaware of itself; but I, the thinking subject, know about it. When I conceive of this being in the abstract, the way it is independently of its being an object for a subject—that is to say, not as a phenomenon for something else—I call it *being in itself.* This being-in-itself is not accessible to me, however, for the mere thought of it will turn it into an object and thus into something that appears to me as being. It is in myself alone that I know a being that not merely appears to, but is for, itself—one in which being and being known go together. My own being differs radically from any being of things because I can say, "I am." But if I objectify my empirical existence, this is not the same as the I-in-itself. I do not know what I am in myself if I am my own object; to find out, I would have to become aware of myself in some way other than cognitive knowledge. And even then the being-in-itself of other things would remain alien to me.

The division of being into objective being, being-in-itself, and subjective being does not give me three kinds of being that exist side by side. It does give me three inseparable poles of the being I find myself in. I may tend to *take one of the three for being as such.* Then I either construe the one and only being as being-in-itself, without noticing that I am making it an object for myself in the process—or I construe it as this object of mine, forgetting in this phenomenal transformation of all being that in objectiveness there must be something which appears, and something it appears to—or I construe it as subjective being, with myself as ultimate reality, without realizing that I can never be otherwise than in a situation, conscious of objects and searching for being-in-itself. Objective being pours out to me in endless variety and infinite abundance; it means the world I can get to know. Subjective being is to me as certain as it is incomprehensible; it can come to be known only to the extent to which it has been objectified as empirical existence and is no longer truly subjective. Being-in-itself defies cognition. It is a boundary concept we cannot help thinking, one that serves to question everything I know objectively—for whenever some objective being should be taken for being proper, in the absolute sense, it will be relativized into a phenomenon by the mere idea of being-in-itself.

Thus we fail to hold fast any being as intrinsic. None of them is being pure and simple, and none can do without the other; each one is a being within being. *The whole eludes us.* There is nothing like a common genus of which the three modes—objective, subjective, and in-itself—might be species; nor is there one source to which they can be traced. They are heterogeneous and repel each other as much as they need each other to be at all—to be, that is, for our consciousness. They almost seem to have dropped out of the unfathomable, three mutual strangers who belong together even though there is no link between them and none of them will help us comprehend another. None may claim precedence, except in some particular perspective. For naïve metaphysics, seeking direct possession of intrinsic being, being-in-itself comes first; but it can only be populated with conceptions from the objective world, which in such metaphysics is supposed to be underlying all existence. Objective being has precedence for all cognition, because objects alone are knowable, and also because in cognition we take being for the sum of knowledge—not including the knower, who is merely added to this being. In illustrative philosophizing, on the other hand, subjective being will come briefly to the fore; from this standpoint of self-comprehension, the questioning and knowing subject tends to accord precedence to itself.

EXISTENCE ANALYSIS AS AN ANALYSIS OF CONSCIOUSNESS

We have found being distinctly conceived in objects, directly grasped in self-reflection and evanescently touched—and recognized as inconceivable—in the boundary idea of being-in-itself.

All of these thoughts spring from *the thinker's existence.* From this common ground, to which the search for being takes me, the modes of being appear as perspectives for my thought. The thought itself comprises all perspectives; what it means by being is simply all there is at a time, comprising whatever may occur to me as being. It is my consciousness of temporal existence in the situation I find myself in.

Since existence is consciousness and I exist as consciousness, things are for me only as objects of consciousness. For me, nothing can be without entering into my consciousness. Consciousness as existence is the medium of all things—although we shall see that it is the mere fluid of being.

To analyze existence is to analyze consciousness.

1. Consciousness of Objects and of Self; Existing Consciousness

To be conscious is not to be the way a thing is. It is a peculiar kind of being, the essence of which is to *be directed at objects we mean.* This basic phenomenon—as self-evident as it is marvelous—has been called intentionality. Consciousness is intentional consciousness, which means that its relation to its object is not the relation of a thing that strikes another, or is struck by another. There is no causal relation, and indeed no interrelation at all, as between two of a kind or two on one level. In consciousness, rather, I have an object before me. The way I have it does not matter. It may be perception, which is biologically based on causal relations between physical phenomena, though the phenomena as such can never cause intentionality but require intentional acts to animate perception. It may be imagination, or recollection. Or it may be thinking, which can be visual or abstract, aimed at real objects or at imaginary ones. One thing always remains: my consciousness is aimed at what I mean.

Consciousness is self-reflexive. It not only aims at objects, but turns back upon itself—that is to say, it is not only conscious but self-conscious at the same time. The reflexion of consciousness upon itself is as self-evident and marvelous as is its intentionality. I aim at myself; I am both one and twofold. I do not exist as a thing exists, but in an inner split, as my own object, and thus in motion and inner unrest. No consciousness can be understood as stable, as merely extant. Because it is not like the being of spatial and ideal things—things I can walk around, things I can hold fast, things I can visualize so that they stand before me—consciousness evaporates when I would take it for being. While I am conscious of objects as of something else, I am also conscious of myself as an object, but so as to coincide with this object that is myself. It is true that what happens in this confrontation when I observe myself psychologically is that the experience I know and my knowledge of this experience will be so aimed at each other as to make me conscious of two different things at once: what I know, and my knowing it. Yet at the core of the process stands my subjective consciousness, with the one identical "I" actually doubled by the thought that "I am conscious of myself." The coincidence of "I think" and "I think that I think" permits neither one to be without the other. A seeming logical absurdity becomes a reality: one is not one but two—and yet it does not become two, but remains precisely this unique one. It is the general, formal concept of the I.

The omnipresent and not otherwise deducible basic phenomenon of consciousness as the split into subject and object means that *self-consciousness and consciousness of objects go together*. True, I become so absorbed in things that I forget myself. But there always remains a last subjective point, an impersonal and purely formal I-point which a thing will confront by existing—that is to say, for which the thing will be an object. Conversely, I cannot so isolate my self-consciousness that I know myself alone: I exist only by confronting other things. There is no subjective consciousness without an objective one, however slight.

Finally there is a consciousness that is neither like the external being of things nor an objectless intentionality. This is the experience of mere inward motion that can light up in sudden intentionality and be known in retrospect, although the lack of any split keeps it dormant and its existence can only be remembered—of experiences had while awakening, for example, and of undefinable sensations. Viewed from the split consciousness, this *merely existing* one is a *limit* that can be empirically illuminated as a start and a transition, and as the encompassing ground; from the viewpoint of things outwardly extant, it is inwardness. Without any splits into subjective and objective consciousness, the merely existing one would be a fulfillment distinguished from an objective, concrete process by the fact that I can recall this experience as existing at a time when I was not myself, and that I can but retrospectively visualize it, that is, make it conscious, objective, and plain.

If existence is consciousness, it is still not just one or all of the definite concepts of consciousness. Opposed to them is *the unconscious*. But if this is to have any being for us, we must either make it conscious or we must be conscious of it as "the unconscious"—in other words, as a phenomenon, an object of consciousness—and thus, for our consciousness, enable it to be.

The several meanings in which we conceive the unconscious correspond to the concepts of consciousness. The unconscious equivalent of intentional, objective consciousness is nonobjectiveness. The unconscious equivalent of self-consciousness is what we have experienced and objectively sensed but not expressly reflected upon and rated as known. The unconscious equivalent of merely existing consciousness is what we have not inwardly experienced in any sense, what lies entirely outside the realms of our consciousness.

The statement that all existence is consciousness does not mean that consciousness is all. It does mean that for us there is only what enters into the consciousness to which it appears. For us the unconscious is as we become conscious of it.

2. Possibilities of Analyzing Consciousness

Real consciousness is always the existence of an individual with other things that exist in time; it has a beginning and an end. As such, consciousness is an object of empirical observation and study. It contains the fullness of the world if the world is only the temporal world of real consciousness.

Our *conscious existence as a temporal reality* is a ceaseless urge to satisfy many desires. Raised from a state of nature by knowledge and the faculty of choice, we consciously envision death and seek to avoid it at all costs. The instinct of self-preservation makes us fear perils and distinguish them so as to meet them. We seek pleasure in the enjoyment of existence and in the sense of its expansion, for which we toil each day. In anticipation of things to come we think of distant possibilities and goals and dangers. Worry, born of this reflection on what lies ahead, forces us to provide for the future. To satisfy the boundless will to live and the power drives of existence, we conquer others and delight in seeing our status reflected in our environment; indeed, it is this mirror that seems to give us our real sense of existence. Yet all this will satisfy our consciousness only for moments. It keeps driving us on. Never really bringing content, it achieves no goal and ceases only when we die.

Such are the descriptions of consciousness as the empirically real existence of an instinctual life. It can also be described as formal *consciousness at large*. In self-consciousness, distinct from other selves and from the objects I mean, I know myself as acting, then, and as identical with myself as time passes; I know I remain the one I. In objective consciousness I have the modes of objective being in the categories; I understand what definite being I encounter, and I know that cognition of all mundane existence is possible in generally valid form. My consciousness at large is interchangeable with that of anyone else who is my kind, even though not numerically identical.

Insofar as consciousness with its world—whether existing reality or consciousness at large—is an object and may thus come to be known, it becomes a topic either of psychology, if it is empirical existence, or of logic, if possessed of generally valid knowledge.

But there is a third way to analyze consciousness: not as naturally given the way it is, but as a fulfilled real consciousness which never remains the same, which undergoes transformations and is thus historic. *Historically changing consciousness* not only happens, as does a natural process; it remembers, it affects itself, it engenders itself in its history. Man actively lives the life of his successive generations, instead of merely suffering it in a repetition of the same.

An *objective study* of these metamorphoses constitutes world orientation—as anthropology and analytical psychology and intellectual history. Beginning with the dull mind of primitive man, such study allows us to glimpse the leaps in human history from one form to the other, to see now how germs unfold slowly, and then again the sudden flash of new origins of consciousness. In the individual we trace the inner changes and analyze them up to the limit where the processes defy analysis. We seek to penetrate the worlds and self-illuminations of the personally and historically strangest and most remote forms of consciousness.

The study of changeable consciousness teaches us that we cannot set up any substantial real consciousness as the "natural consciousness," or its substance as the "natural view of the world." This would be a reduction to the slicked-down form of a distinct phenomenal consciousness—as a society of historically linked individuals will take it for granted—or to the psychological pattern of the drives of living existence in its environment. There is no immediate existence that might be scientifically analyzed, in one exclusively correct way, as the natural one. Objectively, any attempt to construe and characterize such an existence

has only relative significance. The man who takes it for a radical cognition of being determines only what his narrow mind will make him think of himself. We can, of course, try to go back beyond all historicity and all concreteness in pursuit of what we might call "bare existence"—but this will only impoverish us. We may claim that what we know at the end will fit the universal immediacy of existence, but in fact we shall have stated only a very meager and formally empty consciousness of being that will be historically particular and fixed in time. And if we approach the supposedly immediate by construing the seeming genetic priority of primitive tribes as "natural," we find that once we know more about their existence it proves to be not at all natural but specifically artificial and strange.

There is no radical departure for the awaking of consciousness. Nobody begins afresh. I do not step into a primal situation. So, as there is no generally determinable, natural, unveiled existence to be discovered by removing fallacies, what really lies at the root of it cannot be sought by abstracting from acquired traits. It can be sought only by questioning what these traits have led to. An understanding of all that has been acquired and evolved remains the ground on which we understand existence. The utmost clarity about existence that we can achieve comes to depend upon what scientific intellectual history has achieved already. I cannot see through existence if I merely know general structures, but only if I take a concrete part in the historic process of factual, active, and cognitive world orientation.

Thus the existence analysis conceived as preceding any research operation in the world—though actually performed only after the completed operation—will be either a schema for consciousness at large, showing the network of the modes of being and the sense of validity, or it will be a diagram of conscious existence in reality, isolating the psychological forces at work as libido, fear, worry, will to power, fear of death, or death wish; or it will be the historic self-understanding of consciousness as it has evolved.

No way of making existence conscious gets me to the bottom of it. Instead, unless I confine myself artificially and try to use a supposed knowledge as an anchor in existence where it cannot take hold, any existence analysis will leave me suspended in my situation. The fact that efforts to get underneath it all—as if there were an existing ground to penetrate—seem to plunge me into a void indicates that existence is not what counts if I want to get at being. What counts is myself. Constructions of existence will not take me to being. They can only help me get there by a leap; and the approach that may enable me to take this leap is not existence analysis any more; it is elucidation of Existenz.

3. Consciousness as a Boundary

In analyzing consciousness we work out constructive schemata for logic (the formal visualization of what is valid for consciousness at large), for psychology (the study of empirically existing consciousness), and for the history of consciousness (the reproduction of the mental process).

In part, these objectifying analyses are available in magnificent drafts, but they can never be conclusive. They keep encountering limits that make us feel what is beyond the analyses. Logic, then, will turn about into a formal metaphysical transcending (as in the case of Plotinus); psychology, into elucidation of Existenz (as in Kierkegaard's); and the history of consciousness, into consummate metaphysics (as in Hegel's). Philosophizing cannot be consummated in the self-observation of an empirically existing consciousness, nor in the construction of the ever-present consciousness at large, nor in historical knowledge.

Consciousness is a boundary. It is an object of observation, and yet it already defies objective observation. The statement that in philosophizing we start out from consciousness is untrue insofar as it would seem to confirm that the general—logical, psychological, or historical—analyses of the kind of consciousness that anyone can have at any time amount to philosophical thinking. The statement truly refers to the elucidations that begin and end with *existential consciousness.*

DISTINGUISHING EXISTENZ

We saw being as kept in suspension by the inconceivable being-in-itself. We sensed it as a boundary in existence analysis. But while being-in-itself was the utterly other, completely inaccessible to me as nonexistent for thought, I myself, as I exist, am the limit to analyzing existence. Herein lies the next step we must take in our search for being.

1. Empirical Existence; Consciousness at Large; Possible Existenz

What do I mean when I say "I"?

The first answer is that in thinking about myself I have made myself an object. I am this body, this individual, with an indefinite self-consciousness reflected in my impact upon my environment—I am *empirical existence.*

Second, I am a subject essentially identical with every other subject. I am interchangeable. This interchangeability is not the identity of average qualities among empirical individuals; it is subjective being as such, the subjectiveness that is the premise of all objectiveness—I am *consciousness at large.*

Third, I experience myself in potential unconditionality. I not only want to know what exists, reasoning pro and con; I want to know from a source beyond reasoning, and there are moments of action when I feel certain that what I want now, what I am now doing, is what I really want myself. I want to be so that this will and this action are mine. My very essence—which I do not know even though I am sure of it—comes over me in the way I want to know and to act. In this potential freedom of knowledge and action I am *"possible Existenz."*

Thus, instead of an unequivocally determined I, we have several meanings. As consciousness at large I am the subject whose objects are the things of reality and general validity. Every individual shares in this conceptual general consciousness if objectified being appears to him as it does to all men. Next, I am empirical individuality as objectified subjectiveness; as such I am a special and, in this form, singular occurrence in the endless diversity of individuals. Then, again as empirical existence, I am this individual for consciousness at large, which makes me an object for psychology, and an inexhaustible one at that—an object of observation and research, but not of total cognition. Finally, as possible Existenz, I am a being related to its potential and, as such, nonexistent for any consciousness at large. To conceive the meaning of possible Existenz is to break through the circle of all modes of objective and subjective being.

In philosophizing we admit each of the modes of subjective being. We do not lump them together as identical; and in a limited sense we accord a primacy to each one, though reserving the absolute primacy for possible Existenz.

We recognize the primacy of the empirical I as compelled by the needs of existence, but we recognize it relatively, and not for philosophizing itself.

Consciousness at large will be paramount as a requisite of any being for me as the subject. The following two trains of thought may illustrate the meaning of this formal paramountcy that covers all subjectiveness and objectiveness. First, I not only exist like any living thing; I also know that I exist. I can conceive the possibility of my nonexistence. If I try to think of myself as not being at all, however, I notice that in allowing the rest of the world to stand I am involuntarily letting myself stand as well, as a point in consciousness at large for which the world would be. Then I go on to think of the possibility that there were no being at all. But while I can say this, I cannot really think it either, because I still keep thinking as this "I"—as if I had being even though the world had not. Each time, the questioner remains extant as consciousness at large, while it seems that all other being can really be thought out of existence. The thinker's consciousness at large is entitled to its specific primacy in the limited sense that we can temporarily conceive it as the ultimate being without which there is no other.

In philosophizing, the I of possible Existenz has the decidedly dominant function of breaking through the circle of objective and subjective being, toward the being-in-itself which in that circle can be only negatively defined. Possible Existenz may perhaps open the positive way that is closed to consciousness at large in the world of objects. This kind of philosophizing is as nothing for empirical existence, and a groundless figment of the imagination for consciousness at large. But for possible Existenz it is the way to itself, and to being.

2. Existenz

Existenz is the never objectified source of my thoughts and actions. It is that whereof I speak in trains of thought that involve no cognition. It is what relates to itself, and thus to its transcendence.*

––––––––

*No definable concept—which would presuppose some kind of objective being—can express the being of Existenz. The very word is just one of the German synonyms for "being." The philosophical idea began obscurely, as a

Can something be, and yet not be a real object among objects? Obviously it cannot be the "I am" we conceive as empirical existence or consciousness at large, as comprehensible and deducible. The question is whether all the objective and subjective conceptions of being have brought me to the end, or whether my self can be manifested to me in yet another fashion. We are touching what seems to me the pivotal point of the sense of philosophizing.

To be means to decide about being. It is true that, as I observe myself, I am the way I am; although an individual, I am a case of something general, subject to causality or responding to the valid challenge of objectively fixed commandments. But where I am my own origin, everything has not yet been settled in principle, in accordance with general laws. It is not only due to the infinity of conditions that I do not know how it might be, had it been settled. On quite a different plane it is still my own self that decides what it is.

This thought—impossible to conceive objectively—is the sense of *freedom* of possible Existenz. In this sense I cannot think that, after all, everything takes its course, and that I might therefore do just as I please and vindicate my action by whatever general arguments come to hand. Instead, for all the dependence and determinacy of my existence, I feel sure that ultimately something rests with me alone. What I do or forgo, what I want first and foremost, where I cling to options and where I proceed to realizations—all this results neither from general rules I act upon, as right, nor from psychological laws to which I am subject. It does spring, in the restlessness of my existence and by the certainty of self-being, from freedom. Where I stop observing myself psychologically and still do not act with unconscious naïveté; where I act positively, rather, soaring with a bright assurance that gives me nothing to know but sustains my own being—there I decide what I am.

I know a kind of appeal to which my true self inwardly responds by the realization of my being. But it is not as an isolated being that I come to sense what I am. Against my self-will, against the accident of my empirical existence, I experience myself in *communication*. I am never more sure of being myself than at

––––––––

mere inkling of what Kierkegaard's use of the word has since made historically binding upon us.

times of total readiness for another, when I come to myself because the other too comes to himself in our revealing struggle.

As possible Existenz I seize upon the *historicity* of my existence. From the mere diversity of knowable realities it will expand to an existential depth. What is outwardly definite and delimiting is inwardly the appearance of true being. The man who loves mankind only does not love at all, but one who loves a particular human being does. We are not yet faithful if we are rationally consistent and will keep agreements; we are faithful if we accept as our own, and know ourselves bound to, what we have done and loved. A will to reorganize the world properly and permanently is no will at all; a proper will is to seize as my own whatever chances my historic situation offers.

If I am rooted in historicity, my temporal existence carries no weight in and by itself: but it does carry weight in the sense that *in time I decide for eternity.* What is time, then? As the future, it is possibility; as the past, it is the bond of fidelity; as the present, it is decision. Time, then, is not something that merely passes; it is the *phenomenality of Existenz.* Existenz is gained in time, by our own decisions. Once temporality has this weight and I know it, I have overcome temporality—not by replacing it with an abstract timelessness, not by putting myself outside of time, but by the fact that in time I stand above time. In my conscious life, governed by vital urges and the finite will to be happy, I want time to last as though deliverance from the anxieties of existence were found in blind permanence. I can no more eliminate this will from my living consciousness than I can void the sorrows of mortality. They are part of my existence as such. But if, in time, I act and love absolutely, time is eternal. This is something my intellect cannot grasp, something that will light up only at the moment, and afterwards only in doubtful remembrance. It is no outward possession, to have and to hold.

There is a distinguishing formula, meaningless to intellectual consciousness at large, but an appeal to possible Existenz. It goes as follows: real being loses its reality in all objective cognition, turning into endless duration, into laws of nature, or into the nonbeing of mere transience; but Existenz is realized in choices made in temporal historicity. Thus, despite its objective disappearance, Existenz achieves reality as fulfilled time. Eternity is neither timelessness nor duration for all time; it is the depth of time as the historic appearance of Existenz.

3. World and Existenz

Existenz will find itself with other Existenz in the mundane situation, without coming to be recognizable as mundane being. What is in the world appears as being to my consciousness at large, but only a transcending possible Existenz can be sure of Existenz.

Being that compels recognition exists directly. I can take hold of it, can make something of it, and with it—technically with things, or in arguing with myself and with other consciousness. In it lies the *resistance* of anything given, whether the real resistance of empirical reality or the resistance of logical necessities or impossibilities. It is always objective being, an original object or an adequate objectification like the models or types that serve as research tools, for instance.

Existenz, which in itself does not exist, *appears* to possible Existenz as existence. In our minds, of course, we cannot close the gap between world and Existenz, between things we can know and things we can elucidate, between objective being and the free being of Existenz. In fact, however, the two modes of being are so close together that a consciousness which is also possible Existenz will find the distinction an infinite task whose performance combines the cognition of mundane being with the elucidation of Existenz.

It is only abstractly that we can formulate the distinction of objective being and the free being of Existenz. We can say, for instance, that objective being is given as mechanism, life, and consciousness, while I as Existenz am original—not original being, but my own origin in existence. Measured by the being of things, there is no freedom; measured by freedom, the being of things is not true being. Or we can say that extant being and free being are not two antithetical kinds of being which might be coordinated. They are interrelated but flatly incomparable; being in the sense of objectivity and being in the sense of freedom exclude one another. The one steps from time into timelessness or endless duration; the other steps from time into eternity. What is for all time, or valid, is objectiveness; what is evanescent and yet eternal is Existenz. We can say that one is for a thinking subject only, while the other, though never without an object, is real only for communicating Existenz.

From the view of the world, any appearance of Existenz is merely objective being. From that viewpoint we see consciousness and the subjective I, but not Existenz; from there we cannot even understand what is meant by Existenz. *From the point of view of Existenz,* its own being is merely something that appears in existence, an existence that is not an appearance of Existenz, and is not its true self, but is recreant. It is as though originally all existence should be Existenz, and as though whatever part of it is nothing but existence could be understood as depleted, entangled, bereft of Existenz.

There is no pointer to lead us from objective being to another kind of being, unless it be done indirectly, by the disjointness and inconclusiveness of objective being. But Existenz does permeate the forms of that being as media of its realization, and as possibilities of its appearance. Standing *on the borderline of world and Existenz,* possible Existenz views all existence as more than existence. Proceeding from the most remote, from the mechanism, being will approach itself, so to speak, via life and consciousness, seeking to find itself in Existenz as what it is. Or—while consciousness at large conceives existence from this borderline as pure existence—it may be the character of all existence to be potentially relevant for Existenz by providing the impulse for it or serving as its medium.

There can be no Existenz without other Existenz, and yet objectively it makes no sense to speak of it as manifold. For whenever Existenz and Existenz communicate historically in the dark of mundane being, they are one for the other only, invalid for any watching consciousness at large. What is invisible from outside is not surveyable as a being of many.

On the one side, possible Existenz can see the being of the world, split into modes of being, in the medium of consciousness at large; on the other side is every Existenz. *On no side is there a conclusive being,* neither objectively as the one mundane existence nor existentially as a conceivable and surveyable world of all Existenz. If I think of being, it will always be a distinct being, not *the* being. In the ascertainment of possible Existenz I do not have an Existenz for an object, nor do I make sure of an Existenz at all. I only make sure of myself and of the Existenz I communicate with; we are what simply admits of no substitution; we are not cases of a species. Existenz is a sign pointing toward this self-ascertainment of a being that is objectively

neither conceivable nor valid—a being that no man knows or can meaningfully claim, either in himself or in others.

BEING

We have found no one answer to the question we raised at the start: what is being? An answer to this question satisfies the questioner if it allows him to recognize his own being. But the question of being itself is not unequivocal; it depends upon who asks it. It has no original meaning for our existing consciousness at large, which we can break up into the multiplicity of distinct being. It is only with possible Existenz, in transcending all existence and all objective being, that the impassioned search for being-in-itself begins—only to fall short of the goal of definite knowledge. Whatever exists is phenomenal; it is *appearance,* not being. And yet it is not nothing.

1. Appearance and Being

The sense of "appearance" in such statements has its categorial derivation in a particular, objective relationship: between the way something appears from a standpoint, as a phenomenon, and the way it is in itself, regardless of the standpoint. In an objectifying sense, then, phenomenality is the aspect of a mental addendum, of something we have to think as objectively underlying but not yet objective itself—something I conceive as an object only because, in principle, I might come to know it as such (as the atom, for instance).

It is in the category of appearance—using it to transcend this definite objectifying relation of phenomenal and underlying elements—that we conceive all being when we seek being as such.

Even so, the being that appears will remain twofold. In temporal existence we cannot overcome the duality of the inaccessible being-in-itself of *transcendence*—which we cannot conceive as the objectively underlying addendum—and the self-being manifest to Existenz, which is not existing consciousness. Existenz and transcendence are heterogeneous, but interrelated. Their relationship appears in existence.

As an object of science, existence is the appearance of something *theoretically* underlying. Science has no access to Existenz, nor to transcendence. But in a philosophical sense the appearance of being-in-itself results from the scientific cognition of a phenomenon *plus* the conception of the underlying addendum. In the scientific study of phenomena we think up the underlying addendum; in philosophizing we use the phenomena to touch being in our interpretation of *ciphers of transcendence,* and in the thinking that *appeals to Existenz.*

Nor is the consciousness we study the same consciousness in which I am sure of self-being and aware of transcendence. There is no unconscious Existenz, but consciousness as an object of scientific cognition is never that existential consciousness. This is why I, the single living individual existing for objective research, can turn, for myself, into the encompassing medium of all being when my consciousness is the psychologically inaccessible absolute assurance of Existenz. For the same reason, the statement that nothing lies outside consciousness is untrue if I understand consciousness as a mere research object. The statement is true in the sense that for me there is only what becomes phenomenal and thus enters into my consciousness. It is in going beyond its own explorable existence that consciousness begins and ends its contact with the unexplorable. For science this is the unconscious with its many meanings; for Existenz, it is transcendence. Yet this supplement to consciousness will of necessity be conscious again—for science as a theory of the unconscious, and for Existenz as the cipher of being in a self-contradictory and thus evanescent form.

The phrase "appearance of being" must be understood as ambiguous if we are to grasp the thesis that *Existenz appears in its own consciousness.* It means neither the appearance of an underlying objectivity nor of a transcendent being-in-itself.

On the one hand, Existenz cannot be psychologically understood as a conscious phenomenon. Only the forms of the existence of consciousness can be objects of psychology—its causally conditioned and intelligibly motivated experiences, but not its existential ground. Instead, in psychological research we think up an underlying unconscious, which we consider the reality of consciousness. In an objectifying sense, consciousness is the phenomenon of this underlying addendum, the way in which it appears. In an existential sense, however, appearance means a way of becoming conscious, a way of having been objectified,

in which a simultaneously and wholly present being understands itself. I know eternally what in this way is never known objectively. I am what appears in this way—not as something underlying, but as myself. We group the appearance of consciousness as a research object with the underlying, which to us is outright alien. And we group the appearance of Existenz with what we are originally, what we will answer for. The appearance of the underlying objectivity is generally valid for cognition; the appearance of Existenz is manifest in existential communication.

On the other hand, as the appearance in consciousness of its *subjective* being, Existenz can be sure of itself only in relation to transcendent being-in-itself. This it can feel but cannot be. What manifests itself to Existenz is not plain, straightforward being; it is being that addresses Existenz—itself no more than a subjective appearance—as a possibility.

Appearance is heterogeneous. The underlying objectivity appears in phenomena, transcendent being-in-itself in ciphers, Existenz in the assurance of absolute consciousness. In each direction, this heterogeneousness voids the stability of being. In its entirety it will keep being definitively *disjoint for the questioner as possible Existenz in temporal existence,* even at the root of his search.

2. Being and the Many Modes of Being

In thinking about our question, what is being, we may try to *take one thing for being as such* and all other being for derivative. There are many possible ways to try this, but none to carry it through. Suppose, for instance, I were to equate intrinsic being with objective knowability and to regard myself as derived from the objects, thus making a thing of myself and denying all freedom. Or suppose I were to turn the freedom of the subject into original being, and to derive things from that. Each time, the derivation of one from the other would be a fantastic leap. I can neither comprehend myself by the being of things, nor can I take all things to be myself. Instead, I am in the world; there are things that exist for me; I do make original decisions as a possible Existenz that appears to itself in the world. No rudiment of being enables me to comprehend all the being I find myself in. This is my situation, which I must not forget as I philosophize.

Our search for being started out from manifold being and led back to it, as to the modes of being. If we did not find being, there is still the question *why everything is called being* even though it cannot be brought under one principle or derived from one origin.

The fact we face here is that any statement is made in the form of language. Whatever we may be discussing will take the form of a definite sentence with the predicate "is"—even if the sentence refers to no being at all, even if it is an indirect suggestion or if it connects a train of thought that may be illustrative as a whole but that does not define an object as the one referred to.

Language is the phenomenal form of all thought. Whether in objective cognition or in nonobjective elucidation—in either case I am thinking. And what I think I have to think in *categories.* These are basic definitions of all thought; there is no superior category of which the rest might be species or derivations; but what they have in common, what defines them, is that they will always state a being. It is thought itself which in some sense is one and will accordingly call heterogeneous being—though no common concept of it is discoverable—by the one name of being.

As we think in categories, the question is whether our thoughts are adequately or inadequately categorized. We have to distinguish between, on the one hand, what is directly what it is, what is to be discovered and then to be straightforwardly discussed in categories—and on the other hand, what is not such an object but will be discussed just the same, in an indirect way, open to misunderstanding, and necessarily also in categories. Schematically we can formulate the distinction as follows: The *discovery of being* is scientific cognition; it gives us our bearings in the world and will always more or less adequately grasp a definite being. The *ascertainment of being* is philosophizing as the transcending of objectivity; in the medium of categories it grasps inadequately, in substituted objectivities, what can never become objective.

Methodologically, therefore, the genuine philosophical steps are to be grasped as modes of transcending. What they express regarding content, from the existential source of an absolute consciousness, is a being that employs such thought for its self-ascertainment as intrinsic being.

As possible Existenz comes to itself by way of philosophizing, it cannot exchange its freedom for the stifling narrowness of a being known as intrinsic. It will always be freedom, not cognition, that lets us experience what proper being is. The impulse behind our dissection of the concepts of being is to loosen our consciousness, to experiment with possibilities so as to get at the root of true philosophizing and there to *search* for the one being, as being proper.

We can approach being either by its *dilution* into everything of which we can indefinitely say it "is," or by its *fixation* into a categorially *defined* being that is known, or by the accentuation of *true* being, which is ascertained in thought. We differentiate, accordingly, between definite and indefinite being, between the various definitions, and between the true and the trivial.

True being cannot be found in a sense that we might know. It is to be sought in its *transcendence,* to which only Existenz, not consciousness at large, can ever relate.

One might suppose that any meaningful thinking must indirectly aim at this transcendence if it is not to deteriorate into vacuous intellectual gamesmanship and indifferent factuality. It could be that the designation of all being as being, with no noticeable common denominator save the form of language—that this most tenuous appearance of being in our speech indicates how deeply rooted all of it is in the one being. But these are indefinite thoughts, unless they already signify a transcending. For all categories can be used as means to transcend themselves, to dissolve their particularity in a unity that has neither an existence in the world nor a meaning in logic—namely, in the one being of transcendence which enters only the soul of a historic Existenz, if anything. From there it pervades meaning and existence, seeming to confirm them both, and then again to fracture and dissolve them both.

Ontology as a doctrine of being can achieve only one result nowadays: to make us conscious of being by the modes of being that occur to our thought. In the performance of this task it never touches the one being; it only clears the way for its ascertainment. Today's ontology will not be metaphysics any more; it will be a doctrine of categories. Whatever I may be thinking can only make room for the "I" as possible Existenz—which is outside my every thought at the same time. To possible Existenz, thoughts mean relative knowabilities, possibilities, appeals, but no more. In the same way, my partner in communicative thinking will stay outside his thoughts, for himself and for me, in order to move with me in possible thoughts and not to be subjected to absolute ones. To meet in communication is to break through the thought that made the breakthrough possible.

Existenz
from Philosophy

MUNDANE EXISTENCE AND EXISTENZ

If by "world" I mean the sum of all that cognitive orientation can reveal to me as cogently knowable for everyone, the question arises whether the being of the world is all there is. Does cognitive thinking stop with world orientation? What we refer to in mythical terms as the soul and God, and in philosophical language as Existenz and transcendence, is not of this world. Neither one is knowable, in the sense of things in the world. Yet both might have another kind of being. They need not be nothing, even though they are not known. They could be objects of thought, if not of cognition.

What is there, as against all mundane being? In the answer to this question lies the basic decision of philosophy.

We answer: there is the being which in the phenomenality of existence *is not* but *can be, ought to be,* and therefore decides in time whether it is in eternity.

This being is myself as *Existenz.* I am Existenz if I do not become an object for myself. In Existenz I know, without being able to see it, that what I call my "self" is independent. The possibility of Existenz is what I live by; it is only in its realization that I am myself. Attempts to comprehend it make it vanish, for it is not a psychological subject. I feel more deeply rooted in its possibility than in my self-objectifying grasp of my nature and my character. Existenz appears to itself as existence, in the polarity of subjectivity and objectivity; but it is not the appearance of an object given anywhere, or uncoverable as underlying any reflection. It is phenomenal only for itself and for other Existenz.

It is thus not my existence that is Existenz; but, *being human,* I am possible Existenz *in existence.* I exist or I do not exist, but my Existenz, as a possibility, takes a step toward being or away from being, toward nothingness, in every choice or decision I

make. My existence differs from other existence in scope; my world can be broad or narrow. But Existenz differs from other Existenz in essence, because of its freedom. As existence I live and die; my Existenz is unaware of death but soars or declines in relation to its being. Existence exists empirically, Existenz as freedom only. Existence is wholly temporal, while Existenz, in time, is more than time. My existence is finite, since it is not all existence, and yet, for me, it is concluded within itself. Existenz is not everything and not for itself alone either, for its being depends on its relation to other Existenz and to transcendence—the wholly Other that makes it aware of being not by itself alone—but while existence may be termed infinite as a relatively rounded endlessness, the infinity of Existenz is unrounded, an open possibility. Action on the ground of possible Existenz disconcerts me in existence; as existence, concerned with enduring in time, I cannot but turn against the doubtful path of unconditionality that may be costly, even ruinous, in existence. My concern with existence tends to make existential actions conditional upon the preservation of my existence; but to possible Existenz, the unqualified enjoyment of existence is already apostasy; to Existenz, the condition of its reality in existence is that it comprehends itself as unconditional. If I merely want to exist, without qualifications, I am bound to despair when I see that the reality of my existence lies in total foundering.

Existence is fulfilled in *mundane being;* to possible Existenz, the world is the field of its phenomenality.

The *known* world is the alien world. I am *detached* from it. What my intellect can know and what I can experience empirically repulses me as such, and I am irrelevant to it. Subject to overpowering causality in the realm of reality and to logical compulsion in the realm of validity, I am not sheltered in either. I hear no kindred language, and the more determined I am to comprehend the world, the more homeless will it make me feel; as the Other, as nothing but the world, it holds no comfort. Unfeeling, neither merciful nor unmerciful, subject to laws or floundering in coincidence, it is unaware of itself. I cannot grasp it, for it faces me impersonally, explicable in particulars but never intelligible as a whole.

And yet *there is another way in which I know the world.* It is akin to me then; I am at home in it and even sheltered in it. Its laws are the laws of my own reason. I find peace as I adjust to it, as I make my tools and expand my cognition of the world. It will speak to me now; it breathes a life that I share. I give myself up to it, and when I am in it I am with myself. It is familiar in small, present things, and thrilling in its grandeur; it will make me unwary in proximity or tend to sweep me along to its far reaches. Its ways are not the ways I expect, but though it may startle me with undreamed of fulfillments and incomprehensible failures, I shall trust it even as I perish.

This is no longer the world I know about in purely cognitive orientation. But my contentment in dealing with it is ambiguous. I may *crave* the world as the font of my joy of living, may be drawn to it and deceived about it by my blind will to live. I can indeed not exist without this craving, but as an absolute impulse it becomes self-destructive; it is against this impulse that my possible Existenz warns me to detach myself from the world lest I become its prey. Or, *in the world* that is so close to me, so much my kin, I may set out to *transcend* the world. Whether seeing it, thinking about it, acting and loving, producing and developing in it—in all that, then, I deal with something else at the same time, with a phenomenon of the transcendence that speaks to me. This is not a world I know but one that seems to have lost its continuity. It will change according to times and persons, and depending on my inner attitudes; it does not say the same things to all men, and not the same things at all times. I must be ready for it if I want to hear it. If I withhold myself, the very thing I might transcend to will withdraw. For it is only for freedom and by freedom, and there is nothing cogent about it at all.

Possible Existenz thus *sets itself off* from the world in order to find the right way into the world. It cuts loose from the world so that its grasp of the world will give it more than the world can be. The world attracts Existenz as the medium of its realization, and repels it as its possible decay to mere existence. There is a tension between the world and Existenz. They cannot become one, and they cannot separate either.

In philosophizing on the ground of possible Existenz we presuppose this tension. The world, as *what can be known,* and Existenz, as *what must be elucidated,* are dialectically distinguished and then reconsidered as one.

Mundane being, the being we know, is *general* because it is generally valid for everyone. It is the common property of all rational creatures who can agree on its being the same thing they mean. Its validity

applies, in the endlessness of real things, to the definable particular.

Existenz is *never general,* and thus not a case that might be subsumed as particular under a universal. Objectified as a phenomenon, however, Existenz is also the individuality of the historic particular. We still comprehend this under general categories, limited only by the endlessness of individual factuality, which makes the individual inexhaustible and thus ineffable. But individuality as such is not Existenz. All that it is, to begin with, is the visible profusion of mundane existence—a profusion whose existential originality can be examined by the questioner's self-being, but not by any knowledge.

The union of Existenz and the world is the incalculable process of which no one who is a part of it can be sure.

POSSIBLE EXISTENZ UNSATISFIED IN EXISTENCE

1. Doubts of the Being of Existenz

Once we divorce Existenz from existence, from the world, and from a general character, there seems to be nothing left. Unless Existenz becomes an object, it seems a vain hope to think of it; such thinking cannot last or produce results, so the attempted conception of Existenz seems bound to destroy itself. We can doubt the being of Existenz in every respect and let common sense tell us to stick to objectivity as both real and true. Was the attempt the outgrowth of a chimera?

There is no way to remove our doubts about Existenz. It is neither knowable as existence nor extant as validity. We can deny Existenz as we can deny the content of any philosophical thought—as opposed to particular objective cognition, whose object is demonstrable. I can never say of myself what I am, as if I were demonstrably extant. Whatever can be said of me by way of objectification applies to my empirical individuality, and as this can be the phenomenon of my Existenz, it is not a subject to any definitive psychological analysis either—a limit of my self-knowledge which indirectly points to something else, without ever being able to compel that something to become apparent. Hence the elucidation of Existenz is a deliverance but not a fulfillment, as knowledge would be; it widens my scope, but it does not create substance by demonstrating any being that I might objectively comprehend.

Since Existenz is thus inaccessible to one who asks about it in terms of the purely objective intellect, it remains subject to lasting doubt. Yet though no proof can force me to admit its being, my thinking is still not an end: it gets beyond the bounds of objective knowability in a *leap* that exceeds the capacity of rational insight. Philosophizing begins and ends at a point to which that leap takes me. Existenz is the *origin* of existential philosophizing, not its goal. Nor is its origin the same as its beginning, beyond which I would go on asking for an earlier beginning; it is not my license either, which would drive me to despair, and it is not a will resulting from the endlessness of questionable motivations. The origin is free being. This is what I transcend to as *philosophizing, not knowing, brings me to myself.* The helplessness to which philosophizing reduces me when I doubt its origin is an expression of the helplessness of my self-being, and the reality of philosophizing is the incipient upsurge of that self-being. The premise of philosophizing, therefore, is to *take hold* of Existenz—which begins as no more than a dark striving for sense and support, turns into doubt and despair as reminders of its derivation from the realm of possibility, and then appears as the incomprehensible certainty that is elucidated in philosophizing.

2. Being Unsatisfied as an Expression of Possible Existenz

If I reduce all things to mundane existence, either in theory or in practice, I feel unsatisfied. This feeling is a negative origin; in separating Existenz from mundane existence it makes me sense the truth of that separation. As there is no knowledge for which the world is conclusive, no "right" order of existence that could possibly be definitive, and no absolute final goal that all might see as one, I cannot help getting more unsatisfied the clearer I am in my mind about what I know, and the more honest I am about the sense of what I am doing.

No reasons will sufficiently explain this feeling. It expresses the being of possible Existenz, which understands itself, not something else, when it declares itself unsatisfied. What I feel then is not the impotence of knowledge. It is not the emptiness at the end of

all my achievements in a world in which I face the brink of nothingness. Instead, I feel a discontent that eggs me on.

An inexplicable discontent is a step out of mere existence, the step into the *solitude of possibility* where all mundane existence disappears. This solitude is not the resignation of the scientist who buries his hopes for a cognition of intrinsic being. It is not the irritation of the man of action who has come to doubt the point of all action. Nor is it the grief of a man in flight from himself and loath to be alone. Instead, after all these disillusionments, it is my dissatisfaction with existence at large, *my need to have my own origin.* To be unsatisfied is a condition inadequate to existence, and when this condition has opposed me to the world, it is my freedom that conquers all disenchantment and returns me to the world, to my fellow man with whom I ascertain the origin. I do not, however, comprehend all this in thoughtful reflection—which is indeed what fails me—but in the reality of my actions and in total foundering.

This possible conquest alone lends substance and significance to the otherwise irremovable relativity of theoretical *knowledge* and practical *action.*

I may well derive a peculiar and profound satisfaction from a theoretical knowledge of things in general, from surveying world images, from contemplating forms and existence, and from expanding all of this farther and farther, under ideas. But it is my dissatisfaction that makes me feel that this whole world, for all its universality and validity, is not all of being. My attitude in it is not one of curiosity about every particular, shared with a fellow scientist who might be interchangeable according to his function; it is an attitude of original curiosity about being itself, shared with a friend. What grips me is a communion in asking and answering questions, and a communication which within objective validity goes indirectly beyond it.

When I face objective tasks in *practical* life, when I deal with them and ask about their meaning, no meaning that I can grasp in the world will satisfy me. My sense of possible Existenz will not rest even if my conscious comprehension feeds on the idea of a whole in which I have my place and do my job. The thought of fulfillment in an entirety will come to be merely relative, like a temptation to conceal the boundary situations which break up any entirety. Though each idea of the whole is also a step beyond the fission into sheer coincidence, I am never able to survey the whole; eventually it will be back at the mercy of the accidents of mundane existence. A place within the whole, a place that would lend importance to the individual as a member of the body of this kind of being, is always questionable. But what remains to me as an individual is what never fits into a whole: the choice of my tasks and my striving for accomplishment are simultaneous manifestations of *another* origin, unless the annihilating thought that all I do might be senseless makes me shut my eyes. While I devote my empirical individuality to my finite tasks, my possible Existenz is more than that empirical individuality, and more than the objective, realistic impersonality of my political, scientific, or economic achievements. Although its essence is realized solely by this participation in the historic process of mundane existence, Existenz is at war with the lower depths of the encompassing world in which it finds itself. It is against those depths that, failing in the world, it seeks to hold its own in the eternity of intrinsic being.

Not unless it is indeed unsatisfied—both theoretically, with the mere knowledge and contemplation of all things in the world, and practically, with the mere performance of a task in an ideal entirety—can possible Existenz *utter* and understand this dissatisfaction. It is never *motivated* by generally valid reasons; those rather tend to induce contentment and tranquillity in the totality of a mundane existence permeated by the idea and thus spiritualized. The discontent of possible self-being has broken through mundane existence and cast the individual back upon himself, back to the origin that lets him deal with his world and, with his fellow, realize his Existenz.

3. The Breakthrough Ascertained in Existential Elucidation

If I am unsatisfied and want to clarify this not just by setting myself apart but by positive thoughts on what this is all about, I come to existential elucidation.

As Existenz results from the real act of breaking through mundane existence, existential elucidation is the *thinking ascertainment* of that act. The breakthrough goes from possible Existenz to its realization, without being able to leave the borderline of possibility. To have its reality—although it is not objectively

demonstrable—in action itself is the peculiar quality of Existenz. In its philosophical elucidation we pursue each thought that leads to the breakthrough, no matter from what side.

a. The breakthrough occurs at the *limits* of mundane existence. Philosophical thinking leads up to such limits and puts us in mind of the experiences they involve and of the appeal they issue. From the situations in the world, it leads to "boundary situations"; from empirical consciousness, to "absolute consciousness"; from actions qualified by their purposes, to "unconditional actions."

b. But the breakthrough still does not lead us out of the world. It occurs in the world, and so philosophical thought follows the appearance of Existenz in the world, in "historic consciousness" and in the "tension of subjectivity and objectivity" in its existence.

c. The breakthrough is *original*. Events happen in the world, but in the breakthrough something is settled by me. Existenz is certain that no part of intrinsic being can stay unsettled for it as a phenomenon in temporal existence. For either I allow the course of things to decide *about* me—vanishing as myself, since there is no real decision when everything just *happens*—or I deal with being originally, as myself, with the feeling that there must be a decision. My thought, aimed at the origin, seeks to elucidate "freedom."

d. Nothing I know in the world can give me any reasons for my decision; but what I am to decide can be grasped in the medium of that knowledge. Existential elucidation pervades my existence in the world, not in the sense that what matters were now known, but so I can sense possibilities that may give me a grasp on truth—on what is true as I *become* true. "I myself" and "communication" as the premise of self-being are the things we try to cover in the fundamental thoughts of all existential elucidation.

· · ·

MAURICE MERLEAU-PONTY (1908–1961)

Maurice Merleau-Ponty was born in Rochefort-sur-mer. Like Sartre, he was educated at the Ecole Normale Superieure, and with Sartre and de Beauvoir he co-founded *Les Temps Modernes.* Although he was a

Catholic during the first part of his life, he withdrew from the church in the 1930s and became critical of Christianity. After the war, during which he served in the army, he taught at the University of Lyon, the Sorbonne, and the College de France.

In *Phenomenology of Perception* (1945), Merleau-Ponty draws on Gestalt psychology to develop his own account of perception. One of his targets is the sense-datum theory of perception. When I examine (say) a refrigerator at a particular time, the sense-datum theorist would be inclined to say that I have before consciousness a set of images with certain features such as color and shape. I put these images together and infer that there is an object before me with various properties, but what I perceive is limited to sense-data. In particular, it would be on the basis of an inference that I would conclude that the refrigerator has an inside compartment, if I were in no position at the moment to open the door and provide myself with relevant sense-data. Merleau-Ponty suggests a different story. When I examine the refrigerator, I perceive a multidimensional object that has a front, back, interior, and sides. I *perceive* the refrigerator *as having* an interior even though its door is closed at the moment. He draws on Marcel's emphasis that people are bodies in order to explain the fact that we perceive things as having properties that are not apparent. Merleau-Ponty's view is that perception takes the shape it does because we are embodied. Our embodiment allows us to move about and perceive things from different perspectives and predisposes perception to anticipate confronting objects that have properties that are not immediately apparent. Our perception is also shaped by the projects we freely choose. These projects shape the form in which the world of things appears to us and they also are responsible for the significance of the things in the world.

In the preface to his *Phenomenology of Perception* Merleau-Ponty describes the development of phenomenology from the work of Husserl and provides many helpful insights concerning Husserl's thought and the relationship between Husserl and Heidegger. In "Freedom," the final chapter in *Phenomenology of Perception*, Merleau-Ponty points out a consequence of the facts (a) that we freely choose our projects and (b) that these projects shape our world:

There is "ultimately nothing that set limits to freedom, except those limits that freedom itself has set in the form of its various initiatives, so that the subject has simply the external world that he gives himself." [17] He elaborates on the point that some of our free choices limit, and form the backdrop of, others. We freely choose projects and situations that then provide us with motives for further action. "Without the roots which [freedom] thrusts into the world, it would not be freedom at all." [18]

In "The Metaphysical in Man," from *Sense and Non-Sense,* Merleau-Ponty casts doubt on the idea that we may study humanity by taking up the perspective of "an absolute observer in whom all points of view are summed up and, correlatively, a true projection of all perspectives." In sensing another person, we do not posit an object whose features we may come to know through an investigation that will leave those features unaffected. Instead, the two of us enter into a relationship of "exchange and communication." The truth is itself something we decide upon in concert with others. Merleau-Ponty uses his view of knowledge to raise doubts about the common religious idea of a God who stands outside the world and whose observations of it constitute the absolute truth.

Preface
from Phenomenology of Perception

What is phenomenology? It may seem strange that this question has still to be asked half a century after the first works of Husserl. The fact remains that it has by no means been answered. Phenomenology is the study of essences; and according to it, all problems amount to finding definitions of essences: the essence of perception, or the essence of consciousness, for example. But phenomenology is also a philosophy which puts essences back into existence, and does not expect to arrive at an understanding of man and the

----

[17] Maurice Merleau-Ponty, *Phenomenology of Perception,* trans. Colin Smith (London: Routledge & Kegan Paul, 1962), 436.
[18] Ibid., 456.

world from any starting point other than that of their 'facticity'. It is a transcendental philosophy which places in abeyance the assertions arising out of the natural attitude, the better to understand them; but it is also a philosophy for which the world is always 'already there' before reflection begins—as an inalienable presence; and all its efforts are concentrated upon re-achieving a direct and primitive contact with the world, and endowing that contact with a philosophical status. It is the search for a philosophy which shall be a 'rigorous science', but it also offers an account of space, time and the world as we 'live' them. It tries to give a direct description of our experience as it is, without taking account of its psychological origin and the causal explanations which the scientist, the historian or the sociologist may be able to provide. Yet Husserl in his last works mentions a 'genetic phenomenology',* and even a 'constructive phenomenology'.† One may try to do away with these contradictions by making a distinction between Husserl's and Heidegger's phenomenologies; yet the whole of *Sein und Zeit* springs from an indication given by Husserl and amounts to no more than an explicit account of the 'natürlicher Weltbegriff' or the 'Lebenswelt' which Husserl, towards the end of his life, identified as the central theme of phenomenology, with the result that the contradiction re-appears in Husserl's own philosophy. The reader pressed for time will be inclined to give up the idea of covering a doctrine which says everything, and will wonder whether a philosophy which cannot define its scope deserves all the discussion which has gone on around it, and whether he is not faced rather by a myth or a fashion.

Even if this were the case, there would still be a need to understand the prestige of the myth and the origin of the fashion, and the opinion of the responsible philosopher must be that *phenomenology can be practised and identified as a manner or style of thinking, that it existed as a movement before arriving at complete awareness of itself as a philosophy.* It has been long on the way, and its adherents have discovered it in every quarter, certainly in Hegel and Kierkegaard, but equally in Marx, Nietzsche and Freud. A purely linguistic examination of the texts in question would

yield no proof; we find in texts only what we put into them, and if ever any kind of history has suggested the interpretations which should be put on it, it is the history of philosophy. We shall find in ourselves, and nowhere else, the unity and true meaning of phenomenology. It is less a question of counting up quotations than of determining and expressing in concrete form this *phenomenology for ourselves* which has given a number of present-day readers the impression, on reading Husserl or Heidegger, not so much of encountering a new philosophy as of recognizing what they had been waiting for. Phenomenology is accessible only through a phenomenological method. Let us, therefore, try systematically to bring together the celebrated phenomenological themes as they have grown spontaneously together in life. Perhaps we shall then understand why phenomenology has for so long remained at an initial stage, as a problem to be solved and a hope to be realized.

It is a matter of describing, not of explaining or analysing. Husserl's first directive to phenomenology, in its early stages, to be a 'descriptive psychology', or to return to the 'things themselves', is from the start a rejection of science. I am not the outcome or the meeting-point of numerous causal agencies which determine my bodily or psychological make-up. I cannot conceive myself as nothing but a bit of the world, a mere object of biological, psychological or sociological investigation. I cannot shut myself up within the realm of science. All my knowledge of the world, even my scientific knowledge, is gained from my own particular point of view, or from some experience of the world without which the symbols of science would be meaningless. The whole universe of science is built upon the world as directly experienced, and if we want to subject science itself to rigorous scrutiny and arrive at a precise assessment of its meaning and scope, we must begin by reawakening the basic experience of the world of which science is the second-order expression. Science has not and never will have, by its nature, the same significance *qua* form of being as the world which we perceive, for the simple reason that it is a rationale or explanation of that world. I am, not a 'living creature' nor even a 'man', nor again even 'a consciousness' endowed with all the characteristics which zoology, social anatomy or inductive psychology recognize in these various products of the natural or historical process—I am the absolute source, my

---

* *Méditations cartésiennes*, pp. 120 ff.
† See the unpublished *6th Méditation cartésienne*, edited by Eugen Fink, to which G. Berger has kindly referred us.

existence does not stem from my antecedents, from my physical and social environment; instead it moves out towards them and sustains them, for I alone bring into being for myself (and therefore into being in the only sense that the word can have for me) the tradition which I elect to carry on, or the horizon whose distance from me would be abolished—since that distance is not one of its properties—if I were not there to scan it with my gaze. Scientific points of view, according to which my existence is a moment of the world's, are always both naïve and at the same time dishonest, because they take for granted, without explicitly mentioning it, the other point of view, namely that of consciousness, through which from the outset a world forms itself round me and begins to exist for me. To return to things themselves is to return to that world which precedes knowledge, of which knowledge always *speaks,* and in relation to which every scientific schematization is an abstract and derivative sign-language, as is geography in relation to the countryside in which we have learnt beforehand what a forest, a prairie or a river is.

This move is absolutely distinct from the idealist return to consciousness, and the demand for a pure description excludes equally the procedure of analytical reflection on the one hand, and that of scientific explanation on the other. Descartes and particularly Kant *detached* the subject, or consciousness, by showing that I could not possibly apprehend anything as existing unless I first of all experienced myself as existing in the act of apprehending it. They presented consciousness, the absolute certainty of my existence for myself, as the condition of there being anything at all; and the act of relating as the basis of relatedness. It is true that the act of relating is nothing if divorced from the spectacle of the world in which relations are found; the unity of consciousness in Kant is achieved simultaneously with that of the world. And in Descartes methodical doubt does not deprive us of anything, since the whole world, at least in so far as we experience it, is reinstated in the *Cogito,* enjoying equal certainty, and simply labelled 'thought of . . .'. But the relations between subject and world are not strictly bilateral: if they were, the certainty of the world would, in Descartes, be immediately given with that of the *Cogito,* and Kant would not have talked about his 'Copernican revolution'. Analytical reflection starts from our experience of the world and goes back to the subject as to a condition of possibility distinct

from that experience, revealing the all-embracing synthesis as that without which there would be no world. To this extent it ceases to remain part of our experience and offers, in place of an account, a reconstruction. It is understandable, in view of this, that Husserl, having accused Kant of adopting a 'faculty psychologism',* should have urged, in place of a noetic analysis which bases the world on the synthesizing activity of the subject, his own *'noematic reflection'* which remains within the object and, instead of begetting it, brings to light its fundamental unity.

The world is there before any possible analysis of mine, and it would be artificial to make it the outcome of a series of syntheses which link, in the first place sensations, then aspects of the object corresponding to different perspectives, when both are nothing but products of analysis, with no sort of prior reality. Analytical reflection believes that it can trace back the course followed by a prior constituting act and arrive, in the 'inner man'—to use Saint Augustine's expression—at a constituting power which has always been identical with that inner self. Thus reflection is carried away by itself and installs itself in an impregnable subjectivity, as yet untouched by being and time. But this is very ingenuous, or at least it is an incomplete form of reflection which loses sight of its own beginning. When I begin to reflect my reflection bears upon an unreflective experience; moreover my reflection cannot be unaware of itself as an event, and so it appears to itself in the light of a truly creative act, of a changed structure of consciousness, and yet it has to recognize, as having priority over its own operations, the world which is given to the subject because the subject is given to himself. The real has to be described, not constructed or formed. Which means that I cannot put perception into the same category as the syntheses represented by judgements, acts or predications. My field of perception is constantly filled with a play of colours, noises and fleeting tactile sensations which I cannot relate precisely to the context of my clearly perceived world, yet which I nevertheless immediately 'place' in the world, without ever confusing them with my daydreams. Equally constantly I weave dreams round things. I imagine people and things whose presence is not incompatible with

----

Logische Untersuchungen, Prolegomena zur reinen Logik, p. 93.

the context, yet who are not in fact involved in it: they are ahead of reality, in the realm of the imaginary. If the reality of my perception were based solely on the intrinsic coherence of 'representations', it ought to be for ever hesitant and, being wrapped up in my conjectures on probabilities, I ought to be ceaselessly taking apart misleading syntheses, and reinstating in reality stray phenomena which I had excluded in the first place. But this does not happen. The real is a closely woven fabric. It does not await our judgement before incorporating the most surprising phenomena, or before rejecting the most plausible figments of our imagination. Perception is not a science of the world, it is not even an act, a deliberate taking up of a position; it is the background from which all acts stand out, and is presupposed by them. The world is not an object such that I have in my possession the law of its making; it is the natural setting of, and field for, all my thoughts and all my explicit perceptions. Truth does not 'inhabit' only 'the inner man',* or more accurately, there is no inner man, man is in the world, and only in the world does he know himself. When I return to myself from an excursion into the realm of dogmatic common sense or of science, I find, not a source of intrinsic truth, but a subject destined to the world.

All of which reveals the true meaning of the famous phenomenological reduction. There is probably no question over which Husserl spent more time — or to which he more often returned, since the 'problematic of reduction' occupies an important place in his unpublished work. For a long time, and even in recent texts, the reduction is presented as the return to a transcendental consciousness before which the world is spread out and completely transparent, quickened through and through by a series of apperceptions which it is the philosopher's task to reconstitute on the basis of their outcome. Thus my sensation of redness is *perceived as* the manifestation of a certain redness experienced, this in turn as the manifestation of a red surface, which is the manifestation of a piece of red cardboard, and this finally is the manifestation or outline of a red thing, namely this book. We are to understand, then, that it is the apprehension of a certain *hylè,* as indicating a phenomenon of a higher degree, the *Sinngebung,* or active meaning-giving operation which may be said to define consciousness, so that the world is nothing but 'world-as-meaning', and the phenomenological reduction is idealistic, in the sense that there is here a transcendental idealism which treats the world as an indivisible unity of value shared by Peter and Paul, in which their perspectives blend. 'Peter's consciousness' and 'Paul's consciousness' are in communication, the perception of the world 'by Peter' is not Peter's doing any more than its perception 'by Paul' is Paul's doing; in each case it is the doing of pre-personal forms of consciousness, whose communication raises no problem, since it is demanded by the very definition of consciousness, meaning or truth. In so far as I am a consciousness, that is, in so far as something has meaning for me, I am neither here nor there, neither Peter nor Paul; I am in no way distinguishable from an 'other' consciousness, since we are immediately in touch with the world and since the world is, by definition, unique, being the system in which all truths cohere. A logically consistent transcendental idealism rids the world of its opacity and its transcendence. The world is precisely that thing of which we form a representation, not as men or as empirical subjects, but in so far as we are all one light and participate in the One without destroying its unity. Analytical reflection knows nothing of the problem of other minds, or of that of the world, because it insists that with the first glimmer of consciousness there appears in me theoretically the power of reaching some universal truth, and that the other person, being equally without thisness, location or body, the Alter and the Ego are one and the same in the true world which is the unifier of minds. There is no difficulty in understanding how *I* can conceive the Other, because the I and consequently the Other are not conceived as part of the woven stuff of phenomena; they have validity rather than existence. There is nothing hidden behind these faces and gestures, no domain to which I have no access, merely a little shadow which owes its very existence to the light. For Husserl, on the contrary, it is well known that there is a problem of other people, and the *alter ego* is a paradox. If the other is truly for himself alone, beyond his being for me, and if we are for each other and not both for God, we must necessarily have some appearance for each other. He must and I must have an outer appearance, and there must be, besides the

---

* In te redi; in interiore homine habitat veritas (Saint Augustine).

perspective of the For Oneself—my view of myself and the other's of himself—a perspective of For Others—my view of others and theirs of me. Of course, these two perspectives, in each one of us, cannot be simply juxtaposed, *for in that case it is not I that the other would see, nor he that I should see.* I must be the exterior that I present to others, and the body of the other must be the other himself. This paradox and the dialectic of the Ego and the Alter are possible only provided that the Ego and the Alter Ego are defined by their situation and are not freed from all inherence; that is, provided that philosophy does not culminate in a return to the self, and that I discover by reflection not only my presence to myself, but also the possibility of an 'outside spectator'; that is, again, provided that at the very moment when I experience my existence—at the ultimate extremity of reflection—I fall short of the ultimate density which would place me outside time, and that I discover within myself a kind of internal weakness standing in the way of my being totally individualized: a weakness which exposes me to the gaze of others as a man among men or at least as a consciousness among consciousnesses. Hitherto the *Cogito* depreciated the perception of others, teaching me as it did that the I is accessible only to itself, since it defined *me* as the thought which I have of myself, and which clearly I am alone in having, at least in this ultimate sense. For the 'other' to be more than an empty word, it is necessary that my existence should never be reduced to my bare awareness of existing, but that it should take in also the awareness that *one* may have of it, and thus include my incarnation in some nature and the possibility, at least, of a historical situation. The *Cogito* must reveal me in a situation, and it is on this condition alone that transcendental subjectivity can, as Husserl puts it,* be an intersubjectivity. As a meditating Ego, I can clearly distinguish from myself the world and things, since I certainly do not exist in the way in which things exist. I must even set aside from myself my body understood as a thing among things, as a collection of physico-chemical processes. But even if the *cogitatio,* which I thus discover, is without location in objective time and space, it is not without place in the phenomenological world. The world, which I distinguished

from myself as the totality of things or of processes linked by causal relationships, I rediscover 'in me' as the permanent horizon of all my *cogitationes* and as a dimension in relation to which I am constantly situating myself. The true *Cogito* does not define the subject's existence in terms of the thought he has of existing, and furthermore does not convert the indubitability of the world into the indubitability of thought about the world, nor finally does it replace the world itself by the world as meaning. On the contrary it recognizes my thought itself as an inalienable fact, and does away with any kind of idealism in revealing me as 'being-in-the-world'.

It is because we are through and through compounded of relationships with the world that for us the only way to become aware of the fact is to suspend the resultant activity, to refuse it our complicity (to look at it *ohne mitzumachen,* as Husserl often says), or yet again, to put it 'out of play'. Not because we reject the certainties of common sense and a natural attitude to things—they are, on the contrary, the constant theme of philosophy—but because, being the presupposed basis of any thought, they are taken for granted, and go unnoticed, and because in order to arouse them and bring them to view, we have to suspend for a moment our recognition of them. The best formulation of the reduction is probably that given by Eugen Fink, Husserl's assistant, when he spoke of 'wonder' in the face of the world.† Reflection does not withdraw from the world towards the unity of consciousness as the world's basis; it steps back to watch the forms of transcendence fly up like sparks from a fire; it slackens the intentional threads which attach us to the world and thus brings them to our notice; it alone is consciousness of the world because it reveals that world as strange and paradoxical. Husserl's transcendental is not Kant's and Husserl accuses Kant's philosophy of being 'worldly', because it *makes use* of our relation to the world, which is the motive force of the transcendental deduction, and makes the world immanent in the subject, instead of *being filled with wonder* at it and conceiving the subject as a process of transcendence towards the world. All the misunderstandings with his interpreters, with the existentialist 'dissidents' and finally with himself, have

---

* *Die Krisis der europäischen Wissenschaften und die transzendentale Phänomenologie,* III (unpublished).

† *Die phänomenologische Philosophie Edmund Husserls in der gegenwärtigen Kritik,* pp. 331 and ff.

arisen from the fact that in order to see the world and grasp it as paradoxical, we must break with our familiar acceptance of it and, also, from the fact that from this break we can learn nothing but the unmotivated upsurge of the world. The most important lesson which the reduction teaches us is the impossibility of a complete reduction. This is why Husserl is constantly re-examining the possibility of the reduction. If we were absolute mind, the reduction would present no problem. But since, on the contrary, we are in the world, since indeed our reflections are carried out in the temporal flux on to which we are trying to seize (since they *sich einströmen,* as Husserl says), there is no thought which embraces all our thought. The philosopher, as the unpublished works declare, is a perpetual beginner, which means that he takes for granted nothing that men, learned or otherwise, believe they know. It means also that philosophy itself must not take itself for granted, in so far as it may have managed to say something true; that it is an ever-renewed experiment in making its own beginning; that it consists wholly in the description of this beginning, and finally, that radical reflection amounts to a consciousness of its own dependence on an unreflective life which is its initial situation, unchanging, given once and for all. Far from being, as has been thought, a procedure of idealistic philosophy, phenomenological reduction belongs to existential philosophy: Heidegger's 'being-in-the-world' appears only against the background of the phenomenological reduction.

A misunderstanding of a similar kind confuses the notion of the 'essences' in Husserl. Every reduction, says Husserl, as well as being transcendental is necessarily eidetic. That means that we cannot subject our perception of the world to philosophical scrutiny without ceasing to be identified with that act of positing the world, with that interest in it which delimits us, without drawing back from our commitment which is itself thus made to appear as a spectacle, without passing from the *fact* of our existence to its *nature,* from the Dasein to the Wesen. But it is clear that the essence is here not the end, but a means, that our effective involvement in the world is precisely what has to be understood and made amenable to conceptualization, for it is what polarizes all our conceptual particularizations. The need to proceed by way of essences does not mean that philosophy takes them as its object, but, on the contrary, that our existence is

too tightly held in the world to be able to know itself as such at the moment of its involvement, and that it requires the field of ideality in order to become acquainted with and to prevail over its facticity. The Vienna Circle, as is well known, lays it down categorically that we can enter into relations only with meanings. For example, 'consciousness' is not for the Vienna Circle identifiable with what we are. It is a complex meaning which has developed late in time, which should be handled with care, and only after the many meanings which have contributed, throughout the word's semantic development, to the formation of its present one have been made explicit. Logical positivism of this kind is the antithesis of Husserl's thought. Whatever the subtle changes of meaning which have ultimately brought us, as a linguistic acquisition, the word and concept of consciousness, we enjoy direct access to what it designates. For we have the experience of ourselves, of that consciousness which we are, and it is on the basis of this experience that all linguistic connotations are assessed, and precisely through it that language comes to have any meaning at all for us. 'It is that as yet dumb experience . . . which we are concerned to lead to the pure expression of its own meaning.'* Husserl's essences are destined to bring back all the living relationships of experience, as the fisherman's net draws up from the depths of the ocean quivering fish and seaweed. Jean Wahl is is therefore wrong in saying that 'Husserl separates essences from existence'.† The separated essences are those of language. It is the office of language to cause essences to exist in a state of separation which is in fact merely apparent, since through language they still rest upon the ante-predicative life of consciousness. In the silence of primary consciousness can be seen appearing not only what words mean, but also what things mean: the core of primary meaning round which the acts of naming and expression take shape.

Seeking the essence of consciousness will therefore not consist in developing the *Wortbedeutung* of consciousness and escaping from existence into the universe of things said; it will consist in rediscovering my actual presence to myself, the fact of my con-

---

* *Méditations cartésiennes,* p. 33.
† *Réalisme, dialectique et mystère,* l'Arbalète, Autumn, 1942, unpaginated.

sciousness which is in the last resort what the word and the concept of consciousness mean. Looking for the world's essence is not looking for what it is as an idea once it has been reduced to a theme of discourse; it is looking for what it is as a fact for us, before any thematization. Sensationalism 'reduces' the world by noticing that after all we never experience anything but states of ourselves. Transcendental idealism too 'reduces' the world since, in so far as it guarantees the world, it does so by regarding it as thought or consciousness of the world, and as the mere correlative of our knowledge, with the result that it becomes immanent in consciousness and the aseity of things is thereby done away with. The eidetic reduction is, on the other hand, the determination to bring the world to light as it is before any falling back on ourselves has occurred, it is the ambition to make reflection emulate the unreflective life of consciousness. I aim at and perceive a world. If I said, as do the sensationalists, that we have here only 'states of consciousness', and if I tried to distinguish my perceptions from my dreams with the aid of 'criteria', I should overlook the phenomenon of the world. For if I am able to talk about 'dreams' and 'reality', to bother my head about the distinction between imaginary and real, and cast doubt upon the 'real', it is because this distinction is already made by me before any analysis; it is because I have an experience of the real as of the imaginary, and the problem then becomes one not of asking how critical thought can provide for itself secondary equivalents of this distinction, but of making explicit our primordial knowledge of the 'real', of describing our perception of the world as that upon which our idea of truth is forever based. We must not, therefore, wonder whether we really perceive a world, we must instead say: the world is what we perceive. In more general terms we must not wonder whether our self-evident truths are real truths, or whether, through some perversity inherent in our minds, that which is self-evident for us might not be illusory in relation to some truth in itself. For in so far as we talk about illusion, it is because we have identified illusions, and done so solely in the light of some perception which at the same time gave assurance of its own truth. It follows that doubt, or the fear of being mistaken, testifies as soon as it arises to our power of unmasking error, and that it could never finally tear us away from truth. We are in the realm of truth and it is 'the expe-

rience of truth' which is self-evident.* To seek the essence of perception is to declare that perception is, not presumed true, but defined as access to truth. So, if I now wanted, according to idealistic principles, to base this *de facto* self-evident truth, this irresistible belief, on some absolute self-evident truth, that is, on the absolute clarity which my thoughts have for me; if I tried to find in myself a creative thought which bodied forth the framework of the world or illumined it through and through, I should once more prove unfaithful to my experience of the world, and should be looking for what makes that experience possible instead of looking for what it is. The self-evidence of perception is not adequate thought or apodeictic self-evidence.† The world is not what I think, but what I live through. I am open to the world, I have no doubt that I am in communication with it, but I do not possess it; it is inexhaustible. 'There is a world', or rather: 'There is the world'; I can never completely account for this ever-reiterated assertion in my life. This facticity of the world is what constitutes the *Weltlichkeit der Welt*, what causes the world to be the world; just as the facticity of the *cogito* is not an imperfection in itself, but rather what assures me of my existence. The eidetic method is the method of a phenomenological positivism which bases the possible on the real.

We can now consider the notion of intentionality, too often cited as the main discovery of phenomenology, whereas it is understandable only through the reduction. 'All consciousness is consciousness of something'; there is nothing new in that. Kant showed, in the *Refutation of Idealism,* that inner perception is impossible without outer perception, that the world, as a collection of connected phenomena, is anticipated in the consciousness of my unity, and is the means whereby I come into being as a consciousness. What distinguishes intentionality from the Kantian relation to a possible object is that the unity of the world, before being posited by knowledge in a specific act of identification, is 'lived' as ready-made or already there. Kant himself shows in the *Critique of Judge-*

---

* *Das Erlebnis der Wahrheit* (*Logische Untersuchungen, Prolegomena zur reinen Logik*) p. 190.
† There is no apodeictic self-evidence, the *Formale und transzendentale Logik* (p. 142) says in effect.

ment that there exists a unity of the imagination and the understanding and a unity of subjects *before the object,* and that, in experiencing the beautiful, for example, I am aware of a harmony between sensation and concept, between myself and others, which is itself without any concept. Here the subject is no longer the universal thinker of a system of objects rigorously interrelated, the positing power who subjects the manifold to the law of the understanding, in so far as he is to be able to put together a world—he discovers and enjoys his own nature as spontaneously in harmony with the law of the understanding. But if the subject has a nature, then the hidden art of the imagination must condition the categorial activity. It is no longer merely the aesthetic judgement, but knowledge too which rests upon this art, an art which forms the basis of the unity of consciousness and of consciousnesses.

Husserl takes up again the *Critique of Judgement* when he talks about a teleology of consciousness. It is not a matter of duplicating human consciousness with some absolute thought which, from outside, is imagined as assigning to it its aims. It is a question of recognizing consciousness itself as a project of the world, meant for a world which it neither embraces nor possesses, but towards which it is perpetually directed—and the world as this pre-objective individual whose imperious unity decrees what knowledge shall take as its goal. This is why Husserl distinguishes between intentionality of act, which is that of our judgements and of those occasions when we voluntarily take up a position—the only intentionality discussed in the *Critique of Pure Reason*—and operative intentionality (*fungierende Intentionalität*), or that which produces the natural and antepredicative unity of the world and of our life, being apparent in our desires, our evaluations and in the landscape we see, more clearly than in objective knowledge, and furnishing the text which our knowledge tries to translate into precise language. Our relationship to the world, as it is untiringly enunciated within us, is not a thing which can be any further clarified by analysis; philosophy can only place it once more before our eyes and present it for our ratification.

Through this broadened notion of intentionality, phenomenological 'comprehension' is distinguished from traditional 'intellection', which is confined to 'true and immutable natures', and so phenomenology can become a phenomenology of origins. Whether we are concerned with a thing perceived, a historical event or a doctrine, to 'understand' is to take in the total intention—not only what these things are for representation (the 'properties' of the thing perceived, the mass of 'historical facts', the 'ideas' introduced by the doctrine)—but the unique mode of existing expressed in the properties of the pebble, the glass or the piece of wax, in all the events of a revolution, in all the thoughts of a philosopher. It is a matter, in the case of each civilization, of finding the Idea in the Hegelian sense, that is, not a law of the physico-mathematical type, discoverable by objective thought, but that formula which sums up some unique manner of behaviour towards others, towards Nature, time and death: a certain way of patterning the world which the historian should be capable of seizing upon and making his own. These are the *dimensions* of history. In this context there is not a human word, not a gesture, even one which is the outcome of habit or absentmindedness, which has not some meaning. For example, I may have been under the impression that I lapsed into silence through weariness, or some minister may have thought he had uttered merely an appropriate platitude, yet my silence or his words immediately take on a significance, because my fatigue or his falling back upon a ready-made formula are not accidental, for they express a certain lack of interest, and hence some degree of adoption of a definite position in relation to the situation.

When an event is considered at close quarters, at the moment when it is lived through, everything seems subject to chance: one man's ambition, some lucky encounter, some local circumstance or other appears to have been decisive. But chance happenings offset each other, and facts in their multiplicity coalesce and show up a certain way of taking a stand in relation to the human situation, reveal in fact an *event* which has its definite outline and about which we can talk. Should the starting-point for the understanding of history be ideology, or politics, or religion, or economics? Should we try to understand a doctrine from its overt content, or from the psychological make-up and the biography of its author? We must seek an understanding from all these angles simultaneously, everything has meaning, and we shall find this same structure of being underlying all relationships. All these views are true provided that they are not isolated, that we delve deeply into history and reach the unique core of existential meaning which emerges in each perspective. It is true, as Marx says, that history does not walk on its head, but it is also true that it does not think with its feet. Or one should say rather that it is neither its 'head' not its 'feet' that we have to worry about, but its body. All economic and psychological explanations of a doctrine are true, since the thinker never thinks from any starting-point but the one constituted by what he is. Reflection even on a doctrine will be complete only if it succeeds in linking up with the doctrine's history and the extraneous explanations of it, and in putting back the causes and meaning of the doctrine in an existential structure. There is, as Husserl says, a 'genesis of meaning' (*Sinngenesis*),* which alone, in the last resort, teaches us what the doctrine 'means.' Like understanding, criticism must be pursued at all levels, and naturally, it will be insufficient, for the refutation of a doctrine, to relate it to some accidental event in the author's life: its significance goes beyond, and there is no pure accident in existence or in co-existence, since both absorb random events and transmute them into the rational.

Finally, as it is indivisible in the present, history is equally so in its sequences. Considered in the light of its fundamental dimensions, all periods of history appear as manifestations of a single existence, or as episodes in a single drama—without our knowing whether it has an ending. Because we are in the world, we are *condemned to meaning,* and we cannot do or say anything without its acquiring a name in history.

Probably the chief gain from phenomenology is to have united extreme subjectivism and extreme objectivism in its notion of the world or of rationality. Rationality is precisely measured by the experiences in which it is disclosed. To say that there exists rationality is to say that perspectives blend, perceptions confirm each other, a meaning emerges. But it should not be set in a realm apart, transposed into absolute Spirit, or into a world in the realist sense. The phenomenological world is not pure being, but the sense which is revealed where the paths of my various experiences intersect, and also where my own and other people's intersect and engage each other like gears. It is thus inseparable from subjectivity and intersubjectivity, which find their unity when I either take up my past experiences in those of the present, or other people's in my own. For the first time the philosopher's thinking is sufficiently conscious not to anticipate itself and endow its own results with reified form in the world. The philosopher tries to conceive the world, others and himself and their interrelations. But the meditating Ego, the 'impartial spectator' (*uninteressierter Zuschauer*)[†] do not rediscover an already given rationality, they 'establish themselves',[‡] and establish it, by an act of initiative which has no guarantee in being, its justification resting entirely on the effective power which it confers on us of taking our own history upon ourselves.

The phenomenological world is not the bringing to explicit expression of a pre-existing being, but the laying down of being. Philosophy is not the reflection of a pre-existing truth, but, like art, the act of bringing truth into being. One may well ask how this creation is *possible,* and if it does not recapture in things a pre-existing Reason. The answer is that the only pre-existent Logos is the world itself, and that the philosophy which brings it into visible existence does not begin by being *possible;* it is actual or real like the world of which it is a part, and no explanatory hypothesis is clearer than the act whereby we take up this unfinished world in an effort to complete and conceive it. Rationality is not a *problem.* There is behind it no unknown quantity which has to be determined by deduction, or, beginning with it, demonstrated inductively. We witness every minute the miracle of related experiences, and yet nobody knows better than we do how this miracle is worked, for we are ourselves this network of relationships. The world and reason are not problematical. We may say, if we wish, that they are mysterious, but their mystery defines them: there can be no question of dispelling it by some 'solution', it is on the hither side of all solutions. True philosophy consists in re-learning to look at the world, and in this sense a historical account can give meaning to the world quite as 'deeply' as a philosophical treatise. We take our fate in our hands, we be-

---

* The usual term in the unpublished writings. The idea is already to be found in the *Formale und transzendentale Logik,* pp. 184 and ff.

[†] *6th Méditation cartésienne* (unpublished).
[‡] Ibid.

come responsible for our history through reflection, but equally by a decision on which we stake our life, and in both cases what is involved is a violent act which is validated by being performed.

Phenomenology, as a disclosure of the world, rests on itself, or rather provides its own foundation.* All knowledge is sustained by a 'ground' of postulates and finally by our communication with the world as primary embodiment of rationality. Philosophy, as radical reflection, dispenses in principle with this resource. As, however, it too is in history, it too exploits the world and constituted reason. It must therefore put to itself the question which it puts to all branches of knowledge, and so duplicate itself infinitely, being, as Husserl says, a dialogue or infinite meditation, and, in so far as it remains faithful to its intention, never knowing where it is going. The unfinished nature of phenomenology and the inchoative atmosphere which has surrounded it are not to be taken as a sign of failure, they were inevitable because phenomenology's task was to reveal the mystery of the world and of reason.† If phenomenology was a movement before becoming a doctrine or a philosophical system, this was attributable neither to accident, nor to fraudulent intent. It is as painstaking as the works of Balzac, Proust, Valéry or Cézanne—by reason of the same kind of attentiveness and wonder, the same demand for awareness, the same will to seize the meaning of the world or of history as that meaning comes into being. In this way it merges into the general effort of modern thought.

Freedom
from Phenomenology of Perception

Again, it is clear that no causal relationship is conceivable between the subject and his body, his world or his society. Only at the cost of losing the basis of all my certainties can I question what is conveyed to me by my presence to myself. Now the moment I turn to myself in order to describe myself, I have a glimpse of an anonymous flux,‡ a comprehensive project in which there are so far no 'states of consciousness', nor, *a fortiori*, qualifications of any sort. For myself I am neither 'jealous', nor 'inquisitive', nor 'hunchbacked', nor 'a civil servant'. It is often a matter of surprise that the cripple or the invalid can put up with himself. The reason is that such people are not for themselves deformed or at death's door. Until the final coma, the dying man is inhabited by a consciousness, he is all that he sees, and enjoys this much of an outlet. Consciousness can never objectify itself into invalid-consciousness or cripple-consciousness, and even if the old man complains of his age or the cripple of his deformity, they can do so only by comparing themselves with others, or seeing themselves through the eyes of others, that is, by taking a statistical and objective view of themselves, so that such complaints are never absolutely genuine: when he is back in the heart of his own consciousness, each one of us feels beyond his limitations and thereupon resigns himself to them. They are the price which we automatically pay for being in the world, a formality which we take for granted. Hence we may speak disparagingly of our looks and still not want to change our face for another. No idiosyncrasy can, seemingly, be attached to the insuperable generality of consciousness, nor can any limit be set to this immeasurable power of escape. In order to be determined (in the two senses of that word) by an external factor, it is necessary that I should be a thing. Neither my freedom nor my universality can admit of any eclipse. It is inconceivable that I should be free in certain of my actions and determined in others: how should we understand a dormant freedom that gave full scope to determinism? And if it is assumed that it is snuffed out when it is not in action, how could it be rekindled? If *per impossibile* I had once succeeded in *making myself into* a thing, how should I subsequently reconvert myself to consciousness? Once I am free, I am not to be counted among things, and I must then be uninterruptedly free. Once my actions cease to be mine, I shall never recover them, and if I lose my hold on the world, it will never be restored to me. It is equally inconceivable that my liberty should be attenuated; one cannot be to some extent free, and if, as is often said, motives incline

---

* 'Rückbeziehung der Phänomenologie auf sich selbst,' say the unpublished writings.
† We are indebted for this last expression to G. Gusdorf, who may well have used it in another sense.

---

‡ In the sense in which, with Husserl, we have taken this word.

me in a certain direction, one of two things happens: either they are strong enough to force me to act, in which case there is no freedom, or else they are not strong enough, and then freedom is complete, and as great in the worst torments as in the peace of one's home. We ought, therefore, to reject not only the idea of causality, but also that of motivation.* The alleged motive does not burden my decision; on the contrary my decision lends the motive its force. Everything that I 'am' in virtue of nature or history—hunchbacked, handsome or Jewish—I never am completely for myself, as we have just explained: and I may well be these things for other people, nevertheless I remain free to posit another person as a consciousness whose views strike through to my very being, or on the other hand merely as an object. It is also true that this option is itself a form of constraint: if I am ugly, I have the choice between being an object of disapproval or disapproving of others. I am left free to be a masochist or a sadist, but not free to ignore others. But this dilemma, which is given as part of the human lot, is not one for me as pure consciousness: it is still I who makes another to be for me and makes each of us be as human beings. Moreover, even if existence as a human being were imposed upon me, the manner alone being left to my choice, and considering this choice itself and ignoring the small number of forms it might take, it would still be a free choice. If it is said that my temperament inclines me particularly to either sadism or masochism, it is still merely a manner of speaking, for my temperament exists only for the second order knowledge that I gain about myself when I see myself as others see me, and in so far as I recognize it, confer value upon it, and in that sense, choose it. What misleads us on this, is that we often look for freedom in the voluntary deliberation which examines one motive after another and seems to opt for the weightiest or most convincing. In reality the deliberation follows the decision, and it is my secret decision which brings the motives to light, for it would be difficult to conceive what the force of a motive might be in the absence of a decision which it confirms or to which it runs counter. When I have abandoned a project, the motives which I thought held me to it suddenly lose their force and collapse. In order to resuscitate them, an effort is required on my part to reopen time and set me back to the moment preceding the making of the decision. Even while I am deliberating, already I find it an effort to suspend time's flow, and to keep open a situation which I feel is closed by a decision which is already there and which I am holding off. That is why it so often happens that after giving up a plan I experience a feeling of relief: 'After all, I wasn't all that involved'; the debate was purely a matter of form, and the deliberation a mere parody, for I had decided against from the start.

We often see the weakness of the will brought forward as an argument against freedom. And indeed, although I can will myself to adopt a course of conduct and act the part of a warrior or a seducer, it is not within my power to be a warrior or seducer with ease and in a way that 'comes naturally'; really to *be* one, that is. But neither should we seek freedom in the act of will, which is, in its very meaning, something short of an act. We have recourse to an act of will only in order to go against our true decision, and, as it were, for the purpose of proving our powerlessness. If we had really and truly made the conduct of the warrior or the seducer our own, then we should *be* one or the other. Even what are called obstacles to freedom are in reality deployed by it. An unclimbable rock face, a large or small, vertical or slanting rock, are things which have no meaning for anyone who is not intending to surmount them, for a subject whose projects do not carve out such determinate forms from the uniform mass of the *in itself* and cause an orientated world to arise—a significance in things. There is, then, ultimately nothing that can set limits to freedom, except those limits that freedom itself has set in the form of its various initiatives, so that the subject has simply the external world that he gives himself. Since it is the latter who, on coming into being, brings to light significance and value in things, and since no thing can impinge upon it except through acquiring, thanks to it, significance and value, there is no action of things on the subject, but merely a signification (in the active sense), a centrifugal *Sinngebung*. The choice would seem to lie between scientism's conception of causality, which is incompatible with the consciousness which we have of ourselves, and the assertion of an absolute freedom divorced from the outside. It is impossible to decide beyond which point things cease to be ἐφ'ἡμιν. Either they all lie within our power, or none does.

---

* See J. P. Sartre, *L'Être et le Néant*, pp. 508 and ff.

The result, however, of this first reflection on freedom would appear to be to rule it out altogether. If indeed it is the case that our freedom is the same in all our actions, and even in our passions, if it is not to be measured in terms of our conduct, and if the slave displays freedom as much by living in fear as by breaking his chains, then it cannot be held that there is such a thing as *free action,* freedom being anterior to all actions. In any case it will not be possible to declare: 'Here freedom makes its appearance', since free action, in order to be discernible, has to stand out against a background of life from which it is entirely, or almost entirely, absent. We may say in this case that it is everywhere, but equally nowhere. In the name of freedom we reject the idea of acquisition, since freedom has become a primordial acquisition and, as it were, our state of nature. Since we do not have to provide it, it is the gift granted to us of having no gift, it is the nature of consciousness which consists in having no nature, and in no case can it find external expression or a place in our life. The idea of action, therefore, disappears: nothing can pass from us to the world, since we are nothing that can be specified, and since the non-being which constitutes us could not possibly find its way into the world's plenum. There are merely intentions immediately followed by their effects, and we are very near to the Kantian idea of an intention which is tantamount to the act, which Scheler countered with the argument that the cripple who would like to be able to save a drowning man and the good swimmer who actually saves him do not have the same experience of autonomy. The very idea of choice vanishes, for to choose is to choose *something* in which freedom sees, at least for a moment, a symbol of itself. There is free choice only if freedom comes into play in its decision, and posits the situation chosen as a situation of freedom. A freedom which has no need to be exercised because it is already acquired could not commit itself in this way: it knows that the following instant will find it, come what may, just as free and just as indeterminate. The very notion of freedom demands that our decision should plunge into the future, that something should have been *done* by it, that the subsequent instant should benefit from its predecessor and, though not necessitated, should be at least required by it. If freedom is doing, it is necessary that what it does should not be immediately undone by a new freedom. Each instant, therefore, must not be a closed world; one instant must be able to commit its successors and, a decision once taken and action once begun, I must have something acquired at my disposal, I must benefit from my impetus, I must be inclined to carry on, and there must be a bent or propensity of the mind. It was Descartes who held that conservation demands a power as great as does creation; a view which implies a realistic notion of the instant. It is true that the instant is not a philosopher's fiction. It is the point at which one project is brought to fruition and another begun*—the point at which my gaze is transferred from one end to another, it is the *Augen-Blick.* But this break in time cannot occur unless each of the two spans is of a piece. Consciousness, it is said, is, though not atomized into instants, at least haunted by the spectre of the instant which it is obliged continually to exorcise by a free act. We shall soon see that we have indeed always the power to interrupt, but it implies in any case a power to *begin,* for there would be no severance unless freedom had taken up its abode somewhere and were preparing to move it. Unless there are cycles of behaviour, open situations requiring a certain completion and capable of constituting a background to either a confirmatory or transformatory decision, we never experience freedom. The choice of intelligible character is excluded, not only because there is no time anterior to time, but because choice presupposes a prior commitment and because the idea of an initial choice involves a contradiction. If freedom is to have *room*† in which to move, if it is to be describable as freedom, there must be something to hold it away from its objectives, it must have a *field,* which means that there must be for it special possibilities, or realities which tend to cling to being. As J. P. Sartre himself observes, dreaming is incompatible with freedom because, in the realm of imagination, we have no sooner taken a certain significance as our goal than we already believe that we have intuitively brought it into being, in short, because there is no obstacle and nothing *to do.*‡ It is established that freedom is not to be confused with those abstract decisions of will at grips with motives or passions, for the classical conception of deliberation is relevant only to a freedom 'in bad

---

*J. P. Sartre, *L'Être et le Néant,* p. 544.

†'avoir du champ'; in this sentence there is a play on the word 'champ' = field (Translator's note).

‡J. P. Sartre, *L'Être et le Néant,* p. 562.

faith' which secretly harbours antagonistic motives without being prepared to act on them, and so itself manufactures the alleged proofs of its impotence. We can see, beneath these noisy debates and these fruitless efforts to 'construct' ourselves, the tacit decisions whereby we have marked out round ourselves the field of possibility, and it is true that nothing is done as long as we cling to these fixed points, and everything is easy as soon as we have weighed anchor. This is why our freedom is not to be sought in spurious discussion on the conflict between a style of life which we have no wish to reappraise and circumstances suggestive of another: the real choice is that of whole character and our manner of being in the world. But either this total choice is never uttered, since it is the silent upsurge of our being in the world, in which case it is not clear in what sense it could be said to be ours, since this freedom glides over itself and is the equivalent of a fate— or else our choice of ourselves is truly a choice, a conversion involving our whole existence. In this case, however, there is presupposed a previous acquisition which the choice sets out to modify and it founds a new tradition: this leads us to ask whether the perpetual severance in terms of which we initially defined freedom is not simply the negative aspect of our universal commitment to a world, and whether our indifference to each determinate thing does not express merely our involvement in all; whether the ready-made freedom from which we started is not reducible to a power of initiative, which cannot be transformed into *doing* without taking up some proposition of the world, and whether, in short, concrete and actual freedom is not indeed to be found in this exchange. It is true that nothing has *significance* and value for anyone but *me* and through anyone but me, but this proposition remains indeterminate and is still indistinguishable from the Kantian idea of a consciousness which 'finds in things only what it has put into them', and from the idealist refutation of realism, as long as we fail to make clear how we understand significance and the self. By defining ourselves as a universal power of *Sinn-Gebung*, we have reverted to the method of the 'thing without which' and to the analytical reflection of the traditional type, which seeks the conditions of possibility without concerning itself with the conditions of reality. We must therefore resume the analysis of the *Sinngebung*, and show how it can be both centrifugal and centripetal, since it has

been established that there is no freedom without a field.

When I say that this rock is unclimbable, it is certain that this attribute, like that of being big or little, straight and oblique, and indeed like all attributes in general, can be conferred upon it only by the project of climbing it, and by a human presence. It is, therefore, freedom which brings into being the obstacles to freedom, so that the latter can be set over against it as its bounds. However, it is clear that, one and the same project being given, one rock will appear as an obstacle, and another, being more negotiable, as a means. My freedom, then, does not so contrive it that this way there is an obstacle, and that way a way through, it arranges for there to be obstacles and ways through in general; it does not draw the particular outline of this world, but merely lays down its general structures. It may be objected that there is no difference; if my freedom conditions the structure of the 'there is', that of the 'here' and the 'there', it is present wherever these structures arise. We cannot distinguish the quality of 'obstacle' from the obstacle itself, and relate one to freedom and the other to the world in itself which, without freedom, would be merely an amorphous and unnameable mass. It is not, therefore, outside myself that I am able to find a limit to my freedom. But do I not find it in myself? We must indeed distinguish between my express intentions, for example the plan I now make to climb those mountains, and general intentions which evaluate the potentialities of my environment. Whether or not I have decided to climb them, these mountains appear high to me, because they exceed my body's power to take them in its stride, and, even if I have just read *Micromégas*, I cannot so contrive it that they are small for me. Underlying myself as a thinking subject, who am able to take my place at will on Sirius or on the earth's surface, there is, therefore, as it were a natural self which does not budge from its terrestrial situation and which constantly adumbrates absolute valuations. What is more, my projects as a thinking being are clearly modelled on the latter; if I elect to see things from the point of view of Sirius, it is still to my terrestrial experience that I must have recourse in order to do so; I may say, for example, that the Alps are *molehills*. In so far as I have hands, feet, a body, I sustain around me intentions which are not dependent upon my decisions and which affect my surroundings in a way which I do not choose. These intentions are general in a double sense: firstly in the sense that they constitute a system in which all possible objects are simultaneously included; if the mountain appears high and upright, the tree appears small and sloping; and furthermore in the sense that they are not simply mine, they originate from other than myself, and I am not surprised to find them in all psycho-physical subjects organized as I am. Hence, as Gestalt psychology has shown, there are for me certain shapes which are particularly favoured, as they are for other men, and which are capable of giving rise to a psychological science and rigorous laws. The grouping of dots

··   ··   ··   ··   ··   ··

is always perceived as six pairs of dots with two millimetres between each pair, while one figure is always perceived as a cube, and another as a plane mosaic.* It is as if, on the hither side of our judgement and our freedom, someone were assigning such and such a significance to such and such a given grouping. It is indeed true that perceptual structures do not always force themselves upon the observer; there are some which are ambiguous. But these reveal even more effectively the presence within us of spontaneous evaluation: for they are elusive shapes which suggest constantly changing meanings to us. Now a pure consciousness is capable of anything except being ignorant of its intentions, and an absolute freedom cannot choose itself as hesitant, since that amounts to allowing itself to be drawn in several directions, and since, the possibilities being *ex hypothesi* indebted to freedom for all the strength they have, the weight that freedom gives to one is thereby withdrawn from the rest. We *can* break up a shape by looking at it awry, but this too is because freedom uses the gaze along with its spontaneous evaluations. Without the latter, we would not have a world, that is, a collection of things which emerge from a background of formlessness by presenting themselves to our body as 'to be touched', 'to be taken', 'to be climbed over'. We should never be aware of adjusting ourselves to things and reaching them where they are, beyond us, but would be conscious only of restricting our thoughts to the immanent objects of our intentions, and we should not be in the world, ourselves implicated in the spectacle and, so to speak, intermingled with things, we should simply enjoy the spectacle of a universe. It is, therefore, true that there are no obstacles in themselves, but the self which qualifies them as such is not some acosmic subject; it runs ahead of itself in relation to things in order to confer upon them the form of things. There is an autochthonous significance of the world which is constituted in the dealings which our incarnate existence has with it, and which provides the ground of every deliberate *Sinngebung*.

This is true not only of an impersonal and, all in all, abstract function such as 'external perception'. There is something comparable present in all evaluations. It has been perceptively remarked that pain and fatigue can never be regarded as causes which 'act' upon my liberty, and that, in so far as I may experience either at any given moment, they do not have their origin outside me, but always have a significance and express my attitude towards the world. Pain makes me give way and say what I ought to have kept to myself, fatigue makes me break my journey. We all know the moment at which we decide no longer to endure pain or fatigue, and when, simultaneously, they become intolerable in fact. Tiredness does not halt my companion, because he likes the clamminess of his body, the heat of the road and the sun, in short, because he likes to feel himself in the midst of things, to feel their rays converging upon him, to be the cynosure of all this light, and an object of touch for the earth's crust. My own fatigue brings me to a halt because I dislike it, because I have chosen differently my manner of being in the world, because, for instance, I endeavour, not to be in nature, but rather to win the recognition of others. I am free in relation to fatigue to precisely the extent that I am free in relation to my being in the world, free to make my way by transforming it.† But here once more we must recognize a sort of sedimentation of our life: an attitude towards the world, when it has received frequent confirmation, acquires a favoured status for us. Yet since freedom does not tolerate any motive in its path, my habitual being in the world is at each moment equally precarious, and the complexes which I have allowed to develop over the years always remain equally soothing, and the free act can with no difficulty blow them

---

* Footnote omitted—ed.

† J. P. Sartre, *L'Être et le Néant*, pp. 531 and ff.

sky-high. However, having built our life upon an inferiority complex which has been operative for twenty years, it is not *probable* that we shall change. It is clear what a summary rationalism might say in reply to such a hybrid notion: there are no degrees of possibility; either the free act is no longer possible, or it is still possible, in which case freedom is complete. In short, 'probable' is meaningless. It is a notion belonging to statistical thought, which is not thought at all, since it does not concern any particular thing actually existing, any moment of time, any concrete event. 'It is improbable that Paul will give up writing bad books' means nothing, since Paul may well decide to write no more such books. The probable is everywhere and nowhere, a reified fiction, with only a psychological existence; it is not an ingredient of the world. And yet we have already met it a little while ago in the perceived *world*. The mountain is great or small to the extent that, as a perceived thing, it is to be found in the field of my possible actions, and in relation to a level which is not only that of my individual life, but that of 'any man'. Generality and probability are not fictions, but phenomena; we must therefore find a phenomenological basis for statistical thought. It belongs necessarily to a being which is fixed, situated and surrounded by things in the world. 'It is improbable' that I should at this moment destroy an inferiority complex in which I have been content to live for twenty years. That means that I have committed myself to inferiority, that I have made it my abode, that this past, though not a fate, has at least a specific weight and is not a set of events over there, at a distance from me, but the atmosphere of my present. The rationalist's dilemma: either the free act is possible, or it is not—either the event originates in me or is imposed on me from outside, does not apply to our relations with the world and with our past. Our freedom does not destroy our situation, but gears itself to it: as long as we are alive, our situation is open, which implies both that it calls up specially favoured modes of resolution, and also that it is powerless to bring one into being by itself.

. . .

We therefore recognize, around our initiatives and around that strictly individual project which is oneself, a zone of generalized existence and of projects already formed . . . . Already generality intervenes, already our presence to ourselves is mediated by it

and we cease to be pure consciousness, as soon as the natural or social constellation ceases to be an unformulated *this* and crystallizes into a situation, as soon as it has a meaning—in short, as soon as we exist. Every thing appears to us through a medium to which it lends its own fundamental quality; this piece of wood is neither a collection of colours and tactile data, not even their total *Gestalt,* but something from which there emanates a woody essence; these 'sensory givens' modulate a certain theme or illustrate a certain style which is the wood itself, and which creates, round this piece of wood and the perception I have of it, a horizon of significance. The natural world, as we have seen, is nothing other than the place of all possible themes and styles. It is indissolubly an unmatched individual and a significance. Correspondingly, the generality and the individuality of the subject, subjectivity qualified and pure, the anonymity of the One and the anonymity of consciousness are not two conceptions of the subject between which philosophy has to choose, but two stages of a unique structure which is the concrete subject. Let us consider, for example, sense experience. I lose myself in this red which is before me, without in any way qualifying it, and it seems that this experience brings me into contact with a pre-human subject. Who perceives this red? It is nobody who can be named and placed among other perceiving subjects. For, between this experience of red which I have, and that about which other people speak to me, no direct comparison will ever be possible. I am here in my own point of view, and since all experience, in so far as it derives from impression, is in the same way strictly my own, it seems that a unique and unduplicated subject enfolds them all. Suppose I formulate a thought, the God of Spinoza, for example; this thought as it is in my living experience is a certain landscape to which no one will ever have access, even if, moreover, I manage to enter into a discussion with a friend on the subject of Spinoza's God. However, the very individuality of these experiences is not quite unadulterated. For the thickness of this red, its thisness, the power it has of reaching me and saturating me, are attributable to the fact that it requires and obtains from my gaze a certain vibration, and imply that I am familiar with a world of colours of which this one is a particular variation. The concrete colour red, therefore, stands out against a background of generality, and this is why, even without transferring myself to another's point of view, I grasp myself in perception as *a* perceiving subject, and not as unclassifiable consciousness. I feel, all round my perception of red, all the regions of my being unaffected by it, and that region set aside for colours, 'vision', through which the perception finds its way into me. Similarly my thought about the God of Spinoza is only apparently a strictly unique experience, for it is the concretion of a certain cultural world, the Spinozist philosophy, or of a certain philosophic style in which I immediately recognize a 'Spinozist' idea. There is therefore no occasion to ask ourselves why the thinking subject or consciousness perceives itself as a man, or an incarnate or historical subject, nor must we treat this apperception as a second order operation which it somehow performs starting from its absolute existence: the absolute flow takes shape beneath its own gaze as 'a consciousness', or a man, or an incarnate subject, because it is a field of presence—to itself, to others and to the world—and because this presence throws it into the natural and cultural world from which it arrives at an understanding of itself. We must not envisage this flux as absolute contact with oneself, as an absolute density with no internal fault, but on the contrary as a being which is in pursuit of itself outside. If the subject made a constant and at all times peculiar choice of himself, one might wonder why his experience always ties up with itself and presents him with objects and definite historical phases, why we have a general notion of time valid through all times, and why finally the experience of each one of us links up with that of others. But it is the question itself which must be questioned: for what is given, is not one fragment of time followed by another, one individual flux, then another; it is the taking up of each subjectivity by itself, and of subjectivities by each other in the generality of a single nature, the cohesion of an intersubjective life and a world. The present mediates between the For Oneself and the For Others, between individuality and generality. True reflection presents me to myself not as idle and inaccessible subjectivity, but as identical with my presence in the world and to others, as I am now realizing it: I am all that I see, I am an intersubjective field, not despite my body and historical situation, but, on the contrary, by being this body and this situation, and through them, all the rest.

What, then, becomes of the freedom we spoke about at the outset, if this point of view is taken? I can no longer pretend to be a cipher, and to choose my-self continually from the starting point of nothing at all. If it is through subjectivity that nothingness appears in the world, it can equally be said that it is through the world that nothingness comes into being. I am a general refusal to be anything, accompanied surreptitiously by a continual acceptance of such and such a qualified form of being. *For even this general refusal is still one manner of being, and has its place in the world.* It is true that I can at any moment interrupt my projects. But what *is* this power? It is the power to begin something else, for we never remain suspended in nothingness. We are always in a plenum, in being, just as a face, even in repose, even in death, is always doomed to express something (there are people whose faces, in death, bear expressions of surprise, or peace, or discretion), and just as silence is still a modality of the world of sound. I may defy all accepted form, and spurn everything, for there is no case in which I am utterly committed: but in this case I do not withdraw into my freedom, I commit myself elsewhere. Instead of thinking about my bereavement, I look at my nails, or have lunch, or engage in politics. Far from its being the case that my freedom is always unattended, it is never without an accomplice, and its power of perpetually tearing itself away finds its fulcrum in my universal commitment in the world. My actual freedom is not on the hither side of my being, but before me, in things. We must not say that I continually choose myself, on the excuse that I *might* continually refuse what I am. Not to refuse is not the same thing as to choose. We could identify drift and action only by depriving the implicit of all phenomenal value, and at every instant arraying the world before us in perfect transparency, that is, by destroying the world's 'worldliness'. Consciousness holds itself responsible for everything, and takes everything upon itself, but it has nothing of its own and makes its life in the world. We are led to conceive freedom as a choice continually remade as long as we do not bring in the notion of a generalized or natural time. We have seen that there is no natural time, if we understand thereby a time of things without subjectivity. There is, however, at least a generalized time, and this is what the common notion of time envisages. It is the perpetual reiteration of the sequence of past, present and future. It is, as it were, a constant disappointment and failure. This is what is expressed by saying that it is continuous: the present which it brings to us is never a present for good, since it is already over when it appears, and the future has, in it, only the appearance of a goal towards which we make our way, since it quickly comes into the present, whereupon we turn towards a fresh future. This time is the time of our bodily functions, which like it, are cyclic, and it is also that of nature with which we co-exist. It offers us only the adumbration and the abstract form of a commitment, since it continually erodes itself and undoes that which it has just done. As long as we place in opposition, with no mediator, the For Itself and the In Itself, and fail to perceive, between ourselves and the world, this natural foreshadowing of a subjectivity, this prepersonal time which rests upon itself, acts are needed to sustain the upsurge of time, and everything becomes equally a matter of choice, the respiratory reflex no less than the moral decision, conservation no less than creation. As far as we are concerned, consciousness attributes this power of universal constitution to itself only if it ignores the event which upholds it and is the occasion of its birth. A consciousness for which the world 'can be taken for granted', which finds it 'already constituted' and present even in consciousness itself, does not *absolutely* choose either its being or its manner of being.

What then is freedom? To be born is both to be born of the world and to be born into the world. The world is already constituted, but also never completely constituted; in the first case we are acted upon, in the second we are open to an infinite number of possibilities. But this analysis is still abstract, for we exist in both ways *at once*. There is, therefore, never determinism and never absolute choice, I am never a thing and never bare consciousness. In fact, even our own pieces of initiative, even the situations which we have chosen, bear us on, once they have been entered upon by virtue of a state rather than an act. The generality of the 'rôle' and of the situation comes to the aid of decision, and in this exchange between the situation and the person who takes it up, it is impossible to determine precisely the 'share contributed by the situation' and the 'share contributed by freedom'. Let us suppose that a man is tortured to make him talk. If he refuses to give the names and addresses which it is desired to extract from him, this does not arise from a solitary and unsupported decision: the man still feels himself to be with his comrades, and, being still involved in the common struggle, he is as it were incapable of talking. Or else, for months or years, he has, in his mind, faced this test and staked his whole life

upon it. Or finally, he wants to prove, by coming through it, what he has always thought and said about freedom. These motives do not cancel out freedom, but at least ensure that it does not go unbuttressed in being. What withstands pain is not, in short, a bare consciousness, but the prisoner with his comrades or with those he loves and under whose gaze he lives; or else the awareness of his proudly willed solitude, which again is a certain mode of the *Mit-Sein*. And probably the individual in his prison daily reawakens these phantoms, which give back to him the strength he gave to them. But conversely, in so far as he has committed himself to this action, formed a bond with his comrades or adopted this morality, it is because the historical situation, the comrades, the world around him seemed to him to expect that conduct from him. The analysis could be pursued endlessly in this way. We choose our world and the world chooses us. What is certain, in any case, is that we can at no time set aside within ourselves a redoubt to which being does not find its way through, without seeing this freedom, immediately and by the very fact of being a living experience, take on the appearance of being and become a motive and a buttress. Taken concretely, freedom is always a meeting of the inner and the outer—even the prehuman and prehistoric freedom with which we began—and it shrinks without ever disappearing altogether in direct proportion to the lessening of the *tolerance* allowed by the bodily and institutional data of our lives. There is, as Husserl says, on the one hand a 'field of freedom' and on the other a 'conditioned freedom';* not that freedom is absolute within the limits of this field and non-existent outside it (like the perceptual field, this one has no traceable boundaries), but because I enjoy immediate and remote possibilities. Our commitments sustain our power and there is no freedom without some power. Our freedom, it is said, is either total or non-existent. This dilemma belongs to objective thought and its stable-companion, analytical reflection. If indeed we place ourselves within being, it must necessarily be the case that our actions must have their origin outside us, and if we revert to constituting consciousness, they must originate within. But we have learnt precisely to recognize the order of phenomena. We are involved in the world and with others in an

---

*Fink, *Vergegenwärtigung und Bild,* p. 285.

inextricable tangle. The idea of situation rules out absolute freedom at the source of our commitments, and equally, indeed, at their terminus. No commitment, not even commitment in the Hegelian State, can make me leave behind all differences and free me for anything. This universality itself, from the mere fact of its being experienced, would stand out as a particularity against the world's background, for existence both generalizes and particularizes everything at which it aims, and cannot ever be finally complete.

The synthesis of *in itself* and *for itself* which brings Hegelian freedom into being has, however, its truth. In a sense, it is the very definition of existence, since it is effected at every moment before our eyes in the phenomenon of presence, only to be quickly re-enacted, since it does not conjure away our finitude. By taking up a present, I draw together and transform my past, altering its significance, freeing and detaching myself from it. But I do so only by committing myself somewhere else. Psychoanalytical treatment does not bring about its cure by producing direct awareness of the past, but in the first place by binding the subject to his doctor through new existential relationships. It is not a matter of giving scientific assent to the psychoanalytical interpretation, and discovering a notional significance for the past; it is a matter of reliving this or that as significant, and this the patient succeeds in doing only by seeing his past in the perspective of his co-existence with the doctor. The complex is not dissolved by a non-instrumental freedom, but rather displaced by a new pulsation of time with its own supports and motives. The same applies in all cases of coming to awareness: they are real only if they are sustained by a new commitment. Now this commitment too is entered into in the sphere of the implicit, and is therefore valid only for a certain temporal cycle. The choice which we make of our life is always based on a certain givenness. My freedom can draw life away from its spontaneous course, but only by a series of unobtrusive deflections which necessitate first of all following its course—not by any absolute creation. All explanations of my conduct in terms of my past, my temperament and my environment are therefore true, provided that they be regarded not as separable contributions, but as moments of my total being, the significance of which I am entitled to make explicit in various ways, without its ever being possible to say whether I confer their meaning upon them or receive it from them. I am a psychological and his-torical structure, and have received, with existence, a manner of existing, a style. All my actions and thoughts stand in a relationship to this structure, and even a philosopher's thought is merely a way of making explicit his hold on the world, and what he is. The fact remains that I am free, not in spite of, or on the hither side of, these motivations, but by means of them. For this significant life, this certain significance of nature and history which I am, does not limit my access to the world, but on the contrary is my means of entering into communication with it. It is by being unrestrictedly and unreservedly what I am at present that I have a chance of moving forward; it is by living my time that I am able to understand other times, by plunging into the present and the world, by taking on deliberately what I am fortuitously, by willing what I will and doing what I do, that I can go further. I can miss being free only if I try to bypass my natural and social situation by refusing to take it up, in the first place, instead of assuming it in order to join up with the natural and human world. Nothing determines me from outside, not because nothing acts upon me, but, on the contrary, because I am from the start outside myself and open to the world. We are *true* through and through, and have with us, by the mere fact of belonging to the world, and not merely being in the world in the way that things are, all that we need to transcend ourselves. We need have no fear that our choices or actions restrict our liberty, since choice and action alone cut us loose from our anchorage. Just as reflection borrows its wish for absolute sufficiency from the perception which causes a thing to appear, and as in this way idealism tacitly uses that 'primary opinion' which it would like to destroy as opinion, so freedom flounders in the contradictions of commitment, and fails to realize that, without the roots which it thrusts into the world, it would not be freedom at all. Shall I make this promise? Shall I risk my life for so little? Shall I give up my liberty in order to save liberty? There is no theoretical reply to these questions. But there are these *things* which stand, irrefutable, there is before you this person whom you love, there are these men whose existence around you is that of slaves, and *your* freedom cannot be willed without leaving behind its singular relevance, and without willing freedom *for all*. Whether it is a question of things or of historical situations, philosophy has no other function than to teach us to see them clearly once more, and it is true to say that it comes into being by destroying itself as separate philosophy. But what is here required is silence, for only the hero lives out his relation to men and the world. 'Your son is caught in the fire; you are the one who will save him. . . . If there is an obstacle, you would be ready to give your shoulder provided only that you can charge down that obstacle. Your abode is your act itself. Your act is you. . . . You give yourself in exchange. . . . Your significance shows itself, effulgent. It is your duty, your hatred, your love, your steadfastness, your ingenuity. . . . Man is but a network of relationships, and these alone matter to him.'*

The Metaphysical in Man
from Sense and Non-Sense

.   .   .

As presently oriented, the sciences of man are metaphysical or transnatural in that they cause us to rediscover, along with structure and the understanding of structure, a dimension of being and a type of knowledge which man forgets in his natural attitude.[†] It is natural to believe ourselves in the presence of a world and a time over which our thought soars, capable of considering each part at will without modifying the part's objective nature. This belief is taken up and systematized in the beginnings of science, which always takes for granted an absolute observer in whom all points of view are summed up and, correlatively, a true projection of all perspectives. But the sciences of man—not to mention the others—have made it evident that all knowledge of man by man, far from being pure contemplation, is the taking up by each, *as best he can,* of the acts of others, reactivating from ambiguous signs an experience which is not his own, appropriating a structure (e.g., the *a priori* of the species, the sublinguistic schema or spirit of a civilization) of which he forms no distinct concept but which he puts together as an experienced pianist deciphers an unknown piece of music: without himself grasping the motives of each gesture or each operation, without being able to bring to the surface of con-

sciousness all the sediment of knowledge which he is using at that moment. Here we no longer have the positing of an object, but rather we have communication with a way of being. The universality of knowledge is no longer guaranteed in each of us by that stronghold of absolute consciousness in which the Kantian "I think"—although linked to a certain spatio-temporal perspective—was assured *a priori* of being identical to every other possible "I think." The germ of universality or the "natural light" without which there could be no knowledge is to be found ahead of us, in the thing where our perception places us, in the dialogue into which our experience of other people throws us by means of a movement not all of whose sources are known to us. Metaphysics begins from the moment when, ceasing to live in the evidence of the object—whether it is the sensory object or the object of science—we apperceive the radical subjectivity of all our experience as inseparable from its truth value. It means two things to say that our experience is our own: both that it is not the measure of all imaginable being in itself and that it is nonetheless co-extensive with all being of which we can form a notion. This double sense of the *cogito* is the basic fact of metaphysics: I am sure that there is being—on the condition that I do not seek another sort of being than being-for-me. When I am aware of sensing, I am not, on the one hand, conscious of my state and, on the other, of a certain sensuous quality such as red or blue—but red or blue are nothing other than my different ways of running my eyes over what is offered to me and of responding to its solicitation. Likewise, when I say that I see someone, it means that I am moved by sympathy for this behavior of which I am a witness and which holds my own intentions by furnishing them with a visible realization. It is our very difference, the uniqueness of our experience, which attests to our strange ability to enter into others and re-enact their deeds. Thus is founded a truth which, as Pascal said, we can neither reject nor completely accept. Metaphysics is the deliberate intention to describe this paradox of consciousness and truth, exchange and communication, in which science lives and which it encounters in the guise of vanquished difficulties or failures to be made good but which it does not thematize. From the moment I recognize that my experience, precisely insofar as it is my own, makes me accessible to what is not myself, that I am sensitive to the world and to others, all the beings which ob-

---

* A. de Saint-Exupéry, *Pilote de Guerre,* pp. 171, 174, 176.
[†] Some footnotes have been omitted—ed.

jective thought placed at a distance draw singularly nearer to me. Or, conversely, I recognize my affinity with them; I am nothing but an ability to echo them, to understand them, to respond to them. My life seems absolutely individual and absolutely universal to me. This recognition of an individual life which animates all past and contemporary lives and receives its entire life from them, of a light which flashes from them to us contrary to all hope—this is metaphysical consciousness, whose first stage is surprise at discovering the confrontation of opposites and whose second stage is recognition of their identity in the simplicity of *doing*. Metaphysical consciousness has no other objects than those of experience: this world, other people, human history, truth, culture. But instead of taking them as all settled, as consequences with no premises, as if they were self-evident, it rediscovers their fundamental strangeness to me and the miracle of their appearing. The history of mankind is then no longer the inevitable advent of modern man in fixed stages starting with the cave men, that imperious growth of morality and science of which "all too human" textbooks chatter; it is not empirical, successive history but the awareness of the secret bond which causes Plato to be still alive in our midst.

Understood in this way, metaphysics is the opposite of system. If system is an arrangement of concepts which makes all the aspects of experience immediately compatible and compossible, then it suppresses metaphysical consciousness and, moreover, does away with morality at the same time. For example, if we wish to base the fact of rationality or communication on an absolute value or thought, either this absolute does not raise any difficulties and, when everything has been carefully considered, rationality and communication remain based on themselves, or else the absolute descends into them, so to speak—in which case it overturns all human methods of verification and justification. Whether there is or is not an absolute thought and an absolute evaluation in each practical problem, my own opinions, which remain capable of error no matter how rigorously I examine them, are still my only equipment for judging. It remains just as hard to reach agreement with myself and with others, and for all my belief that it is in principle always attainable, I have no other reason to affirm this principle than my experience of certain concordances, so that in the end whatever solidity there is in my belief in the absolute is nothing but my experience of agreement with myself and others. Recourse to an absolute foundation—when it is not useless—destroys the very thing it is supposed to support. As a matter of fact, if I believe that I can rejoin the absolute principle of all thought and all evaluation on the basis of evidence, then I have the right to withdraw my judgments from the control of others on the condition that I have my consciousness for myself; my judgments take on a sacred character; in particular—in the realm of the practical—I have at my disposal a plan of escape in which my actions become transfigured: the suffering I create turns into happiness, ruse becomes reason, and I piously cause my adversaries to perish. Thus, when I place the ground of truth or morality outside ongoing experience, either I continue to hold to the probabilities it offers me (merely devalued by the ideal of absolute knowledge), or I disguise these probabilities as absolute certainties—and then I am letting go of the verifiable for the sake of truth, which is to say I drop the prey to catch its shadow. I waver between uncertainty and presumptuousness without ever finding the precise point of human resolution. If, on the other hand, I have understood that truth and value can be for us nothing but the result of the verifications or evaluations which we make in contact with the world, before other people and in given situations of knowledge and action, that even these notions lose all meaning outside of human perspectives, then the world recovers its texture, the particular acts of verification and evaluation through which I grasp a dispersed experience resume their decisive importance, and knowledge and action, true and false, good and evil have something unquestionable about them precisely because I do not claim to find in them absolute evidence. Metaphysical and moral consciousness dies upon contact with the absolute because, beyond the dull world of habitual or dormant consciousness, this consciousness is itself the living connection between myself and me and myself and others. Metaphysics is not a construction of concepts by which we try to make our paradoxes less noticeable but is the experience we have of these paradoxes in all situations of personal and collective history and the actions which, by assuming them, transform them into reason. One cannot conceive of a response which would eliminate such an inquiry; one thinks only of resolute actions which carry it further. Metaphysics is not a knowledge come to complete the edifice of knowledges but is lucid familiarity with whatever threatens these fields of knowledge and the acute awareness of their worth. The contingency of all that exists and all that has value is not a little truth for which we have somehow or other to make room in some nook or cranny of the system: it is the condition of a metaphysical view of the world.

Such a metaphysics cannot be reconciled with the manifest content of religion and with the positing of an absolute thinker of the world. These affirmations immediately pose the problem of a theodicy which has not taken one step forward since Leibniz and which in the last analysis perhaps consisted—even for Leibniz himself—of evoking the existence of this world as an insurpassable fact which from the first solicits creative actualization and therefore of rejecting the point of view of a worldless God. God then appears, not as the creator of this world—which would immediately entail the difficulty of a sovereign and benevolent power forced to incorporate evil in His works—but rather as an idea in the Kantian and restrictive sense of the word. God becomes a term of reference for a human reflection which, when it considers the world such as it is, condenses in this idea what it would like the world to be. A God who would not be simply for us but for Himself, could, on the contrary, be sought by metaphysics only behind consciousness, beyond our ideas, as the anonymous force which sustains each of our thoughts and experiences.* At this point religion ceases to be a conceptual construct or an ideology and once more becomes part of the experience of interhuman life. The originality of Christianity as the religion of the death of God is its rejection of the God of the philosophers and its herald-

ing of a God who takes on the human condition. The role of religion in culture is not that of a dogma or even of a belief, a cry. But what else could it be and still be effective? The Christian teaching that the Fall is fortunate, that a world without fault would be less good, and, finally, that the creation, which made being fall from its original perfection and sufficiency, is nevertheless more valuable or was all to the good makes Christianity the most resolute negation of the conceived infinite.

Lastly, no matter if metaphysics conceived as system has clashed with scientism, as Bergson saw, there is much more than a concordat between a metaphysics which rejects system as a matter of principle and a science which is forever becoming more exact in measuring how much its formulas diverge from the facts they are supposed to express: there is a spontaneous convergence.† Philosophical self-consciousness does

---

* Any determination one would like to give of this foundation at once becomes contradictory—not with that fertile contradiction of human consciousness but with the inert contradiction of inconsistent concepts. I have the right to consider the contradictions of my life as a thinking and incarnate subject, finite and capable of truth, as ultimate and true because I have experienced them and because they are interconnected in the unquestionable perception of a thing or in the experience of a truth. I can no longer introduce a "transcendence in immanence" behind me as Husserl did (even transcendence qualified as hypothetical), for I am not God, and I cannot verify the co-existence of these two attributes in any indubitable experience.

† Bergson's *Introduction à la métaphysique* shows in a profound way that science should be considered not only with respect to its completed formulas but also with an eye to the margin of indetermination which separates these formulas from the data to be explained and that, taken in this way, it presupposes an intimacy with the still-to-be-determined data. Metaphysics would then be the deliberate exploration of this world prior to the object of science to which science refers. In all these respects it seems to us that Bergson has perfectly defined the metaphysical approach to the world. It remains to be seen whether he was true to this method and did not revert to the system in passing from the "curve of facts" to a vital or spiritual impulse of which they would be the manifestation or the trace and which could be perceived only from the absolute observer's viewpoint, thus transforming the effort and tension he first described into an eternal repose. If, for Bergson, intuition really makes us transcend the world, it is because Bergson is not fully aware of his own presuppositions and of that simple fact that all we live is lived against the background of the world. And if, on the other hand, his philosophy is finally to be understood as a philosophy of immanence, he may be reproached with having described the human world only in its most general structures (e.g., duration, openness to the future); his work lacks a picture of human history which would give a content to these intuitions, which paradoxically remain very general. [English translation of Bergson's book by T. E. Hulme, *An Introduction to Metaphysics* (New York and London, 1912).]

not make science's effort at objectification futile; rather, philosophy pursues this effort at the human level, since all thought is inevitably objectification: only philosophy knows that on this level objectification cannot become carried away and makes us conquer the more fundamental relationship of co-existence. There can be no rivalry between scientific knowledge and the metaphysical knowing which continually confronts the former with its task. A science without philosophy would literally not know what it was talking about. A philosophy without methodical exploration of phenomena would end up with nothing but formal truths, which is to say, errors. To do metaphysics is not to enter a world of isolated knowledge nor to repeat sterile formulas such as we are using here: it is thoroughly to test the paradoxes it indicates; continually to re-verify the discordant functioning of human intersubjectivity; to try to think through to the very end the same phenomena which science lays siege to, only restoring to them their original transcendence and strangeness. When it seems that methodology has incontestably established that all induction is baseless in the absolute sense of the word and that all reflection always carries with it whole vistas of experience which tacitly cooperate to produce the purest of our evidence, it will undoubtedly be in order to revise the classical distinction between induction and reflection and to ask ourselves if two kinds of knowing are really involved or if there is not rather one single way of knowing, with different degrees of naïveté or explicitness.

A certain number of negations were necessary clearly to define the limits of this conception of metaphysics, but, taken in itself, such a conception is the essence of positiveness, and it is impossible to see what it could deprive us of. The glory of the evidence such as that of successful dialogue and communication, the common fate which men share and their oneness, which is not merely a biological resemblance but is a similarity in their most intimate nature—all that science and religion can effectively live is here brought together and rescued from the ambiguities of a double life.

SIMONE DE BEAUVOIR (1908–1986)

Simone de Beauvoir was born in Paris, the daughter of a lawyer. She studied philosophy at the Sorbonne, where she met Sartre. The two remained close friends for life but never married, considering the institution bourgeois. She became an important figure in French intellectual life after the Second World War and co-founded *Les Temps Modernes* with Sartre and Merleau-Ponty. She wrote novels and plays, including *She Came to Stay* (1943), *The Blood of Others* (1944), *All Men Are Mortal* (1946), and *The Mandarins* (1954). Her most influential publication was *The Second Sex* (1949), a feminist classic, and her book *The Ethics of Ambiguity* (1948) is an important attempt to draw out the ethical implications of existentialism.

In *The Ethics of Ambiguity* de Beauvoir argues that philosophers have obscured and oversimplified many aspects of our lives and our world by insisting that there is one view capable of rendering our situation completely intelligible. In fact, the human situation is too complex to be captured by any one consistent view, and invariably philosophers advocate views that "lie to us" and "leave in the shadow certain troubling aspects of a too complex situation."[19]

Our situation is, she says, ambiguous through and through. Simultaneously we are: (1) part of the world and (2) the mere consciousness of the world. We are both individuals and dependent on the collectivity. We have sovereign importance yet we are entirely insignificant. We are subjects for ourselves yet objects to others. We conceive of our lives as continuing indefinitely but know we face death.

De Beauvoir suggests that existentialism has always been a philosophy of ambiguity, and she credits Kierkegaard with initiating existentialism by "affirming the irreducible character of ambiguity,"[20] and Sartre with continuing the theme by treating the human being as "that being whose being is not to be...."[21] However, she also suggests that existentialism appears to have left us with a philosophy of despair in that it seems to deprive us of any "principle for making choices," any ideal by which to live our lives. Sartre in particular has portrayed the

---

[19] Simone de Beauvoir, *The Ethics of Ambiguity,* trans. Bernard Frechtman (Secaucus: Citadel Press, 1948), 8.
[20] Ibid., 9.
[21] Ibid., 10.

human being as engaged in the impossible project of becoming God, who is a synthesis of the in-itself and the for-itself.

Nevertheless, even if Sartre is correct in saying that the human project is impossible to achieve, we can still see a way to affirm human existence and overcome despair. We can do so by *choosing* human existence in all its ambiguity. We can decide to *want* to engage in the tension-filled human project "even with the failure which it involves."[22] Such a choice does not show that human existence is valuable from an objective point of view, a point of view independent of human existence; but then such a point of view does not exist. Instead, the decision to choose human existence shows that it is valuable from the only point of view that exists; namely, the point of view of a person who desires to exist.

But if each of us is a free creator of values, can't we view ourselves as separate from others in a way that entitles us to ignore them when we devise our scheme of values? It might seem so. However, de Beauvoir suggests that even though individuals are genuinely separate from each other, it is possible to set out "an ethics of ambiguity" that "will refuse to deny *a priori* that separate existants can, at the same time, be bound to each other, that their individual freedoms can forge laws valid for all."[23]

In defending her ethics of ambiguity, de Beauvoir claims that whatever else people might want in affirming their existence, they will also want freedom; whatever else people who affirm life might value, they will also value freedom. For we not only have goals, we also have the desire to pursue those goals ourselves. We want to be self-determining. But self-determination is possible only if we possess the freedom to pursue our lives ourselves. It is true that self-determining people will sometimes make mistakes. However, "to prohibit a man from error is to forbid him to fulfill his own existence, it is to deprive him of life."[24] Hence, freedom is considered valuable by everyone, and the prescription of freedom for everyone can be taken as a "law valid for all."

Even if we agree with de Beauvoir to posit the importance of freedom, we might still be unsure about which ethical questions will be resolved thereby. Particularly difficult will be the problem of how to decide on the relative importance of conflicting freedoms. For example, being entirely free to save lives conflicts with being entirely free to conform to one's religion, for sometimes religious groups require people to put their lives in danger, as when Jehovah's Witnesses require their members to refuse blood transfusions. So we must ask "when it is a question of choosing among freedoms, how shall we decide?"[25] And de Beauvoir's answer is that in the final analysis "one finds himself back at the anguish of free decision."[26] One must just *decide* which freedoms are more important, after carefully considering the complex ways in which different freedoms will affect people, for there is no concrete basis on which to base the decision.

In *The Second Sex* (1949), de Beauvoir develops an account of the relationship between the sexes that extends ideas Hegel set out in "Master and Slave." Like Hegel, de Beauvoir sees each person as hostile to all others. Each of us is a subject that would like to make an object of everyone else. Moreover, some of us have largely succeeded in dominating others in this way. Men as a group have managed to dominate women; men as a group have gotten women to accept the view that men are subjects and women are the objects for the male subjects. Men are the "one" and women are the "other." This subordination penetrates every aspect of the relationship between the sexes.

The Ethics of Ambiguity

AMBIGUITY AND FREEDOM

"The continous work of our life," says Montaigne, "is to build death." He quotes the Latin poets: *Prima, quae vitam dedit, hora corpsit.* And again: *Nascentes*

---

[22] Ibid., 13.
[23] Ibid., 18.
[24] Ibid., 138.

[25] Ibid., 145.
[26] Ibid., 148.

morimur. Man knows and thinks this tragic ambivalence which the animal and the plant merely undergo. A new paradox is thereby introduced into his destiny, "Rational animal," "thinking reed," he escapes from his natural condition without, however, freeing himself from it. He is still a part of this world of which he is a consciousness. He asserts himself as a pure internality against which no external power can take hold, and he also experiences himself as a thing crushed by the dark weight of other things. At every moment he can grasp the non-temporal truth of his existence. But between the past which no longer is and the future which is not yet, this moment when he exists is nothing. This privilege, which he alone possesses, of being a sovereign and unique subject amidst a universe of objects, is what he shares with all his fellow-men. In turn an object for others, he is nothing more than an individual in the collectivity on which he depends.

As long as there have been men and they have lived, they have all felt this tragic ambiguity of their condition, but as long as there have been philosophers and they have thought, most of them have tried to mask it. They have striven to reduce mind to matter, or to reabsorb matter into mind, or to merge them within a single substance. Those who have accepted the dualism have established a hierarchy between body and soul which permits of considering as negligible the part of the self which cannot be saved. They have denied death, either by integrating it with life or by promising to man immortality. Or, again they have denied life, considering it as a veil of illusion beneath which is hidden the truth of Nirvana.

And the ethics which they have proposed to their disciples has always pursued the same goal. It has been a matter of eliminating the ambiguity by making oneself pure inwardness or pure externality, by escaping from the sensible world or by being engulfed in it, by yielding to eternity or enclosing oneself in the pure moment. Hegel, with more ingenuity, tried to reject none of the aspects of man's condition and to reconcile them all. According to his system, the moment is preserved in the development of time; Nature asserts itself in the face of Spirit which denies it while assuming it; the individual is again found in the collectivity within which he is lost; and each man's death is fulfilled by being canceled out into the Life of Mankind. One can thus repose in a marvelous optimism where even the bloody wars simply express the fertile restlessness of the Spirit.

At the present time there still exist many doctrines which choose to leave in the shadow certain troubling aspects of a too complex situation. But their attempt to lie to us is in vain. Cowardice doesn't pay. Those reasonable metaphysics, those consoling ethics with which they would like to entice us only accentuate the disorder from which we suffer. Men of today seem to feel more acutely than ever the paradox of their condition. They know themselves to be the supreme end to which all action should be subordinated, but the exigencies of action force them to treat one another as instruments or obstacles, as means. The more widespread their mastery of the world, the more they find themselves crushed by uncontrollable forces. Though they are masters of the atomic bomb, yet it is created only to destroy them. Each one has the incomparable taste in his mouth of his own life, and yet each feels himself more insignificant than an insect within the immense collectivity whose limits are one with the earth's. Perhaps in no other age have they manifested their grandeur more brilliantly, and in no other age has this grandeur been so horribly flouted. In spite of so many stubborn lies, at every moment, at every opportunity, the truth comes to light, the truth of life and death, of my solitude and my bond with the world, of my freedom and my servitude, of the insignificance and the sovereign importance of each man and all men. There was Stalingrad and there was Buchenwald, and neither of the two wipes out the other. Since we do not succeed in fleeing it, let us therefore try to look the truth in the face. Let us try to assume our fundamental ambiguity. It is in the knowledge of the genuine conditions of our life that we must draw our strength to live and our reason for acting. From the very beginning, existentialism defined itself as a philosophy of ambiguity. It was by affirming the irreducible character of ambiguity that Kierkegaard opposed himself to Hegel, and it is by ambiguity that, in our own generation, Sartre, in *Being and Nothingness,* fundamentally defined man, that being whose being is not to be, that subjectivity which realizes itself only as a presence in the world, that engaged freedom, that surging of the for-oneself which is immediately given for others. But it is also claimed that existentialism is a philosophy of the absurd and of despair. It encloses man in a sterile anguish, in an empty subjectivity. It is incapable of furnishing him with any principle for making choices. Let him do as he pleases. In any case, the game is lost. Does not Sartre declare, in effect, that man is a "useless passion," that he tries in vain to realize the synthesis of the for-oneself and the in-oneself, to make himself God? It is true. But it is also true that the most optimistic ethics have all begun by emphasizing the element of failure involved in the condition of man; without failure, no ethics; for a being who, from the very start, would be an exact co-incidence with himself, in a perfect plenitude, the notion of having-to-be would have no meaning. One does not offer an ethics to a God. . . .

Well and good. But it is still necessary for the failure to be surmounted, and existentialist ontology does not allow this hope. Man's passion is useless; he has no means for becoming the being that he is not. That too is true. And it is also true that in *Being and Nothingness* Sartre has insisted above all on the abortive aspect of the human adventure. It is only in the last pages that he opens up the perspective for an ethics. However, if we reflect upon his descriptions of existence, we perceive that they are far from condemning man without recourse.

The failure described in *Being and Nothingness* is definitive, but it is also ambiguous. Man, Sartre tells us, is "a being who *makes himself* a lack of being *in order that there might be* being." That means, first of all, that his passion is not inflicted upon him from without. He chooses it. It is his very being and, as such, does not imply the idea of unhappiness. If this choice is considered as useless, it is because there exists no absolute value before the passion of man, outside of it, in relation to which one might distinguish the useless from the useful. The word "useful" has not yet received a meaning on the level of description where *Being and Nothingness* is situated. It can be defined only in the human world established by man's projects and the ends he sets up. In the original helplessness from which man surges up, nothing is useful, nothing is useless. It must therefore be understood that the passion to which man has acquiesced finds no external justification. No outside appeal, no objective necessity permits of its being called useful. It *has* no reason to will itself. But this does not mean that it can not justify itself, that it can not *give itself* reasons for being that it does not *have*. And indeed Sartre tells us that man makes himself this lack of being *in order that* there might be being. The term *in order that*

clearly indicates an intentionality. It is not in vain that man nullifies being. Thanks to him, being is disclosed and he desires this disclosure. There is an original type of attachment to being which is not the relationship "wanting to be" but rather "wanting to disclose being." Now, here there is not failure, but rather success. This end, which man proposes to himself by making himself lack of being, is, in effect, realized by him. By uprooting himself from the world, man makes himself present to the world and makes the world present to him. I should like to be the landscape which I am contemplating, I should like this sky, this quiet water to think themselves within me, that it might be I whom they express in flesh and bone, and I remain at a distance. But it is also by this distance that the sky and the water exist before me. My contemplation is an excruciation only because it is also a joy. I can not appropriate the snow field where I slide. It remains foreign, forbidden, but I take delight in this very effort toward an impossible possession. I experience it as a triumph, not as a defeat. This means that man, in his vain attempt to *be* God, makes himself exist *as* man, and if he is satisfied with this existence, he coincides exactly with himself. It is not granted him to exist without tending toward this being which he will never be. But it is possible for him to want this tension even with the failure which it involves. His being is lack of being, but this lack has a way of being which is precisely existence. In Hegelian terms it might be said that we have here a negation of the negation by which the positive is re-established. Man makes himself a lack, but he can deny the lack as lack and affirm himself as a positive existence. He then assumes the failure. And the condemned action, insofar as it is an effort to be, finds its validity insofar as it is a manifestation of existence. However, rather than being a Hegelian act of surpassing, it is a matter of a conversion. For in Hegel the surpassed terms are preserved only as abstract moments, whereas we consider that existence still remains a negativity in the positive affirmation of itself. And it does not appear, in its turn, as the term of a further synthesis. The failure is not surpassed, but assumed. Existence asserts itself as an absolute which must seek its justification within itself and not suppress itself even though it may be lost by preserving itself. To attain his truth, man must not attempt to dispel the ambiguity of his being but, on the contrary, accept the task of realizing it. He rejoins himself only to the extent that he agrees to remain at a distance from himself. This conversion is sharply distinguished from the Stoic conversion in that it does not claim to oppose to the sensible universe a formal freedom which is without content. To exist genuinely is not to deny this spontaneous movement of my transcendence, but only to refuse to lose myself in it. Existentialist conversion should rather be compared to Husserlian reduction: let man put his will to be "in parentheses" and he will thereby be brought to the consciousness of his true condition. And just as phenomenological reduction prevents the errors of dogmatism by suspending all affirmation concerning the mode of reality of the external world, whose flesh and bone presence the reduction does not, however, contest, so existentialist conversion does not suppress my instincts, desires, plans, and passions. It merely prevents any possibility of failure by refusing to set up as absolutes the ends toward which my transcendence thrusts itself, and by considering them in their connection with the freedom which projects them.

The first implication of such an attitude is that the genuine man will not agree to recognize any foreign absolute. When a man projects into an ideal heaven that impossible synthesis of the for-itself and the in-itself that is called God, it is because he wishes the regard of this existing Being to change his existence into being; but if he agrees not to be in order to exist genuinely, he will abandon the dream of an inhuman objectivity. He will understand that it is not a matter of being right in the eyes of a God, but of being right in his own eyes. Renouncing the thought of seeking the guarantee for his existence outside of himself, he will also refuse to believe in unconditioned values which would set themselves up athwart his freedom like things. Value is this lacking-being of which freedom *makes itself* a lack; and it is because the latter makes itself a lack that value appears. It is desire which creates the desirable, and the project which sets up the end. It is human existence which makes values spring up in the world on the basis of which it will be able to judge the enterprise in which it will be engaged. But first it locates itself beyond any pessimism, as beyond any optimism, for the fact of its original springing forth is a pure contingency. Before existence there is no more reason to exist than not to exist. The lack of existence can not be evaluated since it is the fact on the basis of which all evaluation is defined. It can not be compared to anything for there

is nothing outside of it to serve as a term of comparison. This rejection of any extrinsic justification also confirms the rejection of an original pessimism which we posited at the beginning. Since it is unjustifiable from without, to declare from without that it is unjustifiable is not to condemn it. And the truth is that outside of existence there is nobody. Man exists. For him it is not a question of wondering whether his presence in the world is useful, whether life is worth the trouble of being lived. These questions make no sense. It is a matter of knowing whether he wants to live and under what conditions.

But if man is free to define for himself the conditions of a life which is valid in his own eyes, can he not choose whatever he likes and act however he likes? Dostoievsky asserted, "If God does not exist, everything is permitted." Today's believers use this formula for their own advantage. To re-establish man at the heart of his destiny is, they claim, to repudiate all ethics. However, far from God's absence authorizing all license, the contrary is the case, because man is abandoned on the earth, because his acts are definitive, absolute engagements. He bears the responsibility for a world which is not the work of a strange power, but of himself, where his defeats are inscribed, and his victories as well. A God can pardon, efface, and compensate. But if God does not exist, man's faults are inexpiable. If it is claimed that, whatever the case may be, this earthly stake has no importance, this is precisely because one invokes that inhuman objectivity which we declined at the start. One can not start by saying that our earthly destiny *has* or *has not* importance, for it depends upon us to give it importance. It is up to man to make it important to be a man, and he alone can feel his success or failure. And if it is again said that nothing forces him to try to justify his being in this way, then one is playing upon the notion of freedom in a dishonest way. The believer is also free to sin. The divine law is imposed upon him only from the moment he decides to save his soul. In the Christian religion, though one speaks very little about them today, there are also the damned. Thus, on the earthly plane, a life which does not seek to ground itself will be a pure contingency. But it is permitted to wish to give itself a meaning and a truth, and it then meets rigorous demands within its own heart.

However, even among the proponents of secular ethics, there are many who charge existentialism with offering no objective content to the moral act. It is said that this philosophy is subjective, even solipsistic. If he is once enclosed within himself, how can man get out? But there too we have a great deal of dishonesty. It is rather well known that the fact of being a subject is a universal fact and that the Cartesian *cogito* expresses both the most individual experience and the most objective truth. By affirming that the source of all values resides in the freedom of man, existentialism merely carries on the tradition of Kant, Fichte, and Hegel, who, in the words of Hegel himself, "have taken for their point of departure the principle according to which the essence of right and duty and the essence of the thinking and willing subject are absolutely identical." The idea that defines all humanism is that the world is not a given world, foreign to man, one to which he has to force himself to yield from without. It is the world willed by man, insofar as his will expresses his genuine reality.

Some will answer, "All well and good. But Kant escapes solipsism because for him genuine reality is the human person insofar as it transcends its empirical embodiment and chooses to be universal." And doubtless Hegel asserted that the "right of individuals to their particularity is equally contained in ethical substantiality, since particularity is the extreme, phenomenal modality in which moral reality exists (*Philosophy of Right*, § 154)." But for him particularity appears only as a moment of the totality in which it must surpass itself. Whereas for existentialism, it is not impersonal universal man who is the source of values, but the plurality of concrete, particular men projecting themselves toward their ends on the basis of situations whose particularity is as radical and as irreducible as subjectivity itself. How could men, originally separated, get together?

And, indeed, we are coming to the real situation of the problem. But to state it is not to demonstrate that it can not be resolved. On the contrary, we must here again invoke the notion of Hegelian "displacement." There is an ethics only if there is a problem to solve. And it can be said, by inverting the preceding line of argument, that the ethics which have given solutions by effacing the fact of the separation of men are not valid precisely because there *is* this separation. An ethics of ambiguity will be one which will refuse to deny *a priori* that separate existants can, at the same time, be bound to each other, that their individual freedoms can forge laws valid for all.

·   ·   ·

Must we grant this curious paradox: that from the moment a man recognizes himself as free, he is prohibited from wishing for anything?

On the contrary, it appears to us that by turning toward this freedom we are going to discover a principle of action whose range will be universal.

·   ·   ·

AMBIGUITY

·   ·   ·

In the first place, it seems to us that the individual as such is one of the ends at which our action must aim. Here we are at one with the point of view of Christian charity, the Epicurean cult of friendship, and Kantian moralism which treats each man as an end. He interests us not merely as a member of a class, a nation, or a collectivity, but as an individual man. This distinguishes us from the systematic politician who cares only about collective destinies; and probably a tramp enjoying his bottle of wine, or a child playing with a balloon, or a Neapolitan lazzarone loafing in the sun in no way helps in the liberation of man; that is why the abstract will of the revolutionary scorns the concrete benevolence which occupies itself in satisfying desires which have no morrow. However, it must not be forgotten that there is a concrete bond between freedom and existence; to will man free is to will there to *be* being, it is to will the disclosure of being in the joy of existence; in order for the idea of liberation to have a concrete meaning, the joy of existence must be asserted in each one, at every instant; the movement toward freedom assumes its real, flesh and blood figure in the world by thickening into pleasure, into happiness. If the satisfaction of an old man drinking a glass of wine counts for nothing, then production and wealth are only hollow myths; they have meaning only if they are capable of being retrieved in individual and living joy. The saving of time and the conquest of leisure have no meaning if we are not moved by the laugh of a child at play. If we do not love life on our own account and through others, it is futile to seek to justify it in any way.

However, politics is right in rejecting benevolence to the extent that the latter thoughtlessly sacrifices the future to the present. The ambiguity of freedom, which very often is occupied only in fleeing from itself, introduces a difficult equivocation into relationships with each individual taken one by one. Just what is meant by the expression "to love others"? What is meant by taking them as ends? In any event, it is evident that we are not going to decide to fulfill the will of every man. There are cases where a man positively wants evil, that is, the enslavement of other men, and he must then be fought. It also happens that, without harming anyone, he flees from his own freedom, seeking passionately and alone to attain the being which constantly eludes him. If he asks for our help, are we to give it to him? We blame a man who helps a drug addict intoxicate himself or a desperate man commit suicide, for we think that rash behavior of this sort is an attempt of the individual against his own freedom; he must be made aware of his error and put in the presence of the real demands of his freedom. Well and good. But what if he persists? Must we then use violence? There again the serious man busies himself dodging the problem; the values of life, of health, and of moral conformism being set up, one does not hesitate to impose them on others. But we know that this pharisaism can cause the worst disasters: lacking drugs, the addict may kill himself. It is no more necessary to serve an abstract ethics obstinately than to yield without due consideration to impulses of pity or generosity; violence is justified only if it opens concrete possibilities to the freedom which I am trying to save; by practising it I am willy-nilly assuming an engagement in relation to others and to myself; a man whom I snatch from the death which he had chosen has the right to come and ask me for means and reasons for living; the tyranny practised against an invalid can be justified only by his getting better; whatever the purity of the intention which animates me, any dictatorship is a fault for which I have to get myself pardoned. Besides, I am in no position to make decisions of this sort indiscriminately; the example of the unknown person who throws himself in to the Seine and whom I hesitate whether or not to fish out is quite abstract; in the absence of a concrete bond with this desperate person my choice will never be anything but a contingent facticity. If I find myself in a position to do violence to a child, or to a melancholic, sick, or distraught person the reason is that I also find myself charged with his upbringing, his happiness, and his health: I am a parent, a teacher, a nurse, a doctor, or a friend. . . So, by a tacit agreement, by the very fact that I am solicited, the strict-

ness of my decision is accepted or even desired; the more seriously I accept my responsibilities, the more justified it is. That is why love authorizes severities which are not granted to indifference. What makes the problem so complex is that, on the one hand, one must not make himself an accomplice of that flight from freedom that is found in heedlessness, caprice, mania, and passion, and that, on the other hand, it is the abortive movement of man toward being which is his very existence, it is through the failure which he has assumed that he asserts himself as a freedom. To want to prohibit a man from error is to forbid him to fulfill his own existence, it is to deprive him of life. At the beginning of Claudel's *The Satin Shoe,* the husband of Dona Prouheze, the Judge, the Just, as the author regards him, explains that every plant needs a gardener in order to grow and that he is the one whom heaven has destined for his young wife; beside the fact that we are shocked by the arrogance of such a thought (for how does he know that he is this enlightened gardener? Isn't he merely a jealous husband?) this likening of a soul to a plant is not acceptable; for, as Kant would say, the value of an act lies not in its *conformity* to an external model, but in its internal truth. We object to the inquisitors who want to create faith and virtue from without; we object to all forms of fascism which seek to fashion the happiness of man from without; and also the paternalism which thinks that it has done something for man by prohibiting him from certain possibilities of temptation, whereas what is necessary is to give him reasons for resisting it.

Thus, violence is not immediately justified when it opposes willful acts which one considers perverted; it becomes inadmissible if it uses the pretext of ignorance to deny a freedom which, as we have seen, can be practised within ignorance itself. Let the "enlightened elites" strive to change the situation of the child, the illiterate, the primitive crushed beneath his superstitions; that is one of their most urgent tasks; but in this very effort they must respect a freedom which, like theirs, is absolute. They are always opposed, for example, to the extension of universal suffrage by adducing the incompetence of the masses, of women, of the natives in the colonies; but this forgetting that man always has to decide by himself in the darkness, that he must want beyond what he knows. If infinite knowledge were necessary (even supposing that it were conceivable), then the colonial administrator himself would not have the right to freedom; he is much further from perfect knowledge than the most backward savage is from him.

. . .

However, the "enlightened elite" objects, one does not let a child dispose of himself, one does not permit him to vote. This is another sophism. To the extent that woman or the happy or resigned slave lives in the infantile world of ready-made values, calling them "an eternal child" or "a grown-up child" has some meaning, but the analogy is only partial. Childhood is a particular sort of situation: it is a natural situation whose limits are not created by other men and which is thereby not comparable to a situation of oppression; it is a situation which is common to all men and which is temporary for all; therefore, it does not represent a limit which cuts off the individual from his possibilities, but, on the contrary, the moment of a development in which new possibilities are won. The child is ignorant because he has not yet had the time to acquire knowledge, not because this time has been refused him. To treat him as a child is not to bar him from the future but to open it to him; he needs to be taken in hand, he invites authority, it is the form which the resistance of facticity, through which all liberation is brought about, takes for him. And on the other hand, even in this situation the child has a right to his freedom and must be respected as a human person. . . .

Thus, we can set up point number one: the good of an individual or a group of individuals requires that it be taken as an absolute end of our action; but we are not authorized to decide upon this end *a priori*. The fact is that no behavior is ever authorized to begin with, and one of the concrete consequences of existentialist ethics is the rejection of all the previous justifications which might be drawn from the civilization, the age, and the culture; it is the rejection of every principle of authority. To put it positively, the precept will be to treat the other (to the extent that he is the only one concerned, which is the moment that we are considering at present) as a freedom so that his end may be freedom; in using this conducting-wire one will have to incur the risk, in each case, of inventing an original solution. Out of disappointment in love a young girl takes an overdose of pheno-barbital; in the morning friends find her dying, they call a doctor, she is saved; later on she becomes a happy mother of a family; her friends were right in considering her

suicide as a hasty and heedless act and in putting her into a position to reject it or return to it freely. But in asylums one sees melancholic patients who have tried to commit suicide twenty times, who devote their freedom to seeking the means of escaping their jailers and of putting an end to their intolerable anguish; the doctor who gives them a friendly pat on the shoulder is their tyrant and their torturer. A friend who is intoxicated by alcohol or drugs asks me for money so that he can go and buy the poison that is necessary to him; I urge him to get cured, I take him to a doctor, I try to help him live; insofar as there is a chance of my being successful, I am acting correctly in refusing him the sum he asks for. But if circumstances prohibit me from doing anything to change the situation in which he is struggling, all I can do is give in; a deprivation of a few hours will do nothing but exasperate his torments uselessly; and he may have recourse to extreme means to get what I do not give him. That is also the problem touched on by Ibsen in *The Wild Duck*. An individual lives in a situation of falsehood; the falsehood is violence, tyranny: shall I tell the truth in order to free the victim? It would first be necessary to create a situation of such a kind that the truth might be bearable and that, though losing his illusions, the deluded individual might again find about him reasons for hoping. What makes the problem more complex is that the freedom of one man almost always concerns that of other individuals. Here is a married couple who persist in living in a hovel; if one does not succeed in giving them the desire to live in a more healthful dwelling, they must be allowed to follow their preferences; but the situation changes if they have children; the freedom of the parents would be the ruin of their sons, and as freedom and the future are on the side of the latter, these are the ones who must first be taken into account. The Other is multiple, and on the basis of this new questions arise.

One might first wonder for whom we are seeking freedom and happiness. When raised in this way, the problem is abstract; the answer will, therefore, be arbitrary, and the arbitrary always involves outrage. It is not entirely the fault of the district social-worker if she is apt to be odious; because, her money and time being limited, she hesitates before distributing it to this one or that one, she appears to others as a pure externality, a blind facticity. Contrary to the formal strictness of Kantianism for whom the more abstract the act is the more virtuous it is, generosity seems to us to be better grounded and therefore more valid the less distinction there is between the other and ourself and the more we fulfill ourself in taking the other as an end. That is what happens if I am engaged in relation to others. The Stoics impugned the ties of family, friendship, and nationality so that they recognized only the universal form of man. But man is man only through situations whose particularity is precisely a universal fact. There are men who expect help from certain men and not from others, and these expectations define privileged lines of action. It is fitting that the negro fight for the negro, the Jew for the Jew, the proletarian for the proletarian, and the Spaniard in Spain. But the assertion of these particular solidarities must not contradict the will for universal solidarity and each finite undertaking must also be open on the totality of men.

But it is then that we find in concrete form the conflicts which we have described abstractly; for the cause of freedom can triumph only through particular sacrifices. And certainly there are hierarchies among the goods desired by men; one will not hesitate to sacrifice the comfort, luxury, and leisure of certain men to assure the liberation of certain others; but when it is a question of choosing among freedoms, how shall we decide?

Let us repeat, one can only indicate a method here. The first point is always to consider what genuine human interest fills the abstract form which one proposes as the action's end. Politics always puts forward Ideas: Nation, Empire, Union, Economy, etc. But none of these forms has value in itself; it has it only insofar as it involves concrete individuals. If a nation can assert itself proudly only to the detriment of its members, if a union can be created only to the detriment of those it is trying to unite, the nation or the union must be rejected. We repudiate all idealisms, mysticisms, etcetera which prefer a Form to man himself. But the matter becomes really agonizing when it is a question of a Cause which genuinely serves man. That is why the question of Stalinist politics, the problem of the relationship of the Party to the masses which it uses in order to serve them, is in the forefront of the preoccupations of all men of good will. However, there are very few who raise it without dishonesty, and we must first try to dispel a few fallacies.

The opponent of the U.S.S.R. is making use of a fallacy when, emphasizing the part of criminal violence assumed by Stalinist politics, he neglects to confront it with the ends pursued. Doubtless, the purges, the deportations, the abuses of the occupation, and the police dictatorship surpass in importance the violences practised by any other country; the very fact that there are a hundred and sixty million inhabitants in Russia multiplies the numerical coefficient of the injustices committed. But these quantitative considerations are insufficient. One can no more judge the means without the end which gives it its meaning than he can detach the end from the means which defines it. . . .

But, on the other hand, the defender of the U.S.S.R. is making use of a fallacy when he unconditionally justifies the sacrifices and the crimes by the ends pursued; it would first be necessary to prove that, on the one hand, the end is unconditioned and that, on the other hand, the crimes committed in its name were strictly necessary.

. . .

Thus, we challenge every condemnation as well as every *a priori* justification of the violence practised with a view to a valid end. They must be legitimized concretely. A calm, mathematical calculation is here impossible. One must attempt to judge the chances of success that are involved in a certain sacrifice; but at the beginning this judgment will always be doubtful; besides, in the face of the immediate reality of the sacrifice, the notion of chance is difficult to think about. On the one hand, one can multiply a probability infinitely without ever reaching certainty; but yet, practically, it ends by merging with this asymptote: in our private life as in our collective life there is no other truth than a statistical one. On the other hand, the interests at stake do not allow themselves to be put into an equation; the suffering of one man, that of a million men, are incommensurable with the conquests realized by millions of others, present death is incommensurable with the life to come. It would be utopian to want to set up on the one hand the chances of success multiplied by the stake one is after, and on the other hand the weight of the immediate sacrifice. One finds himself back at the anguish of free decision. And that is why political choice is an ethical choice: it is a wager as well as a decision; one bets on the chances and risks of the measure under consideration; but whether chances and risks must be assumed or not in the given circumstances must be decided without help, and in so doing one sets up values. . . .

ambiguity wording

Ordinarily, situations are so complex that a long analysis is necessary before being able to pose the ethical moment of the choice. We shall confine ourselves here to the consideration of a few simple examples which will enable us to make our attitude somewhat more precise. In an underground revolutionary movement when one discovers the presence of a stool-pigeon, one does not hesitate to beat him up; he is a present and future danger who has to be gotten rid of; but if a man is merely suspected of treason, the case is more ambiguous. We blame those northern peasants who in the war of 1914–18 massacred an innocent family which was suspected of signaling to the enemy; the reason is that not only were the presumptions vague, but the danger was uncertain; at any rate, it was enough to put the suspects into prison; while waiting for a serious inquiry it was easy to keep them from doing any harm. However, if a questionable individual holds the fate of other men in his hands, if, in order to avoid the risk of killing one innocent man, one runs the risk of letting ten innocent men die, it is reasonable to sacrifice him. We can merely ask that such decisions be not taken hastily and lightly, and that, all things considered, the evil that one inflicts be lesser than that which is being forestalled.

There are cases still more disturbing because there the violence is not immediately efficacious; the violences of the Resistance did not aim at the material weakening of Germany; it happens that their purpose was to create such a state of violence that collaboration would be impossible; in one sense, the burning of a whole French village was too high a price to pay for the elimination of three enemy officers; but those fires and the massacring of hostages were themselves parts of the plan; they created an abyss between the occupiers and the occupied. Likewise, the insurrections in Paris and Lyons at the beginning of the nineteenth century, or the revolts in India, did not aim at shattering the yoke of the oppressor at one blow, but rather at creating and keeping alive the meaning of the revolt and at making the mystifications of conciliation impossible. Attempts which are aware that one by one they are doomed to failure can be legitimized by the whole of the situation which they create. This is also the meaning of Steinbeck's novel *In Dubious Battle* where a communist leader does not hesitate to launch a costly strike of uncertain success but through

which there will be born, along with the solidarity of the workers, the consciousness of exploitation and the will to reject it.

It seems to me interesting to contrast this example with the debate in John Dos Passos' *The Adventures of a Young Man*. Following a strike, some American miners are condemned to death. Their comrades try to have their trial reconsidered. Two methods are put forward: one can act officially, and one knows that they then have an excellent chance of winning their case; one can also work up a sensational trial with the Communist Party taking the affair in hand, stirring up a press campaign and circulating international petitions; but the court will be unwilling to yield to this intimidation. The party will thereby get a tremendous amount of publicity, but the miners will be condemned. What is a man of good will to decide in this case?

Dos Passos' hero chooses to save the miners and we believe that he did right. Certainly, if it were necessary to choose between the whole revolution and the lives of two or three men, no revolutionary would hesitate; but it was merely a matter of helping along the party propaganda, or better, of increasing somewhat its chances of developing within the United States; the immediate interest of the C.P. in that country is only hypothetically tied up with that of the revolution; in fact, a cataclysm like the war has so upset the situation of the world that a great part of the gains and losses of the past have been absolutely swept away. If it is really *men* which the movement claims to be serving, in this case it must prefer saving the lives of three concrete individuals to a very uncertain and weak chance of serving a little more effectively by their sacrifice the mankind to come. If it considers these lives negligible, it is because it too ranges itself on the side of the formal politicians who prefer the Idea to its content; it is because it prefers itself, in its subjectivity, to the goals to which it claims to be dedicated. Besides, whereas in the example chosen by Steinbeck the strike is immediately an appeal to the freedom of the workers and in its very failure is already a liberation, the sacrifice of the miners is a mystification and an oppression; they are duped by being made to believe that an effort is being made to save their lives, and the whole proletariat is duped with them. Thus, in both examples, we find ourselves before the same abstract case: men are going to die so that the party which claims to be serving them will realize a limited gain; but a concrete analysis leads us to opposite moral solutions.

It is apparent that the method we are proposing, analogous in this respect to scientific or aesthetic methods, consists, in each case, of confronting the values realized with the values aimed at, and the meaning of the act with its content. The fact is that the politician, contrary to the scientist and the artist, and although the element of failure which he assumes is much more outrageous, is rarely concerned with making use of it. May it be that there is an irresistible dialectic of power wherein morality has no place? Is the ethical concern, even in its realistic and concrete form, detrimental to the interests of action? The objection will surely be made that hesitation and misgivings only impede victory. Since, in any case, there is an element of failure in all success, since the ambiguity, at any rate, must be surmounted, why not refuse to take notice of it? In the first number of the *Cahiers d'Action* a reader declared that once and for all we should regard the militant communist as "the permanent hero of our time" and should reject the exhausting tension demanded by existentialism; installed in the permanence of heroism, one will blindly direct himself toward an uncontested goal; but one then resembles Colonel de la Roque who unwaveringly went right straight ahead of him without knowing where he was going. Malaparte relates that the young Nazis, in order to become insensitive to the suffering of others, practised by plucking out the eyes of live cats; there is no more radical way of avoiding the pitfalls of ambiguity. But an action which wants to serve man ought to be careful not to forget him on the way; if it chooses to fulfill itself blindly, it will lose its meaning or will take on an unforeseen meaning; for the goal is not fixed once and for all; it is defined all along the road which leads to it. Vigilance alone can keep alive the validity of the goals and the genuine assertion of freedom. Moreover, ambiguity can not fail to appear on the scene; it is felt by the victim, and his revolt or his complaints also make it exist for his tyrant; the latter will then be tempted to put everything into question, to renounce, thus denying both himself and his ends; or, if he persists, he will continue to blind himself only by multiplying crimes and by perverting his original design more and more. The fact is that the man of action becomes a dictator not in respect to his ends but because these ends are necessarily set up through his will. Hegel, in his *Phenomenology,* has emphasized this inextricable confusion between objectivity and subjectivity. A man gives himself to a Cause only by making it *his* Cause; as he fulfills himself within it, it is also through him that it is expressed, and the will to power is not distinguished in such a case from generosity; when an individual or a party chooses to triumph, whatever the cost may be, it is their own triumph which they take for an end. If the fusion of the Commissar and the Yogi were realized, there would be a self-criticism in the man of action which would expose to him the ambiguity of his will, thus arresting the imperious drive of his subjectivity and, by the same token, contesting the unconditioned value of the goal. But the fact is that the politician follows the line of least resistance; it is easy to fall asleep over the unhappiness of others and to count it for very little; it is easier to throw a hundred men, ninety-seven of whom are innocent, into prison, than to discover the three culprits who are hidden among them; it is easier to kill a man than to keep a close watch on him; all politics makes use of the police, which officially flaunts its radical contempt for the individual and which loves violence for its own sake. The thing that goes by the name of political necessity is in part the laziness and brutality of the police. That is why it is incumbent upon ethics not to follow the line of least resistance; an act which is not destined, but rather quite freely consented to; it must make itself effective so that what was at first facility may become difficult. For want of internal criticism, this is the role that an opposition must take upon itself. There are two types of opposition. The first is a rejection of the very ends set up by a regime: it is the opposition of anti-fascism to fascism, of fascism to socialism. In the second type, the oppositionist accepts the objective goal but criticizes the subjective movement which aims at it; he may not even wish for a change of power, but he deems it necessary to bring into play a contestation which will make the subjective appear as such. Thereby he exacts a perpetual contestation of the means by the end and of the end by the means. He must be careful himself not to ruin, by the means which he employs, the end he is aiming at, and above all not to pass into the service of the oppositionists of the first type. But, delicate as it may be, his role is, nevertheless, necessary. Indeed, on the one hand, it would be absurd to oppose a liberating action with the pretext that it implies crime and tyranny; for without crime and tyranny there could be no liberation of man; one can not escape that dialectic which goes from freedom to freedom through dictatorship and oppression. But, on the other hand, he would be guilty of allowing the liberating movement to harden into a moment which is acceptable only if it passes into its opposite; tyranny and crime must be kept from triumphantly establishing themselves in the world; the conquest of freedom is their only justification, and the assertion of freedom against them must therefore be kept alive.

CONCLUSION

Is this kind of ethics individualistic or not? Yes, if one means by that that it accords to the individual an absolute value and that it recognizes in him alone the power of laying the foundations of his own existence. It is individualism in the sense in which the wisdom of the ancients, the Christian ethics of salvation, and the Kantian ideal of virtue also merit this name; it is opposed to the totalitarian doctrines which raise up beyond man the mirage of Mankind. But it is not solipsistic, since the individual is defined only by his relationship to the world and to other individuals; he exists only by transcending himself, and his freedom can be achieved only through the freedom of others. He justifies his existence by a movement which, like freedom, springs from his heart but which leads outside of him.

This individualism does not lead to the anarchy of personal whim. Man is free; but he finds his law in his very freedom. First, he must assume his freedom and not flee it; he assumes it by a constructive movement: one does not exist without doing something; and also by a negative movement which rejects oppression for oneself and others. In construction, as in rejection, it is a matter of reconquering freedom on the contingent facticity of existence, that is, of taking the given, which, at the start, *is there* without any reason, as something willed by man. A conquest of this kind is never finished; the contingency remains, and, so that he may assert his will, man is even obliged to stir up in the world the outrage he does not want. But this element of failure is a very condition of his life; one

can never dream of eliminating it without immediately dreaming of death. This does not mean that one should consent to failure, but rather one must consent to struggle against it without respite.

Yet, isn't this battle without victory pure gullibility? It will be argued that this is only a ruse of transcendance projecting before itself a goal which constantly recedes, running after itself on an endless treadmill; to exist for Mankind is to remain where one is, and it fools itself by calling this turbulent stagnation progress; our whole ethics does nothing but encourage it in this lying enterprise since we are asking each one to confirm existence as a value for all others; isn't it simply a matter of organizing among men a complicity which allows them to substitute a game of illusions for the given world?

We have already attempted to answer this objection. One can formulate it only by placing himself on the grounds of an inhuman and consequently false objectivity; within Mankind men may be fooled; the word "lie" has a meaning by opposition to the truth established by men themselves, but Mankind can not fool itself completely since it is precisely Mankind which creates the criteria of true and false. In Plato, art is mystification because there is the heaven of Ideas; but in the earthly domain all glorification of the earth is true as soon as it is realized. Let men attach value to words, forms, colors, mathematical theorems, physical laws, and athletic prowess; let them accord value to one another in love and friendship, and the objects, the events, and the men immediately *have* this value; they have it absolutely. It is possible that a man may refuse to love anything on earth; he will prove this refusal and he will carry it out by suicide. If he lives, the reason is that, whatever he may say, there still remains in him some attachment to existence; his life will be commensurate with this attachment; it will justify itself to the extent that it genuinely justifies the world.

This justification, though open upon the entire universe through time and space, will always be finite. Whatever one may do, one never realizes anything but a limited work, like existence itself which tries to establish itself through that work and which death also limits. It is the assertion of our finiteness which doubtless gives the doctrine which we have just evoked its austerity and, in some eyes, its sadness. As soon as one considers a system abstractly and theoretically, one puts himself, in effect, on the plane of the universal, thus, of the infinite. That is why reading the Hegelian system is so comforting. I remember having experienced a great feeling of calm on reading Hegel in the impersonal framework of the Bibliotheque Nationale in August 1940. But once I got into the street again, into my life, out of the system, beneath a real sky, the system was no longer of any use to me: what it had offered me, under a show of the infinite, was the consolations of death; and I again wanted to live in the midst of living men. I think that, inversely, existentialism does not offer to the reader the consolations of an abstract evasion: existentialism proposes no evasion. On the contrary, its ethics is experienced in the truth of life, and it then appears as the only proposition of salvation which one can address to men. Taking on its own account Descartes' revolt against the evil genius, the pride of the thinking reed in the face of the universe which crushes him, it asserts that, despite his limits, through them, it is up to each one to fulfill his existence as an absolute. Regardless of the staggering dimensions of the world about us, the density of our ignorance, the risks of catastrophes to come, and our individual weakness within the immense collectivity, the fact remains that we are absolutely free today if we choose to will our existence in its finiteness, a finiteness which is open on the infinite. And in fact, any man who has known real loves, real revolts, real desires, and real will knows quite well that he has no need of any outside guarantee to be sure of his goals; their certitude comes from his own drive. There is a very old saying which goes: "Do what you must, come what may." That amounts to saying in a different way that the result is not external to the good will which fulfills itself in aiming at it. If it came to be that each man did what he must, existence would be saved in each one without there being any need of dreaming of a paradise where all would be reconciled in death.

ALBERT CAMUS (1913–1960)

Albert Camus was born in Algeria and studied philosophy at the University of Algiers. His work as a journalist brought him to Paris, where he was active in the resistance and joined the ranks of the existentialists. His leading publications were *The Stranger* (1942), *The Myth of Sisyphus and Other Essays* (1942), *The Plague* (1947), *The Rebel* (1951), and *The Fall* (1956). Three years before he was killed in a car wreck, he was awarded the Nobel prize for literature.

Should we say that our lives are not worth living if they are ultimately pointless and arbitrary? In "The Myth of Sisyphus" and "An Absurd Reasoning" Camus struggles with this issue. He gives powerful expression to the despair of those who (like Pascal) are struck with how dismal life seems if there is no God who assigns things a purpose and who promises an afterlife, but who (unlike Pascal) wish to face up to the shortcomings of life without falling back on religious faith and other "evasions." Camus finds himself struck with the absurdity of the world. He longs for a world that assigns itself and him an interpretation, a meaning and a value, but finds that the world he lives in does not do so. Those who share Camus' view of the absurdity of the world are alienated from their world; they are unable to think of it as theirs. But what is to be done? Camus asks: Should we continue to live in an absurd world? Doesn't the fact of absurdity entail that life is not worth living? If it did, shouldn't we commit suicide?

In the end Camus suggests that suicide is not the proper response to absurdity. Instead, we should live on with scorn for the world, knowing fully that the world is absurd, and while living, we should remain unresigned to the absurdity of the world. We should live as an act of rebellion. "That revolt," he says, "gives life its value."

The Myth of Sisyphus
from The Myth of Sisyphus and Other Essays

The gods had condemned Sisyphus to ceaselessly rolling a rock to the top of a mountain, whence the stone would fall back of its own weight. They had thought with some reason that there is no more dreadful punishment than futile and hopeless labor.

If one believes Homer, Sisyphus was the wisest and most prudent of mortals. According to another tradition, however, he was disposed to practice the profession of highwayman. I see no contradiction in this. Opinions differ as to the reasons why he became the futile laborer of the underworld. To begin with, he is accused of a certain levity in regard to the gods. He stole their secrets. Ægina, the daughter of Æsopus, was carried off by Jupiter. The father was shocked by that disappearance and complained to Sisyphus. He, who knew of the abduction, offered to tell about it on condition that Æsopus would give water to the citadel of Corinth. To the celestial thunderbolts he preferred the benediction of water. He was punished for this in the underworld. Homer tells us also that Sisyphus had put Death in chains. Pluto could not endure the sight of his deserted, silent empire. He dispatched the god of war, who liberated Death from the hands of her conqueror.

It is said also that Sisyphus, being near to death, rashly wanted to test his wife's love. He ordered her to cast his unburied body into the middle of the public square. Sisyphus woke up in the underworld. And there, annoyed by an obedience so contrary to human love, he obtained from Pluto permission to return to earth in order to chastise his wife. But when he had seen again the face of this world, enjoyed water and sun, warm stones and the sea, he no longer wanted to go back to the infernal darkness. Recalls, signs of anger, warnings were of no avail. Many years more he lived facing the curve of the gulf, the sparkling sea, and the smiles of earth. A decree of the gods was necessary. Mercury came and seized the impudent man by the collar and, snatching him from his joys, led him forcibly back to the underworld, where his rock was ready for him.

You have already grasped that Sisyphus is the absurd hero. He *is*, as much through his passions as through his torture. His scorn of the gods, his hatred of death, and his passion for life won him that unspeakable penalty in which the whole being is exerted toward accomplishing nothing. This is the price that must be paid for the passions of this earth. . . . At the very end of his long effort measured by skyless space and time without depth, the purpose is achieved. Then Sisyphus watches the stone rush down in a few moments toward that lower world whence he will have to push it up again toward the summit. He goes back down to the plain.

It is during that return, that pause, that Sisyphus interests me. A face that toils so close to stones is

already stone itself! I see that man going back down with a heavy yet measured step toward the torment of which he will never know the end. That hour like a breathing-space which returns as surely as his suffering, that is the hour of consciousness. At each of those moments when he leaves the heights and gradually sinks toward the lairs of the gods, he is superior to his fate. He is stronger than his rock.

If this myth is tragic, that is because its hero is conscious. Where would his torture be, indeed, if at every step the hope of succeeding upheld him? The workman of today works every day in his life at the same tasks, and this fate is no less absurd. But it is tragic only at the rare moments when it becomes conscious. Sisyphus, proletarian of the gods, powerless and rebellious, knows the whole extent of his wretched condition: it is what he thinks of during his descent. The lucidity that was to constitute his torture at the same time crowns his victory. There is no fate that cannot be surmounted by scorn.

If the descent is thus sometimes performed in sorrow, it can also take place in joy. This word is not too much. Again I fancy Sisyphus returning toward his rock, and the sorrow was in the beginning. When the images of earth cling too tightly to memory, when the call of happiness becomes too insistent, it happens that melancholy rises in man's heart: this is the rock's victory, this is the rock itself. . . .

Happiness and the absurd are two sons of the same earth. They are inseparable. It would be a mistake to say that happiness necessarily springs from the absurd discovery. It happens as well that the feeling of the absurd springs from happiness. "I conclude that all is well," says Œdipus, and that remark is sacred. It echoes in the wild and limited universe of man. It teaches that all is not, has not been, exhausted. It drives out of this world a god who had come into it with dissatisfaction and a preference for futile sufferings. It makes of fate a human matter, which must be settled among men.

All Sisyphus' silent joy is contained therein. His fate belongs to him. His rock is his thing. . . .

I leave Sisyphus at the foot of the mountain! One always finds one's burden again. But Sisyphus teaches the higher fidelity that negates the gods and raises rocks. He too concludes that all is well. This universe henceforth without a master seems to him neither sterile nor futile. Each atom of that stone, each mineral flake of that night-filled mountain, in itself forms a world. The struggle itself toward the heights is enough to fill a man's heart. One must imagine Sisyphus happy.

ᘒ *An Absurd Reasoning*
from The Myth of Sisyphus and Other Essays

ABSURDITY AND SUICIDE

There is but one truly serious philosophical problem, and that is suicide.* Judging whether life is or is not worth living amounts to answering the fundamental question of philosophy. All the rest—whether or not the world has three dimensions, whether the mind has nine or twelve categories—comes afterwards. These are games; one must first answer. And if it is true, as Nietzsche claims, that a philosopher, to deserve our respect, much preach by example, you can appreciate the importance of that reply, for it will precede the definitive act. These are facts the heart can feel; yet they call for careful study before they become clear to the intellect.

If I ask myself how to judge that this question is more urgent than that, I reply that one judges by the actions it entails. I have never seen anyone die for the ontological argument. Galileo, who held a scientific truth of great importance, abjured it with the greatest ease as soon as it endangered his life. In a certain sense, he did right.† That truth was not worth the stake. Whether the earth or the sun revolves around the other is a matter of profound indifference. To tell the truth, it is a futile question. On the other hand, I see many people die because they judge that life is not worth living. I see others paradoxically getting killed for the ideas or illusions that give them a reason for living (what is called a reason for living is also an excellent reason for dying). I therefore conclude that the meaning of life is the most urgent of questions.

. . .

An act like this is prepared within the silence of the heart, as is a great work of art. The man himself is ignorant of it. One evening he pulls the trigger or jumps. Of an apartment-building manager who had killed himself I was told that he had lost his daughter five years before, that he had changed greatly since, and that that experience had "undermined" him. A more exact word cannot be imagined. Beginning to think is beginning to be undermined. Society has but little connection with such beginnings. The worm is in man's heart. That is where it must be sought. One must follow and understand this fatal game that leads from lucidity in the face of existence to flight from light.

. . .

But if it is hard to fix the precise instant, the subtle step when the mind opted for death, it is easier to deduce from the act itself the consequences it implies. In a sense, and as in melodrama, killing yourself amounts to confessing. It is confessing that life is too much for you or that you do not understand it. Let's not go too far in such analogics, however, but rather return to everyday words. It is merely confessing that that "is not worth the trouble." Living, naturally, is never easy. You continue making the gestures commanded by existence for many reasons, the first of which is habit. Dying voluntarily implies that you have recognized, even instinctively, the ridiculous character of that habit, the absence of any profound reason for living, the insane character of that daily agitation, and the uselessness of suffering.

What, then, is that incalculable feeling that deprives the mind of the sleep necessary to life? A world that can be explained even with bad reasons is a familiar world. But, on the other hand, in a universe suddenly divested of illusions and lights, man feels an alien, a stranger. His exile is without remedy since he is deprived of the memory of a lost home or the hope of a promised land. This divorce between man and his life, the actor and his setting, is properly the feeling of absurdity. All healthy men having thought of their own suicide, it can be seen, without further explanation, that there is a direct connection between this feeling and the longing for death.

The subject of this essay is precisely this relationship between the absurd and suicide, the exact degree to which suicide is a solution to the absurd. The principle can be established that for a man who does not cheat, what he believes to be true must determine his

---

* Some footnotes have been omitted—ed.

† From the point of view of the relative value of truth. On the other hand, from the point of view of virile behavior, this scholar's fragility may well make us smile.

action. Belief in the absurdity of existence must then dictate his conduct. It is legitimate to wonder, clearly and without false pathos, whether a conclusion of this importance requires forsaking as rapidly as possible an incomprehensible condition. I am speaking, of course, of men inclined to be in harmony with themselves.

Stated clearly, this problem may seem both simple and insoluble. But it is wrongly assumed that simple questions involve answers that are no less simple and that evidence implies evidence. *A priori* and reversing the terms of the problem, just as one does or does not kill oneself, it seems that there are but two philosophical solutions, either yes or no. This would be too easy. But allowance must be made for those who, without concluding, continue questioning. Here I am only slightly indulging in irony: this is the majority. I notice also that those who answer "no" act as if they thought "yes." As a matter of fact, if I accept the Nietzschean criterion, they think "yes" in one way or another. On the other hand, it often happens that those who commit suicide were assured of the meaning of life. These contradictions are constant. . . . Schopenhauer is often cited, as a fit subject for laughter, because he praised suicide while seated at a well-set table. This is no subject for joking. That way of not taking the tragic seriously is not so grievous, but it helps to judge a man.

In the face of such contradictions and obscurities must we conclude that there is no relationship between the opinion one has about life and the act one commits to leave it? Let us not exaggerate in this direction. In a man's attachment to life there is something stronger than all the ills in the world. The body's judgment is as good as the mind's, and the body shrinks from annihilation. We get into the habit of living before acquiring the habit of thinking. In that race which daily hastens us toward death, the body maintains its irreparable lead. In short, the essence of that contradiction lies in what I shall call the act of eluding because it is both less and more than diversion in the Pascalian sense. Eluding is the invariable game. The typical act of eluding, the fatal evasion that constitutes the third theme of this essay, is hope. Hope of another life one must "deserve" or trickery of those who live not for life itself but for some great idea that will transcend it, refine it, give it a meaning, and betray it.

Thus everything contributes to spreading confusion. Hitherto, and it has not been wasted effort, people have played on words and pretended to believe that refusing to grant a meaning to life necessarily leads to declaring that it is not worth living. In truth, there is no necessary common measure between these two judgments. One merely has to refuse to be misled by the confusions, divorces, and inconsistencies previously pointed out. One must brush everything aside and go straight to the real problem. One kills oneself because life is not worth living, that is certainly a truth—yet an unfruitful one because it is a truism. But does that insult to existence, that flat denial in which it is plunged come from the fact that it has no meaning? Does its absurdity require one to escape it through hope or suicide—this is what must be clarified, hunted down, and elucidated while brushing aside all the rest. Does the Absurd dictate death? . . . Reflection on suicide gives me an opportunity to raise the only problem to interest me: is there a logic to the point of death? I cannot know unless I pursue, without reckless passion, in the sole light of evidence, the reasoning of which I am here suggesting the source. This is what I call an absurd reasoning. Many have begun it. I do not yet know whether or not they kept to it.

ABSURD WALLS

All great deeds and all great thoughts have a ridiculous beginning. Great works are often born on a street corner or in a restaurant's revolving door. So it is with absurdity. The absurd world more than others derives its nobility from that abject birth. In certain situations, replying "nothing" when asked what one is thinking about may be pretense in a man. Those who are loved are well aware of this. But if that reply is sincere, if it symbolizes that odd state of soul in which the void becomes eloquent, in which the chain of daily gestures is broken, in which the heart vainly seeks the link that will connect it again, then it is as it were the first sign of absurdity.

It happens that the stage sets collapse. Rising, streetcar, four hours in the office or the factory, meal, streetcar, four hours of work, meal, sleep, and Monday Tuesday Wednesday Thursday Friday and Saturday according to the same rhythm—this path is eas-

the daily round

ily followed most of the time. But one day the "why" arises and everything begins in that weariness tinged with amazement. "Begins"—this is important. Weariness comes at the end of the acts of a mechanical life, but at the same time it inaugurates the impulse of consciousness. It awakens consciousness and provokes what follows. What follows is the gradual return into the chain or it is the definitive awakening. At the end of the awakening comes, in time, the consequence: suicide or recovery. In itself weariness has something sickening about it. Here, I must conclude that it is good. For everything begins with consciousness and nothing is worth anything except through it. There is nothing original about these remarks. But they are obvious; that is enough for a while, during a sketchy reconnaissance in the origins of the absurd. Mere "anxiety," as Heidegger says, is at the source of everything.

Likewise and during every day of an unillustrious life, time carries us. But a moment always comes when we have to carry it. We live on the future: "tomorrow," "later on," "when you have made your way," "you will understand when you are old enough." Such irrelevancies are wonderful, for, after all, it's a matter of dying. Yet a day comes when a man notices or says that he is thirty. Thus he asserts his youth. But simultaneously he situates himself in relation to time. He takes his place in it. He admits that he stands at a certain point on a curve that he acknowledges having to travel to its end. He belongs to time, and by the horror that seizes him, he recognizes his worst enemy. Tomorrow, he was longing for tomorrow, whereas everything in him ought to reject it. That revolt of the flesh is the absurd.*

A step lower and strangeness creeps in: perceiving that the world is "dense," sensing to what a degree a stone is foreign and irreducible to us, with what intensity nature or a landscape can negate us. At the heart of all beauty lies something inhuman, and these hills, the softness of the sky, the outline of these trees at this very minute lose the illusory meaning with which we had clothed them, henceforth more remote than a lost paradise. The primitive hostility of the world rises up to face us across millennia. For a second we cease to understand it because for centuries we have understood in it solely the images and designs that we had attributed to it beforehand, because henceforth we lack the power to make use of that artifice. The world evades us because it becomes itself again. . . . Just one thing: that denseness and that strangeness of the world is the absurd.

Men, too, secrete the inhuman. At certain moments of lucidity, the mechanical aspect of their gestures, their meaningless pantomime makes silly everything that surrounds them. A man is talking on the telephone behind a glass partition; you cannot hear him, but you see his incomprehensible dumb show: you wonder why he is alive. This discomfort in the face of man's own inhumanity, this incalculable tumble before the image of what we are, this "nausea," as a writer of today calls it, is also the absurd. Likewise the stranger who at certain seconds comes to meet us in a mirror, the familiar and yet alarming brother we encounter in our own photographs is also the absurd. I come at last to death and to the attitude we have toward it. On this point everything has been said and it is only proper to avoid pathos. Yet one will never be sufficiently surprised that everyone lives as if no one "knew." This is because in reality there is no experience of death. Properly speaking, nothing has been experienced but what has been lived and made conscious. Here, it is barely possible to speak of the experience of others' deaths. It is a substitute, an illusion, and it never quite convinces us. . . . All the pretty speeches about the soul will have their contrary convincingly proved, at least for a time. From this inert body on which a slap makes no mark the soul has disappeared. This elementary and definitive aspect of the adventure constitutes the absurd feeling. . . .

The mind's deepest desire, even in its most elaborate operations, parallels man's unconscious feeling in the face of his universe: it is an insistence upon familiarity, an appetite for clarity. Understanding the world for a man is reducing it to the human, stamping it with his seal. The cat's universe is not the universe of the anthill. The truism "All thought is anthropomorphic" has no other meaning. Likewise, the mind that aims to understand reality can consider itself satisfied only by reducing it to terms of thought. If man realized that the universe like him can love and suffer, he

---

*But not in the proper sense. This is not a definition, but rather an *enumeration* of the feelings that may admit of the absurd. Still, the enumeration finished, the absurd has nevertheless not been exhausted.

would be reconciled. If thought discovered in the shimmering mirrors of phenomena eternal relations capable of summing them up and summing themselves up in a single principle, then would be seen an intellectual joy of which the myth of the blessed would be but a ridiculous imitation. That nostalgia for unity, that appetite for the absolute illustrates the essential impulse of the human drama. . . .

I know another truism: it tells me that man is mortal. One can nevertheless count the minds that have deduced the extreme conclusions from it. It is essential to consider as a constant point of reference in this essay the regular hiatus between what we fancy we know and what we really know, practical assent and simulated ignorance which allows us to live with ideas which, if we truly put them to the test, ought to upset our whole life. Faced with this inextricable contradiction of the mind, we shall fully grasp the divorce separating us from our own creations. So long as the mind keeps silent in the motionless world of its hopes, everything is reflected and arranged in the unity of its nostalgia. But with its first move this world cracks and tumbles: an infinite number of shimmering fragments is offered to the understanding. We must despair of ever reconstructing the familiar, calm surface which would give us peace of heart. . . .

Of whom and of what indeed can I say: "I know that!" This heart within me I can feel, and I judge that it exists. This world I can touch, and I likewise judge that it exists. There ends all my knowledge, and the rest is construction. For if I try to seize this self of which I feel sure, if I try to define and to summarize it, it is nothing but water slipping through my fingers. . . .

In this unintelligible and limited universe, man's fate henceforth assumes its meaning. A horde of irrationals has sprung up and surrounds him until his ultimate end. In his recovered and now studied lucidity, the feeling of the absurd becomes clear and definite. I said that the world is absurd, but I was too hasty. This world in itself is not reasonable, that is all that can be said. But what is absurd is the confrontation of this irrational and the wild longing for clarity whose call echoes in the human heart. The absurd depends as much on man as on the world. For the moment it is all that links them together. It binds them one to the other as only hatred can weld two creatures together. . . .

I want everything to be explained to me or nothing. And the reason is impotent when it hears this cry

from the heart. The mind aroused by this insistence seeks and finds nothing but contradictions and nonsense. What I fail to understand is nonsense. The world is peopled with such irrationals. The world itself, whose single meaning I do not understand, is but a vast irrational. If one could only say just once: "This is clear," all would be saved. . . .

PHILOSOPHICAL SUICIDE

For me the sole datum is the absurd. The first and, after all, the only condition of my inquiry is to preserve the very thing that crushes me, consequently to respect what I consider essential in it. I have just defined it as a confrontation and an unceasing struggle.

And carrying this absurd logic to its conclusion, I must admit that that struggle implies a total absence of hope (which has nothing to do with despair), a continual rejection (which must not be confused with renunciation), and a conscious dissatisfaction (which must not be compared to immature unrest). Everything that destroys, conjures away, or exorcises these requirements (and, to begin with, consent which overthrows divorce) ruins the absurd and devaluates the attitude that may then be proposed. The absurd has meaning only in so far as it is not agreed to. . . .

"But for the Christian death is certainly not the end of everything and it implies infinitely more hope than life implies for us, even when that life is overflowing with health and vigor." Reconciliation through scandal is still reconciliation. It allows one perhaps, as can be seen, to derive hope of its contrary, which is death. But even if fellow-feeling inclines one toward that attitude, still it must be said that excess justifies nothing. That transcends, as the saying goes, the human scale; therefore it must be superhuman. But this "therefore" is superfluous. There is no logical certainty here. There is no experimental probability either. All I can say is that, in fact, that transcends my scale. If I do not draw a negation from it, at least I do not want to found anything on the incomprehensible. I want to know whether I can live with what I know and with that alone. I am told again that here the intelligence must sacrifice its pride and the reason bow down. But if I recognize the limits of the reason, I do not therefore negate it, recognizing its relative powers.

The theme of the irrational, as it is conceived by the existentials, is reason becoming confused and escaping by negating itself. The absurd is lucid reason noting its limits.

My reasoning wants to be faithful to the evidence that aroused it. That evidence is the absurd. It is that divorce between the mind that desires and the world that disappoints, my nostalgia for unity, this fragmented universe and the contradiction that binds them together.... There can be no question of masking the evidence, of suppressing the absurd by denying one of the terms of its equation. It is essential to know whether one can live with it or whether, on the other hand, logic commands one to die of it. I am not interested in philosophical suicide, but rather in plain suicide.... Any other position implies for the absurd mind deceit and the mind's retreat before what the mind itself has brought to light.

ABSURD FREEDOM

I don't know whether this world has a meaning that transcends it. But I know that I do not know that meaning and that it is impossible for me just now to know it. What can a meaning outside my condition mean to me? I can understand only in human terms. What I touch, what resists me—that is what I understand. And these two certainties—my appetite for the absolute and for unity and the impossibility of reducing this world to a rational and reasonable principle—I also know that I cannot reconcile them. What other truth can I admit without lying, without bringing in a hope I lack and which means nothing within the limits of my condition?

If I were a tree among trees, a cat among animals, this life would have a meaning, or rather this problem would not arise, for I should belong to this world. I should *be* this world to which I am now opposed by my whole consciousness and my whole insistence upon familiarity. This ridiculous reason is what sets me in opposition to all creation. I cannot cross it out with a stroke of the pen....

Let us insist again on the method: it is a matter of persisting. At a certain point on his path the absurd man is tempted. History is not lacking in either religions or prophets, even without gods. He is asked to leap. All he can reply is that he doesn't fully understand, that it is not obvious. Indeed, he does not want to do anything but what he fully understands. He is assured that this is the sin of pride, but he does not understand the notion of sin; that perhaps hell is in store, but he has not enough imagination to visualize that strange future; that he is losing immortal life, but that seems to him an idle consideration. An attempt is made to get him to admit his guilt. He feels innocent. To tell the truth, that is all he feels—his irreparable innocence. This is what allows him everything. Hence, what he demands of himself is to live *solely* with what he knows, to accommodate himself to what is, and to bring in nothing that is not certain. He is told that nothing is. But this at least is a certainty. And it is with this that he is concerned: he wants to find out if it is possible to live *without appeal*.

Now I can broach the notion of suicide. It has already been felt what solution might be given. At this point the problem is reversed. It was previously a question of finding out whether or not life had to have a meaning to be lived. It now becomes clear, on the contrary, that it will be lived all the better if it has no meaning. Living an experience, a particular fate, is accepting it fully. Now, no one will live this fate, knowing it to be absurd, unless he does everything to keep before him that absurd brought to light by consciousness. Negating one of the terms of the opposition on which he lives amounts to escaping it. To abolish conscious revolt is to elude the problem. The theme of permanent revolution is thus carried into individual experience. Living is keeping the absurd alive. Keeping it alive is, above all, contemplating it. Unlike Eurydice, the absurd dies only when we turn away from it. One of the only coherent philosophical positions is thus revolt. It is a constant confrontation between man and his own obscurity. It is an insistence upon an impossible transparency. It challenges the world anew every second. Just as danger provided man the unique opportunity of seizing awareness, so metaphysical revolt extends awareness to the whole of experience. It is that constant presence of man in his own eyes. It is not aspiration, for it is devoid of hope. That revolt is the certainty of a crushing fate, without the resignation that ought to accompany it.

This is where it is seen to what a degree absurd experience is remote from suicide. It may be thought that suicide follows revolt—but wrongly. For it does not represent the logical outcome of revolt. It is just the contrary by the consent it presupposes. Suicide, like the leap, is acceptance at its extreme. Everything is over and man returns to his essential history. His future, his unique and dreadful future—he sees and rushes toward it. In its way, suicide settles the absurd. It engulfs the absurd in the same death. But I know that in order to keep alive, the absurd cannot be settled. It escapes suicide to the extent that it is simultaneously awareness and rejection of death. It is, at the extreme limit of the condemned man's last thought, that shoelace that despite everything he sees a few yards away, on the very brink of his dizzying fall. The contrary of suicide, in fact, is the man condemned to death.

That revolt gives life its value. Spread out over the whole length of a life, it restores its majesty to that life. To a man devoid of blinders, there is no finer sight than that of the intelligence at grips with a reality that transcends it. The sight of human pride is unequaled. No disparagement is of any use. That discipline that the mind imposes on itself, that will conjured up out of nothing, that face-to-face struggle have something exceptional about them. To impoverish that reality whose inhumanity constitutes man's majesty is tantamount to impoverishing him himself. I understand then why the doctrines that explain everything to me also debilitate me at the same time. They relieve me of the weight of my own life, and yet I must carry it alone. At this juncture, I cannot conceive that a skeptical metaphysics can be joined to an ethics of renunciation.

Consciousness and revolt, these rejections are the contrary of renunciation. Everything that is indomitable and passionate in a human heart quickens them, on the contrary, with its own life. It is essential to die unreconciled and not of one's own free will. Suicide is a repudiation. The absurd man can only drain everything to the bitter end, and deplete himself. The absurd is his extreme tension, which he maintains constantly by solitary effort, for he knows that in that consciousness and in that day-to-day revolt he gives proof of his only truth, which is defiance. . . .

.   .   .

Belief in the meaning of life always implies a scale of values, a choice, our preferences. Belief in the absurd, according to our definitions, teaches the contrary. But this is worth examining.

Knowing whether or not one can live *without appeal* is all that interests me. I do not want to get out of my depth. This aspect of life being given me, can I adapt myself to it? Now, faced with this particular concern, belief in the absurd is tantamount to substituting the quantity of experiences for the quality. If I convince myself that this life has no other aspect than that of the absurd, if I feel that its whole equilibrium depends on that perpetual opposition between my conscious revolt and the darkness in which it struggles, if I admit that my freedom has no meaning except in relation to its limited fate, then I must say that what counts is not the best living but the most living. It is not up to me to wonder if this is vulgar or revolting, elegant or deplorable. Once and for all, value judgments are discarded here in favor of factual judgments. I have merely to draw the conclusions from what I can see and to risk nothing that is hypothetical. Supposing that living in this way were not honorable, then true propriety would command me to be dishonorable. . . .

How, then, can one fail to do as so many of those men I was speaking of earlier—choose the form of life that brings us the most possible of that human matter, thereby introducing a scale of values that on the other hand one claims to reject?

But again it is the absurd and its contradictory life that teaches us. For the mistake is thinking that that quantity of experiences depends on the circumstances of our life when it depends solely on us. Here we have to be over-simple. To two men living the same number of years, the world always provides the same sum of experiences. It is up to us to be conscious of them. Being aware of one's life, one's revolt, one's freedom, and to the maximum, is living, and to the maximum. Where lucidity dominates, the scale of values becomes useless. Let's be even more simple. Let us say that the sole obstacle, the sole deficiency to be made good, is constituted by premature death. Thus it is that no depth, no emotion, no passion, and no sacrifice could render equal in the eyes of the absurd man (even if he wished it so) a conscious life of forty years and a lucidity spread over sixty years. Madness and death are his irreparables. Man does not choose. The absurd and the extra life it involves *therefore do not depend on man's will,* but on the contrary, which is death. Weighing words carefully, it is altogether a question of luck. One just has to be able to consent to this. There will never be any substitute for twenty years of life and experience. . . .

"Prayer," says Alain, "is when night descends over thought." "But the mind must meet the night," reply the mystics and the existentials. Yes, indeed, but not that night that is born under closed eyelids and through the mere will of man—dark, impenetrable night that the mind calls up in order to plunge into it. If it must encounter a night, let it be rather that of despair, which remains lucid—polar night, vigil of the mind, whence will arise perhaps that white and virginal brightness which outlines every object in the light of the intelligence. At that degree, equivalence encounters passionate understanding. Then it is no longer even a question of judging the existential leap. It resumes its place amid the age-old fresco of human attitudes. For the spectator, if he is conscious, that leap is still absurd. In so far as it thinks it solves the paradox, it reinstates it intact. On this score, it is stirring. On this score, everything resumes its place and the absurd world is reborn in all its splendor and diversity.

But it is bad to stop, hard to be satisfied with a single way of seeing, to go without contradiction, perhaps the most subtle of all spiritual forces. The preceding merely defines a way of thinking. But the point is to live.

MARTIN BUBER (1878–1965)

Martin Buber was born in Vienna. He was raised by his grandfather Solomon Buber, a rabbinic scholar, and educated at several universities in Vienna and Germany. Buber was an active Zionist and began a monthly called *Der Jude.* He taught in Germany until the Nazis came to power and then at the Hebrew University in Palestine.

In *I and Thou* (1922) Buber distinguishes between two relationships: I and it, on the one hand, and I and thou, on the other. In the first a self observes something that that self regards as an object that is part of the causal order and hence understood in terms of that order. In the second a self addresses and is addressed by another self. We may relate to another person as an it or as a thou. To do the former is to understand the person as an object that fits into the causal order of the world at large. To relate to others in the second way is to address them as beings whose freedom precludes their being reduced to the causal order.

Another difference between the I-it and I-thou relationships concerns the I in each case. The I is shaped differently depending on the relationship taken up. The I who observes an object is different from the I who addresses another self. The I-it relationship involves only the self as observer. But the I-thou relationship involves the self as a complete being, vulnerable to the other.

According to Buber, our relationship to God is that of I-thou. Hence, in this relationship we are complete beings who address and stand ready to respond to God, and we regard God as a free person who is distinct from us.

I and Thou

To man the world is twofold, in accordance with his twofold attitude.

The attitude of man is twofold, in accordance with the twofold nature of the primary words which he speaks.

The primary words are not isolated words, but combined words.

The one primary word is the combination *I-Thou.*

The other primary word is the combination *I-It;* wherein, without a change in the primary word, one of the words *He* and *She* can replace *It.*

Hence the *I* of man is also twofold.

For the *I* of the primary word *I-Thou* is a different *I* from that of the primary word *I-It.*

Primary words do not signify things, but they intimate relations.

Primary words do not describe something that might exist independently of them, but being spoken they bring about existence.

Primary words are spoken from the being.

If *Thou* is said, the *I* of the combination *I-Thou* is said along with it.

If *It* is said, the *I* of the combination *I-It* is said along with it.

The primary word *I-Thou* can only be spoken with the whole being.

The primary word *I-It* can never be spoken with the whole being.

There is no *I* taken in itself, but only the *I* of the primary word *I-Thou* and the *I* of the primary word *I-It.*

When a man says *I* he refers to one or other of these. The *I* to which he refers is present when he says *I.* Further, when he says *Thou* or *It,* the *I* of one of the two primary words is present.

The existence of *I* and the speaking of *I* are one and the same thing.

When a primary word is spoken the speaker enters the word and takes his stand in it.

The life of human beings is not passed in the sphere of transitive verbs alone. It does not exist in virtue of activities alone which have some *thing* for their object.

I perceive something. I am sensible of something. I imagine something. I will something. I feel something. I think something. The life of human beings does not consist of all this and the like alone.

This and the like together establish the realm of *It*.

But the realm of *Thou* has a different basis.

When *Thou* is spoken, the speaker has no thing for his object. For where there is a thing there is another thing. Every *It* is bounded by others; *It* exists only through being bounded by others. But when *Thou* is spoken, there is no thing. *Thou* has no bounds.

When *Thou* is spoken, the speaker has no *thing*; he has indeed nothing. But he takes his stand in relation.

It is said that man experiences his world. What does that mean?

Man travels over the surface of things and experiences them. He extracts knowledge about their constitution from them: he wins an experience from them. He experiences what belongs to the things.

But the world is not presented to man by experiences alone. These present him only with a world composed of *It* and *He* and *She* and *It* again.

I experience something.—If we add "inner" to "outer" experiences, nothing in the situation is changed. We are merely following the uneternal division that springs from the lust of the human race to whittle away the secret of death. Inner things or outer things, what are they but things and things!

I experience something.—If we add "secret" to "open" experiences, nothing in the situation is changed. How self-confident is that wisdom which perceives a closed compartment in things, reserved for the initiate and manipulated only with the key. O secrecy without a secret! O accumulation of information! It, always It!

The man who experiences has not part in the world. For it is "in him" and not between him and the world that the experience arises.

The world has no part in the experience. It permits itself to be experienced, but has no concern in the matter. For it does nothing to the experience, and the experience does nothing to it.

As experience, the world belongs to the primary word *I-It.*

The primary word *I-Thou* establishes the world of relation.

The spheres in which the world of relation arises are three.

First, our life with nature. There the relation sways in gloom, beneath the level of speech. Creatures live and move over against us, but cannot come to us, and when we address them as *Thou,* our words cling to the threshold of speech.

Second, our life with men. There the relation is open and in the form of speech. We can give and accept the *Thou.*

Third, our life with spiritual beings. There the relation is clouded, yet it discloses itself; it does not use speech, yet begets it. We perceive no *Thou,* but none the less we feel we are addressed and we answer—forming, thinking, acting. We speak the primary word with our being, though we cannot utter *Thou* with our lips.

But with what right do we draw what lies outside speech into relation with the world of the primary word?

In every sphere in its own way, through each process of becoming that is present to us we look out toward the fringe of the eternal *Thou;* in each we are aware of a breath from the eternal *Thou;* in each *Thou* we address the eternal *Thou.*

I consider a tree.

I can look on it as a picture: stiff column in a shock of light, or splash of green shot with the delicate blue and silver of the background.

I can perceive it as movement: flowing veins on clinging, pressing pith, suck of the roots, breathing of the leaves, ceaseless commerce with earth and air—and the obscure growth itself.

I can classify it in a species and study it as a type in its structure and mode of life.

I can subdue its actual presence and form so sternly that I recognise it only as an expression of law—of the laws in accordance with which a constant opposition of forces is continually adjusted, or of those in accordance with which the component substances mingle and separate.

I can dissipate it and perpetuate it in number, in pure numerical relation.

In all this the tree remains my object, occupies space and time, and has its nature and constitution.

It can, however, also come about, if I have both will and grace, that in considering the tree I become bound up in relation to it. The tree is now no longer *It*. I have been seized by the power of exclusiveness.

To effect this it is not necessary for me to give up any of the ways in which I consider the tree. There is nothing from which I would have to turn my eyes away in order to see, and no knowledge that I would have to forget. Rather is everything, picture and movement, species and type, law and number, indivisibly united in this event.

Everything belonging to the tree is in this: its form and structure, its colours and chemical composition, its intercourse with the elements and with the stars, are all present in a single whole.

The tree is no impression, no play of my imagination, no value depending on my mood; but it is bodied over against me and has to do with me, as I with it—only in a different way.

Let no attempt be made to sap the strength from the meaning of the relation: relation is mutual.

The tree will have a consciousness, then, similar to our own? Of that I have no experience. But do you wish, through seeming to succeed in it with yourself, once again to disintegrate that which cannot be disintegrated? I encounter no soul or dryad of the tree, but the tree itself.

· · ·

PAUL TILLICH (1886–1965)

Paul Tillich was born in Starzeddel, Germany. After receiving training in theology and philosophy he taught at several cities in Germany. When Hitler took over Germany, Tillich came to the United States and taught at the Union Theological Seminary, Harvard University, and the University of Chicago.

In "Courage and Transcendence," chapter 6 of *The Courage to Be* (1952), Tillich suggests that there is an ultimate reality that he calls "being-itself" upon which all things depend for their being and that

includes nonbeing (although "nonbeing does not prevail against it"[27]) but which otherwise is largely ineffable. Being-itself can be identified as God, but there is no reason to suggest that God in this sense is a personal being. Each of us, Tillich says, is interested in being-itself, for every individual has a fundamental concern that gives meaning to that person's existence, and this most basic concern is something presumed to be metaphysically ultimate.

Tillich says that we may become part of being-itself or "the God above the God of theism" because "the power of being acts through the power of the individual selves." We participate in being-itself through faith, thought of as "the state of being grasped by the power of being-itself." By participating in being-itself, we gain the courage to do something that being-itself does: It "affirms itself against nonbeing."[28] Participating in being-itself gives us the courage to affirm our own being in the face of death and other manifestations of nonbeing and the anxiety these manifestations cause.

◎ *Courage and Transcendence* *from* The Courage to Be

Courage is the self-affirmation of being in spite of the fact of nonbeing. It is the act of the individual self in taking the anxiety of nonbeing upon itself by affirming itself either as part of an embracing whole or in its individual selfhood. Courage always includes a risk, it is always threatened by nonbeing, whether the risk of losing oneself and becoming a thing within the whole of things or of losing one's world in an empty self-relatedness. Courage needs the power of being, a power transcending the nonbeing which is experienced in the anxiety of fate and death, which is present in the anxiety of emptiness and meaninglessness, which is effective in the anxiety of guilt and condemnation. . . . Neither self-affirmation as a part nor self-affirmation as oneself is beyond the manifold threat of nonbeing. Those who are mentioned as representatives of these forms of courage try to transcend

---

[27] Paul Tillich, *The Courage to Be* (New Haven: Yale University Press, 1952), 179.

[28] Ibid., 179.

themselves and the world in which they participate in order to find the power of being-itself and a courage to be which is beyond the threat of nonbeing. There are no exceptions to this rule; and this means that every courage to be has an open or hidden religious root. For religion is the state of being grasped by the power of being-itself. In some cases the religious root is carefully covered, in others it is passionately denied; in some it is deeply hidden and in others superficially. But it is never completely absent. For everything that is participates in being-itself, and everybody has some awareness of this participation, especially in the moments in which he experiences the threat of nonbeing. This leads us to a final consideration, the double question: How is the courage to be rooted in being-itself, and how must we understand being-itself in the light of the courage to be? The first question deals with the ground of being as source of the courage to be, the second with courage to be as key to the ground of being.

· · ·

FATE AND THE COURAGE
TO ACCEPT ACCEPTANCE

The popular belief in immortality which in the Western world has largely replaced the Christian symbol of resurrection is a mixture of courage and escape. It tries to maintain one's self-affirmation even in the face of one's having to die. But it does this by continuing one's finitude, that is one's having to die, infinitely, so that the actual death never will occur. This, however, is an illusion and, logically speaking, a contradiction in terms. It makes endless what, by definition, must come to an end. The "immortality of the soul" is a poor symbol for the courage to be in the face of one's having to die.

The courage of Socrates (in Plato's picture) was based not on a doctrine of the immortality of the soul but on the affirmation of himself in his essential, indestructible being. He knows that he belongs to two orders of reality and that the one order is transtemporal. It was the courage of Socrates which more than any philosophical reflection revealed to the ancient world that everyone belongs to two orders.

But there was one presupposition in the Socratic (Stoic and Neo-Stoic) courage to take death upon oneself, namely the ability of every individual to par-

ticipate in both orders, the temporal and the eternal. This presupposition is not accepted by Christianity. According to Christianity we are estranged from our essential being. We are not free to realize our essential being, we are bound to contradict it. Therefore death can be accepted only through a state of confidence in which death has ceased to be the "wages of sin." This, however, is the state of being accepted in spite of being unacceptable. Here is the point in which the ancient world was transformed by Christianity and in which Luther's courage to face death was rooted. It is the being accepted into communion with God that underlies this courage, not a questionable theory of immortality. The encounter with God in Luther is not merely the basis for the courage to take upon oneself sin and condemnation, it is also the basis for taking upon oneself fate and death. For encountering God means encountering transcendent security and transcendent eternity. He who participates in God participates in eternity. But in order to participate in him you must be accepted by him and you must have accepted his acceptance of you.

Luther had experiences which he describes as attacks of utter despair (*Anfechtung*), as the frightful threat of a complete meaninglessness. He felt these moments as satanic attacks in which everything was menaced: his Christian faith, the confidence in his work, the Reformation, the forgiveness of sins. Everything broke down in the extreme moments of this despair, nothing was left of the courage to be. Luther in these moments, and in the descriptions he gives of them, anticipated the descriptions of them by modern Existentialism. But for him this was not the last word. The last word was the first commandment, the statement that God is God. It reminded him of the unconditional element in human experience of which one can be aware even in the abyss of meaninglessness. And this awareness saved him.

It should not be forgotten that the great adversary of Luther, Thomas Münzer, the Anabaptist and religious socialist, describes similar experiences. He speaks of the ultimate situation in which everything finite reveals its finitude, in which the finite has come to its end, in which anxiety grips the heart and all previous meanings fall apart, and in which just for this reason the Divine Spirit can make itself felt and can turn the whole situation into a courage to be whose expression is revolutionary action. While Luther represents ecclesiastical Protestantism, Münzer represents evangelical radicalism. Both men have shaped history, and actually Münzer's views had even more influence in America than Luther's. Both men experienced the anxiety of meaninglessness and described it in terms which had been created by Christian mystics. But in doing so they transcended the courage of confidence which is based on a personal encounter with God. They had to receive elements from the courage to be which is based on mystical union. This leads to a last question: whether the two types of the courage to accept acceptance can be united in view of the all-pervasive presence of the anxiety of doubt and meaninglessness in our own period.

ABSOLUTE FAITH AND THE COURAGE TO BE

We have avoided the concept of faith in our description of the courage to be which is based on mystical union with the ground of being as well as in our description of the courage to be which is based on the personal encounter with God. This is partly because the concept of faith has lost its genuine meaning and has received the connotation of "belief in something unbelievable." But this is not the only reason for the use of terms other than faith. The decisive reason is that I do not think either mystical union or personal encounter fulfills the idea of faith. Certainly there is faith in the elevation of the soul above the finite to the infinite, leading to its union with the ground of being. But more than this is included in the concept of faith. And there is faith in the personal encounter with the personal God. But more than this is included in the concept of faith. Faith is the state of being grasped by the power of being-itself. The courage to be is an expression of faith and what "faith" means must be understood through the courage to be. We have defined courage as the self-affirmation of being in spite of nonbeing. The power of this self-affirmation is the power of being which is effective in every act of courage. Faith is the experience of this power.

But it is an experience which has a paradoxical character, the character of accepting acceptance. Being-itself transcends every finite being infinitely; God in the divine-human encounter transcends man unconditionally. Faith bridges this infinite gap by accepting the fact that in spite of it the power of being is present, that he who is separated is accepted. Faith accepts "in spite of"; and out of the "in spite of" of faith the "in spite of" of courage is born. Faith is not a theoretical affirmation of something uncertain, it is the existential acceptance of something transcending ordinary experience. Faith is not an opinion but a state. It is the state of being grasped by the power of being which transcends everything that is and in which everything that is participates. He who is grasped by this power is able to affirm himself because he knows that he is affirmed by the power of being-itself. In this point mystical experience and personal encounter are identical. In both of them faith is the basis of the courage to be.

This is decisive for a period in which, as in our own, the anxiety of doubt and meaninglessness is dominant. Certainly the anxiety of fate and death is not lacking in our time. The anxiety of fate has increased with the degree to which the schizophrenic split of our world has removed the last remnants of former security. And the anxiety of guilt and condemnation is not lacking either. It is surprising how much anxiety of guilt comes to the surface in psychoanalysis and personal counseling. The centuries of puritan and bourgeois repression of vital strivings have produced almost as many guilt feelings as the preaching of hell and purgatory in the Middle Ages.

But in spite of these restricting considerations one must say that the anxiety which determines our period is the anxiety of doubt and meaninglessness. One is afraid of having lost or of having to lose the meaning of one's existence. The expression of this situation is the Existentialism of today.

Which courage is able to take nonbeing into itself in the form of doubt and meaninglessness? This is the most important and most disturbing question in the quest for the courage to be. For the anxiety of meaninglessness undermines what is still unshaken in the anxiety of fate and death and of guilt and condemnation. In the anxiety of guilt and condemnation doubt has not yet undermined the certainty of an ultimate responsibility. We are threatened but we are not destroyed. If, however, doubt and meaninglessness prevail one experiences an abyss in which the meaning of life and the truth of ultimate responsibility disappear. Both the Stoic who conquers the anxiety of fate with the Socratic courage of wisdom and the Christian who conquers the anxiety of guilt with the Protestant courage of accepting forgiveness are in a different situation. Even in the despair of having to die and the despair of self-condemnation meaning is affirmed and certitude preserved. But in the despair of doubt and meaninglessness both are swallowed by nonbeing.

The question then is this: Is there a courage which can conquer the anxiety of meaninglessness and doubt? Or in other words, can the faith which accepts acceptance resist the power of nonbeing in its most radical form? Can faith resist meaninglessness? Is there a kind of faith which can exist together with doubt and meaninglessness? These questions lead to the last aspect of the problem discussed in these lectures and the one most relevant to our time: How is the courage to be possible if all the ways to create it are barred by the experience of their ultimate insufficiency? If life is as meaningless as death, if guilt is as questionable as perfection, if being is no more meaningful than nonbeing, on what can one base the courage to be?

There is an inclination in some Existentialists to answer these questions by a leap from doubt to dogmatic certitude, from meaninglessness to a set of symbols in which the meaning of a special ecclesiastical or political group is embodied. This leap can be interpreted in different ways. It may be the expression of a desire for safety; it may be as arbitrary as, according to Existentialist principles, every decision is; it may be the feeling that the Christian message is the answer to the questions raised by an analysis of human existence; it may be a genuine conversion, independent of the theoretical situation. In any case it is not a solution of the problem of radical doubt. It gives the courage to be to those who are converted but it does not answer the question as to how such a courage is possible in itself. The answer must accept, as its precondition, the state of meaninglessness. It is not an answer if it demands the removal of this state; for that is just what cannot be done. He who is in the grip of doubt and meaninglessness cannot liberate himself from this grip; but he asks for an answer which is valid within and not outside the situation of his despair. He asks for the ultimate foundation of what we have called the "courage of despair." There is only one possible answer, if one does not try to escape the question: namely that the acceptance of despair is in itself faith and on the boundary line of the courage to be. In this situation the meaning of life is reduced to despair about the meaning of life. But as long as this despair is an act of life it is positive in its negativity. Cynically speaking, one could say that it is true to life to be cynical about

it. Religiously speaking, one would say that one accepts oneself as accepted in spite of one's despair about the meaning of this acceptance. The paradox of every radical negativity, as long as it is an active negativity, is that it must affirm itself in order to be able to negate itself. No actual negation can be without an implicit affirmation. The hidden pleasure produced by despair witnesses to the paradoxical character of self-negation. The negative lives from the positive it negates.

The faith which makes the courage of despair possible is the acceptance of the power of being, even in the grip of nonbeing. Even in the despair about meaning being affirms itself through us. The act of accepting meaninglessness is in itself a meaningful act. It is an act of faith. We have seen that he who has the courage to affirm his being in spite of fate and guilt has not removed them. He remains threatened and hit by them. But he accepts his acceptance by the power of being-itself in which he participates and which gives him the courage to take the anxieties of fate and guilt upon himself. The same is true of doubt and meaninglessness. The faith which creates the courage to take them into itself has no special content. It is simply faith, undirected, absolute. It is undefinable, since everything defined is dissolved by doubt and meaninglessness. Nevertheless, even absolute faith is not an eruption of subjective emotions or a mood without objective foundation.

An analysis of the nature of absolute faith reveals the following elements in it. The first is the experience of the power of being which is present even in face of the most radical manifestation of nonbeing. If one says that in this experience vitality resists despair one must add that vitality in man is proportional to intentionality. The vitality that can stand the abyss of meaninglessness is aware of a hidden meaning within the destruction of meaning. The second element in absolute faith is the dependence of the experience of nonbeing on the experience of being and the dependence of the experience of meaninglessness on the experience of meaning. Even in the state of despair one has enough being to make despair possible. There is a third element in absolute faith, the acceptance of being accepted. Of course, in the state of despair there is nobody and nothing that accepts. But there is the power of acceptance itself which is experienced. Meaninglessness, as long as it is experienced, includes an experience of the "power of acceptance." To accept this power of acceptance consciously is the religious answer of absolute faith, of a faith which has been deprived by doubt of any concrete content, which nevertheless is faith and the source of the most paradoxical manifestation of the courage to be.

This faith transcends both the mystical experience and the divine-human encounter. The mystical experience seems to be nearer to absolute faith but it is not. Absolute faith includes an element of skepticism which one cannot find in the mystical experience. Certainly mysticism also transcends all specific contents, but not because it doubts them or has found them meaningless; rather it deems them to be preliminary. Mysticism uses the specific contents as grades, stepping on them after having used them. The experience of meaninglessness, however, denies them (and everything that goes with them) without having used them. The experience of meaninglessness is more radical than mysticism. Therefore it transcends the mystical experience.

Absolute faith also transcends the divine-human encounter. In this encounter the subject-object scheme is valid: a definite subject (man) meets a definite object (God). One can reverse this statement and say that a definite subject (God) meets a definite object (man). But in both cases the attack of doubt undercuts the subject-object structure. The theologians who speak so strongly and with such self-certainty about the divine-human encounter should be aware of a situation in which this encounter is prevented by radical doubt and nothing is left but absolute faith. The acceptance of such a situation as religiously valid has, however, the consequence that the concrete contents of ordinary faith must be subjected to criticism and transformation. The courage to be in its radical form is a key to an idea of God which transcends both mysticism and the person-to-person encounter.

THE COURAGE TO BE AS THE KEY TO BEING-ITSELF

Nonbeing Opening Up Being

The courage to be in all its forms has, by itself, revelatory character. It shows the nature of being, it shows that the self-affirmation of being is an affirmation that overcomes negation. In a metaphorical statement (and every assertion about being-itself is either metaphorical or symbolic) one could say that being includes nonbeing but nonbeing does not prevail against it. "Including" is a spatial metaphor which indicates that being embraces itself and that which is opposed to it, nonbeing. Nonbeing belongs to being, it cannot be separated from it. We could not even think "being" without a double negation: being must be thought as the negation of the negation of being. This is why we describe being best by the metaphor "power of being." Power is the possibility a being has to actualize itself against the resistance of other beings. If we speak of the power of being-itself we indicate that being affirms itself against nonbeing. In our discussion of courage and life we have mentioned the dynamic understanding of reality by the philosophers of life. Such an understanding is possible only if one accepts the view that nonbeing belongs to being, that being could not be the ground of life without nonbeing. The self-affirmation of being without nonbeing would not even be self-affirmation but an immovable self-identity. Nothing would be manifest, nothing expressed, nothing revealed. But nonbeing drives being out of its seclusion, it forces it to affirm itself dynamically. Philosophy has dealt with the dynamic self-affirmation of being-itself wherever it spoke dialectically, notably in Neoplatonism, Hegel, and the philosophers of life and process. Theology has done the same whenever it took the idea of the living God seriously, most obviously in the trinitarian symbolization of the inner life of God. Spinoza, in spite of his static definition of substance (which is his name for the ultimate power of being), unites philosophical and mystical tendencies when he speaks of the love and knowledge with which God loves and knows himself through the love and knowledge of finite beings. Nonbeing (that in God which makes his self-affirmation dynamic) opens up the divine self-seclusion and reveals him as power and love. Nonbeing makes God a living God. Without the No he has to overcome in himself and in his creature, the divine Yes to himself would be lifeless. There would be no revelation of the ground of being, there would be no life.

But where there is nonbeing there is finitude and anxiety. If we say that nonbeing belongs to being-itself, we say that finitude and anxiety belong to being-itself. Wherever philosophers or theologians have spoken of the divine blessedness they have implicitly (and sometimes explicitly) spoken of the anxiety of finitude which is eternally taken into the blessedness of the divine infinity. The infinite embraces itself and the finite, the Yes includes itself and the No which it takes into itself, blessedness comprises itself and the anxiety of which it is the conquest. All this is implied if one says that being includes nonbeing and that through nonbeing it reveals itself. It is a highly symbolic language which must be used at this point. But its symbolic character does not diminish its truth; on the contrary, it is a condition of its truth. To speak unsymbolically about being-itself is untrue.

The divine self-affirmation is the power that makes the self-affirmation of the finite being, the courage to be, possible. Only because being-itself has the character of self-affirmation inspite of nonbeing is courage possible. Courage participates in the self-affirmation of being-itself, it participates in the power of being which prevails against nonbeing. He who receives this power in an act of mystical or personal or absolute faith is aware of the source of his courage to be.

Man is not necessarily aware of this source. In situations of cynicism and indifference he is not aware of it. But it works in him as long as he maintains the courage to take his anxiety upon himself. In the act of the courage to be the power of being is effective in us, whether we recognize it or not. Every act of courage is a manifestation of the ground of being, however questionable the content of the act may be. The content may hide or distort true being, the courage in it reveals true being. Not arguments but the courage to be reveals the true nature of being-itself. By affirming our being we participate in the self-affirmation of being-itself. There are no valid arguments for the "existence" of God, but there are acts of courage in which we affirm the power of being, whether we know it or not. If we know it, we accept acceptance consciously. If we do not know it, we nevertheless accept it and participate in it. And in our acceptance of that which we do not know the power of being is manifest to us. Courage has revealing power, the courage to be is the key to being-itself.

Theism Transcended

The courage to take meaninglessness into itself presupposes a relation to the ground of being which we have called "absolute faith." It is without a *special* content, yet it is not without content. The content of absolute faith is the "God above God." Absolute faith and its consequence, the courage that takes the radical doubt, the doubt about God, into itself, transcends the theistic idea of God.

Theism can mean the unspecified affirmation of God. Theism in this sense does not say what it means if it uses the name of God. Because of the traditional and psychological connotations of the word God such an empty theism can produce a reverent mood if it speaks of God. Politicians, dictators, and other people who wish to use rhetoric to make an impression on their audience like to use the word God in this sense. It produces the feeling in their listeners that the speaker is serious and morally trustworthy. This is especially successful if they can brand their foes as atheistic. On a higher level people without a definite religious commitment like to call themselves theistic, not for special purposes but because they cannot stand a world without God, whatever this God may be. They need some of the connotations of the word God and they are afraid of what they call atheism. On the highest level of this kind of theism the name of God is used as a poetic or practical symbol, expressing a profound emotional state or the highest ethical idea. It is a theism which stands on the boundary line between the second type of theism and what we call "theism transcended." But it is still too indefinite to cross this boundary line. The atheistic negation of this whole type of theism is as vague as the theism itself. It may produce an irreverent mood and angry reaction of those who take their theistic affirmation seriously. It may even be felt as justified against the rhetorical-political abuse of the name God, but it is ultimately as irrelevant as the theism which it negates. It cannot reach the state of despair any more than the theism against which it fights can reach the state of faith.

Theism can have another meaning, quite contrary to the first one: it can be the name of what we have called the divine-human encounter. In this case it points to those elements in the Jewish-Christian tradition which emphasize the person-to-person relationship with God. Theism in this sense emphasizes the personalistic passages in the Bible and the Protestant creeds, the personalistic image of God, the word as the tool of creation and revelation, the ethical and social character of the kingdom of God, the personal nature of human faith and divine forgiveness, the historical vision of the universe, the idea of a divine purpose, the infinite distance between creator and creature, the absolute separation between God and the world, the conflict between holy God and sinful man, the person-to-person character of prayer and practical devotion. Theism in this sense is the nonmystical side of biblical religion and historical Christianity. Atheism from the point of view of this theism is the human attempt to escape the divine-human encounter. It is an existential—not a theoretical—problem.

Theism has a third meaning, a strictly theological one. Theological theism is, like every theology, dependent on the religious substance which it conceptualizes. It is dependent on theism in the first sense insofar as it tries to prove the necessity of affirming God in some way; it usually develops the so-called arguments for the "existence" of God. But it is more dependent on theism in the second sense insofar as it tries to establish a doctrine of God which transforms the person-to-person encounter with God into a doctrine about two persons who may or may not meet but who have a reality independent of each other.

Now theism in the first sense must be transcended because it is irrelevant, and theism in the second sense must be transcended because it is one-sided. But theism in the third sense must be transcended because it is wrong. It is bad theology. This can be shown by a more penetrating analysis. The God of theological theism is a being beside others and as such a part of the whole of reality. He certainly is considered its most important part, but as a part and therefore as subjected to the structure of the whole. He is supposed to be beyond the ontological elements and categories which constitute reality. But every statement subjects him to them. He is seen as a self which has a world, as an ego which is related to a thou, as a cause which is separated from its effect, as having a definite space and an endless time. He is a being, not being-itself. As such he is bound to the subject-object structure of reality, he is an object for us as subjects. At the same time we are objects for him as a subject. And this is decisive for the necessity of transcending theological theism. For God as a subject makes me into an object which is nothing more than an object. He deprives me of my subjectivity because he is all-powerful and all-knowing. I revolt and try to make *him* into an object, but the revolt fails and becomes desperate. God appears as the invincible tyrant, the being in contrast with whom all other beings are without freedom and subjectivity. He is equated with the recent tyrants who with the help of terror try to transform every-

thing into a mere object, a thing among things, a cog in the machine they control. He becomes the model of everything against which Existentialism revolted. This is the God Nietzsche said had to be killed because nobody can tolerate being made into a mere object of absolute knowledge and absolute control. This is the deepest root of atheism. It is an atheism which is justified as the reaction against theological theism and its disturbing implications. It is also the deepest root of the Existentialist despair and the widespread anxiety of meaninglessness in our period.

Theism in all its forms is transcended in the experience we have called absolute faith. It is the accepting of the acceptance without somebody or something that accepts. It is the power of being-itself that accepts and gives the courage to be. This is the highest point to which our analysis has brought us. It cannot be described in the way the God of all forms of theism can be described. It cannot be described in mystical terms either. It transcends both mysticism and personal encounter, as it transcends both the courage to be as a part and the courage to be as oneself.

The God Above God and the Courage To Be

The ultimate source of the courage to be is the "God above God"; this is the result of our demand to transcend theism. Only if the God of theism is transcended can the anxiety of doubt and meaninglessness be taken into the courage to be. The God above God is the object of all mystical longing, but mysticism also must be transcended in order to reach him. Mysticism does not take seriously the concrete and the doubt concerning the concrete. It plunges directly into the ground of being and meaning, and leaves the concrete, the world of finite values and meanings, behind. Therefore it does not solve the problem of meaninglessness. In terms of the present religious situation this means that Eastern mysticism is not the solution of the problems of Western Existentialism, although many people attempt this solution. The God above the God of theism is not the devaluation of the meanings which doubt has thrown into the abyss of meaninglessness; he is their potential restitution. Nevertheless absolute faith agrees with the faith implied in mysticism in that both transcend the theistic objectivation of a God who is a being. For mysticism such a God is not more real than any finite being, for the courage to be such a God has disappeared in the abyss of meaninglessness with every other value and meaning.

The God above the God of theism is present, although hidden, in every divine-human encounter. Biblical religion as well as Protestant theology are aware of the paradoxical character of this encounter. They are aware that if God encounters man God is neither object nor subject and is therefore above the scheme into which theism has forced him. They are aware that personalism with respect to God is balanced by a transpersonal presence of the divine. They are aware that forgiveness can be accepted only if the power of acceptance is effective in man—biblically speaking, if the power of grace is effective in man. They are aware of the paradoxical character of every prayer, of speaking to somebody to whom you cannot speak because he is not "somebody," of asking somebody of whom you cannot ask anything because he gives or gives not before you ask, of saying "thou" to somebody who is nearer to the I than the I is to itself. Each of these paradoxes drives the religious consciousness toward a God above the God of theism.

The courage to be which is rooted in the experience of the God above the God of theism unites and transcends the courage to be as a part and the courage to be as oneself. It avoids both the loss of oneself by participation and the loss of one's world by individualization. The acceptance of the God above the God of theism makes us a part of that which is not also a part but is the ground of the whole. Therefore our self is not lost in a larger whole, which submerges it in the life of a limited group. If the self participates in the power of being-itself it receives itself back. For the power of being acts through the power of the individual selves. It does not swallow them as every limited whole, every collectivism, and every conformism does. This is why the Church, which stands for the power of being-itself or for the God who transcends the God of the religions, claims to be the mediator of the courage to be. A church which is based on the authority of the God of theism cannot make such a claim. It inescapably develops into a collectivist or semicollectivist system itself.

But a church which raises itself in its message and its devotion to the God above the God of theism without sacrificing its concrete symbols can mediate a courage which takes doubt and meaninglessness into itself. It is the Church under the Cross which alone can do this, the Church which preaches the Crucified who cried to God who remained his God after the God of confidence had left him in the darkness of doubt and meaninglessness. To be as a part in such a church is to receive a courage to be in which one cannot lose one's self and in which one receives one's world.

Absolute faith, or the state of being grasped by the God beyond God, is not a state which appears beside other states of the mind. It never is something separated and definite, an event which could be isolated and described. It is always a movement in, with, and under other states of the mind. It is the situation on the boundary of man's possibilities. It *is* this boundary. Therefore it is both the courage of despair and the courage in and above every courage. It is not a place where one can live, it is without the safety of words and concepts, it is without a name, a church, a cult, a theology. But it is moving in the depth of all of them. It is the power of being, in which they participate and of which they are fragmentary expressions.

One can become aware of it in the anxiety of fate and death when the traditional symbols, which enable men to stand the vicissitudes of fate and the horror of death have lost their power. When "providence" has become a superstition and "immortality" something imaginary that which once was the power in these symbols can still be present and create the courage to be in spite of the experience of a chaotic world and a finite existence. The Stoic courage returns but not as the faith in universal reason. It returns as the absolute faith which says Yes to being without seeing anything concrete which could conquer the nonbeing in fate and death.

And one can become aware of the God above the God of theism in the anxiety of guilt and condemnation when the traditional symbols that enable men to withstand the anxiety of guilt and condemnation have lost their power. When "divine judgment" is interpreted as a psychological complex and forgiveness as a remnant of the "father-image," what once was the power in those symbols can still be present and create the courage to be in spite of the experience of an infinite gap between what we are and what we ought to be. The Lutheran courage returns but not supported by the faith in a judging and forgiving God. It returns in terms of the absolute faith which says Yes although there is no special power that conquers guilt. The courage to take the anxiety of meaninglessness upon oneself is the boundary line up to which the courage to be can go. Beyond it is mere nonbeing. Within it all forms of courage are re-established in the power of the God above the God of theism. *The courage to be is rooted in the God who appears when God has disappeared in the anxiety of doubt.*

QUESTIONS FOR REFLECTION

1. Unamuno says that nothing has value unless it is eternal. Is this why he thinks that being annihilated is a bad thing? Or is it the other way around: Might Unamuno think that nothing finite has value because he thinks being annihilated is a bad thing?

2. To what extent does Unamuno's religiosity overlap with Pascal's? To what extent does it overlap with Kierkegaard's?

3. Compare and contrast Jaspers' idea of transcendent being with Marcel's idea of absolute being and Kant's idea of the noumenal realm.

4. What does Marcel mean by "freedom"? Marcel suggests that freedom is quite distinct from autonomy whereas de Beauvoir tended to equate the two. Why did the two thinkers diverge on this point? Whose view is more accurate?

5. Could Sartre accept de Beauvoir's suggestions for overcoming despair? To what extent does her view call for a revision of Sartre's philosophy?

6. Suppose that each of us invents our values and there is no such thing as objective values. Does de Beauvoir agree that we invent our values? Is this assumption compatible with the claim that we are morally bound to act in various ways?

7. Clarify de Beauvoir's claim that her ethics does not "deny *a priori* that separate existants can, at the same time, be bound to each other, that their individual freedoms can forge laws valid for all." What precisely is meant by "laws valid for all"? When de Beauvoir says that her ethics does not "deny *a priori* that separate existants can . . . be bound to each other," does she mean that her ethics shows that separate "existants" are morally bound to each other?

8. In *Existentialism and Humanism* Sartre says that people are responsible for choosing values that are universalizable in some sense. What precisely does he mean? To what extent is his view compatible with de Beauvoir's?

9. Is femininity part of the essence or identity of a woman? Is masculinity part of the essence or identity of a man? Should femininity and masculinity be transcended? Explain.

10. Why does Camus say that "there is but one truly serious philosophical problem, and that is suicide"? Is he correct?

11. What does Camus mean by "absurdity"? Is absurdity a misfortune? In an essay called "The Absurd,"* Thomas Nagel suggests that "absurdity is one of the most human things about us: a manifestation of our most advanced and interesting characteristics." How would Camus react to Nagel?

12. Is Camus "eluding" or "evading" when he suggests that "to abolish conscious revolt is to elude the problem"?

13. Merleau-Ponty and Marcel both think that it is impossible to grasp the whole of reality, but whereas one thinks our efforts will be repaid with a profound glimpse into the mystery of being, the other thinks our efforts are simply wrongheaded. Explain the reasoning behind each thinker's conclusion.

14. Might people who are normally thought of as nonreligious, such as Sartre, "affirm life" in Tillich's sense? If so, are they religious?

15. According to Buber, our relationship to God is personal. According to Tillich, our relationship to God is impersonal. Which, if either, is correct? Explain.

16. Buber suggests that the self is shaped differently depending on the primary relationship taken to the non-self, *I-it* or *I-thou*. What precisely does he mean? Can't we choose to switch from one relationship to the other? If so, isn't there a single self underlying, and hence, not shaped by the choice?

17. Tillich's view owes a great deal to both Hegel and Kierkegaard. Would Kierkegaard reject Tillich's view in the vehement terms in which he reacts against Hegelianism? Explain.

---

*Nagel's "The Absurd" is reprinted in his *Mortal Questions* (Cambridge: Cambridge University Press, 1979).

FURTHER READINGS

Unamuno

Tragic Sense of Life (1913). Translated by J. E. Crawford Flitch. New York: Dover Publications, 1954.

The Agony of Christianity (1931). Translated by K. F. Reinhardt. New York: F. Ungar Pub. Co., 1960.

Marcel

Metaphysical Journal (1927). Translated by Bernard Wall. Chicago: H. Regnery, 1952.

Being and Having (1935). Translated by Katharine Farrer. New York: Harper Torchbooks, 1949.

Jaspers

Philosophy (1932). Translated by E. B. Ashton. Chicago: University of Chicago Press, 1969.

Reason and Existenz (1935). Translated by W. Earle. London: Routledge & Kegan Paul, 1956.

The Perennial Scope of Philosophy (1948). Translated by R. Manheim. London: Routledge & Kegan Paul, 1950.

The Great Philosophers (1957). Edited by H. Arendt; translated by R. Manheim. New York: Harcourt Brace, 2 vols, 1962.

Merleau-Ponty

Phenomenology of Perception (1945). Translated by Colin Smith. London: Routledge & Kegan Paul, 1962.

Sense and Non-Sense (1948). Translated by Hubert Dreyfus and P. A. Dreyfus. Evanston: Northwestern University Press, 1964.

de Beauvoir

She Came to Stay (1943). Cleveland: World Pub. Co., 1954.

The Blood of Others (1945). New York: Random House, 1948.

The Ethics of Ambiguity (1948). Translated by Bernard Frechtman. Secaucus: Citadel Press, 1948.

The Second Sex (1949). New York: Vintage Press, 1952.

The Mandarins (1954). Cleveland: World Pub. Co., 1956.

Camus

The Stranger (1942). Translated by S. Gilbert. New York: Vintage Books, 1946.

The Myth of Sisyphus (1942). Translated by J. O'Brien. New York: Vintage Books, 1955.

Letters to a German Friend (1945). Translated by J. O'Brien. In *Resistance, Rebellion and Death*. New York: Alfred A. Knopf, 1961.

The Plague (1947). Translated by S. Gilbert. New York: Modern Library, 1948.

The Rebel (1951). Translated by A. Bower. New York: Alfred A. Knopf, 1954.

The Fall (1956). Translated by J. O'Brien. New York: Alfred A. Knopf, 1957.

Buber

I and Thou (1922). Translated by Ronald G. Smith. New York: Charles Scribner's Sons, 1958.

Between Man and Man (1936). Translated by Ronald G. Smith. Boston: Beacon Press, 1947.

Two Types of Faith (1961). Translated by N. P. Goldhawk. New York: Harper, 1961.

Tillich

The Courage to Be (1953). New Haven: Yale University Press, 1952.

WORKS ON THE AUTHORS

Unamuno

Ferrater Mora, Jose. *Unamuno.* Translated by Phillip Silver. Berkeley: University of California Press, 1962.

Rudd, Margaret. *The Lone Heretic.* New York: Gordian Press, 1963.

Marcel

Blackham, H. J. *Six Existential Thinkers.* London: Routledge & Kegan Paul, 1952.

Cain, Seymour. *Gabriel Marcel.* London, 1963.

Jaspers

Olson, A. M., ed. *Heidegger and Jaspers.* Philadelphia: Temple University Press, 1994.

Schilpp, P. A., ed. *The Philosophy of Karl Jaspers.* La Salle, Ill.: Open Court Publishing Co., 1981.

Walraff, C. F. *Karl Jaspers: An Introduction to His Philosophy.* Princeton: Princeton University Press, 1970.

Young-Bruehl, Elizabeth. *Freedom and Karl Jaspers' Philosophy.* New Haven: Yale University Press, 1981.

Merleau-Ponty

Bannan, John F. *The Philosophy of Merleau-Ponty.* New York: Harcourt, Brace & World, 1967.

Coles, Romand. *Self/Power/Other: Political Theory and Dialogical Ethics.* Ithaca, N.Y.: Cornell University Press, 1992.

Whiteside, Kerry H. *Merleau-Ponty and the Foundation of an Existential Politics.* Princeton: Princeton University Press, 1988.

de Beauvoir

Fullbrook, Kate, and Edward Fullbrook. *Simone de Beau-voir and Jean-Paul Sartre.* New York: Basic Books, 1994.

Keefe, Terry. *Simone de Beauvoir: A Study of Her Writings.* London: Harrap, 1983.

Hatcher, Donald L. *Understanding "The Second Sex".* New York: P. Lang, 1984.

Lundgren-Gothlin, Eva. *Sex and Existence: Simone de Beauvoir's The Second Sex.* Hanover, N.H.: University Press of New England, 1996.

Moi, Toril. *Feminist Theory & Simone de Beauvoir.* Oxford: Blackwell Press, 1990.

Camus

Ellison, David R. *Understanding Albert Camus.* Columbia, S.C.: University of South Carolina Press, 1990.

Royle, Peter. *The Sartre-Camus Controversy: A Literary and Philosophical Critique.* Ottawa: University of Ottawa Press, 1982.

Buber

Bergman, Samuel Hugo, 1883–1975. *Dialogical Philosophy from Kierkegaard to Buber.* Albany, N.Y.: State University of New York Press, 1991.

Diamond, Malcolm Luria. *Martin Buber, Jewish Existentialist.* New York: Harper Torchbooks, 1968.

Friedman, Maurice. *Martin Buber: The Life of Dialogue.* Chicago: University of Chicago Press, 1955.

Wood, Robert E. *Martin Buber's Ontology: An Analysis of I and Thou.* Evanston: Northwestern University Press, 1969.

Tillich

Kegley, C. W., and R. W. Bretall, eds. *The Theology of Paul Tillich.* New York: Macmillan, 1952.

Kelsey, David H. *The Fabric of Paul Tillich's Theology.* New Haven: Yale University Press, 1967.

Thatcher, Adrian. *The Ontology of Paul Tillich.* Oxford: Oxford University Press, 1978.

CHAPTER 7

Existentialist Literature

This final chapter gathers together several literary works that call to mind existentialist themes. Many literary forms are represented: plays, fantasy fiction, science fiction, straight fiction, novels, and literary essays.

The first selections are contributions by Fyodor Dostoevsky and Franz Kafka, who are not considered existentialists but who nonetheless share existentialist concerns. In *Notes from Underground*, Part One of which is included here, Dostoevsky records the reflections of a man who finds himself unable to take on an identity from his society and unsatisfied with any he is able to create for himself. In "The Grand Inquisitor," from his novel *The Brothers Karamazov*, Dostoevsky's character Ivan narrates a story in which Christ returns to earth and is taken into custody by the Grand Inquisitor, who raises questions about the relative importance of freedom versus happiness. In "An Imperial Message," Kafka creates characters who strive in vain to come to terms with a world that is absurd.

The next author is an existentialist philosopher: Jean-Paul Sartre. As his work illustrates, writers associated with the term "existentialism" often attempted to communicate their ideas through literary means other than philosophical essays. In the excerpt from his novel *Nausea*, Sartre's character perceives a tree as it is in itself and finds the experience nauseating. Sartre's play *No Exit*, set in hell, explores the idea that our own self-assessment depends on how others see us, so that indeed hell might be other people.

The final set of selections consists of stories that might prove useful in exploring existentialist ideas. The first of these is Jorge Borges' brief fantasy called "Everything and Nothing," about an individual who attempts to become somebody by playing roles and, upon asking God for help in achieving his identity, is surprised to hear God admit to an existential crisis of his own. Next comes Flannery O'Connor's short story "A Good Man Is Hard to Find," in which an ordinary family encounters unusual strangers, which raises the question of whether or not people are responsible for their characters. Last are Philip K. Dick's science fiction story "The Imposter" and John Barth's novel, *The End of the Road,* a chapter of which is included here; both deal with identity crises.

FYODOR DOSTOEVSKY (1821–1881)

Fyodor Mikhailovich Dostoevsky was a Russian novelist whose first novel *Poor Folk* (1846), published when he was in his mid-twenties, won him immediate acclaim. In 1849 he and other members of a secret group called the Petrashevsky Circle were convicted for revolutionary activities and sentenced to death. Nicholas I allowed the prisoners to face a firing squad before commuting the sentence at the last moment. Dostoevsky was sent to a penal colony in Siberia for four years of labor. Already a religious man, his experience in Siberia increased his devotion to Christianity. *Notes from Underground* (1864) was one of the few works he published in a magazine called *Time* that he started with his brother. Aside from *Notes from Underground* and *The Idiot* (1868), Dostoevsky's best known works include *Crime and Punishment* (1866), *The Possessed* (1871), and *The Brothers Karamazov* (1880). "The Grand Inquisitor" is from the last of these novels.

Notes from Underground

Part One
The Mousehole*

I

I'm a sick man . . . a mean man. There's nothing attractive about me. I think there's something wrong with my liver. But, actually, I don't understand a damn thing about my sickness; I'm not even too sure what it is that's ailing me. I'm not under treatment and never have been, although I have great respect for medicine and doctors. Moreover, I'm morbidly superstitious— enough, at least, to respect medicine. With my education I shouldn't be superstitious, but I am just the same. No, I'd say I refuse medical help simply out of contrariness. I don't expect you to understand that, but it's so. Of course, I can't explain whom I'm trying to fool this way. I'm fully aware that I can't spite the doctors by refusing their help. I know very well that I'm harming myself and no one else. But still, it's out of spite that I refuse to ask for the doctors' help. So my liver hurts? Good, let it hurt even more!

I've been living like this for a long time, twenty years or so. I'm forty now. I used to be in government service, but I'm not any more. I was a nasty official. I was rude and enjoyed being rude. Why, since I took no bribes, I had to make up for it somehow. (That's a poor attempt at wit, but I won't delete it now. I wrote it thinking it'd sound very sharp. But now I realize that it's nothing but vulgar showing off, so I'll let it stand if only for that reason.)

---

*It goes without saying that both these *Notes* and their author are fictitious. Nevertheless, people like the author of these notes may, and indeed must, exist in our society, if we think of the circumstances under which that society has been formed. It has been my wish to show the public a character of the recent past more clearly than is usually shown. He belongs to the generation that is now rounding out its days. In the excerpt entitled "The Mousehole," this man introduces himself and presents his views, trying to explain why he has appeared, and could not help but appear, in our midst. The next excerpt consists of this man's actual "notes," relating to certain events in his life.
FYODOR DOSTOYEVSKY

When petitioners came up to my desk for information, I snarled at them and felt indescribably happy whenever I managed to make one of them feel miserable. Being petitioners, they were a meek lot. One, however, wasn't. He was an officer, and I had a special loathing for him. He just wouldn't be subdued. He had a special way of letting his saber rattle. Disgusting. For eighteen months I waged war with him about that saber. I won out in the end, and he stopped the thing from rattling. All this, however, happened when I was still young. But shall I tell you what it was really all about? Well, the real snag, the most repulsive aspect of my nastiness, was that, even when I was at my liverish worst, I was constantly aware that I was not really wicked nor even embittered, that I was simply chasing pigeons, you might say, and thus passing the time. And so I might be frothing at the mouth, but if you had brought me a doll to play with or had offered me a nice cup of tea with sugar, chances are I would have calmed down. I'd even have been deeply touched, although, angry at myself, I would be certain to gnash my teeth later and be unable to sleep for several months. But that's the way it was.

I was lying just now when I said I used to be a nasty official. And I lied out of spite. I was having fun at the expense of the petitioners and that officer, but deep down, I could never be really nasty. I was always aware of many elements in me that were just the opposite of wicked. I felt that they'd been swarming inside me all my life, trying to break out, but I had refused to let them. They tormented me, they drove me into shame and convulsions, and I was fed up with them. Ah, how fed up I was with them! Doesn't it seem to you as if I were trying to justify myself, to ask for your forgiveness? I'm sure you must think that. . . . Well, believe me, I don't care if you do think so.

I couldn't manage to make myself nasty or, for that matter, friendly, crooked or honest, a hero or an insect. Now I'm living out my life in a corner, trying to console myself with the stupid, useless excuse that an intelligent man cannot turn himself into anything, that only a fool can make anything he wants out of himself. It's true that an intelligent man of the nineteenth century is bound to be a spineless creature, while the man of character, the man of action, is, in most cases, of limited intelligence. This is my conviction at the age of forty. I'm forty now, and forty years is a whole life—forty is deep old age. It's indecent, vulgar, and immoral to live beyond forty! Who lives beyond forty? Answer me honestly. Or let me tell you then: fools and good-for-nothings. I'll repeat that to the face of any of those venerable patriarchs, those respected grayheads, for the whole world to hear. And I have a right to say it, for I'll live to be sixty. I'll live to be seventy! I'll live to be eighty! . . . Wait, give me a chance to catch my breath. . . .

Do you think I'm trying to make you laugh? Then you've got me wrong again. I'm not at all the cheerful fellow you think I am, or you may think I am. But if you're irritated by all my babble (I feel you must be by now) and feel like asking me who the hell I am after all, I'll have to answer that I'm a collegiate assessor. I entered the service to have something to eat (and for that only). And so, when a distant relative died, leaving me six thousand rubles, I immediately resigned and installed myself in my corner here. I had lived here even before that, but now I've really settled down. My room is miserable and ugly, on the outskirts of the city. The maid here is a peasant woman, nasty out of sheer stupidity; moreover, there's always a bad smell about her. They tell me that the Petersburg climate is bad for me and that, with my miserable income, it's a very expensive place to live. I know all that myself. I know it better than all my would-be advisers. But I'm going to stay in Petersburg! I won't leave! I won't leave because . . .

Ah, it's really all the same whether I go or stay.

Now then, what does a decent man like to talk about most? Himself, of course. So I'll talk about myself.

II

Now I want to tell you, ladies and gentlemen, whether you like it or not, why I couldn't even become an insect. I must first solemnly declare that I tried many times to become one. But even that was beyond me. I swear that too great a lucidity is a disease, a true, full-fledged disease. For everyday needs, the average person's awareness is more than sufficient, and it is about a half or a quarter of that of the unhappy nineteenth century intellectual, particularly if he's unfortunate enough to live in Petersburg, the most abstract and premeditated city on earth (there are premedi-

tated and unpremeditated cities). The extent of consciousness at the disposal of what may be termed the spontaneous people and the men of action is sufficient. I bet you think I say that just to take a crack at men of action, and that this kind of showing off is just as much in poor taste as the saber rattling of that officer I mentioned. But I ask you, who on earth goes around showing off his sickness, and even glorying in it?

On second thought though, I'd say that everyone does. People do pride themselves on their infirmities and I, probably, more than anyone. So don't let's argue about it—I admit my contention was inane. But I still say that not only too much lucidity, but any amount of it at all is a disease. That's where I stand. But let's leave that for a moment too. Now tell me this: why, just when I was most capable of being conscious of every refinement of the "good and the beautiful," as they used to put it once upon a time, were there moments when I lost my awareness of it, and did such ugly things—things that everyone does probably, but that I did precisely at moments when I was most aware that they shouldn't be done.

The more conscious I was of "the good and the beautiful," the deeper I sank into the mud, and the more likely I was to remain mired in it. But what struck me was the feeling I had that, in my case, it wasn't accidental, that it was intended to be that way, as if that were my normal state rather than a sickness or depravity; so that finally I lost all desire to fight my depravity. In the end, I almost believed (perhaps I even *did* believe) that it actually *was* my normal state.

But, in the beginning, what agonies I went through in this inner struggle! I didn't believe that there were others who went through all that, so I've kept it a secret all my life. I was ashamed (perhaps, even now, I am still ashamed). I reached a point where I felt a secret, unhealthy, base little pleasure in creeping back into my hole after some disgusting night in Petersburg and forcing myself to think that I had again done something filthy, that what was done couldn't be undone. And I inwardly gnawed at myself for it, tore at myself and ate myself away, until the bitterness turned into some shameful, accursed sweetishness and, finally, into a great, unquestionable pleasure. Yes, yes, definitely a pleasure! I mean it! And that's why I started out on this subject: I wanted to find out whether others experience this sort of pleasure too.

I'll explain it to you: I derived pleasure precisely from the blinding realization of my degradation; because I felt I was already up against the wall; that it was horrible but couldn't be otherwise; that there was no way out and it was no longer possible to make myself into a different person; that even if there were still enough time and faith left to become different, I wouldn't want to change myself; and that, even if I wanted to, I still wouldn't have done anything about it, because, actually, there wasn't anything to change into. Finally, the most important point is that there's a set of fundamental laws to which heightened consciousness is subject so that there's no changing oneself or, for that matter, doing anything about it. Thus, as a result of heightened consciousness, a man feels that it's all right if he's bad as long as he knows it—as though that were any consolation. But enough. . . . Ah, what a lot of words! And what have I explained? What's the explanation for this pleasure? But I'll make myself clear! I'll go through with it! That's why I've taken up my pen.

I, for instance, am horribly sensitive. I'm suspicious and easily offended, like a dwarf or a hunchback. But I believe there have been moments when I'd have liked to have my face slapped. I say that in all seriousness—I'd have derived pleasure from this too. Naturally it would be the pleasure of despair. But then, it is in despair that we find the most acute pleasure, especially when we are aware of the hopelessness of the situation. And when one's face is slapped—why, one is bound to be crushed by one's awareness of the pulp into which one has been ground. But the main point is that, whichever way you look at it, I was always guilty in the first place, and what is most vexing is that I was guilty without guilt, by virtue of the laws of nature. Thus, to start with, I'm guilty of being more intelligent than all those around me. (I've always felt that and, believe me, it's weighed on my conscience sometimes. All my life, I have never been able to look people straight in the eye—I always feel a need to avert my face.) And then, I'm also guilty because, even if there had been any forgiveness in me, it would only have increased my torment, because I would have been conscious of its uselessness. I surely would have been unable to do anything with my forgiveness: I wouldn't have been able to forgive because the offender would simply have been obeying the laws of nature in slapping me, and it makes no sense to forgive the laws of nature—but neither could I have forgotten it, because it is humiliating, after all. Finally, even if I hadn't wanted to be forgiving at all, but on the contrary, had wished to avenge myself on the offender, I couldn't have done it, for the chances are I'd never have dared to do anything about it even if there had been something I could do. Why wouldn't I have dared? Well, I'd especially like to say a few words about that.

III

Now let's see how things are with people who are capable of revenge and, in general, of taking care of themselves. When the desire for revenge takes possession of them, they are drained for a time of every other feeling but this desire for revenge. Such a gentleman just rushes straight ahead, horns lowered, like a furious bull, and nothing stops him until he comes up against a stone wall. (Speaking of walls, it must be noted that spontaneous people and men of action have a sincere respect for them. For these people a wall is not the challenge that it is for people like you and me who think and therefore do nothing; it is not an excuse to turn back, an excuse in which one of our kind doesn't really believe—although he always welcomes it. No, their respect is perfectly sincere. A wall has a calming effect upon them; it is as though it solved a moral issue—it is something final and, perhaps, even mystical. . . . But we'll come back to walls later.)

In my view, such a spontaneous man—the real, normal man—is the fulfillment of the wishes of his tender mother, Nature, who so lovingly created him on this earth. I envy that man. I'm bilious with envy. He's stupid, I won't dispute that, but then, maybe a normal man is supposed to be stupid; what makes you think he isn't? Perhaps that's the great beauty of it. And what makes me even more inclined to suspect this is that if we take the antithesis of a normal man, the man of heightened consciousness, who is a test-tube product rather than a child of nature (this is almost mysticism, my friends, but I have a feeling that it is so), we find that this test-tube man is so subdued by his antithesis that he views himself—heightened consciousness and all—as a mouse rather than a man. So, even if he's a mouse with a heightened consciousness, he's still nothing but a mouse, whereas the other is a man. So there. And, what's more, he regards himself as a mouse; no one asks him to do so. This is a very important point.

Now let's look at this mouse in action. Let's assume it has been humiliated (it is constantly being humiliated) and that it wishes to avenge itself. It's possible too that there's even more spite accumulated in it than in *l'homme de la nature et de la vérité*. The nauseating, despicable, petty desire to repay the offender in kind may squeak more disgustingly in the mouse than in the natural man who, because of his innate stupidity, considers revenge as merely justice, whereas the mouse, with its heightened consciousness, is bound to deny the justice of it. Now we come to the act of revenge itself. In addition to being disgraced in the first place, the poor mouse manages to mire itself in more mud as a result of its questions and doubts. And each question brings up so many more unanswered questions that a fatal pool of sticky muck is formed, consisting of the mouse's doubts and torments as well as of the gobs of spit aimed at it by the practical men of action, who stand around like judges and dictators and laugh lustily at it till their throats are sore. Of course, the only thing left for it to do is to shrug its puny shoulders and, affecting a scornful smile, scurry off ignominiously to its mousehole. And there, in its repulsive, evil-smelling nest, the downtrodden, ridiculed mouse plunges immediately into a cold, poisonous, and—most important—never-ending hatred. For forty years, it will remember the humiliation in all its ignominious details, each time adding some new point, more abject still, endlessly taunting and tormenting itself. Although ashamed of its own thoughts, the mouse will remember everything, go over it again and again, then think up possible additional humiliations. It may even try to avenge itself, but then it will do so in spurts, pettily, from behind the stove, anonymously, doubting that its vengeance is right, that it will succeed, and feeling that, as a result, it will hurt itself a hundred times more than it will hurt the one against whom its revenge is directed, who probably won't even feel enough of an itch to scratch himself. Then, on its deathbed, the mouse will remember it all again, plus all the accumulated interest and . . .

But it is precisely this cold, sickening mixture of hope and despair; this deliberate retreat to a tomb under the floor for all these years; this artificially induced hopelessness, of which I'm still not fully convinced; this poison of thwarted desires turned inward; this feverish hesitation; the final resolutions followed a minute later by regrets—all this is the gist of the strange pleasure I've mentioned. This pleasure is so subtle, so evasive, that even slightly limited people, or people who simply have strong nerves, won't understand the first thing about it.

"It may also be difficult to understand for those who've never been slapped around," you may add with a self-satisfied grin.

Thus you may politely suggest that I'm talking like an expert because I've been slapped. I bet that's just what you think. But let me reassure you, ladies and gentlemen: I don't care in the least what you may think, but I haven't really been slapped. But that's enough on this subject that seems to interest you so much.

I'll continue calmly about people with strong nerves who can't understand the somewhat more subtle aspects of pleasure. Although, under other circumstances, these people may roar like furious bulls and this may add immensely to their prestige, they capitulate at once before the impossible, that is, a stone wall. What stone wall? Why, the laws of nature, of course; the conclusions of the natural sciences, of mathematics. When they are through proving to you that you descend from the monkey, it will do you no good to screw up your nose—you'll just have to take it. Trust them to prove to you that a single drop of your own fat is bound to be dearer to you, when you come down to it, than a hundred thousand human lives and that this conclusion is an answer to all this talk about virtue and duty, and other ravings and superstitions. So just take it for what it is—there's nothing else you can do; it's like two and two make four. That's arithmetic. Just try and disprove it!

"Wait a minute," they'll call out to you, "why protest? Two and two do make four. Nature doesn't ask your advice. She isn't interested in your preferences or whether or not you approve of her laws. You must accept nature as she is with all the consequences that that implies. So a wall is a wall, etc., etc. . . ."

But, good Lord, what do I care about the laws of nature and arithmetic if I have my reasons for disliking them, including the one about two and two making four! Of course, I won't be able to breach this wall with my head if I'm not strong enough. But I don't have to accept a stone wall just because it's there and I don't have the strength to breach it.

As if such a wall could really leave me resigned and bring me peace of mind because it's the same as twice two makes four! How stupid can one get? Isn't it much better to recognize the stone walls and the impossibilities for what they are and refuse to accept them if surrendering makes one too sick? Isn't it better, resorting to irrefutable logical constructions, to arrive at the most revolting conclusions on the eternal theme that you too, somehow, share the responsibility for the stone wall, although it's obvious that you're not at all to blame for it; and then, to sink voluptuously into inertia, gnashing your teeth in impotent rage, unable to find someone on whom to vent your rage and hatred, and losing hope of ever finding anyone; feeling that you've been short-changed, cheated, deceived, that everything is a mess in which it is impossible to tell what's what, but that despite this impossibility and deception, it still hurts you, and the less you can understand, the more it hurts.

IV

"Ha!" you may object sarcastically, "this way you'll soon find pleasure in a toothache."

"Well," I'd answer, "there's pleasure in a toothache too."

Once I suffered from a toothache for a whole month, and I can tell you there's pleasure in it. In this instance, of course, people don't rage in silence. They moan. But they are no ordinary moans; they're malicious, and in this maliciousness lies the point. It's this moaning that expresses the pleasure of the sufferer, for if he didn't enjoy it, he wouldn't moan. This is a good example of what I mean, so I'll dwell on it for a while. To start with, these moans express all the humiliating pointlessness of the pain, a pain that obeys certain laws of nature about which you don't give a damn, for you're the one who must suffer, and nature can't feel a thing. Thus, these moans indicate that, although there's no enemy, the pain is there; that you, together with your dentist, are completely at the mercy of your teeth; that if it pleases someone, your toothache will stop, and if it doesn't, it may go on for another three months; and that, finally, if you refuse to resign yourself and go on protesting, all you can do to relieve your feelings is to give yourself a whipping or pound the stone wall with your fists. There's definitely nothing else you can do.

So it is these horrible insults and humiliations, inflicted on us by God knows whom, that generate a pleasure that sometimes reaches the highest degree of voluptuousness. Please, ladies and gentlemen, listen carefully some time to the moans of a nineteenth century intellectual suffering from a toothache. Listen on the second or third day of pain, when he is no longer moaning the way he did on the first day, that is, simply because his tooth ached. His moaning is quite unlike the moaning of a peasant, for he has been affected by education and by European civilization. He moans like a man who, as they say nowadays, "has been uprooted from the soil and lost contact with the people." His moans soon become strident and perverse, and they continue day and night. He certainly knows that he's not helping himself by moaning like that. No one knows better than he that he's tormenting and irritating himself and others for nothing; that his audience, and this includes his family, for whom he's trying so hard, is listening to him with disgust; that they don't believe he's sincere in the least and realize that he could moan differently, more simply, without all these trills and flourishes; and that he's putting it all on out of sheer spite and viciousness.

Well, there's voluptuous pleasure in all this degradation and in the realization of it.

I'm disturbing you? Breaking your heart? Keeping everyone awake? All right, stay awake then, feel every second that my teeth ache. To you, I'm no longer the hero I tried to appear at first, but simply a despicable little man. So be it. I'm very glad you've managed to see through me. It makes you uncomfortable to listen to my cowardly moaning? Well, be uncomfortable. I'll produce one of those moaning flourishes in a minute, then you can tell me how you feel. . . .

You still don't understand what I have in mind? Well, then it looks as if you have to grow up and develop your comprehension so that you can grasp all the twists of this voluptuousness. That makes you laugh? I'm very happy it does. Of course my jokes are in poor taste, inappropriate, and confused; they reveal my lack of security. But that is because I have no respect for myself. After all, how can a man with my lucidity of perception respect himself?

V

How can one, after all, have the slightest respect for a man who tries to find pleasure in the feeling of humiliation itself? I'm not saying that out of any mawkish sense of repentance. In general, I couldn't stand saying "Sorry, Papa, I'll never do it again."

And it wasn't at all because I was incapable of saying it. On the contrary, perhaps it was just because I was only too prone to say it. And you should've seen under what circumstances too! I'd get myself blamed, almost purposely, for something with which I'd had nothing to do even in thought or dream. That's what was most disgusting. But, even so, I was always deeply moved, repented my wickedness, and cried; in this, of course, I was deceiving myself, although I never did so deliberately. It was my heart that let me down here. In this case, I can't even blame the laws of nature, although those laws have oppressed me all my life. It makes me sick to remember all this, but then I was sick at the time too. It took me only a minute or so to recognize that it was all a pack of lies; all that repentance, those emotional outbursts and promises of reform—nothing but pretentious, nauseating lies. I was furious. And if you ask me now why I tortured and tormented myself like that, I'll tell you: I was bored just sitting with my arms folded, so I went in for all those tricks. Believe me, it's true. Just watch yourself carefully and you'll understand that that's the way it works. I made up whole stories about myself and put myself through all sorts of adventures to satisfy, at any price, my need to live. How many times did I convince myself that I was offended, just like that, for no reason at all. And although I knew that I had nothing to be offended about, that I was putting it all on, I'd put myself into such a state that in the end I'd really feel terribly offended. I was so strongly tempted to play tricks of this sort that, in the end, I lost all restraint.

Once, or rather twice, I tried to make myself fall in love. And, believe me, ladies and gentlemen, I certainly suffered! Deep down, of course, I couldn't quite believe in my suffering and felt like laughing. But it was suffering nevertheless—the real stuff, with jealousy, violence, and all the trimmings.

And all that out of sheer boredom, ladies and gentlemen, sheer boredom. I was crushed by inertia. And what would the natural, logical fruit of heightened consciousness be if not inertia, by which I mean consciously sitting with folded arms! I mentioned that before. And I repeat again and again: spontaneous people and men of action can act precisely because they are limited and stupid. How shall I explain? Let me put it this way: because of their limitations, these people mistake the nearest secondary causes for primary ones. This way they become convinced faster and more easily than others that they have found an incontrovertible reason for acting, and they have no further qualms about acting, which, of course, is the important thing. Obviously, in order to act, one must be fully satisfied and free of all misgivings beforehand. But take me: how can I ever be sure? Where will I find the primary reason for action, the justification for it? Where am I to look for it? I exercise my power of reasoning, and in my case, every time I think I have found a primary cause I see another cause that seems to be truly primary, and so on and so forth, indefinitely. This is the very essence of consciousness and thought. It must be another natural law. And what happens in the end? The same thing over again.

Remember when I spoke of vengeance (I bet you didn't follow me too well)? It is said that a man avenges himself because he thinks it is the just thing to do. This implies that he has found the primary reason, the basis for his action, which, in this case, is Justice. This gives him foolproof peace of mind, so he avenges himself without qualms, efficiently, certain throughout that he's acting fairly and honestly.

But I can't see any justice or virtue in vengeance, so if I indulge in it, it is only out of spite and anger. Anger, of course, overcomes all hesitations and can thus replace the primary reason precisely because it is no reason at all. But what can I do if I don't even have anger (that's where I started from, remember)? In me, anger disintegrates chemically like everything else, because of those damned laws of nature. As I think, the anger vanishes, the reasons for it evaporate, the responsible person is never found, the insult becomes an insult no longer but a stroke of fate, just like a toothache, for which no one can be held responsible. And so I find that all I can do is take another whack at the stone wall, then shrug the whole thing off because of my failure to find the primary cause of the evil.

And, if I did try to follow my feeling blindly without thinking about primary causes, if I managed to keep my consciousness out of it, even temporarily, if I did make myself hate or love just to avoid sitting with folded arms—then, within forty-eight hours at the most, I'd loathe myself for deliberately sinking into self-deception. And everything would burst like a soap bubble and end in inertia.

You know, ladies and gentlemen, probably the only reason why I think I'm an intelligent man is that in all my life I've never managed to start or finish anything. I know, I know, I'm just a chatterbox, a harmless, boring chatterbox like all my kind. But how can I help it if it is the inescapable fate of every intelligent man to chatter, like filling an empty glass from an empty bottle?

. . .

VII

. . . Who was it that first said that man does nasty things only because he doesn't know where his real interests lie, that if he were enlightened about his true interests, he would immediately stop acting like a pig and become kind and noble? Being enlightened, the argument goes on, and seeing where his real advantage lay, he would realize that it was in acting virtuously. And, since it is well established that a man will not act deliberately against his own interests, it follows that he would have no choice but to become good. Oh, the innocence of it! Since when, in these past thousands of years, has man acted exclusively out of self-interest? What about the millions of facts that show that men, deliberately and in full knowledge of what their real interests were, spurned them and rushed in a different direction? They did so at their own risk without anyone advising them, refusing to follow the safe, well-trodden path and searching for another path, a difficult one, an unreasonable one, stubbornly working their way along it in the darkness. Doesn't this suggest that stubbornness and willfulness were stronger in these people than their interests?

Interest! What interest? Can you define exactly what is in the interest of a human being? And suppose the interest of a man is not only consistent with but even demands something harmful rather than advantageous? Of course, if such an instance *is* possible, then the whole rule is nothing but dust. Now, you tell me—is such an instance possible? You may laugh if you wish, but I want you to answer me this: is there an accurate scale of human advantages? Aren't there any advantages that are omitted, that cannot possibly be included in any such scale? As far as I can make out, you've based your scale of advantages on statistical averages and scientific formulas thought up by economists. And since your scale consists of such advantages as happiness, prosperity, freedom, security,

and all that, a man who deliberately disregarded that scale would be branded by you—and by me too, as a matter of fact—as an obscurantist and as utterly insane. But what is really remarkable is that all of your statisticians, sages, and humanitarians, when listing human advantages, insist on leaving out one of them. They never even allow for it, thus invalidating all their calculations. One would think it would be easy just to add it to the list. But that's where the trouble lies—it doesn't fit into any scale or chart.

You see, ladies and gentlemen, I have a friend—of course, he's your friend, too, and, in fact, everyone's friend. When he's about to do something, this friend explains pompously and in detail how he must act in accordance with the precepts of justice and reason. Moreover, he becomes passionate as he expostulates upon human interests; heaps scorn on the shortsighted fools who don't know what virtue is or what's good for them. Then, exactly fifteen minutes later, without any apparent external cause, but prompted by something inside him that is stronger than every consideration of interest, he pirouettes and starts saying exactly the opposite of what he was saying before; that is, he discredits the laws of logic and his own advantage; in short, he attacks everything. . . .

Now, since my friend is a composite type, he cannot be dismissed as an odd individual. So perhaps there is something that every man values above the highest individual advantage, or (not to be illogical) there may exist a human advantage that is the most advantageous (and it is precisely the one that is so consistently left out), which is also more important than the others and for the sake of which a man, if need be, will go against reason, honor, security, and prosperity—in short, against all the beautiful and useful things—just to attain it, the most advantageous advantage of the lot, the one which is the dearest to him.

"So," you may interrupt me, "it's an advantage all the same."

Wait a minute. Let me make myself clear. It's not a question of words. The remarkable thing about this advantage is that it makes a shambles of all the classifications and tables drawn up by humanitarians for the happiness of mankind. It crowds them out, as it were. But before I name this advantage, let me go on record and declare that all these lovely systems, all these theories that explain to man what is to his true advantage so that, to achieve it, he will forthwith become good and noble—all these are, in my opinion, nothing but sterile exercises in logic. Yes, that's all there is to it. For instance, propounding the theory of human regeneration through the pursuit of self-interest is, in my opinion, almost like . . . well, like saying with H. T. Buckle that man mellows under the influence of civilization and becomes less bloodthirsty and less prone to war. He appears to be following logical reasoning in arriving at that conclusion. But men love abstract reasoning and neat systematization so much that they think nothing of distorting the truth, closing their eyes and ears to contrary evidence to preserve their logical constructions. I'd say the example I've taken here is really too glaring. You have only to look around you and you'll see blood being spilled, and in the most playful way, just as if it were champagne. Look at the United States, that indissoluble union, plunged into civil war! Look at the Schleswig-Holstein farce . . . And what is it in us that is mellowed by civilization? All it does, I'd say, is to develop in man a capacity to feel a greater variety of sensations. And nothing, absolutely nothing else. And through this development, man will yet learn how to enjoy bloodshed. Why, it has already happened. Have you noticed, for instance, that the most refined, bloodthirsty tyrants, compared to whom the Attilas and Stenka Razins are mere choirboys, are often exquisitely civilized? In fact, if they are not overly conspicuous, it is because there are too many of them and they have become too familiar to us. Civilization has made man, if not always more bloodthirsty, at least more viciously, more horribly bloodthirsty. In the past, he saw justice in bloodshed and slaughtered without any pangs of conscience those he felt had to be slaughtered. Today, though we consider bloodshed terrible, we still practice it—and on a much larger scale than ever before. It was said that Cleopatra—please forgive me this example from ancient history—enjoyed sticking golden pins into the breasts of her slaves, delighting in their screams and writhings. You may object that this happened in relatively barbarous times; or you may say that even now we live in barbarous times (also relatively), that pins are still stuck into people, that even today, although man has learned to be more discerning than in ancient times, he has yet to learn how to follow his reason.

Nevertheless, there's no doubt in your mind that he will learn as soon as he's rid of certain bad old habits and when common sense and science have completely reeducated human nature and directed it along the proper channels. You seem certain that man himself will give up erring *of his own free will* and will stop opposing his will to his interests. You say, moreover, that science itself will teach man (although I say it's a luxury) that he has neither will nor whim—never had, as a matter of fact—that he is something like a piano key or an organ stop; that, on the other hand, there are natural laws in the universe, and whatever happens to him happens outside his will, as it were, by itself, in accordance with the laws of nature. Therefore, all there is left to do is to discover these laws and man will no longer be responsible for his acts. Life will be really easy for him then. All human acts will be listed in something like logarithm tables, say up to the number 108,000, and transferred to a timetable. Or, better still, catalogues will appear, designed to help us in the way our dictionaries and encyclopedias do. They will carry detailed calculations and exact forecasts of everything to come, so that no adventure and no action will remain possible in this world.

Then—it is still you talking—new economic relations will arise, relations ready-made and calculated in advance with mathematical precision, so that all possible questions instantaneously disappear because they receive all the possible answers. Then the utopian palace of crystal will be erected; then . . . well, then, those will be the days of bliss.

Of course, you can't guarantee (it's me speaking now) that it won't be deadly boring (for what will there be to do when everything is predetermined by timetables?). But, on the other hand, everything will be planned very reasonably.

But then, one might do anything out of boredom. Golden pins are stuck into people out of boredom. But that's nothing. What's really bad (this is me speaking again) is that the golden pins will be welcomed then. The trouble with man is that he's stupid. Phenomenally stupid. That is, even if he's not really stupid, he's so ungrateful that another creature as ungrateful cannot be found. I, for one, wouldn't be the least surprised if, in that future age of reason, there suddenly appeared a gentleman with an ungrateful, or shall we say, retrogressive smirk, who, arms akimbo, would say:

"What do you say, folks, let's send all this reason to hell, just to get all these logarithm tables out from under our feet and go back to our own stupid ways."

That isn't so annoying in itself; what's bad is that this gentleman would be sure to find followers. That's the way man is made.

And the explanation for it is so simple that there hardly seems to be any need for it—namely, that a man, always and everywhere, prefers to act in the way he feels like acting and not in the way his reason and interest tell him, for it is very possible for a man to feel like acting against his interests and, in some instances, I say that he *positively* wants to act that way—but that's my personal opinion.

So one's own free, unrestrained choice, one's own whim, be it the wildest, one's own fancy, sometimes worked up to a frenzy—that is the most advantageous advantage that cannot be fitted into any table or scale and that causes every system and every theory to crumble into dust on contact. And where did these sages pick up the notion that man must have something that they feel is a normal and virtuous set of wishes; what makes them think that man's will must be reasonable and in accordance with his own interests? All man actually needs is *independent* will, at all costs and whatever the consequences.

Speaking of will, I'm damned if I—

VIII

"Ha-ha-ha! Strictly speaking there's no such thing as will!" you may interrupt me, guffawing. "Today, science has already succeeded in dissecting a man sufficiently to be able to tell that what we know as desire and free will are nothing but—"

Hold on, hold on a moment! I was coming to that myself. I admit I was even frightened about it. I was about to say that will depended on hell knows what and perhaps we should thank God for that, but then I remembered about science, and that stopped me short. And it was at that point that you spoke up. Now, suppose one day they really find a formula at the root of all our wishes and whims that will tell us what they depend on, what laws they are subject to, how they develop, what they are aiming at in such and such a case, and so on and so forth—that is, a real mathematical equation? Well, chances are that man will then cease to feel desire. Almost surely. What joy will he get out of functioning according to a timetable? Furthermore, he'll change from a man into an organ stop or something like that, for what is a man without will, wishes, and desires, if not an organ stop?

Let's examine the probabilities then—whether or not it's likely to happen. Now, what do *you* say?

"Hm . . ." you say, "our wishes are mostly misguided because of a mistaken evaluation of what's in our interest. If we sometimes desire something that doesn't make sense, it is because, in our stupidity, we believe that it's the easiest way to attain a supposed advantage. But once all this has been explained to us and worked out on a sheet of paper (which is very possible, because it is contemptible and meaningless to maintain that there may exist laws of nature which man will never penetrate), such desires will simply cease to exist. For when desire merges with reason, then we will reason instead of desiring. It will be impossible to retain reason and desire something senseless, that is, harmful. And once all our desires and all our reasoning can be computed (for the day is bound to come when we'll understand what actually governs what we now describe as our free will), then we may really have some sort of tables to guide our desires like everything else. So, if a man sticks out his tongue at someone, it is because he cannot *not* stick it out and has to stick it out holding his head exactly at the angle he does. So what *freedom* is there left in him, especially if he's a learned man, a diploma-holding scientist? Why, he can plot his life thirty years in advance. Anyway, if it comes to that, we've no choice but to accept. We must keep repeating to ourselves that, at no time and in no place, will nature ever ask for our permission; that we must accept it as it is and not as we paint it in our imaginations; that if we're moving toward graphs, timetables, and even test tubes, well, we'll just have to take it all—including, of course, the test tube! And if we do not wish to accept, nature itself will—"

Yes, yes, I know, I know . . . But there's a snag here, as far as I'm concerned. You must excuse me, ladies and gentlemen, if I get entangled in my own thoughts. You must make allowances for the fact that I've spent all the forty years of my life in a mousehole under the floor. So allow me to indulge my fancy.

I will admit that reason is a good thing. No argument about that. But reason is only reason, and it only satisfies man's rational requirements. Desire, on the other hand, is the manifestation of life itself—of all of life—and it encompasses everything from reason down to scratching oneself. And although, when we're guided by our desires, life may often turn into a messy affair, it's still life and not a series of extractions of square roots.

I, for instance, instinctively want to live, to exercise all the aspects of life in me and not only reason, which amounts to perhaps one-twentieth of the whole.

And what does reason know? It knows only what it has had time to learn. Many things will always remain unknown to it. That must be said even if there's nothing encouraging in it.

Now, human nature is just the opposite. It acts as an entity, using everything it has, conscious and unconscious, and even if it deceives us, it lives. I suspect, ladies and gentlemen, that you're looking at me with pity, wondering how I can fail to understand that an enlightened, cultured man, such as the man of the future, could not deliberately wish to harm himself. It's sheer mathematics to you. I agree, it is mathematics. But let me repeat to you for the hundredth time that there is one instance when a man can wish upon himself, in full awareness, something harmful, stupid, and even completely idiotic. He will do it in order to *establish his right* to wish for the most idiotic things and not to be obliged to have only sensible wishes. But what if a quite absurd whim, my friends, turns out to be the most advantageous thing on earth for us, as sometimes happens? Specifically, it may be more advantageous to us than any other advantages, even when it most obviously harms us and goes against all the sensible conclusions of our reason about our interest—because, whatever else, it leaves us our most important, most treasured possession: our individuality.

Some people concede, for instance, that desire may be the thing man treasures most. Desire, of course, can, if it wishes, agree with reason, especially if one uses it sparingly, never going too far. Then desire is quite useful, even praiseworthy.

But in reality, desire usually stubbornly disagrees with reason . . . and . . . and . . . let me tell you that this too is useful and praiseworthy.

. . .

. . . [I]t seems to me that the meaning of man's life consists in proving to himself every minute that he's a man and not a piano key. And man will keep proving it and paying for it with his own skin; he will turn into a troglodyte if need be. And, since this is so, I cannot help rejoicing that things are still the way they are and that, for the time being, nobody knows worth a damn what determines our desires.

Now you scream that no one intends to deprive me of my free will, that they're only trying to arrange things so that my will coincides with what is in my own interest, the laws of nature, and arithmetic.

Ah, ladies and gentlemen, don't talk to me of free will when it comes to timetables and arithmetic, when everything will be deducible from twice two makes four! There's no need for free will to find that twice two is four. That's not what I call free will!

IX

Of course I'm joking, my friends, and I realize my jokes are weak. Still, everything can't be just laughed off. Perhaps I'm joking through clenched teeth. You see, I'm haunted by certain questions, and perhaps you'll allow me to ask them.

Now, you, for instance—you want to cure man of his bad old habits and reshape his will according to the requirements of science and common sense. But what makes you think that man either can or *should* be changed in this way? What leads you to the conclusion that it is absolutely necessary to change man's desires? How do you know that these corrections will actually be to man's advantage? And, if you'll allow me to speak quite openly, what makes you so sure that abstention from acting contrary to one's interests, as determined by reason and arithmetic, is always to one's advantage and that this applies to mankind as a whole?

So far, these are nothing but assumptions on your part. I'll grant you that they conform to the laws of logic. But are they in accordance with human law? In case you think I'm crazy, let me explain. I agree that man is a creative animal, doomed to strive consciously toward a goal, engaged in full-time engineering, as it were, busy building himself roads that lead *somewhere—never mind where*. And perhaps if he feels like straying now and then, it is just because he is *doomed* to build this road; even the man of action, however stupid he may be, must realize from time to time that his road always goes *somewhere* and that the main thing is not *where* it goes but keeping the well-meaning babe at his engineering chores, thus saving him from the deadly snares of idleness, which, as is well known, is the mother of all vice. There's no disputing that man likes creating and building roads. But why does he also like chaos and disorder even into his old age? Explain that if you can! But wait, I myself would like to say a few words on this particular subject. I wonder if he doesn't like chaos and destruction so much just because he's instinctively afraid of reaching the goal he's working for? How do you know, perhaps he likes his objective only from a distance; perhaps he only likes to contemplate it and not to live in it, preferring to leave it, when it comes down to it, to animals such as ants, sheep, and such. Of course, ants are different. They have a wonderful everlasting piece of engineering on which to work—the anthill.

The worthy ants began with their anthill and will most likely end with it, which is greatly to the credit of their single-mindedness and perseverance. But man is frivolous and unaccountable and perhaps, like a chess player, he enjoys the achieving rather than the goal itself.

And who can tell, perhaps the purpose of man's life on earth consists precisely in this uninterrupted striving after a goal. That is to say, the purpose is life itself and not the goal which, of course, must be nothing but twice two makes four. And twice two, ladies and gentlemen, is no longer life but the beginning of death. At least, man has always feared this twice two makes four, and it's what I'm afraid of now.

Let's assume that man does nothing but search for this twice two, that he crosses oceans and sacrifices his life in this quest, while, all the time, he is really afraid of finding that it does make four. He feels that once he has discovered it, he'll have nothing left for which to search. The workers, at least, when they receive their money at the end of the week, go to a tavern and then, perhaps, land in a police station, so there's something to keep them busy. But otherwise, what is a man to do with himself when he achieves one of his objectives? In any case, there is a visible awkwardness in him every time he does. He loves the achieving, but does not particularly enjoy what he achieves. Funny, isn't it? Yes, man is a comical animal, and there's obviously a joke in all this. Still, I say that twice two is an unbearable notion, an arrogant imposition. This twice two image stands there, hands in pockets, in the middle of your road, and spits in your direction. Nevertheless, I'm willing to agree that twice-two-makes-four is a thing of beauty. But, if we're going to praise everything like that, then I say that twice-two-makes-five is also a delightful little item now and then.

And what makes you so cocksure, so positive that only the normal and the positive, that is, only what promotes man's welfare, is to his advantage? Can't reason also be wrong about what's an advantage? Why

can't man like things other than his well-being? Maybe he likes suffering just as much. Maybe suffering is just as much to his advantage as well-being. In fact, man adores suffering. Passionately. It's a fact. For this, there's no need even to go to world history. Just ask yourself, if you've had any kind of experience of life. And, personally, I even feel that it's shameful to like just well-being by itself. Right or wrong, it's very pleasant to break something from time to time.

Actually, I'm not advocating suffering any more than well-being. What I'm for is whim, and I want the right to use it whenever I want to.

I know, for instance, that suffering is inadmissible in light stage plays. In the utopian crystal palace, it'd be inconceivable, for suffering means doubt and denial, and what kind of crystal palace would that be, if people had doubts about it? Nevertheless, I'm certain that man will never give up true suffering, that is, chaos and destruction. Why, suffering is the only cause of consciousness. And, although I declared at the beginning that consciousness is man's greatest plague, I know that he likes it and won't exchange it for any advantage. Consciousness, for instance, is of a much higher order than twice two. After twice two, we'll of course have nothing left either to do or to find out. All that'll be left for us will be to block off our five senses and plunge into contemplation. With consciousness we have nothing much to do either, but we can at least lacerate ourselves from time to time, which does liven us up a bit. It may go against progress, but it's better than nothing.

X

So, you believe in an indestructible crystal palace in which you won't be able to stick out your tongue or blow raspberries even if you cover your mouth with your hand. But I'm afraid of such a palace precisely because it's indestructible and because I won't ever be allowed to stick my tongue out at it.

Try to understand: if, instead of that palace, there were nothing but a chicken house, and if I had to crawl into it to get out of the rain, I wouldn't call it a palace just out of gratitude, because it kept me dry. You may laugh and say that for that purpose it makes no difference whether it is a chicken coop or a palace. I'd agree with you if the only purpose of life was keeping from getting wet.

But suppose I decided that keeping dry is not the only reason for living and that, while we're at it, we'd better try and live in palaces? That's my wish and my choice. You'll change it only when you manage to change my preferences. By all means, do so if you can. But, in the meantime, allow me to distinguish between the chicken coop and the palace.

. . .

. . . [W]hy not stop these notes right here? I feel it was a mistake to start writing them in the first place. However, I've at least felt ashamed all the time I've been writing this story, so it isn't literature, but a punishment and an expiation. Of course, spinning long yarns about how I poisoned my life through moral disintegration in my musty hole, lack of contact with other men, and spite and vanity is not very interesting. I swear it has no literary interest, because what a novel needs is a hero, whereas here I have collected, as if deliberately, all the features of an anti-hero. These notes are bound to produce an extremely unpleasant impression, because we've all lost touch with life and we're all cripples to some degree. We've lost touch to such an extent that we feel a disgust for life as it is really lived and cannot bear to be reminded of it. Why, we've reached a point where we consider real life as work—almost as painful labor—and we are secretly agreed that the way it is presented in literature is much better. And what's all this fuss about? What are we turning our noses up at? What are we demanding? We don't know ourselves. We would be the ones to suffer if our whimsical wishes were granted. Well, try it yourselves—ask for more independence. Take anyone and untie his hands, open up his field of activity, relax discipline, and . . . well, believe me, he'd immediately want that discipline clamped down on him again. I know that what I'm saying is liable to make you angry; that it may make you stamp your feet and scream:

"Talk about yourself and about your own miseries in your stinking hole, but don't you dare say *all of us.*"

But listen to me for a moment. I'm not trying to justify myself by saying *all of us.* As for me, all I did was carry to the limit what you haven't dared to push even halfway—taking your cowardice for reasonableness, thus making yourselves feel better. So I may still turn out to be more *alive* than you in the end. Come on, have another look at it! Why, today we don't even know where real life is, what it is, or what it's called! Left alone without literature, we immediately become entangled and lost—we don't know what to join, what to keep up with; what to love, what to hate; what to respect, what to despise! We even find it painful to be men—real men of flesh and blood, with *our own private bodies;* we're ashamed of it, and we long to turn ourselves into something hypothetical called the average man. We're stillborn, and for a long time we've been brought into the world by parents who are dead themselves; and we like it better and better. We're developing a taste for it, so to speak. Soon we'll invent a way to be begotten by ideas altogether. But that's enough, I've had enough of writing these *Notes from Underground.*

Actually the notes of this lover of paradoxes do not end here. He couldn't resist and went on writing. But we are of the opinion that one might just as well stop here.

The Grand Inquisitor
from The Brothers Karamazov

. . . My story is laid in Spain, in Seville, in the most terrible time of the Inquisition, when fires were lighted every day to the glory of God, and 'in the splendid *auto da fé* the wicked heretics were burnt.' Oh, of course, this was not the coming in which He will appear according to His promise at the end of time in all His heavenly glory, and which will be sudden 'as lightning flashing from east to west.' No, He visited His children only for a moment, and there where the flames were crackling round the heretics. In His infinite mercy He came once more among men in that human shape in which He walked among men for three years fifteen centuries ago. He came down to the 'hot pavements' of the southern town in which on the day before almost a hundred heretics had, *ad majorem gloriam Dei*, been burnt by the cardinal, the Grand Inquisitor, in a magnificent *auto da fé*, in the presence of the king, the court, the knights, the cardinals, the most charming ladies of the court, and the whole population of Seville.

"He came softly, unobserved, and yet, strange to say, every one recognized Him. That might be one of the best passages in the poem. I mean, why they recognized Him. The people are irresistibly drawn to Him, they surround Him, they flock about Him, follow Him. He moves silently in their midst with a gentle smile of infinite compassion. The sun of love burns in His heart, light and power shine from His eyes, and their radiance, shed on the people, stirs their hearts with responsive love. He holds out His hands to them, blesses them, and a healing virtue comes from contact with Him, even with His garments. An old man in the crowd, blind from childhood, cries out, 'O Lord, heal me and I shall see Thee!' and, as it were, scales fall from his eyes and the blind man sees Him. The crowd weeps and kisses the earth under His feet. Children throw flowers before Him, sing, and cry hosannah. 'It is He—it is He!' all repeat. 'It must be He, it can be no one but Him!' He stops at the steps of the Seville cathedral at the moment when the weeping mourners are bringing in a little open white coffin. In it lies a child of seven, the only daughter of a prominent citizen. The dead child lies hidden in flowers. 'He will raise your child,' the crowd shouts to the weeping mother. The priest, coming to meet the coffin, looks perplexed, and frowns, but the mother of the dead child throws herself at His feet with a wail. 'If it is Thou, raise my child!' she cries, holding out her hands to Him. The procession halts, the coffin is laid on the steps at His feet. He looks with compassion, and His lips once more softly pronounce, 'Maiden, arise!' and the maiden arises. The little girl sits up in the coffin and looks round, smiling with wide-open wondering eyes, holding a bunch of white roses they had put in her hand.

"There are cries, sobs, confusion among the people, and at that moment the cardinal himself, the Grand Inquisitor, passes by the cathedral. He is an old man, almost ninety, tall and erect, with a withered face and sunken eyes, in which there is still a gleam of light. He is not dressed in his gorgeous cardinal's robes, as he was the day before, when he was burning the enemies of the Roman Church—at this moment he is wearing his coarse, old, monk's cassock. At a distance behind him come his gloomy assistants and slaves and the 'holy guard.' He stops at the sight of the crowd and watches it from a distance. He sees everything; he sees them set the coffin down at His feet, sees the child rise up, and his face darkens. He knits his thick gray brows and his eyes gleam with a sinister fire. He holds out his finger and bids the guards

take Him. And such is his power, so completely are the people cowed into submission and trembling obedience to him, that the crowd immediately makes way for the guards, and in the midst of deathlike silence they lay hands on Him and lead Him away. The crowd instantly bows down to the earth, like one man, before the old Inquisitor. He blesses the people in silence and passes on. The guards lead their prisoner to the close, gloomy vaulted prison in the ancient palace of the Holy Inquisition and shut Him in it. The day passes and is followed by the dark, burning, 'breathless' night of Seville. The air is 'fragrant with laurel and lemon.' In the pitch darkness the iron door of the prison is suddenly opened and the Grand Inquisitor himself comes in with a light in his hand. He is alone; the door is closed at once behind him. He stands in the doorway and for a minute or two gazes into His face. At last he goes up slowly, sets the light on the table and speaks.

"'Is it Thou? Thou?' but receiving no answer, he adds at once, 'Don't answer, be silent. What canst Thou say, indeed? I know too well what Thou wouldst say. And Thou hast no right to add anything to what Thou hadst said of old. Why, then, art Thou come to hinder us? For Thou hast come to hinder us, and Thou knowest that. But dost Thou know what will be to-morrow? I know not who Thou art and care not to know whether it is Thou or only a semblance of Him, but to-morrow I shall condemn Thee and burn Thee at the stake as the worst of heretics. And the very people who have to-day kissed Thy feet, to-morrow at the faintest sign from me will rush to heap up the embers of Thy fire. Knowest Thou that? Yes, maybe Thou knowest it,' he added with thoughtful penetration, never for a moment taking his eyes off the Prisoner."

"I don't quite understand, Ivan. What does it mean?" Alyosha, who had been listening in silence, said with a smile. "Is it simply a wild fantasy, or a mistake on the part of the old man—some impossible *quiproquo?*"

"Take it as the last," said Ivan, laughing, "if you are so corrupted by modern realism and can't stand anything fantastic. If you like it to be a case of mistaken identity, let it be so. It is true," he went on, laughing, "the old man was ninety, and he might well be crazy over his set idea. He might have been struck by the appearance of the Prisoner. It might, in fact, be simply his ravings, the delusion of an old man of ninety, over-excited by the *auto da fé* of a hundred heretics the day before. But does it matter to us after all whether it was a mistake of identity or a wild fantasy? All that matters is that the old man should speak out, should speak openly of what he has thought in silence for ninety years."

"And the Prisoner too is silent? Does He look at him and not say a word?"

"That's inevitable in any case," Ivan laughed again. "The old man has told Him He hasn't the right to add anything to what He has said of old. One may say it is the most fundamental feature of Roman Catholicism, in my opinion at least. 'All has been given by Thee to the Pope,' they say, 'and all, therefore, is still in the Pope's hands, and there is no need for Thee to come now at all. Thou must not meddle for the time, at least.' That's how they speak and write too—the Jesuits, at any rate. I have read it myself in the works of their theologians. 'Hast Thou the right to reveal to us one of the mysteries of that world from which Thou hast come?' my old man asks Him, and answers the question for Him. 'No, Thou hast not; that Thou mayest not add to what has been said of old, and mayest not take from men the freedom which Thou didst exalt when Thou wast on earth. Whatsoever Thou revealest anew will encroach on men's freedom of faith; for it will be manifest as a miracle, and the freedom of their faith was dearer to Thee than anything in those days fifteen hundred years ago. Didst Thou not often say then, "I will make you free"? But now Thou hast seen these "free" men,' the old man adds suddenly, with a pensive smile. 'Yes, we've paid dearly for it,' he goes on, looking sternly at Him, 'but at last we have completed that work in Thy name. For fifteen centuries we have been wrestling with Thy freedom, but now it is ended and over for good. Dost Thou not believe that it's over for good? Thou lookest meekly at me and deignest not even to be wroth with me. But let me tell Thee that now, to-day, people are more persuaded than ever that they have perfect freedom, yet they have brought their freedom to us and laid it humbly at our feet. But that has been our doing. Was this what Thou didst? Was this Thy freedom?'"

"I don't understand again," Alyosha broke in. "Is he ironical, is he jesting?"

"Not a bit of it! He claims it as a merit for himself and his Church that at last they have vanquished freedom and have done so to make men happy. 'For now' (he is speaking of the Inquisition, of course) 'for the first time it has become possible to think of the happiness of men. Man was created a rebel; and how can rebels be happy? Thou wast warned,' he says to Him. 'Thou hast had no lack of admonitions and warnings, but Thou didst not listen to those warnings; Thou didst reject the only way by which men might be made happy. But, fortunately, departing Thou didst hand on the work to us. Thou hast promised, Thou hast established by Thy word, Thou hast given to us the right to bind and to unbind, and now, of course, Thou canst not think of taking it away. Why, then, hast Thou come to hinder us?'"

"And what's the meaning of 'no lack of admonitions and warnings'?" asked Alyosha.

"Why, that's the chief part of what the old man must say.

"'The wise and dread spirit, the spirit of self-destruction and non-existence,' the old man goes on, 'the great spirit talked with Thee in the wilderness, and we are told in the books that he "tempted" Thee. Is that so? And could anything truer be said than what he revealed to Thee in three questions and what Thou didst reject, and what in the books is called "the temptation"? And yet if there has ever been on earth a real stupendous miracle, it took place on that day, on the day of the three temptations. The statement of those three questions was itself the miracle. If it were possible to imagine simply for the sake of argument that those three questions of the dread spirit had perished utterly from the books, and that we had to restore them and to invent them anew, and to do so had gathered together all the wise men of the earth—rulers, chief priests, learned men, philosophers, poets—and had set them the task to invent three questions, such as would not only fit the occasion, but express in three words, three human phrases, the whole future history of the world and of humanity—dost Thou believe that all the wisdom of the earth united could have invented anything in depth and force equal to the three questions which were actually put to Thee then by the wise and mighty spirit in the wilderness? From those questions alone, from the miracle of their statement, we can see that we have here to do not with the fleeting human intelligence, but with the absolute and eternal. For in those three questions the whole subsequent history of mankind is, as it were, brought together into one whole, and foretold, and in them are united all the unsolved historical contradictions of human nature. At the time it could not be so clear, since the future was unknown; but now that fifteen hundred years have passed, we see that everything in those three questions was so justly divined and foretold, and has been so truly fulfilled, that nothing can be added to them or taken from them.

"'Judge Thyself who was right—Thou or he who questioned Thee then? Remember the first question; its meaning, in other words, was this: "Thou wouldst go into the world, and art going with empty hands, with some promise of freedom which men in their simplicity and their natural unruliness cannot even understand, which they fear and dread—for nothing has ever been more insupportable for a man and a human society than freedom. But seest Thou these stones in this parched and barren wilderness? Turn them into bread, and mankind will run after Thee like a flock of sheep, grateful and obedient, though for ever trembling, lest Thou withdraw Thy hand and deny them Thy bread." But Thou wouldst not deprive man of freedom and didst reject the offer, thinking, what is that freedom worth, if obedience is bought with bread? Thou didst reply that man lives not by bread alone. But dost Thou know that for the sake of that earthly bread the spirit of the earth will rise up against Thee and will strive with Thee and overcome Thee, and all will follow him, crying, "Who can compare with this beast? He has given us fire from heaven!" Dost Thou know that the ages will pass, and humanity will proclaim by the lips of their sages that there is no crime, and therefore no sin; there is only hunger? "Feed men, and then ask of them virtue!" that's what they'll write on the banner, which they will raise against Thee, and with which they will destroy Thy temple. Where Thy temple stood will rise a new building; the terrible tower of Babel will be built again, and though, like the one of old, it will not be finished, yet Thou mightest have prevented that new tower and have cut short the sufferings of men for a thousand years; for they will come back to us after a thousand years of agony with their tower. They will seek us again, hidden underground in the catacombs, for we shall be again persecuted and tortured. They will find us and cry to us, "Feed us, for those who have promised us fire from heaven haven't given it!" And then we shall finish building their tower, for he finishes the building who feeds them. And we alone shall feed them in Thy name, declaring falsely that it is in Thy name. Oh, never, never can they feed themselves without us! No science will give them bread so long as they remain free. In the end they will lay their freedom at our feet, and say to us, "Make us your slaves, but feed us." They will understand themselves, at last, that freedom and bread enough for all are inconceivable together, for never, never will they be able to share between them! They will be convinced, too, that they can never be free, for they are weak, vicious, worthless and rebellious. Thou didst promise them the bread of Heaven, but, I repeat again, can it compare with earthly bread in the eyes of the weak, ever sinful and ignoble race of man? And if for the sake of the bread of Heaven thousands shall follow Thee, what is to become of the millions and tens of thousands of millions of creatures who will not have the strength to forego the earthly bread for the sake of the heavenly? Or dost Thou care only for the tens of thousands of the great and strong, while the millions, numerous as the sands of the sea, who are weak but love Thee, must exist only for the sake of the great and strong? No, we care for the weak too. They are sinful and rebellious, but in the end they too will become obedient. They will marvel at us and look on us as gods, because we are ready to endure the freedom which they have found so dreadful and to rule over them—so awful it will seem to them to be free. But we shall tell them that we are Thy servants and rule them in Thy name. We shall deceive them again, for we will not let Thee come to us again. That deception will be our suffering, for we shall be forced to lie.

"'This is the significance of the first question in the wilderness, and this is what Thou hast rejected for the sake of that freedom which Thou hast exalted above everything. Yet in this question lies hid the great secret of this world. Choosing "bread," Thou wouldst have satisfied the universal and everlasting craving of humanity—to find some one to worship. So long as man remains free he strives for nothing so incessantly and so painfully as to find some one to worship. But man seeks to worship what is established beyond dispute, so that all men would agree at once to worship it. For these pitiful creatures are concerned not only to find what one or the other can worship, but to find something that all would believe in and worship; what is essential is that all may be *together* in it. This craving for *community* of worship is the chief misery of every man individually and of all humanity from the beginning of time. For the sake of common worship they've slain each other with the sword. They have set up gods and challenged one another, "Put away your gods and come and worship ours, or we will kill you and your gods!" And so it will be to the end of the world, even when gods disappear from the earth; they will fall down before idols just the same. Thou didst know, Thou couldst not but have known, this fundamental secret of human nature, but Thou didst reject the one infallible banner which was offered Thee to make all men bow down to Thee alone—the banner of earthly bread; and Thou hast rejected it for the sake of freedom and the bread of Heaven. Behold what Thou didst further. And all again in the name of freedom! I tell Thee that man is tormented by no greater anxiety than to find some one quickly to whom he can hand over that gift of freedom with which the ill-fated creature is born. But only one who can appease their conscience can take over their freedom. In bread there was offered Thee an invincible banner; give bread, and man will worship thee, for nothing is more certain than bread. But if some one else gains possession of his conscience—oh! then he will cast away Thy bread and follow after him who has ensnared his conscience. In that Thou wast right. For the secret of man's being is not only to live but to have something to live for. Without a stable conception of the object of life, man would not consent to go on living, and would rather destroy himself than remain on earth, though he had bread in abundance. That is true. But what happened? Instead of taking men's freedom from them, Thou didst make it greater than ever! Didst Thou forget that man prefers peace, and even death, to freedom of choice in the knowledge of good and evil? Nothing is more seductive for man than his freedom of conscience, but nothing is a greater cause of suffering. And behold, instead of giving a firm foundation for setting the conscience of man at rest for ever, Thou didst choose all that is exceptional, vague and enigmatic; Thou didst choose what was utterly beyond the strength of men, acting as though Thou didst not love them at all—Thou who didst come to give Thy life for them! Instead of taking possession of men's freedom, Thou didst increase it, and burdened the spiritual kingdom of mankind with its sufferings for ever. Thou didst desire man's free love, that he should follow Thee freely, enticed and taken captive by Thee. In place of the rigid ancient law, man must

hereafter with free heart decide for himself what is good and what is evil, having only Thy image before him as his guide. But didst Thou not know that he would at last reject even Thy image and Thy truth, if he is weighed down with the fearful burden of free choice? They will cry aloud at last that the truth is not in Thee, for they could not have been left in greater confusion and suffering than Thou hast caused, laying upon them so many cares and unanswerable problems.

"'So that, in truth, Thou didst Thyself lay the foundation for the destruction of Thy kingdom, and no one is more to blame for it. Yet what was offered Thee? There are three powers, three powers alone, able to conquer and to hold captive for ever the conscience of these impotent rebels for their happiness—those forces are miracle, mystery and authority. Thou hast rejected all three and hast set the example for doing so. When the wise and dread spirit set Thee on the pinnacle of the temple and said to Thee, "If Thou wouldst know whether Thou art the Son of God then cast Thyself down, for it is written: the angels shall hold him up lest he fall and bruise himself, and Thou shalt know then whether Thou art the Son of God and shalt prove then how great is Thy faith in Thy Father." But Thou didst refuse and wouldst not cast Thyself down. Oh, of course, Thou didst proudly and well, like God; but the weak, unruly race of men, are they gods? Oh, Thou didst know then that in taking one step, in making one movement to cast Thyself down, Thou wouldst be tempting God and have lost all Thy faith in Him, and wouldst have been dashed to pieces against that earth which Thou didst come to save. And the wise spirit that tempted Thee would have rejoiced. But I ask again, are there many like Thee? And couldst Thou believe for one moment that men, too, could face such a temptation? Is the nature of men such, that they can reject miracle, and at the great moments of their life, the moments of their deepest, most agonizing spiritual difficulties, cling only to the free verdict of the heart? Oh, Thou didst know that Thy deed would be recorded in books, would be handed down to remote times and the utmost ends of the earth, and Thou didst hope that man, following Thee, would cling to God and not ask for a miracle. But Thou didst not know that when man rejects miracle he rejects God too; for man seeks not so much God as the miraculous. And as man cannot bear to be without the miraculous, he will create new miracles of his own for himself, and will worship deeds of sorcery and witchcraft, though he might be a hundred times over a rebel, heretic and infidel. Thou didst not come down from the Cross when they shouted to Thee, mocking and reviling Thee, "Come down from the cross and we will believe that Thou art He." Thou didst not come down, for again Thou wouldst not enslave man by a miracle, and didst crave faith given freely, not based on miracle. Thou didst crave for free love and not the base raptures of the slave before the might that has overawed him for ever. But Thou didst think too highly of men therein, for they are slaves, of course, though rebellious by nature. Look round and judge; fifteen centuries have passed, look upon them. Whom hast Thou raised up to Thyself? I swear, man is weaker and baser by nature than Thou hast believed him! Can he, can he do what Thou didst? By showing him so much respect, Thou didst, as it were, cease to feel for him, for Thou didst ask far too much from him—Thou who hast loved him more than Thyself! Respecting him less, Thou wouldst have asked less of him. That would have been more like love, for his burden would have been lighter. He is weak and vile. What though he is everywhere now rebelling against our power, and proud of his rebellion? It is the pride of a child and a schoolboy. They are little children rioting and barring out the teacher at school. But their childish delight will end; it will cost them dear. They will cast down temples and drench the earth with blood. But they will see at last, the foolish children, that, though they are rebels, they are impotent rebels, unable to keep up their own rebellion. Bathed in their foolish tears, they will recognize at last that He who created them rebels must have meant to mock at them. They will say this in despair, and their utterance will be a blasphemy which will make them more unhappy still, for man's nature cannot bear blasphemy, and in the end always avenges it on itself. And so unrest, confusion and unhappiness—that is the present lot of man after Thou didst bear so much for their freedom! The great prophet tells in vision and in image, that he saw all those who took part in the first resurrection and that there were of each tribe twelve thousand. But if there were so many of them, they must have been not men but gods. They had borne Thy cross, they had endured scores of years in the barren, hungry wilderness, living upon locusts and roots—and Thou mayest indeed point with pride at those children of freedom, of free love, of free and splendid sacrifice for Thy name. But remember that they were only some thousands; and what of the rest? And how are the other weak ones to blame, because they could not endure what the strong have endured? How is the weak soul to blame that it is unable to receive such terrible gifts? Canst Thou have simply come to the elect and for the elect? But if so, it is a mystery and we cannot understand it. And if it is a mystery, we too have a right to preach a mystery, and to teach them that it's not the free judgment of their hearts, not love that matters, but a mystery which they must follow blindly, even against their conscience. So we have done. We have corrected Thy work and have founded it upon *miracle, mystery* and *authority*. And men rejoiced that they were again led like sheep, and that the terrible gift that had brought them such suffering was, at last, lifted from their hearts. Were we right teaching them this? Speak! Did we not love mankind, so meekly acknowledging their feebleness, lovingly lightening their burden, and permitting their weak nature even sin with our sanction? Why hast Thou come now to hinder us? And why dost Thou look silently and searchingly at me with Thy mild eyes? Be angry. I don't want Thy love, for I love Thee not. And what use is it for me to hide anything from Thee? Don't I know to Whom I am speaking? All that I can say is known to Thee already. And is it for me to conceal from Thee our mystery? Perhaps it is Thy will to hear it from my lips. Listen, then. We are not working with Thee, but with *him*—that is our mystery. It's long—eight centuries—since we have been on *his* side and not on Thine. Just eight centuries ago, we took from him what Thou didst reject with scorn, the last gift he offered Thee, showing Thee all the kingdoms of the earth. We took from him Rome and the sword of Cæsar, and proclaimed ourselves sole rulers of the earth, though hitherto we have not been able to complete our work. But whose fault is that? Oh, the work is only beginning, but it has begun. It has long to await completion and the earth has yet much to suffer, but we shall triumph and shall be Cæsars, and then we shall plan the universal happiness of man. But Thou mightest have taken even then the sword of Cæsar. Why didst Thou reject that last gift? Hadst Thou accepted that last counsel of the mighty spirit, Thou wouldst have accomplished all that man seeks on earth—that is, some one to worship, some one to keep his conscience, and some means of uniting all in one unanimous and harmonious ant-heap, for the craving for universal unity is the third and last anguish of men. Mankind as a whole has always striven to organize a universal state. There have been many great nations with great histories, but the more highly they were developed the more unhappy they were, for they felt more acutely than other people the craving for world-wide union. The great conquerors, Timours and Ghenghis-Khans, whirled like hurricanes over the face of the earth striving to subdue its people, and they too were but the unconscious expression of the same craving for universal unity. Hadst Thou taken the world and Cæsar's purple, Thou wouldst have founded the universal state and have given universal peace. For who can rule men if not he who holds their conscience and their bread in his hands? We have taken the sword of Cæsar, and in taking it, of course, have rejected Thee and followed *him*. Oh, ages are yet to come of the confusion of free thought, of their science and cannibalism. For having begun to build their tower of Babel without us, they will end, of course, with cannibalism. But then the beast will crawl to us and lick our feet and spatter them with tears of blood. And we shall sit upon the beast and raise the cup, and on it will be written, "Mystery." But then, and only then, the reign of peace and happiness will come for men. Thou art proud of Thine elect, but Thou hast only the elect, while we give rest to all. And besides, how many of those elect, those mighty ones who could become elect, have grown weary waiting for Thee, and have transferred and will transfer the powers of their spirit and the warmth of their heart to the other camp, and end by raising their *free* banner against Thee. Thou didst Thyself lift up that banner. But with us all will be happy and will no more rebel nor destroy one another as under Thy freedom. Oh, we shall persuade them that they will only become free when they renounce their freedom to us and submit to us. And shall we be right or shall we be lying? They will be convinced that we are right, for they will remember the horrors of slavery and confusion to which Thy freedom brought them. Freedom, free thought and science, will lead them into such straits and will bring them face to face with such marvels and insoluble mysteries, that some of them, the fierce and rebellious, will destroy themselves, others, rebellious but weak, will destroy one another, while the rest, weak and unhappy, will crawl fawning to our feet and whine to us: "Yes, you were right, you alone possess His mystery, and we come back to you, save us from ourselves!"

"'Receiving bread from us, they will see clearly that we take the bread made by their hands from them, to give it to them, without any miracle. They will see that we do not change the stones to bread, but in truth they will be more thankful for taking it from our hands than for the bread itself! For they will remember only too well that in old days, without our help, even the bread they made turned to stones in their hands, while since they have come back to us, the very stones have turned to bread in their hands. Too, too well will they know the value of complete submission! And until men know that, they will be unhappy. Who is most to blame for their not knowing it?— speak! Who scattered the flock and sent it astray on unknown paths? But the flock will come together again and will submit once more, and then it will be once for all. Then we shall give them the quiet humble happiness of weak creatures such as they are by nature. Oh, we shall persuade them at last not to be proud, for Thou didst lift them up and thereby taught them to be proud. We shall show them that they are weak, that they are only pitiful children, but that childlike happiness is the sweetest of all. They will become timid and will look to us and huddle close to us in fear, as chicks to the hen. They will marvel at us and will be awe-stricken before us, and will be proud at our being so powerful and clever, that we have been able to subdue such a turbulent flock of thousands of millions. They will tremble impotently before our wrath, their minds will grow fearful, they will be quick to shed tears like women and children, but they will be just as ready at a sign from us to pass to laughter and rejoicing, to happy mirth and childish song. Yes, we shall set them to work, but in their leisure hours we shall make their life like a child's game, with children's songs and innocent dance. Oh, we shall allow them even sin, they are weak and helpless, and they will love us like children because we allow them to sin. We shall tell them that every sin will be expiated, if it is done with our permission, that we allow them to sin because we love them, and the punishment for these sins we take upon ourselves. And we shall take it upon ourselves, and they will adore us as their saviors who have taken on themselves their sins before God. And they will have no secrets from us. We shall allow or forbid them to live with their wives and mistresses, to have or not to have children—according to whether they have been obedient or disobedient— and they will submit to us gladly and cheerfully. The most painful secrets of their conscience, all, all they will bring to us, and we shall have an answer for all. And they will be glad to believe our answer, for it will save them from the great anxiety and terrible agony they endure at present in making a free decision for themselves. And all will be happy, all the millions of creatures except the hundred thousand who rule over them. For only we, we who guard the mystery, shall be unhappy. There will be thousands of millions of happy babes, and a hundred thousand sufferers who have taken upon themselves the curse of the knowledge of good and evil. Peacefully they will die, peacefully they will expire in Thy name, and beyond the grave they will find nothing but death. But we shall keep the secret, and for their happiness we shall allure them with the reward of heaven and eternity. Though if there were anything in the other world, it certainly would not be for such as they. It is prophesied that Thou wilt come again in victory, Thou wilt come with Thy chosen, the proud and strong, but we will say that they have only saved themselves, but we have saved all. We are told that the harlot who sits upon the beast, and holds in her hands the *mystery,* shall be put to shame, that the weak will rise up again, and will rend her royal purple and will strip naked her loathsome body. But then I will stand up and point out to Thee the thousand millions of happy children who have known no sin. And we who have taken their sins upon us for their happiness will stand up before Thee and say: "Judge us if Thou canst and darest." Know that I fear Thee not. Know that I too have been in the wilderness, I too have lived on roots and locusts, I too prized the freedom with which Thou hast blessed men, and I too was striving to stand among Thy elect, among the strong and powerful, thirsting "to make up the number." But I awakened and would not serve madness. I turned back and joined the ranks of those *who have corrected Thy work.* I left the proud and went back to the humble, for the happiness of the humble. What I say to Thee will come to pass, and our dominion will be built up. I repeat, to-morrow Thou shalt see that obedient flock who at a sign from me will hasten to heap up the hot cinders about the pile on which I shall burn Thee for coming to hinder us. For if any one has ever deserved our fires, it is Thou. To-morrow I shall burn Thee. *Dixi.*'"

Ivan stopped. He was carried away as he talked, and spoke with excitement; when he had finished, he suddenly smiled.

Alyosha had listened in silence; towards the end he was greatly moved and seemed several times on the point of interrupting, but restrained himself. Now his words came with a rush.

"But . . . that's absurd!" he cried, flushing. "Your poem is in praise of Jesus, not in blame of Him—as you meant it to be. And who will believe you about freedom? Is that the way to understand it? That's not the idea of it in the Orthodox Church. . . . That's Rome, and not even the whole of Rome, it's false—those are the worst of the Catholics, the Inquisitors, the Jesuits! . . . And there could not be such a fantastic creature as your Inquisitor. What are these sins of mankind they take on themselves? Who are these keepers of the mystery who have taken some curse upon themselves for the happiness of mankind? When have they been seen? We know the Jesuits, they are spoken ill of, but surely they are not what you describe? They are not that at all, not at all. . . . They are simply the Romish army for the earthly sovereignty of the world in the future, with the Pontiff of Rome for Emperor . . . that's their ideal, but there's no sort of mystery or lofty melancholy about it. . . . It's simple lust of power, of filthy earthly gain, of domination—something like a universal serfdom with them as masters—that's all they stand for. They don't even believe in God perhaps. Your suffering Inquisitor is a mere fantasy."

"Stay, stay," laughed Ivan, "how hot you are! A fantasy you say, let it be so! Of course it's a fantasy. But allow me to say: do you really think that the Roman Catholic movement of the last centuries is actually nothing but the lust of power, of filthy earthly gain? Is that Father Païssy's teaching?"

"No, no, on the contrary, Father Païssy did once say something rather the same as you . . . but of course it's not the same, not a bit the same," Alyosha hastily corrected himself.

"A precious admission, in spite of your 'not a bit the same.' I ask you why your Jesuits and Inquisitors have united simply for vile material gain? Why can there not be among them one martyr oppressed by great sorrow and loving humanity? You see, only suppose that there was one such man among all those who desire nothing but filthy material gain—if there's only one like my old Inquisitor, who had himself eaten roots in the desert and made frenzied efforts to subdue his flesh to make himself free and perfect. But yet all his life he loved humanity, and suddenly his eyes were opened, and he saw that it is no great moral blessedness to attain perfection and freedom, if at the same time one gains the conviction that millions of

God's creatures have been created as a mockery, that they will never be capable of using their freedom, that these poor rebels can never turn into giants to complete the tower, that it was not for such geese that the great idealist dreamt his dream of harmony. Seeing all that he turned back and joined—the clever people. Surely that could have happened?"

"Joined whom, what clever people?" cried Alyosha, completely carried away. "They have no such great cleverness and no mysteries and secrets. . . . Perhaps nothing but Atheism, that's all their secret. Your Inquisitor does not believe in God, that's his secret!"

"What if it is so! At last you have guessed it. It's perfectly true, it's true that that's the whole secret, but isn't that suffering, at least for a man like that, who has wasted his whole life in the desert and yet could not shake off his incurable love of humanity? In his old age he reached the clear conviction that nothing but the advice of the great dread spirit could build up any tolerable sort of life for the feeble, unruly, 'incomplete, empirical creatures created in jest.' And so, convinced of this, he sees that he must follow the counsel of the wise spirit, the dread spirit of death and destruction, and therefore accept lying and deception, and lead men consciously to death and destruction, and yet deceive them all the way so that they may not notice where they are being led, that the poor blind creatures may at least on the way think themselves happy. And note, the deception is in the name of Him in Whose ideal the old man had so fervently believed all his life long. Is not that tragic? And if only one such stood at the head of the whole army 'filled with the lust of power only for the sake of filthy gain'—would not one such be enough to make a tragedy? More than that, one such standing at the head is enough to create the actual leading idea of the Roman Church with all its armies and Jesuits, its highest idea. I tell you frankly that I firmly believe that there has always been such a man among those who stood at the head of the movement. . . . No doubt it is so, and so it must be indeed. I fancy that even among the Masons there's something of the same mystery at the bottom, and that that's why the Catholics so detest the Masons as their rivals breaking up the unity of the idea, while it is so essential that there should be one flock and one shepherd. . . . But from the way I defend my idea I might be an author impatient of your criticism. Enough of it."

"You are perhaps a Mason yourself!" broke suddenly from Alyosha. "You don't believe in God," he added, speaking this time very sorrowfully. He fancied besides that his brother was looking at him ironically. "How does your poem end?" he asked, suddenly looking down. "Or was it the end?"

"I meant to end it like this. When the Inquisitor ceased speaking he waited some time for his Prisoner to answer him. His silence weighed down upon him. He saw that the Prisoner had listened intently all the time, looking gently in his face and evidently not wishing to reply. The old man longed for Him to say something, however bitter and terrible. But He suddenly approached the old man in silence and softly kissed him on his bloodless aged lips. That was all His answer. The old man shuddered. His lips moved. He went to the door, opened it, and said to Him: 'Go, and come no more . . . come not at all, never, never!' And he let Him out into the dark alleys of the town. The Prisoner went away."

"And the old man?"

"The kiss glows in his heart, but the old man adheres to his idea."

"And you with him, you too?" cried Alyosha, mournfully.

Ivan laughed. . . .

FRANZ KAFKA (1883–1924)

Franz Kafka was born in Prague. He studied law and literature at the University of Prague. After graduating he worked for the Worker's Accident Insurance Institute and spent his evenings writing. His best known works include "The Metamorphosis" (1915), *The Trial* (1925), and *The Castle* (1926). Of these, only the first was completed and published before Kafka died from tuberculosis. It was Kafka's wish that all of his papers, including manuscripts, would be burned, but his friend Max Brod set aside these wishes and published Kafka's novels posthumously.

An Imperial Message
from Parables and Paradoxes

The Emperor, so it runs, has sent a message to you, the humble subject, the insignificant shadow cowering in the remotest distance before the imperial sun; the Emperor from his deathbed has sent a message to you alone. He has commanded the messenger to kneel down by the bed, and has whispered the message to him; so much store did he lay on it that he ordered the messenger to whisper it back into his ear again. Then by a nod of the head he has confirmed that it is right. Yes, before the assembled spectators of his death—all the obstructing walls have been broken down, and on the spacious and loftily-mounting open staircases stand in a ring the great princes of the Empire—before all these he has delivered his message. The messenger immediately sets out on his journey; a powerful, an indefatigable man; now pushing with his right arm, now with his left, he cleaves a way for himself through the throng; if he encounters resistance he points to his breast, where the symbol of the sun glitters; the way, too, is made easier for him than it would be for any other man. But the multitudes are so vast; their numbers have no end. If he could reach the open fields how fast he would fly, and soon doubtless you would hear the welcome hammering of his fists on your door. But instead how vainly does he wear out his strength; still he is only making his way through the chambers of the innermost palace; never will he get to the end of them; and if he succeeded in that nothing would be gained; he must fight his way next down the stair; and if he succeeded in that nothing would be gained; the courts would still have to be crossed; and after the courts the second outer palace; and once more stairs and courts; and once more another palace; and so on for thousands of years; and if at last he should burst through the outermost gate—but never, never can that happen—the imperial capital would lie before him, the center of the world, crammed to bursting with its own refuse. Nobody could fight his way through here, least of all one with a message from a dead man.—But you sit at your window when evening falls and dream it to yourself.

JEAN-PAUL SARTRE (1905–1980)

Sartre published *Nausea* in 1938 and his play *No Exit* in 1944. *Nausea* was his first major work. In the excerpt from *Nausea* reprinted here, Sartre's character Roquentin describes an anguishing episode in which his pre-existing conceptualization of a chestnut tree dissolves and he is confronted with the nauseating, uninterpreted reality of the tree. The play *No Exit* was originally entitled *The Others*. According to Sartre, one force that shaped his play was his experience during the war of being unable to escape the watchful eyes of others. He asked Albert Camus to direct and appear in the play. Sartre was awarded the Nobel prize for literature in 1964, but he declined it for political reasons.

Nausea

So I was in the park just now. The roots of the chestnut tree were sunk in the ground just under my bench. I couldn't remember it was a root any more. The words had vanished and with them the significance of things, their methods of use, and the feeble points of reference which men have traced on their surface. I was sitting, stooping forward, head bowed, alone in front of this black, knotty mass, entirely beastly, which frightened me. Then I had this vision.

It left me breathless. Never, until these last few days, had I understood the meaning of "existence." I was like the others, like the ones walking along the seashore, all dressed in their spring finery. I said, like them, "The ocean *is* green; that white speck up there *is* a seagull," but I didn't feel that it existed or that the seagull was an "existing seagull"; usually existence hides itself. It is there, around us, in us, it is *us,* you can't say two words without mentioning it, but you can never touch it. When I believed I was thinking about it, I must believe that I was thinking nothing, my head was empty, or there was just one word in my head, the word "to be." Or else I was thinking... how can I explain it? I was thinking of *belonging,* I was telling myself that the sea belonged to the class of green objects, or that the green was a part of the quality of the sea. Even when I looked at things, I was miles from dreaming that they existed: they looked like scenery to me. I picked them up in my hands, they served me as tools, I foresaw their resistance. But that all happened on the surface. If anyone had asked me what existence was, I would have answered, in good faith, that it was nothing, simply an empty form which was added to external things without changing anything in their nature. And then all of a sudden, there it was, clear as day: existence had suddenly unveiled itself. It had lost the harmless look of an abstract category: it was the very paste of things, this root was kneaded into existence. Or rather the root, the park gates, the bench, the sparse grass, all that had vanished: the diversity of things, their individuality, were only an appearance, a veneer. This veneer had melted, leaving soft, monstrous masses, all in disorder—naked, in a frightful, obscene nakedness.

. . .

The word absurdity is coming to life under my pen; a little while ago, in the garden, I couldn't find it, but neither was I looking for it, I didn't need it: I thought without words, *on* things, *with* things. Absurdity was not an idea in my head, or the sound of a voice, only this long serpent dead at my feet, this wooden serpent. Serpent or claw or root or vulture's talon, what difference does it make. And without formulating anything clearly, understood that I had found the key to Existence, the key to my Nauseas, to my own life. In fact, all that I could grasp beyond that returns to this fundamental absurdity.

. . .

No Exit

. . .

INEZ [*confronting him fearlessly, but with a look of vast surprise*]: Well, well! [*A pause.*] Ah, I understand now. I know why they've put us three together.

GARCIN: I advise you to—to think twice before you say any more.

INEZ: Wait! You'll see how simple it is. Childishly simple. Obviously there aren't any physical torments—you agree, don't you? And yet we're in hell. And no one else will come here. We'll stay in this room together, the three of us, for ever and ever. . . . In short, there's someone absent here, the official torturer.

GARCIN [*sotto voce*]: I'd noticed that.

INEZ: It's obvious what they're after—an economy of man-power—or devil-power, if you prefer. The same idea as in the cafeteria, where customers serve themselves.

ESTELLE: What ever do you mean?

INEZ: I mean that each of us will act as torturer of the two others.

[*There is a short silence while they digest this information.*]

GARCIN [*gently*]: No, I shall never be your torturer. I wish neither of you any harm, and I've no concern

with you. None at all. So the solution's easy enough; each of us stays put in his or her corner and takes no notice of the others. You here, you here, and I there. Like soldiers at our posts. Also, we mustn't speak. Not one word. That won't be difficult; each of us has plenty of material for self-communings. I think I could stay ten thousand years with only my thoughts for company.

ESTELLE: Have *I* got to keep silent, too?

GARCIN: Yes. And that way we—we'll work out our salvation. Looking into ourselves, never raising our heads. Agreed?

INEZ: Agreed.

ESTELLE [*after some hesitation*]: I agree.

GARCIN: Then—good-by. . . .

ESTELLE: Excuse me, have you a glass? [GARCIN *does not answer.*] Any sort of glass, a pocket-mirror will do. [GARCIN *remains silent.*] Even if you won't speak to me, you might lend me a glass.

[*His head still buried in his hands,* GARCIN *ignores her.*]

INEZ [*eagerly*]: Don't worry. I've a glass in my bag. [*She opens her bag. Angrily*] It's gone! They must have taken it from me at the entrance.

ESTELLE: How tiresome! . . .

INEZ: Suppose I try to be your glass? Come and pay me a visit, dear. Here's a place for you on my sofa.

ESTELLE: But—[*Points to* GARCIN.]

INEZ: Oh, he doesn't count.

ESTELLE: But we're going to—to hurt each other. You said it yourself.

INEZ: Do I look as if I wanted to hurt you?

ESTELLE: One never can tell.

INEZ: Much more likely *you'll* hurt *me.* Still, what does it matter? If I've got to suffer, it may as well be at your hands, your pretty hands. Sit down. Come closer. Closer. Look into my eyes. What do you see?

ESTELLE: Oh, I'm there! But so tiny I can't see myself properly.

INEZ: But *I* can. Every inch of you. Now ask me questions. I'll be as candid as any looking-glass.

ESTELLE: Are you really—attracted by me?

INEZ: Very much indeed.

[*Another short silence.*]

ESTELLE [*indicating* GARCIN *by a slight movement of her head*]: But I wish he'd notice me, too.

INEZ: Of course! Because he's a Man! [*To* GARCIN] You've won. [GARCIN *says nothing.*] But look at her, damn it! [*Still no reply from* GARCIN.] Don't pretend. You haven't missed a word of what we've said.

GARCIN: Quite so; not a word. I stuck my fingers in my ears, but your voices thudded in my brain. Silly chatter. Now will you leave me in peace, you two? I'm not interested in you.

INEZ: Not in me, perhaps—but how about this child? Aren't you interested in her? Oh, I saw through your game; you got on your high horse just to impress her.

GARCIN: I asked you to leave me in peace. There's someone talking about me in the newspaper office and I want to listen. And, if it'll make you any happier, let me tell you that I've no use for the "child," as you call her.

ESTELLE: Thanks.

GARCIN: Oh, I didn't mean it rudely.

ESTELLE: You cad!

[*They confront each other in silence for some moments.*]

GARCIN: So's that's that. [*Pause.*] You know I begged you not to speak.

ESTELLE: It's *her* fault; she started. I didn't ask anything of her and she came and offered me her—her glass.

INEZ: So you say. But all the time you were making up to him, trying every trick to catch his attention.

ESTELLE: Well, why shouldn't I? . . .

GARCIN: I died too soon. I wasn't allowed time to—to do my deeds.

INEZ: One always dies too soon—or too late. And yet one's whole life is complete at that moment, with a line drawn neatly under it, ready for the summing up. You are—your life, and nothing else.

GARCIN: What a poisonous woman you are! With an answer for everything.

INEZ: Now then! Don't lose heart. It shouldn't be so hard, convincing me. Pull yourself together, man, rake up some arguments. [GARCIN *shrugs his shoulders.*] Ah, wasn't I right when I said you were vulnerable? Now you're going to pay the price, and what a price! You're a coward, Garcin, because I wish it. I wish it—do you hear?—I wish it. And yet, just look at me, see how weak I am, a mere breath on the air, a gaze observing you, a formless thought that thinks you. [*He walks towards her, opening her hands.*] Ah, they're open now, those big hands, those coarse, man's hands! But what do you hope

to do? You can't throttle thoughts with hands. So you've no choice, you must convince me, and you're at my mercy.

ESTELLE: Garcin!

GARCIN: What?

ESTELLE Revenge yourself.

GARCIN: How?

ESTELLE: Kiss me, darling—then you'll hear her squeal.

GARCIN: That's true, Inez. I'm at your mercy, but you're at mine as well.

[*He bends over* ESTELLE. INEZ *gives a little cry.*]

INEZ: Oh, you coward, you weakling, running to women to console you!

ESTELLE: That's right, Inez. Squeal away.

INEZ: What a lovely pair you make! If you could see his big paw splayed out on your back, rucking up your skin and creasing the silk. Be careful, though! He's perspiring, his hand will leave a blue stain on your dress.

ESTELLE: Squeal away, Inez, squeal away! . . . Hug me tight, darling; tighter still—that'll finish her off, and a good thing too!

INEZ: Yes, Garcin, she's right. Carry on with it, press her to you till you feel your bodies melting into each other; a lump of warm, throbbing flesh. . . . Love's a grand solace, isn't it, my friend? Deep and dark as sleep. But I'll see you don't sleep.

[GARCIN *makes a slight movement.*]

ESTELLE: Don't listen to her. Press your lips to my mouth. Oh, I'm yours, yours, yours.

INEZ: Well, what are you waiting for? Do as you're told. What a lovely scene: coward Garcin holding babykiller Estelle in his manly arms! Make your stakes, everyone. Will coward Garcin kiss the lady, or won't he dare? What's the betting? I'm watching you, everybody's watching, I'm a crowd all by myself. Do you hear the crowd? Do you hear them muttering, Garcin? Mumbling and muttering. "Coward! Coward! Coward! Coward!"—that's what they're saying. . . . It's no use trying to escape, I'll never let you go. What do you hope to get from her silly lips? Forgetfulness? But I shan't forget you, not I! "It's I you must convince." So come to me. I'm waiting. Come along, now. . . . Look how obedient he is, like a well-trained dog who comes when his mistress calls. You can't hold him, and you never will.

GARCIN: Will night never come?

INEZ: Never.

GARCIN: You will always see me?

INEZ: Always.

[GARCIN *moves away from* ESTELLE *and takes some steps across the room. He goes to the bronze ornament.*]

GARCIN: This bronze. [*Strokes it thoughtfully.*] Yes, now's the moment; I'm looking at this thing on the mantelpiece, and I understand that I'm in hell. I tell you, everything's been thought out beforehand. They knew I'd stand at the fireplace stroking this thing of bronze, with all those eyes intent on me. Devouring me. [*He swings round abruptly.*] What? Only two of you? I thought there were more; many more. [*Laughs.*] So this is hell. I'd never have believed it. You remember all we were told about the torture-chambers, the fire and brimstone, the "burning marl." Old wives' tales! There's no need for red-hot pokers. Hell is—other people!

JORGE LUIS BORGES (1899–1986)

Jorge Luis Borges was born in Buenos Aires, Argentina. Borges' father (a lawyer) and mother both spoke English because his paternal grandfather, Colonel Francisco Borges, married an English-woman. Like his father before him, eventually he lost his sight. As a young boy he attended school in Argentina, but his higher education took place in Geneva, Switzerland, at the College Calvin, where he learned several languages and developed an admiration for the philosophy of Arthur Schopenhauer. Borges' writings include *The Aleph* (1949), *Doctor Brodie's Report* (1970), *The Book of Sand* (1971), and *The Book of Imaginary Beings* (1957).

Everything and Nothing

There was no one in him; behind his face (which even through the bad paintings of those times resembles no other) and his words, which were copious, fantastic and stormy, there was only a bit of coldness, a dream dreamt by no one. At first he thought all people were like him, but the astonishment of a friend to whom he had begun to speak of this emptiness showed him his error and made him feel always that an individual should not differ in outward appearance. Once

he thought that in books he would find a cure for his ill and thus he learned the small Latin and less Greek a contemporary would speak of; later he considered that what he sought might well be found in an elemental rite of humanity, and let himself be initiated by Anne Hathaway one long June afternoon. At the age of twenty-odd years he went to London. Instinctively he had already become proficient in the habit of simulating that he was someone, so that others would not discover his condition as no one; in London he found the profession to which he was predestined, that of the actor, who on a stage plays at being another before a gathering of people who play at taking him for that other person. His histrionic tasks brought him a singular satisfaction, perhaps the first he had ever known; but once the last verse had been acclaimed and the last dead man withdrawn from the stage, the hated flavor of unreality returned to him. He ceased to be Ferrex or Tamerlane and became no one again. Thus hounded, he took to imagining other heroes and other tragic fables. And so, while his flesh fulfilled its destiny as flesh in the taverns and brothels of London, the soul that inhabited him was Caesar, who disregards the augur's admonition, and Juliet, who abhors the lark, and Macbeth, who converses on the plain with the witches who are also Fates. No one has ever been so many men as this man, who like the Egyptian Proteus could exhaust all the guises of reality. At times he would leave a confession hidden away in some corner of his work, certain that it would not be deciphered; Richard affirms that in his person he plays the part of many and Iago claims with curious words "I am not what I am." The fundamental identity of existing, dreaming and acting inspired famous passages of his.

For twenty years he persisted in that controlled hallucination, but one morning he was suddenly gripped by the tedium and the terror of being so many kings who die by the sword and so many suffering lovers who converge, diverge and melodiously expire. That very day he arranged to sell his theater. Within a week he had returned to his native village, where he recovered the trees and rivers of his childhood and did not relate them to the others his muse had celebrated, illustrious with mythological allusions and Latin terms. He had to be someone; he was a retired impressario who had made his fortune and concerned himself with loans, lawsuits and petty usury. It was in this character that he dictated the arid will and testament known to us, from which he deliberately excluded all traces of pathos or literature. His friends from London would visit his retreat and for them he would take up again his role as poet.

History adds that before or after dying he found himself in the presence of God and told Him: "I who have been so many men in vain want to be one and myself." The voice of the Lord answered from a whirlwind: "Neither am I anyone; I have dreamt the world as you dreamt your work, my Shakespeare, and among the forms in my dream are you, who like myself are many and no one."

FLANNERY O'CONNOR (1925–1964)

Flannery O'Connor was born in Savannah, Georgia, where she was raised as a Roman Catholic. She attended the Georgia State College for Women, majoring in English and social science, after which she was awarded a fellowship at the Writers' Workshop at the University of Iowa. She moved to New York in 1948, but in 1950 she was diagnosed as having lupus. In 1951 she returned to Georgia. Among her publications are *Wise Blood* (1952), *Everything that Rises Must Converge* (1965), and *A Good Man Is Hard to Find* (1955).

A Good Man Is Hard to Find

The grandmother didn't want to go to Florida. She wanted to visit some of her connections in east Tennessee and she was seizing at every chance to change Bailey's mind. Bailey was the son she lived with, her only boy. He was sitting on the edge of his chair at the table, bent over the orange sports section of the *Journal.* "Now look here, Bailey," she said, "see here, read this," and she stood with one hand on her thin hip and the other rattling the newspaper at his bald head. "Here this fellow that calls himself The Misfit is aloose from the Federal Pen and headed toward Florida and you read here what it says he did to these people. Just you read it. I wouldn't take my children in any direction with a criminal like that aloose in it. I couldn't answer to my conscience if I did."

Bailey didn't look up from his reading so she wheeled around then and faced the children's mother, a young woman in slacks, whose face was as broad

and innocent as a cabbage and was tied around with a green head-kerchief that had two points on the top like rabbit's ears. She was sitting on the sofa, feeding the baby his apricots out of a jar. "The children have been to Florida before," the old lady said. "You all ought to take them somewhere else for a change so they would see different parts of the world and be broad. They never have been to east Tennessee."

The children's mother didn't seem to hear her but the eight-year-old boy, John Wesley, a stocky child with glasses, said, "If you don't want to go to Florida, why dontcha stay at home?" He and the little girl, June Star, were reading the funny papers on the floor.

"She wouldn't stay at home to be a queen for a day," June Star said without raising her yellow head.

"Yes and what would you do if this fellow, The Misfit, caught you?" the grandmother asked.

"I'd smack his face," John Wesley said.

"She wouldn't stay at home for a million bucks," June Star said. "Afraid she'd miss something. She has to go everywhere we go."

"All right, Miss," the grandmother said. "Just remember that the next time you want me to curl your hair."

June Star said her hair was naturally curly.

The next morning the grandmother was the first one in the car, ready to go. She had her big black valise that looked like the head of a hippopotamus in one corner, and underneath it she was hiding a basket with Pitty Sing, the cat, in it. She didn't intend for the cat to be left alone in the house for three days because he would miss her too much and she was afraid he might brush against one of the gas burners and accidentally asphyxiate himself. Her son, Bailey, didn't like to arrive at a motel with a cat.

She sat in the middle of the back seat with John Wesley and June Star on either side of her. Bailey and the children's mother and the baby sat in front and they left Atlanta at eight forty-five with the mileage on the car at 55890. The grandmother wrote this down because she thought it would be interesting to say how many miles they had been when they got back. It took them twenty minutes to reach the outskirts of the city.

The old lady settled herself comfortably, removing her white cotton gloves and putting them up with her purse on the shelf in front of the back window. The children's mother still had on slacks and still had her head tied up in a green kerchief, but the grandmother had on a navy blue straw sailor hat with a bunch of white violets on the brim and a navy blue dress with a small white dot in the print. Her collar and cuffs were white organdy trimmed with lace and at her neckline she had pinned a purple spray of cloth violets containing a sachet. In case of an accident, anyone seeing her dead on the highway would know at once that she was a lady.

She said she thought it was going to be a good day for driving, neither too hot nor too cold, and she cautioned Bailey that the speed limit was fifty-five miles an hour and that the patrolmen hid themselves behind billboards and small clumps of trees and sped out after you before you had a chance to slow down. She pointed out interesting details of the scenery: Stone Mountain; the blue granite that in some places came up to both sides of the highway; the brilliant red clay banks slightly streaked with purple; and the various crops that made rows of green lace-work on the ground. The trees were full of silver-white sunlight and the meanest of them sparkled. The children were reading comic magazines and their mother had gone back to sleep.

"Let's go through Georgia fast so we won't have to look at it much," John Wesley said.

"If I were a little boy," said the grandmother, "I wouldn't talk about my native state that way. Tennessee has the mountains and Georgia has the hills."

"Tennessee is just a hillbilly dumping ground," John Wesley said, "and Georgia is a lousy state too."

"You said it," June Star said.

"In my time," said the grandmother, folding her thin veined fingers, "children were more respectful of their native states and their parents and everything else. People did right then. Oh look at the cute little pickaninny!" she said and pointed to a Negro child standing in the door of a shack. "Wouldn't that make a picture, now?" she asked and they all turned and looked at the little Negro out of the back window. He waved.

"He didn't have any britches on," June Star said.

"He probably didn't have any," the grandmother explained. "Little niggers in the country don't have things like we do. If I could paint, I'd paint that picture," she said.

The children exchanged comic books.

The grandmother offered to hold the baby and the children's mother passed him over the front seat to her. She set him on her knee and bounced him and told him about the things they were passing. She rolled her eyes and screwed up her mouth and stuck her leathery thin face into his smooth bland one. Occasionally he gave her a faraway smile. They passed a large cotton field with five or six graves fenced in the middle of it, like a small island. "Look at the graveyard!" the grandmother said, pointing it out. "That was the old family burying ground. That belonged to the plantation."

"Where's the plantation?" John Wesley asked.

"Gone With the Wind," said the grandmother, "Ha, Ha."

When the children finished all the comic books they had brought, they opened the lunch and ate it. The grandmother ate a peanut butter sandwich and an olive and would not let the children throw the box and the paper napkins out the window. When there was nothing else to do they played a game by choosing a cloud and making the other two guess what shape it suggested. John Wesley took one the shape of a cow and June Star guessed a cow and John Wesley said, no, an automobile, and June Star said he didn't play fair, and they began to slap each other over the grandmother.

The grandmother said she would tell them a story if they would keep quiet. When she told a story, she rolled her eyes and waved her head and was very dramatic. She said once when she was a maiden lady she had been courted by a Mr. Edgar Atkins Teagarden from Jasper, Georgia. She said he was a very good-looking man and a gentleman and that he brought her a watermelon every Saturday afternoon with his initials cut in it, E. A. T. Well, one Saturday, she said, Mr. Teagarden brought the watermelon and there was nobody at home and he left it on the front porch and returned in his buggy to Jasper, but she never got the watermelon, she said, because a nigger boy ate it when he saw the initials, E. A. T.! This story tickled John Wesley's funny bone and he giggled and giggled but June Star didn't think it was any good. She said she wouldn't marry a man that just brought her a watermelon on Saturday. The grandmother said she would have done well to marry Mr. Teagarden because he was a gentleman and had bought Coca-Cola stock when it first came out and that he had died only a few years ago, a very wealthy man.

They stopped at The Tower for barbecued sandwiches. The Tower was a part stucco and part wood filling station and dance hall set in a clearing outside of Timothy. A fat man named Red Sammy Butts ran it and there were signs stuck here and there on the building and for miles up and down the highway saying, TRY RED SAMMY'S FAMOUS BARBECUE. NONE LIKE FAMOUS RED SAMMY'S! RED SAM! THE FAT BOY WITH THE HAPPY LAUGH. A VETERAN! RED SAMMY'S YOUR MAN!

Red Sammy was lying on the bare ground outside The Tower with his head under a truck while a gray monkey about a foot high, chained to a small chinaberry tree, chattered nearby. The monkey sprang back into the tree and got on the highest limb as soon as he saw the children jump out of the car and run toward him.

Inside, The Tower was a long dark room with a counter at one end and tables at the other and dancing space in the middle. They all sat down at a board table next to the nickelodeon and Red Sam's wife, a tall burnt-brown woman with hair and eyes lighter than her skin, came and took their order. The children's mother put a dime in the machine and played "The Tennessee Waltz," and the grandmother said that tune always made her want to dance. She asked Bailey if he would like to dance but he only glared at her. He didn't have a naturally sunny disposition like she did and trips made him nervous. The grandmother's brown eyes were very bright. She swayed her head from side to side and pretended she was dancing in her chair. June Star said play something she could tap to so the children's mother put in another dime and played a fast number and June Star stepped out onto the dance floor and did her tap routine.

"Ain't she cute?" Red Sam's wife said, leaning over the counter. "Would you like to come be my little girl?"

"No I certainly wouldn't," June Star said. "I wouldn't live in a broken-down place like this for a million bucks!" and she ran back to the table.

"Ain't she cute?" the woman repeated, stretching her mouth politely.

"Arn't you ashamed?" hissed the grandmother.

Red Sam came in and told his wife to quit lounging on the counter and hurry up with these people's order. His khaki trousers reached just to his hip bones and his stomach hung over them like a sack of meal swaying under his shirt. He came over and sat down at a table nearby and let out a combination sigh and yodel. "You can't win," he said. "You can't win," and he wiped his sweating red face off with a gray handkerchief. "These days you don't know who to trust," he said. "Ain't that the truth?"

"People are certainly not nice like they used to be," said the grandmother.

"Two fellers came in here last week," Red Sammy said, "driving a Chrysler. It was a old beat-up car but it was a good one and these boys looked all right to me. Said they worked at the mill and you know I let them fellers charge the gas they bought? Now why did I do that?"

"Because you're a good man!" the grandmother said at once.

"Yes'm, I suppose so," Red Sam said as if he were struck with this answer.

His wife brought the orders, carrying the five plates all at once without a tray, two in each hand and one balanced on her arm. "It isn't a soul in this green world of God's that you can trust," she said. "And I don't count nobody out of that, not nobody," she repeated, looking at Red Sammy.

"Did you read about that criminal, The Misfit, that's escaped?" asked the grandmother.

"I wouldn't be a bit surprised if he didn't attack this place right here," said the woman. "If he hears about it being here, I wouldn't be none surprised to see him. If he hears it's two cent in the cash register, I wouldn't be a tall surprised if he . . ."

"That'll do," Red Sam said. "Go bring these people their Co'-Colas," and the woman went off to get the rest of the order.

"A good man is hard to find," Red Sammy said. "Everything is getting terrible. I remember the day you could go off and leave your screen door unlatched. Not no more.

He and the grandmother discussed better times. The old lady said that in her opinion Europe was entirely to blame for the way things were now. She said the way Europe acted you would think we were made of money and Red Sam said it was no use talking about it, she was exactly right. The children ran outside into the white sunlight and looked at the monkey in the lacy chinaberry tree. He was busy catching fleas on himself and biting each one carefully between his teeth as if it were a delicacy.

They drove off again into the hot afternoon. The grandmother took cat naps and woke up every few minutes with her own snoring. Outside of Toombsboro she woke up and recalled an old plantation that she had visited in this neighborhood once when she was a young lady. She said the house had six columns across the front and that there was an avenue of oaks leading up to it and two little wooden trellis arbors on either side in front where you sat down with your suitor after a stroll in the garden. She recalled exactly which road to turn off to get to it. She knew that Bailey would not be willing to lose any time looking at an old house, but the more she talked about it, the more she wanted to see it once again and find out if the little twin arbors were still standing. "There was a secret panel in this house," she said craftily, not telling the truth but wishing that she were, "and the story went that all the family silver was hidden in it when Sherman came through but it was never found . . ."

"Hey!" John Wesley said. "Let's go see it! We'll find it! We'll poke all the woodwork and find it! Who lives there? Where do you turn off at? Hey Pop, can't we turn off there?"

"We never have seen a house with a secret panel!" June Star shrieked. "Let's go to the house with the secret panel! Hey Pop, can't we go see the house with the secret panel!"

"It's not far from here, I know," the grandmother said. "It wouldn't take over twenty minutes."

Bailey was looking straight ahead. His jaw was as rigid as a horseshoe. "No," he said.

The children began to yell and scream that they wanted to see the house with the secret panel. John Wesley kicked the back of the front seat and June Star hung over her mother's shoulder and whined desperately into her ear that they never had any fun even on their vacation, that they could never do what THEY wanted to do. The baby began to scream and John Wesley kicked the back of the seat so hard that his father could feel the blows in his kidney.

"All right!" he shouted and drew the car to a stop at the side of the road. "Will you all shut up? Will you all just shut up for one second? If you don't shut up, we won't go anywhere."

"It would be very educational for them," the grandmother murmured.

"All right," Bailey said, "but get this: this is the only time we're going to stop for anything like this. This is the one and only time."

"The dirt road that you have to turn down is about a mile back," the grandmother directed. "I marked it when we passed."

"A dirt road," Bailey groaned.

After they had turned around and were headed toward the dirt road, the grandmother recalled other points about the house, the beautiful glass over the front doorway and the candle-lamp in the hall. John Wesley said that the secret panel was probably in the fireplace.

"You can't go inside this house," Bailey said. "You don't know who lives there."

"While you all talk to the people in front, I'll run around behind and get in a window," John Wesley suggested.

"We'll all stay in the car," his mother said.

They turned onto the dirt road and the car raced roughly along in a swirl of pink dust. The grandmother recalled the times when there were no paved roads and thirty miles was a day's journey. The dirt road was hilly and there were sudden washes in it and sharp curves on dangerous embankments. All at once they would be on a hill, looking down over the blue tops of trees for miles around, then the next minute, they would be in a red depression with the dust-coated trees looking down on them.

"This place had better turn up in a minute," Bailey said, "or I'm going to turn around."

The road looked as if no one had traveled on it in months.

"It's not much farther," the grandmother said and just as she said it, a horrible thought came to her. The thought was so embarrassing that she turned red in the face and her eyes dilated and her feet jumped up, upsetting her valise in the corner. The instant the valise moved, the newspaper top she had over the basket under it rose with a snarl and Pitty Sing, the cat, sprang onto Bailey's shoulder.

The children were thrown to the floor and their mother, clutching the baby, was thrown out the door onto the ground; the old lady was thrown into the front seat. The car turned over once and landed right-side-up in a gulch off the side of the road. Bailey remained in the driver's seat with the cat—gray-striped with a broad white face and an orange nose—clinging to his neck like a caterpillar.

As soon as the children saw they could move their arms and legs, they scrambled out of the car, shouting, "We had an ACCIDENT!" The grandmother was curled up under the dashboard, hoping she was injured so that Bailey's wrath would not come down on her all at once. The horrible thought she had had before the accident was that the house she had remembered so vividly was not in Georgia but in Tennessee.

Bailey removed the cat from his neck with both hands and flung it out the window against the side of a pine tree. Then he got out of the car and started looking for the children's mother. She was sitting against the side of the red gutted ditch, holding the screaming baby, but she only had a cut down her face and a broken shoulder. "We've had an ACCIDENT!" the children screamed in a frenzy of delight.

"But nobody's killed," June Star said with disappointment as the grandmother limped out of the car, her hat still pinned to her head but the broken front brim standing up at a jaunty angle and the violet spray hanging off the side. They all sat down in the ditch, except the children, to recover from the shock. They were all shaking.

"Maybe a car will come along," said the children's mother hoarsely.

"I believe I have injured an organ," said the grandmother, pressing her side, but no one answered her. Bailey's teeth were clattering. He had on a yellow sport shirt with bright blue parrots designed in it and his face was as yellow as the shirt. The grandmother decided that she would not mention that the house was in Tennessee.

The road was about ten feet above and they could see only the tops of the trees on the other side of it. Behind the ditch they were sitting in there were more woods, tall and dark and deep. In a few minutes they saw a car some distance away on top of a hill, coming slowly as if the occupants were watching them. The grandmother stood up and waved both arms dramatically to attract their attention. The car continued to come on slowly, disappeared around a bend and appeared again, moving even slower, on top of the hill they had gone over. It was a big black battered hearse-like automobile. There were three men in it.

It came to a stop just over them and for some minutes, the driver looked down with a steady expressionless gaze to where they were sitting, and didn't speak. Then he turned his head and muttered something to the other two and they got out. One was a fat boy in black trousers and a red sweat shirt with a silver stallion embossed on the front of it. He moved around on the right side of them and stood staring, his mouth partly open in a kind of loose grin. The other had on khaki pants and a blue striped coat and a gray hat pulled down very low, hiding most of his face. He came around slowly on the left side. Neither spoke.

The driver got out of the car and stood by the side of it, looking down at them. He was an older man than the other two. His hair was just beginning to gray and he wore silver-rimmed spectacles that give him a scholarly look. He had a long creased face and didn't

have on any shirt or undershirt. He had on blue jeans that were too tight for him and was holding a black hat and a gun. The two boys also had guns.

"We've had an ACCIDENT!" the children screamed.

The grandmother had the peculiar feeling that the bespectacled man was someone she knew. His face was as familiar to her as if she had known him all her life but she could not recall who he was. He moved away from the car and began to come down the embankment, placing his feet carefully so that he wouldn't slip. He had on tan and white shoes and no socks, and his ankles were red and thin. "Good afternoon," he said. "I see you all had you a little spill."

"We turned over twice!" said the grandmother.

"Oncet," he corrected. "We seen it happen. Try their car and see will it run, Hiram," he said quietly to the boy with the gray hat.

"What you got that gun for?" John Wesley asked. "Whatcha gonna do with that gun?"

"Lady," the man said to the children's mother, "would you mind calling them children to sit down by you? Children make me nervous. I want you all to sit down right together there where you're at."

"What are you telling US what to do for?" June Star asked.

Behind them the line of woods gaped like a dark open mouth. "Come here," said their mother.

"Look here now," Bailey began suddenly, "we're in a predicament! We're in . . ."

The grandmother shrieked. She scrambled to her feet and stood staring. "You're The Misfit!" she said. "I recognized you at once!"

"Yes'm," the man said, smiling slightly as if he were pleased in spite of himself to be known, "but it would have been better for all of you, lady, if you hadn't of reckernized me."

Bailey turned his head sharply and said something to his mother that shocked even the children. The old lady began to cry and The Misfit reddened.

"Lady," he said, "don't you get upset. Sometimes a man says things he don't mean. I don't reckon he meant to talk to you thataway."

"You wouldn't shoot a lady, would you?" the grandmother said and removed a clean handkerchief from her cuff and began to slap at her eyes with it.

The Misfit pointed the toe of his shoe into the ground and made a little hole and then covered it up again. "I would hate to have to," he said.

"Listen," the grandmother almost screamed, "I know you're a good man. You don't look a bit like you have common blood. I know you must come from nice people!"

"Yes mam," he said, "finest people in the world." When he smiled he showed a row of strong white teeth. "God never made a finer woman than my mother and my daddy's heart was pure gold," he said. The boy with the red sweat shirt had come around behind them and was standing with his gun at his hip. The Misfit squatted down on the ground. "Watch them children, Bobby Lee," he said. "You know they make me nervous." He looked at the six of them huddled together in front of him and he seemed to be embarrassed as if he couldn't think of anything to say. "Ain't a cloud in the sky," he remarked, looking up at it. "Don't see no sun but don't see no cloud neither."

"Yes, it's a beautiful day," said the grandmother. "Listen," she said, "you shouldn't call yourself The Misfit because I know you're a good man at heart. I can just look at you and tell.

"Hush!" Bailey yelled. "Hush! Everybody shut up and let me handle this!" He was squatting in the position of a runner about to sprint forward but he didn't move.

"I per-chate that, lady," The Misfit said and drew a little circle in the ground with the butt of his gun.

"It'll take a half a hour to fix this here car," Hiram called, looking over the raised hood of it.

"Well, first you and Bobby Lee get him and that little boy to step over yonder with you," The Misfit said, pointing to Bailey and John Wesley. "The boys want to ast you something," he said to Bailey. "Would you mind stepping back in them woods there with them?"

"Listen," Bailey began, "were in a terrible predicament! Nobody realizes what this is," and his voice cracked. His eyes were as blue and intense as the parrots in his shirt and he remained perfectly still.

The grandmother reached up to adjust her hat brim as if she were going to the woods with him but it came off in her hand. She stood staring at it and after a second she let it fall on the ground. Hiram pulled Bailey up by the arm as if he were assisting an old man. John Wesley caught hold of his father's hand and Bobby Lee followed. They went off toward the woods and just as they reached the dark edge, Bailey turned and supporting himself against a gray naked pine trunk, he shouted, "I'll be back in a minute, Mamma, wait on me!"

"Come back this instant!" his mother shrilled but they all disappeared into the woods.

"Bailey Boy!" the grandmother called in a tragic voice but she found she was looking at The Misfit squatting on the ground in front of her. "I just know you're a good man," she said desperately. "You're not a bit common!"

"Nome, I ain't a good man," The Misfit said after a second as if he had considered her statement carefully, "but I ain't the worst in the world neither. My daddy said I was a different breed of dog from my brothers and sisters. 'You know,' Daddy said, 'it's some that can live their whole life out without asking about it and it's others has to know why it is, and this boy is one of the latters. He's going to be into everything!'" He put on his black hat and looked up suddenly and then away deep into the woods as if he were embarrassed again. "I'm sorry I don't have on a shirt before you ladies," he said, hunching his shoulders slightly. "We buried our clothes that we had on when we escaped and we're just making do until we can get better. We borrowed these from some folks we met," he explained.

"That's perfectly all right," the grandmother said. "Maybe Bailey has an extra shirt in his suitcase."

"I'll look and see terrectly," The Misfit said.

"Where are they taking him?" the children's mother screamed.

"Daddy was a card himself," The Misfit said. "You couldn't put anything over on him. He never got in trouble with the Authorities though. Just had the knack of handling them."

"You could be honest too if you'd only try," said the grandmother. "Think how wonderful it would be to settle down and live a comfortable life and not have to think about somebody chasing you all the time."

The Misfit kept scratching in the ground with the butt of his gun as if he were thinking about it. "Yes'm, somebody is always after you," he mumured.

The grandmother noticed how thin his shoulder blades were just behind his hat because she was standing up looking down on him. "Do you ever pray?" she asked.

He shook his head. All she saw was the black hat wiggle between his shoulder blades. "Nome," he said.

There was a pistol shot from the woods, followed closely by another. Then silence. The old lady's head jerked around. She could hear the wind move through the tree tops like a long satisfied insuck of breath. "Bailey Boy!" she called.

"I was a gospel singer for a while," The Misfit said. "I been most everything. Been in the arm services, both land and sea, at home and abroad, been twict married, been an undertaker, been with the railroads, plowed Mother Earth, been in a tornado, seen a man burnt alive oncet," and he looked up at the children's mother and the little girl who were sitting close together, their faces white and their eyes glassy; "I even seen a woman flogged," he said.

"Pray, pray," the grandmother began, "pray, pray . . ."

"I never was a bad boy that I remember of," The Misfit said in an almost dreamy voice, "but somewheres along the line I done something wrong and got sent to the penitentiary. I was buried alive," and he looked up and held her attention to him by a steady stare.

"That's when you should have started to pray," she said. "What did you do to get sent to the penitentiary that first time?"

"Turn to the right, it was a wall," The Misfit said, looking up again at the cloudless sky. "Turn to the left, it was a wall. Look up it was a ceiling, look down it was a floor. I forgot what I done, lady. I set there and set there, trying to remember what it was I done and I ain't recalled it to this day. Oncet in a while, I would think it was coming to me, but it never come."

"Maybe they put you in by mistake," the old lady said vaguely.

"Nome," he said. "It wasn't no mistake. They had the papers on me."

"You must have stolen something," she said.

The Misfit sneered slightly. "Nobody had nothing I wanted," he said. "It was a head-doctor at the penitentiary said what I had done was kill my daddy but I known that for a lie. My daddy died in nineteen ought nineteen of the epidemic flu and I never had a thing to do with it. He was buried in the Mount Hopewell Baptist churchyard and you can go there and see for yourself."

"If you would pray," the old lady said, "Jesus would help you."

"That's right," The Misfit said.

"Well then, why don't you pray?" she asked trembling with delight suddenly.

"I don't want no hep," he said. "I'm doing all right by myself."

Bobby Lee and Hiram came ambling back from the woods. Bobby Lee was dragging a yellow shirt with bright blue parrots in it.

"Thow me that shirt, Bobby Lee," The Misfit said. The shirt came flying at him and landed on his shoulder and he put it on. The grandmother couldn't name what the shirt reminded her of. "No, lady," The Misfit said while he was buttoning it up, "I found out the crime don't matter. You can do one thing or you can do another, kill a man or take a tire off his car, because sooner or later you're going to forget what it was you done and just be punished for it."

The children's mother had begun to make heaving noises as if she couldn't get her breath. "Lady," he asked, "would you and that little girl like to step off yonder with Bobby Lee and Hiram and join your husband?"

"Yes, thank you," the mother said faintly. Her left arm dangled helplessly and she was holding the baby, who had gone to sleep, in the other. "Hep that lady up, Hiram," The Misfit said as she struggled to climb out of the ditch, "and Bobby Lee, you hold onto that little girl's hand."

"I don't want to hold hands with him," June Star said. "He reminds me of a pig."

The fat boy blushed and laughed and caught her by the arm and pulled her off into the woods after Hiram and her mother.

Alone with The Misfit, the grandmother found that she had lost her voice. There was not a cloud in the sky nor any sun. There was nothing around her but woods. She wanted to tell him that he must pray. She opened and closed her mouth several times before anything came out. Finally she found herself saying, "Jesus. Jesus," meaning, Jesus will help you, but the way she was saying it, it sounded as if she might be cursing.

"Yes'm," The Misfit said as if he agreed. "Jesus thrown everything off balance. It was the same case with Him as with me except He hadn't committed any crime and they could prove I had committed one because they had the papers on me. Of course," he said, "they never shown me my papers. That's why I sign myself now. I said long ago, you get a signature and sign everything you do and keep a copy of it. Then you'll know what you done and you can hold up the crime to the punishment and see do they match and in the end you'll have something to prove you ain't been treated right. I call myself The Misfit," he said, "because I can't make what all I done wrong fit what all I gone through in punishment."

There was a piercing scream from the woods, followed closely by a pistol report. "Does it seem right to you, lady, that one is punished a heap and another ain't punished at all?"

"Jesus!" the old lady cried. "You've got good blood! I know you wouldn't shoot a lady! I know you come from nice people! Pray! Jesus, you ought not to shoot a lady. I'll give you all the money I've got!"

"Lady," The Misfit said, looking beyond her far into the woods, "there never was a body that give the undertaker a tip."

There were two more pistol reports and the grandmother raised her head like a parched old turkey hen crying for water and called, "Bailey Boy, Bailey Boy!" as if her heart would break.

"Jesus was the only One that ever raised the dead," The Misfit continued, "and He shouldn't have done it. He thrown everything off balance. If He did what He said, then it's nothing for you to do but throw away everything and follow Him, and if He didn't, then it's nothing for you to do but enjoy the few minutes you got left the best way you can—by killing somebody or burning down his house or doing some other meanness to him. No pleasure but meanness," he said and his voice had become almost a snarl.

"Maybe He didn't raise the dead," the old lady mumbled, not knowing what she was saying and feeling so dizzy that she sank down in the ditch with her legs twisted under her.

"I wasn't there so I can't say He didn't," The Misfit said. "I wisht I had of been there," he said, hitting the ground with his fist. "It ain't right I wasn't there because if I had of been there I would of known. Listen lady," he said in a high voice, "if I had of been there I would of known and I wouldn't be like I am now." His voice seemed about to crack and the grandmother's head cleared for an instant. She saw the man's face twisted close to her own as if he were going to cry and she murmured, "Why you're one of my babies. You're one of my own children!" She reached out and touched him on the shoulder. The Misfit sprang back as if a snake had bitten him and shot her three times through the chest. Then he put his gun down on the ground and took off his glasses and began to clean them.

Hiram and Bobby Lee returned from the woods and stood over the ditch, looking down at the grandmother who half sat and half lay in a puddle of blood with her legs crossed under her like a child's and her face smiling up at the cloudless sky.

Without his glasses, The Misfit's eyes were red-rimmed and pale and defenseless-looking. "Take her off and thow her where you thown the others," he said, picking up the cat that was rubbing itself against his leg.

"She was a talker, wasn't she?" Bobby Lee said, sliding down the ditch with a yodel.

"She would of been a good woman," The Misfit said, "if it had been somebody there to shoot her every minute of her life."

"Some fun!" Bobby Lee said.

"Shut up, Bobby Lee," The Misfit said. "It's no real pleasure in life."

PHILIP K. DICK (1928–1982)

Philip K. Dick, a well-known science-fiction writer, was born in Chicago and lived in Berkeley, California. He attended the University of California at Berkeley for only one year before dropping out. He worked as a disc jockey and managed a record store, writing science fiction in his spare time, until he was able to subsist in relative poverty while writing full time. Some of his novels reflect his own experience with psychedelic drugs. Two of his better known publications are *Do Androids Dream of Electric Sheep?* (1968), on which the movie *Blade Runner* was based, and *The Man in the High Castle* (1962).

Imposter

"One of these days I'm going to take time off," Spence Olham said at first-meal. He looked around at his wife. "I think I've earned a rest. Ten years is a long time."

"And the Project?"

"The war will be won without me. This ball of clay of ours isn't really in much danger." Olham sat down at the table and lit a cigarette. "The news-machines alter dispatches to make it appear the Outspacers are right on top of us. You know what I'd like to do on my vacation? I'd like to take a camping trip to those mountains outside of town, where we went that time. Remember? I got poison oak and you almost stepped on a gopher snake."

"Sutton Wood?" Mary began to clear away the food dishes. "The Wood was burned a few weeks ago. I thought you knew. Some kind of a flash fire."

Olham sagged. "Didn't they even try to find the cause?" His lips twisted. "No one cares anymore. All they can think of is the war." He clamped his jaws together, the whole picture coming up in his mind, the Outspacers, the war, the needle-ships.

"How can we think about anything else?"

Olham nodded. She was right, of course. The dark little ships out of Alpha Centauri had bypassed the Earth cruisers easily, leaving them like helpless turtles. It had been one-way fights, all the way back to Terra.

All the way, until the protec-bubble was demonstrated by Westinghouse Labs. Thrown around the major Earth cities and finally the planet itself, the bubble was the first real defense, the first legitimate answer to the Outspacers—as the news-machines labeled them.

But to win the war, that was another thing. Every lab, every project was working night and day, endlessly, to find something more: a weapon for positive combat. His own project, for example. All day long, year after year.

Olham stood up, putting out his cigarette. "Like the Sword of Damocles. Always hanging over us. I'm getting tired. All I want to do is take a long rest. But I guess everybody feels that way."

He got his jacket from the closet and went out on the front porch. The shoot would be along any moment, the fast little bug that would carry him to the Project.

"I hope Nelson isn't late." He looked at his watch. "It's almost seven."

"Here the bug comes," Mary said, gazing between the rows of houses. The sun glittered behind the roofs, reflecting against the heavy lead plates. The settlement was quiet; only a few people were stirring. "I'll see you later. Try not to work beyond your shift, Spence."

Olham opened the car door and slid inside, leaning back against the seat with a sigh. There was an older man with Nelson.

"Well?" Olham said, as the bug shot ahead. "Heard any interesting news?"

"The usual," Nelson said. "A few Outspace ships hit, another asteroid abandoned for strategic reasons."

"It'll be good when we get the Project into final stage. Maybe it's just the propaganda from the news-machines, but in the last month I've gotten weary of all this. Everything seems so grim and serious, no color to life."

"Do you think the war is in vain?" the older man said suddenly. "You are an integral part of it, yourself."

"This is Major Peters," Nelson said. Olham and Peters shook hands. Olham studied the older man.

"What brings you along so early?" he said. "I don't remember seeing you at the Project before."

"No, I'm not with the Project," Peters said, "but I know something about what you're doing. My own work is altogether different."

A look passed between him and Nelson. Olham noticed it and he frowned. The bug was gaining speed, flashing across the barren, lifeless ground toward the distant rim of the Project building.

"What is your business?" Olham said. "Or aren't you permitted to talk about it?"

"I'm with the government," Peters said. "With FSA, the security organ."

"Oh?" Olham raised an eyebrow. "Is there any enemy infiltration in this region?"

"As a matter of fact I'm here to see you, Mr. Olham."

Olham was puzzled. He considered Peters' words, but he could make nothing of them. "To see me? Why?"

"I'm here to arrest you as an Outspace spy. That's why I'm up so early this morning. *Grab him, Nelson—*"

The gun drove into Olham's ribs. Nelson's hands were shaking, trembling with released emotion, his face pale. He took a deep breath and let it out again.

"Shall we kill him now?" he whispered to Peters. "I think we should kill him now. We can't wait."

Olham stared into his friend's face. He opened his mouth to speak, but no words came. Both men were staring at him steadily, rigid and grim with fright. Olham felt dizzy. His head ached and spun.

"I don't understand," he murmured.

At that moment the shoot car left the ground and rushed up, heading into space. Below them the Project fell away, smaller and smaller, disappearing. Olham shut his mouth.

"We can wait a little," Peters said. "I want to ask him some questions first."

Olham gazed dully ahead as the bug rushed through space.

"The arrest was made all right," Peters said into the vidscreen. On the screen the features of the security chief showed. "It should be a load off everyone's mind."

"Any complications?"

"None. He entered the bug without suspicion. He didn't seem to think my presence was too unusual."

"Where are you now?"

"On our way out, just inside the protec-bubble. We're moving at a maximum speed. You can assume that the critical period is past. I'm glad the takeoff jets in this craft were in good working order. If there had been any failure at that point—"

"Let me see him," the security chief said. He gazed directly at Olham where he sat, his hands in his lap, staring ahead.

"So that's the man." He looked at Olham for a time. Olham said nothing. At last the chief nodded to Peters. "All right. That's enough." A faint trace of disgust wrinkled his features. "I've seen all I want. You've done something that will be remembered for a long time. They're preparing some sort of citation for both of you."

"That's not necessary," Peters said.

"How much danger is there now? Is there still much chance that—"

"There is some chance, but not too much. According to my understanding it requires a verbal key phrase. In any case we'll have to take the risk."

"I'll have the Moon base notified you're coming."

"No." Peters shook his head. "I'll land the ship outside, beyond the base. I don't want it in jeopardy."

"Just as you like." The chief's eyes flickered as he glanced again at Olham. Then his image faded. The screen blanked.

Olham shifted his gaze to the window. The ship was already through the protec-bubble, rushing with greater and greater speed all the time. Peters was in a hurry; below him, rumbling under the floor, the jets were wide open. They were afraid, hurrying frantically, because of him.

Next to him on the seat, Nelson shifted uneasily. "I think we should do it now," he said. "I'd give anything if we could get it over with."

"Take it easy," Peters said. "I want you to guide the ship for a while so I can talk to him."

He slid over beside Olham, looking into his face. Presently he reached out and touched him gingerly, on the arm and then on the cheek.

Olham said nothing. *If I could let Mary know,* he thought again. *If I could find some way of letting her know.* He looked around the ship. How? The vidscreen? Nelson was sitting by the board, holding the gun. There was nothing he could do. He was caught, trapped.

But why?

"Listen," Peters said, "I want to ask you some questions. You know where we're going. We're moving Moonward. In an hour we'll land on the far side, on the desolate side. After we land you'll be turned over immediately to a team of men waiting there. Your body will be destroyed at once. Do you understand that?" He looked at his watch. "Within two hours your parts will be strewn over the landscape. There won't be anything left of you."

Olham struggled out of his lethargy. "Can't you tell me—"

"Certainly, I'll tell you." Peters nodded. "Two days ago we received a report that an Outspace ship had penetrated the protec-bubble. The ship let off a spy in the form of a humanoid robot. The robot was to destroy a particular human being and take his place."

Peters looked calmly at Olham.

"Inside the robot was a U-Bomb. Our agent did not know how the bomb was to be detonated, but he conjectured that it might be by a particular spoken phrase, a certain group of words. The robot would live the life of the person he killed, entering into his usual activities, his job, his social life. He had been constructed to resemble that person. No one would know the difference."

Olham's face went sickly chalk.

"The person whom the robot was to impersonate was Spence Olham, a high-ranking official at one of the research Projects. Because this particular Project was approaching crucial stage, the presence of an animate bomb, moving toward the center of the Project—"

Olham stared down at his hands. *"But I'm Olham!"*

"Once the robot had located and killed Olham it was a simple matter to take over his life. The robot was probably released from the ship eight days ago. The substitution was probably accomplished over the last weekend, when Olham went for a short walk in the hills."

"But I'm Olham." He turned to Nelson, sitting at the controls. "Don't you recognize me? You've known me for twenty years. Don't you remember how we went to college together?" He stood up. "You and I were at the University. We had the same room." He went toward Nelson.

"Stay away from me!" Nelson snarled.

"Listen. Remember our second year? Remember that girl? What was her name—" He rubbed his forehead. "The one with the dark hair. The one we met over at Ted's place."

"Stop!" Nelson waved the gun frantically. "I don't want to hear any more. You killed him! You . . . machine."

Olham looked at Nelson. "You're wrong. I don't know what happened, but the robot never reached me. Something must have gone wrong. Maybe the ship crashed." He turned to Peters. "I'm Olham. I know it. No transfer was made. I'm the same as I've always been."

He touched himself, running his hands over his body. "There must be some way to prove it. Take me back to Earth. An X-ray examination, a neurological study, anything like that will show you. Or maybe we can find the crashed ship."

Neither Peters nor Nelson spoke.

"I am Olham," he said again. "I know I am. But I can't prove it."

"The robot," Peters said, "would be unaware that he was not the real Spence Olham. He would become Olham in mind as well as body. He was given an artificial memory system, false recall. He would look like him, have his memories, his thoughts and interests, perform his job.

"But there would be one difference. Inside the robot is a U-Bomb, ready to explode at the trigger phrase." Peters moved a little away. "That's the one difference. That's why we're taking you to the Moon. They'll disassemble you and remove the bomb. Maybe it will explode, but it won't matter, not there."

Olham sat down slowly.

"We'll be there soon," Nelson said.

He lay back, thinking frantically, as the ship dropped slowly down. Under them was the pitted surface of the Moon, the endless expanse of ruin. What could he do? What would save him?

"Get ready," Peters said.

In a few minutes he would be dead. Down below he could see a tiny dot, a building of some kind. There were men in the building, the demolition team, waiting to tear him to bits. They would rip him open, pull off his arms and legs, break him apart. When they found no bomb they would be surprised; they would know, but it would be too late.

Olham looked around the small cabin. Nelson was still holding the gun. There was no chance there. If he could get to a doctor, have an examination made— that was the only way. Mary could help him. He thought frantically, his mind racing. Only a few minutes, just a little time left. If he could contact her, get word to her some way.

"Easy," Peters said. The ship came down slowly, bumping on the rough ground. There was silence.

"Listen," Olham said thickly. "I can prove I'm Spence Olham. Get a doctor. Bring him here—"

"There's the squad," Nelson pointed. "They're coming." He glanced nervously at Olham. "I hope nothing happens."

"We'll be gone before they start work," Peters said. "We'll be out of here in a moment." He put on his pressure suit. When he had finished he took the gun from Nelson. "I'll watch him for a moment."

Nelson put on his pressure suit, hurrying awkwardly. "How about him?" He indicated Olham. "Will he need one?"

"No." Peters shook his head. "Robots probably don't require oxygen."

The group of men were almost to the ship. They halted, waiting. Peters signaled to them.

"Come on!" He waved his hand and the men approached warily; stiff, grotesque figures in their inflated suits.

"If you open the door," Olham said, "it means my death. It will be murder."

"Open the door," Nelson said. He reached for the handle.

Olham watched him. He saw the man's hand tighten around the metal rod. In a moment the door would swing back, the air in the ship would rush out. He would die, and presently they would realize their mistake. Perhaps at some other time, when there was no war, men might not act this way, hurrying an individual to his death because they were afraid. Everyone was frightened, everyone was willing to sacrifice the individual because of the group fear.

He was being killed because they could not wait to be sure of his guilt. There was not enough time.

He looked at Nelson. Nelson had been his friend for years. They had gone to school together. He had been best man at his wedding. Now Nelson was going to kill him. But Nelson was not wicked; it was not his fault. It was the times. Perhaps it had been the same way during the plagues. When men had shown a spot they probably had been killed, too, without a moment's hesitation, without proof, on suspicion alone. In times of danger there was no other way.

He did not blame them. But he had to live. His life was too precious to be sacrificed. Olham thought quickly. What could he do? Was there anything? He looked around.

"Here goes," Nelson said.

"You're right," Olham said. The sound of his own voice surprised him. It was the strength of desperation. "I have no need of air. Open the door."

They paused, looking at him in curious alarm.

"Go ahead. Open it. It makes no difference." Olham's hand disappeared inside his jacket. "I wonder how far you two can run?"

"Run?"

"You have fifteen seconds to live." Inside his jacket his fingers twisted, his arm suddenly rigid. He relaxed, smiling a little. "You were wrong about the trigger phrase. In that respect you were mistaken. Fourteen seconds, now."

Two shocked faces stared at him from the pressure suits. Then they were struggling, running, tearing the door open. The air shrieked out, spilling into the void. Peters and Nelson bolted out of the ship. Olham came after them. He grasped the door and dragged it shut. The automatic pressure system chugged furiously, restoring the air. Olham let his breath out with a shudder.

One more second—

Beyond the window the two men had joined the group. The group scattered, running in all direction. One by one they threw themselves down, prone on the ground. Olham seated himself at the control board. He moved the dials into place. As the ship rose up into the air the men below scrambled to their feet and stared up, their mouths open.

"Sorry," Olham murmured, "but I've got to get back to Earth."

He headed the ship back the way it had come.

It was night. All around the ship crickets chirped, disturbing the chill darkness. Olham bent over the vidscreen. Gradually the image formed; the call had gone through without trouble. He breathed a sigh of relief.

"Mary," he said. The woman stared at him. She gasped.

"Spence! Where are you? What's happened?"

"I can't tell you. Listen, I have to talk fast. They may break this call off any minute. Go to the Project grounds and get Dr. Chamberlain. If he isn't there, get any doctor. Bring him to the house and have him stay there. Have him bring equipment, X-ray, fluoroscope, everything."

"But—"

"Do as I say. Hurry. Have him get it ready in an hour." Olham leaned toward the screen. "Is everything all right? Are you alone?"

"Alone?"

"Is anyone with you? Has . . . has Nelson or anyone contacted you?"

"No. Spence, I don't understand."

"All right. I'll see you at the house in an hour. And don't tell anyone anything. Get Chamberlain there on any pretext. Say you're very ill."

He broke the connection and looked at his watch. A moment later he left the ship, stepping down into the darkness. He had a half mile to go.

He began to walk.

One light showed in the window, the study light. He watched it, kneeling against the fence. There was no sound, no movement of any kind. He held his watch up and read it by starlight. Almost an hour had passed.

Along the street a shoot bug came. It went on.

Olham looked toward the house. The doctor should have already come. He should be inside, waiting with Mary. A thought struck him. Had she been able to leave the house? Perhaps they had intercepted her. Maybe he was moving into a trap.

But what else could he do?

With a doctor's records, photographs and reports, there was a chance, a chance of proof. If he could be examined, if he could remain alive long enough for them to study him—

He could prove it that way. It was probably the only way. His one hope lay inside the house. Dr. Chamberlain was a respected man. He was the staff doctor for the Project. He would know, his word on the matter would have meaning. He could overcome their hysteria, their madness, with facts.

Madness—That was what it was. If only they would wait, act slowly, take their time. But they could not wait. He had to die, die at once, without proof, without any kind of trial or examination. The simplest test would tell, but they had no time for the simplest test. They could think only of the danger. Danger, and nothing more.

He stood up and moved toward the house. He came up on the porch. At the door he paused, listening. Still no sound. The house was absolutely still.

Too still.

Olham stood on the porch, unmoving. They were trying to be silent inside. Why? It was a small house; only a few feet away, beyond the door, Mary and Dr. Chamberlain should be standing. Yet he could hear nothing, no sound of voices, nothing at all. He looked at the door. It was a door he had opened and closed a thousand times, every morning and every night.

He put his hand on the knob. Then, all at once, he reached out and touched the bell instead. The bell pealed, off some place in the back of the house. Olham smiled. He could hear movement.

Mary opened the door. As soon as he saw her face he knew.

He ran, throwing himself into the bushes. A security officer shoved Mary out of the way, firing past her. The bushes burst apart. Olham wriggled around the side of the house. He leaped up and ran, racing frantically into the darkness. A searchlight snapped on, a beam of light circling past him.

He crossed the road and squeezed over a fence. He jumped down and made his way across a backyard. Behind him men were coming, security officers, shouting to each other as they came. Olham gasped for breath, his chest rising and falling.

Her face—He had known at once. The set lips, the terrified, wretched eyes. Suppose he had gone ahead, pushed open the door and entered! They had tapped the call and come at once, as soon as he had broken off. Probably she believed their account. No doubt she thought he was the robot, too.

Olham ran on and on. He was losing the officers, dropping them behind. Apparently they were not much good at running. He climbed a hill and made his way down the other side. In a moment he would be back at the ship. But where to, this time? He slowed down, stopping. He could see the ship already, outlined against the sky, where he had parked it. The settlement was behind him; he was on the outskirts of the wilderness between the inhabited places, where the forests and desolation began. He crossed a barren field and entered the trees.

As he came toward it, the door of the ship opened.

Peters stepped out, framed against the light. In his arms was a heavy Boris gun. Olham stopped, rigid. Peters stared around him, into the darkness. "I know you're there, some place," he said. "Come on up here, Olham. There are security men all around you."

Olham did not move.

"Listen to me. We will catch you very shortly. Apparently you still do not believe you're the robot. Your call to the woman indicates that you are still under the illusion created by your artificial memories.

"But you *are* the robot. You are the robot, and inside you is the bomb. Any moment the trigger phrase may be spoken, by you, by someone else, by anyone. When that happens the bomb will destroy everything for miles around. The Project, the woman, all of us will be killed. Do you understand?"

Olham said nothing. He was listening. Men were moving toward him, slipping through the woods.

"If you don't come out, we'll catch you. It will be only a matter of time. We no longer plan to remove you to the Moon base. You will be destroyed on sight, and we will have to take the chance that the bomb will detonate. I have ordered every available security officer into the area. The whole county is being searched, inch by inch. There is no place you can go. Around this wood is a cordon of armed men. You have about six hours left before the last inch is covered."

Olham moved away. Peters went on speaking; he had not seen him at all. It was too dark to see anyone. But Peters was right. There was no place he could go. He was beyond the settlement, on the outskirts where the woods began. He could hide for a time, but eventually they would catch him.

Only a matter of time.

Olham walked quietly through the wood. Mile by mile, each part of the county was being measured off, laid bare, searched, studied, examined. The cordon was coming all the time, squeezing him into a smaller and smaller space.

What was there left? He had lost the ship, the one hope of escape. They were at his home; his wife was with them, believing, no doubt, that the real Olham had been killed. He clenched his fists. Some place there was a wrecked Outspace needle-ship, and in it the remains of the robot. Somewhere nearby the ship had crashed and broken up.

And the robot lay inside, destroyed.

A faint hope stirred him. What if he could find the remains? If he could show them the wreckage, the remains of the ship, the robot—

But where? Where would he find it?

He walked on, lost in thought. Some place, not too far off, probably. The ship would have landed close to the Project; the robot would have expected to go the rest of the way on foot. He went up the side of a hill and looked around. Crashed and burned. Was there some clue, some hint? Had he read anything, heard anything? Some place close by, within walking distance. Some wild place, a remote spot where there would be no people.

Suddenly Olham smiled. Crashed and burned—

Sutton Wood.

He increased his pace.

It was morning. Sunlight filtered down through the broken trees, onto the man crouching at the edge of the clearing. Olham glanced up from time to time, listening. They were not far off, only a few minutes away. He smiled.

Down below him, strewn across the clearing and into the charred stumps that had been Sutton Wood, lay a tangled mass of wreckage. In the sunlight it glittered a little, gleaming darkly. He had not had too much trouble finding it. Sutton Wood was a place he knew well; he had climbed around it many times in his life, when he was younger. He had known where he would find the remains. There was one peak that jutted up suddenly, without a warning.

A descending ship, unfamiliar with the Wood, had little chance of missing it. And now he squatted, looking down at the ship, or what remained of it.

Olham stood up. He could hear them, only a little distance away, coming together, talking in low tones. He tensed himself. Everything depended on who first saw him. If it was Nelson, he had no chance. Nelson would fire at once. He would be dead before they saw the ship. But if he had time to call out, hold them off

for a moment—That was all he needed. Once they saw the ship he would be safe.

But if they fired first—

A charred branch cracked. A figure appeared, coming forward uncertainly. Olham took a deep breath. Only a few seconds remained, perhaps the last seconds of his life. He raised his arms, peering intently.

It was Peters.

"Peters!" Olham waved his arms. Peters lifted his gun, aiming. "Don't fire!" His voice shook. "Wait a minute. Look past me, across the clearing."

"I've found him," Peters shouted. Security men came pouring out of the burned woods around him.

"Don't shoot. Look past me. The ship, the needle-ship. The Outspace ship. Look!"

Peters hesitated. The gun wavered.

"It's down there," Olham said rapidly. "I knew I'd find it here. The burned wood. Now you believe me. You'll find the remains of the robot in the ship. Look, will you?"

"There is something down there," one of the men said nervously.

"Shoot him!" a voice said. It was Nelson.

"Wait." Peters turned sharply. "I'm in charge. Don't anyone fire. Maybe he's telling the truth."

"Shoot him," Nelson said. "He killed Olham. Any minute he may kill us all. If the bomb goes off—"

"Shut up." Peters advanced toward the slope. He stared down. "Look at that." He waved two men up to him. "Go down there and see what that is."

The men raced down the slope, across the clearing. They bent down, poking in the ruins of the ship.

"Well?" Peters called.

Olham held his breath. He smiled a little. It must be there; he had not had time to look, himself, but it had to be there. Suddenly doubt assailed him. Suppose the robot had lived long enough to wander away? Suppose his body had been completely destroyed, burned to ashes by the fire?

He licked his lips. Perspiration came out on his forehead. Nelson was staring at him, his face still livid. His chest rose and fell.

"Kill him," Nelson said. "Before he kills us."

The two men stood up.

"What have you found?" Peters said. He held the gun steady. "Is there anything there?"

"Looks like something. It's a needle-ship, all right. There's something beside it."

"I'll look." Peters strode past Olham. Olham watched him go down the hill and up to the men. The others were following after him, peering to see.

"It's a body of some sort," Peters said. "Look at it!"

Olham came along with them. They stood around in a circle, staring down.

On the ground, bent and twisted in a strange shape, was a grotesque form. It looked human, perhaps; except that it was bent so strangely, the arms and legs flung off in all directions. The mouth was open; the eyes stared glassily.

"Like a machine that's run down," Peters murmured. Olham smiled feebly. "Well?" he said.

Peters looked at him. "I can't believe it. You were telling the truth all the time."

"The robot never reached me," Olham said. He took out a cigarette and lit it. "It was destroyed when the ship crashed. You were all too busy with the war to wonder why an out-of-the-way woods would suddenly catch fire and burn. Now you know."

He stood smoking, watching the men. They were dragging the grotesque remains from the ship. The body was stiff, the arms and legs rigid.

"You'll find the bomb now," Olham said. The men laid the body on the ground. Peters bent down.

"I think I see the corner of it." He reached out, touching the body.

The chest of the corpse had been laid open. Within the gaping tear something glinted, something metal. The men stared at the metal without speaking.

"That would have destroyed us all, if it had lived," Peters said. "That metal box there."

There was silence.

"I think we owe you something," Peters said to Olham. "This must have been a nightmare to you. If you hadn't escaped, we would have—" He broke off.

Olham put out his cigarette. "I knew, of course, that the robot had never reached me. But I had no way of proving it. Sometimes it isn't possible to prove a thing right away. That was the whole trouble. There wasn't any way I could demonstrate that I was myself."

"How about a vacation?" Peters said. "I think we might work out a month's vacation for you. You could take it easy, relax."

"I think right now I want to go home," Olham said.

"All right, then," Peters said. "Whatever you say."

Nelson had squatted down on the ground, beside the corpse. He reached out toward the glint of metal visible within the chest.

"Don't touch it," Olham said. "It might still go off. We better let the demolition squad take care of it later on."

Nelson said nothing. Suddenly he grabbed hold of the metal, reaching his hand inside the chest. He pulled.

"What are you doing?" Olham cried.

Nelson stood up. He was holding on to the metal object. His face was blank with terror. It was a metal knife, an Outspace needle-knife, covered with blood.

"This killed him," Nelson whispered. "My friend was killed with this." He looked at Olham. "You killed him with this and left him beside the ship."

Olham was trembling. His teeth chattered. He looked from the knife to the body. "This can't be Olham," he said. His mind spun, everything was whirling. "Was I wrong?"

He gaped.

"But if that's Olham, then I must be—"

He did not complete the sentence, only the first phrase. The blast was visible all the way to Alpha Centauri.

JOHN BARTH (1930–)

John Barth was born in Maryland. After failing to become a jazz drummer while studying at the Julliard, he studied journalism at Johns Hopkins University. He teaches English at the State University of New York in Buffalo. Two of his books are *The End of the Road* (1958) and *Chimera* (1972).

The End of the Road

. . .

6. IN SEPTEMBER IT WAS TIME TO SEE THE DOCTOR

I had first met the Doctor quite by chance—a fortunate chance—on the morning of March 17, 1951, in what passes for the grand concourse of the Pennsylvania Railroad Station in Baltimore. It happened to be the day after my twenty-eighth birthday, and I was sitting on one of the benches in the station with my suitcase beside me. I was in an unusual condition: I couldn't move. . . .

If you look like a vagrant it is difficult to occupy a train-station bench all night long, even in a busy terminal, but if you are reasonably well dressed, have a suitcase at your side, and sit erect, policemen and railroad employees will not disturb you. I was sitting in the same place, in the same position, when the sun struck the grimy station windows next morning, and in the nature of the case I suppose I would have remained thus indefinitely, but about nine o'clock a small, dapper fellow in his fifties stopped in front of me and stared directly into my eyes. He was bald, dark-eyed, and dignified, a Negro, and wore a graying mustache and a trim tweed suit to match. The fact that I did not stir even the pupils of my eyes under his gaze is an index to my condition, for ordinarily I find it next to impossible to return the stare of a stranger.

"Weren't you sitting here like this last night?" he asked me sharply. I did not reply. He came close, bent his face down toward mine, and moved an upthrust finger back and forth about two inches from my eyes. But my eyes did not follow his finger. He stepped back and regarded me critically, then suddenly snapped his fingers almost on the point of my nose. I blinked involuntarily, although my head did not jerk back.

"Ah," he said, and regarded me again. "Does this happen to you often, young man?"

Perhaps because of the brisk assuredness of his voice, the *no* welled up in me like a belch. And I realized as soon as I deliberately held my tongue (there being in the last analysis no reason to answer his question at all) that as of that moment I was artificially prolonging what had been a genuine physical immobility. Not to choose at all is unthinkable: what I had done before was simply choose not to act, since I had been at rest when the situation arose. Now, however, it was harder—"more of a choice"—to hold my tongue than to croak out something that filled my mouth, and so after a moment I said, "No." . . .

"You'll have to come over to the farm—my Remobilization Farm over near Wicomico—for a day or so, for observation," he explained coldly. "You don't have anything else to do, do you?"

"Well, I should get back to the university, I guess. I'm a student."

"Oh," he chuckled. "Might as well forget about that for a while. You can come back in a few days if you want to." . . .

The Doctor spent two or three one-hour sessions with me each day. He asked me virtually nothing about myself; the conversations consisted mostly of harangues against the medical profession for its stupidity in matters of paralysis, and imputations that my condition was the result of defective character and intelligence.

"You claim to be unable to choose in many situations," he said once. "Well, I claim that that inability is only theoretically inherent in situations, when there's no chooser. Given a particular chooser, it's unthinkable. So, since the inability *was* displayed in your case, the fault lies not in the situation but in the fact that there was no chooser. Choosing is existence: to the extent that you don't choose, you don't exist. Now, everything we do must be oriented toward choice and action. It doesn't matter whether this action is more or less reasonable than inaction; the point is that it is its opposite."

"But why should anyone prefer it?" I asked.

"There's no reason why you should prefer it," he said, "and no reason why you shouldn't. One is a patient simply because one chooses a condition that only therapy can bring one to, not because any one condition is inherently better than another. All my therapies for a while will be directed toward making you conscious of your existence. It doesn't matter whether you act constructively or even consistently, so long as you act. It doesn't matter to the case whether your character is admirable or not, so long as you think you have one."

"I don't understand why you should choose to treat anyone, Doctor," I said.

"That's my business, not yours."

And so it went. I was charged, directly or indirectly, with everything from intellectual dishonesty and vanity to nonexistence. If I protested, the Doctor observed that my protests indicated my belief in the truth of his statements. If I only listened glumly, he observed that my glumness indicated my belief in the truth of his statements.

"All right, then," I said at last, giving up. "Everything you say is true. All of it is the truth."

The Doctor listened calmly. "You don't know what you're talking about," he said. "There's no such thing as truth as you conceive it."

These apparently pointless interviews did not constitute my only activity at the farm. Before every meal the other patients and I were made to perform various calisthenics under the direction of Mrs. Dockey. For the older patients these were usually very simple— perhaps a mere nodding of the head or flexing of the arms—although some of the old folks could execute really surprising feats: one gentleman in his seventies was an excellent rope climber, and two old ladies turned agile somersaults. For each Mrs. Dockey prescribed different activities; my own special prescription was to keep some sort of visible motion going all the time. If nothing else, I was constrained to keep a finger wiggling or a foot tapping, say, during mealtimes, when more involved movements would have made eating difficult. And I was told to rock from side to side in my bed all night long: not an unreasonable request, as it happened, for I did this habitually anyhow, even in my sleep—a habit carried over from childhood.

"Motion! Motion!" the Doctor would say, almost exalted. "You must be always *conscious* of motion!"

There were special diets and, for many patients, special drugs. I learned of Nutritional Therapy, Medicinal Therapy, Surgical Therapy, Dynamic Therapy, Informational Therapy, Conversational Therapy, Sexual Therapy, Devotional Therapy, Occupational and Preoccupational Therapy, Virtue and Vice Therapy, Theotherapy and Atheotherapy—and, later, Mythotherapy, Philosophical Therapy, Scriptotherapy, and many, many other therapies practiced in various combinations and sequences by the patients. Everything, to the Doctor, is either therapeutic, anti-therapeutic, or irrelevant. He is a kind of super-pragmatist.

At the end of my last session—it had been decided that I was to return to Baltimore experimentally, to see whether and how soon my immobility might recur—the Doctor gave me some parting instructions.

"It would not be well in your particular case to believe in God," he said. "Religion will only make you despondent. But until we work out something for you it will be useful to subscribe to some philosophy. Why don't you read Sartre and become an existentialist? It will keep you moving until we find something more suitable for you. Study the *World Almanac:* it is to be your breviary for a while. Take a day job, preferably factory work, but not so simple that you are able to think coherently while working. Something involving sequential operations would be nice. Go out in the evenings; play cards with people. I don't recommend buying a television set just yet. If you read anything outside the *Almanac,* read nothing but plays—no novels or non-fiction. Exercise frequently. Take long walks, but always to a previously determined destination, and when you get there, walk right home again, briskly. And move out of your present quarters; the association is unhealthy for you. Don't get married or have love affairs yet: if you aren't courageous enough to hire prostitutes, then take up masturbation temporarily. Above all, act impulsively: don't let yourself get stuck between alternatives, or you're lost. You're not that strong. If the alternatives are side by side, choose the one on the left; if they're consecutive in time, choose the earlier. If neither of these applies, choose the alternative whose name begins with the earlier letter of the alphabet. These are the principles of Sinistrality, Antecedence, and Alphabetical Priority—there are others, and they're arbitrary, but useful. Good-by."

"Good-by, Doctor," I said, a little breathless, and prepared to leave. . . .

A most extraordinary Doctor. Although I kept telling myself that I was just going along with the joke, I actually did move down to East Chase Street. I took a job as an assembler on the line of the Chevrolet factory out on Broening Highway, where I operated an air wrench that bolted leaf springs on the left side of Chevrolet chassis, and I joined the U.A.W. I read Sartre but had difficulty deciding how to apply him to specific situations (How did existentialism help one decide whether to carry one's lunch to work or buy it in the factory cafeteria? I had no head for philosophy). . . .

I left myself sitting in the Progress and Advice Room, I believe, in September of 1953, waiting for the Doctor. . . .

"How are you these days, Horner?" the Doctor asked affably as he entered the room.

"Just fine, Doctor," I replied breezily. "How's yourself?"

The Doctor took his seat, spread his knees, and regarded me critically, not answering my question.

"Have you begun teaching yet?"

"Nope. Start next week. Two sections of grammar and two of composition." . . .

"Who is this confident fellow you've befriended?" he asked. "One of the other teachers? He's terribly sure of himself!"

I blushed: it occurred to me that I *was* imitating Joe Morgan. "Why do you say I'm imitating somebody?"

"I didn't," the Doctor smiled. "I only asked who was the forceful fellow you've obviously met."

"None of your business, sir."

"Oh, my. Very good. It's a pity you can't take over that manner consistently—you'd never need my services again! But you're not stable enough for that yet, Jacob. Besides, you couldn't act like him when you're in his company, could you? Anyway I'm pleased to see you assuming a role. You do it, evidently, in order to face up to me: a character like your friend's would never allow itself to be insulted by some crank with his string of implausible therapies, eh?"

"That's right, Doctor," I said, but much of the fire had gone out of me under his analysis.

"This indicates to me that you're ready for Mythotherapy, since you seem to be already practicing it without knowing it, and therapeutically, too. But it's best you be aware of what you're doing, so that you won't break down through ignorance. Some time ago I told you to become an existentialist. Did you read Sartre?"

"Some things. Frankly I really didn't get to be an existentialist."

"No? Well, no matter now. Mythotherapy is based on two assumptions: that human existence precedes human essence, if either of the two terms really signifies anything; and that a man is free not only to choose his own essence but to change it at will. Those are both good existentialist premises, and whether they're true or false is of no concern to us—they're *useful* in your case."

He went on to explain Mythotherapy.

"In life," he said, "there are no essentially major or minor characters. To that extent, all fiction and biography, and most historiography, are a lie. Everyone is necessarily the hero of his own life story. *Hamlet* could be told from Polonius's point of view and called *The Tragedy of Polonius, Lord Chamberlain of Denmark.* He didn't think he was a minor character in anything, I daresay. Or suppose you're an usher in a wedding. From the groom's viewpoint he's the major character; the others play supporting parts, even the bride. From your viewpoint, though, the wedding is a minor episode in the very interesting history of *your* life, and the bride and groom both are minor figures. What you've done is choose to *play the part* of a minor character: it can be pleasant for you to *pretend to be* less important than you know you are, as Odysseus does when he disguises as a swineherd. And every member of the congregation at the wedding sees himself as the major character, condescending to witness the spectacle. So in this sense fiction isn't a lie at all, but a true representation of the distortion that everyone makes of life.

"Now, not only are we the heroes of our own life stories—we're the ones who conceive the story, and give other people the essences of minor characters. But since no man's life story as a rule is ever one story with a coherent plot, we're always reconceiving just the sort of hero we are, and consequently just the sort of minor roles that other people are supposed to play. This is generally true. If any man displays almost the same character day in and day out, all day long, it's either because he has no imagination, like an actor who can play only one role, or because he has an imagination so comprehensive that he sees each particular situation of his life as an episode in some grand overall plot, and can so distort the situations that the same type of hero can deal with them all. But this is most unusual.

"This kind of role-assigning is myth-making, and when it's done consciously or unconsciously for the purpose of aggrandizing or protecting your ego—and it's probably done for this purpose all the time—it becomes Mythotherapy. Here's the point: an immobility such as you experienced that time in Penn Station is possible only to a person who for some reason or other has ceased to participate in Mythotherapy. At that time on the bench you were neither a major nor a minor character: you were no character at all. It's because this has happened once that it's necessary for me to explain to you something that comes quite naturally to everyone else. It's like teaching a paralytic how to walk again.

"Now many crises in people's lives occur because the hero role that they've assumed for one situation or set of situations no longer applies to some new situation that comes up, or—the same thing in effect—because they haven't the imagination to distort the new situation to fit their old role. This happens to parents, for instance, when their children grow older, and to lovers when one of them begins to dislike the other. If the new situation is too overpowering to ignore, and they can't find a mask to meet it with, they may become schizophrenic—a last-resort mask—or simply shattered. All questions of integrity involve this consideration, because a man's integrity consists in being faithful to the script he's written for himself.

"I've said you're too unstable to play any one part all the time—you're also too unimaginative—so for you these crises had better be met by changing scripts as often as necessary. This should come naturally to you; the important thing for you is to realize what you're doing so you won't get caught without a script, or with the wrong script in a given situation. You did quite well, for example, for a beginner, to walk in here so confidently and almost arrogantly a while ago, and assign me the role of a quack. But you must be able to change masks at once if by some means or other I'm able to make the one you walked in with untenable.

"It's extremely important that you learn to assume these masks wholeheartedly. Don't think there's anything behind them: *ego* means *I,* and *I* means *ego,* and the ego by definition is a mask. Where there's no ego—this is you on the bench—there's no *I.* If you sometimes have the feeling that your mask is *insincere*—impossible word!—it's only because one of your masks is incompatible with another. You mustn't put on two at a time. There's a source of conflict, and conflict between masks, like absence of masks, is a source of immobility. The more sharply you can dramatize your situation, and define your own role and everybody else's role, the safer you'll be. It doesn't matter in Mythotherapy for paralytics whether your role is major or minor, as long as it's clearly conceived, but in the nature of things it'll normally always be major. Now say something."

I could not.

"Say something!" the Doctor ordered. "Move! Take a role!"

I tried hard to think of one, but I could not.

"Damn you!" the Doctor cried. He kicked back his chair and leaped upon me, throwing me to the floor and pounding me roughly.

"Hey!" I hollered, entirely startled by his attack. "Cut it out! What the hell!" I struggled with him and, being both larger and stronger than he, soon had him off me. We stood facing each other warily, panting from the exertion.

"You watch that stuff!" I said belligerently. "I could make plenty of trouble for you if I wanted to, I'll bet!"

"Anything wrong?" asked Mrs. Dockey, sticking her head into the room. I would not want to tangle with her.

"No, not now," the Doctor smiled, brushing the knees of his white trousers. "A little Pugilistic Therapy for Jacob Horner. No trouble." She closed the door.

"Shall we continue our talk?" he asked me, his eyes twinkling. "You were speaking in a manly way about making trouble."

But I was no longer in a mood to go along with the whole ridiculous business. I'd had enough of the old lunatic for this quarter.

"Or perhaps you've had enough of The Old Crank for today, eh?"